THE COMPLETE PRACTICAL ENCYCLOPEDIA OF
ARCHAEOLOGY

THE COMPLETE PRACTICAL ENCYCLOPEDIA OF
ARCHAEOLOGY

THE KEY SITES, WHO DISCOVERED THEM, AND HOW TO BECOME AN ARCHAEOLOGIST

HERMES HOUSE

This edition is published by Hermes House,
an imprint of Anness Publishing Ltd,
Hermes House, 88–89 Blackfriars Road,
London SE1 8HA;
tel. 020 7401 2077;
fax 020 7633 9499

www.hermeshouse.com;
www.annesspublishing.com

Anness Publishing has a new picture agency outlet for images for
publishing, promotions or advertising. Please visit our website
www.practicalpictures.com for more information.

Publisher: Joanna Lorenz
Project Editors: Catherine Stuart, Melanie Hibbert and Dan Hurst
Production Controller: Wendy Lawson
Photographers: Robert Pickett and Mark Wood
Jacket Design: Nigel Partridge

ETHICAL TRADING POLICY
At Anness Publishing we believe that business should be conducted in an
ethical and ecologically sustainable way, with respect for the
environment and a proper regard to the replacement of the natural
resources we employ.
   As a publisher, we use a lot of wood pulp to make high-quality paper
for printing, and that wood commonly comes from spruce trees. We
are therefore currently growing more than 750,000 trees in three
Scottish forest plantations: Berrymoss (130 hectares/320 acres), West
Touxhill (125 hectares/305 acres) and Deveron Forest (75
hectares/185 acres). The forests we manage contain more than 3.5
times the number of trees employed each year in making paper for the
books we manufacture.
   Because of this ongoing ecological investment programme, you, as
our customer, can have the pleasure and reassurance of knowing that a
tree is being cultivated on your behalf to naturally replace the materials
used to make the book you are holding.
   Our forestry programme is run in accordance with the UK
Woodland Assurance Scheme (UKWAS) and will be certified by the
internationally recognized Forest Stewardship Council (FSC). The FSC
is a non-government organization dedicated to promoting responsible
management of the world's forests. Certification ensures forests are
managed in an environmentally sustainable and socially responsible
way. For further information about this scheme, go to
www.annesspublishing.com/trees

Previously published in two separate volumes,
The Illustrated World Encyclopedia of Archaeology and Practical Archaeology

PUBLISHER'S NOTE
Although the advice and information in this book are believed to be
accurate and true at the time of going to press, neither the authors nor
the publisher can accept any legal responsiblity or liability for any
errors or omissions that may be made.

CONTENTS

Introduction

From the great pyramids of Egypt to the eerily beautiful standing stones at Stonehenge, some of the world's most iconic buildings serve as a bridge to the past that can be spanned with archaeology, opening a link with history and allowing us privileged access into the lives of our ancestors.

Archaeology is a truly vast subject, encompassing all that has been made or done by humans, from the first known stone tools about 2.6 million years ago up to events in recent history. The whole world is available for study to the archaeologist, from mountains to jungle, from remote islands to big cities, and from deserts to shipwrecks. Few fields of learning can match such geographical and chronological depth.

This book will take you on a journey back in time to different cultures and landscapes, and offer valuable practical advice to those looking to develop an active interest in archaeology or even embark on a career as an archaeologist.

The first section of the book looks at practical archaeology, exploring what is actually involved in being an archaeologist. Discover the tools that archaeologists use, how they record their findings and the painstaking processes involved in sensitive excavation. It is in this section that the budding archaeologist will find out how to get involved in volunteering at local digs and become familiar with the complex tools and practices of the archaeologist's trade. Sensitive issues such as the excavation of human remains are looked at in depth, and illustrated case studies of actual digs demonstrate the techniques and theories of archaeology in practice.

For the amateur archaeologist or keen enthusiast, there is essential information on how to read maps and landscapes, how to begin excavating a

Above An impressive stone tomb forms part of an intricate labyrinth of catacombs that lie beneath the Egyptian city of Alexandria.

site and how to accurately analyze, date and identify any finds that you make. The various specialist branches of archaeology are explored, from coastal and marine archaeology, through to battlefield and forensic archaeology, so that the student or enthusiast can learn about the options available to them.

The second part of the book is a fascinating journey through the history of archaeology that takes a look at the world's most important archaeological discoveries and the dedicated people who uncovered them. World-famous archaeologists are presented in detail, from the pioneers of archaeology such

Below The excavation of human remains allows archaeologists' unique access into the habits of early man. Careful excavation can reveal much about diet, health and even how a person died.

Below A well preserved Aboriginal rock painting in the Kakadu National Park, Australia. The image depicts the evil spirit Nabulwinjbulwinj and is estimated to be around 20,000 years old.

Below Modern tools, such as this electronic distance equipment (EDM), is used to help archaeologists carefully plot a potential dig site prior to excavation.

as Henry Layard and Howard Carter to modern archaeologists such as Gertrude Caton-Thompson. These fascinating profiles offer detailed insights into the unique methods and personal histories that drove these archaeologists to uncover some of the world's greatest archaeological finds.

The final section of the book is a comprehensive visual directory of some of the world's most important archaeological sites. This global exploration highlights the impressive pyramids at Giza, the stunning rock-hewn temples of Petra, the remarkably well preserved ruined city of Pompeii, the baffling standing stones of Stonehenge and the immense and beautiful temple complex of Angkor in Cambodia, among many others.

This comprehensive guide will take the reader on an inspiring and instructive journey through the fascinating world of archaeology, demonstrating that it is only by uncovering the technological and social marvels of our ancestors that we can truly understand our inherited cultural history and form an accurate picture of the ancient world.

Above At Medinet Habu, the mortuary temple of Ramesses III, the pharoah is depicted standing upright in stone as Osiris, the Egyptian god of the afterlife.

Right An intricately carved ceremonial nail found in the foundations of the great ziggurat at Ur, in modern day Iraq, excavated by Sir Leonard Wooley in 1923.

Below Greece's Parthanon has been undergoing an intensive restoration and preservation process since 1975.

ARCHAEOLOGY IN PRACTICE

Image Archaeologists use brushes to remove soil from artifacts at a First Dynasty grave in Abydos, Egypt.

What Drives Archaeologists?

Some people become so obsessed with ancient pots and standing stones that they devote their lives to archaeology. They are motivated by the challenge of trying to deduce how our ancestors lived and what they thought and believed.

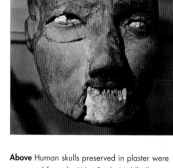

Above Human skulls preserved in plaster were recovered from the West Bank, Middle East, where they were buried some 7,000 year ago.

Archaeologists are not driven by money. While they are not treasure hunters, there isn't an archaeologist alive whose pulse would not quicken at the sight of a beautiful brooch emerging from the soil. However, an archaeologist would not ask 'how much is it worth?', but 'how old is it, why is it here and what can we learn about the maker and the owner?'

Archaeology is rooted in curiosity rather than dreams of wealth, and anybody can be an archaeologist – it isn't necessary to have a university degree or a special licence. If you have ever wondered 'how old is my house, how did the previous inhabitants use the rooms and what did the rooms look like?', you are already asking the right questions.

Riddle solvers

Being interested in the past can be frustrating because the record is so incomplete. Materials tend to survive only if they are durable, such as stone or pottery, or if special conditions prevail, such as permafrost (which acts like a deep freeze to preserve organic remains) or extreme aridity, (where the air is too dry for the survival of microbes that cause wood, paper, grass, cloth or hair to rot). That is why archaeologists have devised ingenious ways to extract information and

meaning from the detritus and surviving remnants of the past. Being unashamed scavengers, archaeologists are also willing to borrow ideas from other disciplines. They have raided the tool chests of historians and linguists, soil scientists and geologists, botanists and anatomists, anthropologists and geographers, and art and architectural historians. More recently, huge strides in archaeological knowledge have been

achieved by using scientific and medical technologies – carbon-14 dating, CAT scanning or DNA analysis – as tools for dating the past, looking inside mummified human remains or tracing the genetic origins of people, animals and food plants.

A winning occupation

All these factors answer the question of why archaeology is so fascinating: it combines intellectual stimulation with physical exercise, it is an integrative subject that draws on many other disciplines, it is a subject that touches on all our lives and asks questions about our ancestor's origins and development, and it leads to a deeper understanding of the world in which we live.

There is plenty of pleasure and knowledge to be gained from taking part in archaeology, and this part of the book will achieve its aim if it shows you how easy it is to turn from an armchair archaeologist, watching other people doing archaeology on television, into an active archaeologist doing your own research.

Above Archaeologists can provide dates for ancient ceramics, like this Chinese Ming dynasty vase (1367–1644), by studying glazing techniques and manufacturing methods.

Right The temple of Tholos at Delphi, Greece (380–360BC). Such complete monuments are rare – more often, archaeologists have to work with fragments of past lives.

Above What all archaeologists have in common is that they study the physical remains of the human past, from whole landscapes to microscopic objects, or the symbols left by previous peoples, such as this Aboriginal cave art at Bungle Bungle, Western Australia.

What is archaeology?

There are numerous definitions of archaeology: so many that some people talk about 'archaeologies' in the plural. Some argue that archaeology is a way of thinking, a creative process, others say it is a set of questions about the past, while some define it as the study of human experience – how people have lived in the past and responded to their environment.

There are also many different kinds of archaeologist: some that dig and some that study the results of other people's digs; archaeologists that specialize in a period, a culture, a region or a type of artefact – flint tools or Roman coins, for example. There are landscape archaeologists, terrestrial archaeologists and marine archaeologists (there are no extraterrestrial archaeologists yet, though NASA does employ an archaeologist to study satellite images!).

Archaeology versus history

Historians also study the past, but they do so by using written and oral records. Archaeologists can delve deeper into the past to study the thousands of years of human endeavour that occurred before written or oral records began. Archaeology can also supplement history by looking for material evidence that doesn't appear in the historical record.

For example, history tells us that Shakespeare's plays were performed at London's Rose Theatre. Only by excavating the theatre have we been able to reconstruct its original appearance. Finds from the theatre site, such as bottles, fruit remains, nutshells, shellfish and tobacco pipes, tell us that the audience smoked, drank and chomped their way through snacks throughout the performances – facts that add a human element to the historical record.

What Do Archaeologists Really Do?

The popular image of the archaeologist is of an intrepid hole digger looking for buried treasure, probably dressed in eccentric clothes. Though there are some archaeologists that cultivate this image, there are many archaeologists who wear suits to work and might never have held a trowel in their lives.

Above The ethical treatment of human remains is an important part of responsible excavation.

There are archaeologists in a surprising number of fields: they work in the media, in schools, in parliaments and the civil service, in museums, engineering, publishing and the travel and tourism industries. Some run large public companies or institutions (for example, the UK's Big Lottery Fund); others are employed by the army, the police and the secret services. Yet others have a day job as a banker or farmer, and turn to archaeology as a weekend hobby. There are even rock star archaeologists (former Rolling Stones guitarist Bill Wyman has published archaeology books, as has singer Julian Cope, while ex-Beatle Sir Paul McCartney sponsors the UK's annual Conservation Awards).

Training for life

It is archaeology's proud boast that it is democratic, classless and integrative, and that the skills involved in archaeology are the ones that make for a successful career in many walks of life – these skills include team building, problem solving, communication, empirical observation and deduction, and human resource management.

There are also many different fields in which to specialize, from field archaeologists, who do actually dig holes, to those who master the skills of blacksmithing to understand the techniques used by Roman armourers, or those who devote their lives to identifying the diseases of past populations through bone remains.

This book shows how 'practical archaeology' is a process of many stages, from data gathering and initial field survey to taking a decision to dig (or not to dig), analysing finds, reporting the results, pinning down dates, conducting specialized research and reporting the results. Throughout the book, we will continually encounter two main approaches to fieldwork: research archaeology, where the aim is to find answers for specific questions, and rescue archaeology, where the digger makes a record of archaeology being threatened by development or some other destructive force, such as coastal erosion. It is therefore worth looking at both in greater detail here.

Research archaeology

Whether amateur or professional, student or professor, research archaeologists can select and define their own field of study, choose their own sites to investigate and frame their own set of questions. These might be as simple as 'what can I find out about the lives of the people that have lived on this plot of land in the past?' or they can be as complex as 'what do the features of this landscape tell us about the religious practice and beliefs of our ancestors?'

Research might focus on a site as small as a single house plot or garden, or a whole town, or on a landscape that might range in scale from a village to a whole river system of hundreds of miles. Alternatively, the aim might be

Above Rescue excavations often take place on development sites where their trowelling contrasts with earth-moving on a huge scale.

Above Archaeologists often study traditional crafts such as blacksmithing to understand the development of ancient industry.

Above Thanks to television programmes that feature 'live digs', many of us are now more familiar with what archaeologists do.

to study a particular type of monument, such as rock art, burial mounds, shrines or medieval gardens, or to tackle complex thematic questions, examining religion, the countryside, industry, trade, transport, diet or cultural change.

Rescue archaeology

By contrast, rescue archaeology involves salvaging information before it is destroyed. In some parts of the world it is impossible to put a spade into the ground without stumbling upon archaeological remains. It isn't practical to preserve all the archaeology – to attempt to do so would freeze development in just about every major city in the world.

Instead, rescue archaeologists work with developers who build new roads, houses, factories, pipelines, schools or hospitals. In many countries planning laws require developers to consult experts and assess the likely impact of the development on the environment – both on the natural environment, with its delicate ecosystems, and on the historic environment, consisting of

Above Students often volunteer at excavations as part of a further education course.

Opportunities for volunteers

The techniques that are used in research archaeology and rescue archaeology are largely identical, but the working conditions can be different. Volunteers are rarely allowed to take part in rescue archaeology because of the training and experience required to work on building sites – where there are often numerous hazards – and archaeologists often need to work against the clock. The archaeologists are contractually obliged to complete their work within a set period of days to avoid holding up the development.

Research-led excavations are often conducted at a slower pace over several years by university archaeology departments or a local archaeology society. Many are run as community digs, perhaps organized by the local museum, or as training excavations for university archaeology students and anyone else who is interested. You are usually expected to stay for at least a week, and you may have to pay a small fee to cover the costs of training, food and accommodation.

existing historic buildings and buried remains. Highly skilled rescue archaeologists work in an environment more akin to that of a consultant architect, builder, surveyor or engineer. Their task is to make an objective assessment of the importance of the archaeological remains, deciding what can be sacrificed to the development and when it is necessary to carry

out an excavation to 'rescue' what will otherwise be lost.

Put crudely, archaeology is viewed by many developers as a 'contaminant' that has to be removed before the site can legally be developed. However, for the rescue archaeologist, removing that contaminant is a lucky-dip activity. They don't get to choose, but have to tackle whatever comes up.

INVESTIGATING THE PAST WITHOUT DIGGING

One of the ironies of archaeology is that it destroys the material on which it depends. Digging a site, no matter how painstakingly it is done, involves removing soil and the materials within it for examination. Once this is done, the site can never be returned to its original state: the stratigraphy, which is vital for dating the remains, will have been irrevocably disturbed. Instead, the excavator's records of what they found is all that is left.

So, contrary to the popular belief, digging is not the defining activity of archaeology. Any digging is preceded by a huge amount of information gathering. This includes studying historical maps and noting the changes over time, analysing placenames for clues to past uses, assessing patterns in the landscape, especially as seen from the air, and compiling any other archive information about a site.

Opposite The dusting of snow in this aerial view of Stonehenge highlights some of the less obvious features.

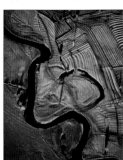

Above This aerial photograph of the River Dove taken in Uttoxeter, central England, shows a buried lake and ancient ploughmarks.

Above Research into the previous history of a site is being made easier by the increasing amount of data accessible on the internet.

Above These ship-shaped stone settings at Anundshög, Sweden, offer visible evidence of medieval burial practice.

Non-invasive Archaeology

Archaeology is never about leaping in and digging at random, just to see what might be there. Instead, all archaeology begins by defining what is already known about a site and then asking what are the gaps in this knowledge that can be filled by further investigation.

Above Your local library, records offices and local history archives are a good place to begin when searching for a record of the past. They are often very helpful to new users.

It sounds counter-intuitive for an archaeologist to say 'don't touch the archaeology'. Surely the best way to push forward the frontiers of our archaeological knowledge is to dig? In some circumstances this is indeed true, and future chapters will examine when and why archaeologists do undertake excavations. However, like a doctor who does not want to subject a patient to the trauma of surgery unless absolutely necessary, archaeologists

Below Maps record landscape features that are themselves evidence of past activities. Archaeologists look for shapes and patterns that look like the result of human activity, rather than natural forces, such as circular burial mounds, terracing or ditched enclosures.

strive to avoid causing any harm or damage to the buried archaeology if they can extract information by some other means. Instead, the aim is to use the least harmful and least costly research techniques to answer your questions efficiently, which is why the starting point for much archaeological enquiry is a desk in a library or records office, looking at maps and aerial photographs or following up clues in old photographs or archives, rather than out in the open air with a trowel.

Desktop analysis

The first phase of information gathering is referred to as 'desktop analysis' or 'desktop assessment'. You might think that this involves analysing

the debris scattered across your desk! In fact, to do so would be an archaeological exercise in its own right, treating the objects on the desk and their relation to each other as clues to your personality, lifestyle and interests. In fact, desktop analysis is the term that archaeologists use to draw a distinction between office-based research and research carried out on site, which is called 'fieldwork'.

Among the resources that are typically analysed and summarized as part of a desktop assessment are modern and historic maps, place names, records of past finds from the study area, published and unpublished excavation reports, research papers in archaeological journals, university dissertations and theses. The excavation and finds records held by planning authorities or museums (sometimes called 'Sites and Monuments Records' or 'Historic Environment Records'), aerial photographs and the maps, documents and photographs held in records offices and local history archives are analysed, too.

Making a start

Desktop analysis is often a good way for a novice to start out in archaeology because it is an area where you cannot make damaging mistakes. Libraries, records offices and local history archives strongly encourage private research and most of them are keen

to attract new users. Many run short introductory sessions explaining what resources they have and how to get the most from them.

When you embark on desktop research, it is best to start small and work outward. You might start by finding out as much as you can about your own house before you expand outward to look at the street, the neighbourhood, village or town. Most archives are organized according to geographical location, so to find your way into the records, you will need to know the grid reference for your house, or a settlement, parish or street name. At this early stage, you might wish to compile a summary of all that is known about a particular area.

Building up an analysis

Working from the known to the unknown, you can then see what information gaps there are that you might try to investigate. Here is one example: you know from comparing two maps that a house in Jackson Lane was built before 1930 (it is shown on a map of that date, so it already existed when that map was surveyed) and after 1902 (because it is not shown on a map of that date). It is part of a group of houses of similar style in the same street, which suggests that they were all built as a single development. By studying the index of the local newspaper, you might just discover an advertisement for newly built houses in

Below Past and present may be reflected in a street name: once a place where bricks were made, now famously the focus of London's Bangladeshi community.

Above Sand dredger on the River Thames near to London's Waterloo Bridge, c. 1825. Dredgermen sometimes found items in rivers that were later sold on to antiquarians.

Cabinets of curiosity

Early archaeologists were less concerned about the destructive nature of their activities than they are today. Aristocratic landowners would open up a barrow on their land to entertain their guests. To avoid possible disappointment, the barrow was sometimes excavated in advance by servants and finds put back into the soil so that the guests, journeying out to the site on horseback after lunch, could witness their 'discovery'.

Cremation urns, skulls, Roman coins or brooches excavated in this way were then placed in 'cabinets of curiosity', the forerunner to our modern museums. Road labourers, canal diggers and farm workers who made chance finds could earn a handsome bonus by selling these to local clergymen and aristocrats eager to extend their private collections. There was also a thriving trade in forging antiquities to sell at a high price to credulous antiquaries.

the street dating from 1910. The advert gives the builder's name – Thomas Jackson – which gives an explanation for the street name. You might also learn from the newspaper that he was a well-known builder of the time, so you may be able to find out what else he built in the area. Next, you could study the carved stone details that he incorporated as a signature above the front doors of his houses. They look as if they might have originally come from a much older building, so did he salvage older masonry? If so, what building or buildings did they come from and where were they? And so, as you gather more information, a fuller picture of the street's past evolves.

Below Archaeologists rely on digital maps a great deal.

Types of Maps

Accurate mapping was born out of the needs of navigation in the great age of the explorers from the 15th century. Prior to that, most surviving maps were created to facilitate the tithe system of taxation. Attempts to map the landscape in detail were mainly due to military needs arising from wars.

Above An archaeologist looks for clues on an historic county map of Wiltshire, England.

There are many reasons for the archaeologist's love affair with maps. One is that the features shown on maps – rivers, roads, settlements, woods, fields and boundaries – are exactly the same features that archaeologists study in their attempts to understand the historic environment. In other words, how people have interacted with and shaped their environment in the past, as distinct from the natural environment, which is shaped by natural forces rather than adapted by human hands.

Tithe maps and land tax

The first national British mapping agencies were established in the 18th century. Most of the maps that survive in records offices from before then are to do with land tenure and taxation. In Europe, the Church was a major landowner, and it derived much of its wealth from the tithe system, whereby landowners obeyed the Biblical instruction to pay to the Church a tithe (or one-tenth) of their income. Until the mid-19th century tithes were paid in the form of agricultural produce, such as grain, hay, timber, wine, farm animals or butter and cheese. Large tithe barns still survive in some parts of Europe for storing this produce, which then had to be sold in order to raise money for the Church. Later laws enabled the Church to convert tithes paid in kind into a financial tax, alternatively landowners could donate a piece of land to the church in perpetuity to free themselves from the annual charge.

As a result, some of the earliest maps to survive, which show details such as land boundaries, field names and the names of landowners and tenants, take the form of tithe maps. They provide a detailed picture of the countryside at the time they were surveyed, as do similar, though often less detailed, maps produced to assess landowners' liabilities to poor rates and Church rates (taxes used to pay for hospitals, almshouses, asylums and workhouses).

Enclosure, canals and railways

Another source of information is the enclosure map. It charts the change from open-field systems of farming, common throughout Europe up until the Middle Ages, to smaller hedged fields. The medieval system of common pasture that anyone could use and large fields divided into narrow strips, where each tenant grew a different crop, gave way to a system whereby the land was divided into regularly shaped fields, bounded by walls or hedges. Following an enquiry carried out by commissioners, fields were given to those individuals with demonstrable rights of land ownership within the parish. Many social injustices resulted from this system, taking land away

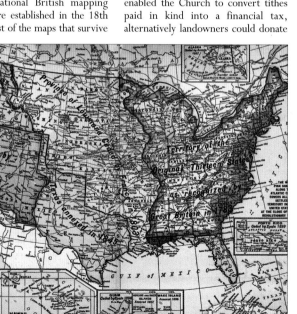

Left A 19th-century map showing the growth of the USA from its original 13 colonies.

Left Early mapping in the 20th century was often driven by military need. Here, an American soldier maps fire operations while sheltering in a fox hole.

National mapping agencies

The Ordnance Survey – or OS, as it is known – published its first large-scale map in 1801, and produced maps of the whole of England, Wales, Scotland and Ireland over subsequent decades. These maps are extraordinarily accurate and are at the large scale of 1:500. Published between 1855 and 1895, they are so detailed that they even show garden paths and flower-beds.

Many other countries established similar mapping agencies during the World Wars I and II, when military units mapped much of Europe and Africa. In those countries not involved in these wars, national surveys also took place, motivated by a desire to chart natural resources – such as minerals, building stone, oil and gas – and potential threats from such natural hazards as earthquakes. This was the momentum behind the mapping of the United States from 1879, of Canada from 1906, and of Australia from 1946.

from those who could not prove their title to it. However, the enclosure system did produce a legacy of maps that date from as early as the 16th century to the late 19th century.

This was also the age when trusts and companies were established to build turnpike (toll) roads, canals (England's first canal opened in 1761, the United States' in 1790) and railways (built from the 1830s in England, the United States and Australia). In each case, the production of accurate maps was an essential part of the legal process, whereby land was acquired and developed for these transport systems, and also of the engineering process to find the most efficient routes, and build tunnels, viaducts, cuttings and embankments.

Where to find historic maps online

Thanks to digitization, more and more maps are available on the Internet. For example, there are libraries such as the Perry-Castañeda Library Map Collection at the University of Texas in Austin that not only provide access to their own collections, but also provide links to tens of thousands of historic maps from all over the world. The link to the univeristy's website is www.lib.utexas.edu/maps/

Many national mapping agencies also have services on their website specifically for historians and archaeologists interested in historic maps:
- Australia, Geoscience Australia: www.ga.gov.au/
- Canada, Natural Resources Canada: atlas.nrcan.gc.ca/site/english/index.html
- New Zealand, Land Information New Zealand: www.linz.govt.nz
- South Africa, Chief Directorate, Surveys and Mapping: w3sli.wcape.gov.za
- UK, Ordnance Survey: www.ordnancesurvey.co.uk
- USA, the United States Geological Survey's National Map: nationalmap.gov/
- A complete list of the world's national mapping agencies can be found at whc.unesco.org/en/mapagencies/

Above The German National Library Museum in Leipzig holds an exhaustive collection of maps covering German-speaking territories during the 20th and 21st centuries. Over 200,000 items, including giant wall maps, have been collected since 1913.

Map Regression

Comparing maps of different dates is a key archaeological technique. Known as map regression, it involves peeling away the layers of change from today's landscape and working back to the landscapes of the past to build up a picture of the ways in which settlements and landscapes have changed.

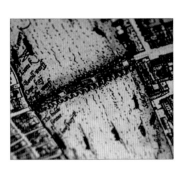

The way in which comparing maps of different periods can help to chart a period of change is perfectly illustrated by the case study of Sheffield. This industrial city in northern England, transformed from a small market town of 5,000 people, built around a Norman castle, into England's fifth largest city with a population of 1.8 million. Much of Sheffield's expansion took place during the Industrial Revolution, when the city developed an

Above Ancient property boundaries and riverside areas such as wharfs and 'bogs' are visible in this map of the Tower Bridge area of the Thames in 16th-century London.

international reputation for the quality of its iron and steel edge tools (such as files, knives and chisels) and cutlery.

Sheffield: from a rural town to a centre of industry

Above The map of Sheffield drawn by Gosling in 1736, mapping a hilltop town on the banks of the River Don, with just a few streets.

Above The Fairbank map of 1796 shows the original medieval core of to the east, still connected to the expanding city in the west.

Above This OS map, not published until 1909, is based on a survey of 1887, when the city was again in a phase of rapid expansion.

Above Aerial view of modern Sheffield. The town hall *(centre)* sits just south of the site that originally contained the medieval castle.

Map regression of Sheffield

By starting with Ralph Gosling's map of Sheffield in 1736, you can see a typical rural town that is still essentially medieval in character, set on a hill above the River Don. The pattern of streets reflects the shape of the hilltop, which is oval in shape, with a long ridge spreading westward. The streets coming into the town from a number of directions follow ancient trackways across the surrounding hills, and they converge on the site of the Norman castle, church and market square.

The map of Sheffield published by Wm Fairbank and Son in 1796, and that of the Town and Environs of Sheffield published by W and J Fairbank in 1808, show how the city began to expand westward from its medieval core in the early 18th century. Growth was limited by the hilly topography, with the result that the city grew more by infilling gardens, orchards and open spaces than by outward expansion. By the mid-18th century, all of the available land within the city centre had been built upon. The first deliberately planned extensions to the city date from the 1750s: these two maps show the old western boundary of the city at Coalpit Lane and the new area of development along Division Street, with its characteristic grid-like street pattern contrasting with the more sinuous medieval streets and alleys.

In a 1903 Ordnance Survey map, you can see how the overcrowded medieval core of the city survived well into the 19th century, when comprehensive rebuilding began in 1875 – much of it was completed in time for Sheffield to be granted city status in 1893. Street widening and rebuilding gave the city centre its current character, but left key elements in the medieval street pattern intact, including narrow lanes, which vary the pattern of the city from open squares and wide boulevards to pedestrian alleyways.

Amsterdam's Canal Circle

A celebrated example of town development that can be reconstructed from maps is Amsterdam's famous *Grachtengordel*, or Canal Circle. A 16th-century aerial view of Amsterdam drawn by Cornelius Anthoniszoon (now in the Amsterdams Historische Museum) shows the medieval city, built around the dam across the River Amstel, after which the city is named. The drawing also shows the city walls and towers, separated from the strip fields beyond by a moat: the modern streets that follow the line of these defences are still called Voorburgwal and Achterburgwal, meaning 'before' and 'behind' the 'town wall'.

Amsterdam prospered on trade with Africa and the Far East to become one of Europe's biggest trading ports (along with Venice, Genoa, Lisbon, London and Antwerp). From 1609, the city council embarked on an ambitious scheme to expand the city. Three further concentric canals were dug around the medieval moat to provide space for ships to berth, warehouses and the homes of the city's merchants and bankers.

The progress of this scheme can be traced in two maps published in the 1640s, the earliest of which (see below right) shows that the first stretch of the canal circle has been constructed to the east of the medieval city centre, as has the new Jordaan quarter, built as an

Amsterdam: an expanding trading centre

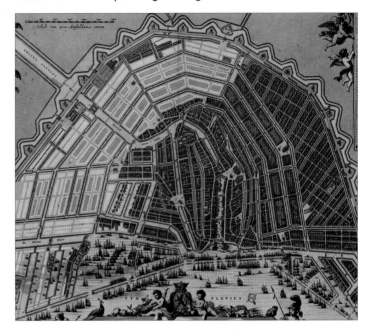

Above This map of Amsterdam shows the scheme designed by city architect Daniel Stalpaert for wrapping the Canal Circle around the original medieval heart of the city. Ships arriving at the port of Amsterdam (shown at the bottom of the map) unloaded their cargoes into barges which transported produce through the city via the canals. The coloured area of the map to the east shows how far construction had reached by the time the map was surveyed, with the western half laid out, but yet to be built.

artisans' suburb further east again, so that the prevailing westerly winds would take the smells of tanning, brewing and butchery away from the inhabited areas. A slightly later map (see above) shows the next stage of the canal circle dug but not yet built up, wrapping round to the north and west of the city, and terminating in an area of public parks, which are still known as Plantage ('the Plantation').

The 17th-century city has survived remarkably intact, so maps can be used to date the stylistic development of architecture in Amsterdam and create a

Above An earlier map of the city, drawn by the cartographer Joan Blaeu in the early 1640s, shows the situation before the canals were fully excavated, with long fields (called polders) to the north and west of the medieval city. The newly built Jordaan industrial quarter, planned in 1612, appears to the east.

dated archaeological-type series of gable styles, beginning with the early stepped gables, moving to bell-shaped gables and gables shaped like the shoulders and neck of a wine bottle, ending with the ornate French-style gables fashionable in the 18th century.

Maps for Dating Individual Houses

Map regression allows you to track the development of whole towns and landscapes, but equally you can compare maps to learn about the history of a specific plot or property. Whether you live in a recently built home or one that has been around for years, you're likely to find it in town plans.

Any home that has been standing for the last 100 years should be shown on a map, and possibly a copy of this will be attached to your house deeds. This is because in many parts of the world, town planning and land registers were established at the beginning of the 20th century. Sometimes there are earlier town maps to draw upon if your aim is to research an older property.

Town plans

The keeping of these records was probably thought of as intrusive and bureaucratic by some American, Australian or South African pioneers, but in retrospect they now allow researchers to trace the settlement of the US Midwest, for example, or of the earliest streets and houses in Johannesburg, in South Africa, where permission was needed from the government in Pretoria to build a house from the late 19th century. Because of this bureacracy, the maps of towns made 100 years ago are available for scrutiny and comparison with the same plots today.

In an older town, early maps and views might still exist that can take you back in time — early town plans are, for example, often found in the local history books, which were first published in reasonable quantities from the beginning of the 18th century. Such maps and engravings might appear at first sight to be crude: map makers were rarely accomplished artists and they often tried to draw a three-dimensional topographical view without the necessary skill to produce a polished perspective. Buildings are often stylized or drawn roughly, and it is tempting to dismiss many of these as inaccurate or stylized to the point where they can tell us little.

In fact, early map makers often went to great lengths to achieve accuracy, and they can be trusted to get right such details as whether the buildings they show were timber framed or built of brick or stone, whether they had gardens and back extensions, stables and orchards, and even whether they had shop fronts or inn signs.

Cirencester comparison

One town map made in 1715, by the Dutch artist and engraver Johannes Kip (1653–1722), shows part of a view of Cirencester (*see opposite page*). By comparing it with a modern photograph of the same street, it is clear from the shape of the gables and placing of the windows that the building shown in the photograph and

Above Sometimes historic maps of buildings are used as the basis of ongoing development. A project to extend the height of buildings in Wynyard Square, Sydney, incorporated information from an 1880s plan as well as a modern commercial fire-risk map.

Left Buda, the oldest part of Hungary's capital Budapest, which is divided by the River Danube, has fine examples of medieval housing.

A hidden medieval suburb

Sometimes a map shows more than what survives above ground today. Visiting the Hare Lane parking lot in Gloucester, a cathedral town by the River Severn in the west of England, you would be forgiven for thinking that the site had escaped development until recently. However, visit the local museum and you will see early maps and paintings showing that it was once a densely built-up suburb, lined by flamboyant 16th-century timber framed buildings – only two of which survive. It was flattened as part of a slum clearance programme in the 1930s and there was little subsequent development on the site, so this is an area of great interest to archaeologists looking for surviving Roman remains. Because there has been no intrusive development, with deep piles or underground parking lots, there is likely to be a rich deposit of medieval archaeology surviving below ground.

Left The Raven Inn, painted by Robert Swan in 1942 and later pulled down as part of an urban scheme, is a fine example of Hare Lane's original medieval heritage.

the one in Kip's engraving are the same. Thus, we can say with some confidence that the building must date from before 1715.

Applying this same principle to all the houses in Cirencester, you could produce a map of every building in the town shown on Kip's engraving and, therefore, existing in 1715 – in effect, making a map of the oldest buildings to survive in the town. However, more than that: having pinned down the oldest buildings, which make up about 10 per cent of all Cirencester's buildings, you can then use later maps to allocate a timespan to all the rest of the buildings, based on the date at which every building in the town makes its first appearance on a map.

As well as producing a phased series of maps that shows the town's development, map regression can also help you track the history of a particular site, looking to see what earlier buildings stood there that have since been demolished, or finding out what a building might have been used for in the past – sometimes a simple cottage might turn out to have been a public house, a place of worship, a school or even a mill.

The archaeological value of gardens

In the case of towns with a long history, map regression can help to identify areas that might have undisturbed

Above This house (*shown centre*), with its four distinctive gables, is shown on Johannes Kip's early 18th-century engraving of Cirencester, UK, at the western edge of the town.

archaeology. The Roman town of Corinium Dobunorum in England (modern-day Cirencester) had a walled area that was second only in extent to that of the Roman capital, Londinium. This large town in Roman times shrank to one-quarter of its size in the Middle Ages and did not expand again to fill the area occupied by the Roman town until the late 19th century.

Archaeologists studying the town are especially interested in houses with generous gardens that have not been touched or built upon since Roman times. In fact, that is exactly the sort of site that some of the finest mosaic pavements have been found in recent decades – on the sites of gardens, allotments and school playing fields.

Above Little changed in appearance, here is the same building today. The fact that it is on Kip's map means that the house must date from before 1715, the year the map was published.

Below Although at first glance they may seem uniform in style, Amsterdam's different types of gable can help to date the city's buildings.

Placename Evidence

Maps are covered in writing as well as symbols, and the writing — mainly consisting of placenames — is an important source of archaeological information in its own right. Placename analysis grew from the study of linguistics in the 19th century and is now an international activity.

Specialists in toponomastics (the term for 'the study of placenames') aim to explain the origin and meaning of settlement names, and many provide dates and manuscript sources for the earliest known use of that name. Some scholars even look at the names of individual houses, farms, fields, roads, tracks and hills, woods and forests, brooks, rivers and estuaries and pubs — any topographical feature in the landscape that has a recorded name.

Prehistoric names

In some parts of Europe, placenames can be traced back to prehistory. In France, the cities of Amiens, Rheims and Soissons are examples of places that have preserved their pre-Roman

Below Roman architecture in Saintes, southern France, whose name is a corruption of the Roman name Mediolanum Santonum, meaning 'the central town of the Santones', the pre-Roman tribe that inhabited the region.

Gaulish tribal names (the homes, respectively, of the Ambiani, the Remi and the Suesiones).

In the 'Celtic fringe' of Europe — north-west Spain, western France, Cornwall, Wales, Ireland and parts of Scotland — hundreds of prehistoric names survive because these regions escaped colonization by Romans and post-Roman invaders from Central Europe. One of the most common placename elements in such names is the prefix *tre*, meaning 'hamlet', 'homestead' or 'settlement'. The second element often tells us the founder's name — for example, Tregavethan is Gavethan's homestead — or describes the local topography — Tregair is the hamlet of the *caer* ('hillfort').

In Scotland, placenames have been used to map the Kingdom of the Picts, the people who lived in northern and central Scotland in the post-Roman period. Some Pictish placenames are similar to names found in Wales — *aber*, for example, meaning 'river mouth', as in Aberdeen, or *lhan*, as in Lhanbryde, meaning 'churchyard' — but pure Pictish names include *pit* (a 'farm' or 'land-holding'), as in Pittodrie and Pittenween, *fin* ('hill'), as in Findochty, *pert* ('hedge'), as in Perth and Larbert and *carden* ('wood'), as in Kincardine.

European conquerors

In Europe and many parts of the Mediterranean, the Romans had a huge influence on placenames, either because they created cities that had not existed before (London, or the Roman Londinium, being a famous example) or because the monuments they built

Above Pictish placenames, as well as their standing stones, characterize central Scotland.

were so durable that later people named the place after the Roman remains: Chester, Lancaster and Manchester, for example, from the Latin *castra*, or 'fort'; Cirencester, from 'the *castra* on the River Churn'; Eccles, from *ecclesia* ('church'), Portchester combines Latin *portus* ('harbour') and *castra*, and all the placenames beginning with 'pont' are from *pontus* ('bridge'), such as Pontefract or Pontypool.

Once Roman rule broke down in Europe, Germanic, central European and Slavic people migrated into the former empire and brought their own linguistic contribution to placenames, introducing elements such as *wald* ('wood'), *ey* ('island') and *feld* ('field'). Placenames that are distinctive to a particular group of invaders help us to identify the areas where they settled. In southern England, many places tell us that they owe their origins to the Anglo-Saxons because they include elements such as *ton* and *wic* or *wick*, which means 'settlement'. Other common Saxon placenames feature *bourne* ('stream'), *coombe* ('valley'), *worth* ('fenced enclosure'), *den* or *ling* ('hill') and *ham* ('village').

There is a clear boundary between southern names and northerly names of Viking origin that appear throughout Lincolnshire and Yorkshire up to the Scottish borders, where placenames include the elements *gate* ('road'), *beck* ('stream'), *thwaite* ('forest clearing'), *tarn* ('lake'), *garth* ('enclosure'), *fell* ('hill') and *booth* ('summer pasture').

Some well-known placenames

• Den Haag (The Hague) means 'the hedge', a reference to the fact that this used to be a royal park used for hunting, surrounded by a substantial hedge to keep the deer inside.
• Paris is named after the Parisii, the pre-Roman tribe that occupied the region where the city now lies.
• New York is named after the Duke of York, later King James II of England, but Manhattan comes from the Native American name 'Man a ha tonh', meaning the place for gathering bows.
• The Americas are either named after the Florentine explorer, Amerigo Vespucci, who first surveyed the coastline of the New World or after the Bristol merchant Richard Amerike, who funded John Cabot's voyage of discovery to North America in 1497.

Above Spike Island, Ireland, the penal colony which lent its name to a particularly spartan housing development in the mid- to late-19th century in Sawston, Cambridgeshire, England.

Placenames with French elements do not mean that they were founded after the Norman Conquest, as they are often blended with older placename elements, as in Chester le Street, which combines French and Latin (*castra*, 'fort', and *street*, 'a paved road').

The New World

Placenames can also give us a clue to the origins of settlers and migrants in other parts of the world. Migrants have taken the names of their original homes and spread them around the world, from New England and Harlem to New Zealand and New South Wales. Although placenames can provide clues to the origin of the settlers, as in New Plymouth, this is not a consistent principle and some cities are named after a founder, patron or monarch, as in Jamestown (named after King James I of England).

In the United States, the colonization process can be traced in the European origins of placenames for the earlier settlements. The 21 states along the eastern side of the country have names derived from Latin, English, Spanish or French personal or placenames; for example, Vermont (French for 'green mountain'), Florida (Spanish for 'flowery') or Virginia (named after Elizabeth I, Queen of England).

The further west you travel, the more you will encounter placenames derived from the indigenous languages of the Native American people living in those lands, as in Missouri, from *mihsoori*, 'dugout canoe', Utah, meaning 'high land' or Mississippi, derived from the native American Ojibwe word *misi-ziibi* meaning 'great river'.

In some parts of the world, our more enlightened age has decided to revert to indigenous names, as in Mount Cook in New Zealand, named in honour of Captain James Cook, who first circumnavigated New Zealand in 1770, but now called Aoraki, meaning 'cloud piercer', in the Kai Tahu dialect of the Maori language.

Recent names

Names do not have to be old to convey information: street names and house names can help with dating, from the numerous places all over the former British Empire that commemorate Queen Victoria, to those that remind us of battles and military leaders, or have origins in folklore. For example, 'The Spike' in the Cambridgeshire village of Sawston is named after Spike Island, an Irish open prison used between 1847 and 1883; Sawston's 'Spike' can be dated to this period. The name tells us what the tanning factory workers of Sawston, who named the district, thought of their new homes.

Below Migrants from the Old World to the New found many familiar placenames on arrival in their new environments.

Patterns in the Landscape

As well as being a useful tool for charting and dating the growth in settlements, maps also have another important function to archaeologists. These representations of the landscape can help to identify patterns and shapes that might be of archaeological significance once interpreted.

The landscape is an amalgam of natural and human actions. Contours and gradients, watercourses and vegetation are mainly the result of natural processes, but much else in the landscape is the result of human activity, whether it be in the form of planted woodland, cultivated fields, field boundaries, ditches and artificial watercourses, or quarries, harbours, roads and buildings. An archaeologist, reading a map, is interested in the patterns that indicate human interaction with the landscape. Though many landscape alterations will be modern, there are a surprising number that are far older.

Below Roman roads, like the Appian Way in Puglia, southern Italy, are easy to distinguish on maps because of their straightness.

Patterns with meaning

Over time, archaeologists (especially those who specialize in landscape history) have become skilled at interpreting maps to find the older patterns that tell a story of settlement growth and land use. Their work is based on the assumption that certain basic principles underlie the way that people have used the landscape in the past, and that many of these uses leave distinctive patterns.

Property boundaries and hedge lines generally leave behind noticeable patterns. Historic railways and canals, ancient droveways and Roman roads are also easy to spot on a map, even where they have been closed or abandoned for years, because their linear character survives and is

Above Ancient walled boundaries and gently sloping banks in Dartmoor, southern England.

apparent in the property boundaries or hedge alignments that remain.

Boundaries as a whole are a rich field of study, and some archaeologists, by combining fieldwork and map study, have been able to show that some types of field patterns survive from the prehistoric period in Europe, especially in upland areas that were once cultivated, but are now used for grazing. These ancient land divisions were first recognized on Dartmoor, the extensive area of granite upland at the centre of the English county of Devon. In Dartmoor the low walls and banks, known locally as 'reaves', run in parallel lines down valley slopes, dividing the land into narrow strips. They have been excavated and dated to the Bronze Age. Similar land divisions dating from approximately the same period are now being discovered in other upland areas of Europe — in the Causse Méjan region of south-central France, for example.

Other patterns might be based on topographical principles. One example would be that springs occur at specific places where the underlying geology changes: find those springs and you will probably also find archaeological sites because springs have often been regarded as sacred places in the past. Roman farms and villas are also located close to a spring, and are often built halfway up a gentle south-facing slope, aligned east to west.

Some patterns are characteristic of a particular time or culture. All over

Right The sheer size of Long Bredy in Dorset, southern England, makes it a striking landmark – it is a Neolithic barrow some 197m (645ft) long and 1.8m (6ft) high. However, its immediate surroundings reveal other interesting, less obvious archaeology from different periods, such as circular Bronze Age round barrows, ditches and cross-dykes that marked out ancient pasture.

Europe and the Mediterranean, archaeologists have worked out the extent of Roman colonization simply by looking at maps for the tell-tale signs of straight roads and towns with a strict rectilinear street plan aligned on the cardinal points of the compass. Even the extent of Roman farming can be plotted by looking for rectilinear fields aligned with the course of Roman roads characteristic of the Roman system of land division known as 'centuriation'. This pattern can still be seen clearly, for example, in the flatlands of the Po River delta in northern Italy, east of Ferrara and north of Ravenna.

Mysterious patterns

Other patterns are more subtle and there is not always an explanation. Archaeologists are still trying to uncover the principles that might underlie the positioning of prehistoric burial mounds in the landscape. An archaeologist might question what made people choose this spot rather than that? Once it was thought that burial mounds were placed on hilltops and ridges to be visible from afar. Studying the map suggests that this might be true – where you find clusters of mounds along the escarpment of the Cotswolds in England, for example. However, many mounds have been found in low-lying areas, and environmental evidence from ancient pollens in the soil of the burial mound tells us that some were built in woodland clearings, where they wouldn't be seen by anyone who didn't know where to look.

The archaeologist, therefore, has to be careful when studying maps to avoid producing patterns where there are none. These sites might have been

Above The Po River delta in Itay has a flat landscape and a system of lagoons (or polders) that has seen a history of intensive farming.

chosen by divination or there might have been no rational pattern at all. Or is there some other pattern? Some archaeologists have observed that some classes of mound have been found precisely 1.6km (1 mile) in a south-easterly direction from the nearest contemporary settlement.

Another challenge to the map interpreter is the fact that the landscape is dynamic and might have looked different in the past. Rivers in particular have a habit of changing their course, especially if there are wide plains that offer a choice of routes, or where glaciation has

The elephant-shaped hill
Not all patterns have an archaeological explanation. The British Library has a map of Africa's Gold Coast surveyed in 1923 with a hill that looks like an elephant. In fact, that is exactly what it is. Toiling under the tropical sun all day, the soldiers responsible for surveying this inaccessible region must have decided that they had done enough. Rather than survey the blank area on the map, they filled it in by drawing round a picture in a magazine, creating contours in the form of an elephant. Perhaps because so few people visit this part of Africa, the elephant-shaped hill remained undetected for many years.

significantly changed the shape of the landscape. Some archaeologists – called palaeo-environmentalists – specialize in creating maps of the ancient landscape. They look for the typical contours that mark sites of earlier curves of the rivers, or of ancient lakes, such as Lake Mungo and the Willandra lakes in Australia, where evidence of early human settlement might be found.

Aerial Views of Buried Features

Early aerial photography was designed to give earthbound archaeologists a better view of standing monuments, but it also reveals buried features. Archaeologists routinely use photographs taken from the air to look for soil marks, shadows and crop marks reflecting what lies beneath the soil.

Above This crater-like landscape in eastern England is evidence of Neolithic flint mining.

Experimenting with balloons, scaffolds and kites, and then using aeroplanes as a vantage point, archaeologists have been taking photographs from the air for more than a century, motivated initially by the desire to see large monuments in their entirety and within their wider setting. However, a very different revolution was born once archaeologists realized that not only could they see standing monuments, but they could also detect buried features and sites barely recognizable from the ground.

How buried features shape the land

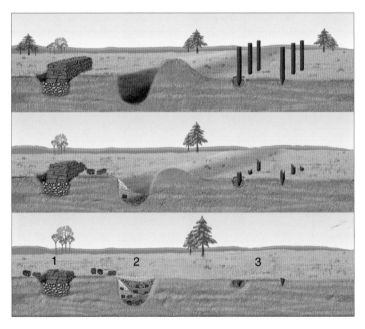

Above This series of illustrations demonstrates how the gradual decay of features impacts on the landscape. **1** Buried walls lead to stunted crops because the roots lack moisture and cannot penetrate the deeper soil. **2** Ditches have the opposite effect, providing deep moist soil and taller crops. **3** Post holes and post pits produce taller crops, and a pattern of shadows all in a row.

Revealing new archaeological sites

Until the 1920s, the only way to find archaeological sites was by chance – builders stumbling across a Roman mosaic or farmer's ploughing up flint tools – or through the ditches, banks, walls and mounds, monuments and materials that happened to survive above ground. With the arrival of aerial photography, the archaeologist has been given the ability to see beneath the soil and detect buried features from the air, the equivalent of giving an archaeologist X-ray vision. One immediate consequence was a huge rise in the number of known archaeological sites. Slowly, maps that had been virtually empty of archaeological sites, began to fill. For the first time ever in human history, people began to realize just how intensively the landscape had been used in the past, how many sites there were, and how large past populations might have been.

Weather and soil patterns

There are many different reasons why buried features can, under certain conditions, be seen from the air. Soil marks are the simplest to see, and they depend on the contrast in colour, between the natural geology and buried features, that is revealed when a site is ploughed. Such contrasts are especially noticeable in chalky soils, where the dark rings of ditches and burial mounds, pits, hut circles or enclosure ditches contrast vividly with the white colour of the surrounding topsoil.

Parch marks

Apart from soil colour differences, most of the other features visible on aerial photographs have to do with weather and soil depth and their effects on natural or cultivated vegetation. Parch marks, for example, often tell us where stone walls, floors, paths or burial chambers can be found, because the grass growing above is denuded of moisture and turns yellow when the spring rains cease, temperatures rise and moisture in the soil evaporates under the dehydrating effects of the sun. Such colour differences might only last a few days, before all the grass begins to parch and turn yellow, but if you happen to catch the fleeting moment of maximum contrast, the amount of detail revealed can be astonishing. Lost and buried towns, villages, churches, villas, farmsteads, garden terraces and paths, cemeteries, forts and monastic complexes have all been discovered in this way.

Crop marks

Another way to find archaeological remains is through crop marks. Minor colour differences can result from differential crop germination and access to water. Seed planted over pits and

Below Patterns made by parch marks and ditches reveal the remains of an entire ancient settlement – in this case, the deserted medieval village of Middle Ditchford in the Cotswolds area of western England. The long shadows indicate the low angle of the sun at the time of photography.

Above O.G.S. Crawford combined extensive flying experience and archaeology to become the pioneer of aerial archaeology.

Pioneer of aerial photography

O.G.S. (Osbert Guy Stanhope) Crawford (1886–1957) served as an observer with the Royal Flying Corps in Europe in World War I. He was shot down in 1918, but survived and was appointed the first Archaeology Officer of the Ordnance Survey in 1920, responsible for compiling the archaeological information that appears on British Ordnance Survey maps.

Crawford combined his love of photography with his flying experience to create a new discipline. He wrote *Air Survey and Archaeology* (1924) and *Air Photography for Archaeologists* (1929), which brought his work to the attention of archaeologists in other parts of the world. Previously unsuspected discoveries began to be made worldwide – from the astonishing Nasca (Nazca) Lines of Peru, rediscovered in 1939 by the US archaeologists Dr Paul Kosok and Maria Reiche, to the subtle remains of prehistoric footpaths and roads in Central America and the 6,000 surviving Maori earthwork fortifications (called pā in Maori) that have now been mapped from the air in New Zealand.

ditches will often germinate slightly earlier than neighbouring plants, resulting in subtle colour differences at certain points in the growing season, as the plants mature at different rates. Crops that germinate earlier will be darker in the three weeks or so before they begin to ripen and vice versa: seed sown on the stony ground of a burial mound, cairn, bank or buried wall will be lighter and later to mature.

In addition, deep features such as pits and ditches act as a sump, attracting and retaining moisture, while shallower soil dries out under the sun. This can further exaggerate colour differences in the crop, or even result in taller crops that throw a slight shadow if photographed when the sun is low in the sky, revealing the presence, location and shape of buried archaeology (*see opposite page*).

The effects of shadow

Parch marks produce 'negative' marks that appear as lighter lines on photographs, whereas crop marks are visible as 'positive', or darker, lines. Parch marks and crop marks are usually most numerous from late spring to early autumn, but winter brings an entirely new set of conditions because lush vegetation that might disguise the presence of mounds and hollows dies down, and the low angle of the sun produces shadow marks revealing slight differences in contour. In full sunlight, for example, a buried farmstead might simply look like a rectangular platform; low winter sun can reveal individual buildings grouped around a courtyard.

Snow and flooding

Flooding, snow and frost can produce similar effects to shadows. Water lying in the shallow features of a field can reveal buried pits, ditches, ploughing lines, boundaries, ponds and water scoops; while frost and snow that collects, drifts and melts at different rates can emphasize subtle differences in height between features. Garden archaeology, for example, often involves studying winter photographs to detect ponds and mounds, alleys and terraces, paths and beds, wild and cultivated ground.

Mapping the Results

To maximize the benefits of aerial photography, archaeologists need to be able to transcribe the features they can see on to a map. To do this means using various pieces of equipment and various techniques that minimize the distortions of contour, angle and perspective.

Purely for reconnaissance purposes – just recording what is visible on the ground – 'oblique' photographs will do, and many air photographic collections have huge collections of such pictures, which can be taken simply by pointing a hand-held camera through the window of a light aircraft. They are called 'oblique' because they are taken at an oblique, or slanting, angle to the landscape.

However, if the features are to be mapped, it is necessary to take 'vertical' photographs, which requires a plate camera to be mounted on or within the plane. Gyroscopes and levelling instruments ensure that the camera stays level, even if the aeroplane itself tilts, and the camera is set to photograph a block of landscape directly below the plane. Sometimes pairs of cameras are mounted side by side to take stereoscopic pictures that almost overlap, which produces a three-dimensional image when looked at through a special viewfinder.

Photogrammetry

Even vertical photography has to be rectified before the features that are visible on the print can be super-imposed on to a base map, because the ground itself is very rarely completely flat. When measuring how long a wall or ditch might be, for example, compensation has to be made for the effect of landscape relief as the wall or ditch runs uphill or down a valley. Specialist plotting machines and computer programmes have been developed that take on much of the repetitive arithmetic involved in transcription work (technically known as 'photogrammetry' – the conversion of vertical photographs into accurate scaled plans).

Above In 2000, an initiative to incorporate the archaeological heritage of Australia's second mainland settlement, Parramatta, into plans for the city's development used GIS to align and display current streets and boundaries, archaeological features and a sequence of historic maps and aerial photographs. The resulting plan was then incorporated into a heritage inventory database.

Film types

Black-and-white film is much used in aerial photography because it is inexpensive and easy to process, as well as because it gives good clear results that can be manipulated easily to heighten contrasts.

Infrared film is also used because it heightens the contrast in colours – such as the colours in crop marks – so that very slight variations can be seen more clearly than they would appear in 'true' colour or in black and white photography. However, when inter-preting infrared prints, you have to get used to the counter-intuitive fact that green represents plough soil and red represents crops.

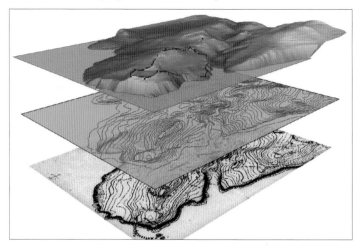

Left Topographic information and GIS are used to construct a three-dimensional view of a Hellenistic fort on the island of Antekythera, Greece. The topographic data (including contours and other details of the landscape), shown at the bottom level, is 'traced' and integrated with a plan of the fort created by walking around the ruins with a global positioning system. This tracing appears as the middle level. Using GIS, the tracing is projected onto three dimensions to give an idea of what the walls and towers, in red, would have looked like (top level).

Geographical Information Systems

One of the biggest innovations in mapping of recent years has to be the use of computerized Geographical Information Systems (GIS), a computer system for storing and displaying mapped data. Although GIS sounds complex, it is really a simple idea. Instead of storing information on a computer by placename or monument type, it is labelled with map coordinates – degrees of longitude and latitude – so that it can be stored spatially. This allows the information to be superimposed upon a base map, which makes it is easier for you to find what you are interested in, simply by locating the specific area you want on the computer map and selecting from a menu of information.

The work of transcribing archaeological data from photographs on to maps and interpreting the features on the basis of their shape and size and relationship to each other is a highly skilled activity that requires training and expensive equipment. However, once the different features are coded, they are stored as different layers of information, and the data from hundreds of photographs can be brought together in one GIS system. At that point anyone can use the system to produce richly detailed pictures of the landscape and its archaeological features at different periods in time.

Revealing continuity

This data in a GIS system can be superimposed over the top of the modern landscape, often with fascinating results. Sometimes the landscape has been so radically transformed by later activity that there is no discernible link between the present and the past, but equally it is often the case that features visible above ground – hedges, walls, ditches, and other boundary markers, for example – line up with buried features, revealing, for example, that a particular wall marking a parish boundary dates back hundreds, if not thousands, of years.

Mapping Angkor Wat's historic canal system

The restoration of Angkor Wat, Cambodia, including original canals and roadways, formed the basis of a UNESCO-funded survey during the mid-1990s. More recently, the Archaeological Computing Laboratory at the University of Sydney imported this information, along with aerial photography and remote sensed images (such as satellite images and airborne radar imagery), into a GIS system to identify archaeological features at the site.

Above An aerial photograph of Angkor reveals a landscape of modern fields and roads, mounds and *trapeang* (ponds).

Above At ground level, measurements of individual buildings are taken to check the accuracy of earlier drawings.

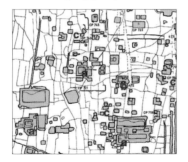

Above Archaeological features are traced from remote sensed data. The blue areas are the *trapeang* and moats; the brown areas are mounds; black lines show field boundaries.

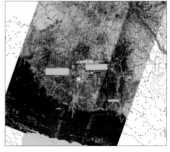

Above A digitized map combining information on contours, radar imagery and archaeological features. The pale blue rectangles are Angkorean period reservoirs.

The future lies with Lidar

The use of digital aerial photography is in its infancy, but promises astonishing results, especially when associated with light detection and ranging (Lidar) technology. Lidar uses laser pulses bouncing off the surface of the earth to detect solid bodies, just as radar uses radio waves. Mounted on an aeroplane, Lidar scanners measure the time it takes for the signal to bounce back from the earth, scanning the ground surface to an accuracy of 154mm (6in).

Lidar can see through clouds and thick woodland or vegetation and can be used year round, day and night. Its ability to see through jungle foliage has made a huge difference to archaeology in South America, where normal aerial photography is impossible. Lidar, however, is not invincible: it is not as effective in areas with peaty soils and gravels that do not reflect laser pulses well.

The Value of Inventories

Although they are little more than lists of known sites and monuments, inventories provide varying levels of descriptive and analytical detail. They are another important resource for anyone trying to find out as much as possible about the archaeology of a particular area.

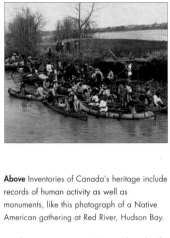

Above Inventories of Canada's heritage include records of human activity as well as monuments, like this photograph of a Native American gathering at Red River, Hudson Bay.

Archaeologists have been making lists since the earliest days of the discipline. When the venerable Society of Antiquaries was founded in London in 1707, one of its first tasks was to compile 'a comprehensive survey of the nation's antiquities'. This goal, of creating a definitive list, or inventory, of all known archaeological sites has proved to be elusive: not only are sites discovered (and destroyed) faster than people can record them, the definition of 'archaeology' continues to widen.

In the last 50 years, we have seen the rise of industrial and marine archaeology (*see Industrial Archaeology*), and prisons, cold-war military sites, shops and suburban houses are a few examples of what are now classed as heritage sites.

Legal duty

Inventories are so fundamental to archaeology that new laws are currently being drafted in Britain, making it a legal duty for all planning authorities to maintain accurate and up

to date inventories. Many already do so, and they are known as Sites and Monuments Records (SMRs) or by the more modern name of Historic Environment Records (HERs).

These records play a critical role in ensuring that nobody destroys an archaeological site out of ignorance. When somebody applies for planning permission to build on a site, the register is checked to see if anything archaeological has ever been found there in the past. As well as having this practical application within the planning system, SMRs or HERs are also of great value to anyone researching any part of the historic landscape. Anyone can ask to see them, although usually this involves making an appointment, and some local authorities are keen to see greater use made of their inventories in academic and voluntary research.

SMRs and HERs seek to record all the known sites in a defined geographical area, so your first task as a researcher interested in a particular site is to find out where the relevant list is held – a good starting point is to look at the website of your local planning authority, under 'Planning' or 'Conservation Services'.

Other national inventories

Britain is exceptional in having such comprehensive local and regional coverage, though Australia, Canada and

Above and right Some inventories are set up by organizations keen to recover traditional knowledge, for example on ancient hunting techniques or water conservation. The structures shown here formed part of Italian researcher Pietro Laureano's 'Water Atlas' project.

New Zealand, along with some American states, also have similar regional record systems, and most countries in the world have inventories at national level of the sites and monuments that are of sufficient importance to be 'listed' or 'designated' (*see Conservation and Research*).

Studying inventories

The site you are interested in might also feature a number of other inventories that have been compiled by archaeologists over the last century or more as part of research into a particular monument type. For example, you might find inventories that are devoted to standing stones, rock art, burial mounds, hillforts, Roman villas, early Christian churches, medieval deer parks, battlefields, windmills, munitions factories or hospitals and asylums.

If you are lucky, the task of consulting all these inventories might be made easier for you by cross references from one source to another. In a good modern inventory, individual entries will not only describe what is known about the site, it will also include a list of references to published and unpublished records – for example, excavation reports or other inventories.

The quality of inventories will vary greatly, and you might find looking through inventories for information about a site something of a lucky dip.

Where to find inventories

To find out what archaeological databases and inventories exist and where they can be consulted, it is best to start with the website of the relevant government agency: it might be a national state heritage service, or it might be the heritage and planning department of the state, regional, county or district government. The websites of state heritage services will often point you toward other local and regional sources of information.

• Australia: The Department of the Environment and Heritage (DEH) www.deh.gov.au/
• Canada: The Canadian Heritage Information Network: www.chin.gc.ca/English/index.html
• England, English Heritage: www.english-heritage.org.uk/ (the National Monuments Resource Centre run by English Heritage in Swindon is a good starting point as it has its own inventories resulting from 100 years of fieldwork and it works in partnership with a number of other archive and record-holding bodies and so has indexes to the records that they hold)
• England, the Archaeology Data Service: ads.ahds.ac.uk/ (the ADS has a large and growing range of databases, including HEIRNET, which has details of National Monuments Records, Sites and Monuments Records, national thematic inventories, specialist resources and other information sources held by organisations from across the UK)
• New Zealand, The Ministry for Culture and Heritage: www.mch.govt.nz/; New Zealand Archaelogical Association: www.nzarchaeology.org.uk/
• Northern Ireland, The Environment and Heritage Service: www.ehsni.gov.uk/
• Republic of Ireland, The Department of the Environment, Heritage and Local Government: www.heritagedata.ie/en/
• Scotland, The Royal Commission on the Ancient and Historical Monuments of Scotland: www.rcahms.gov.uk/
• South Africa, South African Heritage Resources Agency: www.sahra.org.za/intro.htm
• Wales, The Royal Commission on the Ancient and Historical Monuments of Wales: www.rcahmw.org.uk/

Just as it is impossible to compile a definitive inventory, so it is impossible to consult every inventory that exists on the off-chance that it might throw light on your site.

A good example of an inventory is the site recording scheme run by the New Zealand Archaeological Association (*see box above*). It will enable anyone — amateur, academic or professional – to consult or contribute to a growing database of sites, ranging from Maori settlements and houses to shipwrecks and whaling industry remains. Their inventory includes, for example, comprehensive coverage

Left Maori wood carvings, such as this one at Paihia, are among the artefacts listed as Protected in New Zealand's national inventory.

of MÇori pÇ (pronounced *pah*), which are vital defended hilltop settlements surrounded by earthen ramparts.

Remember, too, that compiling inventories is an important activity for archaeologists in its own right and one where amateurs can make a significant contribution. There are active groups all over the world that record everything from church monuments and tombstone inscriptions to war memorials or defensive structures surviving from World Wars I and II. In fact, for every class of world heritage, from historic millstones to early examples of chapels and houses built from corrugated iron, there is more than likely to be a club or society devoted to making an inventory of surviving examples.

Miscellaneous Records

*As well as consulting inventories to find out what is already known about a
site, a conscientious archaeologist will comb through a huge and bewildering
array of archives, books, journals and digital databases, and check the
holdings of museums, local studies libraries and records offices.*

People who use and manage heritage
information systems dream of the day
when comprehensive and fully indexed
records are available on-line, so that all
you have to do is enter a placename or
grid coordinate into a search engine to
retrieve everything that is known about
a site. However, we are a long way yet
from the day when the world's
archaeological data can be consulted in
one big seamless on-line database.
Until that happens, learning about a

Above Museums with sizeable archaeological
collections may be able to give information
on many artefacts not actually on display.

particular site more often means
making an appointment to go and visit
a museum, records office or a local
library and trawling through the
records that they maintain.

Museum archives

If the house, street, settlement or
landscape you are studying is the site of
a major archaeological monument, it is
likely that you will be following in the
trail of several previous archaeologists
who will probably have left plenty of
information to follow up. Looking for

Above and left Prior to excavating part of the
grounds at Berkeley Castle, western England,
archaeologists at the University of Bristol used
existing historical records to research the
original landscape, including a Tudor map
(Moyle's 1544 survey of Berkeley, *left*) and a
1712 town plan (by Jan Kip, *above*).

Below This 17th-century painting of Berkeley
Castle by Hendrick Dankerts provided further
clues to the castle's geography and the
possible location of a medieval road.

Footnotes and bibliographies

Archaeology is a scientific discipline, and like all sciences, it proceeds on the basis of a separation between data and interpretation. In the case of archaeology, the data often consists of material that has already been published somewhere else. Rather than repeat what is already available, footnotes and bibliographies are used to show where that data can be found.

This academic practice is of enormous benefit to anyone trying to finding a way through the maze of material that might exist for the area being studied. The footnotes and bibliography will give leads worth following up, and each one will have its own footnotes and bibliography, pointing you in all sorts of directions for further research.

Above A recently published article or book will list the sources or archives the author has consulted in the footnotes and bibliography.

Above Public libraries and records offices may have a computerized database of maps, deeds, wills and other valuable sources.

information is more of a challenge if you are the first to study an area, or if the finds are not spectacular enough to feature in published literature or museum displays – bones and flints, for example, rather than fine brooches or pottery. Most museums have room after room of these less glamorous finds, and the amount of material stored in basements and back rooms is often several times greater than the amount on display.

Some museums are now pursuing the enlightened path of opening up their stores and encouraging their use. Anyone researching the archaeology of Greater London, for example, can visit the London Archaeological Archive Resource Centre (LAARC; www.museumoflondon.org.uk/laarc/new/default.asp) and look at material and records from over 5,000 projects in the city, dating back to the beginning of the 20th century.

LAARC is a pioneer in providing free public access to a rich body of material; more commonly, museums are not geared to the needs of researchers and the quality and completeness of their archives can vary. In some cases, records may consist of little more than a shoebox full of card indexes with handwritten details of accidental finds, such as a Roman coin found by someone digging their vegetable patch and brought to the museum for

identification. At the other end of the scale, records can consist of detailed computerized records linked to finds, photographs, maps, plans, excavation reports, analyses and references to other books and sources for further information about the site.

Records and local archives

Though archaeology, in its emphasis on the study of material remains, is a separate discipline from local history, based on documentary research, it would be foolish to ignore what historical records might be able to tell you about a site or landscape. There are no hard and fast boundaries between archaeological and historical methodology at the desktop assessment phase of the research process – the differences come to the fore once archaeologists move into the field. So a desktop assessment will include a search through records that are held in a records office or a local history library.

These might include copies of old newspapers, historic photographs, census returns, deeds and wills, parish registers, charters and grants of land, and possibly diaries and antiquarian field notes, paintings and engravings that show streets, buildings, towns or monuments as they looked in the past, or the papers of large estates or ecclesiastical authorities.

None of this should be neglected as a possible source of information, even if it takes time to work systematically through the indexes looking for relevant material. Such a search is more likely to prove rewarding if you are studying the comparatively recent past, especially if you want to add a human dimension to your knowledge. Archaeologists in London, for example, excavating houses that were destroyed by wartime bombing, were able to date the construction of buildings from newspaper reports, put names to the people who lived in the houses, find out what their occupations were, excavate the pipes that previous inhabitants had smoked, the toys that their children played with and even reconstruct what they might have had for tea from the jars and bottles found in their refuse tips.

What are you looking for and why?

How far you go toward building up a complete picture depends on your field of research – some researchers become obsessive collectors of data, while others look at only recent research on the grounds that current archaeological methods yield more reliable data than past antiquarian pursuits. The aim in either case is to become familiar with the grain and character of the area you are studying. It takes time to do this – sometimes many months or years – but developing an archaeological feel for the landscape is satisfying and rewarding, as your mental picture begins to build up detail and nuance.

Case Study: a Cotswold Upland Farm, England

In 2007, the School of Conservation Sciences at Bournemouth University, England, organized a line excavation at a farm in Wiggold, Gloucestershire. The dig was preceded by a detailed desktop assessment designed to reveal as much as possible about the farm's archaeological history.

Above Geophysical equipment is used to find the precise location of buried ditches and pits.

The location of the excavation site at Wiggold was an important factor. Nearby Cirencester, south-west of the site, was a major Roman town linked to other Roman administration centres by a network of roads, some of which are still in use.

Placenames and documents

Akeman Street, the main Roman road from Cirencester to London, forms the farm's southern boundary, and the Fosse Way, linking Exeter to Lincoln via Bath, Cirencester and Leicester, runs north to south through the middle of

the farm holding. It is possible that both roads have changed their course over time, so the farm might well have original Roman roads preserved beneath its fields, as well as possible roadside buildings.

White Way is another road of Roman, or possibly prehistoric, date that forms the western boundary of the farm. 'White Way' is a medieval name that refers to the salt that was carried

Below Archives held at the National Monuments Record Centre, Swindon, produced this aerial photograph of a mysterious circular feature, which might be an Iron Age (pre-Roman) enclosure, or the remains of a ditch and bank built to keep deer out of woodland in the Middle Ages.

along this road after being extracted from the brine wells beneath the town of Droitwich, at the northern end of this road. Welsh Way, forming the northern boundary of the farm, is named after the Welsh drovers who brought their sheep and cattle along this road heading east toward the markets of London, having crossed the River Severn at Gloucester.

Wiggold itself is a Saxon name, which means the *wold* ('wood') of someone named Wiga – perhaps the same Wiga who is recorded in the Domesday book as the owner of land in Pauntley, in Gloucestershire, and at Kilcot, on the River Thames further east in Oxfordshire. The Domesday book also records that William Fitz Osbern, Earl of Hereford, who owned Cirencester manor from 1066 to 1070, detached two hides (206ha (514 acres)) of land and bestowed them on a tenant to create the Manor of Wigwold, but the Saxon name suggests that the farm at Wiggold has origins that go back to before the Norman Conquest.

Aerial photographs

The National Monuments Record Centre houses aerial photographs that were taken over a period of 50 years. These reveal that the farm has many buried archaeological features, including the lines of medieval field boundaries, hedges and ditches that were removed in the 1950s to make larger fields, and the remains of medieval ridge and furrow cultivation, as well as many ditches and pits whose shapes suggest prehistoric enclosures.

Inventories and archives

No less than 95 known sites have been recorded in the immediate vicinity of the farm. These include burial mounds dating from the Bronze and Iron Ages and prehistoric pits, through to more recent quarries and lime kilns.

A visit to the local museum revealed that large numbers of prehistoric flints have been found at seven different parts of the farm. Additionally, Roman pottery and building material has been reported from an area of the farm that lies along the route of the old Midland and South Western Junction Railway, which ceased to operate in the 1960s and has since been turned into a farm track.

Conclusion

In the case of the Cotswold's upland farm project, desktop analysis has demonstrated that there can be a huge amount of archaeological information to be found in maps and photographs, or buried away in archives and inventories. From the analysis, it is now known that this farm has a rich

Above Field walking prior to excavation was used to identify areas in which flint tools had been made and used.

multi-period archaeological landscape, with many potentially important sites located within it.

Desktop analysis can result in a cascade of data or a complete blank. If you do draw a blank, you might worry that the area you have chosen to study lacks archaeology – in reality, it can mean that nobody has yet been out to look. Absence of data doesn't always mean absence of archaeology, so you need to move on to the next stage and undertake investigations in the field.

However, too much data might lead you to ask whether there is anything left to be discovered. The answer is yes, because most of what you find will be raw material that has yet to be digested and analysed. This data doesn't become information until someone brings it all together in one place and adds it all up into a coherent picture.

Gathering together the disparate strands of what is already known is the first step toward writing a history of the place that you live in, and all archaeological research is based on this pattern of enquiry – working from the known to the unknown. Desktop analysis – pinning down what we already know – is essential for framing the next stage in the archaeological process, when we move from the desk and the computer into the field.

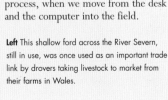

Left This shallow ford across the River Severn, still in use, was once used as an important trade link by drovers taking livestock to market from their farms in Wales.

LOOKING FOR EVIDENCE IN THE FIELD

In the previous chapter, we have seen that the purpose of desktop analysis is to gather as complete a picture as possible about the site or area being studied. The next stage is to leave the desk and look at the evidence on the ground. This chapter looks at the techniques involved for getting to know your site in more detail before deciding whether or not to excavate. Although several types of high-tech equipment are used to access the landscape, the archaeologist also relies heavily on observation to help with the analysis of the site, and by simply walking across the land, there is plenty to be discovered. These first two stages – desktop analysis and looking for evidence in the field – often go hand in hand. It's often only after giving proper consideration to the evidence gathered from both stages, that a decision to dig, or not to dig, is finally made.

Opposite Archaeology students learn how to operate a global positioning system (GPS).

Above Many archaeologists now use hand-held GPS in conjunction with maps to locate earthworks as part of a field survey.

Above Heritage conservationists conducting a survey of surviving archaeology in Hampshire, UK, record their observations.

Above Walking a site where the earth has been recently tilled may turn up anything from ancient pottery shards to Roman mosaics.

From the Desk to the Field

Studying landscapes without visiting the area you are studying is like trying to write a travel guide to Vienna without visiting the city. You need to get a feel for the city's unique atmosphere, and the same is true of archaeological sites — knowing them on paper is no substitute for walking the site.

Above Archaeologists may use GPS to determine a precise area to be fieldwalked.

In reality desktop analysis and field survey go together — the two techniques are not used separately — rather, they complement each other. Archaeologists involved in archival research will constantly visit the site they are studying to compare what they have discovered from maps and photographs with what they can see on the ground, and vice versa. Looking at the landscape in the field will often suggest new questions or lines of enquiry that need to be researched using maps and databases.

High-tech surveying

Some of these techniques used to survey the field are based on remote sensing technology — using instruments such as metal detectors, global positioning systems (GPS), resistivity meters and magnetometers. This equipment was

Stone for Stonehenge

In 2004 archaeologists Geoff Wainwright and Tim Darvill set out to study the hilltop of Carn Meini in South Wales, from where the bluestones of the inner circle at Stonehenge were quarried around 2600BC. Their desktop analysis of the site produced a blank archaeological map. However, after three seasons of fieldwork they discovered hundreds of examples of prehistoric activity. Their archaeological map of the area is now crowded with cairns, causewayed enclosures, chambered long barrows, stone circles, dolmens, single standing stones and rock art, along with large areas of prehistoric quarry debris, littered with hammer stones and flake tools. The lesson is that you should never assume that because an area is well known that it has been well studied — and that simply looking at the landscape with an enquiring mind can produce rich rewards.

Right The hilltop of Carn Meini is in the Presili Hills of Pembrokeshire, South Wales.

Above Among the more visible features are prehistoric standing stones, such as the Kermario stones near Carnac, northern France, which date from the third millennium BC.

once so expensive and technical that it was used by only a handful of specialists working in university departments of archaeological science, but it is now becoming standard equipment used by all archaeologists. With the fall in price has come an equally important change – ease of use.

Walking the fields

As well as high-tech survey techniques, archaeologists also use some very simple tried-and-tested field survey methods that require very little by way of equipment and are the backbone of much amateur field archaeology. Walking over fields systematically after ploughing to look for scatters of pottery, flint, tile or bone is another commonly deployed technique for discovering sites, as is metal detecting, which has a valuable role to play in archaeology if used with respect for the archaeology rather than as a treasure-hunting device (*see* Geophysical Surveys).

Rock art

In the parts of the world where nomadic people build shelters from organic materials that leave little archaeological trace, much of our knowledge about past societies has come from 'above ground' archaeology. One important area of study is rock art, whether painted or carved. It is one of the oldest forms of human expression and one of the most widespread – from Northumberland, England, to North Africa, from South Africa to Australia, and from Chile to Ottawa. There are enthusiastic groups dedicated to finding, recording and conserving the astonishing range of what are technically called 'petroglyphs' if they are incised, 'pictographs' if painted and 'petroforms', if they consist of rocks and stones deliberately arranged to make a pattern.

Above Detail of a bison head from a Paleolithic cave mural painting in Lascaux II grotto, France.

Simply walking across the landscape with an observant and enquiring mind can lead to the discovery of archaeological features such as ditches, banks and mounds. There is a surprising amount of archaeology, known as 'above ground' archaeology, all around us that isn't buried and doesn't require

digging – field boundaries, crosses, boundary markers, early grave stones and rock art, for example. Studying these examples is a form of archaeology that is open to anyone to undertake – all the more so as it is non-invasive, and does little harm to the landscapes and objects being studied.

Reading the Landscape

One form of fieldwork is simply to go for a walk, known as 'a walkover', to explore and read the landscape, searching for remains that survive above the ground. These can be ancient earthworks, or 'humps and bumps', or they can be the evidence of more recent activity, such as canals, mills and mines.

Once bitten by the archaeology bug, life becomes one long field survey: whenever you travel, you'll habitually and instinctively scan the landscape for archaeological clues – whether walking to work through town, travelling by car or train or walking for exercise and leisure. With practice and familiarity, archaeologists learn to distinguish between features in the landscape that are natural and those that are the result of human intervention. It isn't easy, and some people have more of a gift than others. The changing seasons and, as we have already seen, varying times of day have an impact on what you see, as do different types of light and alternative states of vegetation. People who regularly find new sites tend to be those who have lived in an area for a long time, and who walk the same ground regularly.

Thinking you already know everything there is to learn about a street, building or landscape will never lead to new discoveries. You need to keep looking at the landscape with fresh eyes and asking questions, until one day, seen in a different light, something sings out that you haven't noticed before, such as an alignment of stones that looks deliberate rather than natural, or the slight scratches on a boulder that suddenly form a pattern when seen in the raking light of the winter sun, or the ditch that you suddenly realized was dug to divert water to some long vanished mill.

Systematic survey

You can do better than to make accidental discoveries: by selecting an area of the landscape and walking across it systematically, you can look

for evidence – or even record evidence that is staring you in the face but that nobody has recorded before. In many parts of Europe, for example, projects have been set up to record the fast-disappearing relics of twentieth-century warfare, from tank traps and gun emplacements hidden in woodland to decaying prisoner-of-war camps and gunpowder factories or the forgotten nuclear bunkers and rocket test sites of the Cold War.

Although there is a place for simply walking the landscape just to 'see what is there', patterns and meaning often do not emerge unless field survey is undertaken in a more systematic way. Some of the survey work undertaken by archaeologists is led by the desktop research they do, and is concerned, for example, with inspecting on the ground sites that they have found on aerial photographs. They may also plot the rise and fall of the land using electronic distance measurement (EDM) equipment. Three people are needed to operate the equipment, and this must be done in an area of open field with a clear view of the surroundings (*see opposite*). EDM is also used to plot excavated features during an actual dig, this is explained in chapter three (*see* Breaking New Ground).

Left The eroded banks of ditches and streams might also reveal buried remains, as can tracks and gates cut through banks or other earthworks – and long shadows.

Alternatively, you might set out to look for and compile maps of some very specific type of feature – books have recently been published on sheep pens and animal pounds, on medieval rabbit warrens and on water meadows and meadow management, all of which have resulted from systematic field survey work. In Northumberland, England, local volunteers have been scouring the upland moors for examples of prehistoric rock art, and they have added hundreds of new finds to the database of known examples.

In France an archaeologist on a walking holiday became fascinated with the boundary walls and marker stones, along with cairns (heaps of stone created by clearing the land for ploughing) that he noticed on the hills he was exploring. He returned later to study them using a systematic approach and has proved that they are the remains of intensive prehistoric agriculture on what is now a wild upland nature park.

Mole hills and cuttings

When you are out in the field, never miss the opportunity to examine disturbed ground. Countless sites have been discovered through nothing more sophisticated than the examination of soil thrown up by rabbits, moles, foxes, badgers and other ground-burrowing creatures. Archaeologists taking part in 'Time Team', the British television programme, discovered a splendid Roman villa with bath suite and mosaic floors after the landowner discovered the small stone cubes (tesserae) used by Roman mosaic makers in the soil turned up by moles burrowing in his field (*see* The Importance of Location).

However, the most common form of disturbance to buried archaeology has to be ploughing. The systematic walking of ploughed fields is an activity that is of huge importance to all archaeologists – but especially to local amateur societies, because it is one of the easiest and least expensive ways to contribute to archaeological knowledge, as well as to satisfy that thirst for new discovery that provides motivation for all archaeologists.

Conducting an earthworks survey using EDM

1 The reflector is fixed to a staff marked with a vertical scale, and is placed at the point where the ground rises or falls.

2 The EDM operator checks the spirit level to ensure the tripod is level, then looks through the lens at the reflector.

3 A small knob beside the lens adjusts the focus. The EDM then records the vertical and horizontal scale.

4 A third person then plots the distance on a graph, recording the rise and fall of the landscape.

Above Kenyan-based archaeologist Richard Leakey with one of the African fossils that has provided vital clues to early human history.

Looking for the first humans in Africa

Many a time, discoveries have been made in circumstances where someone less dedicated and less familiar with the terrain might have seen nothing. Richard and Maeve Leakey are well known for their systematic quest for fossil bones in Kenya. In August 1984, a member of the Leakey's survey team, Kamoya Kimeu, spotted a fragment of blackened bone, which was almost undistinguishable in colour from the surrounding black basalt pebbles of a dry river bed. However, he and the Leakeys were determined and continued searching the same spot for another four years. Their reward was to find numerous fragments of bone that eventually added up to the nearly complete skeleton of a teenager who lived 1.6 million years ago, now called 'the Turkana Boy' after nearby Lake Turkana.

The Importance of Location

Perhaps the most important piece of information that can be given about any archaeological site is its precise location. Any artefact taken out of the ground will lose the greater part of its archaeological value if there is no record of where it came from.

Above Recording location is crucial to placing a site within its wider historical context.

It is important to describe and analyse an archaeological site as fully as possible, but no single piece of information is quite so critical as saying where the site is, because that is the vital piece of data that allows other archaeologists to locate the site and study it further.

Location, location

To illustrate just how easy it is for sites to get lost, consider the subject of a UK 'Time Team' television programme, filmed in August 2005 at Withington, Gloucestershire. Withington is the site of a villa excavated in 1811 by the antiquarian, Samuel Lysons, after a ploughman discovered Roman remains in a field on which he was working. Excavations revealed some very fine mosaics (now in the British Museum), however no record was made at the time of exactly where the villa was

Left and below Archaeologists walking a site with a hand-held GPS (*left*) can import their track data – or 'waypoints' – into software such as Google Earth to produce a clear geographical profile. The Phoenecian port of Sabratha, Libya (*below*), was mapped in this way by Charlene Brown in 2006. Note that satellite maps are subject to continual updates.

located. Experts from 'Time Team' took two whole days before they managed to find it.

Location is also a very crucial piece of evidence in its own right, because it enables any one site to be located within a larger geographical context. As we have seen, the distribution of hill-forts, causewayed enclosures, temples, stone alignments or henges can tell us something about the influence of the people who built such monuments. The distribution of rock art in the landscape might give us clues about links between a certain rock-art pattern and ancient water sources, for example.

Pinpointing a site

For all these reasons, field survey work always begins by linking the area to be studied with a precise map location. This is easy enough at the macroscopic level – most of us can find where we live on a road map – but field work requires much greater precision.

Achieving that precision requires specialist surveying skills, though the principles are simple enough to understand. National mapping agencies have established certain fixed points on the earth's surface, known in different parts of the world as 'benchmarks', 'trig points', 'trigonometrical stations' or 'triangulation pillars'. These are points whose precise location has been measured in three dimensions – longitude, latitude and height above sea level. Starting from this known point, you can then work to the unknown

Above 'Benchmarks' are managed by the Ordnance Survey in the UK.

Above Using a total station needs clear and open terrain; woods and steep hills present real challenges to the surveyor.

point that you want to survey by using tape measures or surveying chains to measure distances, and you can use a special tripod-mounted optical instrument, called a theodolite, for measuring variations in height.

Similar equipment and techniques were used by the first map makers and the mathematical basis of surveying was understood by pyramid and temple builders in the distant past. Surveying by this method involves taking endless measurements and making a series of mathematical calculations. Over long distances, in difficult and overgrown terrain, mistakes are easily made, and yet skilled surveyors can plot precise locations with pinpoint accuracy.

The age of the GPS

All of this arcane knowledge is in the process of being made redundant with the advent of the Global Positioning System (GPS), a device that enables any point on the earth to be pinpointed by bouncing radio signals to a series of satellites orbiting the earth. There are many different types of GPS – from cheap hand-held devices that are accurate to within a metre or so, to large 'total stations', which have enough memory to store huge quantities of data in the field and are accurate to about 2mm ($\frac{2}{25}$in).

Hand-held devices are useful for pinpointing the location of discrete monuments – a boulder with cup and ring marks, for example, or a standing stone. You can also use them to plot a

series of alignments – for example, tracing the locations of boundary marker stones or of a water course, irrigation canal or track.

The GPS is so easy to use that the biggest challenge now is to remember to carry spare batteries if you are working for long periods in the field – and even this problem can be overcome by using solar-powered equipment.

Total stations

Commercial units, surveyors and academic research groups use total stations to produce a terrain model. To do this involves first setting up a base station, whose position on the globe is located by satellite. An archaeologist wearing a backpack with an aerial and transmitter/receiver then walks across the site, guided by flags or poles set into the ground at intervals of 3–5m (10–16ft). The base station keeps a three-dimensional record of the entire walk, which can then be read by a computer and converted into graphic information. Usually this takes the form of a contoured plan of the site, accurate to within 3mm ($\frac{1}{10}$in) in the case of the most sophisticated systems. Thus, long hours (if not days) of surveying complex earthworks can now be reduced to a day of walking back and forth across the site, and the plotting of the results, which once also took several days, is now achieved using software that takes longer to print out than to process.

However, this system is not foolproof – dense woodland can defeat GPS signals, as can tall buildings – but having said that, surveying in such environments is challenging even when using conventional equipment.

Above The backpack worn by this archaeologist communicates with satellites in orbit around the earth to provide locational data with pinpoint accuracy.

Field Walking

The field survey techniques described so far have been concerned with understanding landscape use at a broad level. Having walked over a tract of landscape to identify sites of past activity, the next stage is to return to specific places for a closer examination of any surface finds.

Above The systematic inspection of land is an essential part of field survey.

The best time to do detailed field walking is after the site has been ploughed and after rain or frost has broken down the soil, which helps to wash out any archaeological material brought to the surface by cultivation. Mostly the finds exposed in this way will consist of fairly robust and durable materials – such as pottery, flint, building stone, brick or tile. Metal objects, such as nails or coins, might also be exposed, and these are best located using metal-detecting equipment (*see Metal Detecting*).

In an ideal world, this material should be left exactly where you find it, as a resource for other archaeologists to study. However, in reality it might be necessary to take the material away for adequate cleaning and analysis, so it follows that there are some important ground rules that archaeologists are expected to observe when they do this sort of work.

Know what is legal

First it is essential to check whether field walking is legal or not and obtain the necessary permits. In many European countries, the heritage is deemed to be publicly owned, and nobody is allowed to undertake archaeological work of any kind unless they have applied for and obtained a licence from the relevant state department. It is illegal almost everywhere in the world to take objects from protected monuments, and this can include sites that are designated for their wildlife and biodiversity as well as their archaeological value, since disturbing rocks and vegetation can have an impact on rare wildlife habitat.

Meet the landowner

In all circumstances, it is essential to gain the permission of the landowner for field walking, because, quite apart from the fact that it is common courtesy to do so, the landowner has a legal interest in any objects that are found on the land. Building a good relationship with the landowner can be vital to the success of a project in other ways, such as the timing of the work. You need the farmer to tell you when ploughing is going to take place, as the best time to sample ploughed fields is within the first three to four weeks after the soil has been turned, and before it has become compacted by heavy rain or by harrowing.

Few landowners object to non-intrusive archaeological activity on their land, if the purpose of the work is explained to them. On the contrary, many farmers have an intimate relationship with the land they cultivate, and they may have a deep and genuine

Left Field walking requires the co-operation of the landowner, so that crops are not harmed.

Protecting the land

The increasing power of farm machinery and more intensive agricultural practices mean that archaeological sites that have survived for many centuries are now being destroyed in a few short hours. Government agencies in Great Britain estimate that the landscape has been transformed by mechanized farming in the last 50 years, and that the landscapes known to our predecessors bore many more marks of past activity than the flat fields of today. The truth of this can be seen in landscapes used for army training on the Salisbury Plain, in central southern England, where, despite the destructive impact of tanks and explosives, there are thousands of above ground monuments within the Ministry of Defence estate, and almost none on adjoining properties which have been farmed.

Left Ancient field patterns and boundaries, which provide vital clues as to the archaeology beneath, can be destroyed when trees, hedges, banks and ditches are levelled to create a larger field for agricultural use.

interest in learning more about the people who were there before them. They often know the land better than anyone, and may be able to guide you toward areas where they have made finds in the past. They might also have maps and records relating to the history of the land and even, in some cases, a few bags or boxes full of the pottery they have found themselves. They can also prevent you from making embarrassing mistakes: archaeologists in Herefordshire, England, recently became excited by a large feature showing up on a geophysical scan, and were planning to investigate until the farmer told them that was where his father had buried a pile of rusty old wire some years previously.

Informing the landowner

Rather than demonize farmers for the destructive effects of ploughing, archaeologists try to prevent damage simply by telling farmers about the archaeology that can be found on their land. Although there are some farmers that are not interested, most are very happy to cease ploughing sensitive areas once they understand what lies beneath their soil. New grant regimes that reward farmers for sustainable farming and the protection of the historic environment are also beginning to have a beneficial effect on buried archaeology.

Above Few people understand the land so well as those who farm it. A farmer may be aware of fragments of pottery of other historic artefacts found on their land, and advise on where best to look for them.

Left Not all landscapes are easy to walk; searching for tell-tale signs in rocky or steep landscape requires skill and stamina.

Field Walking Techniques

Generally there are two stages to field walking: first, systematically walking across the ground in lines to identify where most of the material is located, then setting out grids to examine the most productive areas in more detail and determine the results of the field walk.

By using a group of people walking carefully in lines, a large field can be surveyed fairly rapidly. Lines can be laid out at 15, 20 or 30m (50, 65 or 100ft) intervals, depending on how many people there are; however, at more than 30m (50ft), there is the risk of missing small scatters of material.

To ensure that people do not wander off line, ranging rods are used to mark out the walking lines. It is common practice to walk in a southerly to northerly direction across a field, simply because this aids plotting 'find' spots on a map (by convention, maps are always drawn with north at the top). The aim is to walk slowly along

the line, scanning a metre or so along each side, looking for concentrations of finds lying on the surface of the ground, which are then marked using flags or poles. At this stage the aim is not to collect material so much as to identify where it is.

Grids and timing

The next stage is to examine the more productive areas in greater detail by dividing the site into squares. The size of the squares can vary from as small as 5 x 5m (16 x 16ft) to as large as 20 x 20m (65 x 65ft), depending on the scale of the site and the number of people involved. As the aim is not to

Above Ploughing turns over a 'sample' of what lies buried beneath farmed land.

collect absolutely everything, but rather to sample the site, larger squares are normally preferable.

The grids should be laid out on the ground using tapes, poles and strings, and they need to be plotted precisely on a base map, with each square given a unique number. Field walkers then spend a finite amount of time – perhaps 5 minutes for a small square and 15 minutes for a larger one – looking for surface finds in each square of the grid. Limiting the amount of time spent in each grid square is intended to counteract the fact that a field walker becomes much better at spotting objects the longer the patch of ground is studied. Tempting as it is to try and find every object within the grid, it is vital to move on to the next square once the allotted time is up to avoid bias information in favour of one square over another.

Team work

This work is usually done as a team effort, with some members doing the field walking, others identifying the finds and others recording them using a plan of the site and recording sheets.

At a very basic level, the finds from each grid should be sorted into basic types of material, such as worked flint, worked stone, shell, bone, brick, pottery, metal and so on. Each type of

Left A large area can be surveyed as part of a team effort, with everyone walking in straight lines at designated distances apart.

Right The finds from each area are bagged separately for later analysis: concentration of finds in one area might indicate a buried site.

material is then counted and weighed, and the result is recorded on the site survey sheet, leaving the material itself behind where it was found. Done in this way, nothing is taken away from the site.

However, sometimes a find needs to be taken away for cleaning and further examination by an expert, so one member of the team will bag such finds and label them with the correct grid reference. The sorts of material that might be taken away include pottery and bone. In the case of pottery, the shape of the vessel, the decoration, the colour and the inclusions in the clay of the vessel can all be used by experts in dating the piece and assessing what the vessel might have been used for, whether it was for cooking, tableware or for the burial of cremated remains. In pieces of bone, experts will identify the type of animal, its age, the specific bone type and any butchery marks as evidence of farming practices, diet and ritual, refuse disposal or industrial processes, such as tanning.

Graphic results

The results can be presented graphically by using graded sized dots or by colour coding each grid, using a different colour for each artefact type and showing what percentage of each artefact type was found in the grid. The patterns that emerge from looking at the relative density of finds across a site can show where the activity was focused and, thus, where any buildings, pits or structures might be.

Concentrations of different materials can provide clues to the nature of the buried remains. For example, slag and burnt material might indicate an area of industrial activity, while tile and brick might indicate the location of a building; pottery might indicate a dwelling and large amounts of pottery of one type might suggest a warehouse or storage area. Animal bones or shell might indicate refuse pits, and large shards the waste from a kiln site.

Above On hillsides, rain and soil 'creep' can carry material a long way.

Questioning the results

There are many reasons why finds should be treated with caution. One is the effect known as 'hill wash', where rain carries soil and the objects in it slowly downhill over many years. This can lead to an accumulation of material at the bottom of a slope, far away from the true settlement or activity site higher up the hill. Or it can lead to sites in the valley bottom becoming invisible – because the deposits are buried under a deep layer of soil, below the level of the plough. Some material can also arrive on site mixed up in manure from a farm or settlement some distance away – often the pottery that has arrived in this way is small and abraded, with rounded rather than sharp edges. So surface sampling is useful in helping to locate possible sites, but like all archaeological techniques, it often raises as many questions as it answers, and answering those questions involves further investigation, using electronic survey techniques that can look below ground and tell us what might be going on.

Metal Detecting

Metal detecting has often received bad press among archaeologists because inappropriate metal-detector use can cause irreversible harm. However, when used appropriately, metal detecting can make a valuable contribution toward archaeological techniques.

The chief accusations made against metal detectorists is that they can be unwilling to reveal the location of their finds in case other detectorists visit 'their' sites, and that they dig for 'treasure' rather than for knowledge, often destroying the contextual evidence that archaeologists need to reconstruct the past. Sometimes material is stolen from sites without being reported or given to the landowner, to whom it legally belongs, and there are particularly ruthless gangs of metal detectorists who raid monuments that are protected by law.

Reporting finds

To illustrate the loss of archaeological knowledge that can occur, imagine that a detectorist finds a bronze cup.

Left Underwater metal detectors prove extremely useful when surveying wrecks.

Below An Anglo-Saxon gold pendant is excavated with great care.

That vessel will have a monetary value, because there are people who collect antiquities and are willing to pay for good examples. However, the cup has no archaeological value unless a lot more is known about where it was buried, how it got into the soil and what else was buried with it.

In fact, something similar to this happened in March 2001 in the UK when Steve Bolger, a metal detectorist, discovered a beautiful Saxon drinking vessel. He reported the find even though he didn't have to (UK law requires only gold and silver finds to be reported: not bronze unless it is prehistoric), so archaeologists were able to visit the find spot and the subsequent excavation was captured on the UK television programme 'Time

Above This copper harness decoration was unearthed during an excavation at Weedon Hill, Buckinghamshire, UK.

Team'. The vessel was the merest hint of what lay beneath the soil. A rare and unusual Saxon cemetery dating from around AD500, with bodies laid to rest along with their spears and shields, was subsequently uncovered.

Through further tests, archaeologists are hoping to find out where these people came from. This will help to fill the gaps in our knowledge about 'the Dark Ages', a name given to this period in European history because little is known about what happened at a time when Roman rule had collapsed and there were huge political and social upheavals in Europe, Africa and Asia.

The Nebra Sky Disc

Compare this with the equally true story of the spectacular Nebra Sky Disc – hailed as the world's oldest depiction of the cosmos. This circular bronze disc depicts the autumn sky, with crescent moon, sun and a cluster of stars – probably the Pleiades, or Seven Sisters, constellation. We now know that the disc was illegally excavated by metal detectorists in 1999 and sold several times before being seized by police in Switzerland, along with two metal-hilted swords dating from 1600BC, which were found close to the disc. Because the detectorists gave misleading information about the find site, it took an enormous amount of detective work before police and archaeologists arrived at the place where the disk was found, at Nebra, in Saxony-Anhalt,

Above A metal dectectorist scans a mountain site for significant finds.

Codes of practice

In most countries, using a metal detector without a licence is illegal, yet the law is often ignored as there is no effective policing. Where it is allowed, the law requires you to obtain the landowner's permission and to operate within certain legal constraints. In Great Britain, for example, certain types of finds have to be reported to the District Coroner, including gold and silver objects, prehistoric metalwork and coins over 300 years old. For full details and The Metal Detecting Code of Practice visit the website of the Portable Antiquities Scheme, which is run by the British Museum:
• www.finds.org.uk/index.php
• www.finds.org.uk/documents/ CofP1.pdf

Another code of practice is available from English Heritage:
• www.english-heritage.org.uk/ upload/pdf/Our-Portable-Past.pdf
Information on metal detecting in the United States is available from the Federation of Metal Detector and Archaeological Clubs at:
• www.fmdac.org/

Germany. Excavation here led to the finding of a hilltop sanctuary, which is now thought to be an astronomical observatory, like Stonehenge.

Common-sense guidelines

These are two contrasting examples of metal detecting: one involving naked theft of the heritage for personal gain and the other involving the responsible reporting of finds. In order to encourage more people to behave responsibly, archaeologists and metal detector clubs have drawn up codes of conduct that are full of common-sense guidance. The codes explain, for example, that permission must be gained in writing from the landowner before metal-detecting equipment is used. Detectorists are asked only to work on ground that has already been disturbed (such as ploughed land or land that has been ploughed in the past) and never to dig stratified archaeological deposits. Keeping an accurate record of finds and the spot where they were found is essential, and finds should always be reported to the local museum (in a perfect world, finds

Above Inlaid with gold and around 30cm (12in) in diameter, the spectacular bronze 'sky disc' of Nebra is the oldest known depiction of the heavens.

should be donated to that museum, rather than sold for personal gain).

On the positive side, detectorists can also do a huge amount of good: dedicated metal-detector users who follow best practice guidelines have uncovered thousands of objects that might never have been known to archaeology. In Great Britain, more than 67,000 archaeological items and 427 pieces of treasure were discovered and reported by members of the public in 2005 alone. Some of the more spectacular examples, from Viking gold arm bands to medieval brooches, can be seen on the British Museum's Portable Antiquities Scheme website (*see box*).

Archaeological research

Of course, metal detecting also has a place within archaeological research. Most archaeologists now use metal detectors as part of surface sampling, simply because mud-coated metal

objects in ploughed soil are easy to miss when scanning by eye. For the same reason, metal detectors are used in excavations, to detect metal objects that diggers might miss when they clear soil from a site. It can also help locate buried metal so that a digger knows it is there in advance and can excavate it carefully to avoid accidental damage to the buried object.

Geophysical Surveys

'Geofizz' is the shorthand name for 'geophysical survey'. This involves using a battery of remote sensing devices linked to computers to show what lies beneath the soil. Geophysics is one of the most useful developments in archaeology of recent years.

Where once archaeologists had to guess at what lay under the soil from the evidence of aerial photographs and surface sampling, now they can use various devices that detect differences in the electrical or magnetic properties of features below the surface of the soil, provided it is not water-logged. As a result they know in advance not only where to dig, but also what they are likely to find. Drawing on clues from their research, archaeologists choose the most suitable method for that site.

Resistivity

One type of equipment is an electrical resistance meter, which has probes that measure higher or lower resistance to the flow of electricity. A stone wall, for example, impedes the flow and registers as an area of high resistance, whereas a pit or ditch conducts electricity more effectively and is registered as an area of low resistance.

These areas of higher and lower resistance are recorded as signals by the resistivity meter and can be converted,

Above A seismic survey can be used to detect the depth of buried features below ground.

using a computer programme, into a graphic image, showing areas of high (black or dark grey) and low (light grey to white) impedance. It is usually possible to interpret this pattern and see the clear outlines of buildings or ditches, but often it is only when the digging begins that it is possible to say what it is exactly that has produced the pattern of variations. There are plenty

Which type of geophysical survey equipment to use?

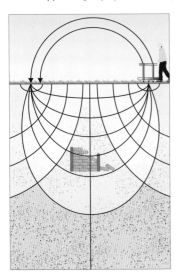

Above A resistivity meter records the levels of resistance encountered when a weak electrical current passes through the ground. Walls tend to resist current; pits and ditches show low resistance.

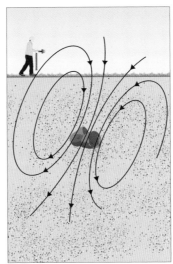

Above Magnetometry detects buried features whose magnetic field differs from the natural background field – often this is because the polarity has been altered through heat, so the technique is good for finding kilns and pottery.

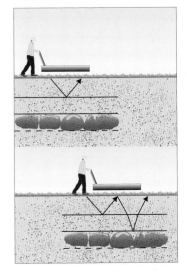

Above Ground-penetrating radar detects the speed with which radar signals bounce back when sent from the surface; the differences can be used to detect rock, soil, water, walls, pavements and voids.

of non-archaeological possibilities, ranging from buried pipes or electrical cables, to natural pockets of iron-rich soil or buried rubbish. Waterlogged soils are also difficult to survey because the ubiquity of such a good conductor of electricity swamps any minor fluctuations that might otherwise be detected from buried features.

For this reason, the technicians who specialize in geophysical survey are always guarded in their interpretation of the results. Scientifically, all that a resistivity survey can tell you is that there is an anomaly, in other words, something below the soil that is causing a pattern different to that of the normal electrical resistance properties of the soil. Even so, such surveys are very helpful in pinpointing precisely where the buried features are, and in showing areas that are empty of features.

Resistance meters are good at detecting solid features, such as the streets and buildings of a Roman town. This makes resistivity survey more useful to archaeologists dealing with classical sites in Italy, for example, and less so for those looking for the temporary camping sites of nomadic hunters.

Magnetometry

By contrast, the excavator of a camp site might gain better results from the use of a magnetometer. This measures the normal or natural magnetic field for the soil on the site being investigated. Sensors can then detect objects or areas below the soil that have a different polarity. That difference might indicate the presence of alien geology – for example, flints or worked stone with a stronger magnetic field than the background geology. Often it indicates areas of burning, which has the effect of fixing the direction of the magnetic field of the burnt earth at the place and time of the firing. Thus a hearth or a barbecue pit, or clay objects such as bricks or pottery, will show up as having a different magnetic field to the surrounding soil – and might thus indicate the presence below the soil of pits or ditches holding burnt material.

Great Britain's biggest geophysical survey

In 2002, the Landscape Research Centre completed work on a 220-ha (545-acre) geophysical survey of Yorkshire's Vale of Pickering, which involved members of the survey team walking an average of 10km (6 miles) a day, every day for two years. The results, plotted at a scale of 1:1000, filled a 3.5m- (11½ft-)long piece of paper. Geophysical survey was chosen because of the area's unusual geomorphology, with blown sand overlying buried archaeological deposits, preventing sites being visible as crop marks. The results showed that this 'empty' landscape was covered in archaeology, including Bronze Age tracks, dense Iron Age and Roman settlements, as well as Anglo-Saxon settlements and a cemetery.

Above A geophysical survey at the Vale showed part of a Late Iron Age and Roman period 'ladder settlement', comprising a ditched trackway with a series of overlapping settlement enclosures at the top of the image, and distinctive sub-rectangular anomalies. These indicate the presence of Early Anglo-Saxon cavity floor buildings incorporating deep pits, designed to provide a dry air space beneath the floors of the buildings and invariably used as rubbish tips when they went out of use. The enhanced magnetic susceptibility of the discarded rubbish makes these features stand out quite distinctively in this type of survey.

However, there is one main deficiency of magnetometry – subtle differences in a magnetic field can easily be swamped by a large object or an object that is highly magnetic, or by one that is made of a metallic material that distorts the natural background polarity. This means that buried cables and metal pipes can make it impossible to conduct an accurate survey, as can a metal fence, a pylon or overhead electrical cables.

Ground penetrating radar

Because of the cost of the equipment, ground penetrating radar (GPR) is not as widely applied in archaeology as it is in oil prospecting, engineering or geological survey. The great advantage it has for archaeologists is in showing the depth of buried objects, adding the third dimension of depth to the two-dimensional plan view obtained from resistivity and magnetometry survey.

With GPR, a radar signal is sent into the ground, which bounces back to a receiver at different strengths and different time intervals. This signal is then converted to data about the solidity and nature of the soil and features within it. In some soils the results can be startlingly clear. Used in the uniformly sandy soils of a desert, small objects such as flint tools can be detected and pinpointed precisely. However, some types of subsoil such as clay are far less easy to penetrate than others and rocky soils scatter the signal, creating lots of meaningless feedback noise.

Geophysical Survey Methods

Geophysical surveys are now commonplace in archaeology because they are non-invasive (they produce useful data without destroying or harming the archaeology) and they enable large areas of ground to be surveyed at speed – at a fraction of the cost of stripping and excavating the same area.

Above A 'gradiometer' records magnetic variations to pinpoint buried archaeology.

The same basic methods are used to perform a geophysical survey, regardless of which type of equipment is being used (and the same basic approach also applies to field surveys, field walking and the use of metal detectors). Because survey techniques often produce better results when used in combination, archaeologists will usually deploy a whole battery of remote-sensing techniques combined with field walking when beginning their work of understanding a site (*see* Breaking New Ground).

The long walk

Doing a geophysical survey involves the somewhat tedious process of walking in straight lines backward and forward across the site, following guided tape measures and string lines that are set out in advance to mark out the survey area. In the case of resistivity or magnetometry equipment, the surveyor carries a pair of probes mounted on a frame. The probes are inserted into the ground over and again at intervals of about one stride's length, or 1m (3ft), until the whole site is covered. One small site – say a suspected burial mound – might require the surveyor to walk up and down 100 times along a 50m (165ft) line, spaced at 1m (3ft) intervals – a

Above (top) Readings can be taken quickly and easily to log the position of features.

Above (bottom) Data logged by the resistivity meter is processed by computer to produce a map of buried ditches, pits and walls.

Below Seeing beneath the soil with a resistivity meter: following a grid line marked out with string, readings are taken at 1m (3ft) intervals.

total of 5km (3 miles). With ground penetrating radar, the effort is not quite so demanding because the survey equipment is pulled across the ground on wheels.

Data analysis

The data that is captured by the survey instruments includes global positioning coordinates that pinpoint precisely where on the earth the readings were taken, plus the data from the ground, which then has to be interpreted. The data is transferred to a computer and converted, using specially designed software, into a series of contour lines, dots or grey-scale tones that are displayed on the screen or printed out.

The challenge is to interpret this pattern and understand what it is showing. This is where it is essential to be familiar with the shapes and patterns of typical archaeological sites and features. Identifying a Roman villa, for example, is relatively easy, but it takes skill and local knowledge to distinguish between a buried ditch and a buried bank, or between the circular ditch that surrounds a Bronze-Age burial mound and one of similar size surrounding an Iron-Age round house.

Often this is impossible unless you combine the data from a geophysical survey with finds from field walking or information from an aerial survey. Indeed, it is sometimes said that remote sensing works best if you already know what you are looking for! This is not as contradictory as it might sound. You might, for example, know from field walking that there is a kiln site somewhere in the vicinity, but not precisely where. Doing a geophysical survey will help to determine the exact location of an archaeological site that is known to exist.

Successes and failures

An example of the potentially misleading results of a geophysical survey comes from Leominster, Herefordshire, where local archaeologists used ground penetrating radar (GPR) to investigate an area close to the town's historic priory church, which was due

Locating royal burials

In 2006 GPR was used with great success when archaeologists surveyed the floor of Edward the Confessor's Chapel at Westminster Abbey. The chapel was used as a mausoleum by the medieval kings and queens of England until the 14th century. GPR was deployed to locate graves, which could then be attributed to various members of the royal family by reference to medieval documents. Using GPR enabled this to be done without disturbing the splendid mosaic marble pavement that covers the chapel floor.

Left View of the shrine floor; image generated using ground-penetrating radar. These results show traces of a number of burials but the main image is the dark area – this is the packing used to seal the tomb entrance.

Right An image of a shipwreck was created from a sonar geophysical device. The data is collected as thousands of 'echo points'.

Below The torpedo-shaped echolocation device is known informally as a 'fish'.

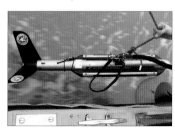

to be developed for use as a parking lot. The GPR survey revealed a circular structure beneath the soil that was the right shape and in the right position to be a baptistery. Excited archaeologists went into print in leading journals predicting the discovery of an important religious building. Sadly, it was not to be: when the soil was removed, the feature turned out to be a circular stone wall around flowerbeds and a flagpole built in the 1930s.

However, GPR was used rather more successfully at New York State's West Point Foundry, where only the

foundation walls survive. This is where railway engineers built the United States' first locomotive, dubbed *The Best Friend*. Although archaeologists knew that the machinery in the foundry was driven by a giant waterwheel, they were not able to locate the water channels that supplied the wheel. Rather than excavating large areas, ground penetrating radar (GPR) was used to search for the channels, which led them to the buried pipework and stone lined culverts that underlie the cobbled foundry floor. They were able to find the source and preserve the floor.

The Message in the Hedges

Not all archaeological survey techniques involve high-tech equipment: some archaeologists use hedges and vegetation as a clue to the way that the landscape was used in the past. Hedge survey is one of the more intriguing developments in archaeology in recent decades.

Above Hawthorn is quick growing and much used in modern hedges.

In the 1970s amateur and professional archaeologists expressed great excitement when claims were made that a simple dating formula had been created based on counting species. According to this theory, all you had to do was count the woodland tree species in a 91.5-m (100-yd) stretch of hedge, and each species was said to represent an additional 100 years in the age of the hedge. This means that a species-rich hedge with a mix of elm, oak, blackthorn, hawthorn, holly, ash, willow, wild pear, elderflower and field maple might be a 1,000-year-old Saxon hedge, whereas a hawthorn hedge with few other species is likely to have been planted more recently during the 19th or 20th centuries.

Woodland origins

The assumption behind this formula was that older hedges started out as woodland, however, bit by bit the timber from the wood was cleared, leaving a new field bound by such trees as the farmer chose to leave as a cattle barrier or property line. There was another theory, which held that the hedges gained species through time as wind-born or bird-born seeds became trapped by the hedge, germinated, grew and seeded to become an established part of the matrix.

Of course, nothing in life is ever that simple, and hedge specialists working in Norfolk, Shropshire and Northumbria have now concluded, after studying thousands of miles of hedge, that the truth to the origins of a species-rich hedge is more complex and more interesting than the 100-year formula suggests. (For more indepth coverage of the subject, see *Hedgerow History: Ecology, History and Landscape Character* by Gerry Barnes and Tom Williamson).

Challenging assumptions

Long-established hedges were often replanted and realigned in the 18th and 19th centuries to conform more closely to the ideals of agricultural improvers – crooked hedges were straightened and ancient hedges with large timbers or mature trees were cropped and replaced by quickthorn. Diaries and farm records show that species-rich hedges can be very recent, because farmers used the local woods as a source for hedging material, taking seedlings of any variety they could find. Archdeacon Plymley, writing in the 18th century, wrote, for example: 'I enclosed a small common…a trench

Above The lush landscape of the Arenal region, Costa Rica, has been subject to intensive aerial and ground survey.

Tracing ancient footpaths

Satellite imaging has recently been used to spot changes in vegetation that indicate the routes of 2,000-year-old processional pathways. They are in the Arenal region of present-day Costa Rica, and are invisible to observers on the ground. The repeated use of these paths to navigate rugged terrain between small villages and ancestral cemeteries over several centuries created shallow trenches, which now collect moisture. The lusher growth produced by vegetation in response to the extra water can be detected in infrared satellite photography, even in places where thick vegetation prevents archaeologists from treading today, or where the trenches are now hidden after being filled in by layers of ash from prehistoric volcanic eruptions.

Since studying these processional routes, archaeologists have found pottery that suggests they were used for more than 1,000 years, from roughly 500BC to AD600. People returned to them year after year for ritual feasts, despite abandoning their villages because of eruptions from the nearby Arenal Volcano.

Above When excavating historic buildings, such as farmhouses, archaeologists pay close attention to the vegetation of the site.

was dug of considerable width and depth. Strong bushes of hazel, willow, hawthorn or whatever could be met with in a neighbouring wood, were planted in this trench…young hawthorns or hollies or their berries, were [then] put between the stems.'

However, although archaeologists have to treat the results of hedge survey with some caution, they don't have to throw hedge study out of their toolbox altogether. If a combination of indicators are found – multiple species, sinuous hedges, planted on a bank, perhaps beside a sunken lane, and perhaps also forming the boundary of a parish or farm – the accumulation of detail begins to suggest that the hedge, or its ancestors, have been around for some time. Studies in France, Germany and the Netherlands suggest that the hedges used to separate fields from lanes are typically 700 years old, and the word 'hedge' itself is derived from the Anglo Saxon word *hecg* (*hecke* in Old German, *haag* in Dutch).

Revelations from plants

In recent years, archaeologists have also begun to pay close attention to the types of plants growing on ancient sites

and on the differences in vegetation density. Using geochemical analysis, they have discovered that where animals have been kept or where manure – of human or animal origin – has been stored or deliberately buried, chemicals in the soil encourage taller growth of plants that like a high phosphate level, such as nettles. This effect can persist not for years or decades but for centuries. On medieval village sites, for example, this phenomenon has been used to distinguish between houses built for humans and byres for cattle; or to determine which end of a longhouse the humans lived in and which end housed the animals.

Some plants, by contrast, favour very thin, poor soils, where they thrive because of the lack of competition from more vigorous competitors.

Above Nettles with nitrogen-rich disturbed soil and dense growth often indicate places where animals have been fed in the past.

Clover is one such plant, and in summer, when the clover is more obvious because it is in flower, it is possible to survey buried walls and solid features simply by looking for the lines of white clover flowers.

Below Woods rich in hazel were once planted to provide timber for fences, baskets and thatching materials.

Above Slow-growing holly is often found in older hedges: in folklore, the prickly leaves were said to guard property from evil spirits.

Case Study: Survey at Portus Romae

The British and Italian archaeologists who studied Portus Romae, the ancient port of imperial Rome, set out with the deliberate intention of seeing how much information they could gather without doing any excavation – they were met with great success.

Above Reconstruction of warehouse fronts at Portus, where shipped goods were stored.

Passengers flying into Rome's Fiumicino Airport might be forgiven for thinking that the lake they can see from the left-hand side of the aeroplane, just south of the runway on the northern bank of the River Tiber, is a natural salt-water lagoon of the type that is very common along this stretch of the Italian coast. However, if they look again they will see that it is actually hexagonal (with six straight sides) in shape.

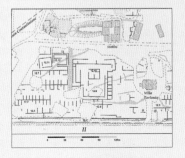

Evidence found in a name and location

This unnatural shape, spotted on maps and aerial photographs, alerted the archaeologists to the presence of something unusual at the mouth of the Tiber, and placename research revealed that it was known as Portus – Latin for 'door' or 'gateway', but also the word for a harbour that has given us the English word 'port'.

Searching through archives revealed that excavations had taken place in 1867/8, in the 1930s and again in the 1960s. These revealed that Emperor Claudius (who ruled from AD41–54) had built an offshore harbour at the

Left and below Magnetometer survey evidence for the location of the temple and warehouses at Portus (*below*), with magnetic anomalies appearing as solid dark lines. The drawn plan (*left*) interprets this data, plotting the location and possible structure of these buried features.

Tiber mouth, but as Rome grew it proved to be too small to cope with the volume of shipping bringing grain and oil from various parts of the Empire, especially from North Africa, to feed the citizens of Rome. One of Cladius's successors, Emperor Trajan (AD98–117), built the huge hexagonal inner harbour, which is 700m (3,000ft) across, with sides of 358m (1,175ft) in length. In doing so, Trajan did what Rome had done on other occasions and borrowed ideas from its bitter enemy, the Carthaginians – the source of the hexagonal form of the inland port.

Discovering a large port complex

Previous excavations had looked at only a fraction of the site, so geophysical survey techniques were used to see just how much else remained below ground. Magnetometry was used as the primary survey technique because this can generally be undertaken more rapidly. Resistivity was also deployed to explore areas of particular interest or uncertainty.

The magnetometer survey revealed that the port complex was a massive 1,000ha (2,470 acres) in extent. The survey also led to several major new discoveries. One of these finds was the existence of a large canal 40m (130ft) wide linking the hexagonal harbour to the River Tiber. The survey team also discovered the buried remains of a large and imposing columned building placed where it

would be clearly visible to every ship entering the port. A suggestion is that perhaps the building was a temple, which might have been fronted by a statue of the emperor, emphasizing to travellers from the far-flung corners of the Empire that they had now arrived in the capital, Rome.

A massive sorting task

Scores of structures were located by the magnetometer survey, and they were all associated with the bustling public, commercial and industrial life of the harbour, so the team used field walking to try and sort out which buildings were used for what purpose. A huge quantity of pottery, tile, brick and iron had been brought up to the surface by ploughing, and the sheer amount of material that needed to be weighed and measured presented the archaeologists with a major task, but it proved to be an effective way of allowing significant patterns and differences to emerge.

The pottery and building materials collected by the survey team were sorted by class into fine tablewares, coarser cooking and storage wares and amphorae – the distinctive tall two-handled jars used by the Romans for transporting oil, wine, olives and fish sauce – and the building materials were sorted by function into roof tiles, brick, floor tiles, column fragments, and so on. The relative densities of these different materials across the site were then mapped by computer.

This enabled the team to guess which buildings might have been warehouses (large quantities of amphorae used as storage jars), which might have been industrial complexes (large quantities of iron slag) and which ones might have been grain warehouses (almost no finds), shops (a wide variety of different types of pottery) or offices and customs buildings (cubes of tesserae from mosaic floors). Some buildings produced lots of marble

Right Hypothetical computer reconstruction of late 2nd century AD warehouses (Grande Magazzini di Settimio Severo) at Portus.

Reconstructing the development of Portus

Right The Port of Claudius originated in the 1st century AD. Connected to the River Tiber by canals, it was an unusual choice of location due to poor shelter and a tendency to silt up.

Below The distinctive hexagonal pool (*below right*) took shape during the reign of Trajan (98–117BC). It had good storage capacity and was lined with warehouses. The later antique port (*below*), which survived until the 6th century AD, remained fortified, although building activity had slackened by this period.

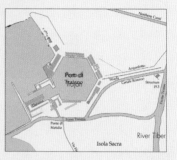

fragments, suggesting that raw marble was shipped to Portus from elsewhere, turned into columns and other architectural elements on site, then shipped up river to Rome.

A thriving trading centre

Looking at the origin of the pottery found on site, it was clear that most of the imports shipped into Portus and bound for Rome came from Africa and the eastern Mediterranean. Dating of the finds revealed a further surprise:

it was evident that the port continued in use at least into the early 7th century. This ties up with the historical evidence for Portus as the seat of a bishopric in the 4th century, granted municipal status under the Emperor Constantine, when the Basilica of Sant' Ippolito was built on the site. And if Portus was thriving then, perhaps Rome – the imperial capital – was thriving, too, despite the picture of barbarian attack and sacking that has come down to us from history.

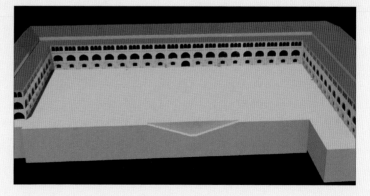

BREAKING NEW GROUND

The moment that an archaeologist puts a spade into the ground and begins to dig, he or she enters into a whole series of professional and academic obligations – to dig scientifically, to record accurately what is found, to treat all the archaeology with equal respect (rather than, as in the past, disregarding recent material in favour of Roman, for example), to make proper arrangements for the conservation, study and future storage of all the finds, to publish a record of what was found and to make provision for archiving the results of the excavation so that future archaeologists have access to them. To this onerous list, add another of health and safety responsibilities and legal obligations. Yet, still there is the sheer excitement of digging, and the sense of embarking on a voyage of discovery. No matter how thoroughly the desktop analysis was done that precedes the excavation, it is almost always the case that there is more below the ground than anyone predicted.

Opposite Archaeologists use small trowels to excavate the boundary wall to a historic harbour site.

Above The earth is delicately prised away from two skulls lying in situ in a burial site.

Above An archaeology student practises trowelling techniques during a research excavation.

Above Unravelling the history of this Roman site requires careful excavation and observation.

Excavation Strategies

Archaeology is complex, so it is not surprising that there is not one simple method of digging. There are many excavation strategies, some or all of which might be used on a site. The differences between rescue and research-led archaeology can account for the way in which a site is excavated.

As mentioned earlier, development-led 'rescue' archaeology is performed in response to the imminent destruction of archaeological remains that are being threatened by new development. This means that development-led archaeologists are more constrained than research archaeologists – the site of the excavation is not one that they have chosen to investigate to answer research questions, but one that has been dictated by the planning and development process. They have very little time to rescue any archaeology that may be present.

By contrast, research archaeology is elective – it is something chosen to answer important questions that can only be answered through excavating a particular site that has been identified as capable of yielding those answers.

Engineering solutions

Developers do everything they can to avoid the costs involved in large-scale excavation, and archaeologists have a similar desire to dig only as much as is absolutely necessary, because of the destructive nature of archaeology. Working together, developers and archaeologists aim to design buildings and structures that will avoid harming the archaeology.

One way to do this is by simply avoiding the archaeology. If the planned route of a gas pipeline is heading straight for a field that looks, from aerial photography, as if it contains a prehistoric enclosure, every effort will be made to change the pipeline route. On an urban development site, engineers will try to place the piles and foundations needed to support the new

Above If topsoil has previously been disturbed it can be removed by a mechnical digger.

building well away from archaeologically sensitive areas. One common strategy is to build a raft of recycled concrete over the top of the archaeological remains and build on top of the raft, without disturbing the soil below. Another is to use 'flying foundations', which are designed to carry the weight of the building on relatively slender piles that only disturb, say, 10 per cent of the buried archaeology rather than 25 per cent.

Preservation *in situ*

One strategy is known in the archaeological trade by the acronym PARIS, for 'Preserving Archaeology *In Situ*' – *in situ* being Latin for 'in place', or 'not removed'. It aims to preserve as much archaeology as possible in the place and in the state in which it was originally formed or deposited. However, because it is rarely possible to leave 100 per cent of the archaeology *in situ*, archaeologists often deal with various situations where very small areas of the site are excavated – using techniques that are often described as 'keyhole archaeology'.

Keyhole archaeology

A 'watching brief' might be one part of keyhole archaeology. It involves being on site as engineers dig foundation trenches or drill piles into the soil, to

Left At their most successful, test pits function as a small-scale excavation, presenting a microcosm of the whole site.

Right An archaeologist watches as heavy machinery opens a trench for inspection. He has marked the traces of a feature in the soil and must monitor digging carefully.

Right An archaeologist watches as heavy machinery opens a trench for inspection. He has marked the traces of a feature in the soil and must monitor digging carefully.

see if anything archaeological turns up in the excavated soil. Watching briefs are only used in circumstances where prior desktop research suggests there isn't any archaeology; in other words it is a back-up strategy. In theory, if the excavating machinery starts to produce archaeological remains, engineering work can stop while a proper investigation is carried out. In practice, it is often very difficult to interpret the odd finds that might emerge in the bucket of a digger, no matter how carefully the digger driver tries to be, so this is a ham-fisted form of excavation compared with the precision of a trowel wielded by an experienced archaeologist.

Test pits

Preferable to a watching brief is the opportunity to sink test pits or trial trenches into the ground, targeting the areas that will be destroyed in later construction work, such as the areas where piles are to be sunk. Yet this can be a frustrating type of archaeology, too, because small-scale excavation nearly always raises more questions than it answers. Imagine trying to understand the picture depicted in a complex jigsaw when you only have a few small pieces to go on. The problem with both test pits and trial trenches is that, however carefully they are sited, they might miss significant parts of the archaeology. One example occurred when the Eton Rowing Lake was excavated at Dorney, along the River Thames near Windsor in southern England. Numerous trial trenches missed an enormous deposit of worked Neolithic flint that was found once the engineering work began.

However, test pits do have a value. They can be used to examine the nature and extent of any archaeological remains, and to make judgements about whether further large-scale excavation is needed.

Research excavation

Although rescue and research-led excavation techniques are not mutually exclusive, there are often important differences in how an excavation proceeds. The director of a research excavation is less constrained in terms of time or the choice of technique, and the placing of trenches can be dictated by the nature of the archaeology and the questions that are being asked, rather than by engineering decisions about where to place shafts, piles or trenches for service pipes.

The research archaeologist is often in the fortunate position of being able to plan several seasons of work at one site, and the time between one season and the next can be used as important thinking time, during which finds can be analysed and excavation aims modified in the light of feedback from specialists. In commercial work, the tight time constraints that apply on a building site demand fast work by the archaeologist and little time for second thoughts or to go back and rethink any interpretations.

Rescuing London's heritage

Preservation in situ normally means preserving archaeological remains without excavating them, on the basis that it is better to preserve than to destroy. Sometimes it can also mean excavating the remains and then preserving what was found, rather than, as often happens, digging a big hole and taking away all the archaeology to allow an underground parking lot or plant room to be built.

In 1988 Museum of London archaeologists made an unexpected discovery in London when they unearthed the city's Roman amphitheatre on the site of a new art gallery. These

Above Excavating a Roman timber box from a drain during the rescue excavation at London's buried Roman amphitheatre.

2,000-year-old remains were so important that the site was declared a protected monument, and the masonry of the amphitheatre was incorporated into the design of the art gallery's basement, where it is now a popular visitor attraction.

Large-scale Excavation

The most satisfying archaeology, and the most rewarding, is the excavation of a large area, so that a part of the landscape can be investigated in its entirety, leading to an understanding of continuity and change over time. This can occur in both development-led and research-led archaeology.

Sometimes, the scale of development is so large that substantial resources are allocated to a project, enabling work to be done that is the envy of research-based archaeologists. This is especially the case when the developer wants to be seen as acting responsibly toward the natural and historic environment and goes beyond the minimum that is legally required, giving archaeologists the money and time to do the best possible job.

This has been the case in England, for example, with the construction of new industrial, commercial and housing estates around the new town of Peterborough, and in the Cotswold Water Park, where huge areas of countryside have been excavated for sand and gravel. Within cities, the equivalent is the development of a whole block, involving deep excavations, as occurred in London during the construction of new underground stations on the Jubilee Line, or in Istanbul, during the construction of a new railway tunnel beneath the Bosporus, linking Europe and Asia.

Total archaeology

Excavations of large areas are at the extreme end of the archaeological scale and are extremely expensive to mount, not just because of the costs of hiring skilled people and all the necessary equipment, but because the excavation costs typically amount to only 40 per cent of the total cost of the project. Post-excavation costs – for conserving and studying all the material found during excavation, and for publishing and archiving the results – account for the balance, and these can be considerably higher if the results are so important that a decision is made to fund a permanent visitor centre or museum on the site.

Total excavation is, therefore, rare. It is often the case that such archaeology is funded by public utilities or govern-

Above Large-scale excavation may involve dividing a site, such as the ancient farm shown above, into several smaller sub-sites.

mental bodies as part of the infra-structural cost of achieving a publicly desirable objective such as new transport systems, pipelines, Olympic facilities or mineral extraction.

Putting things into context

Where such opportunities occur, they offer an important counterbalance to small-scale excavation, which gives in-depth information about a particular site. From the information gained during a small-scale excavation, archaeologists try to develop general theories that apply to all monuments of that type. So excavating one Romano-British farmstead, for example, can provide data about the accommodation for humans and animals, field size and number, crops grown and storage methods, whether the farm was self-sufficient or involved in specialized production for trade, how and when the farm was founded, evolved and was abandoned, and what changes occurred during the period that it was in use. (*For a case-study example, see Frocester Court.*)

Large-scale archaeology can then put this information into context and reveal patterns at the level of a whole landscape. Is the Romano-British farmstead typical or unusual, what came before and after, what can be learnt about the use of the landscape over a long period of time, does the

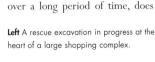

Left A rescue excavation in progress at the heart of a large shopping complex.

Right Excavations at the site of London Heathrow Airport's Terminal 5 uncovered the straight line of Roman field ditches and the post pits of a prehistoric timber monument.

pattern revealed by the landscape suggest slow steady continuity of people and culture, and are there distinct episodes of change and innovation, war and conquest, culture succeeding culture?

Excavation at Heathrow

The site of London Heathrow Airport's Terminal 5 building was the location for one of Great Britain's largest-ever excavations. The site, over 100ha (250 acres), took 18 months to investigate and the story that emerged perhaps represents the potted history of a large part of England.

The first evidence of human activity in the heavily forested landscape of 8,000 years ago (the Mesolithic, or Middle Stone Age) consists of cooking pits that were visited again and again and used for many generations – evidence, perhaps, of regular ritual gatherings. Bigger monuments were then constructed in the Neolithic period (4000–3600BC), consisting of rows of posts and long ditches and banks, built in such a way as to suggest that the builders were aware of the older pits and wished to incorporate them into their own structures.

These monuments continued in use for hundreds of years as people slowly cleared the woodland landscape, creating fields and permanent settlements, with trackways, houses, food storage pits and waterholes. Before this, land was probably shared by the whole community, but with settlement came the first boundaries (ditches and banks with hedges or timber palisades) dating from 2000BC (the Early Bronze Age), which show that people were claiming ownership of specific areas of land for the first time.

Right In a classic rescue project, a Christian funeral basilica from the 5th century AD was excavated in 2004 in Marseille, France, prior to the construction of a parking lot on the site.

Above After stripping the topsoil by machine, more delicate excavation begins.

Above On such large sites as Heathrow, digital recording comes to the fore.

In the Middle Bronze Age (1500–1100BC), landholdings begin to consolidate into fewer but larger settlements. This process of nucleation continues through the early Iron Age (from 700BC), when there are only two settlements. By the time of the Roman conquest, there was just one large settlement at the centre of the block. From this period into the Roman period, there was no fundamental change to the architecture of the landscape. New land divisions respect older monuments and there is no sense that the past was forgotten or ignored, until the 3rd century AD, when a ladder-like field system was imposed on the landscape without reference to anything that had been before. The Romans simply transformed the world they found and made it new, but only after two centuries of occupation. Their field systems and settlements lasted only a short time. The village of the Roman era died out and was replaced by a new village in the 12th century.

Setting up a Research Project

Keyhole archaeology and total excavation represent the extremes of archaeological practice, but most excavations lie in the middle ground. Here is a more typical approach to how a research project is set up, staffed by a mix of experienced archaeologists and students, trainees and volunteers.

Above These archaeologists are setting up an excavation site in Kazakhstan.

The logistics involved in setting up an excavation are very complex, and television programmes based on the idea that archaeological problems can be resolved in a long weekend are misleading. Those programmes actually involve many weeks of preparation work beforehand, involving a team of producers employed on a regular basis, and they often show only a small part of what is, in reality, a much longer programme of archaeological research.

Before digging begins

Digs are usually run by a director (often with one or more deputies to share the load). The first task facing the director of a research-based excavation is to gain permission to dig. Legal constraints and property laws mean that you cannot simply dig at will. In many countries, a licence to excavate is required, especially if the site to be investigated is legally classified as a protected monument. Gaining a licence often involves a great deal of previous research to convince the relevant state heritage authorities that excavation really is necessary, because the site is under threat or because digging is the only way to answer key research questions.

As well as undertaking a very thorough desktop assessment and proving that the site fits established and agreed research strategies, a common tactic is to form a project steering group and invite fellow researchers to act as advisers to the project. That way they can validate your work, act as referees and vouch for the value and necessity of the work. The same experts might also agree to be part of the post-excavation team, providing invaluable expertise in identifying and analysing the finds.

The end result of this initial process is a formal document known as a 'Project Design', which sets out clearly what is known about the site, why excavation is justified, what the aims of the excavation are and what contribution will be made to the knowledge of the past through excavation of the site.

Paying the bills

Another essential and time-consuming task is ensuring that the costs of the excavation are planned for and that funding is in place to meet all the expenses. Excavations are often funded by a mosaic of small grants from archaeological societies, charitable trusts, donations and sponsorship. Or they might be funded by academic institutions, learned societies and research academies, such as the internationals schools of archaeology maintained by various governments in parts of the world that are the major

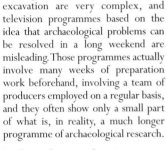

Left The ongoing Tayinat Archaeological Project, abbreviated to TAP, is an initiative by the University of Toronto to chart the rise of urban civilizations in ancient Turkey.

Right University students will sometimes work in pairs on a research dig, one to excavate and the other to record what is found.

focus for archaeological research. (The UK, German, United States, Swiss, Norwegian, Dutch and Finnish governments all have research schools in Rome, Athens, Ankara, Nairobi, Tehran, Amman and Jerusalem.) Once again, this is where forward planning is essential, because grant applications have to be made months in advance of the dig and approaches need to be made well in advance to potential donors of equipment and money.

Multi-tasking skills

The director has to be a person of many skills, because while research and financial management abilities are essential to the dig's viability, there are many mundane tasks to attend to as well. When will the dig take place? If the dig depends on volunteers, then it has to take place at a time when volunteers are available, and that usually means timing it for university holiday periods. In fact much research archaeology takes place in the summer for this reason.

How many people are needed and how will they be recruited? Students of archaeology form the backbone of the workforce, simply because it is a requirement of many university courses that students spend a minimum period of time gaining fieldwork experience. This core workforce can be augmented by volunteers from the community, including members of a local archaeology society.

In either case, the excavation might be advertised months ahead in archaeological magazines and websites. Before advertising the excavation, key decisions have to be made about how long will be needed for the dig to take place, the number of people required and their skill levels, and where the diggers will be accommodated and fed and how much they will be charged. The fees that participants pay for training and daily sustenance are a vital part of the business plan for any dig.

Human resources

Typically, a research dig will take place over a 4- to 6-week period, employing a workforce of 30 people or more. Some excavations provide accommodation and food, while others may provide no more than a campsite and a water supply.

If that sounds rather bohemian, it is often the case that digs can be very memorable experiences that live in people's memories for the rest of their lives. Working as a member of a team on a project that might be located in a beautiful part of the countryside, often with good weather (possibly also with excellent local food) and involving a mix of physical and intellectual challenges is a powerful formula for enticing participants. The social side of

Above With large numbers of people on a project, briefing meetings are essential. These are held on a regular basis during excavation – usually at the start and/or close of the day.

an excavation also plays an important role (which is one reason why archaeologists who dig together often become close friends).

A participant might find him or herself working as part of a multi-cultural, multinational team, working in a part of the world where he or she becomes part of the local community for a period of time. Even if a participant is not planning to become a professional archaeologist, going on a dig is an excellent way to get close to other cultures and meet people from other backgrounds.

The Tools for the Job

Having sorted out the human and financial resources, the next task a director faces is that of bringing together the many tools that are needed on an average excavation. The precise list of tools and equipment will depend on the scale, character and duration of the dig.

Even a small simple excavation that needs only the basic resources can require a long checklist of equipment. To start with, there is the equipment used for doing the actual digging, string, nails and tape measures for marking out the trenches, a turfing tool for cutting and skimming off the turf, and spades, picks and shovels for moving earth. On top of that the digging process will call for brushes, hand shovels, buckets, the wheelbarrow and planks used for taking the excavated soil away from the site for wet and dry sieving (sifting) and for building a safe spoil tip (heap).

As the site begins to yield archaeological material, waterproof labels and pens will be necessary for labelling finds and soil changes, and bags will be required for storing finds and soil samples. Every find and soil type has to be recorded using previously prepared record sheets. Further detailed records of the site might also need to be captured, and this can involve using a camera and drawing plans and sections using grids, graph paper, tape measures and pencils.

The digger's pride and joy

Most of the tools used in archaeology can be acquired from other people's toolkits – the builder, surveyor, gardener or artist. However, there is one tool that is distinctively archaeological: the trowel. This has to be a special sort of trowel, not the curved

Above The ubiquitous trowel is the key tool in an archaeologist's fieldwork kit. Seasoned archaeologists may carry more than one, choosing the best tool for the job in hand.

type used by gardeners or the large flat trowels preferred by bricklayers, masons or plasterers. Working with archaeologists over many years, the British tool manufacturer Spear & Jackson has developed a specially designed tool, called the WHS (named after the tool's original manufacturers, William Hunt & Sons), that is forged from steel with a 10cm (4in) blade and a comfortable rubber handle and finger guard.

However, as with all things, trowel preferences can be cultural: while British archaeologists favour the WHS model, many mainland European archaeologists prefer the slightly shorter and broader Italian-made Battiferro pointing trowel. In North America, the slightly longer 11.4cm (4½in) Marshalltown pointing trowel is the preferred choice of many archaeologists, and though it might be much more expensive than its European counterparts, it does come with its own belt holster, so there is less risk of putting it down somewhere and forgetting where.

Trowels have many functions. Used as a blade, lever and scraper, trowels represent the archaeological equivalent

Left The volunteer archaeologist is likely to encounter a selection of tools, including creature comforts such as a thermal flask or sun hat to plastic ties for 'bagging and tagging' archaeological finds.

Sun hat and water bottle to prevent dehydration

Tape measure for drawing plans

String for marking out the edges of a site

Trowels

Metal pegs for securing labels and string lines

Plasterer's leaf

Plastic ties for securing bags

Gloves to prevent blisters

Dental toothpick for delicate excavation

The purpose of test pits

Prior to opening up the main part of a site, the director might use test pits, measuring 1 x 1m (3 x 3ft), as a training exercise to familiarize the diggers with the soil conditions and the nature of the local geology. Test pits can also be used to investigate how deep the deposits are, or how well preserved they are – especially in fields that might have been ploughed or in soils that corrode bone or organic remains. Test pitting can help a director decide whether the topsoil contains archaeological material and needs to be excavated by hand, or whether it is so disturbed that machine excavation can be used. Another common practice is to dig a sequence of test pits across a site or around the perimeter to find out just how far the site extends; for example, to see whether there are any burials outside a cemetery wall or enclosure ditch.

Left A small area of turf and topsoil are removed to create a test pit. The content of the pit, which is recorded, may affect the decision on how and where to dig.

of the surgeon's scalpel, used for precise and delicate tasks on site. However, they can also perform all the tasks that are involved in excavating and cleaning archaeological features. On some types of excavation site, where absolute precision is needed to preserve the finds, trowels are the only 'large' tool permitted on site, along with plastic scrapers, dental tools and even modified cutlery.

Trowel etiquette

Whatever the model, size or shape of the trowel when it is new, the trowel will change shape and size over time, especially if it has been used over time for digging abrasive surfaces, such as stone. Seasoned archaeologists usually carry their trowels with pride: wear and tear is seen as a symbol of experience and prowess, and each trowel, once worn, has its own character. In fact, some archaeologists often carry more than one trowel and will select a different tool for fairly robust work and another for the precision needed to excavate bones or metalwork, or complete pots.

Because trowels are so personal, archaeologists are fiercely protective of them. It is very much a taboo to borrow someone's trowel – and certainly not without the owner's express permission, so bear this in mind if you are working on a site for the first time.

Large machinery

Archaeologists are equally willing to use large machinery on sites. Once you have ascertained, usually by test pits or trial trenches, that there is nothing of archaeological value in the topsoil, this can be cleared from the site by bringing in a tractor with scraper bucket or back hoe. Pneumatic hammers are often necessary to break through concrete floors or other solid obstructions on urban sites.

Needless to say, the use of such heavy equipment is expensive, requires trained operators and has health and

Above Earth-moving machinery is carefully monitored by archaeologists and camera crew at a live televised dig, Windsor Castle, England.

safety and insurance implications, but such costs have to be weighed against the time saved in opening up the site and getting down to the real task in hand. Some archaeologists even provide a specialist contracting service and will undertake this kind of work with delicacy and skill, and an understanding of archaeological objectives that might be missing in a general contractor.

Risk Assessment and Security

The director's list of pre-excavation tasks is not finished yet: archaeological excavation also involves a whole additional set of management and organizational responsibilities that are to do with the health and safety of the diggers and of the security of the site.

Above Excavating this well presents a large range of challenges and possible risks.

As a volunteer taking part in an excavation, it is easy to take for granted the work that will have gone into the preparation before the dig begins. Someone will have sent joining instructions and maps to the volunteers, along with equipment lists and information about the excavation and its objectives. On their arrival volunteers will find accommodation or a campsite, toilets and (if lucky) hot water and a shower. On site there might be a marquee where diggers can take shelter in bad weather, and which they can use for morning, lunch and afternoon tea breaks.

Several lockable huts, similar to those used on building sites, will have been rented and delivered to the site for use as site offices and stores. They will be used to store all the paperwork and recording materials used on site, for meetings, for storing equipment and for processing and storing finds. Valuable equipment and finds need to be taken off site every night, and some electronic equipment such as cameras, computers and electronic measuring equipment will need access to an electricity supply because batteries will need to be recharged overnight.

In some countries, these facilities will be set up within a secure compound. Sometimes diggers are accommodated in a school or hostel, while some long-term excavations have their own purpose-built dig houses and offices.

Security and the public

Archaeologists have to walk a delicate line between involving the public in their work and ensuring that the site is not damaged by vandals, metal detectorists or people who walk all

Left and below Reflector jackets are vital to the safety of archaeologists at a dig, particularly on sites where machinery is present.

Below Children are often invited to take part in small research excavations, but they should be monitored carefully by an adult at all times.

over the site unaware of the damage they are doing to delicate remains. If the dig is in a remote part of the countryside, this can be less of a problem, but in or on the edge of populated areas and on publicly accessible land it will be necessary to hire and install security fencing, inform the police and perhaps hire a security team to watch the site – otherwise you might return to the site the next day to find that your scientifically precise work has been wrecked by treasure hunters during the night. In some countries, armed guards are a necessity, posted day and night.

Every archaeologist is an evangelist for their cause, and it is natural to want to share information about the site with the public, through the local media and through site tours. However, these are best planned for the last days of the excavation, when most of the work has been completed. It is never a good idea to broadcast to the world that you have found something 'rare, valuable or unusual' unless you want to attract the wrong kind of visitor and sadly, some journalists seem to know of only one kind of headline when it comes to archaeology – one that screams out the monetary value of a find rather than its archaeological value as a piece of information. 'What is it worth?' is a question journalists ask too often about archaeological finds rather than 'what does it mean?'.

Health and safety

Over and above the common-sense issues of site security, there might well be a number of additional reasons why special measures need to be taken to meet the terms of insurance policies and health and safety legislation.

Undertaking a formal risk assessment before working on a site might well seem a long way from the excitement of archaeological research, however it is necessary to make sure that people are safe when they work on site and that adequate measures are in place to ensure that they are not harmed by tools and machinery, by falling sections, by soil heaps that

Above Archaeological work usually carries on even when adverse weather threatens.

Weather and its influence

The local climate can be a decisive factor in the excavation regime. In hot weather conditions, the dig might begin at dawn, involving a very early start to the day, but finishing before noon and the hottest period of the day. After lunch and a siesta, staff might use the afternoons for laboratory work, analysing soil samples or cleaning finds. Excavation does not always stop for rain: gentle rain can produce good working conditions because changes in soil colour are easier to see when the soil is damp and the sunlight is diffused by cloud.

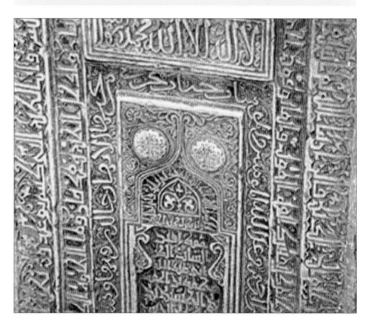

collapse, or by insects, wildlife, dehydration and too much exposure to the sun – to name just a few of the many potential hazards.

As part of the risk assessment, decisions have to be made about where machinery will operate, with clear working zones that nobody else is allowed to enter and a site supervisor to prevent anyone entering that area while machinery, such as dumper trucks and tractors, are operating.

Above This 900-year-old Persian tombstone was stolen from a mosque in Tehran, Iran, and later recovered from a British antiques dealer.

Professional archaeologists usually work on site wearing high-visibility clothing and protective helmets and footwear. Health and safety legislation requires that a first-aid box is available, that a trained first-aider knows how to use it and that everyone on site knows what to do if there is an accident.

Removing the Topsoil

*Before the serious archaeology begins, the site has to be prepared by
removing the disturbed topsoil and cleaning the site to reveal the
undisturbed archaeological features below. Cleaning will help the diggers
to get a feel for the site and to answer key questions about where to dig.*

Undisturbed archaeology is sometimes
found right on the surface of the site,
especially in the case of sites that have
remained untouched by subsequent
agriculture, in which case there is no
need to strip turf and topsoil from the
site. However, there is often a layer of
turf or scrubby vegetation that needs to
be removed, and there might also be a
layer of plough spoil that has been
turned and mixed so many times
over the centuries that any material

it contains is of little value to
the archaeologist. Test pitting (*see*
Excavation Strategies) will help to
establish whether or not this is the case.

Stripping the topsoil

On a small excavation, turf and topsoil
removal is all done by hand, using a
spade, pickaxe and shovel. On larger
excavations, the overburden is stripped
off by a machine – a task that is often
done before the diggers arrive on site.

Above Removal of turf prior to an excavation
on the Scottish island of Dun Eistean.

There is a great skill to stripping a
site so that archaeological features are
cleanly revealed but not damaged. The
archaeologist who supervises the
stripping of the site needs to have a
good understanding of the local soils
and geology to be able to tell the
difference between disturbed plough
soil, 'natural' features and those that
are archeologically significant. This is
easy enough on a flat site with an even
depth of plough soil, or a site on chalk
where black soil-filled archaeological
features are highlighted against the
white of the underlying geology, but it
is far less easy when dealing with sticky
clay on a hillside. In such circumstances, the rule is to err on the side of
caution, grading the site little by little
and checking the newly revealed
surface at each scrape of the tractor
bucket to see whether the soil changes
colour or character or whether there
are any finds in the soil.

It is better to take off too little over
the site overburden than too much –
you cannot reconstruct features that
are scraped up in a metal tractor
bucket. More and more archaeologists
enlist the help of metal detectorists at
this stage in the opening up of a site, to
search the topsoil for metal objects that
might be hidden in the soil. These can

Left Hoes are used to penetrate to the next
level of a site in the Sudanese desert.
Topsoiling becomes more complex when
dealing with fine sediment and ditches that
tend to fill as quickly as they are dug.

range from discarded bits of tractor and modern nails, to lost children's toys, coins, keys, brooches or buttons. Many will have been lost casually – by someone working or walking in the field – but some might also add important information about the nature of the deposits that form the history of the site.

Cleaning

Before any decisions can be made about where to begin digging, the site is cleaned up and planned. While archaeologists are sometimes accused of taking a relaxed attitude to their own personal appearance, they are obsessive about site cleanliness. 'Spoil' – the soil that has been extracted from the site and is regarded as no longer of any informational use – has to be constantly removed because it gets in the way of those careful observations about change in soil colour on which decisions are made.

So having opened up the site, the next stage for the diggers, while the supervisors and directors ponder the excavation strategy, is to clean all the loose soil and make a drawn and photographic record of the site. Cleaning is best done in dry conditions, because wet soils will smear and obscure the edges of features. Cleaning tools include a trowel and a hoe and – like any house-proud home owner – an old-fashioned brush and dustpan. Archaeologists soon learn particular techniques for cleaning the loose soil away from features. They use the brush to flick it from the surface into the hand shovel or dustpan rather than dragging soil and stone across the feature, which can cause damage.

Spoil tips

The spoil tip (heap), is where all the waste material excavated from the site is placed. To restore the site after the excavation, different parts of the site might have their own separate spoil tips. The first is used to store the turf (if any), which will eventually be put back when the site is refilled. The second might be used to store topsoil – that is the humus-rich soil into which farmers plant their crops, as distinct from the less fertile subsoil that lies underneath, which might make a third tip. All three tips are located well away from areas that might need excavating, but not so far away as to create a long trek for the diggers who empty their buckets and barrows at regular intervals.

Some archaeologists regard creating a good spoil tip as an art, and they design them with all the care of a landscape architect. Grading the spoil tip is critical, so that there is no risk of a landslip. Ergonomic solutions to lifting and transporting soil from the site are considered to avoid back and joint injuries or the risk of diggers slipping off planks – that is why experienced diggers often create spoil tips that resemble archaeological features such as barrows and ziggurats (the terraced temples of ancient Mesopotamia, with ramps that run at a gentle gradient up the sides to the summit).

Above If the ground is particularly solid, you may need to hack to the next level with a pickaxe. This should be used with care.

Above Small finds may be 'missed' and end up submerged in spoil. It is wise to check the spoil heap regularly with a metal detector.

Above (top) Systematic topsoiling requires the turf to be removed in neat slices. These are then replaced when the site is backfilled at the end of the excavation.

Above (bottom) Site features begin to emerge once the top level of soil is removed.

Datum Points and Site Grids

In order to create an overall plan of the site, a 'datum point' is set up that will be used as the reference point for all the other measurements. These measurements are taken to pinpoint the precise location of every feature of an excavation, and to note the exact positions of the key finds.

Above An archaeologist measures the height of a wall from the fixed datum point.

While the initial cleaning of the site is in progress, other archaeologists will be busy selecting the particular point on the site that will be used as the datum point – that is, a fixed location from which all the other measurements on the site are made.

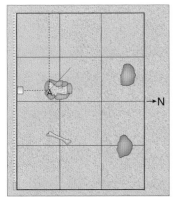

Locating a datum point

Using conventions established by 18th-century surveyors working for the Ordnance Survey, it is established practice to locate the datum point on the south-western edge of the site. Measurements will be taken from that point in an easterly direction first, then in a northerly direction.

The datum point is normally located in a place that gives an uninterrupted view of the whole site, because tape measures will be run from it, and various optical measuring instruments

Left and below Once the datum points are set up at the corners of the site, a tape can be run around the edges, from one corner to the next. The position of features can be plotted by running another tape at right angles to this. In this example, point A is 0.75m (2¹/₂ ft) from the western edge of the site, and 1.75m (5¹/₄ ft) from the southern edge.

rely on it to provide their measurements. If the site is steep, terraced or hilly, several datum points are set up, each overlooking an area of the site. The datum points are sited somewhere that is not likely to be excavated for the duration of dig (which might be several years) or in the future. It is a fixed point that should survive for decades afterward, in the case of research digs, so that archaeologists can revisit the site in the future and locate its features precisely. If no obvious landscape features suggest themselves, such as a building, gate post or fence line, archaeologists will sometimes create their own datum point by hammering a long metal or concrete post into the

Below On this large industrial site, mini-datum points marked with red flags have been set up to help plot the features in the south-western area of the excavation.

ground, a strategy often deployed if the team expects to revisit the site over a number of years and can be sure that the field won't be cultivated.

Although Global Positioning Systems (GPS; *see* The Importance of Location) now allow archaeologists to pinpoint where on the planet the datum point is, these systems don't make datum points entirely redundant. There are extremely accurate GPS systems that can guide unmanned tractors across a field, ploughing, sowing or harvesting crops without human intervention, however, most systems can pinpoint a location to only within 300mm (12in) – and that is a margin that is large enough to lead to some serious errors on an archaeological site.

Total stations, or EDMs

Achieving pinpoint accuracy and recording in three dimensions once required surveying skills and mathematical dexterity acquired through long practice, using tape measures, a theodolite, measuring staffs and ranging rods – equipment that had not changed much since Greek and Roman road builders or medieval church builders developed their crafts. Fortunately, anyone can now do the same job using a battery-operated device called a total station, also known as electronic distance measuring equipment (EDM; *see* The Importance of Location). The only limitation is that these devices tend to work best in open terrain.

The EDM is placed on the datum point, and its position is fixed using co-ordinates from the GPS (or it might have its own inbuilt GPS). The reflector is taken to the spot on the site where the position needs to be fixed. The EDM bounces a beam of infrared light off the reflector, and the total station's software is then able to produce a set of three dimensional coordinates: it calculates latitude and longitude by combining data from the angle of the beam in relation to the north point and the time it takes for the light to go out and come back, and it calculates heights by taking a reading from the reflector scale.

Site grids

If an EDM is not available, the alternative is to set up a site grid, which will use the datum point as the starting point (*see illustration opposite*). Typically, the grid is marked out using tape measures and by hammering iron pegs into the ground to mark out the grid squares, usually at 5m (16ft) intervals. The pegs themselves are used throughout the excavation as mini datum points, from which measurements can be taken within that 5m/16ft grid square.

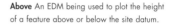

Above An EDM being used to plot the height of a feature above or below the site datum.

This grid might be used to produce an initial plan of the site by plotting the edges of all the features, using a six-figure grid system. If the coordinates of the datum point are 100/100, the grid is used to measure how many metres to the east, then to the north of the datum point the feature lies. If the written grid reference for a pit is 270/065, the pit is 27m (88ft) east of the datum point and 6.5m (21ft) north.

Above A datum point is being set up on Mount Erebus, Antarctica.

National grids

Some countries have a national grid system that archaeologists can use as the basis for pinpointing the location of their site datum. Datum base points, from which all heights above and below sea level are measured, are located around the world – at Newlyn in Cornwall, for example, at Cardona Island Lighthouse in Puerto Rico, and at Kortright in Sierra Leone. In countries with no national grid, archaeologists depend on local grids established at some past date for military or engineering use, or on GPS.

The Initial Site Plan

Once the grid is in place, it then becomes possible to create an accurate plan of the site, which will show the features that have been revealed through cleaning. A detailed plan of the site is important before the dig begins, because it will be a record of the original conditions of the site.

Field archaeology consists of a series of repetitive processes, one of which is maintaining a drawn and photographic record of the site while it is being excavated – in effect, making as accurate a copy as possible on paper and on camera of the site that is about to be destroyed. This may sound brutal, but it is the truth – as soon as undisturbed archaeological material is removed from a site, it is impossible to put it back in the same way that it was found. As most people cannot rely on having an accurate memory, drawing and photography are the tools that archaeologists have developed as

the means by which a site can be 'reconstructed' at a later stage – albeit in the virtual reality of a computer model rather than physically.

Drawing equipment

Although archaeologists like the drawings to look clean, clear and pleasing, this is essentially a technical activity rather than an aesthetic one. Archaeologists do not sit by the side of the trench and seek to create a three-dimensional sketch of the site using shading and perspective. Instead, the plan is strictly two dimensional, and it is achieved by using a combination of

Above Archaeologists continually refer to their plans of the site throughout the excavation.

the site grid and a sheet of graph paper as a guide. Graph paper is covered in a grid of lines, and these will correspond to the lines of the site grid that has already been laid out using pegs hammered into the ground.

To start making a plan, a drawing board – a light but firm rectangle of wood – is necessary. A drawing board is typically 750mm (30in) in length and 500mm (20in) or so in width, so it is small enough to be carried around and to work with on site, but large enough

Above The drawn record begins as soon as features begin to appear. Working as a pair, one archaeologist measures the position and dimensions of a visible feature within the squares of the drawing grid, while the other records this on a scaled drawing.

Left A simple scale can be applied to the drawing by correlating the squares of the graph paper to the drawing grid.

The result is a two-dimensional plan of the outline of the features visible at this stage, which will be the top of the features, before excavation begins. Further information is added to the plan once it has been drawn. Reference numbers are allocated to each feature, and these numbers are then written by the corresponding feature on the plan, along with the height of the top of the feature above sea level, which is measured using a theodolite and site datum or EDM.

Site photography

Finally, everything that has been drawn is also photographed as a further record of the site. In preparation for photography, the site may be given a final cleaning, which will include the removal of all tools and people from the site so that they do not appear in the photograph. However, what must appear in the photographs is a scale, usually consisting of a pair of surveyor's ranging rods, which are 2-m (6½-ft) long poles, divided into four 500mm (20in) segments, alternately painted red and white. One of these is laid on the site to line up with the vertical axis of the photograph, and another is laid parallel to the horizontal axis. These will give an approximate sense of the size of the site and features in the resulting photograph.

Below Each feature on the site is photographed as well as drawn.

to accommodate a sheet of metric graph paper, which measures about 594mm (23in) x 420mm (28in).

The graph paper is secured to the drawing board using a masking tape or adhesive tape that will be easy to remove at a later stage without tearing the paper. A sheet of heavy-grade weatherproof tracing paper is laid over the graph paper, secured to the drawing board with the same type of tape. For drawing, an HB pencil and a good non-smudging eraser is suitable.

Tapes and grids

For taking measurements, both a long 20m (65ft) tape measure and a short 3m (10ft) one will be necessary, as well as a drawing grid, an invaluable aid. The drawing grid consists of a frame, measuring 1m (3ft) x 1m (3ft), with wires or strings subdividing the frame into 100mm (40in) squares.

The grid is laid on the ground on top of the features that you want to draw; the grid squares correspond to the squares on the graph paper on your drawing board, and planning the site is a question of transferring the outlines of the features that you can see on the ground on to the tracing paper, using the underlying graph paper as a guide.

Making the plan

The drawing grid is used for drawing smaller details, but first it is best to draw the outlines of the major features using the site grid. This is achieved by running the long tape measure between two pegs on opposite sides of the site and marking on your tracing paper the precise points at which the tape intersects the edges of the feature. The only way to achieve the required degree of accuracy is to stand directly over the point, looking vertically down on to the tape measure – standing to take measurements at an oblique angle will result in a reading that could be out by 100mm/4in or more.

Having marked on the tracing paper the point where the tape and feature coincide, you can then use the shorter tape measure to take further spot measurements from the tape at intervals of 100mm (4in), 200mm (8in), 300mm (12in), 400mm (16in) or 500mm (20in). How many measurements you take will depend on the shape and complexity of the feature. Straight-sided ditches, for example, will need fewer spot measurements than a serpentine one. The shape of the feature is then sketched in using the measured points as a guide.

Typical Site Features

*Once a site is cleaned up, what is found should not come as too much of a
surprise to the archaeologists if the preparation work was done in advance.
In addition, some common features are often encountered on a typical
archaeological site, and these can provide clues to the site before digging.*

Opening up the site involves removing
soil that has been disturbed by natural,
human or animal activity, such as tree-
root disturbance, ploughing or
burrowing, to expose features that have
not been disturbed. What survives will
depend on the age of the deposits, and
on climate and soil conditions. For
example, in waterlogged dry or cold
conditions (*see* Vulnerable Finds), more
organic material survives, such as
clothing, basketry, paper and flesh,
whereas in acidic conditions bones
might not survive but wood does. This
is why few human remains are
associated with Hadrian's Wall; the
moorland soil destroys bone, but there

are well-preserved written records,
consisting of tablets of wood. Knowing
the soil and weather conditions will
provide information to archaeologists.

Colours in the soil

On a typical site, surviving structures
are mostly the remains of buildings and
property boundaries, pits and hearths,
tracks and roadways, and industrial
remains, such as kilns or debris. There
are also burial sites, as well as sites
interpreted as 'ritual', often because
their purpose is not understood.

In most cases, these are visible in the
ground as circles, rectangles or lines of
soil that are different in colour from

Above This site is recognizable as a Roman fort
from the 'playing card' shape of the outer walls
and the barrack blocks within.

the 'natural', or background, soil.
These colour differences are often the
result of the slow rotting of organic
remains, such as timber posts or beams
that once stood in the ground.

The importance of simple soil stains
and subtle colour differences is
spectacularly demonstrated at Sutton
Hoo, in Suffolk, England. This site is
renowned for its two Anglo-Saxon
cemeteries of the 6th and early 7th
centuries. One of these cemeteries,
when excavated in the 1930s, was

Above This area of raised ground at Great
Burwood Estate, Essex, England, puzzled
archaeologists, who sunk two trial trenches into
the earth following an initial survey. They found
the remains of a prominent 17th-century
dwelling, which they were able to date partly
from the trading goods found at the site.

Left The excavation of the burial ship at Sutton
Hoo, East Anglia, UK, in 1939.

Right Kalut-e Gird, a circular fortress close to the Afghan border, was buried beneath creeping sand dunes for many years.

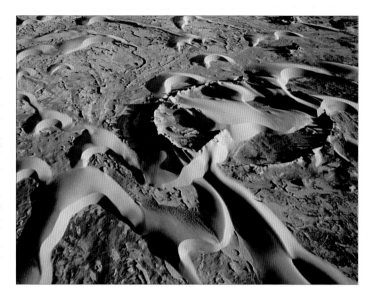

found to contain an undisturbed ship burial and a wealth of brooches, shoulder claps and royal regalia of gold inlaid with red garnet, all of which can now be seen in the British Museum. Photographs of the 27m- (88½ft-) long ship at the heart of the cemetery show what appears to be a complete hull with all its planks in place. In fact, the timber had disappeared, and everything known about the boat results from the painstaking care with which the excavators traced barely discernible stains from the rotted wood that survived in the sand in which the boat was laid upon.

Explaining the differences

After a site has been abandoned by its original users, ditches and pits slowly accumulate silt, leaves, grass and weeds as they fill through the natural processes of wind, rain and soil erosion. Ditches might, for example, provide a habitat for wetland plants that rot to a darker colour than the surrounding grassland; finer silts are washed into the hollow by rain or the slow collapse of the sides.

Experimental archaeology has been conducted that involved excavating pits and monitoring the speed in which they fill and what they fill with. It has been established that the process is fast to begin with, but slows down over time, so that distinctive hollows marking the position of a pit or a ditch might be visible for many decades after the abandonment of the site. The implication of this work is that our ancestors had to keep their ditches and gullies well-maintained if they were to be effective in draining water, or to keep out animals. Seasonal recutting of ditches must have been the norm.

What do they mean?

Looked at in plan, without any further excavation, the shape of the features will often tell archaeologists a great deal about the nature and age of the

Above Post holes are evidence of former boundaries on this Bronze Age track.

The archaeology of a post hole

Post holes are a common find in archaeology. They represent the remains of timber posts set into the ground, usually as part of a fence or wall. Some posts have sharp, pencil-shaped ends and are hammered straight into the ground. Bigger, flat-bottomed posts are usually set into a specially dug hole or pit; the space between the post and the edges of the hole is then backfilled with soil and small rocks, which are rammed hard to ensure that the post stays upright. When archaeologists excavate post holes they typically find the packing material, represented by soil of a different colour to the post itself. The post will either show up as an area of dark organic soil, if the post rotted within the hole, or as a ghost of the post, if the post was deliberately pulled out of the post hole to be reused elsewhere as part of the dismantling of the structure. In the latter case, the soil filling the space once occupied by the post will be derived from the slow process of the natural erosion and worm action, gradually filling the hole.

site. Archaeologists have dug enough sites to recognize common types: circular ditches, depending on their diameter, might be evidence of a burial mound, or of a hut. Long lines of small stake holes might represent a fence or palisade. Larger post holes could be a house, hut, byre or workshop, if set in a rectangular pattern, perhaps with smaller stake holes representing internal divisions.

Some or all of these could represent human activity from any time between the Mesolithic and the later medieval period, but clues such as the size of the features and the overall assemblage – the mix of features that are found in association with each other – enable a seasoned archaeologist to make a good guess at what the site contains just from looking at the overall pattern of feature, even before excavation.

Contexts and Site Codes

Archaeologists use certain terms to describe the features found during an excavation. It is important that a digger understands this terminology to make sure records are kept accurately. Because the terminology can be confusing, sometimes reference numbers are used.

Some archaeologists object to the use of descriptive terms such as 'ditch', 'feature', 'fill', 'deposit', 'layer' or 'soil'. They try to be as objective and as scientific as possible and use neutral terms to describe the material they excavate. Avoiding evaluative terms is not a question of slavish adherence to an archaeological orthodoxy; it is often the case that the interpretation of a site or a feature changes as you excavate it. Rather than rewriting the site notes each time a feature that was initially

described as a pit turns into a grave, it is better to use neutral terminology during the data-gathering stage and reserve judgement about the function or meaning of the context until all the evidence is available, as part of the analytical post-excavation phase.

Use of the term 'context'

The neutral term increasingly used to describe the material that archaeologists excavate is 'context', and every context is given a unique

Above The first trench sunk at a dig may reveal numerous 'contexts'.

identification number, or 'site code', as it is excavated. The word is a good one because the deposits or layers that we excavate are quite literally the contexts, or containers, for the finds that lie within them.

However, the term context is also used for a phase in the site's history that might not have any physical counterpart. For example, in between the digging of a ditch, which leaves a physical cut in the surrounding soil and rock, and the filling of the ditch, which is represented by stones and soil that wash into the ditch from the top and sides, there is a period when the ditch is open. This open phase might last for many years, but if the ditch is kept clean and periodically recut, that passage of time is not represented by a physical imprint. However, the passage of time is recognized by archaeologists by allocating a context number to the open ditch. Technically, anything that represents a unique event in the sequence of events that makes up the history of the site is a context – because a period of time passes between the digging of the ditch and the next stage in its history, the open ditch has its own context number.

Other archaeologists use a variety of terms to distinguish different types of context. Some use the word 'locus' to describe a soil deposit, and some

Left The layers of soil excavated from a section of the site each represent an individual 'context', reflecting the passage of time.

Right Using EDM, site surveyors can pinpoint the location of a demarcated feature, or a 'section' marked out to excavate that feature, before the dig gets fully underway. The supplies a basic 'context' for any finds unearthed in that spot.

avoid the issue simply by referring to every context by its reference number, which might be prefixed with a letter indicating whether it is soil, a wall or a floor. Perhaps the most common practice is a combination of the two: using context numbers as a scientifically neutral record of the site, but using more easily understood descriptive words as an aid to communicating with fellow diggers and for interpreting the site as it is excavated. Hence, the supervisor might refer to 'that deposit' to describe a 'layer' of 'soil' forming part of the 'fill' of a 'cut', such as a 'ditch'. You might also hear the word 'feature' used to describe a post hole or solid structures, such as walls, floors, cobbled yards or roads. With these philosophical and terminological thoughts to ponder, our first time archaeologist finally gets the go ahead to begin to dig.

Who does what on site?

Within the digging hierarchy, some or all of the tasks involved in excavating and documenting the site might be entrusted to a specialist, to ensure an accurate record is made.

For example, a site photographer will only be involved in taking pictures, while an illustrator or draughtsperson will be primarily responsible for all the site plans and section drawings. There might also be a surveyor, whose job is to compile and maintain a log of all the grid measurements taken on site. There will almost certainly be a finds specialist, whose job is to ensure that all finds are labelled, conserved and securely stored – though volunteers from among the diggers are often recruited for a day or so in the finds shed to help with this work and learn how finds are treated on site. If the excavation requires it, there might be an environmentalist with the equipment and skills to take and analyse soil samples on site.

On smaller digs, some or all of these tasks might be the responsibility of the site supervisor or the director. Supervisors will often be keen to train individual diggers to do their own recording, on the grounds that the person who knows the material best is the person who has the intimate understanding of the feature that comes from having excavated it.

Above A supervisor is always there to monitor the diggers. Typically, one is assigned to manage each of the main areas of the site, such as individual trenches.

Preparing to Dig a Section

A 'section' dig will allow archaeologists to have an interior look at a site before the real excavation begins. Archaeologists use certain terms to describe the features that might be found in this and other digs, and it is important that a digger understands them to make sure records are kept accurately.

Above A feature being excavated in two sections, each of which will have its own code.

The site as a whole has been cleaned up, gridded and planned, and the initial excavation strategy discussed. Sometimes the excavators will decide to put sections through some of the features in order to investigate their stratigraphy and contents.

A section is a vertical incision cut through an archaeological feature, such as a ditch or a pit. Like a slice through a layer cake, it reveals the different colours and textures of soil that fill the feature, and the sequence and contents help archaeologists to date and understand past human activity on the site.

Preparing a section

A first-time digger may be asked to dig a section of a small ditch. The first task will be to do a mini site preparation exactly like the one that has already been done for the site as a whole, including cleaning it up once again. Archaeologists are obsessive about keeping their working areas clean, treating a site as if it were a scientific laboratory for the systematic gathering of data, and ensuring that the subtle differences in soil colour that mark the edges of features are not obscured by loose or trampled soil.

The next step will be to demarcate a length of ditch to excavate. An area that will be comfortable to work in will need to be marked out, but it shouldn't be so large that it will involve extra work without gaining additional information – a 2m (6½ft) stretch of ditch will usually suffice. Both ends of the area to be excavated should be marked using nails and string. These represent the points at which the sections will later be drawn. They need to be at precise right angles to the line of the ditch and parallel to each other, otherwise the section that is revealed will be distorted and will not represent the relationships between the different deposits filling the ditch.

Photographs and codes

Before excavation, photographs are taken of the ditch. A scale is included in the picture, consisting of a pole or rod typically 50cm (20in) or 1m (3¼ft) in length, divided like a ruler into 100mm intervals by red and white coloured bands. Without the scale, it will be difficult for anyone to judge how big the ditch is from a photograph: with it, the width and depth can be estimated.

Every photograph taken is logged in a register, and a unique code for the area of the site will be issued. This code will be used to identify everything that

Left With the topsoil removed, and features revealed by the changing colours in the soil, decisions can be made about where to dig a section in order to take a closer look.

Above An opened trench, like every feature on the site, will also have its own unique code. For example, if the trench is the ninth area to be opened on the site, it might be called Trench 9. That unique number is also recorded on the master plan of the site and entered into a 'context register', along with the location of the trench.

Above (top) The multiple features visible in this Roman burial site are individual graves.

Above (bottom) Excavators work in pairs to uncover the remains of an ancient road.

results from the excavation of the ditch – not just the photographs, but also the various recording sheets (these will be explained later), plans, section drawings, grid coordinates, finds and soil samples.

The site itself will have its own unique code. In the UK this usually consists of three letters derived from the name of the site and then two numbers, denoting the year in which the work commenced. So the whole of the dig might be known as AHF07, meaning Abbey Home Farm 2007.

Digging a section

In order to reveal the section, it is necessary to remove the soil that is filling the feature. However, that soil itself is a vital part of the evidence for the history of the site, so the soil has to be removed systematically, layer by layer. As the soil is loosened with a trowel it is vital to collect all the visible finds from the layer. On some sites, the loose soil is also sieved (sifted) to look for finds trapped in unbroken clumps or too small to be seen by the excavator, including microscopic environmental finds such as seeds, pollens, insects and snails, charcoal and fish bones.

Knowing exactly where to place a section takes great skill, but there is no foolproof method of ensuring that the section you decide to cut will recover all the data. For example, when excavating a section of ditch, you might find that the ditch itself contains several additional features: perhaps a post hole from a gate post, or perhaps a layer of burnt stones and charcoal. Unless by sheer luck the vertical section happens to coincide with these features, the section alone will miss them and thus not be a complete record of the ditch. For that reason, every feature that is

found within another feature is also planned and sectioned, and a record is made of the vertical and horizontal extent of every layer that the excavator encounters, to ensure a full record.

The excavator's aim, therefore, is to record all the features in three dimensions: vertical section records show how deep each layer is and how each one relates to adjacent layers; plan records show how far each layer extends in a horizontal direction. Sections and plans form two of the most important records that result from modern scientific archaeology.

85

Excavating a Ditch

After all the preparation work, which may have involved section digging, the aim for the team is to begin excavating the first context in its entirety. This involves the very difficult task of judging where the existing layer stops and where a new one begins.

The go-ahead has finally been given to make a start on excavating the first ditch. The first deposit is removed, using a trowel to remove the surface of the fill. Beginning at one end of the ditch, a mini trench is cut into the soil, loosening the earth with a scraping action, with the pointed heel of the trowel pulled toward the digger. Proceeding with care until it becomes clear what the fill is like, small amounts of soil are removed, with the loose trowelled soil regularly swept up with a hand shovel and put into a container, such as a plastic bucket.

Depending on the nature of the material being excavated, the bucket might simply be emptied into a wheelbarrow – and when that is full, it might be wheeled away and the material dumped on the spoil tip. However, if the site is likely to yield small finds, the material might be sieved before it is discarded. The sieving (sifting) process involves breaking down the soil and passing it through a series of sieves (screens) of finer and finer mesh size. Some soils simply will not break down into finer particles when wet, and become as hard as concrete when dry. Such soils might be wet sieved using a hose, after they have first been soaked by standing them in a bucket of water.

As the digger gets to know the soil being worked, the speed of excavation will pick up. Heavier tools, such as a mattock or hoe, might be used if the layer is empty of finds and of monotonous consistency – which is the norm for many ditch fills. The way the

Above When systematic line trowelling is in action, it is important that the excavated part of the trench is not walked across.

dig proceeds reflects the expectations of what the dig fill is like. Even so, the digger should be constantly alert for finds, or for any change in soil colour and consistency that marks a transition from one layer to another, or perhaps a separate feature within a ditch.

Looking for interfaces

The places where a digger is most likely to encounter the first signs of a change are at the edges of the ditch, because this is where the deposit is often the shallowest. When a ditch begins to fill up after it has fallen out of use, soil from the sides falls to the bottom first and tends to form deeper layers in the middle of the ditch, trailing to shallower layers at the sides.

The blunt reality of archaeology, however, is that diggers very often dig through the next layer without recognizing the change. The division between one layer and the next is called the horizon, and sometimes this can be quite sharp, especially when dealing with pits that are filled manually over a period of time, with clear changes from a brown to a black layer, or from silt to fine gravel. Just as

Left Ditches are one of the commonest types of feature found on archaeological sites: this one at Pattnam in Kerala, southern India, marks a boundary in the historic trading port of Muziris and it yielded pottery evidence of ancient trade between India and Rome dating back some 3,000 years.

often, however, this interface is gradual rather than abrupt, especially if the soil has been well and truly mixed up by centuries of worm and root activity.

Excavating in spits

To minimize the risk of going too deep and penetrating a separate layer within the ditch fill, a digger usually takes the soil down in 'spits', by first removing a depth of 30mm (1in) to 50mm (2in) at one end of the trench. If no change in the soil is detected in that small area of the trench, the same depth of soil is taken out again across the whole of the trench. Then the whole process begins again – taking down another 30mm (1in) to 50mm (2in) in a small area of the trench before excavating a bigger area.

The digger will keep checking the sections that mark the two ends of the trench, and the vertical slice through the ditch that gets deeper as digging continues downward. This provides additional vital clues to the character of the soil being taken out, and will show clearly whether the digger has gone too far and dug into a new layer.

A nervous first-time digger shouldn't worry over the risks of doing the job wrong: the site supervisor's job is to keep checking the work and to help the digger interpret what is being found. With their knowledge and experience they will also help the digger distinguish between the fill of the ditch and the 'natural' surface, which is to say the virgin soil or gravel or rock into which the ditch was cut. It is this natural surface that will form the sides and bottom of the emptied-out ditch, once it is fully excavated.

Once emptied, the ditch will then be revealed again in the shape and form that it was when it began to fill up: excavating the ditch will help to reveal past, long-buried landscape features. How long that ditch was a feature of the landscape, why it was dug, how it was filled and how it relates to other site features are questions that the digger ultimately hopes to help answer.

Right Spit excavation is in progress amid the cramped surroundings of an inner-city site.

The basics of line trowelling

1 The purpose of line trowelling is to clean the site and reveal colour changes in the soil.

2 Using the edge of the trowel, soil is loosened and drawn back toward the diggers.

3 Colour changes may indicate buried archaeology, so loose soil is routinely cleared from the trowelled area.

4 This resulting 'spoil' is collected in a bucket for dry sieving (sifting) for any small finds the digger did not spot.

Describing Deposits

The physical appearance of the deposit needs to be recorded accurately and in detail as it is excavated, with additional observations or amendments being added as the digging proceeds. Paperwork rules an excavation just as much as any other sphere of life.

Before digging for very long, the site supervisor will arrive with a context recording sheet and sit down with the digger to explain the procedures for recording the excavation. The examples given here are taken from the practice commonly used by British archaeologists, but similar recording systems are widely used all over the world, perhaps with slightly different terminology.

Increasingly, as electronic equipment becomes less expensive, more reliable and easy to use, laptops or hand-held computers are used to record information about a context. However, even where data is captured digitally in the field, a paper record is also kept, on the belt and braces principle that if a computer disc is lost, stolen or destroyed, there is always another back-up record.

Allocating context numbers

As a digger excavates a trench or ditch, every deposit or feature encountered will be given its own unique context number. This number is obtained from the context register, and is allocated in numerical sequence – so the upper-most layer of, for example, Trench 9 will be given the context number 900 (the next layer will be 901, the next 902 and so on). The context number is written at the head of the recording sheet, along with the name of the trench and its grid references.

Right Regularly spraying the sides of an open trench with water will help to bring out the different colours of the soil layers.

The rest of the sheet is used to record any observations about the physical appearance of the deposit. But rather than leave the description of the deposit to the subjective judgement of the digger, the sheet has a number of tick boxes that serve as prompts for recording the main characteristics.

Soil colour

As it dries, soil changes colour, so the deposit is ideally described when it is damp: sprucing it up with a light spray is permitted – in fact, diggers working on sunny dry conditions keep a sprayer handy for this purpose, delivering a fine mist of water to the surface of the soil sufficient to restore its colour, but not to wash the particles away.

Above Accurate description is key to the recording of archaeological features.

First, the digger will describe the basic colour of the deposit: black, brown, white, yellow, orange, and so on. However, soils are rarely all of one simple colour, so archaeologists tend to describe the predominant hue, using such terms as blackish, whitish, yellowish, orangey. The description might also note if the soil is con-sistently of that colour, or whether it grades from light to dark, or vice versa. As the digger excavates the site, he or she will also be asked to note how easy it is to distinguish the layer from adjoining layers – whether the 'horizon clarity' is good, medium or poor.

Above Rolling the earth between fingers will help to assess soil compaction.

Above The shape and content of a feature are recorded on a context recording sheet.

Soil composition

Composition relates to the size of the particles that make up the deposit, ranging from the finest – clay and silt – to middling – sand (particles up to 2mm (⅒in) in size) and gravel (2–4mm (⅒–³⁄₁₆in)) – to the largest – pebbles (4–60mm (³⁄₁₆–2⅜in)), cobbles (60–250mm (2⅜–10in)) and boulders (more than 250mm (10in)). Once again, it is not common for soils to have a consistent composition, and archaeologists often end up using descriptions that combine two or more terms, such as silty sand (a sandy deposit with some silt) or sandy silt (vice versa). With larger material, such as gravels, pebbles, cobbles and boulders, it is useful to note the particle size range and the roundedness – whether sharp and angular, rounded and smooth or in between.

Soil compaction

Compaction describes the strength of the deposit when placed under pressure. For fine-grained deposits such as clay, silt or sand, the test is to try to mould a moist sample with your fingers. If it crumbles it is friable, and if its easily moulded, mouldable with strong pressure or resistant to moulding it is described as soft, firm and hard, respectively. Coarser-grained deposits, such as gravels, pebbles and so on are described as loose if they are not self-supporting, friable if they crumble easily, firm if they keep their form under pressure and compact if they are impossible to break.

Variations can occur even within one layer – for example, a road surface or a cobbled yard might have different patterns of composition and compaction, reflecting wear and tear from the use and erosion of the surface. This fact will be brought out in the plans and photographs of the feature, but it also needs to be described on the context recording sheet.

Inclusions

The term 'inclusions' describes any other material in the layer, and this can include natural materials, such as snail shells, or materials resulting from human activity, such as charcoal, bone fragments, shell, worked flint, 'alien' stone that is different from the natural geology, pottery, daub, baked clay, tile, brick and so on. These are described in terms of their frequency (rare 1–3 per cent, sparse 3–7 per cent, moderate 10–20 per cent, common 20–30 per cent, very common 30–40 per cent and abundant 40–50 per cent), and in terms of their size (smears, flecks, and small, medium or large inclusions).

A typical recording sheet

Every organization has its own design when it comes to context recording sheets, but they all record the same core information about the context:

• The character of the deposit e.g. colour and article size.

• The context number and its relationship to other contexts.

• An interpretation and discussion saying how you think the context was formed.

• Reference numbers of any soil samples, photographs, drawings and finds, such as, pot, bone, wood or leather.

Right A context recording sheet from the Museum of London Archaeology Service.

Above Students at an archaeology open day practice recording a scatter of 'inclusions' such as worked flints, using a drawing grid.

Finds in Context

As a layer is carefully excavated, the digger will try to recover all the
artefacts it contains, layer by layer, and the finds from each context will be
recorded and stored separately. The individual finds have the potential to
help archaeologists understand more about the history of the site.

After a couple of hours excavating the first layer of a ditch, the work for a digger can become a little bit routine and monotonous. This is when a digger may become a little careless and, for example, might inadvertently clip the edge of a piece of pottery with a trowel, causing it to flake, with spots of orange flecks appearing in the soil. A digger should always trowel with care – it is difficult to know when you might come across a find.

Finds trays

The supervisor might send the digger to see the finds supervisor, who will explain what happens to the material found during the excavation. First the digger will be given a plastic container, such as a tray or a bucket, and a waterproof label, on which the site code and context number is written in waterproof ink. The tray is where the digger will store all the finds that come from that context; as soon as another

Above This pot 'chimney' uncovered on a site at Heywoods, Barbados, will be painstakingly taken apart, and the relationship between each piece carefully recorded.

deposit is encountered, a new number and tray will be supplied to keep the finds from each layer separate.

Depending on the nature of the site, finds such as pottery, brick, tile, bone or iron slag are regarded as routine – the context recording sheet enables the

Below The recovered bones in the tray were found during an excavation at a medieval burial site. The markers in the earth indicate the position of individual graves.

Right Special bagged finds are tagged into the earth at the exact position in which they were found. The location can then be recorded using a total station or by taking measurements manually.

Dealing with uncommon finds

1 If you find something out of the ordinary, ask your supervisor to take a look. The find may need to be placed in a sealed bag for labelling.

2 Label the bag with the site name, day number and context number before placing it in the tray with the other finds from that context.

Above A 3,500-year-old wooden bridge support is surrounded by layers of tagged stratigraphy.

digger to comment on the quantity and variety of material from the deposit, but no further action is required on the digger's part, other than to deliver the labelled trays to the finds shed at the end of the day. (*For more about the finds shed, see* Processing Finds on Site.)

Special finds

Some finds are regarded as 'special', though the definition of special varies from site to site. On some sites, artefacts are so rare that every single find is recorded in detail. On sites that are rich in material, perhaps only the diagnostically significant finds will be given special treatment: for example, finds that can be dated in absolute terms (coins) or in relative terms (brooches). Alternatively, objects might be given a privileged status if their precise position might be important for the interpretation of the site – for example, objects in a grave, carefully laid out in a significant position around the body of the deceased, or a pit whose contents might have been deposited in a significant order as part of a ritual.

In all cases, special finds (which are sometimes referred to as 'small finds') are treated to a higher level of recording and description. As well as being given a unique number, the precise find spot will be recorded in three dimensions, using EDM equipment or a theodolite and tape measures (*see* The Initial Site Plan), and the details will be entered into a special finds register and noted on the context recording sheet.

As the site is excavated, the digger will learn what is commonplace and what is special, and if something unusual is encountered, the digger will seek guidance before going any further. Special techniques apply to the extraction of fragile materials, metal objects and material that might be subjected to DNA testing or carbon dating.

Describing relationships

Back at the ditch, the digger will find a new layer emerging, which might be of a different colour and consistency to the one that was being trowelled. The entire first layer from the ditch has been removed, so the digger plans, photographs and assigns a number to the new deposit. In recording the new context, the digger has to decide what relationship exists between this deposit and the first. The relationship can be very simple: in this case the second deposit is entirely covered by the first. But there are several other possibilities that a digger might encounter: two deposits can abut each other, and one can entirely surround another (this is called a lenticular deposit). Most importantly of all for phasing, one context can cut through another.

Being honest about what you find

Sometimes the precise relationship of one deposit to another isn't always crystal clear. You might not even be entirely certain that there are two separate layers, because one blends gradually into another or one is similar to the next – just with fewer inclusions. It is here that experience counts for so much: what is puzzling to a first-time digger might be something that a seasoned digger has seen many times before.

For this reason, context recording sheets have an area for discussion of the evidence, which allows the digger to record comments and changing interpretations as he or she works. This can be used to make observations arising from an intimate relationship with that patch of soil. Relevant observations that might affect the interpretation of the evidence and its reliability might be to note the methods and conditions under which the digger worked (for example, rapid work under salvage conditions, heavy rain, poor light), what the weather and soil conditions were like (waterlogged, frozen, baked hard by the sun), or whether there was evidence of tree-root disturbance or animal burrowing.

Reaching 'the Natural'

The aim of excavation is to unravel the history of archaeological features by removing and examining the deposits one at a time, in the reverse order from that in which they were laid down. This process continues until the only material left is the natural geological surface.

It can take a few days of digging before a digger is nearly finished excavating a ditch (*see* Excavating a Ditch). This will be a process of discovery for someone who is a novice, finding out how to excavate and record the site and what secrets lie hidden in the ground. Sometimes an unexpected surprise might appear at the base of the ditch. For example, a water channel constructed of stone called a 'box culvert'.

Seeking the natural

If there is a surprise at the base of the ditch, such as a box culvert, it won't have reached a fully excavated stage. To do so will involve dismantling the culvert or other structure, but first it has to be given a context number, cleaned, drawn and photographed, and its coordinates plotted — the same repetitive pattern that is part of every context, deposit and feature.

Above The layers of an opened context are ready for examination by an archaeologist.

After filling in the context sheet describing the structure, the digger can begin to take it apart. This can be a sad task because it often involves the destruction of something that had been beautifully constructed; in the case of a box culvert, it will have flat stones forming the base and top, and supporting stones running along the length of the ditch to form a rectangular channel, or conduit.

Removing the conduit is necessary to confirm whether or not there are any further deposits beneath the culvert, including any finds that might help to date it. Although the digger is destroying something that has survived for many centuries, that person might be consoled with the thought that plenty more of it survives below the ground. Once there are no further finds and the supervisor is satisfied that the digger has reached what archaeologists call 'the natural' — meaning the natural geological surface that has been unmodified by human activity — the excavation will reach a conclusion.

Recording the cut

Before the digger prepares to clean up, photograph and draw the empty ditch, it is important to remember that empty features also need a context number. The open empty ditch itself represents a stage in the history of the

Left Archaeologists penetrate to the Bronze-Age level of an ancient site in Sinop, Turkey.

The archaeology of a box culvert

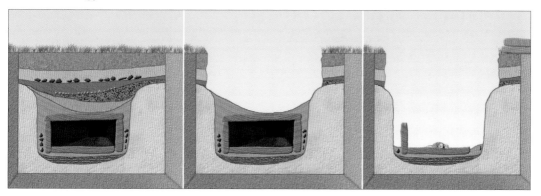

1 This section through a Roman culvert, used to take water from a spring to a water tank, shows the ditch originally dug to lay down the culvert, the culvert itself, made from stone, and the fill above.

2 By this stage, the top levels have been excavated and recorded: the top two layers are cultivated topsoil and a layer of subsoil directly below. Next comes the Roman ditch fill, dated by the pottery fragments in the soil.

3 By the third and final stage, the culvert has been opened to see what lies within: perhaps nothing, perhaps a coin lost by the person who made the culvert, or perhaps the skeleton of a long dead frog or rat!

site. This type of feature is described as a 'cut', naturally enough, because it cuts through another feature – in this case the natural geology.

Various terms are used to record cuts, starting with basic dimensions, such as length, width and depth (with maximum, minimum and average measurements if these vary). The shape can be linear, or it can be square, rectangular, circular, oval, sub-circular or sub-oval or irregular. Linear and irregular features can sometimes also be described as straight, curving or curvilinear. The orientation of the cut should also be recorded.

If the cut has discernible corners, they are described as straight, rounded or irregular. The sides can be vertical, U-shaped, V-shaped or irregular. The opposing side of the cut might be symmetrical or asymmetrical, and the gradient can be shallow (less than 45 degrees), moderate (45 degrees) or steep (more than 45 degrees). The sides can also be stepped, and the base can be flat, tapered or curved (concave or convex).

The digger's observations

Free text areas of the recording sheet can be used to make interpretative observations: for example, what, at the end of the day, does the digger think of the site? In discussion with the site supervisor, the conclusion might be that the ditch was dug to house the stone culvert, which itself was constructed to carry water from a spring that has yet to be located somewhere higher up the hill. Water was channelled

Left The remains of a Victorian drainage system were uncovered on an industrial site.

from the spring to a group of buildings that are being excavated lower down the hillside site.

The interpretation should include all the evidence that supports the theory about the construction, use and disuse of the feature, based on the information gained from its shape. In this example, the ditch is narrow, with steep regular sides and flat bottom, and there is a shallow gradient, suggesting that it was dug specifically as a channel to house the culvert – it was not dug for another purpose and later used as a culvert. If the ditch had remained open for any period of time, the sides would be more eroded and would have a shallower gradient.

The digger will also try to explain the origin of the deposits in the ditch: whether they are the result of deliberate deposition or from a natural process. The fact that the fill of the ditch is uniform supports the conclusion that the ditch was cut, the culvert laid and the ditch filled again in a short period of time. If the ditch had been left open, there would have been a slow build up of silts and vegetation that would leave distinct bands of soil of different colours and compositions.

Section Drawings and Photographs

Once features are fully excavated, the vertical sections are drawn and photographed to show how the excavated deposits fit together and as a permanent record of what was removed from the site. Section drawings are one of the most informative components of a site's recording.

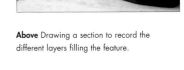

Above Drawing a section to record the different layers filling the feature.

In many ways the section drawing encapsulates the story of the feature by capturing a slice through its contents. However, in some cases it will provide only a partial story – in the ditch with the box culvert (*see* Reaching the 'Natural'), for example, it only tells about events that happened after the ditch or pit began to fill. This is often the point at which it ceased to be used for its original purpose – although this final stage can have its own interesting story, because sometimes pits or ditches are deliberately closed by filling them with ritual deposits. All this information is captured in the drawing of the section.

Preparing for a drawing

In preparation for the drawing, first the vertical face is trowelled to ensure that it is as straight as possible. Next, a datum line, or base line, is created, from which to take measurements. At the top of the section, a string is nailed to one side of the ditch and stretched across to the other side . It is kept tight and a mini spirit level is used to make sure that it is perfectly horizontal and isn't catching on any protruding stone or potshard, before the other side of the string is nailed to the opposite side of the ditch. The site surveyor will provide EDM readings for the two ends of the datum string, which will need to be adjusted if they turn out not to be the same height – they should be the same height for the string to be absolutely level. A tape

measure can now be run along this string, attaching it to the nails with clips (not the string, or it will droop). This tape gives the horizontal scale for the drawing, and a hand tape measure can be used to take vertical readings above and below the string.

Making the drawing

To represent the string, one of the thicker lines on the graph paper is chosen, and to indicate it as the base line, arrows are drawn on either side of the section drawing. Next, the sides of the ditch are measured and drawn in in relation to the base line, with measurements being transferred to the tracing paper by the means of dots

and then joining the dots to represent as accurately as possible the shape of the ditch sides.

The horizons of the layers that fill the ditch are then drawn, along with the stones of the culvert and the fill below and above. Larger inclusions, such as stones in the ditch fill, are also drawn in as accurately as possible. Finally, the drawing is labelled to show the context numbers that were allocated to each layer and feature as the ditch was excavated, along with the site and trench reference numbers, a note of the scale at which

Below A large, opened context is measured and recorded here with the aid of a crane.

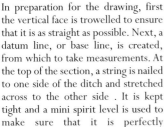

Recording the stratigraphic layers of a context

1 The 'horizons' of each discernible level of the sides of the ditch are measured and readings noted.

2 Readings are then drawn to scale on graph paper and joined up to form a record of the stratigraphy.

the drawing has been made, the orientation (the direction in which the section is facing) and the digger's initials and date, to indicate who made the drawing in case questions need to be asked at a later stage. If stylized conventions are used to indicate differences in ditch fill – for example, dots to indicate gravel – a key also needs to be supplied.

Photography

As well as making a drawn plan of the site, a photographic record is maintained of the site at every stage in its excavation. This photographic record is a valuable additional check for future archaeologists who might want to use the site data. Some photographs are taken specifically as an integral part of the site record, along with the drawings, finds and context sheets. Others are taken to place features and the site as a whole into its wider context. It is also useful to have some general site shots taken during the course of the dig, including diggers at work. As well as being useful for future publications and for illustrating lectures, there is a great nostalgic value in being able to look back a decade or more hence on what will, hopefully, have been a memorable excavation.

If the site is large, photographing the site in its entirety is not always easy; if the director anticipates the need to gain a high view of the site, scaffolding towers or an elevated platform known as a 'cherry picker' can be rented and used for taking aerial views. Some archaeologists have tried attaching cameras to kites and helium balloons, but these are rarely as easy to control and manoeuvre as one might like. Aerial photographs of the site are a great bonus, and might be obtainable if there is an airstrip in the vicinity and light aircraft owners willing to fly over your site with a camera.

Film and digital

Although digital photography is now widely used, some archaeologists still use 35mm film, and the different requirements of site archives, publication and lectures means that some also like to take black-and-white pictures as well as colour.

Digital photography is increasingly used as the price of good quality digital cameras comes down. Digital cameras are also excellent for making a 'social' record of the site – especially for use in lectures and on websites because they are easily integrated into computer-based applications.

Shot composition

Lighting is critical for all site photography. The whole of the subject needs to be lit by the same light, not half in bright sunshine and the other in shade. It is also important that record shots taken of features and deposits or finds before they are removed from the ground have a scale and a north arrow.

The area to be photographed must be impeccably clean and free of debris, spoil, tools, labels, clothes, and so on – hence the sections are photographed last, after the section drawing has been completed and the section string, nails and labels have been removed. At the last moment the area to be photographed can be sprayed with water to enhance colours and contrasts.

Above After the site has been drawn, labels, pins and tapes are removed and the site cleaned for photography.

95

Revealing the Layers

The excavation of a site is an exciting time for archaeologists, but also a testing one. Having revealed in plan – that is in bird's eye view – what features appear to exist on the site, it is usual for the diggers to pause and think about a number of questions.

The key concepts that need to be addressed mainly relate to 'phasing' and 'stratigraphy' of the site. These concepts are central to all archaeology – they are the main analytical tools that we have for understanding the phases of activity that have taken place in the past on the site.

Phasing is a shorthand term for questions such as: how old are these features, are they all of one period, or do they represent several periods of activity? Can we put these features into some kind of relative chronological order, from the newest features on the site to the oldest? Can we tell whether these different phases of use were continuous and evolutionary, or were there periods of use and abandonment –

maybe seasonal (used in summer, not in winter), maybe separated by much longer periods of time?

Stratigraphy

Answering those questions is only possible if we can investigate the stratigraphy, a concept derived from geology that involves the analysis of the different layers found in soil sections. Geologists study sections that can be many metres deep and that represent millions of years of titanic geological processes, such as volcanic eruption, flooding and the deposition of sands and gravels, or the folding, heating and compression of rocks. Archaeologists tend to work with much smaller soil sections, which represent the smaller

Above On urban sites, the phasing is often complex due to repeated use through history.

chunks of time that result from small-scale human activity. Even so, the basic principles are the same, and they are based on the logical premise that the lowest layers in any section through the earth are the oldest and the highest ones are the most recent.

Phasing

Using this relatively basic concept, it is not difficult to understand the phasing of a simple ditch that has slowly filled from the bottom up. However, stratigraphic analysis is more complex when you begin to look at the intersections of two or more different

Above The layers of a cliffside context have been tagged in Wyoming, USA.

Left Recording a section through layers of peats and gravels at an intertidal location.

Cowdery's Down

No matter how carefully you prepare in advance, occasionally archaeology has the power to throw up something unexpected. At Cowdery's Down, in Hampshire, England, archaeologists turned up in the late 1970s to excavate what they thought from aerial photographs and trial excavation was the site of a Civil War fortification. They thought it was where parliamentary forces had set up gun platforms on the hillside to blast away at the Royalist-held Basing House on the opposite side of the valley, which would date the site to the mid-17th century. However, that guess was proven to be wrong by 1,000 years.

Once the site was opened up in full, archaeologists found a complete Saxon village – the first of its kind ever to be found in England – with a number of large hall houses, each sitting in its own fenced yard, amid a maze of ditches and pits. The challenge that then faced

Above The phasing at this Anglo-Saxon village was based on painstaking excavation of the post holes, representing the remains of fences and property boundaries.

the archaeologists was to answer the question: are these houses and other features all of the same date? The only way to tell was to look for the points where the post holes left by the rotten timbers of one house or fence cut through another. A very small number of such post holes were found, forming a sort of '8' shape rather than an 'O'. Delicate excavation of soil at the point where the two post holes met established which one was the oldest and which the newest of the two.

Archaeologist then used this critical stratigraphical evidence and correlated it with other evidence that was found at the site – slight differences in the alignments of the fences and huts, for example, or in the style of the construction, or in the internal layout – to phase the site's many different periods. Some of the ditches and fences were proven to be Iron Age and Roman, and the hall houses themselves were proven to have been rebuilt and replaced several times during the period from the late 5th to the early 8th century.

phases of activity. In an urban environment, for example, where people have lived on the same site for hundreds – or thousands – of years, adapting what they find or building new houses on top of old, the resulting stratigraphy is a mind-bending mix of deposits. Some will lie on top of others, some will cut through others, while some will abut others and some are entirely contained within others (this is called a lens).

Vital clues to the phasing of the site can be found in those superimpositions and juxtapositions of layers, some of which can be very slight and easily destroyed during excavation. It is perhaps the most difficult challenge any archaeologist faces, deciding where exactly to dig in order to find those critical diagnostic intersections that tell the story of the phasing of the site.

Left Deep contexts, such as this medieval well, provide a rich stratigraphic record.

The Site Matrix

Before a digger leaves a ditch after it has finally been excavated, it is essential to try to place the ditch itself within the wider context of the whole site, showing how it relates to the other features that have also been dug up and recorded.

Distinguishing between contexts and understanding their relationships can be the most challenging and difficult part of any excavation, because it is a matter of judgement and interpretation. Fortunately, establishing stratigraphical relationships does not need to be a solitary activity or a one-time event. Diggers are encouraged to discuss their thoughts with fellow diggers and supervisors – indeed, much of the conversation that takes place at the end of a long hard day over dinner or around the camp fire is about

the overall interpretation of the site and how the various pieces fit together. It is often the case that preliminary thoughts are revised over and over again, as more evidence begins to emerge that might help the digger move from tentative to firmer ground.

Creating a matrix

Understanding the site as a whole is made easier by the use of a series of conventions that were devised by the Bermuda-born archaeologist Ed Harris, while working on excavations

Above Chaotic as it looks, the site matrix will reduce this site to a clear chronological record.

in Winchester, England, in 1973. His set of conventions, known as the Harris Matrix, or (less often) the Winchester seriation diagram, are now used all over the world as a means of describing stratigraphy relationships. However, many other archaeologists were involved in refining the basic approach through work undertaken in Cirencester and in London during the 1970s and 1980s.

The matrix for any site will look like a family tree diagram, with boxes that have context numbers instead of people's names. The uppermost context is at the top – it represents the most recent deposit. Different types of feature are represented by different shaped boxes – to distinguish between deposits, cuts and hard features. In the case of a simple ditch, the diagram will show a basic linear progression, of one context lying over another. However, if another feature is encountered within the ditch – for example, a post hole cut into the fill of the ditch, with its own cut and fill – that would be shown as a separate branch off the main tree.

Floating and fixed matrices

The matrix for the ditch is a complete representation of the ditch and its fill, but it is floating without a wider context unless the ditch matrix is joined to a larger diagram of the site,

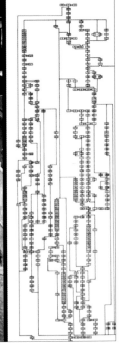

Left The extensive matrix to the right can be read by an archaeologist as a timeline of features at the Roman wall site on the left.

showing the relationships of every feature to another. This can be done only if a section of the ditch is found that cuts or is cut by another feature, enabling archaeologists to show a relationship between the two features. Bit by bit the floating matrices can be joined together like a jigsaw to create a phased matrix for the whole site; at least, in the ideal world, for it is one of the frustrating facts of archaeology that it is not always possible to define a clear physical relationship between one context and another, although similarities in the fill and in the finds from each context might suggest they belong to the same phase.

The example of the box culvert, right, shows how multiple contexts can be placed into a logical sequence.

Creating a Harris Matrix

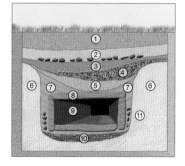

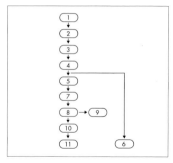

1 Every context has a number, including the cut itself (11), each number representing the physical counterpart to an event or action in the life of the culvert.

2 These events or actions are then represented in a chronological diagram, with recent events appearing at the top and the oldest events at the bottom.

The excavation record

The process that a digger will go through to excavate a ditch is one that quickly becomes familiar, and that will be repeated many times during the course of the excavation. Here is a quick summary of the basic steps:

• Clean the area to define the extent of the context
• Assign a number to the context
• Take photographs of the context
• Plan the context
• Survey the context to pinpoint its position
• Excavate the context and in doing so define the limits of the next context
• Recover artefacts (and environmental samples) from the context and record 'special' finds
• Describe the context on a recording sheet, including its physical relationship to other contexts
• Survey the context to give its height in relation to the site datum
• Repeat the process until the context has been excavated in its entirety
• Draw the resulting section

• Define and describe the 'cut' represented by the feature
• Survey in the base/natural layer of the feature.

Site archive

The collective result of this activity will be a set of data that records all the excavated material and that consist of:

• Notebooks listing all the site coordinates, context numbers, photographs, drawings, finds and special finds
• Plans and section drawings of the whole site as well as of individual contexts
• Context record sheets and matrices
• Black-and-white and colour photographs
• Finds and environmental samples.

All of the items in these lists are now familiar with the exception of the finds and the environmental samples. (*For more on these, see* Rich Finds and Humbler Finds.)

Below Excavating and recording is a repetitive activity, but the thrill of discovering and sharing knowledge of finds is never dull.

Case Study: Frocester Court

Frocester Court is the site of one of Britain's longest-running continuous excavations. Since 1961, enthusiasts have been excavating a 2.8-ha (7-acre) site with thorough and painstaking care in order to try and understand the 4,000-year history of Frocester parish, starting in the Bronze Age.

Above One of Frocester's Roman finds – the rim and base of a cooking jar dating from the 4th century.

Mr Eddie Price, the owner of Frocester Court, knew that there was something in the field opposite his farmhouse because there were stony areas that were difficult to plough, where he picked up a large amount of pottery. Mr Price showed the pottery to Captain Gracie, a local archaeologist, who visited Frocester in 1961, dug a trench and found a Roman mosaic pavement. Captain Gracie returned every year until 1978 when he became too ill to continue, and Mr Price took over as the director of excavations.

Frocester's story

The mosaic pavement turned out to be the floor of a long corridor running the length of a Roman villa, dating from

Left This plan of part of the site points out some of the early Roman buildings.

the end of the 3rd century. However, careful excavation of the area around the villa made Mr Price realize that this was just one phase of the history of the site, and he made it his mission to excavate the field and gradually unpick the archaeology in order to follow the fortunes of human activity at Frocester right from first beginnings to the present day.

The Bronze Age

The earliest evidence that could be found at the site for human occupation was a well, with a timber post set in the centre – perhaps as a marker, perhaps used as a ladder. The post was radiocarbon dated (*see* Radiocarbon Dating) to 1600BC, the early Bronze Age.

Typical early Bronze Age pottery was found in a territorial boundary ditch that ran for some 300m/985ft across the site, joining a hollow trackway. It was fenced on either side, so it was probably used as a droveway for moving cattle from site to site.

The Iron Age

By the Iron Age (from 700BC), the sunken droveway had been abandoned, but a new track has developed alongside it, leading to a very large enclosure surrounded by a 3-m (10-ft) deep ditch, perhaps filled with water like a moat. Within the enclosure were some large round buildings, as well as

an elaborate arrangement of fences and stock pens, designed for sorting sheep or cattle into different groups. While humans and beasts co-existed happily inside the farmyard enclosure, there was also a large external garden area, deliberately kept separate from the farmyard to prevent animals trampling or eating the crops.

Toward the end of the Iron Age (say 200BC), the interior of the farm enclosure was divided up into smaller pens, which Mr Price thinks were for smaller animals – hens, pigs, sheep and goats – with rectangular granaries for storing grain. During the same time the external garden had grown to include arable fields. The round houses had been rebuilt even larger, with one main house and two smaller ones – perhaps the homes of an extended family or perhaps, Mr Price suggests, for the farmer and his two wives.

A beautiful bronze neck ring, or torque, was discovered in the foundations of the bigger house, perhaps placed there as a foundation offering. Other finds include horse bones and the moulds for casting the type of lynch pins found on Iron Age chariots, suggesting that the farmer was prosperous enough to own the equivalent of a luxury car.

Dramatic change

By AD100 the moated enclosure, the garden and fields were still there, however, the round houses and internal fences had been swept away and

Reconstructing the history of Frocester Court

Above This reconstruction draws on the earliest evidence from Frocester, and shows a Bronze Age track, wells and boundary ditch.

Above The enclosed site and large circular buildings of this phase characterize the early Iron Age farm.

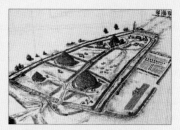

Above By the late Iron Age, the round houses have grown in stature, and the interior has been subdivided into distinct 'pens'.

Above The first Roman farm of 100–275AD, with internal divisions removed and rectangular timbered buildings in place.

Above The grand Roman villa of Frocester Court was built in the 4th century AD, and was set among extended grounds.

Above By the post-Roman phase the villa has declined, but the site continued to be farmed from the 5th century onward.

replaced by Roman-style rectangular buildings made of timber and thatch. Farming was still going on, but also some industrial activity, to judge from the iron and bronze working hearths.

By the 3rd century AD, the evidence suggests that the farm had become a larger estate, with the main centre of occupation elsewhere. Large numbers of 'goads' for guiding oxen were found from this period – evidence that oxcarts were used to bring the crops in from the fields. Behind one of the barns is a cemetery containing the remains of 40 infants – a sad reminder of the high rate of child mortality at this period.

Living in luxury

Some time in the last quarter of the third century the site ceased to be a working farmyard, and a substantial Roman style villa was constructed with massive walls, suggesting that it was several storeys high. Archaeologists found the evidence for the demolition of the older barns, and for the first time in 1,000 years, the moat enclosing the site was filled in and the site appears to have expanded beyond its Iron Age limits.

About 100 years later, the villa was given a makeover and became even more luxurious, with underfloor heating, mosaic floors, a bath house, and a beautiful formal garden. All of this might well be evidence for the prosperity that might have occurred once Roman control of the countryside began to weaken.

After the Romans

Unfortunately, all good things must end. For a while, weaker Roman rule brought prosperity, and those good solid Roman roads meant that it was possible to take goods to markets in still-thriving towns. However, little by little, the infrastructure of late Roman Britain began to break down and life at the villa became more and more impoverished. Refuse that was found in and around the villa suggests that fewer and fewer rooms were used, and there is evidence that parts of the villa were used to house animals. Within only two centuries, the grand villa was abandoned, robbed of useful building materials and ironwork, and parts were burned down. Even so, the site continued as a farm centre until being abandoned before c. 800AD in favour of the present estate centre and the developing Saxon village.

By the late 7th century the Roman villa had been entirely abandoned, and a new area of Saxon settlement had grown up in a different part of Frocester parish. As Frocester Court entered consecutive periods of open-field farming, the farmhouse that is on the site today was built during the 16th century, and a magnificent medieval barn constructed when Frocester was part of the estate owned by the monks of Gloucester Abbey.

RICH FINDS AND HUMBLER FINDS

It is reasonable to think that archaeologists are principally concerned with finding things, especially gold and silver jewellery, sculptures, pots full of coins or spectacular mummies and tombs because that is what is often displayed in museums. It is also what gets the media's attention; for example, the 25- to 30-year-old Anglo-Saxon woman found at Butler's Field in Gloucestershire, England, was nicknamed 'Mrs Getty' by the press because of the rich finds from her grave, whereas they ignored the graves of humbler people, which are just as interesting to archaeologists. Analysis of their teeth or bones can tell us what they ate, how old they were, what ailments they had and whether they were local people who adopted Saxon lifestyles or migrants from the Netherlands, Denmark or Germany. In fact, what interests an archaeologist is any material that can yield information. This chapter looks at the ingenious ways in which archaeologists extract knowledge from even the humblest of finds.

Opposite Pottery urns from a cremation cemetery in Languedoc-Rousillon, used from 11th–7th century BC.

Above The head of Archaeological Reserves of Ecuador examines a pre-Columbian statuette in a storage site in Quito.

Above Sandy deposits from the Çatalhöyük site in Turkey are sifted through a large circular mesh in the search for microscopic finds.

Above Microscopic remains of plants or charred earth are examined as part of the evidence-gathering process.

Artefacts and Ecofacts

Archaeological finds are broadly classified into two categories: artefacts that are the result of human craft, and ecofacts, which are of natural origin and help us understand the environment and landscape surrounding any site being studied. Different recovery and study methods apply to each category.

The excavation of an archaeological site involves the removal of layers of soil in the reverse order from that in which they were deposited, so archaeologists can understand the physical features of a site. Most of that soil gets left behind when the archaeologists depart, but not the finds that come from the soil. Instead, as the site is excavated, the digger will be expected to keep a sharp eye open for finds, which are removed from the soil, placed in a labelled tray and sent to the finds shed for further work.

What is a find?

What counts as a 'find' very much depends on the nature of the site and the recovery strategy that the site director has established. Some sites are so rich in finds that to take everything away for study would require a very large vehicle; these are called common, or bulk, finds. The ancient Roman buildings found all over Europe, the Mediterranean and North Africa are often constructed of durable materials, such as stone, brick and tile. Even if they were 'robbed' in the past by later people, who wanted to reuse the materials in their own structures, the mess and debris left by a collapsed or demolished Roman building is often substantial. In such cases, it is normal to keep a basic record of the quantity and weight of building material from the site, but to keep only examples that are special, because they are intact, or

Above Charred munitions found at the Roman settlement at Farafra, Egypt, which was fortified to protect the routes to other oases.

because the clay tile bears a manufacturer's stamp, the maker's thumb print or some idly scratched graffiti.

By contrast, there are sites that are so insubstantial that every effort is taken to record and salvage the slightest find. Tracking down the camp fires of our earliest nomadic ancestors is a challenging task in which no piece of evidence – even charcoal flecks, bone fragments and pollen – is taken for granted.

Below Palmyra in Syria, one of the most important Roman sites of the Middle East, is rich in architectural remains.

Above (clockwise from top) Carved wooden projectile point from the Hoko wet site; hafted microlith with green stone cutting edge, *in situ*; part of a stone bowl from the dry site.

The Hoko River archaeological site

A dramatic example of the way that environmental conditions can effect the survival rate of artefacts and ecofacts comes from the Hoko River Rockshelter and shell midden (a rubbish heap of shells), in Washington, an American site that straddles both dry land and wet land locations. The list of materials recovered from the waterlogged deposits, where the conditions preserve organic material, include baskets, hats, mats, fishing lines and nets, wooden fishhooks, needles and garment pins. We would know little about the life of the Hoko River people, or their fishing and weaving skills, if we only had the artefacts from the dry side, consisting largely of stone tools and blades.

Man-made or natural finds

The contrast between the Roman and the prehistoric site also highlights the two main types of find that archaeologists collect and study: typically referred to as 'artefacts' and 'ecofacts'.

Artefacts are objects that have been used, modified or made by humans. The ones archaeologists find tend to be of durable materials, such as stone, metal and ceramic, although frozen, arid and waterlogged sites might also yield artefacts made of organic materials, such as leather, wood, woven

Above Preparation of samples during soil and sediment analysis.

straw or reed, paper and cloth. Ecofacts, by contrast, tend to be floral and faunal – that is, they consist of plant material, such as pollen, or of the remains of once-living organisms, such as snail shell or beetle wings.

Different techniques

Artefacts and ecofacts are often different in size. Whereas artefacts are usually visible to the naked eye, many ecofacts are so small that a microscope is needed for their study. This means that the collection strategy for each is different. Artefacts can be separated from the soil deposits in which they are found and are recoverable during the process of excavation or through sieving (sifting) through a coarse mesh. However, ecofacts are often recovered by means of soil sampling; the soil is then washed and filtered through a fine mesh – sometimes in an on-site laboratory, and sometimes away from the site at a later date.

Artefacts and ecofacts are often studied in different ways, too. Ecofacts in particular are the realm of the trained scientist, often using laboratory equipment, such as microscopes and spectrometers, where classifying

pollens or identifying the species from which bone fragments have come requires years of training and familiarity with the material. Artefacts can be appreciated more easily for what they are because they correspond more directly with the everyday objects that we still use. Yet they also have a scientific side, because the microscopic inclusions in the clay in pottery, for example, can help pin down exactly where the pot was made and food residues on the sides or in the porous body of the vessel can tell us what the pot was used for.

No hard boundaries

These are all generalizations, of course, because there is no very hard boundary between artefact and ecofact – where, for example, does charcoal fit, a material modified by humans but also the by-product of natural processes, such as forest fires. In fact, archaeologists do argue among themselves about what exactly is natural and what is artificial, although one of the great achievements of archaeologists in recent years has been to extend hugely the amount of information that can be extracted from all types of find – and not just those that are freshly dug. Unravelling the diets of Bronze Age people from studying the chemistry of their tooth enamel, or reconstructing the DNA of Neanderthals from fossilized bones can bring new relevance to material stored away in archives from decades-old excavations.

Above Excavating a relatively modern lime kiln from the 18th–19th century.

Processing Finds on Site

As finds are recovered from the archaeological site, they are taken to the finds shed or an on-site laboratory for processing. Here, finds are logged, inspected, cleaned and perhaps given emergency conservation treatment before they are stored for future study.

The task of running the finds lab is usually entrusted to a specialist with some knowledge of basic conservation practice. However, on a busy site there can be more finds than one person can cope with, and this is where volunteers are often able to help, taking a day off from digging to learn what happens to finds when they reach the finds shed.

Much finds work is routine and repetitive. By long-established tradition, archaeologists usually store finds in plastic trays, buckets or paper bags.

Below Common finds are placed in a labelled tray to be cleaned; special finds are bagged and their precise find spot recorded.

A popular option among British archaeologists is a shallow rectangular kind of plastic tray that gardeners often use for seed propagation.

Diggers are given a new finds tray at the beginning of every day. One key task is to ensure that every tray has a waterproof label with the site code and context number written on it so that there is a record of where the finds have come from. Those same diggers hand in their finds trays at the end of every day, or when they are full. The person receiving the trays must check that the labels are still intact and have not been mislaid or blown away – if so, they will require relabelling.

Above These pieces of pottery found at the Constantinople excavations in Istanbul, Turkey, will stand up to robust cleaning, but other finds are much more vulnerable.

Cleaning finds

The finds handed in at the end of the previous day now require sorting and cleaning. Once it was common practice to clean every find thoroughly in water and detergent, perhaps using a toothbrush or nailbrush to remove stubborn mud or stains. However, today there is an increasing awareness that the cleaning process can destroy vital evidence, such as food residues sticking to the surfaces of unglazed cooking pots or absorbed by the porous body of an earthenware storage jar, or soot from the cooking process that can be carbon dated. Overzealous cleaning can wash away bloodstains, paint, pigments, fabric, wood and other organic remains, and one scientist has recently warned archaeologists that they risk losing vital DNA evidence if they immerse bones in water.

Consequently, the site director will decide on a general strategy for salvaging and cleaning finds, in consultation with the finds supervisor. The decision about what to wash, what

Below A puppy's paw-print made on the drying clay of a Roman roof tile.

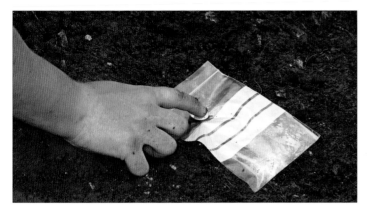

Above The soft bristles of a toothbrush are ideal for cleaning flint and bone.

Above The find is bagged, labelled and pinned to the spot where it was found so that it can, in due course, be plotted on the site plan.

to keep and what to weigh, measure and discard, will depend on the type of site and the type of finds and what sort of evidence the finds can reasonably be expected to yield.

How much to keep?

In an ideal world, everything from the site should be kept. In reality, the costs of storing and studying what are known as 'common finds' or 'bulk finds' can be so great that a balance has to be struck between the investment of time and money and the likely result in terms of information.

Often a decision is made by the director to keep just a sample of the finds, selecting material that is more likely to prove significant or diagnostic in the interpretation and understanding of the site. This strategy can be justified on the grounds that any excavation is, by definition, a sampling exercise. Rarely does an archaeologist get the opportunity to dig a site in its entirety, so the finds from one stretch of ditch are already just a random selection of a small percentage of the artefacts that might have survived.

However, archaeologists have a habit of discovering new ways of extracting information from finds that were once regarded as uninformative. Because of this, increasingly some archaeologists opt for the 'just in case'

strategy of keeping everything – although this can cause a major storage problem in due course.

Where bulk finds are not kept, they are still washed and laid out to dry in the sunshine, usually on old newspaper. Washing or gentle brushing removes mud that might conceal details that can elevate the find to a higher category. Roman roof tiles are routine and utilitarian objects, but occasionally one will have an animal footprint – made by a dog, for example, that has stepped

Above The southern gate of the Roman remains at Silchester, near the town of Reading, UK, has been continually excavated since the 19th century, and the site tells us as much about past excavations as about the settlers who built the town.

onto the drying clay while it was still soft enough to take a paw print. Such marks are popular in museum exhibits or as educational material, because they help to bring the past to life.

Bulk finds are then counted, weighed and described before being discarded. A good strategy is to bury them in a place on the site where they are likely to be undisturbed and to record the burial site in the site archive, so that future archaeologists can go back and recover them if a future need arises.

Going back at a later date

Bulk finds that are reburied at the end of a dig will lose their context and provenance, so they are of less value to future archaeologists. However, they do not entirely lose their value as a source of information. Archaeologists excavating the Roman town of Silchester, in central southern England, have been exploring the dumps left in 1893.

By analysing the contents of the pits, archaeologists were able to develop an insight into the excavation techniques and retrieval strategies of their 19th-century predecessors, learning, for example, what type and proportion of finds had been kept for further study and what was discarded. The pit contents also gave an insight into the range of refreshments that were consumed on site (mineral water, whisky and beer from Amsterdam) and even from which local baker and pastry cook they obtained some of their food supplies.

Activity in the Finds Shed

When a volunteer is asked to help in the finds shed for the day, the finds supervisor will explain the routine and some of the basic principles for dealing with finds. The routine will consist of sorting, packing and labelling the finds, all of which are important in keeping accurate records.

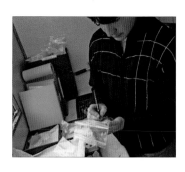

At the start of the day, the find supervisor will ask a volunteer to line up all the finds trays from the previous day's excavation, so that the director and site supervisors can review what has been found. Supervisors can easily become detached from what is happening on other parts of the site, so ideally the director will hold a meeting – perhaps at the beginning or the end of the day – where everyone can review progress on the site as a whole.

The supervisors also constantly monitor the finds that come out of features as they are excavated, because this is primary information that affects the interpretation of the site and the excavation strategy. In addition, special finds – in particular any finds that might help with the dating of features on the site (*see* Finds in Context) – are looked at as soon as they are found.

Below Finds are reviewed daily because they give clues to the interpretation and dating of the features being excavated.

Reviewing and comparing

By reviewing the finds, the supervisors can spot patterns and anomalies. For example, whether or not the various pits in different parts of the site have the same type of finds or different ones – perhaps more or less bone, or bone of different types of animal. Each of the supervisors may have a different area of expertise. The pottery expert can share his or her thoughts on the dating and significance of the pottery from the site, while a zooarchaeologist, who specializes in animal bone, can give a view on the meaning of the material that is found. Does it represent one animal type or many, one cut of meat, such as leg bones, or whole carcasses, are the bones from young or mature animals? The answers to these and other questions all provide information about the site.

Below Archaeology students are shown how to remove particles of earth clinging to the fragments of human skulls.

Above All these special finds are entered into a register to ensure that they do not get lost.

Sorting and packing finds

Once the team meeting has finished, the volunteer's task will be sorting the previous day's finds into different materials. Robust finds are bagged by context and according to type – so all the pottery, for example, from context 901 is put into one bag, all the shell into another, all the bone into a third, and so on.

Strong paper bags are generally used for this purpose, but the volunteer might also be asked to use resealable plastic bags, which come in a variety of sizes and, most importantly, have perforations punched into them. These holes allow moisture to escape, rather than being trapped in the bag. This is vital to the integrity of the find because moisture can cause unstable objects to corrode or crumble, and it encourages mould to form, damaging the material beyond repair.

WIG 07
C 1
Trench B.

Right Here, the animal bones from an excavation are carefully sorted by type and context.

Labelling

The finds supervisor is obsessive about labelling everything – not just once, but twice. First, the volunteer will be asked to write the site code, trench number and context number on the outside of the bag using a waterproof permanent marking pen – resealable plastic bags sometimes have white panels specifically designed for being written on by a pen – and then the volunteer places a waterproof label into the bag with the finds. So the pottery found in a ditch yesterday (*see* Finds in Context) is labelled with the site code AHF07 (*see* Preparing to Dig a Section), the trench code Trench 9 and a code (901) for the context or locus, along with the date when the finds were made.

Finds from different contexts in the same trench are kept together, usually in large stackable plastic boxes. The volunteer should put heavy and robust finds at the bottom of the box and more delicate finds at the top, thereby avoiding delicate pottery being crushed by heavy tile or brick.

Breaking the routine

The bagging and labelling can become a boring routine, but sometimes the routine is broken. For example, one of the supervisors might come into the finds shed to report that a coin has been found. Archaeologists love coins because they can help with the dating of site features. To everyone's disappointment, the finds supervisor insists that nobody rubs the coin to remove the green corrosion covering the coin's surface, because this can damage the coin (*see* Vulnerable Finds).

Instead, the spot where the coin was found is recorded (*see* Finds in Context) and the coin is given a unique find number, which is recorded in the finds log and written on the context sheet, so that everyone will know that special find number 85 came from context 179, and that it was found at this very specific spot on the earth.

Although the significance of its precise location will be unknown at the time, it is worthwhile recording the details carefully in case future digging reveals other artefacts that are associated with the special find.

Above The discovery of this Roman copper cauldron is rare because metals were often melted down and reused.

Archaeologists always work on the principle of recording everything because you never know what information can be useful in the future – and it is impossible to travel back in time if you don't record something.

Special finds

In some parts of the world, special finds are called 'archaeological objects' – however, neither term is satisfactory because all finds are archaeological objects and 'special' is a subjective term (*see* Finds in Context), and archaeologists, as scientists, try not to use value-laden words. Whatever they are called, they can have a legal dimension. Some countries will not permit the export of archaeological objects of a certain age or type, so if a visiting archaeological team is studying and conserving such finds, the work must be done in the host country. There can also be a legal duty to report such finds to a local museum or antiquities authority.

Vulnerable Finds

Common finds, such as tile, brick and stone, tend to be durable and robust, so they do not need special care. However, many finds are more delicate and will need proper first-aid treatment if they are to be preserved from damage for further study.

Once they are taken out of the ground, finds that have enjoyed stable conditions for centuries – if not thousands of years – will suddenly undergo a dramatic change in their environment. Woken from their long sleep, finds can undergo rapid deterioration when exposed to the air, sunlight and the physical handling of a curious sweaty-palmed archaeologist. In fact, these finds would probably shriek with pain if they had nerves and senses.

Minimal handling

Another key principle with all finds is to minimize how much they are handled. Depending on what type of site a volunteer is working on, this principle might even extend to a ban on handling finds with bare hands or on using sharp tools for excavation or cleaning. On a waterlogged site, for example, where wood can survive but might have the texture and consistency of a sponge cake, plastic spatulas are used to handle the finds, and surgical gloves are worn at all times.

Metal is especially vulnerable to decay from handling, so no matter how strong the desire is to clean the corrosion from the surface of that newly discovered coin to see how old it is, the urge has to be resisted. Rubbing the surface damages the patina – the

Right Some finds are too delicate to excavate on site, where microscopic evidence would be missed. Instead, such finds are lifted from the site as a block of soil which is protected from damage by a plaster of Paris wrapping. The find is then transported to a laboratory for detailed examination.

stable layer of corrosion that covers the surface. Removing this exposes the uncorroded metal beneath and starts the corrosion process all over again, so that important details, such as the lettering of an inscription or the mark of the mint where the coin was made, can be lost.

How rapidly finds deteriorate will depend on the nature of the material from which they are made and how great the contrast is between their buried environment and the one to which they are newly exposed. The greatest harm comes from the desiccation of materials that were previously wet or damp, and vice versa – for example, atmospheric moisture causing corrosion to metal objects. Therefore, the aim is to try to replicate the

Above Slipware dish dating from the early–mid 16th century is excavated with great care.

atmosphere from which the finds have just come, or to provide an alternative environment that is better for the finds.

Dry materials

Because damp and humidity can cause metals to decay, a coin will be allowed to air dry naturally (in a secure place) for 24 hours. The same treatment is good for all metal finds, including iron, copper, bronze, lead, tin and pewter (*see* Pottery as Evidence of Everyday Life). Finds made of these metals might well be brittle, so after drying out, they are laid on a supporting bed of crumpled-up acid-free tissue paper, in a rigid polystyrene box. The box is

Above Iron Age bronze shears, probably used for cutting textiles, with their carved container which is made from ash. The container also held a whetstone used for sharpening the shears. These finds were conserved at Flag Fen, UK, using a freeze-drying process.

Above A wooden barge from 100BC is found in the middle of a Netherlands town. It was once used to supply a Roman military base.

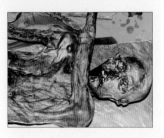

Above The well-preserved remains of Ötzi the Iceman are stored in a freezer.

packed with roughly the same weight of silica gel as the object weighs, along with a relative humidity indicator card, which has a coloured scale that reacts to damp. The relative humidity needs to be maintained at less than 15 per cent, which is achieved by sealing the box tightly, and checking at regular intervals, so that the silica gel bags can be replenished if necessary.

Silver and gold are stable metals, but they are rarely found as solid objects. More often one of these precious metals is applied as an outer layer to another material, such as wood, which might have deteriorated, or as gilding. In each case, the metal is likely to be thin and fragile and it too needs supporting and protecting from any external pressure.

The only exception is where it is thought that preserved organic remains are attached to a metal object – for example, a bone or wood handle to a knife, or leather or textile bindings. In this case, the object should be treated as if it were damp, and conservation advice sought immediately.

Damp and wet materials

By contrast, rapid drying is the enemy of materials that have ancient traces of paint – wall plaster, painted stone and sculpture, for example – or of natural materials, such as worked bone, wood,

ivory, shale, jet or amber, or the kind of fragile pottery that has been fired at a low temperature and that crumbles or breaks easily. Here, the aim is to maintain moisture levels by packing them with wet foam in a plastic box that has a tightly sealed lid.

Objects that are excavated from a waterlogged environment need more than damp foam to maintain moisture levels. They should be stored in a sealed box in distilled water to exclude atmospheric oxygen. Both damp and wet items should be refrigerated if possible – and they should certainly be kept cool and out of the sun to help prevent mould growth.

Wet finds

Flag Fen, near Peterborough, in eastern England, is a Bronze Age site, excavated from 1982, that produced very large quantities of well-preserved timber, so a special facility was built for preserving wet finds. Once excavated, the finds were placed in large tanks, where they were soaked in a solution of water and a wax called polyethylene glycol. It takes several years of immersion for the wax to fill the porous structure of the wood, after which the object can be slowly dried. The wax provides the support that prevents the object from shrinking or cracking as it dries.

Frozen finds

Occasionally archaeologists find frozen environmental evidence in permafrost, glaciers or on mountain tops, where the ground temperature never rises above freezing point. Spectacular discoveries from cold environments include the remains of humans, including the 5,300-year-old body of Ötzi the Iceman, found emerging from a melting glacier in the Italian Alps in 1991, and the 'Ice Maiden'. She was a 12- to 14-year-old girl apparently sacrificed by Inca priests on top of Mount Ambato near Arequipa in the Peruvian Andes in about 1480 – her frozen and well-preserved body was discovered in 1995. In both cases, the bodies were preserved by maintaining the cold conditions that had prevented the normal decay process, storing the remains at a maximum of -6°C (21°F).

Environmental Finds

One of the biggest changes in archaeological practice of the last few decades is the realization that sites contain far more finds than can be seen with the naked eye. These finds are recovered by taking and processing samples of the material from pits, ditches and other landscape features.

Biological or environmental remains are capable of telling archaeologists about many aspects of a site that they might not be able to deduce from more obvious finds. In particular, these remains are valuable for casting light on the type of environment that prevailed at the time the site was in use. Remember that landscapes change with use and weather patterns vary, with much still to be learned about their cycles. So although the archaeological site that is being excavated today might be in the middle of a grassy field surrounded by farmland, the scene might well have looked different in the past, and environmental remains can help provide clues to that past.

Past environments and weather

Pollens, plant remains, snail shells and insects are all materials capable of being used as evidence for reconstructing the environment at the time that the site was in use. Large amounts of tree pollen, for example, can indicate that the site was surrounded by woodland – perhaps it occupied a woodland clearing. The type of pollen and its relative abundance can also tell archaeologists whether the trees were being deliberately managed as coppice – that can be the case where hazel and willow pollen predominates, by contrast with a mixed woodland of oak, ash, alder, birch and so on.

Above Wet sieving stony earth for small finds and environmental evidence.

Some pollens are more indicative of grassland, or wetland environments (reeds and aquatic plants), just as many insects have specific habitat requirements and can thus tell archaeologists whether the environment was wet, dry, wild or cultivated. In wetland sites, plant and insect remains can further refine the picture of the past by telling archaeologists whether the site was on an ancient coastline, estuary, river, lake or pond. The sensitivity of some plants and insects to specific climatic conditions can also fill in a picture of the prevailing weather,

Above Peat cores are extracted from the Bogwater Copse in the Sandhills of North Carolina, as part of a project to reconstruct the hunter-gatherer history of this location. Pollens from surrounding vegetation were also sampled.

Left Students scan sifted soil looking for environmental plant and soil remains. The white background of the tray makes this easier.

which has long been a very important influence on human survival, migration and activity.

Economic information

Environmental remains can also give archaeologists an insight into the economy of the site, and the way that the people who lived there made use of their environment. Plant, bone, food and insect remains can, for example, demonstrate what types of crops were grown, what types of animals were kept and eaten, and whether the site was a smallholding, or a larger-scale farm, for example, processing pigs on an industrial scale.

These remains can tell archaeologists what type of diet the inhabitants enjoyed – whether, for example, it included wild foods, fish or shellfish, or even exotic imported foods from an entirely different part of the world. The remains can also tell archaeologists something about the health of the animals and humans – this information can be determined from the remains of insects and parasites.

One further and vital use for environmental remains is to provide material that can be used for dating parts of the site (*see* Selecting Samples for Carbon Dating). Material that is suitable for carbon dating – such as wood, charcoal or plant material – is often obtained as a result of environmental sampling.

Right Durable remains, such as discarded oyster shells, are an excellent source of evidence of ancient diets.

Below These marigold seed cases, or 'burs', tell archaeologists about the ancient weeds and plant life of the site.

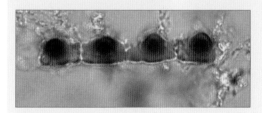

Above The phytoliths of these banana leaves are 'volcano-shaped', and distinguishable from those of a related genus on account of their specific physical form.

The first bananas in Africa

Soil samples have recently been used to trace the origin and spread of bananas from their botanical place of origin in New Guinea, where they were cultivated as early as 5000BC. Bananas do not preserve well, but it is possible to detect their presence through the study of phytoliths. These are microscopic particles produced by plants through interaction with minerals in the soil. They are commonly formed from silicon or calcium – hence their name (*phytolith* means 'plant stone'). The shape of the phytolith is unique to the plant, so it is easy to tell the difference between banana and strawberry phytoliths, for example. As minerals, they survive for a long time and can be dated using carbon-dating techniques.

Looking for phytoliths in soil samples from around the Indian Ocean, scientists at California State University in San Bernardino have established that bananas reached India and Pakistan by 3000BC, probably via Vietnam and Thailand. From India they quickly reached Africa: banana phytoliths have been found near the Uganda–Rwanda border dating from 3000BC. The implication is that Indian Ocean trading was already established by this date. We also know that African crops spread in the opposite direction, because sorghum and millet, cereal grains of the traditional African diet, had reached Korea by 1400BC.

Sampling Strategy

To decide how much material to save, the site director and site supervisors have to consider what sorts of deposits are most likely to yield well-preserved environmental materials. They then attempt to develop a logical sampling strategy appropriate to the site they are excavating.

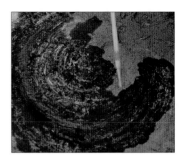

The term 'bulk sample' is usually used to describe large samples taken away from a site and examined for environmental evidence in the laboratory. The material sampled in this way can include soil, hearth contents, peat and wood, and mineralized deposits, such as tufa – the calcium carbonate deposit that forms around springs, cisterns and wells, similar to the limescale that forms in hard-water areas.

Bulk samples can range in size from 10 litres (2½ gallons) – a bucketful – to as much as 100 litres (26½ gallons). This is a large amount of material to process, and sampling every context without a clear reason would not be a good use of limited resources.

If a site is thought to be rich in ecofacts, or environmental finds, an environmental specialist may be included as part of the excavation team. Bulk samples can then be processed on site, using sieves (screens) and flotation tanks (*see* Processing Soil Samples). This allows the environmental archaeologist to quickly identify where the best results are being obtained, so that the scale of the sampling can be increased accordingly and the maximum amount of material can be recovered.

The alternative is to seek specialist advice before the dig starts and agree to a site sampling strategy based on such factors as the likely survival rates of different kinds of environmental

Above Phytoliths are also found in artefacts made of plant matter. At the ancient site of Çatalhöyük in Turkey, samples were taken from baskets buried with the dead.

remains, given the geology of the site and the type of site that it is. The initial strategy should be regularly reviewed in the light of the material that is found as the dig progresses.

What survives where

The background geology might be favourable or hostile to the survival of ecofacts. For example, fewer environmental remains survive in acidic conditions than in alkaline or neutral ones. Charred deposits (the remains of

Above These pottery 'wasters' (a term referring to flawed pottery), found in a 2nd century AD pit, will provide a useful source of mineral evidence.

Left This grave site has an enormous amount of archaeological matter, from large and small finds to organic remains.

hearths, kilns or grain drying activity) yield valuable charcoals and charred plant remains, but destroy insect remains, pollens, spores and plant remains. Waterlogged deposits are the best for the survival of all types of organic material, followed closely by the type of soils that result from an accumulation of human or animal manure – what archaeologists politely call 'cess'. By contrast, fine silt contains fewer organic remains because the alluvial soil formation process leaves behind the heavier biological materials and deposits only fine clay particles.

The sampling strategy should also consider an evaluation of the probable types of feature that will be found on site. Bulk samples will always be taken from burials and cremation sites, if only because of the possibility of recovering small artefacts or artefact fragments that might help with the dating of the burials. Samples are also taken from bone-rich deposits to ensure that all bone is recovered, including smaller bones and fragments. (*For more on excavating human remains, see* The Study of Human Remains.)

Below Analysis of human remains reveals much about diet and disease.

Samples for reconstructing the economy of the site will be taken from any feature thought to be a floor surface, because this is where archaeologists hope to find microscopic debris from any occupational or industrial activities that took place on that floor. Samples from storage pits can tell us what was stored in them, and refuse pits are a gold mine for archaeologists, as are cess pits, middens (ancient refuse heaps), wells and moats.

For environmental reconstruction, the best sources for plant, insect and snail remains are ditches, buried turf lines, peat and the fill of water channels and gulleys, watering holes and ponds.

Environmental controls

As well as collecting material that will be used for working out what the climate and vegetation was like in the past, environmental archaeologists will also collect material from the current environment to provide comparative data. One way to do this is to dig holes around the site being excavated just large enough to hold a plastic drinking cup. The cups are inspected regularly to see what insects fall into the trap, and after counting and identification, they are released. The data collected in this

way will tell archaeologists what types of insects are at home in the ecological niche provided by the present environment, for comparison with the material from excavated samples. Material from the uppermost (or the most recent) layers might be similar in its insect life, while earlier layers might differ. If the archaeologist is lucky, it might be possible to identify the precise contexts in which the transition from, say, a woodland to a grassland environment took place, and perhaps even provide a date based on the site stratigraphy and phasing.

Above Samples were taken from the clay sediments using a 40cm (16in) long plastic down-(drain-) pipe, with the back cut off. They were later analysed for organic content.

The lions in the Tower

A plan to put water back into the moat surrounding the Tower of London was considered in the mid 1990s. As part of the feasibility study, archaeologists excavated sections of the moat. Among the remains they found were the bones of lions, bears and other exotic animal species, dating from the reign of King John (1199–1216) and confirming documentary references to his Royal Menagerie – medieval London's first zoo.

Soil Sampling Techniques

Although it might appear that taking a soil sample is a simple and straightforward procedure – as easy as shovelling earth into a bucket – this is often not the case. Different techniques are necesssary, depending on the nature of the material being sampled.

There are several different types of sample. Bulk sampling and column sampling are the two most likely to be entrusted to a volunteer – monolith and Kubiena samples (*see* Special Recovery Techniques) are the realm of the trained specialist.

The most common approach is single context sampling, where material is extracted from one context (unlike column sampling, where samples are taken from a sequence of related deposits). With single context sampling, care has to be taken to ensure that the sample is representative of the context it comes from. It must be taken from a part of the deposit that is free from potential contamination from surrounding layers or modern activity.

Below To ensure consistency in recording soil colour, a geological soil colour chart is used as a reference.

How much to take

The amount of material taken from the context will depend on various factors. Environmental archaeologists say that the finds from one standard bucket full of soil (a 10-litre (2½-gallon) sample) are statistically valid – they are typical of the feature as a whole. Even so, they recommend taking four buckets (40 litres (10 gallons)) of material.

If there are facilities on site for assessing the presence or absence of biological remains, a 10-litre (2½-gallon) sample is processed at once, and a further 30 litres (7½ gallons) retrieved if the first sample is positive. In the absence of such facilities, 40 litres (10 gallons) are taken, but when the time comes to process the sample, 10 litres

Below Peat bogs often take centuries to form and may be rich in evidence of past climates and ancient vegetation.

Above Boreholes are drilled on a river plain to extract samples of ancient river sediments.

(2½ gallons) will be assessed, and if the results are negative, the remaining material will be discarded.

Sometimes the deposit is slight, in which case the archaeologist might aim for 100 per cent recovery, even if it is less than the recommended minimum sample size of 10 litres (2½ gallons). In particular, this might be the case for a deposit that has been chosen for sampling because it is important in understanding the development, sequencing or dating of the site, such as a layer of burnt material in the fill of a ditch or pit, which could contain material suitable for carbon-14 dating, or that might represent the remains of a cremation, and could contain fragments of dateable material, such as glass beads or brooch fragments.

Left It is vital to record as much information as possible about the origins of ecofinds, in order to build a picture of the natural environment.

Right An example of an Environmental Sample Sheet as used by the Museum of London Archaeology Service. It is designed to be self-explanatory so that volunteers and inexperienced archaeologists can record samples fully and accurately for further investigation and interpretation.

However, an archaeologist might aim for a larger sample of a deposit that appears to be particularly rich in environmental remains – a judgement based on visual criteria, such as the presence of larger biological remains (charred grain or charcoal, for example) or its colour and composition (black, organic and peaty), or from its character as a floor bottom, hearth or pit-edge deposit.

What to take

Although purists might argue that soil samples should be truly representative of the deposit, in reality, there isn't much point in keeping non-diagnostic pebbles or stones, so those should be discarded (once entered on the context record sheets, plans and sections), and

Above Smaller samples should be bagged and labelled with information relating to site, date and context, and placed with the bulk deposits taken from the same location.

all artefactual finds should also be removed and treated as finds, rather than as part of the environmental sample.

Sample recording sheets

Soil samples are recorded using sample recording sheets and a sample register. As well as fixing the location and character of the sample, it should state why the sample was taken and from where, and what questions the sample might answer about the site or feature from which it came. These notes can affect the way the sample is processed in the laboratory. A distinction needs to be made between samples collected from occupational deposits that might have material evidence of people and their activities, and material from environmental deposits, where the aim is to understand the natural environment and exclude human debris.

It is also useful to estimate the size of the deposit and what percentage of the total deposit the sample represents. Fixing the precise location of the samples is important, especially when they have been taken from different points across a floor surface to see whether the finds can determine the segregation of different activities within the building – were specific parts used for food preparation, for example?

Finally, samples are labelled. One waterproof label is placed inside the bag/bucket with the site code, date, square/trench code, locus/context number, sample number (from the sample register) and type of sample. Another label, with the same information, is taped to the outside of the sample bucket, or placed in a plastic bag and tied to the handle.

The magic of metalwork

Evidence for early ironwork was recovered in bulk samples taken from two roundhouses at a site in Berkshire, southern England. Pottery and radiocarbon dating confirmed the site as a Late Bronze Age settlement of the 10th century BC. When the samples were later analysed, they were found to contain thousands of tiny metal fragments of a type known as hammerscale, which is the waste material created when raw iron is hammered to remove slag from the ore-smelting process, or when the metal is repeatedly heated and hammered to produce wrought iron.

By studying the concentrations of hammerscale in the soil, it was possible to work out precisely where in each roundhouse this work was taking place. Furthermore, it provided clear evidence that iron was being produced in the Late Bronze Age. The ironworking huts were located in a separate area from the main settlement, screened by an almost solid fence of closely spaced posts. Perhaps these prehistoric metalworkers were trying to ensure that no-one else witnessed their 'magical' transformation of rocks into metal.

Special Recovery Techniques

There are several methods of taking bulk soil samples. One involves extracting a whole vertical column of material, thus preserving the precise stratigraphy, others involve taking a carefully controlled sample of every layer in a series of deposits, to preserve the precise relationships of different soils for analysis.

Above Washed samples are dried in a heated cabinet before being examined.

Single-context samples are typically taken from selected contexts, such as floor surfaces or the primary (the earliest) fills of pits or ditches, because it is here that archaeologists expect to find the best evidence for the site when it was in use. However, sometimes it is useful to take samples from every deposit in a ditch or from a section through a feature. These will allow archaeologists to study the changes that have occurred over time.

Environmental interest

Not all features are suitable for this type of approach, but environmental archaeologists are particularly keen on finding deep sections that can result from long sequences of natural or human deposition, where the biological remains can potentially provide information on changes in culture or the environment over hundreds of years. They also love soils and turf lines that have been buried and preserved by later sedimentation or activity, because these can tell archaeologists what the environment was like immediately prior to the event that resulted in the burial of the soil.

Continuity or transition

Sometimes the story told by deep deposits is one of continuity and the absence of change. Sometimes, by contrast, the story is one of abrupt change or of gradual transition. For example, the earthen bank of a fortification or enclosure might be constructed on top of the existing turf, thereby preserving environmental data from the moment of the construction, which can be used to compare with later data. Such comparisons become especially relevant if, for example, the fortification was constructed by invaders – say, Roman conquerors of an Iron-Age territory in mainland Europe, or European colonialists arriving in the Americas, Australia, Canada, India or New Zealand. The buried soils thus potentially capture a moment of transition from one economy or set of lifestyles to another, and the study of the impacts of one culture on another are what academic archaeologists strive to understand.

Above Environmental samples are examined in a laboratory, with the aid of identification tools.

Left Archaeologists removing cores from a sea bed in an area that once existed as dry, inhabited land during the Mesolithic period.

Monoliths and Kubienas

Where suitable sections are found that fulfil these various criteria, there are two possible methods for salvaging material: one is to use monolith or Kubiena-type boxes, which are simply devices made by different manufacturers for collecting an intact block of soil without disturbing its structure. Made of brass, zinc or tin, like long rectangular bread or cake tins (typically 500mm (20in) in length, 140mm (5½in) in width and 100mm (4in) in depth). Many research digs abroad actually manufacture the similar sampling receptacles from locally available food canisters, although specially manufactured tins have the advantage of handles to enable their removal from the section complete with the soil block inside.

The tins are pushed into the exposed section or banged in using a rubber hammer. Several tins are used for deep sections. Each tin is numbered in sequence, and the tins are overlapped by 50mm (2in) or so, to ensure that a complete column is sampled without gaps. This method works best in softer soils, such as peat, where the tins can be cut out. However, the tins often have to be dug out of the section using a sharp spade to slice through the soil at the open end of the tins, which are then tightly wrapped to ensure that the soil block remains intact. After removal, the tins are carefully labelled.

Columns

The second sampling method does not require pre-manufactured tins – this is the columnar method, where accurately measured blocks of sediment are cut from each deposit using a trowel. The aim is to collect a sample size of 250mm (10in) x 250mm (10in) x 60mm (2½in), but the depth and thickness can vary, according to the nature of the deposit. The result from columnar sampling is a series of discrete samples, and although the relationships with adjacent deposits are not preserved, they are recorded on paper. Depending on the soil type, the sample might break up during

extraction and storage, so some vertical information is lost as a result of mixing. However, the method is still effective for sampling layers of particularly rich or interesting stratigraphy.

Above Archaeologists take soil samples from the burial site of a Roman stone coffin.

Left These Kubiena tins have been positioned to remove core samples, undisturbed, from different strata, effectively building a picture of how sediments were laid down over time.

Above 'Archaeomagnetic sampling' is often used to date burnt materials, which, upon cooling, retain a magnetization proportional to the direction and intensity of the Earth's magnetic field at that time. Ancient fired objects can thus be dated by comparison with the known record of the Earth's magnetic field.

The significance of age

The age of a site may dictate whether or not there will be a full-time environmentalist on the team and how many samples are taken. We know relatively little about the economies and environments of prehistoric peoples, and some of the big research questions in archaeology specifically concern the development of different forms of agriculture, animal husbandry, horticulture, medicine, food storage, diet, and so on, so all evidence is potentially valuable.

Samples from medieval and post-medieval sites – of which more is known – are taken in quantity only if exceptionally rich deposits are encountered that can help answer specific economic or dietary questions, because there are other sources of data for environmental conditions, including tree-ring data (see Dendrochronology and Other Dating Methods) and historical records. The exception to the rule of 'the older the better' are periods for which we have little archaeological data, such as the post-Roman to early medieval period in Europe, because little has survived from what was an organic era, where wood, vegetation, fibre and animal products were the main materials for homes, tools, vessels, transport and religious structures.

Processing Soil Samples

Environmental finds are recovered from bulk and column samples by sieving, or sifting, the soil. This action separates the soil from the larger materials, which are then washed to skim off the lighter materials that will float on the water's surface, making them easier to collect.

Both bulk and column samples can be processed on the archaeological site, while under the supervision of an environmental archaeologist, or at some later date in a laboratory. In either situation, the techniques for recovering environmental samples are the same – however, the advantage of processing on site is that the feedback is immediate. Deposits that are rich in material can be sampled further and blank samples can be disposed of, saving on effort and storage costs. If samples are not to be processed immediately, they will need storing in an appropriate manner, ideally keeping them in the cold and dark to prevent mould and fungal infection and to ensure that the samples do not dry out.

Flotation

The separation of biological remains from soil works on the principle that the remains are less dense than water, so they will float on the water's surface rather than sinking to the bottom, as do the denser residues. Flotation tanks come in a variety of forms, including versions that constantly recycle the water used in the flotation process, so that they are less wasteful of this precious resource and can be used in situations where the supply of fresh water is limited to what can be brought to the site in containers. Obviously, using water from a pond or stream would be counterproductive because it will contaminate the archaeological samples with modern material.

Above Small-scale sieving (sifting), of washed samples can be done with a bucket and mesh.

Whatever form they take, flotation tanks all consist of a mesh that sits on top of a water tank. Soil is placed in the mesh and water is added to the tank so that it rises through the mesh from below. The water has to rise slowly enough for the soil in the mesh to break down and release materials trapped within the lumps and crumbs. The lighter material floats and is carried out of the tank by means of a lip or spillway near the top of the tank. The water that spills over this is then passed through a series of fine sieves (screens) or filters, trapping environmental samples and allowing the water through.

The material caught in the sieves is known as the 'flot', or light fraction, and it consists of plant remains, bone fragments, the smaller and lighter bones of fish, birds, mice, voles or reptiles, insect remains, molluscs and charcoal. The material that is left behind in the floation tank is known as 'heavy fraction', or residue.

Sieving or sifting

Flotation is the technique recommended for capturing smaller and lighter ecofacts, but the heavy fraction might still contain heavier materials, so this is now passed through a series of sieves using running water to help move the soil through the mesh, leaving behind larger particles, including any finds. Sieving – or sifting, as it is also known – can start with a relatively course mesh size of 2mm (²⁄₂₅in), which will retrieve charcoal,

Above Screened microscopic finds are suspended in fine mesh bags and left to dry at Çatalhöyük.

Recovering ancient beads

Among the materials that might be missed during excavation but recovered during wet sieving, or wet screening, are the tiny beads that are found in western Asia from the Neolithic period. They are the subject of a research project that is looking at the techniques of early beadmaking at sites that include Wadi Jilat, Jordan, and Çatalhöyük, Turkey, among others.

Analysis involves recovering and studying not just the beads themselves, but also what is known as debitage, the waste flakes and debris that result from bead manufacture. At Çatalhöyük, stone, clay, shell and bone beads have been recovered in quantity from burial sites, and two houses have been identified as possible bead factories on the basis of the quantities of micro-debitage from the obsidian and flint tools that were used to drill holes in the beads.

mollusc shells, small bones and artefacts that might have been hidden in lumps of clay or soil. The remaining soil can then be further sifted, reducing the sieve size each time to 1mm (⅟₂₅in), 0.5mm (⅟₅₀in) and 0.25mm (⅟₁₀₀in). The types of remains trapped at each stage vary: at 1mm/⅟₂₅in, the sieve should trap fish scales, eggshell, marine molluscs and bone; reducing the mesh size picks up seeds, pollens and insect remains, which can vary in size from beetle wing cases to microscopic eggs and parasites.

One of the great advantages of wet sieving over dry sieving is that colour contrasts are heightened by water — soil and dust covered artefacts and ecofacts can be easily missed in a dry state but the ivory colour of bone, the black of charcoal, the iridescence of beetle wings or the calcium white of snail shells is far easier to see when water washes away the dust coating.

Breaking up clumps

In both sieving and flotation, some soil lumps will resist being broken down — especially clay. Wet clay that has formed clumps and then been baked for weeks by high temperatures and hot sun is difficult to break up. In this case, prior to processing, samples of dry material can be soaked in a solution of hydrogen peroxide, using protective gloves. A less effective dispersant that must be used with samples from waterlogged remains is the water softener known as Calgon (sodium hexametaphosphate, or amorphous sodium polyphospate), which, unlike hydrogen peroxide, does not harm plant remains.

Storage

Material collected by both processes of sieving and flotation is usually laid out to dry. Care must be taken to ensure that any light material does not blow away if being dried outdoors. The dry materials are then bagged and labelled. Any plant remains from waterlogged sites are the exception. The residue from these samples is placed in a jar and covered with water.

Wet sieving finds

1 Water is used in wet sieving to break up larger lumps of soil and find the very small objects that might be hidden inside.

3 The resulting mud is then poured through a series of sieves with a finer and finer mesh, leaving a residue in each sieve.

5 Each of the sieves is then laid out in the sunshine to dry; at this stage the contents consist of a mix of stones and small finds.

2 First the soil from the area being sampled is mixed with water to break down the clods and make a runny mud mixture.

4 This is messy work, and it is often necessary to break up stubborn lumps by hand to make sure all the soil passes through the mesh.

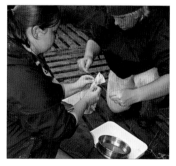

6 Once dry, the residue is bagged and labelled for lab analysis; the final stage is to pick out finds, such as seeds, bones and beads.

The Study of Human Remains

Human remains can tell archaeologists an enormous amount about past lives and cultures. The many beliefs that people have about the sanctity of the grave, which affected how they were buried, give an insight into their cultures – and the bones themselves provide archaeological information.

Above Strong beliefs about life and death mean human remains must be treated with care.

It is precisely because so many different beliefs surround the treatment of the dead that human remains are of such importance to archaeologists. Respect for the dead is a fundamental trait that defines the human species and distinguishes us from most of our closest cousins in the evolutionary tree. Much of what archaeologists know about the very early development of human characteristics comes from burials.

Body and soul

People have in the past treated the deceased in an extraordinary variety of ways that give us glimpses of their beliefs. Some expose their dead, believing that the birds that feed on flesh carry the soul to heaven (archaeologists call this 'excarnation'); others bury the dead with a variety of gifts and possessions ('articulated' or 'extended' burial), while others bind up the dead using cloth or cord so that they resemble a foetus in the womb ('flexed' or 'crouch' burials), perhaps placing them in a stone-lined chamber ('cist' burial), while others again practise cremation and bury the ashes in a specially made urn, or scatter them on the surface of a river.

Some religions believe that body and soul are indivisible, and that to disturb the dead is to cause them distress; others believe that only the soul survives after death, and that the physical body is unimportant – in medieval Europe bodies were routinely dug up after a period of time and the bones stored in charnel houses, making room for new graves. By contrast, some cultures practised ritual embalming or mummification – the ancient Egyptians preserved humans, birds and animals in this way, as did the Christian Church during the Middle Ages, to preserve the bodies of saints, and more

Below Mummified human remains uncovered in the Egyptian desert are covered with a protective mesh.

recently, the Soviet Union afforded the same treatment to its leader Vladimir Lenin (1870–1924).

From studying prehistoric burial practice, archaeologists also think that some people believed in a third transitional state between life and death. Archaeological evidence suggest that some people in the past stored the remains of their dead relatives for a year or more, before taking them to large ritual gatherings where the 'half-dead' were ritually reunited with their ancestors, after which the physical remains were discarded by being placed in pits, burned or placed on rafts and sent down rivers. Other cultures place an entirely different value on the human remains. In southern Asia, people visit the graves of their ancestors several times a year, clean the grave, polish the bones and put out food, money and gifts for the dead.

The value of human remains

Apart from the value to archaeologists of human remains as a cultural indicator, providing details about the lifestyles and beliefs of the community whose dead are being studied, the remains themselves can tell us much about life in the past. Scientific analysis of human remains (*see* Radiocarbon Dating) can tell archaeologists about the age of the deceased, their diet, their state of health and any diseases, injuries or chronic conditions they suffered from, what sort of lifestyle they led – sedentary or active, for example – and whether they show evidence of battle wounds or hunting injuries. Adding all this data together brings a wealth of information about populations and communities – whether the people of a Roman town, a medieval village, the monks of a monastic community, the victims of a plague or epidemic, or the dead of a defeated army.

In recent years, even more exciting developments in the study of genetic material from human remains is opening up new lines of research about human origins and the migration of peoples to all parts of the globe. We are

Above Recovering graves from the 1st–3rd centuries AD in Beirut, Libya.

Science needs human remains

Archaeologists treat the excavation of human remains as an opportunity to learn about the past. However, they now excavate according to codes of practice that have been developed in consultation with governments and communities to avoid causing offence or transgressing community rights and beliefs. As a general rule, human remains are usually excavated because they are found accidentally or because they are under threat anyway from development or natural erosion. In one case, a parish church wanted to extend its graveyard into an adjoining field. Imagine the surprise of the local community when archaeologists checked the field for remains and found that it was already a cemetery – filled with the remains of the people who had lived in the same parish 1,500 years ago.

Above One of the tombs of the Merowe site in Sudan, where the remains of ancient Kushan rulers from 250BC–AD300 are housed in spectacular fashion.

Above A mummified body is excavated at the Bahariya oasis, Egypt, a site rich in Romano–Egyptian human remains and dubbed 'The Valley of the Golden Mummies'.

beginning at last to be able to answer some of the really big questions in archaeology. For example, do humans have a single point of origin (Africa) or did humans evolve independently in different parts of the world (including China, Russia and Indonesia)? When did humans arrive in America and from where? Did the transition from a nomadic hunting and gathering existence to a more settled agricultural lifestyle spread because people

migrated and took domesticated seeds and animals with them, or because the idea of agriculture spread rapidly, without any human migration? Similarly, how many of the great seismic changes in society have occurred because people have imposed those ideas on a society that they have invaded, defeated or colonized, and how much are they due to the fact that good ideas, like fashion trends, are rapidly adopted by everybody?

Human Remains: Legal and Ethical Issues

Finding human remains during an excavation can open up all types of legal and ethical issues, which archaeologists need to be aware of before they excavate. In some cultures, there is a need to honour the dead and ensure that their spirits remain at peace by not disturbing their graves.

Above The 13th-century remains of this infant, found in Lebanon, testify to mummification skills.

The laws relating to the discovery of human remains vary from country to country, but usually the site director is required to inform a civil authority, such as a coroner, when a grave or burial is found. The coroner will consider the evidence and decide whether or not a forensic investigation is needed. If the archaeological evidence points to this being an ancient burial, and not a more recent crime, permission will be given, usually as a written licence, to enable the remains to be excavated – to do so before the licence is issued might be illegal.

Below Twelve skeletons discovered in 2004 at the Azetc Teotihuacan site, near Mexico City, are believed to be the remains of warriors who were captured and sacrificed in around AD 200–250.

The issuing of a licence doesn't mean that the remains will be dug up. As a rule, archaeologists try not to disturb human remains. They will only do so if the remains are to be destroyed anyway – for example, because the site is to be developed – or because the potential scientific value of studying the remains is judged to outweigh the importance of leaving the human remains at rest.

Links with the past

As well as having a general duty to ensure that all human remains are treated with respect and dignity,

Below This mummified hand is part of a headless mummy that was excavated in Lima, Peru, in 2005. The mummy is believed to have belonged to the Wari culture, and date back some 4,000 years.

archaeologists have a specific duty to take into account the views of living descendants, whose views are accorded considerable weight in any discussions concerning the excavation and treatment of remains.

The need to consult descendants can occur where a cemetery is excavated that contains relatively recent burials. This happened in London, where the route of the Channel Tunnel Rail Link passed through the site of the church-yard of St Pancras Church. The decision to route the rail link through the cemetery was controversial and was not one that archaeologists supported, however, once planners and engineers decided to go ahead, archaeologists used parish burial registers and coffin labels to identify as many of the dead as possible so that relatives could be

Right A more or less complete skeleton, some 4,000 years old, is recovered at Ikiztepe, Turkey.

consulted about reburial arrangements. Many of the graves identified turned out to be French aristocrats who had fled the French Revolution, which began in 1789, including the Archbishop of Narbonne and Primate of Languedoc.

Indigenous people

As well as specific named relatives, the definition of descendants might also include a broad class of people, as is the case in the Americas, Canada and Australia, where First Nations, or indigenous people, have to be consulted by law when ancient human remains are discovered. In the United States, the Native American Graves Protection and Repatriation Act specifically prohibits the excavation of sites likely to contain human remains, funerary or sacred objects, or items of cultural and religious importance to Native American or Native Hawaiian people. The law extends to any other ethnic group or community that historically ascribes cultural or symbolic value to the site and might object to the site's excavation.

Reburial

One area of public debate surrounding the study of human remains is the question of reburial once scientific laboratory work as been completed. The Anglican Church advocates reburial, unless there is 'significant future research potential', in which case they argue for the storage of human remains in a suitable holding institution, such as a disused church. In the United Kingdom, the archaeologists who excavated the disused Anglo Saxon church of St Peter, Barton upon Humber, North Lincolnshire, have now built a specially designed chapel to house the remains of the 3,000 individuals exhumed during the excavation. The excavated remains can rest on consecrated ground, but are still accessible to researchers.

Above An interpretation of how Kennewick Man might have looked, reconstructed from remains found on a river bank in 1996.

Kennewick Man

One celebrated example of a discovery that has tested the United States' laws on the treatment of human remains is the case of 'Kennewick Man'. The bones of Kennewick Man were found in 1996, emerging from an eroded river bank along a stretch of the Columbia River near Kennewick, Washington, by an archaeologist called Jim Chatters, who had been systematically studying the river's archaeology over a period of time. The sediments in which the bones were found suggested that the remains were unusually ancient – and scientific tests later indicated that Kennewick man had died at the age of 40 in around 8000BC.

The date places Kennewick Man as an early settler in North America, but archaeologists were hampered from further study by a law requiring them to hand the remains over to American First Nation groups for reburial. Chatters appealed against the law, and, after ten years of legal process, won the right to conduct further scientific tests. He argued from the skeletal evidence and the skull shape that Kennewick Man was descended from an entirely different group of migrants from those that account for today's First Nation people, and that they were not, therefore, his descendants. He also argued that the universal value of the information likely to be gained from studying Kennewick Man outweighed First Nation religious sensitivities.

Human Remains: Excavation Techniques

Some sites are known in advance to be cemeteries or graveyards. However, human remains can also turn up in some unexpected places, so all archaeologists have to be aware of the relevant codes of practice and the correct excavation procedures.

Above A dental pick is being used to remove soil around human vertebrae.

Taking into account religious and ethical issues, public attitudes, and the value and benefit of scientific study, archaeologists try to ensure that the work of excavating and removing human remains is not visible to the general public. This is not a concern on excavations where the public are not permitted and cannot see the site, but in publicly accessible areas, the site might be screened off or the grave area screened with a tent.

Health and safety

The health of the archaeologists working with human remains is also considered, and they might need to wear protective clothing. This is true when working with recent human remains, especially those buried in

airtight coffins where soft tissue can survive – and with it the threat of disease – or, in the case of lead coffins, which can cause lead poisoning.

Archaeologists working on the excavation of a church crypt in London, for example, were glad that they had taken the necessary precautions to avoid contact with disease. Some of the skeletons they found were diagnosed, from characteristic lesions around the knees, to have died from smallpox, a dangerous and highly contagious disease. Another advantage of wearing protective clothing and breathing equipment in such circumstances is that they protect the remains themselves from contamination, which is important if ancient DNA material is to be recovered.

Excavation considerations

The strategy for recovering the human remains and any associated artefacts will depend on the nature of the site, the state of preservation and the likely knowledge to be gained by excavation. One basic decision is if the remains should be excavated on site or block-lifted by cutting around and under the remains. This preserves the surrounding soil so that the coffin, cremation urn or grave contents can be excavated under laboratory conditions.

This was done, for example, in the case of a Roman lead coffin found in London in 1999, which was brought to the Museum of London for opening, an event witnessed by TV cameras. Among the finds that might have been lost under less controlled conditions

Above During the famous excavation of the 'Spanish lady of Spitalfields' by archaeologists in London, broadcast live on television, the threat of active 'plague' bacteria required full protective gear to be worn.

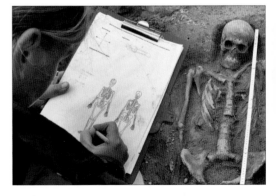

Above These human remains, which are being measured and recorded, were excavated at a 13th-century village – part of a rescue project preceding extension of Berlin's Schoenfeld Airport, Germany.

Lifting and packaging human remains

Recent research at Bristol University, England, has perfected luminescence techniques for dating human remains by measuring the decay of various elements in the bone, and in the quartz of sand in the surrounding soil.

Above Volcano victims from Pompeii are displayed to museum visitors in Italy.

1 Rather than clean the remains on site, skulls are lifted using gloves to prevent contamination from modern matter.

2 The intact skull is potentially full of information about dates, diet and possible injuries.

3 The skull is carefully packed in acid-free tissue paper to prevent damage during transit to the laboratory.

were leaves and flowers placed in the coffin as a funeral garland, along with the remains of a glass flask, which probably held perfumed ointments.

Recording the excavation

Unless there are reasons for preserving the find intact, it is more normal to record the grave through photography and written records. These will note key diagnostic details about the burial practice, such as the orientation (which way the head and feet are facing in relation to the compass points), and whether the skeleton is laid out fully extended or crouched, flexed (with the knees up against the chest and hands

near the chin), or supine (face upward, lying on the back) or prone (on the front, face downward).

Rather than drawing the skeleton, which requires a good knowledge of human anatomy, pre-printed skeleton diagrams can be used to record features of the burial, such as the position of arms, hands, legs and feet, any visible grave goods, the condition of the bone, any missing parts, any parts in unusual positions, any disturbances to the burial, and, of course, the stratigraphical relationships of the grave to any other archaeological features. However, pre-printed sheets are of no use when dealing with multiple burials, or with animal remains, so the excavation and recording of human remains is normally entrusted to someone with a good knowledge of anatomy.

Experienced staff can often excavate, record and lift a skeleton in half a day. They will systematically place the bones in labelled plastic bags according to the body's anatomy, so that the skull, torso, legs and arms are lifted and bagged up separately, with hand and foot bones being bagged with the corresponding leg or arm bones. Soil samples will also be taken to recover small artefacts or biological remains. Particular attention is given to the abdominal, chest and

What does the public think?

In 2005, researchers at Cambridge University, England, carried out a survey to find out what members of the public thought about the excavation of human remains and their display in museums. The result was that 88 per cent believed it was appropriate for human remains to be used for scientific study. More than 70 per cent felt that eventual reburial was desirable, but only when such studies were completed. Only 5 per cent wanted immediate reburial.

The views of archaeologists and the general public seem to be broadly in line, but there are some areas where there was a surprising degree of divergence. Of those questioned, 56 per cent believed that the assumed religion of the deceased should affect how the skeleton was reburied, despite the fact that we cannot know with any certainty what our prehistoric ancestors believed. This raises the difficult question of who, if anyone, has the right to speak for prehistoric people? Is it right to use neo-Pagan or Christian burial rites for people whose religious practices can only be guessed at?

head areas of the body to retrieve evidence of gallstones, food remains or parasites.

Case Study: the Prittlewell Prince

A well-preserved and unrobbed 7th-century burial chamber – packed with the possessions of the deceased – was excavated at Priory Crescent, Prittlewell, Essex, in the south-east of England, in the autumn of 2003. The sheer quality of the finds was outstanding.

Above A gold belt buckle, one of the princely treasures found at Prittlewell, being excavated.

The excavation of this site was special not only for the quality of the finds, but also because the archaeological team displayed an enormous amount of skill in extracting the maximum amount of information from a site that consisted of little but sand. The site was found by a team from the Museum of London Archaeology Service (MoLAS) on a piece of land that was due to be destroyed by a road widening scheme.

Before excavation began, the team used desktop research to establish that Anglo-Saxon graves had been found on the site on three previous occasions: in the 1880s, during the building of the London to Southend railway line; in 1923, when the houses of Priory Crescent were built; and in 1930, when workmen noticed the remains of Saxon and Roman burials in the railway cutting. The objects found in these graves suggested that the cemetery was in use between AD500 and AD700.

A vanished tomb

Nothing, however, suggested the likely burial of a man of power and wealth, which is what the MoLAS team found in 2003. At the south end of the site, where archaeologists were trowelling over the sandy subsoil, they found a rectangular area of soil, subtly different in colour from the surrounding soil.

After three months of painstaking excavation, the MoLAS team were able to reveal that this was the site of an intact and undisturbed chamber grave, measuring 4m (13ft) long and wide, and 1.5m (5ft) deep. The chamber had been dug and then lined with wooden planks, to resemble the appearance of a timber hall. A roof of timber covered the grave, which was then covered by a large burial mound, in typical Anglo-Saxon fashion.

Over time, the timber roof of the buried chamber began to rot and sand trickled through and into the hollow chamber beneath, eventually filling the chamber to the brim. The high acidity of the sand filling in the chamber meant that organic materials, including the body, did not survive – however, they had left their imprint in the form of slight staining in the Essex sand.

With remarkable precision, the sand was excavated to reveal not only the outline of the bed on which the deceased was laid upon the chamber floor, but also the remains of his possessions. These had remained in their original positions, pinned in place by the sand from the mound above.

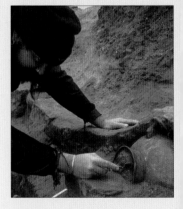

Left and above The bronze bowl is typical of styles known from eastern England in the 7th century. By contrast, a bronze flagon (drinking vessel) from the same period, bearing embossed medallions (see opposite page, top right), was almost certainly a Mediterranean import.

Above This 'folding stool' probably originated from territory in modern-day Slovakia, which was at that time part of Lombardic Italy.

Because of the fragility of the finds, many of them were lifted from the grave in large blocks of soil for later excavation in the laboratory. By making use of this technique, archaeologists doubled the number of finds initially recovered from the site from 60 to 120.

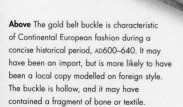

Above The gold belt buckle is characteristic of Continental European fashion during a concise historical period, AD600–640. It may have been an import, but is more likely to have been a local copy modelled on foreign style. The buckle is hollow, and it may have contained a fragment of bone or textile.

Treasured possessions

The finds included a sword and shoe buckles found at the side and foot of the coffin bed. Bronze cauldrons and flagons were found hanging from iron nails hammered into the walls of the house-like tomb, and equipment for feasting was carefully arranged around the body, including glass bowls from Asia Minor, a Byzantine flagon, decorated hanging bowls from Ireland, buckets and drinking horns with gilded mounts. Valued personal possessions laid with the deceased included a gaming board, folded textiles, a solid gold belt buckle, gold coins from Merovingian France, a sword and shield, and a lyre and a folding throne of Italian design.

Most tellingly, a pair of small, gold-foil crosses were found on the body, indicating that the tomb's occupant might have been a Christian, and this combination of pagan burial practice (furnishing the deceased with goods for use in the next world) and Christian symbol held the clues to the possible identity of the deceased.

Identifying the deceased

From historical records we know that St Augustine of Canterbury was sent to England in AD596 by Pope Gregory the Great with the task of converting the Anglo-Saxon tribes to Christianity. There are records of two East Saxon kings who adopted Christianity: King Saebert, who died in AD616, and his grandson, Sigebert II, who was murdered in 653. Possibly, this could be the grave of either Saebert or Sigebehrt, although neither name fits with the name found on a silver spoon that was recovered from the tomb. It was engraved with two incomplete and very worn inscriptions, one of which reads 'FAB...' and the other 'RONAM...'. Perhaps the inscriptions on the spoon form part of the new name that one of these two kings chose as a Christian name when being baptized.

Above Each of the three embossed medallions on the cast bronze flagon shows a figure, thought to be a saint on horseback – in a style that suggests Mediterranean origins.

Other discoveries made in the Museum of London laboratory include a set of 57 plain bone pieces and two large deer-antler dice from some kind of game, as well as a lyre, which is being described as the most complete lyre of the period yet seen in Britain. These artefacts have prompted the popular press to speculate that 'the Prince of Prittlewell', a high-ranking aristocrat who lived in Essex 1,400 years ago, was not only a Christian, but was also fond of music and board games.

Below Two gold foil crosses were among the most significant of the finds in the burial chamber. Of Latin origin, they suggest a strong allegiance to Christianity and are likely to have been grave goods customized specially for the burial ceremony.

AFTER THE DIG IS OVER

The excavation is over and the diggers depart with happy memories of a summer spent in the sun, of new friends made and new skills learned, perhaps with a determination to learn more about some aspect of archaeology. However, for the site director, closing the excavation down – which involves restoring the site by filling holes and replacing topsoil and turf – is not the end of the process at all, but merely the completion of another stage. It has been estimated that about 10 per cent of the effort involved in understanding and researching any one site will go into the desktop assessment phase and another 40 per cent into the excavation, so at this stage the process is now only halfway through. What still lies ahead is the work involved in making sense of everything that has been found. All the information still needs to be linked together into a story that other archaeologists will find useful and that pushes archaeological knowledge forward.

Opposite Carbon-14 tests dated this 'shicra' (woven reed) bag from Lima, Peru, to the 5th century BC.

Above Dendrochronologists date wooden objects by examining the pattern of tree rings and matching them to a dated master sequence.

Above A piece of what is claimed to be Herod's tomb is displayed by archaeologists at a Jerusalem press conference.

Above Coffin furniture, such as these metal spurs retrieved from a grave, may be valuable in dating any bodies found there.

Beginning the Post-Excavation Process

The director now has to make some kind of sense of the catalogue of record sheets, drawings and photographs, not to mention the boxes and bags filled with things found during the excavation. Fortunately, an array of specialists can help analyse the finds and contribute to an understanding of the site.

Above Finds from past excavations in London form a vast study collection for research.

Of course, the director does not simply sit down the day after the dig is over and say 'what does all this mean', because the excavation process itself is an interpretative process. Judgements about what to dig, for example, are based on discussions with diggers and supervisors about the emerging history of the site, its stratigraphy, its phasing and the relationships between features. Finds will have emerged that will have established a broad time period for the use of the site. All of this information is part of the interpretative process.

Because of this process, most directors or project managers will emerge from an excavation with a provisional framework of ideas about the site. The next task is to write about these ideas, while they are still fresh in the mind, and to support the interpretation of the site with evidence from dating, stratigraphy and artefact and ecofact analyses.

Regrettably, there are several reasons why this next stage does not always happen as it should. The director might take a well-deserved vacation, then go back to his or her main job as a university teacher. Some archaeologists write short interim papers and reports featuring the juiciest headline-grabbing findings from the dig, but then lose the will to do the hard work of writing the detailed report. There are also some archaeologists who have never written up the results of major sites that they excavated 30 or more years ago – and the greater the delay the more difficult it is to make a start. It is always easy to put off writing up the site because of 'lack of time or funds'.

The role of the specialist

Perhaps one of the greatest causes of delay in writing up reports is the real shortage of specialists with the knowledge to take material from an excavation, catalogue and analyse it, and produce a report that describes what was found and makes some attempt at saying what it means. Those specialists who are able to do work of this kind are never short of clients; thus the director who approaches a coin or pottery expert for help with the report can expect to have to join a waiting list, and might not know the results for a year or more.

This shortage of specialists is also an opportunity, of course, and it means that any budding pottery, bone, metalwork or coin enthusiast who wants to master the topic will not lack encouragement and help from established specialists. This is a field where there will almost be a guarantee of plenty of future work.

Left Archaeologists at the Arzhan-2 site in the Republic of Tuva, Russia, excavate horse bones from the graves of ancient Scythians, who are known to have revered these animals.

Above Ceramic specialists examine all the finds from an excavation to build up a picture of pottery use at the location.

Presenting the material

The post-excavation process often involves presenting the information learned about the find to other archaeologists and the public. This can include putting some of the material on display in a local museum, giving lectures and writing articles about the site and its finds, presenting the results at academic conferences, perhaps producing a popular publication as well as an academic one, and even taking part in educational initiatives. It will also involve arranging the long-term storage and archiving of all the finds and records so that they are well preserved and are available for other researchers to study.

Above The results of an excavation are presented at an open day.

The post-excavation team

The director will need to call upon the skills and inputs of all types of other people to write up and publish the results of the dig – like many scientific disciplines, archaeology is a highly collaborative process and the director needs to be able to work with, motivate, inspire and manage a wide range of academic, technical and professional specialists. The team that brings all this work to fruition will include photographers and graphics specialists, writers, editors, proofreaders and indexers, layout artists and printers, database experts and web designers, museum curators and education officers, conservators and archivists.

Some of these people have skills that are not specific to archaeology, and increasingly there are opportunities for people who want to pursue a career in archaeology to switch from another skill. For example, people who have trained as editors are in great demand as publications project managers, responsible for resolving any copyright issues that can occur and making sure that all contributors are properly

Right Volunteers and specialists often work together when the excavated find is quite special, as with this cremation burial urn.

acknowledged. Trained teachers are also in demand because of the educational work carried out by many museums, and graphic artists may contribute to the layout of the reports, or perhaps create finished drawings and reconstructions of what the site might have looked like in the past.

The result of this collaboration will be one or more publications – either printed or accessible on the internet –

that tell other archaeologists what has been found. If this is an excavation that is going to continue for several years, the director might publish an interim report, highlighting the year's work and discussing its implications. If the excavation has been completed, the director might publish a definitive report, describing and analysing the site and its significance, with all the supporting evidence.

Creating a Chronological Framework

A main role of the director or project manager is to explain the development of the site over time. This is often a two-stage process: stage one is to place key changes in the site's history into an order using the site matrix; stage two involves establishing precise dates for the different phases of activity.

Above Careful examination of a potentially dateable timber at the base of a large pit.

In order to tell a coherent story about an excavated site, the director needs to establish a chronological framework – in other words, to be able to say what happened first, what happened next, and so on. Even the simplest of sites has a time dimension: people arrived, cleared the woodland, made fires and inhabited it for a time, then moved on. Many sites have a much more complex history – especially places that have been occupied by people continuously for thousands of years, such as some of the classic sites of the Mediterranean or of the Fertile Crescent region between the Nile, Tigris and Euphrates.

The first key to establishing a chronological framework is the site matrix, which was created during the excavation process by recording every deposit, cut or context. At the end of the excavation, the matrix might consist of numerous jigsaw pieces that have to be fitted together to make a complete picture.

For example, the ditch with the stone culvert that was excavated in the chapter 'Breaking New Ground' forms one piece of the jigsaw. The matrix diagram for that ditch will show a series of numbers (*see* The Site Matrix), each of which represents an event in the process of excavating the ditch, constructing the culvert and refilling the ditch, and corresponds to the strata shown in the section diagram.

However, although the matrix shows the relative sequence of events, three other vital pieces of information are missing: what period of time does each stage in the matrix represent; when did the activity represented by each stage actually take place (what archaeologists call an 'absolute' date); and how do the activities represented by the ditch construction, filling and use relate to all the other events and features that were recorded across the whole of the site? (By confirming this, archaeologists might then ask how the activity on this site fits into the regional, cultural, national or global sequence of events.)

Relative dates

Those are big questions for a site matrix to answer, but that is the challenge. One way the director can fit the jigsaw pieces together is to look for stratigraphic relationships at the points where one feature cuts through another. At the simplest level, anything that is found at the bottom of a ditch will have got into the ditch before anything that is found in the middle, and the contents of the middle layers will have got into the ditch before those of the upper layers. Thus, any

Forming a complete picture of a site

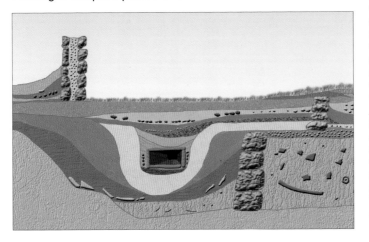

Left By examining other contexts immediately surrounding the stone culvert, archaeologists might conclude that it had been constructed within the natural dip of a silted section of river, to supply a Roman building and jetty (the remains of which are shown buried, right). When the whole area eventually silted up, the site reverted to agricultural land. The ruins of a medieval barn stand above ground, to the left.

Right The remnants of this 13th-century Jewish ritual bath in England forms part of complex foundations relating to London's water supply. Earlier wells, dug during the Roman occupation of the city, were also uncovered during the same rescue excavation, at the site of Blossom's Inn in the east of the city.

layer that lies under another layer must be earlier than that layer and vice versa – the layers at the top are later than those underneath.

At the next level of complexity, one ditch might cross the path of another. Archaeologists will need to know which ditch came first. This can be discovered by using the stratigraphic principles: any feature that is cut by another has to be older and vice versa. The intersection of these two ditches will enable archaeologists to establish a relative sequence: there is now an earlier and later ditch. If either of those ditches intersects with another feature, archaeologists can again establish which came first, so creating relative phasing for three of the sites features – and this process can be used for all the stratigraphic relationships on the site.

Isolated features

In reality, it is rare to pin down the relative chronology of every feature. Most sites have features that exist in isolation – pits, for example – that have no stratigraphic relationship to any other part of the site. Their relationship has to be inferred by other means – if three pits have similar shapes, produce similar pottery and have similar soils, we can hypothesize that they are of similar date, and if one of those pits can be tied stratigraphically to the matrix because it is cut by another feature, all the pits can be given a tentative home in the sequence.

Pinning down key parts of the sequence in relative terms is the first step toward answering the big questions. The next step is to try finding precise dates for parts of the sequence.

Right Examining intersecting contexts in larger, complex sites is a major part of building a complete history of a site.

Using Artefacts as Dating Evidence

There is an unofficial hierarchy in archaeology that places greater emphasis on finds that are capable of yielding dates that can help with the phasing of the site. This often means valuing coins, inscriptions, fine pottery and metalwork above humbler finds.

Above Metal artefacts bearing visible inscriptions, such as this farmer's button, are ideal dating material.

Some types of find – for example, coins, clay tablets, hieroglyphs and inscriptions – incorporate a date as part of their inscription. Or they are inscribed with something that is as good as a date, such as the name of the king or emperor who was on the throne when the object was made. These make it easy to date the piece.

Datable artefacts

For the first 200 years of archaeology, starting in the early 18th century when the discipline first began to form, great effort was invested in building up dated sequences of the most distinctive pottery, jewellery and metalwork forms by looking at the datable objects that they are found with. Initially, this meant focusing on cultures that produced datable material, such as ancient Egypt, Greece, Rome, Byzantium and Arabia.

After establishing chronologies for the materials produced by those civilizations, archaeologists moved out to other cultures, dating their products by looking for deposits that included known and dated products from elsewhere. For example, Egyptian pottery of a known date is often found with late Minoan pottery on Crete, enabling the Minoan pottery to be dated on the assumption that it is contemporary with the Egyptian material. Similarly, pottery exported from Europe to the new world during colonial expansion from the 15th century onward can be used to date the indigenous artefacts found with them in archaeological contexts. After many decades of study, archaeologists have worked out dated sequences for many

Above The Roman coin top-left was minted during the reign of Vespasian (who ruled from AD69–79), and recovered from the city of Dorchester in southern England, indicating a very early date for the city's foundation, shortly after the Roman conquest of Britain in AD43. The two other coins date from the third century AD, indicating Dorchester's continuing usage.

Left This Peruvian grave of a warrior-prince contains precious gold finds (the oxidization has turned them green), and associated pottery – both of which may prove datable.

Above Datable finds (*clockwise from top-left*): a broken medieval gaming counter; a Viking brooch; a Roman bone weaving tablet set; and a near-complete dish in Beauvais Sgraffito, luxury French tableware, dated to 16th century.

Above Ripon Cathedral in Yorkshire, England, built using recycled masonry.

different styles of pottery, metalwork, jewellery and sculpture. This has enabled them to say with some certainty when an object was manufactured or when it was in fashion.

Residual material

In seeking to pin down dates for the site matrix, the director will start by looking for this type of datable find, while also being wary of making the simplistic assumption that the date of the object provides a date for the context in which it is found. There are all sorts of reasons why this might not be the case, and archaeologists are well aware of the dangers of 'residual' material as well as 'intrusive' material (*see box, right*) misleading them.

By residual, archaeologists mean material that is far older than its context. In February 2007, for example, a metal detectorist unearthed a silver denarius near Fowey in Cornwall, England. Because the coin dated from 146BC – some 189 years before the Romans conquered Britain in AD43 – the find sparked much speculation about whether trade contacts existed between Iron-Age Britain and Roman Europe at the time. They might well have done, because Iron-Age Cornwall was an important source of metals, such as tin and lead, which were mined at the time. However, the coin simply could not prove, on its own, that such trade took place. The participants in the debate all assumed that the coin arrived in Cornwall around 146BC, whereas it might have been lost hundreds of years later – it might even, for example, have been lost by a modern collector.

Silver and gold objects, jewellery and works of art – all the datable objects that archaeologists like – are the same type of object that people have hoarded for various reasons. They might be passed down the generations as heirlooms, treasured as lucky charms, or simply kept as a safeguard against inflation – silver and gold retain their value better than bronze. Collectors and museum curators from the 19th and 20th centuries are not alone in valuing objects from the past. Many ancient societies placed a value on objects associated with ancestors, and it is common to find old objects placed in coffins and buried with the deceased. Neolithic axes sometimes turn up on Roman sites, and archaeologists sampling the Thames embankment once found the antlers of exotic deer that certainly did not get there on their own.

Intrusive material

A less common and more easily recognized problem is that of intrusive material, where material from a later date finds its way into earlier contexts. Usually this is the result of some kind of disturbance – for example, animal burrowing is one cause. Wormholes can have a similar effect by creating channels in the soil through which later material drops down through the stratigraphy from the top to the bottom of a ditch. This common phenomenon, where material from one period appears in a connect of a different date, is what motivated astronomers to give the name 'wormholes' to the theoretical corridors in time and space that would allow for the possibility of time travel.

Ancient farming also contributes to the confusion because of the jumble of broken pottery and material from all sorts of dates that accumulates in trash piles and manure heaps that are later taken out and spread on the soil. Some of this material can end up being washed into ditches and pits.

Even what archaeologists call 'robbing' – although in reality the process might be considered 'recycling' – can introduce misleading material into a new context. In medieval Europe, many churches were built from masonry salvaged from ruined Roman buildings.

Earliest and Latest Dates

Two key concepts — terminus post quem (or 'earliest possible date') and terminus ante quem ('latest possible date') — have been developed to enable archaeologists to use artefacts as dating evidence, taking into account the possible longevity of some types of find.

Datable artefacts are treated cautiously, but archaeologists can make statements about them that make logical sense. As a general principle, the different deposits of soil filling a ditch, pit or post hole are likely to be of the same age and date as the artefacts they contain. As long as the fill of the ditch has not been churned up by animal burrowing or ploughing, it would be difficult to think of a scenario to account for interpreting the fill of the ditch as prehistoric if it contained Roman pottery.

Terminus post quem

However, if a datable object, such as a coin, is found within the fill of a ditch, pit or post hole, it is possible to think of various scenarios that might account for its presence in the deposit that should make archaeologists cautious about assuming that it provides a secure date. It is common enough in archaeology to find an object that has been deliberately placed in a ditch, pit or post hole as an offering to the gods and ancestors — such practices continue up to the present day, with 'time capsules' sometimes being included in the foundations of a building.

A Roman coin found at the base of a post hole provides what archaeologists call a *terminus post quem*, meaning that the hole must be later in date than the date at which the coin was struck. In other words, it provides the earliest date in which it is possible for the coin

Above Egyptian mummies entombed in wooden sarcophagi and wearing funerary masks, discovered at the Valley of the Kings, Egypt.

to have got into the post hole. If we know that coins of this type were not struck until AD120, the post hole cannot be earlier than that date, so the building of which the post is part must have been built after AD120.

However, there is another possible scenario that an archaeologist must look out for when using finds as dating evidence. The coin might have got into the fill of the post hole after the building was abandoned. The post itself might have been the central post of a late Iron-Age roundhouse that constructed in the 1st century BC, but that was, 200 years later, considered old fashioned, smoky and draughty by comparison with the new style of architecture introduced by the Romans. A new stone house was built close by and the old one abandoned, left to collapse or even dismantled, during which time the coin was dropped and rolled into the hole left by the decayed or dismantled post. In this scenario, the coin doesn't date the digging of the post hole, nor the period when it was in use, only the decay of the post. Deciding which of these two scenarios is the correct one will depend on the archaeologists' skill in interpreting the layers that fill the excavated post hole.

Left A poignant image of the remains at Pompeii, near Rome, Italy, where bodies mummified in the ash of a Mount Vesuvius eruption in AD79 are being excavated.

Terminus ante quem

Perhaps of considerably greater value to an archaeologist, although occurring more rarely, is the *terminus ante quem*, which means a date before which an event must have taken place. For example, all the material found beneath the ashes and lava that buried Pompeii in August AD79 must date to before that catastrophic eruption of the volcano of Mount Vesuvius.

Other disasters provide a similar seal on events that enables archaeologists to say that material lower down in the stratigraphic sequence must be older. In London, for example, archaeologists often encounter the deep layer of burning that resulted from the Great Fire of September 1666, while another layer of burning found on many London sites is evidence for the Boudiccan revolt of AD60, when native Britons led by Boudicca attacked and set fire to the Roman city.

Stratified finds

For finds to be of any great value in archaeology as dating evidence, it helps if they come from a sealed context – that is to say, if they come from an undisturbed soil deposit that lies beneath another deposit that is demonstrably ancient – for example, from beneath a Roman mosaic floor. Throughout the excavation, the diggers will have been looking out for exactly this sort of dating evidence. It is not often found, but when it is, it can be the pivot around which the dating and phasing of the site will hinge.

More often, the presence of a datable object in the archaeological record is capable of multiple explanations. Such scenarios should stimulate the archaeologists' powers of imagination and explanation. They are a warning against complacency and the drawing of simplistic conclusions. In response, archaeologists look for patterns of finds across a number of features on the site that are consistent, that reinforce each other, and that seem to tell the same story. They also look for similar patterns on other sites, either in the area or of a similar type elsewhere.

Archaeologists will usually talk about likely scenarios rather than certain ones. In order to see those patterns at all, they need to gather data as objectively as possible, so that other archaeologists can look at the same data subsequently and either agree with their interpretation or argue for a different scenario.

Above The Great Fire of London has left an indelible mark on the archaeological record, in the form of a substantial depth of ash and charred timbers.

The Great Fire

The breadth of charred material buried beneath the modern City of London suggests that, when the owners of destroyed properties built their new homes and shops, they did not bother to tidy away the remains of the old but simply built on top. This is consistent with what we know of the post-Fire history of London. Sir Christopher Wren was asked to create a masterplan for a new city to rise from the ashes of the old, with long straight boulevards and open squares in place of the cramped medieval alleys of pre-Fire London. His plan was never executed because London's merchants, keen to get back to making money, quickly rebuilt their premises using the same property boundaries of old.

Above A Roman mosaic under the foundations of a modern-day hospital is being excavated.

Left The 50-year Belvedere time capsule project, sunk into the ground in 1957, is raised again in Tulsa, Oklahoma.

Radiocarbon Dating

One way to achieve greater certainty in dating is to use radiocarbon dating (also known as carbon-14 dating), which enables organic materials to be dated with an increasing degree of accuracy. Radiocarbon dating literally revolutionized prehistoric archaeology when it emerged in the 1940s.

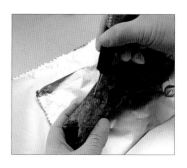

Wartime research into nuclear weaponry led to the development of a peaceful by-product: radiocarbon dating. Until then, prehistoric sites were dated in broad slices of time on the basis of pottery and metalwork typologies, whose accuracy was measured in hundreds or thousands of years. Fragments of a collared urn can tell archaeologists that the site was of a Bronze Age date, but it could not tell precisely when this distinctive type of pottery was made in the Bronze Age – a period spanning 1,500 years or more.

So, for the huge period of time represented by prehistory – literally thousands of years – it was not possible

Below Carbon 14 absorbed by living organisms decays after death (shown top right) at a constant rate; measuring the amount left tells us how long it was since the animal or person died or the plant was cut down.

to do more than make intelligent guesses about the absolute and relative dates of individual sites and their relationships. That inability to say whether one site was earlier or later than another was a major drawback, because one of the key questions in archaeology is how ideas spread – ideas such as agriculture, art, religion, living in cities, kingship, metal-working or fashions in pottery, jewellery or architectural styles – and to provide answers, archaeologists need to have a chronological framework.

The science of radiocarbon dating

That framework fell into place with the discovery that the radioactive isotope of carbon called carbon-14 (which scientists abbreviate to 14C) can be used as a chemical calendar. Carbon-14 is produced by the effects of sunlight

Above Samples from a human femur (thigh) being taken for radiocarbon dating.

on the atmosphere, on the oceans and on plant life. It is in the air we breathe and in the food we eat. All living things absorb it while they are alive – so that animals and plants end up with the same amount of carbon-14 in their cells as there is in the atmosphere.

The moment an organism dies it stops absorbing carbon-14. From that moment on, carbon-14 decays, breaking down chemically and turning into simpler chemicals. Fortunately for archaeologists, carbon-14 decays at a constant and measurable rate. In effect, it provides a clock that starts ticking at

Below Food and drink residues from vessels like this Chinese 'gui' pot, used for making offerings to the gods, can provide organic materials that can be used for carbon dating.

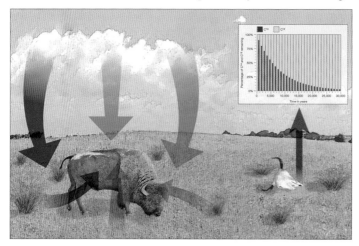

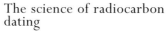

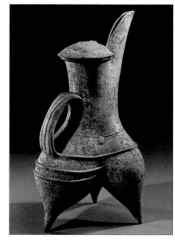

Above A pestle and stone block 'bins', 12th-century corn-grinding equipment found at the Navajo Ancient Monument site in the south-western United States, provide dating material.

Above Willard Libby stands with the equipment he designed for distilling carbon.

Willard Libby, the father of radiocarbon dating

Willard Frank Libby (1908–80), Professor of Chemistry at the University of Chicago, Illinois, was awarded the Nobel Prize in 1960 for leading the team that cracked the rate at which the radioactive isotope carbon-14 decays. The team developed a technique for measuring carbon-14, which they did by building a sensitive Geiger counter. The team then needed to find some way of calibrating the results they got from measuring the amount of remaining carbon-14 they found in organic materials. They did this by creating tables of carbon-14 in objects of a known date. To go as far back in time as possible, they used timbers from the tombs of ancient Egyptians whose date at death was known from tomb hieroglyphs. Once a sequence of dates was pinned down, it was possible to predict the likely decay rates of carbon-14 for objects up to 50,000 years old.

the moment of death, so in theory archaeologists can determine the date at which a tree was cut down or an animal slaughtered by measuring the amount of radiocarbon in a sample of wood or bone and comparing this to the amount of radiocarbon in the atmosphere (which, at the time when radiocarbon dating was first developed, was assumed to be constant).

The dating revolution

With this discovery, bone, antler and plant material, such as charred wood or grain, took on a new significance in the archaeological record. The immediate effect of radiocarbon dating was to enable archaeologists to revisit classical sites – from Jericho to Stonehenge – seeking material suitable for dating. Early carbon dating was slow, expensive and dependent on a handful of specialists working in nuclear laboratories with priorities other than helping archaeology – such as nuclear power generation and weapons development. Despite this, progress was made and the results overturned many old ideas. Sites were shown to be much older than had been thought and to have been occupied for longer; key developments, such as farming, were shown to have occurred earlier than previously thought, often by thousands of years. Sites that were thought to be younger or older than each other were often proved to be contemporaneous, or vice versa.

Above Archaeologists remove samples from charcoal pits for radiocarbon dating.

A key finding was that farming began in several different parts of the world – as far apart as Africa, Asia and the Americas – at about the same time – opening up all sorts of new questions. Once firm dates could be obtained relatively easily, archaeologists became less obsessed with questions about when things happened and instead began to ask why and how. Did new developments and ideas spread across the globe because people migrated and took new ideas with them? Or did their development of agriculture or metal-

working give them an advantage that enabled them to conquer neighbouring peoples, or to colonize the wilderness more effectively? Did people invent these ideas independently of each other in several places at once? Or do good ideas simply travel very fast, implying that there was a network of contacts and links between different people that effectively spread around the inhabited parts of the world?

Selecting Samples for Carbon Dating

Obtaining radiocarbon dates is no longer a technique that archaeologists employ in only rare and exceptional circumstances. It is now the most commonly used form of scientific dating, so it is vital for archaeologists to know what makes a good sample for the test.

Above These samples are stored in phials to prevent contamination before carbon dating.

From being a very expensive and time-consuming process, radiocarbon dating has now become a routine aspect of archaeological practice, with specialized laboratories providing a fast and relatively inexpensive radiocarbon dating service. Samples for testing are chosen in consultation with a specialist, who will advise on the suitability of the material. A variety of organic materials can be tested, including wood and charcoal, nuts and charred grain, animal and human bone, food remains and shell, cloth, pollen, peat and some soils, and even iron and slag if it contains carbon impurities.

Secure stratification

Experience and judgement are necessary to ensure that the material selected for dating will be able to yield a useful date. The material must come from a securely stratified context – one that excludes intrusive material of a later date. It must have been collected under conditions that will prevent contamination by modern material, which means that it should not be handled or washed.

Residual material – or material that is older than the deposit – must also be excluded. Charcoal twigs or nuts are perfect because they contain carbon-14

that has been absorbed over a very short time period – a year in the case of nuts – and can thus give archaeologists a date that is very close to the date at which the nuts were consumed or the twigs were cut and burned in a fire.

By contrast, wood that comes from the central part of the trunk of a very old tree might give a misleading date because it could have been several centuries old when it was cut down and used – it could then have survived in use – perhaps as part of a building – for several more centuries before being salvaged and used as firewood.

Equally, one must bear in mind that radiocarbon dating gives us a date for the object, and not for its context. For example, a date obtained from pig bones that have been consumed as part of a feast will tell archaeologists the date at which the pig was killed and the meat consumed; it will not necessarily tell the date of the pit, because the bones could have been placed in the pit at a much later date. That is why it is very important to obtain more than one sample from each context. The consistency of the dating from several different samples tells a more convincing story than one date on its own, and this is a problem that has dogged the understanding of the different construction phases at major monuments, such as Stonehenge, where the

Left These remains of a prehistoric cow burial, likely to have been part of a sacrificial ceremony, may provide valuable dates.

Right Helge Stine points at the Newfoundland location containing the remains of a Viking village, which predated Columbus' arrival by some 500 years.

dating rests on isolated samples from antler picks, which might be later than the pits they are found in.

The first American invasion

Sometimes radiocarbon dating can be the conclusive piece of evidence that proves an event that has divided archaeological opinion. The 'Saga of the Greenlanders', for example, is an Icelandic poem that describes the colonization of Greenland by the Norwegian Erik the Red. The saga is preserved in a late 14th century manuscript but describes events that took place around AD970 to 1030. How much of the saga is true and how much is fiction? In particular, did Eric and his followers discover and colonize a part of North America, which they called Vinland (*vin* in Old Icelandic means 'flat' – hence 'flat land', or 'land of plains'), which the saga describes as a land of grassy meadows and salmon-filled rivers?

The evidence needed to authenticate the events described in the saga was found in 1960 when the remains of a Viking village were discovered by the Norwegian explorers and archaeologists, Helge and Anne Stine Ingstad at L'Anse aux Meadows, which is now a National Historical Park on the northernmost tip of the island of Newfoundland, in Canada. Carbon-14 dating of the bone needles and knitting tools was used to date the site to around AD1000.

The saga was shown to be a true account of actual events, and the poem also contained evidence that this early colonial settlement might have been abandoned because of a misunderstanding between the Vikings and the local Algonquin people – the milk served to the Native Canadians by the Vikings at a feast made them sick (probably from lactose intolerance) and so the Vikings were suspected of attempting to poison their guests.

Turin Shroud

Carbon dating is used to date any objects where precision is required, not just objects from the very distant past. The Catholic Church gave permission in 1988 for a piece of ancient linen from the Turin Shroud to be tested, and that gave a direct date for the shroud of between 1260 and 1390. This accords very well with the first documented account of the Shroud, which dates from 1357, and suggests that the shroud is not that of the historical Jesus. However, scientists remain intrigued by the skill of the medieval makers of the shroud, and have wondered about the exact technique used to create the ghostly image that it preserves.

Below This sample of the Turin Shroud was carbon dated by scientists at Oxford University, England.

Below Though we now know the Turin Shroud is medieval, we still do not know how the haunting image was produced.

Advanced Dating Strategies

Over the last 50 years, carbon-dating techniques have become more and more refined. Accelerator mass spectrometry has developed as a means of dating exceptionally old deposits, and statistical methods have been developed for achieving greater accuracy.

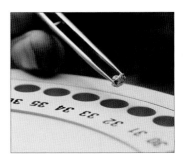

Above A sample about to be incinerated via AMS to measure the degree of carbon decay.

Although most organic materials can be tested for their carbon-14 content, a considerable weight of material might be necessary to yield meaningful results using conventional carbon-dating techniques. Dating laboratories specify a minimum weight of 1g (⅕oz) of wood or charcoal, 5g (⅕oz) of peat or 50g (1¾oz) of bone – but ideally they prefer much more than this: 12g (⅖oz) of wood, 10g (⅓oz) of charcoal and 100g (3½oz) of bone are the ideal. What is more, dating specialists prefer to have two separate samples whenever possible to act as a control. If both samples yield a similar date, you can have some confidence that the samples are uncontaminated by residual or intrusive material.

Splitting atoms

However, what if you only have a tiny amount of material. For example, a single carbonized grain of wheat from a hearth that you think might represent the last human activity before the abandonment of a site. The answer is to use the more expensive and sophisticated accelerator mass spectrometry (AMS) technique, which can yield results from as little as 10mg of material – equivalent to the weight of one cereal grain, or the residues of food contained in the porous vessel walls of a pot.

In basic terms, this works by bursting the atoms apart that make up the sample, and measuring the different amounts of each element. To do this requires equipment that is expensive to build and run, but it is a much more sensitive technique for measuring carbon-14 and can extend the time period for dating ancient material back to 70,000 years ago.

Beyond this date the amount of residual carbon-14 in any sample is so low that it cannot be distinguished from the natural background radiation that exists all around us. Even so, AMS is an important technique for dating early hominid migrations and activities – for example, the spread of our ancestors, Homo sapiens, into Asia and Australia – and for dating the last populations of Neanderthals to survive in Europe, before their final extinction, which is currently dated to around 24,000BC.

New dates for old

Every so often, carbon dating undergoes a mini-revolution when new tests are carried out on material that has already been dated using methods that have been superseded. Much of the redating activity of the last decade has been necessary to eliminate errors in the formulae previously used to turn radio-carbon data into calendar dates. Scientists now know, for example, that the rate of decay of carbon-14 is slower than the figures used by Libby's team when they first developed carbon-dating in the 1940s. The half life of

Left A scientist using computerized equipment to control an AMS experiment.

carbon-14 (the time it takes for the amount of the radioactive isotope carbon-14 to decay) is 5,730 years rather than 5,568 years.

Scientists also know that the amount of carbon-14 in the atmosphere is not constant, but fluctuates, sometimes as the result of sunspot activity and sometimes for reasons that can be observed but that are not understood. Scientists have discovered, too, that not all organisms absorb carbon-14 at the same rate, and that some organisms (especially fish and shellfish) are capable of continuing to absorb carbon in sea water even after death.

Dates derived from measuring carbon-14 have been calibrated with dates from other scientific techniques to investigate and iron out these discrepancies. Armed with all this mass of new data, archaeological scientists have been able to reduce the level of error, at the same time increasing the level of certainty that the dates they provide are accurate.

The meaning of carbon-14 dates in archaeology

Dates are usually expressed in archaeological reports according to a standard format. In general, the report will give the name of the laboratory that under-took the tests, the unique sample number, an archaeological reference number that ties the sample to the site and context from which it was excavated, and then a date.

The date itself is written in a form that expresses the likelihood of the date falling within a certain range. For example, the date 1770–1630BC given in the laboratory report means that there is a 95 per cent certainty that the date falls within the range 1770 to 1630BC. An alternative might be to give the date as 1700±70 (give or take 70 years), which means there is a 95 per cent chance that it lies in the range 1770 to 1630BC. The 140 date range is there because radiocarbon dating is not a pinpoint accurate science. Alternatively, those same dates might be expressed as 3650±70 BP, where BP stands for 'before present' –

Dating America's Clovis culture

Archaeologists believe that the first migrants to arrive in the Americas belonged to the Clovis culture – hunter-gatherers with distinctively shaped spear points first found in Clovis, New Mexico. However, when did they arrive? Clovis artefacts were first dated in the 1960s and 1970s, using carbon-dating techniques that are now obsolete, and gave a date of 13,600 years ago. However, those same artefacts were redated in 2006 using AMS. The results show that Clovis technology is younger than previously thought – 13,100 years old – and lasted only 200 to 350 years. The result introduces all kinds of new questions: is 350 years long enough for those people to have spread from the Siberian land bridge all the way to the tip of South America? Some say 'yes', while others argue it would take 1,000 years. If so, this raises the intriguing possibility that

there were people already in the Amercias before the Clovis people arrived, and that the rapid dissemination of Clovis spear points is explained by these earlier people adopting Clovis technology.

Left Clovis spear points, made of fine-grained stone called 'chert'.

however, 'present' doesn't mean today but rather 1950, the date at which this dating convention was established.

Bayesian statistics

A recent development – so recent that its implications are still being assessed – is the use of Bayesian statistical techniques, designed to reduce the errors in probability calculations. Named after the 18th-century mathematician Thomas Bayes, the theory behind Bayesian statistical techniques is far from new. However, the application of these methods has had to wait for the availability of computers with sufficient speed and power to do the vast amounts of repetitive calculations, or number crunching, involved.

The benefit is that it is becoming possible to give precise calendar dates to radiocarbon samples, rather than date ranges, and some surprising results have already been achieved. For example, Neolithic long barrows in Europe are now thought to have been fashionable for a very short period of time – perhaps no more than 100 years – rather than, as was previously thought, having been a burial practice in use for more than 1,000 years.

Above Carbon dating tells us that 'Wayland's Smithy' chamber tomb, in Oxfordshire, England, was built around 3700BC.

Above Scientists can get dates from a single cereal grain using sophisticated equipment like the mass spectrometer.

Dendrochronology and Other Dating Methods

Trees are especially responsive to environmental fluctuations, and differences in temperature, sunlight and rainfall from one year to the next are reflected in their annual growth rings. As a result, tree-ring dating has become the second most important dating method commonly used in archaeology.

Above Wet or dry summers create unique and dateable patterns of wide and narrow tree rings.

The knowledge that trees have annual growth rings existed as far back as the 15th century, which is when the first historical records speak of counting rings to gauge the age of a tree. However, the use of these rings as a means of giving precise dates to buildings and archaeological sites did not develop until the 1920s. This practice is known as dendrochronology.

One of the pioneers of the technique was A.E. (Andrew Ellicott) Douglass (1867–1962), an American astronomer who looked for evidence of the way that plants might respond to sunspot activity and found a correlation between tree-ring width and solar variation. He did this by looking at the tree rings in timbers from ancient Native American villages in Arizona and New Mexico, and comparing them with sunspot activity records dating back to the 17th century. These records were found in journals kept by scientists such as William Herschel.

Tree-ring research

Douglass subsequently established the Laboratory of Tree-Ring Research at the University of Arizona. He then compared tree-ring evidence from 4,000 year old bristle-cone pine tree trunks preserved in the White Mountains of California with climate records from ice cores, glaciers, lake and seabed deposits and volcanic events. As the research became international in scale, ancient wood from all kinds of sources was added into the study, with samples coming from bog oak – ancient tree trunks preserved in peat bogs in northern Europe – and timbers from ancient buildings, such as the great cathedrals built in Europe.

Little by little a sequence of annual rings was built up that now covers the period back to 10,000BC. There are gaps in the record, and there are many regional variations, due to localized forest fires, volcanic eruptions or periods of severe cold, that are not fully charted. However, despite these problems, master sequences have been built up for whole regions of the world for trees growing in the same geographical zone and under similar climatic conditions. Thus, it is now possible to date ancient timbers with a high degree of precision by taking a sample and matching the pattern of narrow and thick rings from the sample to the regional sequence.

Understanding the results

As always with archaeological dating, the result cannot always be taken at face value. Exact dates for the felling of a tree can be given only if the bark survives or one of the five outer rings just below the bark. This is the part of a tree that is often trimmed off before the timber is used for building purposes. Where it has been removed, or where the timber comes from the central part of the tree, it is better to

Left Tree rings have been used to date the construction of London's medieval waterfront to the early 13th century.

Above Slivers of wood examined by microscope reveal their unique ring pattern.

date the timber by using radiocarbon dating, because that will provide a more accurate date for the felling. Fortunately, bark does often survive in structures that are not intended to be seen – hidden in roofs or buried below ground. Waterlogged timbers from Roman bridges and forts in Germany and the Netherlands have been dated precisely, as have timbers from medieval and Roman waterfronts in London and several Russian and Scandinavian cities. In London, for example, dendro dating has changed the accepted date of the founding of Roman London's timber quays to before the Boudiccan revolt of AD60, rather than after.

Other dating techniques

Archaeologists of today are in a privileged position, because scientists have developed a battery of techniques for dating glass, volcanic ash, obsidian, burnt flint and stone, tooth enamel, pottery and burnt clay, wood, shell, plants and seeds – to name just some of the possibilities. There is a repertoire of dating techniques that, in theory, can be used to obtain absolute dates for any of the sites being excavated. Archaeologists need to know what works best given the age of the site and the type of material available for testing. Tree-ring dating provides the most accurate results for relatively recent sites, while carbon dating is best for older sites, and others – such as potassium-argon dating – are better for very old sites.

Above Archaeologists look for timbers with some bark left on them because the outer five layers tell you exactly when the tree was felled.

A number of specialized dating techniques are based on heating samples of material, then detecting the presence of different elements and their isotopes in the resulting gases. This is the basis of potassium-argon and argon-argon dating, which are used for dating ash, lava and volcanic materials, and also for fossilized bones found in volcanic rocks. For example, potassium-argon dating was used to date Lucy – the famous hominid found in Ethiopia – and the early hominids found in Tanzania's Olduvai Gorge.

Another method used for dating objects is optical, or luminescence, dating. This technique looks for electrons that are trapped or fixed into minerals at the very precise moment that they are exposed to intense light or heat – for example, when clay is fired to create pottery. These can be released and measured either by heating them again, known as thermoluminescence (TL) dating, or by stimulating specific electrons using blue, green or infrared light, which is called optically stimulated luminescence (OSL) dating or photoluminescence (PL) dating.

Above Sand from this hearth in Mungo National Park, Australia, was used for dating the ancient settlement site.

Grains of truth

PL dating has been used effectively to date layers of sand in Australia that cover deposits containing human artefacts. It has shown that people were present at the site up to 60,000 years ago. TL dating has also been used to detect ceramic pieces fraudulently claimed to be ancient. These forgeries lack the trapped electrons that should be there if the ceramic piece had genuinely been fired in antiquity.

147

Finds and Typologies

Long before the scientific techniques were developed for dating organic materials by physical and chemical means, archaeologists adopted the idea of taxonomy – the classification of objects on the basis of their similarities and differences – from botany and the natural sciences.

Taxonomy remains a key technique in archaeology for establishing what the finds from a site can tell us. Once the director or project manager has made decisions about which samples from the site should be packed up and sent to the dating laboratory, the next task is to tackle the rest of the finds from the site. It is unlikely that a director will have the detailed knowledge to analyse the finds without help, so an army of finds specialists will be recruited.

Some archaeologists have built their career not on digging but on getting to know a particular type of find, such as pottery, metalwork, bone, snail and shell, pollens or plant material. Others specialize in ancient building materials,

worked stone, woodwork, coins, leather or textiles, jewellery and personal adornments, glass, statuary or painted wall plaster. Within these broad categories, there might be sub-specialities: some pottery experts only study fine tablewares, amphorae (storage jars), clay lamps, glazed pottery or grass-tempered wares. The skills they possess might have been established by studying a particular class of find for a university research thesis, and then working with that material as a museum curator. They can be depended on to identify accurately the material they are sent, a skill that takes years to develop, through constant handling of the material.

Above Some of the finds from the Royal Arsenal site at Woolwich, UK, include these shot cases as well as lead shot and pottery.

The critical task for the director is to harness the expertise of the best people available. The specialist will normally charge a fee for the work based on an assessment of how many days of work are involved and the complexity of the task.

Typologies

Once the boxes of finds land on the desk of the finds specialist, there are all kinds of questions to be asked. The first and most essential task is to describe what has been found, and to compare

Left and above Specific sites yield very particular categories of find. The 'common finds' pictured above (from the industrial site, *shown left*) are well documented. Existing typologies categorizing styles of metals, leather goods, earthenware, pottery and glassware enable archaeologists to identify and date similar artefacts recovered on site very quickly.

the material from the particular site with what has been found on similar sites elsewhere.

It is rare that a site will yield any finds that are truly new and unique, although this can happen, especially when dealing with sites whose special environment (cold, dry or water-logged) preserves organic remains. More typically, every single find from the site can be placed within an existing framework, or 'typology'. Borrowing principles of classification from the biological sciences, archaeologists have been building up these typologies for the last 150 years, classifying the most common finds from excavations according to their characteristics and their stratigraphic relationships.

Changes over time

Stratigraphy is one of the key principles of archaeological classification because it prevents archaeologists from making simplistic judgements about the material and sorting it according to subjective ideas, such as the commonly

held belief that objects become more complex over time. Faced with a pile of unstratified pottery, it would be tempting to sort them on the assumption that the crudest and simplest shapes might be the earliest, and that as potters became more skilled at their craft, the pottery would become more sophisticated, better made, more elaborate and more diverse in form. This was indeed the sort of assumption that was made by early antiquaries in the 17th and 18th centuries.

However, careful scientific recording of what is found in each layer or context on the site can lead to a different conclusion. Putting the pottery in stratigraphic order, from the earliest layers to the latest, will show how shapes, decoration and materials really change over time. This will reveal the true pattern of development, which is often more interesting than simplistic 'evolutionary' notions based on aesthetic judgements about what looks most sophisticated to the modern eye. Using this scientific

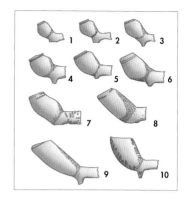

Above This typology of clay pipes spans some 260 years; note how the style of the 'bowls' becomes larger as tobacco becomes cheaper. Dates are as follows: **1:** 1580–1610; **2–5:** 1610–40; **6–7:** 1640–60; **8:** 1660–1710; **9:** 1690–1710; **10:** 1820–40.

approach, archaeologists have been able to build typologies for most of the common types of find – and in some cases have been able to give precise dates to those sequences.

Left Finds recovered at the site of the Roman imperial baths of Kaiserthermen in German's Rhineland suggested continued usage from the Neolithic to the Classical period.

Rediscovering Roman Germany

The classification of armour, brooches and fine tableware from early Roman military sites in Germany has had a significant impact on archaeologists' understanding of Roman artefacts. The campaigns that the Romans fought in their attempts to conquer Germany between the late 1st and late 2nd centuries were recorded by historians, such as Tacitus, and are represented by the remains of forts and frontiers established season by season, according to the fortunes of the army as they advanced or retreated along the banks of the Rivers Rhine and Danube.

This unique combination of historical and archaeological evidence has enabled German scholars, many of them working at the Deutsches Archäologisches Institut founded in 1902, to build the typologies that are still being used by archaeologists studying the Roman Empire for dating commonly found Roman objects, such as Samian pottery, military weapons, belt fittings and the shoulder brooches used to pin cloaks and tunics.

Building Typologies

The task of creating typologies is one of the great ongoing tasks of archaeology; and archaeologists who specialize in finds are always on the lookout for opportunities to make their name by contributing new forms, new dates or revisions to existing typologies.

Much of the work that a specialist does is routine and repetitive, and involves classifying and describing finds that are mostly familiar and commonplace. However, the work also has some challenges, because the placing of objects within a typographical scheme involves familiarity with scores of often-obscure reports and articles in archaeological journals. Although typologies are critical to archaeological analysis, a specialist cannot simply buy a book called 'Everything you might want to know about Bronze-Age axe heads'. Instead, the typology for axe heads is widely dispersed in articles and papers that have been published over the last 100 years, and part of the training that the (often self-educated)

specialist undergoes is to master the scores of reports in which bits of the typology are described.

Every so often someone might bring the current state of knowledge together in a 'corpus' – a definitive statement of all that is currently known about a class of object. Yet that corpus will be out of date before it is printed, because archaeological knowledge is constantly being refined by new discoveries – and that is what motivates the specialists to do the routine work. Every excavation has the potential to refine the sequence, fill in missing gaps, to provide firm dates for parts of the sequence or even to start an entirely new typology, classifying a neglected or little-studied type of find.

Above Beads were recovered during an excavation in Sinai, Egypt. Samples of lava taken from the same site have been linked to a catastrophic eruption on Santorini in 1500BC, which wreaked havoc along the Egyptian coast.

Contributing to new knowledge

People who are steeped in knowledge about their particular field are always looking for material that could lead to a new research project or help them make their mark by publishing a new class of objects. For example, archaeologists specializing in metalwork have in recent years begun to realize that some of the finds that they have described as having an unknown function might have been made to decorate furniture, such as chairs, chests and couches. This realization has led to a new search through the archaeological record for similar material, along with the creation of new typographies.

Finds made by metal detectorists have also sparked new lines of specialist study into medieval shoe buckles, cap badges, belt fittings and ornate metal dress hooks. The latter is a type of fastening that preceded buttons and is known about from 16th-century portraits of well-dressed ladies and gentleman; however, they have only recently been recovered from archaeological contexts.

Left Hunter-gatherer artefacts are tagged in Spila Cave, Croatia. Finds associated with this location have contributed to knowledge about the ancient Illyrian people, who inhabited the Adriatic site during the Hellenic period.

Right This Romano–British brooch, cleverly cast from a single piece of bronze, reflects the style known as the 'Colchester-type' jewellery.

The refinement of typographies is the basis of much of the research that occurs in universities. The excavation director, when looking for specialists to describe and interpret the finds, will often turn to research graduates for help. The director knows that these researchers can, in turn, call on their supervisors and other experienced professionals for assistance if necessary.

Assemblages

Whereas the specialist is concerned with one type of material and its typologies, the person who writes the overall site report has to think in terms of the totality of the evidence — what archaeologists call the 'assemblage'. Assemblage simply means a collection of objects found in association with one another. The word is used to describe not just the contents of one pit, but also the contents of the entire site, and it can also be used to describe bigger collections of related materials. Archaeologists will sometimes talk about regional assemblages of material that reflect cultural differences, or period assemblages — meaning the typical mix of finds that tells archaeologists that the site is from the Neolithic Age rather than the Bronze Age.

Like the specialist, the director will be seeking to compare the assemblage from this particular site with others that are similar. Whether a specialist or project manager, the focus will be continually shifting back and forth between the one site and the larger picture of all similar sites, in order to try to pin down as clearly as possible the sequence of activity at the particular site. During the process, stratigraphy will be used to work out relative dates and scientific dating techniques will give precise dates to parts of the sequence wherever possible, filling out the picture by drawing on dating evidence from other sites that are similar in terms of their individual finds or their assemblages.

Above This assemblage of flint tools, all from the same excavation site, includes material that dates from the Mesolithic, Neolithic and Bronze Ages.

Archaeology is a combination of collaborative work and solo study, and perhaps the loneliest task of all is that faced by the director when it comes to combining the evidence from all of the specialist reports and understanding what they mean for the site as a whole.

Above A reconstruction of a typical Anglo-Saxon settlement based on information from assemblages.

Assemblages and diet

When archaeologists study assemblages, it is not the presence or absence of a type of material that is diagnostic so much as the relative proportions. For example, a list of animal bones from a pit will provide an archaeologist with some idea of the main sources of animal protein in the diet, but the proportions of pig to sheep to cow will tell more about the respective contribution that each makes to the diet — perhaps showing that sheep is the main meat consumed and that pig is rare. The assemblage can be further defined in terms of the types of bone from each animal. If whole animals are consumed, perhaps this is a subsistence household, eating all they produce, whereas selective cuts might suggest a household that can select its meat and perhaps buys from a butcher rather than rearing their own animals. Another refinement might be to look at the age of the animals at slaughter, which can indicate a preference for young animals, such as suckling pig or goat, or that most of the meat is consumed in the winter, perhaps as part of a ritual.

Assemblages also yield important information when compared to other assemblages of a similar date. In one example, the study of food remains has been used to identify pockets of people of different ethnicity on the basis of the presence or absence of specific herbs and seasonings. In another example, regional differences in diet have been detected from the difference in cooking pots, with one region favouring slow-cooked casseroles and another preferring grilled foods.

Seriation and Trends

What happens if an archaeologist is working on an excavation site that consists of separate features, that do not appear to have any stratigraphic relationships, and no material has been found that can be used for absolute dating? The answer is to deploy mathematics.

Above Sir Flinders Petrie (1853–1942) with pottery he recovered from southern Palestine.

Classical sites in Europe are rich in the kinds of finds that can be dated by stratigraphic relationships, scientific dating, typography or assemblage. However, this isn't a luxury that every archaeologist can count on. In the United States and Australia, for example, the evidence from a site can consist entirely of a scattering of finds from the surface of the soil – with no stratigraphy and no intersecting features to provide clues about the phasing or dating of the site.

Faced with such situations, archaeologists have developed the techniques of seriation based on multi-variate analysis. As the latter term suggests, this involves looking at the many variable characteristics that distinguish one assemblage of finds from another – instead of placing one type of find into a typology – for example, a bronze brooch, a coin, or a piece of decorated Samian ware – seriation tries to place the whole assemblage into a typographical sequence.

Fickle fashion

This idea was pioneered by Sir William Flinders Petrie (1853–1942), one of the founders of modern archaeological method. Digging a cemetery at Diospolis Parva in Upper Egypt in 1928, he devised a new system for analysing the contents of the graves that contained nothing that could be dated using the methods of his day and that could not be dated relatively through their stratigraphy because none of the graves touched or cut any of the others.

Instead, Flinders Petrie decided to look at the percentage of each type of artefact in each grave, and then to look for patterns. He represented each grave on a piece of paper and shuffled the papers until he had a sequence that

made sense to him, based on the underlying assumption that pottery styles come in and out of fashion, one style being pushed out by another. Instead of assuming that a style could be in fashion for a long time, and that many styles can co-exist, he assumed that fashions were fickle and short lived, and looked for patterns based on the shortest period of time between the appearance of a style and its replacement by another.

To give a simplified example, if grave 1 contains 10 per cent of pottery style A and 90 per cent of pottery style B, grave 2 contains 90 per cent of pottery style A and 10 per cent of pottery style B, and grave 3 contains 50 per cent of each, Flinders Petrie reasoned that grave 3 overlapped into the two other periods, and the correct date sequence was either 1–3–2 (pottery style A is in the ascendancy) or 2–3–1 (pottery style B is growing in popularity). Adding data from further graves might indicate which is the case, as would analysing not just two pottery variables, but several distinctive artefact

Left Based on the clay pipes typology (*see page 143*), this imaginary scenario reflects how assemblages of pipes recovered from three riverside locations can be used to date those sites. Here, the excavation beneath the bridge revealed the greatest percentage of the earlier styles of pipe, so this is probably the oldest location. The pub ruins are perhaps the newest location, with the greatest percentage of pipes reflecting later styles.

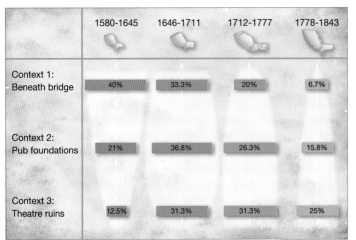

	1580-1645	1646-1711	1712-1777	1778-1843
Context 1: Beneath bridge	40%	33.3%	20%	6.7%
Context 2: Pub foundations	21%	36.8%	26.3%	15.8%
Context 3: Theatre ruins	12.5%	31.3%	31.3%	25%

types and characteristics – flint blades as well as pottery, for example, and decorative motifs and vessel shape.

Computer analysis

What Sir Flinders Petrie did in his head with slips of paper is now done by computer, swapping the mind-bending effort of detecting patterns in multi-dimensional data for computer programs that can define and compare assemblages swiftly, accurately and comprehensively. There is also now the benefit of carbon dating, so that some assemblages can be given an absolute date because of their association with a camp fire, hearth or kiln.

Many such analyses have proven that Sir Flinders Petrie was essentially correct in his assumptions about fashion. The typical result of seriation analysis is the so-called battleship curve – the graphic representation of the frequency with which an object, such as an arrowhead or a pottery shard occurs over time as a percentage of various assemblages. The curve is narrow when the object first appears, widens as it grows in popularity and then tapers off again to a point as it slowly declines in frequency.

The transition from one style to another is not abrupt – different types overlap as one slowly replaces another. One archaeologist has likened this to what you see every day on the streets. Count the number of cars that are one, two, three and four years old and work out the percentage that each makes of the total. The result is likely to be a similar battleship curve, with very few brand new models, a growing proportion of cars that are two, three, and four years old, perhaps reaching the bulge of the curve at between four and five-year-old models, followed by a declining number of six, seven, eight and nine year old models and very few cars over ten years old.

Right An archaeologist examines pottery goods from the oldest-known Mayan royal tomb, found in Guatemala. The tomb dates from 150BC.

Pottery from prehistoric Barbados

Trying to set up a sequence of pottery for prehistoric Barbados, archaeologists looked for various indicators that might have chronological significance. Decoration was one clue, but that was confined to a very small number of shards, so other characteristics were studied, leading to the conclusion that the thickness of the pottery was a vital clue, along with the shape and thickness of the rim of the vessel. The thicker the shards the later they were likely to be, and the finer the earlier (perhaps the reverse of what a crude evolutionary belief might suggest, which is that pottery gets finer as time advances).

The archaeologists then looked at the slip – a type of coloured liquid clay – used to coat the pottery, in combination with decoration. They sorted shards into combinations of finger-marking with cream slip, finger-marking with red slip and finger-marking with polychrome (more than one colour) slip. Comparison with similar pottery from neighbouring islands has suggested that this is a sequence that holds true for a substantial part of the Caribbean and the next stage of research is to try and detect what influence the styles of one island might have on the styles of another.

Above Pottery from Port St Charles, Barbados, both dating from AD600–800. (*Top*) cream slip with red and black slip decoration; (*bottom*) cream slip with red and white slip decoration.

Ancient Environments

So far, the value of finds has been described largely in terms of what they can tell archaeologists about the date of the site from which they were recovered. However, objects contain many different levels of meaning that go well beyond their value as dating evidence.

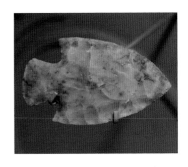

Using finds to provide dates – or date ranges – enables the director to phase the various activities and events that went on at the site. He or she can look at the site's history, from its first use through various changes and peaks and troughs in activity, can look for any gaps in occupation and use, and can look for evidence of continuity of use or eventual abandonment. However, looking for chronological evidence of this kind cannot be divorced from answering a set of questions about what exactly was the nature of the activity that went on at the site and what was the relationship between the people who used the site and their environment, and between the site and its wider landscape setting.

Starting with the environment

Some archaeologists believe that the environment can be a critical factor in determining how people live. For example, a stressful environment can encourage innovative responses and evolutionary change, or it can make life so difficult that populations plummet and people migrate in search of better conditions. Conversely, a benign climate might lead to the plentiful food resources that foster wealth creation, hierarchies, patronage and art, fashion and innovation.

Proving any of these hypotheses will require data about the climate and vegetation. Extracting such information is the task of the environmental

Above Prehistoric hunting tools were recovered from the Arctic tundra on the coast of Alaska in the United States.

archaeologist, whose post-excavation activity will consist of examining and identifying the organic materials recovered from the site. These include the snails, seeds and pollens and any diagnostic elements in the soil that can indicate fires, human occupation or animal husbandry.

Analysing pollen

Pollen samples from a site can be used to create a pollen profile. However, because pollen is so light and can be carried considerable distances by the breeze, archaeologists cannot always

Right Inca storehouses in Peru held emergency supplies of clothing, weaponry and food for times of war or famine.

Above The task for the environmental archaeologist is to present a picture of life at the location by analysing pollen profiles and geological evidence.

be very precise about the specific character of a small plot of land, but it can show what plants were growing in the vicinity of the site and in what quantities. This can serve as a powerful corrective to any ideas about the site that might be derived from its current environment. Many prehistoric burial mounds and henge monuments, for example, are now highly visible structures that can be viewed from afar across fields or pasture – but was this always the case? How would it effect our interpretation if archaeologists discovered that Stonehenge was originally built not on a chalk plain but in a clearing in the dense forest?

Pollen analysis will show whether or not the area was wooded, and whether the woodland species were typical of the so-called 'wildwood', the indigenous natural vegetation of the region, or whether the species were typically of forest clearance and the selection of trees for food (hazel) or basket making (willow), or fencing and building materials (elm, hazel or oak).

Because weeds and wildflowers are specific to certain habitats – woodland, woodland margin, open pasture, cultivated soils, wet, dry, sunny or shady – the weed seed assemblage contributes to the picture of the environment. Snails are habitat specific, too, so their presence is another element that can be considered.

The bigger picture

Broadening out from the immediate environment of the site itself, an environmental archaeologist will try to set the local environmental data into the wider context of what is known about the climatic and vegetational conditions at the time. The picture of ancient weather patterns has been derived from studying ice cores – taken from glaciers or ice caps that have taken centuries to build up, with a new layer of snow being added every year, capturing data about the weather and vegetational conditions that year. Similar data can be obtained from lake and sea-bed sediments, tree-ring data, and volcanic debris. All of this data can be

Above A collection of Minoan pottery was recovered from the island of Crete.

Minoan Crete

The most controversial example of changes within a society due to environmental changes is the rapid collapse of the Minoan civilization on Crete. This has been blamed on the eruption of Thera – a volcanic island 100km (62 miles) from Crete – causing tsunamis, blotting out the sun and choking off plant life. There is no doubt that the eruption would have caused a significant climate upset for the eastern Mediterranean region, but the theory has been challenged because of the gap of a century or more in the date of the eruption and the date for the collapse of the major palace cultures of Minoan Crete.

An alternative theory is that Minoan palace culture ended in a series of co-ordinated palace coups, in which formerly obedient subjects turned on their priest rulers because they were no longer able to guarantee plentiful harvests (and there is evidence for this in the number of palaces that seem to have been deliberately set on fire). Another theory says that the main effect of the eruption was to disrupt trade so that grain could no longer be imported to the island of Crete from other parts of the eastern Mediterranean to feed the population, resulting in mass starvation. Whatever is the explanation, we know that child sacrifice was practised in the final days of the Minoan palace culture, suggesting a degree of desperation and a desire to placate the angry gods.

used to detect climatic differences, especially the very large and cataclysmic events, such as volcanic eruptions, whose effects on weather and crops has often been linked directly to archaeological events and the collapse of whole civilizations.

Climate change is also one of the favoured theories for the evolution of our ancestors, the bipedal apes. They left the protection of jungle canopy, where they used their arms and knuckles for movement, and adapted to the savannah, where they walked on two feet, because the rainforest began to contract.

Further environmental stress might lie behind the migration of humans out of their eastern African homeland. Because arid desert conditions spread, populations began to compete for food and water, travelling further to hunt or gather food.

Above Exceptionally well-preserved early Bronze-Age beaker, wristguard, flint knife, awl and bronze dagger from a burial site at Ferry Fryston in Yorkshire, England. These were excavated during motorway construction work.

The Human Response to Climate Change

As well as reconstructing the immediate environment around the site, archaeologists can understand how the site evolved during a period of time by looking for clues about the way that humans responded to their environment and modified what they found.

Above Today's remote and hostile environments may once have been more accessible.

It can be easily argued that one of the defining characteristics of human beings is that we modify our environment to a far greater degree than any other life form. It is true that birds build nests, beavers cut down trees and make lodges and dams, and other primates use tools. However, *Homo sapiens* has responded to the environment in far more complex ways, in terms of the variety and scale of our buildings, settlements, agricultural practices and industries, religious rites and burial practices. It is the job of the site director writing the results of an excavation to try to explain clearly what the specific site represents in terms of human activity and the ways that humans modified the landscape and environment that they inhabited.

Camp fires

Sometimes that modification is simple: some sites consist of only a patch of burnt earth. In fact, the earliest evidence of humans in the landscape often comes from nothing more tangible than an area of burnt earth,

said to represent hearths or camp fires. Part of the evidence for early migration into the Americas comes from such hearths, some of which have been dated to 15,000BC or even earlier.

This dating contradicts the widely accepted date of roughly 13,000 years ago for the first migrants crossing into North America via the land bridge linking Siberia and Alaska. The land bridge was created by ice-age conditions, where sea levels fell because atmospheric moisture fell as snow, creating the ice sheets and glaciers that reindeer crossed in search of food, followed by Asian hunters. For humans to have arrived before the land bridge existed implies the ability to cross large expanses of ocean, so debate rages about whether these areas of burning really are the result of human activity or of lightening strikes and forest fires.

Stone scatters

More demonstrably human in origin are the scatters of debris from tool-making – often in association with food remains, such as bone. These represent some of the earliest material evidence of human habitation. The Qinghai-Tibetan Plateau is one of the most inhospitable places on the earth, yet archaeologists surveying the shores of the Qinghai Lake, at an elevation of

Left Despite its seemingly barren and impenetrable landscape, the Qinghai-Tibetan mountain range in China was once home to many prehistoric lakeland communities.

3,200m (10,500ft), have found hearths dating from 13,000 years ago along with burnt cobbles used for boiling and degreasing, debris from toolmaking and the bones of a gazelle-sized animals.

Archaeologists excavating in Edmonton, Canada, have also found evidence of butchery, this time from about 10,000 years ago, in what has been dubbed the Quarry of the Ancestors. It is located approximately 75km (50 miles) north of Fort McMurray, one of the first places where humans put down roots in Alberta after the retreat of the glaciers. The quarry has been identified as the source of the sandstone tools that are found at hundreds of sites in northern Alberta and Saskatchewan, including spear points, knives, scrapers, stone flakes and micro-blades.

Right Seeking ancient tools at Fort Calgary in the Quarry of the Ancestors, Alberta, Canada.

Above A Neanderthal skull (*left*) is shown alongside that of a Cro-Magnon skull – an early *Homo sapiens* (*right*).

The gender division debate

It is understandable to think that the informational potential of the scanty remains of early human activity will be rapidly exhausted. What more could an archaeologist excavating a site with human remains have to say once the bones, flints and hearth debris have been dated and described? These tough robust things that endure as evidence of human activity when slighter, more fragile and more interesting materials rot and fade away, can seem unpromising as evidence for human thought and activity, yet, thanks to the ingenuity and creativity of archaeologists who think hard about the meaning of finds, that is exactly what they can be encouraged to yield.

One of the great debates in archaeology concerns the fate of the Neanderthals, who flourished in Europe 130,000 years ago but became extinct about 24,000 years ago. Theories to account for their demise include competition from our own species – *Homo sapiens* – perhaps including deliberate genocide on our part, and the lack of survival strategies to cope with the bitterly cold conditions of the last ice age, which drove Neanderthals to seek refuge in caves in southern Spain.

However, if cold weather is to blame, surely *Homo sapiens* faced exactly the same conditions? Why did we survive and not them? By thinking about this problem, Steven L. Kuhn and Mary C. Stiner of the University of Arizona have theorized that it was the division of labour by gender that gave modern humans an advantage over Neanderthals. The archaeologists noted that discarded animal bones found at Neanderthal sites show that their diets depended on large game. They also considered the presence of healed fractures on female and juvenile Neanderthal skeletons, suggesting that women and children shared the task of hunting game and were injured as a result. The food remains of *Homo sapiens* of the same period include bones from small animals and birds, as well as milling stones for grinding nuts and seeds. Women and children don't exhibit the same serious injures, and cave deposits include bone awls and needles used for making clothes and shelters. All of this is seen as evidence for the emergence of 'female' roles and crafts among Homo sapiens, allowing them to exploit the environment more efficiently and enjoy the advantages of co-operation and complementary roles for men, women and children.

Metalwork Finds

The metalwork that is found on archaeological sites is usually corroded and is often unidentifiable. Nevertheless, metalwork finds can still yield important information – but first they have to be subjected to conservation, specialist cleaning and analytical tests.

Above This hammered bronze disk from Ireland is typical of the 'Celtic' style.

Silver and gold are two of the more stable elements and are less subject to the oxidization that causes rust and corrosion in many other metals. Everyone who has ever come across precious metal during an excavation testifies to the special thrill of finding that tell-tale glint of sunlike colour in the ground that indicates gold coinage or jewellery. However, that experience is a rare one, and the metal that archaeologists routinely find is usually of a different order – more often an unpromising lump of rust or corrosion that hides the original shape of the object, which is only revealed when it has been X-rayed. Fortunately, modern

Below This example of the phenomenal Benin bronze work from West Africa (1440–1897), depicts the head of an Oba king.

X-ray equipment is quick and easy to use and is non-destructive, and so it is now routinely used in archaeological laboratories to analyse corroded metalwork before the objects are cleaned and conserved.

Humble metalwork

Metalwork from archaeological sites tends to be either very routine or very special. Particularly common types of metalwork include nails – used for every type of construction, from boxes to buildings – and parts of buckets and containers, horse harnesses, buckles, and belt fittings, as well as hobnails for boots and sandals.

However, even the functional and humble can have a surprising cultural significance. Archaeologists recently excavated one of the largest burial sites in north-east Cuba, at El Chorro de Maíta, which dates from the period immediately after the Spanish conquest of the island. In many of the graves, archaeologists found necklaces made of small metal tubes. Analysis revealed that these were brass aglets, from European clothing, used from the 15th century onward to prevent fraying on the ends of laces used to fasten clothes, such as doublets and hose, and shoes. Because gold was such a commonplace metal for the indigenous Cubans, they elevated functional European brass to the level of something precious and turned it into an ornament.

Early metallurgy

Perhaps because there is something magical about the transformation of ore into metal, it is often the case that

some of the most spectacular finds of all are metal – and not just of gold. In many different cultures – European, African and Asian – bronze and iron have been used in spectacularly effective ways to create decorative objects. These are as varied as the engraved and enamelled mirrors of the Iron Age La Tène culture, the reliefs and scenes from courtly life of the bronzes from the Kingdom of Benin, in Africa, and the bronze bells and tripods of ancient China.

In the European Bronze Age, the magic of metal has been reflected in the deliberate destruction of costly metalwork, and its offering to the gods through deposition in rivers and pools. A celebrated example is a late Bronze-Age shield made from a sheet of bronze that was beaten into a circular shape, stamped with 29 concentric circles and decorated with rows of small bosses and raised ribs. The shield was found by Dr Ferris 'in a peat moss' in about 1780 at Lugtonridge, near Beith, in Ayrshire, Scotland, along with five other similar shields (sadly all now lost), buried deep in the peat and arranged vertically in a ring. It is assumed that the shields were deposited in the bog as a ceremonial offering – and several holes had been punched through the sheet of bronze as a form of ritual 'killing' of the shield before it was placed in the boggy pool.

The Lugtonridge shield is by no means an isolated example; bogs, fens and pools, rivers and streams have yielded up an astonishing array of very

Above A pair of gold earrings (*top*) and a gold hair ornament (*bottom*) were found in the Archer's grave.

fine metalwork, in the form of axes, shields, cups and cauldrons, suggesting that the makers of such complex and sophisticated objects felt they needed to give something back to the earth from whence the magic metal substance originally came.

Metals and trade

Typologies have long been established for many common metalwork types, as they have been for pottery. For example, the ubiquitous bronze brooches from Iron Age, Roman and early medieval sites that were used to fasten clothes together. Recent research has concentrated on analysing the metal to understand the range of alloy types employed and relate this to

Above A bronze urn at China's Forbidden City, Beijing. The palace was built by the Mongols from 1406–1420, and achieved its full splendour under the Ming dynasty. The palace name refers to the fact that occupants required the emperor's permission to leave.

brooch type and decoration. By mapping alloys to known sources of iron, copper, zinc, tin, aluminium, silicon, nickel, lead and other trace elements, such as mercury, arsenic, phosphorus and manganese, it is hoped that this will lead to identifying the location of the mines and of individual workshops.

What archaeologists already know is that the mastery of metalworking skills has led to power and status. This can be seen by studying the rise of civilizations, such as the ancient Etruscans, whose exploitation of the mineral wealth of the island of Elba and the Colline Metallifere (literally 'Metal-bearing hills') of Tuscany helped them dominate central Italy from 800BC until they were conquered by the Romans.

Left Metal detectors at shipwreck sites can reveal rare artefacts of great historical significance. These colonial Spanish silver coins were recovered from the *Whydah*, a ship that sunk off Cape Cod in 1717.

Amesbury Archer

The finds in the grave of the 'Amesbury Archer', discovered 5km/3 miles from Stonehenge, is the richest of any individual grave found in Great Britain from the Early Bronze Age (2,400–1,500BC). The archer was buried with two gold hair tresses, the oldest securely dated gold found in Britain (from about 2,400BC). Tools from the grave showed that he possessed metalworking skills and might have been regarded by his community as a man with magical powers, hence his special treatment in the grave.

Below An artist's impression of how the Amesbury Archer may have looked.

Pottery as Evidence of Everyday Life

In the debris of day-to-day life, archaeologists can find evidence for social and economic activity, symbols of thought, details about lifestyles, fashions, beliefs, agricultural practice and foods consumed, clothing, art, industry, allegiances, warfare and kinship — and this is a far from exhaustive list.

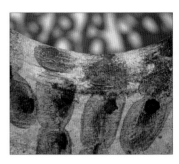

Above Finger marks made on a clay object are the remnants of work by a Roman potter.

Typically, the archaeologist is faced with describing unromantic holes in the ground, and explaining the patterns they make. Post holes and timber slots become houses of various shapes and internal arrangements. Ditches become drainage gullies, defensive enclosures and irrigation canals, associated with water scoops, ponds, wells, field boundaries and trackways. Pits become grain stores or refuse sites, and other types of evidence can be explained as industrial sites where pottery and iron making went on, quarrying sites where raw materials were extracted and worked, mills where materials such as grain or pigments were ground, butchery sites where animals were slaughtered and converted to meat, leather, horn or bone tools. This run-of-the-mill catalogue of basic human activities and site types is what makes up the majority of the archaeological record, with its evidence of the human struggle to survive.

The invention of pottery

Where the archaeologist can begin to get an insight into the life of ancient people beyond mundane subsistence is in the pottery record. Pottery is one of those inventions that is taken for granted and is assumed to have been with humans since the dawn of time, although the earliest clay objects found

so far consist of figurines, such as the so-called Venus of Dolní Vûstonice, a nude female figure dating to between 29,000 and 25,000BC.

The earliest pottery vessels come from Japan and have been dated by thermoluminescence to 11,000BC. China had pottery by 8,000BC and by 3,000BC ceramic vessels can be found everywhere in the world, either spread by trade and diffusion from eastern to western Asia, or invented independently, as is the case in North Africa during the 8th millennium BC and in South America during the 5th millennium BC.

Pottery from excavation

One of the most common forms of ancient material to be found surviving on any archaeological site is pottery. Excavation reports often contain pages

of drawings and descriptions of the different types of vessel, which the pottery specialist can reconstruct from diagnostic fragments, such as shard from a rim or base.

The technique is relatively straightforward because pottery typologies have been built up for just about all the known pottery types recovered from archaeological sites. The colour of the pot is one important clue, along with the character of its 'fabric', the material from which the vessel is made, as well as such inclusions as sand, grit, shell, or ground-up pottery.

The shape of a vessel can often be guessed by measuring the diameter of the rim or base along with the curvature of the body. An experienced pottery expert will often be able to date a piece of pottery at a glance, identify the vessel type (such as

Right Authentic sculpted earthenware from the Kanto Province of Japan has been dated to the Jomon period (14,000–4,000BC).

Above Some Japanese ceramicists have been designated 'Living National Treasures' in recognition of their efforts to revitalize and emulate the intricate craft of ancient dynasties.

cooking pot, storage jar, cremation urn or water jug) and say where it might have been made.

Daily life, fashions and trade

For the expert, identifying the pottery is only the starting point for an exploration of the wider meaning of the pottery assemblage from the site. The range of vessel types represented in that assemblage will tell an expert about the status and wealth of the people who lived there. For example, are these the basic cooking and storage pots of peasant life or specialized vessels with fine fabric and decoration associated with wealthier lifestyles? Are these the products of local pottery kilns, or are they exotic imports? Are they utilitarian in design, or decorated, and is the fabric coarse or fine? All these are potential clues to the quality of life of the owners, of the degree to which the site is linked into wider trading networks, of whether the site is part of the backwater or the mainstream of the prevailing fashions and trends in pottery.

The existence of coarse wear and fine wear side by side in these assemblages also warns experts not to interpret fine tablewares as evidence for a growing expertise in pot making – instead it can indicate differing usages. Up until the recent past, people often had a mix of pottery types in their homes. As well as fine pottery – such as the ubiquitous 'Willow pattern' wares found all over Europe, North America and the 'colonies' from the 19th century, they might also buy more functional wares, such as storage jars and cooking pots, from local potters, who sold their wares using itinerant pedlars, going from door to door.

Debris from a king?

A classic example of pottery as an indicator of status and trade is the case of Tintagel, in Cornwall, Great Britain. Major excavations undertaken by Ralegh Radford in the 1930s uncovered remains of 5th- to 6th-century buildings, where significant volumes of eastern Mediterranean and North African pottery suggested a site with trade links stretching to Constantinople, the capital and hub of the late Roman and early Byzantine world. Radford interpreted Tintagel as the site of either a Celtic monastery or the fortress of a wealthy and powerful king or tribal leader – reinforcing the popular (but archaeologically incorrect) belief that Tintagel is one possible location for the court of King Arthur and his Knights of the Round Table.

Above Fired pottery was found at a Bronze-Age Aegean site at Akrotiri, Greece.

Kiln sites

Pottery experts can pinpoint where a pot was made by examining the minerals in the fabric of the shard under a microscope and matching the clays and inclusions to known clay sources. Given the spectacular nature of Greek pottery, with its many pottery shapes and decorative motifs, it is not surprising that one of the main areas for this kind of work is Athens, where research institutes are mapping the main clay sources and kiln sites for Aegean pottery production back to the Early Bronze Age (or Early Helladic) period, which dates from 2800–2100BC. The results suggest a sophisticated knowledge of sources of clay suitable for ceramic production. By mapping the distribution of pottery around the islands from these kilns, important clues have been given to the far-ranging trade networks of the region, involving raw materials, such as tin, copper and charcoal, but also finished goods, such as bronze and ceramics.

Above These castle ruins at Tintagel, Cornwall, date to the 12th century, but lie on top of a 5th-century palace that has long been associated with the court of King Arthur, the fictional Camelot.

Pottery: the Key to Food Preparation

Pottery can tell archaeologists something about the owner's wealth, social status and trading links, but what about the food they contained? This is a question that a number of specialists will try to address as part of their study of the finds from the site.

Above Bread- and beer-making are depicted on an Egyptian 5th-dynasty tomb mural.

Some types of pottery can offer clues to the foods eaten in the past because their shape is very specific and reflects their function. Round-bottomed vessels, or vessels with short legs, were shaped like that so that they could be embedded in embers and ash, where the contents would slowly cook, whereas pottery and metal braziers have been found that are indicative of broiling or grilling over a barbecue and bakestones are indicative of flatbreads, bannocks, griddle cakes and pancakes, and domed clay ovens indicate the baking of raised loaves.

Lipid analysis

As well as vessel shape, the food residues trapped within the vessel or coating its surface can provide specific information. Since the early 1990s,

specialists in biomolecular archaeology have been looking through their microscopes to search for ancient traces of blood, lipids (fats and fatty acids), proteins, carbohydrates and plant molecules, which survive on the surfaces and within the vessel walls of unglazed – and therefore porous – pottery.

One aim of this research is to seek the origins of foods that are known to be ancient. There is now evidence, for example, of cultured milk products – including yogurts, butter and cheese – all being produced as food for at least 8,000 years, perhaps as an accidental result of storing milk in bags made from sheep or goat stomachs. Beekeeping and honey production is perhaps even older – milk and honey are among the first foodstuffs that are mentioned in the Bible.

Beer might also be an accidental discovery, as the by-product of breadmaking. Beer residues have been found on a pottery vessel dating to 3500BC, which was found at the site of Godin Tepe in the Zagros Mountains of western Iran. Similar residues have been found in Bronze Age pottery (2100–1400BC) from northern Spain, but mixed with hemlock. This is a poisonous plant that ancient Greeks were forced to drink as a form of capital punishment.

Left A beaker recovered from the grave of the Amesbury Archer, probably used in rituals involving beer.

However, the presence of hemlock in small amounts can also indicate ritual use. In small quantities hemlock can have an hallucinogenic effect without being toxic.

Food preservation

Butter- and cheese-making is one way of converting a food that deteriorates rapidly – milk – into forms that are stable and long lasting, which can ensure a food supply through the lean months of winter. Archaeologists know from bone assemblages that milk-producing animals are present in some quantity in most human cultures. However, for evidence of the specific conversion of raw milk into butter or cheese for longer term

Below A Neolithic clay dish from the Czech region of Moravia, known as 'spiral-meander' pottery due to the pattern in the clay and the culture that produced it. Used as drinking vessels, handles were later added to make them portable.

Above These Iron-Age storage pots, recovered from the Czech Republic, would have been used to store liquids (the smaller vessels in the foreground) and food (the larger vessels).

storage, they need to look for pottery types specific to that process. This includes strainers, which are vessels with holes in the base to allow liquid to drain away when milk separates into solid curds and liquid whey during cheese-making.

Because salt can preserve food, it was seen as a precious commodity. The methods people have used to obtain salt can leave distinctive archaeological evidence, such as in the form of salterns — shallow tanks or scoops in the ground where sea water is left to evaporate slowly, leaving crystalline salt behind. This evidence is also found in a type of pottery called briquetage, large shallow vessels in which sea water or brine from salt springs is boiled to evaporate the water, leaving the salt behind.

Salt mines in Austria

There is intriguing early evidence of salt-meat production on an industrial scale at the ancient Dürnberg salt mines in Austria, dating from 800BC, if not earlier. Here, a massive amount of pig bone has been found in association with the mine workings, suggesting that pigs were herded to the mines and slaughtered, then preserved on site using rock salt extracted from the mine. Maybe the reason for bringing the pigs to the mines rather than selling salt to farmers, who would salt their own animals, was to retain a monopoly over the precious commodity of salt.

The discovery and exploitation of the mines corresponds to the rise of the La Tène culture in central Europe, an Iron-Age culture that is renowned for the astonishing complexity, richness and intricacy of its geometrical art, manifested in jewellery and polished bronze mirrors. Some archaeologists have suggested that the grave goods found in La Tène burials indicate the rise of a princely class based on the monopoly over salted products.

Digging deep

The Iron-Age salt mines at Dürnberg, in Austria, Europe, are remarkable for the preservation of organic remains — the salinity is so concentrated there that destructive microbes cannot survive. This means that pieces of ancient clothing, discarded and lost by workers, have survived in the mines, as have their faeces, or coprolites, which can also be found in ancient cess pits or preserved in waterlogged sites. Careful examination in laboratory conditions has identified the parasites that our ancestors had, and the medicines that they took to rid themselves of afflictions. Wormwood bark and coriander seeds were found to be commonly used as purgatives.

Above Portrait of workers at the Dürnberg mine, the oldest salt mine in Europe.

Ancient Diets

Looking even further back into ancient diets, bones, lipids and isotopes can provide broad clues about the origins of food and drink staples. Direct evidence for diet comes from the numerous food bones that are usually found on archaeological sites.

Food bones – the discarded bones of animals eaten by humans – suggest that our ancestors had a very varied diet and were willing to eat a much wider range of wild foods than we might now contemplate. In addition to domestic cattle, sheep, goat and pig bones, archaeologists have found wild red deer, boar, beaver, hare, heron, swan, plover, various types of duck and wildfowl, freshwater and sea fish, and even hedgehog, otter and badger at European sites dating from the last three millennia.

One of the ways that specialists can distinguish between bones that have formed part of a meal is by looking for butchery marks. Food bones are often found chopped up and fragmented, whereas animals hunted for fur but not for food (martens and wildcats, for example) occur as complete skeletons, being discarded whole after skinning and regarded as having no food value.

Food or medicine?

No doubt some of these animals were eaten experimentally, or in extremis, when poverty or deep winter offered no alternative source of food. Archaeologists also know that some foods were eaten for medicinal purposes. Beavers, for example, were driven to extinction in Europe mainly because the salicylin contained in their scent glands was a staple of medicine into the 19th century, used to relieve pain and fever and to treat inflammatory conditions, such as arthritis and rheumatism, which was only superseded with

Above Olives excavated at Pompeii, which survived the onslaught of lava and hot ash.

the discovery of aspirin. This association between the beavers' favourite food (willow twigs) and pain relief was made in the ancient past and was certainly known to the 5th century BC physician, Hypocrites, who stated that the bitter liquid extracted from soaking willow bark could ease aches and pains and reduce fevers.

Shopping lists

Written records can also help archaeologists understand ancient diets. A remarkable cache of writing tablets found on Hadrian's Wall, the Roman frontier between Britain and the land of the 'barbarians', to the north in Scotland, has revealed shopping lists and household inventories. The soldiers garrisoned there in the 1st and 2nd centuries AD enjoyed home-brewed beer and wine imported from Spain and Italy, some of which was sweetened with honey or flavoured with spices, including anise, caraway and lovage.

Samples from waterlogged pits at Hadrian's Wall shows that the military diet included figs, grapes, cherries, blackberries, apples, pears, raspberries and strawberries and even astringent fruits such as elderberries and sloes.

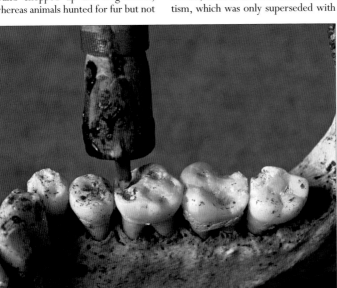

Left Adult teeth found at the site of Mehrgahr in Pakistan contain drilled holes and are evidence of the earliest known practice of dentistry. Archaeologists believe the holes were made 9,000 years ago to ease toothache using a tiny stone blade like the one shown in this reconstruction.

Olive and date stones, or pits, are commonly found, as are hazelnuts, along with peas, beans, lentils, beets and turnips – and plenty of seeds from nettle, suggesting that nettle soup was a part of the soldiers' diet.

Trade and imports

Some of these foods were clearly traded and carried long distances, because although the late Iron Age and Roman period was one of warm dry weather, with grapes and figs being cultivated in northern Europe, dates and olives from Asia must have been transported long distances by land and sea, as were some of the spices found in ancient deposits that can only have come from Asia via the spice routes – black pepper, for example, which turns up at Hadrian's Wall along with less exotic herbs, such as coriander, poppy seed, fennel and dill.

Some sense of the importance of pepper in the ancient diet can be gauged by the recipes in the oldest complete cookbook in possession. Called *De Re Coquinaria* (On Culinary Matters), it is usually attributed to a Roman author called Apicius, but it is more probably a compilation of recipes by several people. Pepper was used in 349 of the 468 recipes in the book, including dormice stuffed with pepper and pine nuts. The pepper and spice trade survived the collapse of the western Roman Empire and, pepper in the medieval period carried associations of ancient luxury and civility.

Isotopes in teeth and bones

Reaching even further back into time, archaeological scientists have begun examining ancient bone collagen in an attempt to understand ancient diets as far back as the Neolithic in Europe (prior to 3000BC). Measuring the ratios of nitrogen to carbon to sulphur isotopes in the collagen cannot tell scientists precisely what people ate, but it can be used to distinguish groups of people with a plant-rich, meat-rich, marine-rich or omnivorous diet. Archaeologists hope eventually to be able to pinpoint the rise of diets based

Right This Roman painting shows the contents of a fishmonger's shop as it would have appeared to customers in the 1st century AD, with squid, crab and bream for sale.

on domesticated animals and plants rather than wild foods, and perhaps to distinguish from the isotopes in tooth enamel what kind of minerals they ingested in drinking water in their childhood, and hence whether they are local people, or migrants to the region in which they spent the remainder of their years and were buried.

Above The excavation of the olive oil processing area at Tell es Sa'idiyeh, Jordan. This early Bronze-Age industrial complex, a hub for passing trade, was destroyed by fire around 2750BC, leaving archaeologists a wealth of charred organic remains to examine and date.

An ancient trading crossroads

Fieldwork can help archaeologists understand how far back in time some staples go. Excavations at Tell es Sa'idiyeh, in central Jordan, sits above the crossroads of two major trade routes among fertile agricultural land. This was the site of a prosperous city in 2900BC, and at that early age there is evidence of areas being set aside for olive oil production and storage, wine-making and textile preparation on an industrial scale, showing that the inhabitants were producing goods for trade.

A fire that swept through part of the city left behind a rich variety of charred plant material. Scientific study of the charred remains shows that the everyday ingredients of the Early Bronze Age diet were wheat and barley, lentils, chickpeas and fava beans, along with grapes, figs, olives and pomegranates, some of which were eaten fresh and some of which were dried to produce raisins and dried figs. What is remarkable about this list of staples is the extent to which it continues to underlie the modern diet of the region, suggesting that in matters of food, people are relatively conservative.

Analysing Human Remains

The analysis of human remains is an exciting field that is branching into many directions, from the study of disease to understanding the ancient beliefs and rituals that led to the building of striking monuments. Many archaeological reports have substantial sections of human remains.

Above A complete skeleton of an old man lies in situ in its place of burial.

Human bodies can turn up virtually anywhere. Ancient burial mounds, tombs and cemeteries are one of the most common forms of monument to survive, and they have long been a focus of archaeological curiosity, from the earliest days of antiquarian digging.

Bones and diseases

Many bone specialists trained as doctors, so they are able to look at bones with professional eyes and can diagnose the many injuries and diseases to which humans were – and still are – vulnerable – not only battle wounds and the conditions of old age, but more esoteric complaints, such as gout, a condition that is erroneously associated with a rich diet and a fondness for after-dinner port. A high

incidence of gout was found in Romano–British people excavated from a cemetery in Cirencester, Gloucestershire. One theory is that the ingestion of lead could be a factor in the onset of gout, and Romans were exposed to lead through the pipes that supplied their water and through the cooking vessels used to prepare a sweetener called defrutum, made by boiling grape juice to form a syrup. However, Roman citizens all over the Roman Empire faced the same exposure to lead, so osteo-archaeologists (those who specialize in bone) now think gout could be related to the high levels of calcium in the local limestone-filtered water rather than a fondness for the yet-to-be-invented fortified wine.

The evidence of poor diet, lacking in essential vitamins and minerals, can be seen in the bone and teeth deformations associated with rickets and scurvy, but just as often archaeologists find indications of indulgence and dietary excess, and it is interesting to see which parts of the population are healthy and which are the gluttons. A study published in 2004 revealed, for example, that obesity was five times more prevalent among monks than among their secular contemporaries, including wealthy merchants or courtiers. Although gluttony is one of the Seven Deadly Sins, and is in direct contravention of the Rule of

Below Mass burial sites usually indicate a large, sudden loss of life due to war or disease.

Below An infant crouch burial in the Boscombe Down Roman cemetery, UK.

Grave goods

Even if archaeologists don't fully understand ancient ritual and religion, they know that it is responsible for some of our most enduring monuments – from pyramids and the tomb of Tutankhamun, to the terracotta warriors of the Chinese Emperor Xing, to the stone circles of Europe and the temples of southern America. Respect for the dead is not unique to *Homo sapiens*: Neanderthal graves have been found in Iraq dating back 80,000 years, in which flowers have been placed in the grave of the deceased, as well as grave goods, such as food, in the form of the bones of bison and auroch, stone tools and pieces of ochre pigment.

Above and left Farming and warfare are reflected in the sickle and spears found in the graves of ancient Greeks during the excavation of a 5th to 3rd century BC site at Édessa, in Macedonia. It is believed that the pottery might have contained food for the deceased on their journey to the afterlife.

St Benedict, which states that 'there is nothing so opposed to Christian life as overeating', archaeologists found numerous cases of medical conditions triggered by a fat-rich diet. For example, the bone condition known as diffuse idiopathic skeletal hyperostosis (DISH, or Forestier's disease), which is commonly associated with type 2 (late onset) diabetes, caused by a diet rich in suet, lard and butter.

Normal and deviant burials

The manner in which the dead are buried reveals a lot about ancient beliefs. Burial practice can be specific to a culture, such as the mummification of the ancient Egyptians, the east to west orientation of Christian burial, or the coin in the mouth that typifies Roman burial custom (to pay the ferryman who takes the spirit across the River Hades).

Archaeologists are far from understanding the meaning of much burial practice, especially when it departs from normal practice. For example, the graves of the Lapita people, the first settlers of the western Pacific, all contain headless skeletons, and some graves had cone shell rings in lieu of the skulls, indicating that the graves were reopened after burial and the heads removed. Sometimes the heads are separately buried nearby and sometimes they are moved to other graves. In one grave, three skulls were found on a man's chest – none of the skulls were his.

Although this treatment of skulls was normal practice for the Lapita people, it would be unusual in a European context – which is why the 30 Roman skeletons found recently in York, England, with their heads removed and placed between their knees, on their chests or by their feet is a mystery.

Even more unusual is the mass grave at Evreux, in Normandy, France, found in 2006. It dates from the 3rd century, and bones of some 40 people have been deliberately mixed with the remains of 100 horses. Normally, graves of this period are organized and orderly, but this strange example defies explanation. In such cases, archaeologists often use the word 'ritual' to describe what they do not understand.

Below and left Archaeologists draw human remains and grave goods at a Lapita burial site. Skulls were typically removed from the skeletons and placed in a ceremonial container (*left*).

The Information in our Genes

Today's archaeological headlines are usually dominated by studies that involve extracting genetic material from bone. These archaeologists are looking for diagnostic genes that can help answer big questions about human origins and the peopling of the world.

Above Forensic scientists examining human bones look first for obvious signs of trauma.

Whenever human remains are found today, the director of the site will always bear in mind the potential information that can be found by doing a DNA study. One example that caught the popular imagination occurred in the late 1990s, when DNA was extracted from a tooth belonging to Cheddar Man – the oldest complete human skeleton yet found in England.

Migration or diffusion?

Cheddar Man was found in Gough's Cave in Cheddar Gorge, Somerset, and dates back to 7150BC. The DNA from his tooth was compared with DNA from saliva taken from people living in the village today. The comparison turned up two exact matches – both among local schoolchildren – and there is one very close match, with someone who by coincidence turned out to be a history teacher.

The serious archaeological issue behind this discovery was the question that has preoccupied archaeologists for decades. How stable have human populations been in the past, and is cultural innovation the result of migration or diffusion – of people moving into new territories and bringing ideas with them, or of ideas spreading through the network of contacts that exist between stable populations? One hundred years ago, when war and conquest was part of the diet fed to school pupils as a part of the national history, it was natural to favour the idea that conquerors brought innovation. However, DNA studies have suggested different answers. In the Cheddar example, there isn't a lot of evidence in the genetic record for foreign genes, showing that the populations have remained largely stable for thousands of years.

The big picture

This large view of populations is always open to small-scale exceptions, and one excavation can easily produce a thought-provoking result. Current archaeological theory suggests that human beings are all derived from migrants who began to spread out of eastern Africa about 100,000 years ago. Travelling along coastal routes and feeding on marine species, these emigrants spread to the rest of the world, reaching Asia and Australia at least 50,000 years ago, replacing other hominids that had spread across the world as a result of earlier migrations, such as the Neanderthals and Java and Peking man.

This theory has been based on two key assumptions. One is the so-called genetic clock, which is based on the finding that genes will mutate at a fairly regular rate, and this is the basis for the dating of the various migrations. The other assumption is the so-called genetic gateway, which says that when a population moves on to a new location (for example, from Siberia to North America) the gene pool of that population will be a subset of the gene pool of the parent population, and that

Above The fossilized cranium of the *Homo erectus* specimen known as 'Java Man' was discovered in 1969 in Indonesia.

Left The indigenous people of Papua New Guinea's Trobriand Islands bury their dead in open-air cemeteries, so when archaeologists found burials from around AD1500 inside caves (for example at Selai Cave, shown here), they suspected migration by Polynesians, arriving in Melanesia from the east, bringing a different burial practice. Reflecting this migration, the physical appearance and culture of the Trobriand Islands people today is more Polynesian than Melanesian in character.

interbreeding in the new population will create a new gene pool with different characteristics from the parent population.

Above Archaeologists examine skulls belonging to human ancestors at the Laboratory of Prehistory in Nice, France.

Above A sample phial containing human DNA is selected for analysis at a laboratory specializing in human evidence.

Exceptions from the norm

As with much archaeology, specialists in ancient DNA seek to establish a body of data to describe what is normal or typical, then once the mainstream pattern is understood, they then begin to look for the exceptions – the tell-tale details that depart from the norm and require explanation.

For example, theories have been published recently to explain what appears to be a pattern of genetic differences between the western and eastern halves of Britain. Such differences have been detected in the archaeological record, and were once believed to be the result of continental invaders – Romans, Saxons, Angles and later Vikings. It has been thought that these invaders pushed the native British population westward into what is now Wales, Cornwall and western Scotland. Now a new, more complex picture is emerging of a post ice-age migration of genetically distinct people from northern Spain into the western side of Britain up the Atlantic and of a similar migration of genetically distinct people from the Germanic near Continent – hence the east-west divide might be 13,000 years old, rather than a recent and historic event.

Above Cerveteri, near Rome, is famed for its well-preserved ancient Etruscan tombs.

The origin of the mysterious Etruscans

The Etruscan civilization in Italy has long been a mystery, but the question of where the ancient Etruscans came from might have been solved through two separate genetic studies. The first looked at the genes of cattle in north, south and central Italy. Specialists in animal genetics have found that Tuscan white cattle are genetically close to Near Eastern cows, whereas there was no genetic convergence between cows from the north and south of Italy and those from the Near East. If correct, this confirms the hypothesis of an eastern origin for the Etruscans, first claimed by the classic historians Herodotus and Thucydides.

A second study involved taking genetic samples from three present-day Tuscan populations living in Murlo, Volterra and Casentino, chosen because they are three of the most archaeologically important Etruscan sites in a region that is known for having Etruscan-derived placenames and its own local dialect. The Tuscan samples were taken from individuals who had lived in the area for at least three generations, and whose surnames were unique to the region. These DNA samples were compared with samples taken from males living in northern Italy, the southern Balkans, the island of Lemnos in Greece, the Italian islands of Sicily and Sardinia and from several modern Turkish and Middle-Eastern populations. The scientists found that the Tuscan and Turkish samples were a close match and that both were different from the other Italian samples. The results reinforce the cattle gene study, reinforcing the idea that the ancient Etruscans migrated to Tuscany from the Near East.

Preparing the Publication and the Archive

Once all this information has been assembled in the form of a series of specialist reports, it is the director's task to weave them into a narrative that — along with supporting pictures, drawings and data — can be published so that other archaeologists can learn from what has been found at the site.

Above Compiling the results of an excavation is very complex when the data is this extensive.

Traditionally, the results of an excavation are published as a report in an archaeological journal or as a book. Many archaeologists still aspire to publish their excavations in this way, because publication in book or journal form is perceived as having a certain status. This is reinforced by the fact that many university funding systems assess the quality and productivity of their research staff on the basis of the books they write and the papers they publish in leading international journals, and review this regularly.

However, the volume of data being generated by modern archaeology is so great that the idea of publishing a complete record of the site is being challenged as the norm for archaeological report writing. Increasingly,

Below and below right Reported finds, such as this coffin 'furniture' (*left*) and Saxon comb made of antler (*right*), are described, dated and placed in their historical context.

archaeologists are being encouraged to think of the results of an excavation in terms of 'data' and 'synthesis'.

By data, archaeologists mean the record of what was found – the site matrix and context record sheets, the plans, sections and photographs, and the artefacts and ecofacts, along with records, drawings and the reports of specialists identifying, describing and dating those finds. Synthesis means an interpretative narrative, which seeks to explain the meaning of the data – what it represents in terms of a chronological sequence of human events and activities at the site.

Not all archaeologists accept the validity of this separation of raw data from its explanation. Others disagree about which is more important. Some archaeologists argue that the interpretation is subjective and will soon be superseded by new thinking, and so should form only a small part of any report. They argue that the data takes

priority and should be published in full so that it is accessible to other archaeologists who can study it and form their own views about what it means. The implication of this position is that the data is capable of multiple interpretations, all of which might be equally valid until tested by debate at conferences and in teaching seminars or by further excavation and research.

Using digital data

This debate would have reached a stalemate but for the advent of digital technologies that enable excavation data to be presented in ways that printed publications cannot emulate. Computer-based graphics and design programmes now allow the data from excavations to be represented in three dimensions. Instead of wasting words in tedious descriptions of the site, the measurements that were recorded on site can be fed into computer-aided design (CAD) software that presents the data visually, in three dimensions, showing the stratigraphy and the precise find spot of every artefact or soil sample. By recording this data as a series of layers, and by using colours and shading, the site can effectively be brought back to life.

What is more, archaeologists who then study the material can subsequently make their own enquiries of the data and explore it in ways that might not have been in the mind of the original excavator. For example, someone interested in the archaeology of

gender might look at the results of a cemetery excavation and analyse the finds in a number of ways, looking to see if any differences between men and women can be discerned in the positioning of graves within the cemetery – are there, perhaps, separate areas for man and women? Or the archaeologist may examine the objects placed in their graves – do keys, brooches, scissors, shears or combs distinguish female burials, and knifes, shields and hobnail shoes distinguish men, and what might it mean if a man is found buried with keys? And are there any skeletal differences evident that could be the result of differences between female and male diets, activities or susceptibility to disease?

Producing a digital report

In the case of digital publishing, some of the work of preparing the publication will require someone with

expertise in computer-aided design, database design and management, as well as Relational or Geographical Information Systems (GIS) and graphics packages for manipulating drawings and photographs.

In larger commercial exaction units, the management of all of these activities might fall to a professional managing editor, whose responsibilities include finding a publisher and negotiating terms, applying for grants to help with the cost of the publication and handling the marketing, sales and distribution of the report. However, it often falls to the site director to undertake all of these tasks.

Conservation and archiving

In addition to publishing skills, a career in archaeology can also be combined with work in conservation, record keeping, archiving and information management. Once such work was relatively limited in scope: archaeological archivists would spend their days in dark basements, cleaning

Below When presenting the results of an excavation as a publication or lecture, many archaeologists will now try to include images of how the environment may have looked.

Why keep the archive?

Storing excavation material is expensive and it is tempting to ask why bother? Digital technology allows for creating virtual versions of the evidence we destroy. However, when new, unexpected technological and scientific developments come along, a virtual record will not help. The revolution in understanding human origins has come about because of our ability to extract DNA from fossilized bones dug up 100 years ago. If they hadn't been kept, it would be necessary to search for new material to dig up and test. In the case of a piece of wood excavated in 1945 from a Mesolithic site in Yorkshire, England, and saved in a glass jar in the Department of Archaeology in Cambridge, England, 60 years later an archaeologist recognized the strange markings on the wood as early evidence for the existence of beavers in post-ice age Britain.

objects, labelling them, conserving them and guarding them against harm – which some of them interpreted as meaning that nobody else should be allowed to touch them.

In recent times, however, more progressive organizations actively promote their archives as teaching and learning resources, and people are encouraged to take full advantage of them. When faced with the problem of storing the vast amounts of material that have been excavated in London, England, over the last 100 years, the Museum of London Archaeology Service set up the innovative London Archaeological Archive Resource Centre (www.museumoflondon.org.uk/laarc/new/default.asp) as a place where anyone can study the primary records and finds. Similar public facilities exist at Colonial Williamsburg, in the United States, for example, and at many other university archives around the world, helping to make archaeology more accessible.

Case Study: Aegean Dendrochronology Project

One good example of the way that excavation directors and specialists can work together has been demonstrated by the Aegean Dendrochronology Project. Finds from individual excavation sites have been amalgamated to build up a database of material of value to everyone working in the region.

The Aegean Sea, which separates the mainlands of Greece and Turkey, is remarkable for its archeologically rich islands, bearing testimony to some of the world's earliest civilizations. It is the focus of numerous excavations and research projects every year.

Archaeologists working in the region know that if they find wood that can be dated using dendrochronology, or tree-ring dating, they need look no further for specialist help than the Malcolm and Carolyn Wiener Laboratory for Aegean and Near Eastern Dendrochronology, based at Cornell University, in the United States. This laboratory is home to the Aegean Dendrochronology Project, founded by Peter Ian Kuniholm, and now directed by Sturt Manning. The project team has spent three decades scouring sites in the Aegean (and from Italy to the Near East region) for samples of ancient wood to try to create a tree-ring

sequence for the last 10,000 years of human and environmental history. The aim is to provide a dating method for the study of history and prehistory in the Aegean that is so accurate that it can date ancient timbers to the precise year in which they were cut down and used as construction material.

The Port of Theodosius

During the 2006 and 2007 seasons the laboratory has been busy in Istanbul, where the construction of a new railway tunnel beneath the Bosporus, linking Europe and Asia, has led to the discovery of a series of harbours dubbed the 'Port of Theodosius', dating from the reign of Emperor Theodosius in AD408. Archaeologists in Istanbul, led by Metin Gokcay, have found a church, a gated entrance to the city and several dozen sunken ships, as well as a series of stone- and timber-built harbours on a huge site that is four city blocks long by three wide. Work on some of the ships is in collaboration with Dr Cemal Pulak, of Texas A&M University and the Institute of Nautical Archaeology. The Istanbul archaeologists called in the Cornell Laboratory (Kuhiholm and group in 2006; Manning and group in 2007), who took samples across this vast site from

Left Sampling oak timbers at the Yenikapi site, Istanbul Harbour, Turkey.

most of the many timber pilings from a series of 4th- to 19th-century piers or docks and structures. Some samples and structures have already been dendro-dated as a result and, critically, some timbers belong to a key 4th- to 7th-century period – which the Aegean Dendrochronology Project needed to fill in the 'Roman Gap' in its sequence, and which may then in the future permit exact dendro-dating in Byzantine to Roman contexts in the region.

The more than 500 samples that the Cornell Laboratory teams have collected to establish the phasing of the various construction projects in the harbour will be added to a huge database of more than 40,000 existing wood samples that comprise the raw data for the Aegean master sequence.

The eruption of Thera

Apart from the value of the project as a crucial resource for dating Aegean and west Asian sites, the project can also pinpoint key environmental events by looking for patterns or signs that indicate vegetation under stress. One such event that had a major impact on the whole world's environment was the eruption of the volcano on the Aegean island of Thera (also known as Santorini); debris or evidence of the eruption has been found as far away as China, Greenland and the United

States. Dating the event would provide a marker, like the burial of Pompeii, for dating excavated sites in the region and for aligning Aegean, Egyptian, Cypriot and Asian chronology, however, the precise date for the eruption has proved hard to pin down.

Traditionally, the event has been dated to about 1500BC, based on similarities between pottery found buried in the volcanic ash in Akrotiri, a town on Thera destroyed by the blast, with similar styles of pottery in the rest of the Aegean, and the correlation of these styles with exchanges of Aegean/ Egyptian objects and influences against the historical dates for the Egyptian kings of the New Kingdom period.

In 2006, Sturt Manning and his team rewrote ancient history by arguing that the eruption occurred 100 years earlier, in 1660–1613BC. To reach this conclusion, Manning and his colleagues analysed 127 tree-ring samples and seeds from Santorini, Crete, Rhodes and Turkey, testing them by radiocarbon dating and tree-ring analysis.

Coincidentally, the Cornell results were reinforced by a separate dendrochronology and radiocarbon study, led by Danish geologist Walter Friedrich, which dated an olive branch severed during the Santorini eruption and arrived independently at a late 17th-century BC date.

Rethinking the region's archeaology

The two sets of findings mean a shift of the dates for the Aegean civilization and its cultures and a new timeline that places a number of events earlier than previously thought, including the formation and high point of the New Palace period on Crete, the Shaft Grave period on the Greek mainland, and the Middle to late Cypriot period on Cyprus. The re-dating of the eruption also raises a number of questions about previously hypothesized dates and associations, and about the precise trading relationships and influences of one culture on another, with major ramifications for the archaeology and art history of the region.

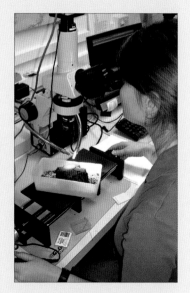

Above Timber samples are analysed at the Cornell Tree-Ring Laboratory. The project has now amassed some 10 million separate samples, providing chronologies for more than 9,000 years.

Sturt Manning has said the results 'call for a critical rethinking of hypotheses that have stood for nearly a century... the earlier chronology would frame a different context, and a longer era, for the very genesis of Western civilization. The 17th century BC may become a very important period'.

Above Core samples are taken from a timbered house on the island of Crete.

Above Tree-ring samples from Cyprus contain vital information about the Santorini eruption.

CHRONOLOGIES

Until the mid-19th century, people only had a vague sense of the ancient past, derived mainly from the Bible, the epics of Homer, and the classical Greek and Latin authors, such as Thucydides and Herodotus, two of the first historians to write down the stories of past deeds and battles that had been hitherto handed down by word of mouth. This changed about 150 years ago with the development of scientific archaeological techniques borrowed in part from geology. Antiquarians did not suddenly become archaeologists overnight, and there were (and remain) religious objections to the new time frames that have emerged, but little by little the study of ancient bones and stone tools has given new insights into the origins of the human species and our development and interaction with the environment. This chapter explains in broad terms what archaeologists have learned over these last 150 years, and what they currently think about human origins and the development of world civilizations.

Opposite Passages linking houses of a Neolithic village at Skara Brae, Orkney Islands, occupied 3100–2500BC.

Above Archaeologists still have much to learn about the construction of megalithic Stonehenge, on Salisbury Plain, Britain.

Above Hieroglyphs and stone reliefs in The Valley of the Kings show the extraordinary craftmanship of ancient Egypt.

Above Machu Picchu – often referred to as the 'Lost City of the Incas' – was once the seat of a great emperor.

Defining the Ages

Much prehistoric archaeology is still based on the three-age system that divides prehistory into three main periods — the Stone Age, Bronze Age and Iron Age. However, the relevance of this framework to ancient civilizations outside of Europe is disputed territory.

The three-age chronology was first proposed by Nicholas Mahudel (1704–47), who observed from his excavation of multi-period burial mounds that bronze tools were found in the lower and earlier burials and iron in the later upper layers. He deduced that stone tools were easier to produce and, therefore, likely to be earlier, and he was one of the first antiquaries to argue convincingly that shaped flints were the work of human activity and not some form of fossil.

Mahudel's book *Three Successive Ages of Stone, Bronze, and Iron* (1734) was ahead of its time and only in the early decades of the 19th century did the three-age chronology become an accepted classi-fication tool, when it was adopted by Christian Jürgensen Thomsen, founder of the Royal (now National) Museum of Denmark as the basis for classifying artefacts in the collection. Thomsen tends to get the credit for the idea, because he, and his protégé, Jens Jacob Worsaae, were such evangelists for the 'Copenhagen arrangement', writing books and giving lectures to learned societies all over Europe.

Growing complexity

Latin and Greek were used as universal languages for scientific communication in the 19th century, so the Old and New Stone Age subdivisions were called the Palaeolithic and the Neo-lithic when the British banker John Lubbock (1834–1913), later Lord Avebury, first proposed these subdivisons in his book *Prehistoric Times* (1865), the first being characterized by simple all-purpose tools, such as axes, clubs and scrapers, and the later period by specialized stone tools, including chisels and reaping hooks. Recognition in the 1930s of a distinctive Middle Stone Age period, characterized by arrowheads and spear points, led to the naming of the Middle Stone Age, or Mesolithic.

This simple subdivision then took on greater and greater complexity over succeeding decades, as archaeologists began to realize that there were other toolmaking technologies intermediate between the three big subdivisions. Thus the Copper Age (also known as the Chalcolithic, from the Greek for 'copper stone') has since been added to the system as an intermediate phase in the early use of metal tools between the Stone and Bronze Ages, and key stages within each age are now marked by further subdivisions into early, middle and late periods. Not all archaeologists agree with such rigid slices of time, and some argue endlessly about the precise point at which one period ends and another begins — or whether there is any fundamental difference between the Late Neolithic and the early Bronze Age (the term 'LaNeBrA' has been coined to describe this critical transition).

Above Can ancient cultures, like that of Cambodia, be classified on the basis of simple materials?

Below This Olmec statue dates from the Formative period (c. 600BC) in Mexico. The Olmecs were a precursor of the great Mesoamerican civilizations.

Right John Lubbock, a close acquaintance of Charles Darwin, was the first to publicly subdivide the Stone Age into new ('Neolithic') and old ('Palaeolithic') eras.

Old World vs New World

With the spread of archaeological research from Europe to other parts of the world, the universality of the three- (or four-) age system began to be questioned. It provided a good framework for European prehistory, but technology has never developed beyond the Stone Age in some parts of the world, while in other parts, technology went from the Stone to the Iron Ages with no Copper or Bronze Ages. In some parts of Asia, iron technology predated bronze, while ceramics, another key technology, vary in pre-dating and postdating the metal phases. And where, some archaeologists ask, does wood, a material of importance to all societies, feature in all of this?

To complicate matters further, the duration of each phase varies from one part of the world to another. Dating each of these phases is a science in itself (*see* Radiocarbon Dating), but in some places the switch from one innovative metal technology (copper) to another (bronze) is fast, and in some cases there are long periods of conservatism. Neither is each phase exclusive: metal objects were made and used in the Neolithic, iron was made and used in the Bronze Age and bronze continued to be used in the Iron Age and beyond (in jewellery and coinage, for example).

Some archaeologists have argued that the three-age system has now outlived its usefulness. In the United States, the three-age system is recognized as having a value for Old World archaeology, but for the New World, a different five-stage framework was proposed in 1958 by Gordon Willey and Philip Phillips – the Lithic stage (hunting), the Archaic stage (gathering of wild resources), the Formative stage (early agriculture), the Classic stage (early civilizations) and the Post-Classic stage (later pre-Hispanic civilizations). Others have argued that we need to think in terms of cultures – the assemblages of tool types and other objects that distinguish one group of people living in a particular region from another – rather than the mechanistic technology of one tool type.

However, the system is still used because cultures do have something in common that enables them to be grouped according to tool type. These big archaeological ages also coincide with geological time systems and periods of glacial and climate change.

Above The 4th-century BC Ficoroni Cist (or cremation urn), decorated with mythical figures, shows the astonishing skill of Etruscan metal-workers during the European Bronze Age.

Below Traditional practices in which materials such as wood, ropes and woven leaves are utilized still survive in many parts of the world, demonstrating the difficulty in defining and separating archaeological periods. This woman uses a shoulder yoke in modern-day Burma.

The Earliest Humans

Darwin's theory of evolution changed our perception of prehistory.
However, many questions remained unanswered until the advent of scientific
dating techniques in the post-war period, now supplemented by the study
of DNA, which have afforded accurate dating to early human remains.

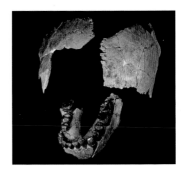

Above These *Homo habilis* skull bones were found in Olduvai Gorge, Tanzinia in 1960. They are estimated to be 1.75 million years old.

In the first half of the 19th century, knowledge gained from the emerging science of geology led to the growing awareness that the world was much older than the chronology worked out by James Ussher (1581–1656), the Anglican Archbishop of Armagh (now in Northern Ireland), who deduced from events and genealogies in the Bible that the earth was created on Sunday 23 October 4004BC.

Darwin's theory (published in 1859) that life forms are continually evolving in response to environmental stimuli then led to the idea that the human species was not created fully formed, but had evolved through potentially many different earlier stages of life. In 1863 Thomas Huxley (1825–95), a biologist and advocate of Darwin's theory of evolution, demonstrated the close similarities between the skulls and anatomy of humans and gorillas – attracting the derisory question from Archbishop Samuel Wilberforce of whether 'it was through his grandfather or grandmother that he claimed descent from a monkey.'

How accurate Huxley was in his deductions has only been proven in the 1960s, with the sequencing of primate and human genes to create a family tree that shows the hominid development from the early primates of 60 million years ago to the modern humans of today (the term 'hominid' includes apes and humans, whereas the term 'hominin' refers to the human lineage, including chimpanzees). The search for further evidence of human ancestry continues because there are many gaps still to be filled in the human family tree. This work is focused in areas of the world that are of the right geological time period to yield finds of fossil bones – in the Eastern Rift Valley of east Africa, in South Africa and in north African countries, such as Libya and Morocco.

Physical attributes

Until recently the study of human evolution was based almost exclusively on examining the physical attributes of skulls and skeletal material, much like archaeologists classify pots and metal-work into typologies. Before the advent of scientific dating techniques, people made assumptions about the chronology based on stratigraphy and on a simplistic interpretation of

Darwinian evolution, which saw adaptation as moving always from crude to sophisticated, from primitive to modern. In the case of skeletal remains, this led to some odd theories mixed up with ideas about racial superiority. In the 19th century, for example, it was commonly held that people could be classified as primitive or superior depending on whether they had rounded or elongated skulls.

What helped to put the study of human origins on a more scientific basis in the 1960s was the development

Above Thomas Huxley publicly advocated Darwinism against some of the most important theorists of 19th-century England. He coined the term 'agnostic', based on his own beliefs.

Above Archaeologists look for human evidence at Fejej in Ethiopia – a site that is currently recognized as the oldest human encampment in the world.

present day

4 million years ago

Above There is much interest in how our ancestors may have looked. This illustration shows the evolution of hominids from our distant ape-like ancestors through three groups of species, each one indicated by a different coloured line, to *Homo sapiens*.

of potassium-argon dating. This measures the ratios of the isotopes potassium 40 and argon 40 in the volcanic rocks or sediments in which the fossil bones are found, and is based on the fact that potassium 40 decays to form argon 40 at a steady rate. Added to this, microbiologists have discovered that DNA, the genetic material present in all living cells, is constantly mutating, and does so at a steady rate, serving as a genetic clock that enables scientists to calculate the likely dates of key stages in hominid development.

Our earliest ancestors

A consensus has developed over the core dates and developments that mark human evolution. Genetic scientists estimate that the split between hominids and apes occurred ten to eight million years ago. The discovery of the six- to seven-million year-old skull of *Sahelanthropus tchadensis* in the Djurab desert in northern Chad in 2002 takes archaeologists close to the point of human origin. This skull has a chimpanzee-like braincase but the flat face, prominent brow ridges and small teeth of a hominid.

Before that discovery, the oldest known hominid was the six-million-year-old *Orrorin tugenensis*, a bipedal

ape (using feet instead of knuckles and feet to bear the skeleton's weight). One challenge facing archaeologists is to identify when bipedalism occurred, marking the evolution from tree-dwelling to ground-dwelling hominids. Within the human family tree, the Australopithecines (literally 'Southern ape men', so-called because the first example was found in South African mining deposits by Raymond Dart, the Australian Professor of Anatomy at Witwatersrand University) occupies a pivotal position as the first demonstrably upright walking direct ancestor of modern humans.

Above Donald Johnson, discoverer of the Australopithecine 'Lucy', holds the skull that marks one of archaeology's greatest finds.

Above The 'Lucy's Legacy' exhibit at Houston, Texas, raised protests in 2007 from those who argued the fossil was too fragile to transport beyond Ethiopia.

Lucy and Little Lucy

The best-known Australopithecus specimen is 'Lucy' (her scientific name is AL 288-1), the 40 per cent complete skeleton of a female of the species A. afarensis, who lived 3.2 million years ago in Ethiopia's Awash Valley, and whose fossil remains were found in 1974 by the International Afar Research Expedition. Lucy was 1.1m (3ft 8in) tall, weighed 29kg (65lb) and looked like an upright walking chimpanzee. Her species was the last before the human and chimpanzee lines split.

In 2000, the remains were found of another member of the same species, the near complete skeleton of a three-year-old A. afarensis female named Selam (Ethiopian for 'Peace'), but also known as 'Little Lucy' or 'Lucy's Baby' (although she lived 3.3 million years ago and is 120,000 years older than Lucy).

The Palaeolithic Era

Archaeologists studying human behaviour in the Palaeolithic era, or 'Old Stone Age', look for sites where bones and tools are found together, perhaps with evidence of fire and cooking. In fact, some researchers argue that the study of archaeology only begins with the first evidence of tool use.

There is an argument that the study of early hominid species, before the first evidence of tool use some 2.5 million years ago, is really a branch of palaeontology (the study of fossils), or of biology, anatomy, geology, geography or physical anthropology. It is true that many of the key figures in the field of human origins research have a background in some other discipline, but there is undoubtedly a considerable overlap between those anthropologists who study early hominid developments during the huge sweep of time spanning the last ten million years and the archaeologists who are more concerned with the last 2.5 million years – the date of the dividing line between the australopithecenes, which are, in many ways, more like primates than humans, and the first hominins, which are more like humans of today than they are like other primates. It is during this latter period that great changes in behaviour took place that mark the beginning of 'human' (instead of instinctive) thought and behaviour.

The Old Stone Age

An important marker in the development of human behaviour is the use of tools made from stone. The period when tool use develops is known as the Palaeolithic era, which is also known as the Old Stone Age. It corresponds to the geological era known as the

Above Palaeolithic axe heads are studied at an ancient site in Libya.

Pleistocene, a period of glacial episodes, or ice ages, fluctuating with warmer intervals, called interglacials. Climatic stress might have been the reason why human ancestors left the tree canopy to explore the open spaces of the savannah, why tool use developed about 2.5 million years ago and why fire was domesticated around 1.5 million years ago.

Once it was thought that only *Homo sapiens* had the conceptual capacity for tool use and fire making, but now archaeologists know that the other great apes (members of the biological

Above 45,000-year-old Neanderthal bones lie in situ at La Chapelle-aux-Saintes, France.

Left An artist's impression shows how a family of *Homo erectus* hominins might have appeared in their natural environment. This species, who were in existence 800,000 to 30,000 years ago, used stone tools and cooked with fire.

family Hominidae, which includes humans, chimpanzees, gorillas and orangutangs) also exhibit social behaviour and language use and will modify natural materials to make tools. A major difference between humans and other hominids is that the great apes are opportunistic – they will use a tool if it happens to be lying around – but do not think ahead and store or carry tools. Crucially, too, humans adapted the stones that they found to create specialist tools, some of them of great aesthetic beauty, with symmetrical profiles, rather than simply using rocks as they were found.

In fact, the current definition of what makes humans different from their primate cousins is the human's capacity to live in the world of the imagination, although, as will be seen, other hominids, all now extinct, also had this capacity. Archaeologists also now know that some of these extinct hominins, such as the Australopithecines, not only made tools but also developed lifestyles of increasing sophistication, and that some of them travelled long distances and colonized large parts of the world.

The Olduvai Gorge

In Tanzania, the Olduvai Gorge – which is known as 'The Cradle of Mankind' – occupies an iconic place in early hominid research. It is the place where so many important discoveries have been made, first by the German prehistorian Hans Reck from 1913, then by members of the Leakey family – Louis and Mary from the 1930s and their son Richard from the 1960s.

The gorge is 50km (30 miles) long and 100m (330ft) deep. Erosion by ancient rivers has revealed deep stratigraphy, with layer upon layer of ancient volcanic deposits that date back 2.5 million years. Named after this site are the very earliest tools, which are known as Oldowan, and consist of cobbles used as hammerstones and sharp-edged flakes that have been deliberately struck from a larger stone to make a variety of tools, such as scrapers, axe-shaped choppers and pointed awls.

First fire

Finding evidence of burning is not necessarily evidence that the fire was made deliberately. Archaeologists looking for the early domestication of fire look for hearth structures, areas of burning that are small and discrete (wild fires will usually scorch a large area) and for fires that are also associated with a concentration of burnt bones, stone tools, or bones that have been butchered and have cut marks or fractures.

So far the earliest generally accepted evidence of controlled fire use comes from fossil hearths and burnt animal bones from sites in Kenya and from the Swartkrans cave in South Africa, both dating from 1.5 million years ago.

Above Archaeologists search for human prehistory at the edge of Olduvai Gorge in Tanzania.

Below The elongated skull of an Australopithecene (*left*) adjacent to the more rounded skull of *Homo habilis* (*right*).

The Paleolithic era: key dates

Dates often overlap because new species and new tools co-existed alongside archaic species and tools for a period of time.

• Lower Palaeolithic (2.5 million to 120,000 years ago): Australopithecines (*Australopithecus africanus*, *A. aethipicus*, *A. garhi*, *A. boisei* and *A. robustus*) and hominins (*Homo habilis*, *H. rudolfensis* and *H. ergaster*) are all using tools, which have been found in Ethiopia, Kenya, Tanzania, Uganda and South Africa. *H. ergaster* migrates out of East Africa and adapts to a wide range of environments in Eurasia.

• Middle Palaeolithic (800,000 years ago to 30,000 years ago): Flake tools are made and used by *H. erectus*, *H. antecessor* and *H. heidelbergensis*. These are the species who populate the world as part of the first 'out of Africa' wave of migration.

• Upper Palaeolithic (100,000 years ago to 12,000 years ago): Modern humans begin the second 'out of Africa' migration and spread across the world to reach Australia and the Americas. Competition between modern humans and other hominins leads to the extinction of Neanderthals in Europe and *H. erectus* in Asia, leaving *H. sapiens* as the only surviving hominin species.

Populating the World

Although archaeologists believe that all hominin species evolved from African ancestors, their fossil remains are found all over the world, testimony to the fact that early hominins were capable of travelling long distances in search of the food that they needed for survival.

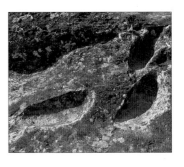

The earliest evidence of human behaviour comes from sites in Africa, but the geographical field widens once early hominins embark on what has been called 'the Great Adventure' of populating the world. In reality, it is unlikely that hominin dispersal out of Africa was the result of a decision to explore what lay beyond the horizon. Instead, archaeologists believe that rapid climate change led to the food-rich African savannah drying up about 1.9 million years ago, forcing the hominins of southern and eastern Africa to travel in search of food.

Working Man

One species in particular seems to have travelled further than the others. *Homo ergaster* ('Working Man') was given his name because of the more varied and sophisticated range of stone tools that this species made. Typically, *H. ergaster* bones and tools are found at sites in Kenya. The most spectacular find to date is the near-complete skeleton of the 'Turkana Boy', so-called because he was found on the shores of Lake Turkana, where he died around 1.5 million years ago.

H. ergaster more closely resembles modern humans than any previous hominin, with his considerably larger brain. His invention of new kinds of stone tools – hand axes, cleavers, flakes, scrapers and chopping tools – points to a new evolutionary phase, as does the wide geographical range of the sites where these tools are found. They are called Acheulian, after the first site where they were found, at Saint-Acheul in France, but they are also found right across the continent of Africa, as far east as India and as far north as southern England.

From Africa to Indonesia, China and Europe

From 1.9 million years ago, when no hominin remains or tools are found outside Africa, it is not long before we find the Acheulian-type tools associated with *H. ergaster* in use at sites in the Jordan Rift Valley, as well as in the former Soviet republic of Georgia, bordering Turkey. It has been calculated that the spread of *H. ergaster* out of Africa represents a journey of 50km (30 miles) a year – not such a big step, if that is translated into a daily average, although, of course, the landscape would have presented numerous barriers and challenges. Travelling along the coast and feeding on shellfish was probably easier than hacking a path through dense jungle, which might explain why the rainforest around the River Congo, for example, has no evidence of colonization by *H. ergaster*, whereas coastal caves and rock shelters have such evidence in relative abundance.

Those first migrants did not stop evolving. Exactly how and when is still

Above Only the discovery of more fossils will enable archaeologists to place *Homo floresiensis* within the hominin family tree.

Homo floresiensis

Scientists continue to make discoveries that suggest that other species of hominin survived until relatively recent times. The skeletal remains of *Homo floresiensis* (dubbed 'the Hobbit' by the media because of its small stature) were discovered on the Indonesian island of Flores in 2003. It was declared to be an entirely new tool-using species that had evolved from *H. erectus*, and that had survived in isolation on this island until about 18,000 years ago, making it the last hominin species other than our own to survive on the planet. However, some scientists do not accept that *H. floresiensis* is a new species. They believe the remains found on the island are those of a modern human with a neurological disorder, called microcephaly, in which the head is much smaller than average for the person's age.

a subject for research (the small amount of skeletal evidence we have for this early phase of hominid evolution would easily fit into a single laboratory) but it is thought that *H. ergaster* evolved into *H. erectus* ('Upright Man'), a species found in south-east Asia (named 'Java Man' and 'Peking Man' after their find sites) while *H. antecessor* ('Pioneer Man') appears in Europe roughly about 800,000 years ago followed by *H. heidelbergensis* ('Heidelberg Man') roughly 600,000 years ago.

Multi-regional evolution

Java Man, Peking Man, Heidelberg Man and several other hominins distinctive to a particular region of the world were once thought to be the co-equal ancestors of the different people of the world – Java Man of the south-east Asian people, Peking Man of the modern Chinese and Heidelberg Man of modern Europeans. In other words, evolutionary scientists once believed that differences in skin colour, body shape, skull shape, hair and eye type and colour could be explained as the result of the evolution of modern humans not once, but several times over, independently and in different parts of the world.

This multi-regional evolutionary theory was based on the science of morphology, which is the study of shapes and forms. Today, the study of genes

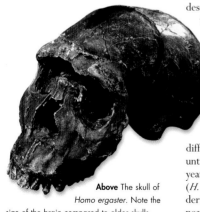

Above The skull of *Homo ergaster*. Note the size of the brain compared to older skulls.

KEY
Major fossil sites
•
Migratory routes
•••••••••

Fossil bones and genetic data have been used to trace the steps of our ancestors in their global journey.

has revolutionized the classification of organic life, and the extraction of ancient DNA from fossil bones has enabled specialists in genetics to examine the degree to which modern humans are really related to these archaic species.

They have concluded that none of us is descended from Java Man, Peking Man or Heidelberg Man, and that, instead, all human beings alive today are descended from an entirely new species that evolved in Africa about 400,000 years ago – *Homo sapiens*. Although the other hominin species were very successful in colonizing their own part of the world, they are now all extinct and contributed nothing to humans' genetic inheritance. Java Man and Peking Man (*H. erectus*) continued to evolve on a different evolutionary track in Asia until becoming extinct around 60,000 years ago. In Europe, Heidelberg Man (*H. heidelbergensis*) evolved into Neanderthal Man (*H. neanderthalensis*), but neanderthals then became extinct

Above This colour coded map, with major fossil sites marked, shows how far each species is known to have migrated on the basis of skeletal finds. *Homo erectus* travelled an extraordinary distance, reaching at least as far as the Indonesian island of Java, then part of a continuous land mass stretching from northern Europe almost to the shores of Australia.

about 23,000 years ago, leaving modern humans as the dominant hominin species.

It is possible that our species caused the extinction of these other hominins, because, like *H. ergaster*, *H. sapiens* was also a great explorer. The species began to migrate out of Africa about 100,000 years ago and, wherever it went, it encountered other hominins. It is likely that *H. sapiens* would have competed with them for food and shelter, either directly, by fighting and killing them, or indirectly, by being better hunters and depriving them of food. The latter was, in fact, becoming increasingly scarce as climate change transformed food-rich savannah into the deserts we know in Africa today.

Caves and Colonization

By carefully excavating evidence from caves and rock shelters, archaeologists have been able to track the human migrations of the Middle and Upper Paleolithic eras, which have extended from East Africa to Australia — and ultimately to the Americas.

What was it that made our *Homo sapiens* ancestors get up and leave their original home in East Africa? As with so many evolutionary developments, it seems that climate change might have been the cause. Ancient pollen evidence from sediments taken from the beds of Lakes Malawi and Tanganyika in East Africa, and from Lake Bosumtwi in Ghana, show that East Africa was subject to a prolonged drought between 100,000 and 75,000 years ago. The drought was so severe that Lake Malawi — on whose shores many early hominins lived, and now some 550km (340 miles) long and 700m (2,300ft) deep — was reduced to a couple of small lakes, no more than 10km (6 miles) across and 200m (650ft) deep. Lake Bosumtwi, currently 10km (6 miles) wide, lost all of its water.

Such a prolonged period of dry, hot weather must have had a profound impact on the landscape and on the availability of food resources. It is likely that this was what motivated some of the 10,000 or so *H. sapiens* who lived in East Africa at the time — and from whom we are all descended — to begin their global journey.

Drowned landscapes

Tracking their migrations is not easy. Early hunter-gatherers left little by way of an imprint on the earth, just as the people who live in the Amazon or in the dense rainforests of south-east Asia today leave little trace of their presence. It is probable that early migrants followed coasts and rivers — perhaps using log boats — to avoid the barriers and hazards of land-based journeys.

Left The first occupants of the Great Cave of Niah in Sarawak, Borneo, were Palaeolithic hunter-gatherers – but excavations have revealed usage up to 4,000 years ago.

Below The skull of *Australopithecus africanus* found at the Sterkfontein cave complex, South Africa, is the most complete specimen to date.

Above Louis and Mary Leakey examine hominin remains on the shores of Lake Tanganyika.

Sea levels were considerably lower than they are today because so much more of the earth's water was locked up in glaciers and the polar ice caps. Places that are now islands in south-east Asia, such as Java, Sumatra and Borneo, were once part of a continuous land mass. Much of the evidence for the earliest human journeys now lies drowned beneath the sea.

Cave archaeology

Such evidence that archaeologists do have for hominin dispersal comes from the painstaking excavation of cave sites, some of which have become famous among archaeologists: the Swartskrans, Sterkfontein and Blombos Caves (*see* The Origins of Art and Ornament) in South Africa, or the Niah Cave in Sarawak, on the island of Borneo.

Very often such cave sites were used as a natural shelter for hundreds of thousands of years, slowly building deposits. Typically, what archaeologists find is a mass of bone and stone tools, and evidence of fire. The bones found in cave deposits cannot always be assumed to be those consumed by humans. Scavengers, such as hyenas, will drag food (including humans) into caves to eat, so cave deposits often consist of a complex mix of human and animal activity.

That explains why archaeological projects at cave sites painstakingly record every find in three dimensions, aiming to reconstruct on computer the exact relationships of all the finds, looking for patterns that might indicate a hearth, a tool manufacturing site, a butchery area, an area where skins are converted to clothing or areas where people slept, or deposited their dead, or carried out their rituals. The search for such evidence can take years and even last for a lifetime, as archaeologists continually revisit important sites to reassess the evidence or excavate new areas – often small areas, but ones that are capable of yielding enough material for years of analysis.

Migration to Australia

Mostly what is found in caves sites is very ordinary to the non-specialist. Typical of the sort of evidence that archaeologists look for when dealing with the early migration period is the Jerimalai limestone cave site on the eastern tip of the island of East Timor. This is being excavated by Sue O'Connor, Head of Archaeology and Natural History at the Australian National University, who hopes the site will answer questions about the routes taken by ancient migrants from southeast Asia to Australia – did they, as she believes, travel south, via Timor, or north, via Borneo and Sulawesi and down through Papua New Guinea?

Until now, all the habitation sites found on these 'stepping stone' islands are later in date than the earliest sites in Australia, but the Jerimalai site has yielded finds dating from 42,000 years old, and could be older. Finds from the cave indicate that the people who sheltered here ate turtles and giant rats – but also tuna fish, which implies that boat-building and fishing skills were established at that date.

Below Jerimalai Cave in East Timor is a site that represents a missing link in the great hominid migration.

Colonizing the world

All the evidence suggests that *Homo sapiens* was on the move 100,000 years ago and migrated northward first from East Africa into North Africa and the Nile region, then eastward into south-west Asia 100,000 years ago and from there eastward into northern India, and then southward down through the Malay peninsula into Indonesia and on to Australia, which was reached 50,000 years ago. Various groups then continued the human journey westward into Europe, northward into China and Russia, eastward into Borneo and New Guinea and southward into Tasmania, all of which show signs of human presence within 40,000 years.

Above As indicated by the arrows in this world map, it is believed that *Homo sapiens* originated in eastern Africa (see nucleus), later migrating mainly to the north and east.

The Americas remained the last uncolonized continents, and there is considerable debate about the origins of their people. The genes of some southern American people suggest that they are part of a group that broke away from Australasian populations up to 35,000 years ago, suggesting that their ancestors made a hazardous ocean voyage across the Pacific to South America. This remains a controversial theory. More certain is the genetic and physical evidence that humans were present in Siberia and Japan 25,000 years ago and that the ancestors of today's Native Americans came from this part of Asia, crossing into North America in several migrations from 15,000 years ago.

The Origins of Art and Ornament

Art, in the form of sculpture, and ornament in the form of jewellery, are among the first evidence of that capacity for imagination and the use of symbols that truly distinguish humans from other forms of life. New finds keep giving earlier dates for the invention of these creative activities.

Above The Blombos Cave 'beads' are actually the pierced shells of Nassarius, or mud snails, still native to that region.

The site at Kostenki, on the banks of the River Don, 155km (250 miles) south of Moscow, has long been one of the classical sites for early human remains. However, new finds from the site indicate that it is older than first thought, dating back 47,000 years to the Upper Palaeolithic era. This makes it one of the earliest places with evidence of modern humans in Europe.

Recent finds not only include the oldest dated bone and ivory needles with eyelets yet found in Europe – probably used for tailoring animal furs to protect the settlers from the harsh climate – they also include an ivory carving that appears to show the head of a human being and marks an early attempt at figurative art. Bones from the site include hare and Arctic fox and fish, implying the use of snares and nets. Reindeer and horses were also hunted and eaten.

Large numbers of tools show that this was a well-used site. Among the tools found were a rotary drill, awls, blades, scrapers and antlers. Shells from the Black Sea – 480km (300 miles) away –

were used to make ornaments and most of the stone used for tool-making at the site came from 160km (100 miles) away, implying that the people who lived at Kostenki might have been trading with other groups, or that they travelled great distances to obtain raw materials.

First evidence of art

If people were carving ivory and making shell jewellery 47,000 years ago, how much further back can we

Below Neolithic rock painting of giraffes from the Tin Abaniora rock-shelter, Iherir Plateau, Tassili n'Ajjer, in Algeria *c.* 3500BC.

Below The 'Venus' of Dolní, Vestonice, Czech Republic, is one of the oldest representations of the human figure dating from 29,000BC.

Right The El-Wad Cave site, Mount Carmel, Israel, has been in use for 200,000 years, and includes some of the earliest human burials ever found.

push these creative activities? Every time archaeologists think they have the answer, someone makes a discovery that pushes the date further back still. In 2004, archaeologists thought the answer had been found in a string of pierced shells found in South Africa's Blombos Cave, 300km (187 miles) east of Cape Town in South Africa, on the Indian Ocean coast. The 41 Nassarius shells found date from 75,000 years ago and had been collected from a river bank (the nearest river then being 20km (12 miles) away). The shells appeared to have been selected for size and had been deliberately perforated for threading on to a string. Traces of red ochre suggest they had been coloured or were worn by someone with red ochre on their body. Two years previously, at the same cave, archaeologists found two rectangular blocks of ochre inscribed with a complex geometric pattern of rectangles and diamond shapes, dating from 77,000 years ago.

New discoveries

Then, in 2006, pierced shells from two separate sites were found whose dating pushes back the date for bead-working to at least 100,000 years ago. The shells were excavated between 1931 and 1932 from the Middle Palaeolithic site at Es-Skhul, Mount Carmel, Israel, and from Oued Djebbana, Bir-el-Ater, Algeria. The original excavators had concentrated on human remains and tools, so the significance of the shells had not been appreciated at the time. Microscopic analysis shows that the shells had been artificially pierced, probably with flint tools, and may have been hung on sinew, fibres or leather for use as pendants or in necklaces.

As for body art, archaeologists now have evidence that rock tools from the Twin Rivers hilltop cave near Lusaka in Zambia were used for grinding pigments 300,000 years ago – before

Homo sapiens even began their migrations – and not just the red of ochre, but a whole repertoire of colours that include yellow, brown, black and purple.

So archaeologists know that people in Africa were capable of the kinds of thinking that lead to the deliberate creation of patterns and jewellery and

the use of minerals for body ornament as far back as the Middle Palaeolithic era. No doubt future finds will push the date for artistic and ornamental behaviour back further still, along with the origins of the key survival skills – boat-building, fishing, clothes-making, hunting and trade – implied by finds from Australia and Russia.

Left This reconstruction shows how three holes pierced at regular intervals might have converted the hollow femur bone of a bear into the world's earliest known flute. The remains of the third hole can be seen on the left.

Creative Neanderthals

What should not be forgotten is that *Homo sapiens* were not the only hominins capable of complex thought, religious belief and artistic creativity. There is a growing body of evidence to show that *Homo heidelbergensis* used ochre as body decoration and that Neanderthals buried their dead in graves, along with offerings of pierced shell jewellery.

Neanderthals might even have developed musical instruments. What is claimed to be the world's oldest flute was found in 1995 in the Divje Babe I cave in western Slovenia. Found in 43,000-year-old Neanderthal occupation layers, it consists of the femur (upper leg bone) of a cave bear punctuated by three holes. It is almost impossible to say whether this really is a musical instrument or, as some academics believe, whether the holes were made by a carnivorous animal simply chewing on the bone.

The Mesolithic Period

Also referred to as the Middle Stone Age, the Mesolithic period is an archaeological period that bridges the Old (Palaeolithic) and New (Neolithic) Stone Ages. It is a period in which the pace of technological development speeds up.

During the Mesolithic period, the 'toolkit' becomes more varied and specialist in function and humans begin to have a bigger impact on the landscape, with the first evidence of tree clearance and monument building. The Mesolithic period is also one in which the climate plays an important part in human development. It is an archaeological period that equates to the Holocene in geology – that is, the period during which the repeated glaciations of the previous era (the Palaeolithic in archaeology, the Pleistocene in geology) begin to give way to longer periods of warm weather – interglacials – during which the glaciers melt and sea levels rise.

With the Mesolithic period, archaeologists have reached the point in human

Below This ancient Mesopotamian relief depicts the mytical flood saga of Gilgamesh.

history where it is no longer possible to talk about changes that take place simultaneously and on a global scale – from now on, archaeology is increasingly varied and regional, with different people living at different levels of development. Early humans living in sites furthest from the Equator had to overcome greater challenges to survive. By contrast, people in Africa, Asia and Australia were far less affected by glacial cold, and the transitional period from the nomadic hunter-gatherer lifestyle of the Palaeolithic period to the settled agricultural life of the Neolithic period is faster and earlier than the same transition in Europe. In south-west Asia, the period between the Old and New Stone Ages is so brief that it is called the Epipaleolithic (meaning 'beyond' the Old Stone Age) rather than the Mesolithic, or Middle Stone Age.

Above The rising water levels of interglacial periods meant that land masses, and with them entire communities, were suddenly lost.

A different world

What also adds to the growing complexity of this period is the way that the map of the world was redrawn as the ice melted. This was not a single smooth event, but instead consisted of a series of cold and warmer periods, during which the glaciers retreated and advanced several times, although each time the cold snaps were less severe than the last.

As the ice melted, the world began to change in ways that created the more familiar geography of today. Instead of a slow rise in the average sea level, there were various tipping points when sudden flooding drowned very large areas of land. In fact, this was how the Mediterranean Sea was created, and

Below Remains found at Star Carr, northern England, including a frontlet (*top*) and the jawbone (*bottom*) of a red deer, tell us something of prehistoric diets.

how the islands of Indonesia, Malaysia, Papua New Guinea and Japan were separated from the mainland and from each other. Tasmania became separated from Australia and the British Isles were cut off from the European continent when water poured into the marshy plains south and east of England, thereby creating the North Sea and English Channel.

The distant mythologized memory of such cataclysmic events is recorded in the Bible, as are the many other traumas of the past — including drought, plague, famine, sickness and plagues of locusts — that early human society suffered as a consequence. There is another echo of these difficult times in the flood story in the ancient Mesopotamian Epic of Gilgamesh, which was written down in the third millennium BC.

Ritual and religion

The Mesolithic period is thus a time in which people had to respond to change and uncertainty, as the landscape in which they lived was transformed, sometimes with astonishing and violent rapidity. Perhaps it is no surprise that this is a period in which archaeologists find increasing amounts of evidence for ritualistic or religious practice and for a growing sense of social organization — which could be interpreted as a banding together to form a common front against an uncertain world.

Archaeologists have many examples of the burial of individuals in isolated graves from the Palaeolithic period, but the Mesolithic period sees the first cemeteries — communal burial places that are used over several generations — in Russia and Ukraine. The grave goods from Oleneostrovski Mogilnik, in Russia, include carved figures — material evidence for the growing importance of the symbolic and spiritual dimensions to life.

People were beginning at this time not just to live in the landscape, but also to modify it for their own use — and not just for economic reasons. As recently as 2007, 12 massive post pits at Warren Field in Crathes, south-west of Aberdeen, in Scotland, have been radiocarbon dated to the Mesolithic period (8000–7500BC). This dating proves that Mesolithic people built big monuments — the size of the pits implies a row of massive tree-trunk sized columns — and challenges the idea that monument building is a later Neolithic innovation. Three similarly massive post holes dating from 8000BC are the earliest evidence of monument making, and these are at the site of Stonehenge in southern England.

Mesolithic ritual seems to have included feasting. Excavating the site of Heathrow Terminal 5, in southern England, archaeologists have found large pits filled with burnt bone and stones that were interpreted as evidence of ritual feasting. The quantity of stones suggests that the site was used for this purpose over many years. And at Star Carr, a Mesolithic site buried beneath a bog in Yorkshire, England — once a lake-edge settlement — excavators found red deer skulls and antlers that had been pierced to be worn as headdresses — nobody is sure whether the antlers were worn by hunters as a disguise, or as some sort of religious or ceremonial costume.

Right The skeleton of an 18-year-old male who was buried with a shell hat and necklace at the Mesolithic site of Arene Candide in Italy.

Above One of the flints found at Pakefield in eastern England.

The settlement of the British Isles

Humans tried to colonize Britain seven times over a 700,000-year period before the ancestors of today's population put down roots some 12,000 years ago. From 32 flint tools found in sediments exposed by erosion at the bottom of a cliff in Pakefield, near the Suffolk seaside town of Lowestoft, archaeologists know that there were tool-using hominins in East Anglia 700,000 years ago, but there were also long periods — of 100,000 years in duration — when the climate was too cold for anyone to live in northern Europe.

189

Drowned Landscapes

Because so much of the evidence for the Mesolithic period lies beneath the sea, finding it presents all kinds of challenges. Archaeologists have responded by borrowing techniques from seismology, by digging bogs and by wading in coastal mud.

The drowned landscapes that hold so much information about our past are not entirely lost forever. For example, cod fishing fleets working the Dogger Bank in the North Sea have been trawling up worked flints, antler tools, and the bones of reindeer, mammoth and woolly rhino for centuries. Yet, only now has the marshy land mass – 22,000km sq (8,500 miles sq) in extent – that once connected the present east coast of England with northern Germany, Denmark and Norway been explored in more detail.

A hidden landscape

Geological surveying in the North Sea in the search for oil has produced a mass of seismic evidence that archaeologists at Birmingham University have turned into a map of Doggerland, an entire European country that has not been seen for 8,500 years or more. So detailed is the seismic data that the archaeologists have been able to reconstruct the rivers, streams, lakes and coastlines of a uniquely preserved Mesolithic landscape covering an area the size of Wales.

The results of this North Sea Palaeolandscapes project ('palaeo' here does not relate to the period – it is used as the term for 'old') have excited archaeologists in all the countries that bound the North Sea basin. Their next big challenge is to look for likely areas of Mesolithic settlement and come up with ways of exploring these underwater sites. Two such sites have already begun to be excavated. One lies 11m (36ft) beneath the sea off the Isle of Wight's Bouldnor Cliff. Divers have already found hundreds of worked flints, charred stones from two hearths and a possible log canoe. The other is in Denmark, where the construction of a major road and rail bridge in the Storebælt region led to the excavation of a wealth of new archaeological evidence for this period, including one

Above Archaeologists are rising to the challenge of reconstructing historic landscapes now hidden beneath sea or salt marsh.

of the defining characteristics of Mesolithic sites, the 'composite' tool, so-called because it is made of more than one material – for example, a flint blade inserted into a bone handle, or a spearhead set into a wooden shaft, or a series of small flints (called 'microliths' or 'microblades') set into a shaft for use as barbed harpoons or arrows.

Seabed prehistory

Another technique archaeologists use to probe beneath the sea is to push tubes known as Vibrocores deep into the seabed. The tubes capture columns of sediment, including layers of ancient soil that can be analysed for evidence of human activity. The sediment can also be correlated with geological evidence to reconstruct the terrain, and it can be analysed for trapped seeds, pollen and mollusc shells to recreate ancient environments and habitats before the sea drowned the landscape.

The results of one such investigation have been used to recreate the Mesolithic landscape of the Arun Estuary in West Sussex (*see opposite page*). You can see the animated results by visiting Wessex Archaeology: www.wessexarch.co.uk/projects/marine/alsf/seabed_prehistory/computer models.html.

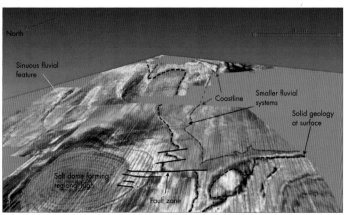

North

Sinuous fluvial feature

Coastline

Smaller fluvial systems

Solid geology at surface

Salt dome forming regional high

Fault zone

Left This seismic map of Doggerland shows the Mesolithic coastline along with river valleys ('fluvial systems') which would have attracted animals and their hunters.

Left At the end of the last ice age, the River Arun, Sussex, UK, flowed a further 13km (8 miles) out into the English Channel than it does today. To fully recreate the valley settlement, Wessex Archaeology created models of human activity and of the likely vegetation.

Intertidal archaeology

Rising sea levels caused by melting glaciers have drowned some low-lying landscapes, which is an obvious effect. However, there is an unexpected effect of the melting glaciers that is not so obvious: some landscapes actually rose upward as the weight and pressure of the ice cap was removed. For example, the ancient shorelines in Scotland, Scandinavia and Canada are now some 8m (26ft) higher than the current average sea level, and that is why the skeletons of sea mammals are sometimes found at sites that are well above, rather then below, the present-day waterline.

Today, the sea levels are rising again, scouring soft and vulnerable coastlines and inland estuaries. This action is revealing long-buried ancient sites at a rate that worries many archaeologists who lack the resources to record all the material that is being revealed before it is destroyed by the rising sea levels.

Ancient bogs

Sometimes evidence is found on land that has become waterlogged. At the Star Carr early Mesolithic site in Yorkshire, England, first excavated by Grahame Clark in the 1950s, the waterlogged conditions of the peat bog covering the site had preserved the wood, bone and antlers that had been used to make arrows and knifes,

mattocks and chisels around 8770BC. Other finds included birch bark, used in tanning animal hides, a wooden platform made of split poplar planks, and even a wooden paddle, used to propel a boat or canoe.

Clark's analysis of the site had far-reaching implications. He found charcoal from burnt reed and birch as evidence for the deliberate clearance of the lakeside site not once but repeatedly over a period of years, which he interpreted as seasonal occupation and use of the site for hunting the deer, elk, pig and aurochs

Right This mesolithic blade, measuring 100mm (4in) long, was an effective tool for butchery and food preparation.

(primitive cattle) and wildfowl whose bones were also found at the site. This is evidence that some groups of people were already tending toward the more settled way of life that defines the Neolithic period: of deliberate exploitation of the landscape on a planned basis; of organized craft and industry; and of social organization over and above that of the immediate family members.

Star Carr can be paralleled by other sites representing other cultures in transition. Dating from 18,000BC is a similar site that was found in Israel in 1989 when the waters of the Sea of Galilee fell to a very low level, thereby revealing the submerged remains of wooden huts made of oak, and a wealth of animal bone and plant remains. However, what made this site Epipaleolithic rather than Neolithic was the discovery that the food remains found there – including wheat, barley and beans – were still being gathered from wild plants, rather than being from domesticated varieties.

Footprints in the mud

Intertidal archaeology involves the strenuous work of monitoring shorelines and estuary margins for the evidence of human activity. The work is demanding because it often involves wading through thick mud in all weathers to record evidence that is only revealed for a short period of time before being covered up again. Some of the evidence is only revealed for a few days before being eroded away by scouring tides.

The result can be the most intimate of encounters with our human ancestors. For example, one site on the River Severn estuary at Goldcliff, near Newport, Gwent, south Wales, has revealed the footprints of children playing on a river bank one sunny day in the Mesolithic period. Mixed in with the children's footprints were those of cranes, aurochs and the deer that their parents were no doubt hunting when they were not fishing for eels.

The Neolithic Period

The era in which people began to grow crops and keep animals is known as the Neolithic, or New Stone Age, period. It led to a huge shift in lifestyles, from a nomadic, opportunistic existence based on hunting and gathering wild food to land clearance and semi-permanent settlements.

In areas of the world less affected by ice age glaciations something new and revolutionary was beginning to happen. Blessed with a climate that encourages rich biodiversity – including animals, such as horses, and plants, such as apples, that were unknown to the Mesolithic hunter-gatherers in northern Europe – the people of south-west Asia began to select and domesticate some animal species, to cultivate certain types of seed and plant, and to lead more settled lives, clearing the landscape of its wild vegetation, living in villages, herding animals, tilling and irrigating fields.

As with so many innovations, such activities are not exclusive to the Neolithic period and can be traced back to a much earlier era. Dogs were first domesticated as hunting partners perhaps 35,000 years ago, and they are found buried with humans in pre-agricultural cemeteries in many parts of the world, from Mesolithic Skateholm in Sweden to the Koster site in Illinois. The careful management of food sources probably dates back thousands of years. The indigenous people of Australia, for example, while living a hunter-gatherer lifestyle, always return part of the plant tubers they dig up to the ground. The earliest known oven and the earliest evidence of grain milling come from a site called Ohalo II, situated on the south-western shore of the Sea of Galilee and date back 15,000 years, around 4,000 years before either wheat or barley were domesticated.

Above Cultivated crops brought about a revolution in human behaviour.

However, the Neolithic period sees an intensification of such behaviour, and an acceleration of the range of animals and crops that are managed. In addition, it is called the Neolithic – the New Stone Age – because of the innovative stone tools that become more common at this time, such as sickles and grindstones specifically connected with agriculture and cereal use.

The Fertile Crescent

The credit for the development of agriculture is traditionally given to the Fertile Crescent region of the Middle East. The term was coined by James Henry Breasted (1865–1935), the first

Above Excavating a dog at the Neolithic site of Ashqelon, Israel. Although the domestication of these animals gained momentum in the Neolithic, the origins of the practice are much earlier.

Above The huge city of Tel Hazor in Galilee began life as a prehistoric farming community.

Right The well-preserved floor of a 'brush hut', where food preparation would have taken place, excavated at the Neolithic site Ohalo II, Israel (*right*), and a gazelle horn core (*far right*), discovered close to a hearth at the site. An artist's reconstruction of a Neolithic brush hut (*below right*).

Above Two of the figs discovered at the Gilgal I site in Jordan.

Founder crops

Nine small figs recently discovered in a house in the early Neolithic village called Gilgal I, in the Jordan Valley, might be the earliest evidence yet of agriculture. The carbonized fruits come from a variety of fig that produces large but sterile fruits. Such mutations occur in the wild, but since they produce no seed, the plant will eventually die without offspring – they can only survive if a human being recognizes the value of the larger fruits and deliberately removes shoots or roots and plants them. Radiocarbon dating dated these figs to 11,400 years ago, and they are the earliest evidence so far of the consumption of a domestic crop, rather than a wild plant.

Figs are one of the so-called 'founder crops' that grow wild in the Fertile Crescent. The others include emmer wheat, einkorn, barley, flax, chickpea, pea, lentil and bitter vetch (a plant with lentil-like seeds). All are relatively easy to grow and it is possible that wild seed was gathered and sown in cultivated fields long before people had the idea of selective breeding.

American to earn a university doctorate in the study of ancient Egypt and the first Professor of Egyptology and Oriental History in the United States (appointed in 1905 by the University of Chicago). He used the term to describe a region that includes the Nile, Jordan, Euphrates and Tigris Rivers and stretches from the eastern shores of the Mediterranean to the Persian Gulf, taking in present-day Egypt, Israel, the West Bank, the Gaza Strip, Lebanon, parts of Jordan, Syria and Iraq and south-eastern Turkey and south-western Iran. Breasted recognized the natural fertility of the region's soils and their seasonal irrigation by region's rivers. He and other archaeologists noted that this was the home of some of the earliest complex societies. It is commonly known, from its shape on the map, as 'The Fertile Crescent'.

Multiple origins

However, this classic view of the Fertile Crescent as the source of all that we associate with the Neolithic revolution has since been challenged, as archaeologists in other parts of the world have found evidence that domesticated crops were developed by different people in geographically distant places.

If each domesticated animal or food plant derived from a single point of origin (as humans do), each species would have a homogeneous gene profile. In fact, ancient crops show distinct regional variations. Grains from Neolithic deposits in the Fertile Crescent have been compared to barley of the similar age from 3,000km (1,875 miles) further east in Central Asia. In every case there was close match between the domesticated barley and its local wild version, and

far less of a match between the two domesticated strains. This means that the farmed varieties were developed independently, many times over.

Similarly, archaeologists have found evidence for the invention of farming in parts of the world with no possibility of contact with people who already had the skill. When Europeans reached the New World, for example, they found steep hillsides carved into terraces where people cultivated potato, tomato, pepper, squash, several varieties of bean, maize, manioc and tobacco, and recent research has suggested that some of these crops were first domesticated in the Americas around 5200BC.

Finds from China give a date of around 7500BC for the earliest example of domesticated rice yet found, though it was not until 5000BC that domesticated rice strains are the dominant form of food consumed. As new finds are made, the traditional view that rice was domesticated in China's Yangtze Delta and spread from there is being challenged by evidence of early rice cultivation in Korea, Japan and northern India, while an entirely different strain of rice was first cultivated in the Sahel region of Africa, along with the sorghum, one of the staple grains of the modern African diet, before 5000BC.

The Spread of Agriculture

Gordon Childe, the Australian archaeologist who was one of the first to try to understand the origins and spread of agriculture, coined the phrase 'Neolithic Revolution' to imply that this was a sudden and all-changing phenomenon. Archaeologists now know that the picture is more complex.

Above Wild wheat growing in the Near East. It was first cultivated 11,000 years ago.

Not only is the development of agriculture far more complex than the idea of a single invention, it also seems to have been a protracted process. Wheat spikelets from Neolithic settlements in northern Syria and south-eastern Turkey have recently been analysed to compare the ratio of wild to domesticated wheat at various dates. At the 10,500-year-old site called Nevali Çori in Turkey, 90 per cent of the spikelets were from wild varieties, while 64 per cent were still wild at the 8,500-year-old site at el Kerkh in Syria and only 36 per cent were wild at 7,500-year-old Kosak Shamali, also in Syria.

This suggests that the cultivation of wild plants began 10,000 to 12,000 years ago, when farmers began saving the seed from selected plants with desirable characteristics and planting them as cultivated crops, but that they also continued to harvest wild wheat, and to consume both in their diet. There was no sudden replacement of wild varieties with selected ones – in fact, it was another 3,000 years before domesticated varieties began to be the dominant choice.

How did it spread?

Similarly, long periods of time separate the development of farming in south-west Asia and its spread to the distant reaches of Europe. Pinning down exactly how long it took has also shed light on how farming practices were spread. One hypothesis is that successful farmers moved out from south-west Asia in search of new land, colonizing new territory at the expense of indigenous hunter-gatherer communities. Another entirely different hypothesis proposes that successful ideas spread rapidly, therefore, farming techniques were adopted by indigenous hunter-gatherer communities once they could see the clear advantages that it brought to their farming neighbours.

If agriculture was spread by the movement of people, archaeologists would expect to find clear evidence of this in the DNA record. They could look for the evidence of Asian genes in the European population, representing the legacy of people whose successful strategies for survival enabled them to migrate and colonize new territories.

Recent studies have indeed found that south-west Asian genes account for about 12 per cent of Europe's population. However, it found that most of the people with such genes live within a 1,000-km (625-mile) radius of the Fertile Crescent (*see The Iron Age*). The number drops by half at 2,000km (1,250 miles) and is negligible by 3,000km (1,875 miles). In other words, it is entirely possible that small pioneer groups could have carried farming into those areas of Europe closest to the Middle East – and we can pinpoint places, such as Crete, that we know to have been directly colonized

Left An ear of wild wheat (*right*), which sheds its grains on reaching maturity, in contrast to cultivated 'einkorn' wheat (*left*), which retains its grains and has to be threshed. Distribution of both has been studied at Middle Eastern sites, to assess how, where and when cultivation took over from the gathering of wild wheat.

Left The remains of charred wheat at Neolithic farming sites in the Middle East have supplied a wealth of material for studying and carbon dating ancient agricultural produce.

Above Each of the Neolithic houses at Skara Brae, on Orkney, Scotland, has a large square central hearth for heating and cooking.

Above Poulnabrone Dolmen, the Burren, Ireland; such monuments act as statements of ancestral land ownership.

Monuments and land ownership

The rise of farming is associated with the building of majestic monuments, many of them so well constructed that they have survived several millennia to be designated as World Heritage Sites, including the impressive chamber tombs of Ireland and Spain, the remarkable stone rows and megalithic structures of Brittany and the large Neolithic settlement at Skara Brae on the west coast of mainland Orkney, Scotland, which Gordon Childe excavated in between 1928 and 1930.

One explanation for the simultaneous rise of farming and monument building is the need to stamp your claim to ownership on the landscape. Once people stop regarding the whole of the landscape as a resource for all, once they begin to clear the wilderness and create fields, once they begin to invest time and effort in the building of houses, an important threshold has been crossed – one begins to develop proprietorial feelings based in the investment of labour and the resources used in creating that fertile landscape.

For all these and many other reasons, archaeologists can speculate that the consolidation of farming as a way of life led to the construction of new forms of communal structure that are used for burial, ritual and for the reinforcement of kinship ties through feasting and betrothals – and for making a visible public statement about the community's entitlement to the land.

in this way because the plants and animals and even the female figurines are the same as those in Neolithic Turkey. However, the uptake of agriculture deeper into northern and western Europe has to be the result of people copying their neighbours and learning from them – the so-called diffusion model for the spread of

innovative ideas, instead of the displacement model based on the mass movement of people.

A slow journey

Attempts to trace the path and chronology of agriculture by carbon dating suggests that agriculture arrived in Europe by two routes – via the

Balkans and via the Mediterranean – and that it spread across Europe in fits and starts, in a long, slow process that took several thousand years. For a long time, agriculture spread no further than the Carpathian Plain in Hungary.

This so-called halt on the onward journey of farming has been explained by biologists as a period during which cereals from Asia had to undergo further selection to find strains better adapted to the colder, wetter environments of Europe. Some archaeologists argue that the hunter-gatherer communities had to become domesticated – in other words, to overcome their resistance to farming, and to adopt the settled lifestyles that go with it.

Left Crop threshing techniques still used by pre-industrial societies help archaeobotanists to understand how prehistoric peoples processed their crops. This Nepalese community continues to rely upon this ancient agricultural method.

Metallurgy

In the three-age system, the Neolithic period gives way to the Bronze Age, but this is a term that needs some explanation, because the Copper Age comes before the Bronze Age in some parts of the world and in other parts the Iron Age follows the Stone Age with no copper or bronze phases.

Above The Trundholm sun chariot (1400BC): a spectacular example of Bronze-Age technology.

Like agriculture, metallurgy seems to have been discovered independently in many different regions. Archaeologists have found copper tools dating from 4800BC at Mehrgarh, in Baluchistan, Pakistan, a site that has also produced some of the earliest evidence of farming (7000BC) in the Middle East. Of similar date is Wadi Faynan, in Jordan, where slag and ore has been found close to a known source of copper, and in the Timna Valley in Israel, currently held to be the oldest known copper mine in the world. In addition, raw unprocessed copper was also beaten into tools and weapons as early as 4000BC at the Old Copper Complex, in present-day Michigan and Wisconsin in the United States.

Left Ancient Egyptian copper mining at Timna Park, in modern Israel, left these formations named 'King Solomon's Pillars'.

The earliest appearance of true bronze (a stronger metal than copper, which is made by adding tin and arsenic to the copper ore) occurs in sites in Iran in the late 4th and the beginning of the 3rd millennium BC. By the mid-3rd millennium BC the skill of making bronze has been acquired by people living in a large area extending from the Persian Gulf to the Aegean.

The transition from stone to copper, and from copper to bronze, was not a one-way street – it did not lead to the immediate replacement of obsolescent stone tools with modern shiny metal. On the contrary, early metal objects deliberately copy their stone and wooden antecedents, while stone battle-axes are found in the graves of the northern European Corded Ware culture of 3,200BC onward that are modelled on copper axes, with lines carved to imitate the appearance of the mould marks on cast metal axes.

The magic of metal

The earliest use of metal consists of jewellery made from gold and copper – visible metallic elements that can be mined relatively easily. Many of the objects that define the earliest of the metal-using civilizations seem to be designed for ornamental use, as gifts for the gods and for use in ceremonies, rather than as work tools or weapons.

Left This roundhouse at Flag Fen, near the town of Peterborough, UK, reconstructs a typical Bronze-Age dwelling.

Above This Bronze-Age stone circle on Machrie Moor, Isle of Arran, Scotland, replaced an earlier Neolithic timber circle.

In 18th and 19th century Europe, some of the most spectacular finds from the Bronze Age were dug or ploughed up by farmers and peat cutters, and today early metalwork is often found by metal detectorists, especially in watery landscapes that have since dried up, or on river foreshores such as the Thames in London, England. Rivers and lakes seem to have been favoured places for objects to be deposited as gifts to the gods – and not just any old gifts – some of the finds from peat bogs and fens include objects of the highest craftsmanship, unique pieces that would have needed skill and patience to create, such as the astonishing sun chariot of Trundholm, in Denmark, a bronze statue of a horse pulling the sun across the sky in a chariot, deposited in a bog sometime in the 15th century BC. It is as if there is a belief that metal, obtained by the transforming power of fire on rock, is regarded as something mystical and god-given, a gift that demands in return something back from its human beneficiaries.

Landscape clearance

In time, however, the development of more utilitarian metalwork led to a speeding up of the process by which the wilderness was tamed. Environmental archaeologists now believe that the Bronze Age (from about 3500BC) was the period in which the process of landscape clearance, which began in the Neolithic period, finally sped up. The Bronze Age is when there was a transformation of large tracts of woodland – interspersed with occasional clearings – into a settled landscape consisting of farms and the occasional woods, as well as fields, hedges, tracks, cattle enclosures, ponds and water scapes and drove roads.

Below The caves at Qumran result from early mining and were later used as a hiding place for the jars containing the Dead Sea Scrolls.

The trees that were cut down to create fields were not wasted, but were used for constructing houses and trackways — some of which provide access into the watery landscapes of fen and lakes, where wildfowl and fish can be trapped. The huge effort involved in taming and farming the landscape is based on the availability of sharp-edged lightweight and portable metal tools in the form of axes, adzes and chisels, and the evidence for this comes from dateable timbers found preserved in waterlogged sites, where the size and shape of the cut marks used to shape the timbers for causeways and house platforms exactly match the axes found at the site.

Above Nordic Bronze-Age petroglyphs depicting a ship on the Vitlyckehäll stone near Tanumshede, in western Sweden.

Specialization

The significance of metallurgy does not lie only in the availability of new technologies, new weapons, and new forms of defence (shields and armour), nor in finely wrought luxury goods, such as jewellery, ritual bowls, cauldrons, bells and incense burners. Just as importantly, it is in this period that some archaeologists believe there is a rise of specialist functions – in which some people make their living from their craft, as metalworkers, potters or farmers – in which trade plays a part, and in which there is the opportunity for accumulating wealth through the exercise of a particular skill, through trade or the monopolistic control of the resources for making metal.

The Iron Age

The last of the three traditional divisions of Old World prehistory is the Iron Age (from 1200BC). It stretches back to the first farmers and continues to the classical cultures of Greece and Rome in Europe and the complex societies of Africa, Asia and the Americas.

One of the insights that archaeologists are beginning to develop through the study of whole landscapes rather than isolated sites is the degree of continuity that can mark the long sweep of prehistory. This is evident in the way that succeeding generations respect the monuments of the past when they build new monuments.

Stonehenge in the south of England, for example, has been built and rebuilt many times. Although the circle of giant trilithons – the sets of three stones consisting of two uprights joined by a horizontal lintel – that defines the most popular image of Stonehenge dates from the Neolithic of 2500BC, there are earlier structures and circles on the site dating back to the first Mesolithic post holes of

Below The loops on these Iron-Age axes from Spain were used to tie the axe head to a wooden shaft.

around 8000BC. In addition, the circle itself is surrounded by hundreds of Bronze- and Iron-Age burial mounds.

Another example of this innate conservatism and respect for tradition is the slow rate at which iron was adopted as a material for tools and weapons. There is evidence to show that iron-making was practised in the Middle Bronze Age. Simple iron tools are known in the Netherlands by soon after 1300BC, and evidence for early iron-making in Britain, at the Bronze Age village of Hartshill Quarry in Berkshire, England, has recently been dated to 1260BC. Ironically, the earliest iron tools in Europe are punches and engraving tools that were probably used for cutting decoration onto the surface of bronze objects.

Below The Castro de Barona Iron-Age hillfort, the home of an Iberian Celtic clan, sits on a peninsula jutting out into the sea.

Above Reconstructions of Iron-Age roundhouses of wood and reed suggest they were surprisingly comfortable.

Trade and inflation

Perhaps what caused the switch from bronze to iron as the predominant metal was some sort of disruption to the trade routes through which tin – an essential material for making bronze – was obtained and distributed from various mines as far apart as Cornwall, Brittany, Galicia and the Italian island of Elba. Evidence for disruption, or an escalation in the price of such materials, can be found in the large numbers of hoards of broken bronze objects that are found in late Bronze Age contexts, probably saved for recycling.

Many more societies had access to supplies of the relatively abundant iron ore than had access to tin. Bronze continued to be used for coinage, brooches, jewellery, military equipment,

bells and horse harnesses for another 2,000 years but the cheaper, stronger and more abundant iron became the metal of choice for tools and weaponry. Robust iron ploughs and spades enabled heavier soils to be cultivated, and something as humble and ordinary as the iron nail made it easier to construct durable buildings.

Warfare and control

It has been argued that the greater availability of iron also led to the rise of warfare during this period, because those cultures that possessed iron-making skills were able to equip larger armies. Equally, it could be argued that the equipping of armies was not the cause of war, but rather the symptom of an age of increasing conflict, perhaps related to population growth and competition for resources.

The Roman answer to competition was conquest. From small beginnings as a small Iron-Age settlement on the River Tiber, the Romans began by conquering their neighbours, including the Etruscans, descendants of metal-working migrants who had settled in Italy to exploit the rich ores there, and then went on to carve out a massive empire taking in much of modern Europe and western Asia.

Above Ancient weaponry is reconstructed and used as part of an investigation into the lives of Iron-Age people living in Denmark.

The Iron Age continued well into the post-Roman period in parts of Europe that lay outside the Roman Empire, and it is in many ways more enigmatic to archaeologists than the more distant past. In their desire to explain, archaeologists often simplify and overlook facts that do not fit their story. For a long time, accounts of the Iron Age have portrayed this as a period of growing homogenization – that is, the beginning of a process that we now call globalization, when we all became more alike in our lifestyles.

Now, archaeologists are looking at the Iron Age again and finding evidence of the contrary – a period of diversity and experimentation, some of which is backward looking (ancient religious sites were reused in the Iron Age after

Above This La Tène pot discovered at a burial mound in Brittany, northern France, has typical geometric patterning, and would have been used as a cremation urn.

being abandoned for up to 1,000 years) and some of which is progressive – for example, literary and archaeological sources show that the Romans prized and imported geese, soap, amber, hides and clothing and wagons manufactured by the Iron-Age people of Germany.

Below A refuge and a fishing base: the Araisi Lake fortress at Gauja, Latvia.

Who were the Celts?

The dominant Iron-Age culture of Europe found north of the Alps is often called Celtic, a culture that is instantly linked with the curvilinear patterning that decorates metalwork items, such as mirrors and shields (such as the Battersea shield, found in the River Thames at Battersea, London, and now in the British Museum), and other objects.

The idea that the people of northern Europe were all Celts seems to have arisen from confusion among 18th- and 19th-century linguistic scholars who noted the overlap between Celtic art and its survival into the Dark-Age Gaelic speaking parts of Atlantic Europe. They hypothesized the Celtic decorative style and the so-called Celtic languages were part of the same cultural package – Celtic speakers produced Celtic art – which, in turn, was used to suggest that the Celts were a people who migrated and spread from some point of origin in Europe, who spread to dominate northern Europe but then were pushed to the margins of western Europe by the Romans.

Now archaeologists believe that so-called Celtic art (also known as La Tène art) originated in the Rhineland, the border region between the Germanic east and the Gallic west of Europe, and that it spread because it was fashionable among the different native people of Europe, rather than through the migration of people. As for the Celtic languages, they were perhaps only spoken by the people of the Atlantic west, restricted to the inhabitants of west Gaul, western Iberia, Ireland, Wales, Scotland and the west of England. In other words, there was no Celtic migration, no Celtic race that once dominated Europe; instead Celticity is all about those phenomena of markets, fashion and consumption.

Complex Societies

The more archaeologists have learnt about the past, the more obvious it has become that human cultures are far more complex than can be conveyed by the three-age system and the use of such simple terms as stone, copper, bronze and iron to describe a specific age, or era, in our past.

The three-age system is based on the observation that simple technologies tell archaeologists something about our ancestor's lifestyles and interactions. Their toolkits are a good indication of their core activities and capabilities, and when these same toolkits are found in association with dwellings of a particular size and shape or pottery of a specific design, it is not unreasonable to deduce that this represents a related group of people, even if they are spread out over a vast geographic terrain.

However, to characterize our own age as simply the 'Silicon Age' would tell archaeologists of the future nothing about the rich lives that people often lead today. Likewise, the terms applied in a similar way to past eras, such as the Stone Age, tell archaeologists little about the many differences that exist between the Bronze Ages in various region, such as China, the Aegean, Ireland, Pakistan or Wisconsin.

Subdivisions

Today, there is an increasing tendency for archaeologists to distinguish these regional subcategories and qualify their use of the three-age system by writing about the Aegean Bronze Age, the Atlantic Bronze Age or the Andean Bronze Age. These regional categories are then further subdivided into periods – for example, Early, Middle and Late Bronze Age. Archaeologists can distinguish further subcultures on the basis of tool shape or pottery variations – hence the distinction in the Neolithic of western Europe between 'Beaker' culture (pottery with a distinctive inverted bell-shaped profile)

and the Corded Ware culture (pottery decorated by pressing woven cord into the semi-dry pottery before firing).

However, for some archaeologists, even these distinctions are too broad and blunt. They reject the notion that cultures can be classified in such simplistic terms and prefer to highlight the unique characteristics of individual sites. There is some validity to this approach. Stonehenge is genuinely unique in that no other henge in the world has trilithons. Conversely, henges, as a monument type, are found all over Neolithic Europe, so many archaeologists accept that the sites they study have characteristics that are unique but also that enable them to be compared and classified.

Above Pottery excavated at Delos, the mythical birthplace of Apollo, Greek god of light, medicine and music.

Above Early temples on Gozo, Malta, suggest the rise of a priestly elite.

Classical civilizations

Many archaeological chronologies now consist of a complex matrix of period, tool type, region and other cultural characteristics – codes that can seem complex to the non-specialist. Cutting across this complexity, however, are the monolithic terms that many of us are familiar with from the media – indeed, they are the classical civilizations and empires out of which the study of archaeology in all its complexity was to emerge: Babylonia, Assyria, Persia, the ancient Greeks, ancient Egypt, the Macedonian Empire, the Roman Empire, the Carthaginian Empire, the Mongol Empire, the Mayans, Aztecs and Incas, the Chinese Empire and so on.

Above Ancient Minoan records of grain, olive oil and dried fruit stores were inscribed on discs such as this one.

What distinguishes these cultures and empires is politics. Prehistorians tend to think about the societies they study as politically neutral – groups of roughly equal people co-existing and trading. However, complex stratified societies begin to emerge in the Neolithic era, in which some people are more equal than others – priests, potters and traders, for example. The Copper and Bronze Ages see the rise of hierarchical societies in which there is a growing difference between the homes of subsistence farmers living on what they can produce to feed and clothe themselves, and the palatial structures that mark out the elite – those who control mines, workshops or trade networks. Examples include some of the most famous of the world's arch-aeological sites, such as the palace of Knossos on Minoan Crete and the great cities of Ur, Uruk and Babylon.

The beginning of history

Associated with the rise of complex societies is the invention of writing and record keeping. Archaeologists make a distinction between proto-writing, which is the use of symbols (such as those found in ancient rock art, which convey information to those who have been initiated into their meaning) and writing systems consisting of signs that have a verbal or linguistic equivalent – each sign representing a vowel, consonant, syllable or word – and that follow the same grammatical rules as the spoken language.

Above The palace at Knossos was one of the largest Minoan palaces: in 1700BC, the whole complex contained some 14,000 rooms.

Right Was Stonehenge built by an egalitarian culture of co-operating families, or by a powerful leader using slaves or hired labour?

Above Tablets written in ancient Sumerian cuneiform script record the distribution of food.

The inventors of writing

To date, ancient Sumerians are acknowledged as the inventors of writing. This Bronze-Age culture of the late 4th millennium BC consisted of some 12 settlements in lower Mesopotamia (modern Iraq), each centred on a temple, and ruled by a king or priestly elite. Large numbers of records dating from 3500BC have been excavated from these temples. Written on clay tablets, in a script that later develops into cuneiform (meaning 'wedge-shaped', from the shape of the stylus used to form the letters), they relate to the storage and distribution of the city's food supplies.

Written records mark the essential boundary between what is considered archaeology and history. For many centuries, archaeology was thought to be an inferior tool for understanding the past – the blunt instrument that you used if no finer tool was available – and where archaeological evidence was used in the historical period, it was made to fit the written records. Only recently has archaeology begun to break away to the extent that archaeologists are now prepared to challenge what the history books say, and characterize much ancient history as fictional, poetic, dramatic, symbolic, rhetorical and biased – and not by any means a definitive and literal account of the past.

Today, the historian and the archaeologist bring different perspectives to this shared territory in which one studies written records and the other the material remains of the past to shed light on the complex cultures and civilizations of the past, their origins, rise, fall and demise, and the essential continuities that link them at the basic level of how ordinary people subsist and survive.

Ancient Civilizations

One way to try to come to terms with the sheer intricacy of complex stratified societies is to look at what was happening in different parts of the world at particular points in time to compare their technological development and social behaviour.

Around 3500BC, in the region known as Mesopotamia (Greek for 'between the rivers', referring to the fertile lands watered by the Rivers Tigris and Euphrates, now mainly in Iraq), city-states begin to develop, in which land and livestock were not owned by individuals, but were communally owned. They were managed by a governor or king, who also had a priestly function and lived in a complex that combined temple and palace.

Mesopotamian cities, such as Ur and Uruk, had populations of up to 65,000 people, and traded widely. The 'Royal Standard of Ur', found by British archaeologist Sir Leonard Woolley in the 1920s and dating from about 2600BC (now in London's British Museum), is a wooden box inlaid with scenes of war and peace made from shell and lapis lazuli from as far away as Afghanistan.

It is likely that Ur got its precious materials through trade with the walled towns of the valley of the Indus,

the longest and most important river in modern Pakistan, where the Harappan civilization (named after Harappa, one of the first Indus Valley settlements to be excavated) flourished from 3300 to 1900BC. Planned towns developed about 2600BC, with populations in the thousands and segregated residential and industrial areas, piped water, drains and sewers and houses built of standard-sized bricks, suggesting mass production and centralized control.

Other early developments

At about the same time, the potter's wheel was first invented in eastern China by the people of the Longshan culture, who are also noted for astonishingly delicate black vessels known as egg-shell pottery. In 2650BC in Egypt, the first pyramid was built (the Great Pyramid of Khufu), and in 2440BC in Europe the massive sarsen stone circle of upright stones capped by a lintel that we associate with today's

Above Some archaeologists argue that Olmec art suggests a strong link with African culture.

Stonehenge were erected – possibly using technology based on wheels or rollers. From pottery figurines found in graves in Mesopotamia and the Indus Valley, we know that wheeled sledges and bullock carts were in use in Asia and India at this date.

In North America, the slow transition from a hunting and gathering society to farming is under way, but on the west coast of South America, the people of the Valdivia culture (modern Ecuador) are already farming maize, kidney beans, squash, cassava and peppers for food, and cotton plants for clothing and living in circular dwellings around a central plaza. They produced

Above Modern Iraq occupies the same lands as ancient Mesopotamia, known as the 'Cradle of civilization', from whose palace at Ur this statue was found.

Left The familiar profile of the Sphinx with the first pyramid of Khufu in the background.

the earliest sculptures of the human figure yet found in the Americas and appear, from similarities in pottery styles, to be in contact with the ancient Jÿmon culture of Kyÿshü, Japan – suggesting trans-Pacific trade.

From 2500 to 1250BC

The trends set in motion 1,000 years earlier – cities, long distance trade, writing and wheeled transport – are now part of world culture, in a swathe from the Pacific to the Atlantic, and Egyptian art, religion, prosperity and influence reach their height under the pharaohs. Minoan palace culture is established on the island of Crete with the building of the fresco-decorated palace at Knossos from 2000BC. Meanwhile, Chinese civilization as we know it today has its roots in the establishment of the Shang dynasty, with its hereditary rulers, fully developed writing systems, divination, astronomy, musical instruments and astonishing skill in casting ceremonial bronze vessels.

At 1500BC, boat-borne migrants known as the Lapita people begin to spread out from south-east Asia, travelling eastward to colonize the islands of the Pacific. In the Americas, there is evidence of similar long-distance sea and coastal journeys in the trade links between the people of the Great Lakes region in North America and those in Central America.

From 1250 to 500BC

The Olmec civilization of Mexico, believed to have been the progenitor of later Mesoamerican civilizations, such as the Maya, can be traced to cities and ceremonial centres established around 1200BC along the coast of Mexico, prospering on the trade in rare minerals used for toolmaking, including obsidian, basalt and jade. Metallurgy is the basis for wealth creation that accounts for the rise of the ancient Etruscans in Italy, the Phoenicians in north Africa and the people of mainland and island Greece. Long-distance trade is built on mastery of the sea, and the ancient Greeks

Right The ruins of Troy, whose story is told in Homer's *Iliad*, probably composed in the 8th century BC and one of earliest complete works of ancient literature to have survived.

develop mass-production techniques for building fast and manoeuvrable galleys, which proved an effective war machine in the constant battles that are depicted on their painted pottery. This decoration evolved from simple geometrical designs in the tenth millennium BC to depictions of Homeric epics 200 years later. Those epics, perhaps recorded from older oral poetry in the 8th century BC, tell of a historical conflict that dates from

City founders

A key debate in archaeology is the question of whether cities result from the decree of a single powerful leader or political entity ordering their construction, around a central palace or temple, or whether they arise from the organic growth of smaller groups or individuals who elect to live together. The theory of a singular leader as the catalyst for urbanization is reinforced by the Gilgamesh epic, the story of a powerful leader who built the city of Uruk, in what is today southern Iraq, the world's oldest named city.

Recent research carried out at Tell Brak, located in northern Mesopotamia (today's northern Iraq and north-eastern Syria) suggests that cities have more complex origins. The pattern of surface finds suggests that the city consisted of a central mound surrounded by settlement clusters. These clusters were separated from one another, indicating social distance among the groups. The patterns of settlement and distance from the central mound also signified autonomy from the political centre of the city.

between 1194BC and 1184BC, the dates of the major burning layers at the city of Troy (period VIIa). Warrior training and prowess are also the basis for the Olympic games, which were established in 776BC at the sanctuary of Zeus, in the ancient city of Olympia.

The books of the Old Testament date from this period, having been written down during the 11th to 2nd centuries BC, although describing events, such as the Exodus of the Jewish people from Egypt to the Promised Land, that probably took place between 1444 and 1290BC. However, the Jewish religion itself probably dates back further still – Abraham, the father of the Jewish people, is thought to have lived around 2000BC.

Measurement

Many cultures have contributed to the mathematical systems used as the basis for calendars, weights and measures. Evidence that humans first used fingers for counting comes from the fact that many numerical systems are based on patterns of tens. However, the ancient Sumerians used 60 as their base, which accounts for the 30 days of the month and the division of time into 60 seconds and minutes – these systems were adopted in ancient Egypt and passed to much of the Old World. Arabic numerals and the concept of zero were introduced to the West via trade between Europe and north Africa, but ultimately they derive from far older counting systems developed in India.

Ancient to Recent Past

From 500BC, the world as we know it today began to take shape. This is the era of emperors and heroes, but just as important is the role of religion in creating new forms of society, art and architecture, and of globalization – the merging of cultures that began with a voyage to the New World.

The Classical Age refers to the ancient Greek and Roman civilizations. Greece reached its peak in the 5th century BC, and in 336BC Alexander the Great of Macedon embarked on his conquest of the Persian Empire that led to the spread of Hellenic ideas from Greece to the borders of Tibet and India. The conquering Romans saw themselves as the heirs of Greek civilization, and adopted their deities, art and buildings styles. Virgil's national foundation myth – the *Aeneid* – mimics the ancient Greek poet Homer in its epic form and claims that Rome was founded by refugees from the burning city of Troy. At the peak of its power, the Roman Empire spread further still than Alexander's, its conquests stretching from Ireland in the west to the port towns of western India.

Just as importantly, these empires opened up trade routes along which ideas flowed as well as commodities,

and mystic eastern religions, including Mithraism and Christianity, challenged the cult of the emperor worship during the 1st and 2nd centuries AD. This led to the Edict of Milan (AD313), the decree of the Roman emperor Constantine the Great (c. 280–337) that established religious tolerance within the empire and ended the state persecution of Christians.

The Middle Ages

Constantine's reign marks the beginning of the Middle Ages in Europe – the intermediate period between the Classical Age and the Modern Era. It is a period in which religion has as big an impact on the archaeological record as the emperors and warriors of the

Above The Dharmarajika, Pakistan, one of the oldest stupas (dome-shaped Buddhist monuments or relic houses) in the world.

classical world, not only in Europe but all over the world, leading to new building types – the temples, mosques, monasteries and cathedrals that represent some of the oldest surviving monuments still in active use.

Although Hinduism (whose origins can be traced to the 3rd millennium BC), Zoroastrianism (16th century BC), Buddhism and Janeism (both 6th century BC) and Shinto (300BC) are all older than Christianity, it is not until the 1st century AD that these world religions begin to expand geographically and to make a significant

Above The Villa Adriana, Italy, the country palace of the Roman Emperor Hadrian.

Above Chichén Itzá, Yucatan, Mexico, seat of Mayan culture from 600–1000AD.

Left This medieval sculpture from Gandhara, Pakistan, shows knowledge of Roman classical art and suggests trade with the West.

mark in the archaeological record. Their expansion and influence are intimately connected to state sponsorship. It is with the adoption of these religions by leaders and elites that they spread and flower as major influences not just on the culture but also on the politics of the era. The so-called 'Donation of Constantine', the document in which the Roman emperor bequeathed his powers and territories to the Catholic Church and nominates the Pope as his heir, is now known to be a medieval forgery, but it typifies the connection between religion and politics that characterizes the Middle Ages in Europe. When Islam is founded by the followers of the holy prophet Muhammad (c. 570–632), it too makes no distinction between the religious and the political realms.

Similarly, the great cities of the Maya in Central America result from the fusion of religion and politics, constructed around pyramidal structures that serve both as religious centres and as the palaces of the Mayan rulers, including the renowned complex at Chichen Itza, which has its Asian counterpart in the stupendous Hindu (and later Buddhist) state temple and Khmer capital at Angkor Wat.

The Modern Era

Different cultures and people have different dates for when the Modern Era begins, but many scholars and university departments have adopted

Left This tobacco pipe symbolizes the post-Columban era when gold, potatoes and tobacco became the first New World exports.

the date of 1500 as a convenient starting point for what is variously called post-medieval or historical archaeology. The Modern Era has its roots in the Florentine Renaissance of the previous century, when scholars sponsored by the Medici family of bankers began to rediscover the works of ancient Greek and Roman authors by scouring the monasteries and libraries of Christian Europe as well as Islamic north Africa for forgotten manuscripts. The first crude excavations of Hadrian's villa and sites in Rome produced astonishing sculptures that had a profound effect on the art of the day, and on contemporary thinking, as Christian theologians began to absorb pagan classical ideals.

It was through this contact with the Islamic world, which until 1492 included the Emirate of Granada in southern Spain, that Europe learnt the mathematical and navigational ideas that underpinned their voyages of discovery and that led to that key date of 1492, when Columbus undertook his five-week voyage across the Atlantic Ocean from the Canary Islands to the Bahamas.

Above The tomb of Columbus, Granada, Spain, honours the father of globalization.

Globalization

That one small voyage began the process of European expansion that characterizes the Modern Era. It is a process that has left a number of signatures in the archaeological record: including the large numbers of people who died from measles and smallpox imported from Europe to which they lacked immunity, the ubiquity of the clay pipes and the mass-produced ceramics that are found on sites from Australia to the Americas, and in the archaeology of the Transatlantic slave trade, where archaeologists in Africa, Europe and the Americas have sought to recover the evidence of a shameful period in our history.

Globalization has also had an important impact on archaeology. The roots of the discipline can be traced to the activities of 17th- and 18th-century antiquaries curious about the objects dug up from burial mounds or the ruins of ancient Greece and Rome, but the modern subject owes a great deal to the study of the many different people and cultures of the world. In fact, in some American universities, archaeology is not a separate subject, but one of four identified sub-disciplines of anthropology, the study of humanity.

Above Buddha statues recovered from the jungle which overran Angkor Wat, Cambodia.

Continental Africa

Nowhere else in the world can match Africa for the sheer longevity and diversity of its archaeology, nor for its range of contemporary cultures that have much to teach ethno-archaeologists about the diversity of people's art, beliefs and lifestyles.

Africa and archaeology are intertwined in many ways, and the discipline can trace many of its roots to the activities of Egyptologists who were sent out from European capitals to explore the ancient Nile. They often came back laden with the treasures that now fill many national museums – and not just mummies and temple facades. Some of the most fascinating finds from ancient Egypt are the everyday items that have survived remarkably unblemished, such as clothing, basketry and wooden furniture made during a period that saw the rise of Egypt as an international power, from 1550 to 1070BC.

Everyday life in Egypt

Thanks to its arid conditions, which help to preserve organic materials, ancient Egypt is still capable of surprising archaeologists, such as the discovery in 2006 of the timbers and rigging of the world's oldest sea-going vessels, dating from the middle of the second millennium BC, in caves at the Red Sea port of Marsa Gawasis. Stone anchors, limestone blocks, cedar and acacia wood beams, oar blades and over 80 perfectly preserved coils of different-sized ropes were discovered in the 4 caves. The extensive damage to the timbers by marine worms provided

Above Built in the 11th century, Great Zimbabwe has some of the oldest stone structures in Southern Africa.

clear evidence of their use as sea-going vessels, which disproved the long-held belief that the ancient Egyptians did not travel long distances by sea because of poor naval technology.

The sheer quantity and scale of Egyptian archaeological remains – such as the astonishing Great Pyramid of Giza, which was finished around 2560BC and is the only one of the Seven Wonders of the Ancient World – have so dominated our view of ancient Africa, that they led to the mistaken notion that the rest of the continent's past was backward and primitive.

However, even as Howard Carter was busy excavating the best-preserved pharaonic tomb ever found in the Valley of the Kings – that of Tutankhamun – over the winter of 1922 and 1923, German and British archaeologists were beginning to explore the fossil rich Olduvai Gorge in eastern Africa's Great Rift Valley, and their discoveries would soon open archaeologists' eyes to the African origins of the human race.

Bantu expansion

Accounting for the vast periods of time since the birth of toolmaking and hunter-gatherer society in Africa has proven to be a challenging task for archaeologists. However, underlying the complexity of the several hundred

Left Giza's Great Pyramid fascinated antiquaries and gave birth to Egyptian studies.

different peoples found in modern sub-Saharan Africa, they have detected a common language and culture, which is known as Bantu (a word that simply means 'the people' in many Bantu-derived languages).

As with the spread of agriculture in Europe and Asia, archaeologists argue over whether the physical migration of people led to the spread of the Bantu language and with it the adoption of farming from 7000BC and of copper-, bronze- and iron-working between 4000 and 500BC, or whether this knowledge was spread organically through contact with new ideas. Equally, there is much debate about the origins of Bantu culture, and whether it comes from south-eastern Nigeria, or further west, in Zambia and the Congo.

Aksum and Ethiopia

What is not in doubt is that the wide-spread adoption of farming, the use of iron for making tools and weapons, and of trade with Europe and Asia, led to the creation of some rich and powerful empires, such as the Aksumite Empire of northern Ethiopia and Eritrea.

Above Bantu oath-taking figure: Bantu languages and culture underlie the diversity of modern Africa.

It flourished from the 4th century BC and thrived on trade with Arabia, India and ancient Rome, exporting ivory, tortoiseshell, gold and emeralds, and trading in silk and spices. As well as its characteristic giant obelisks, used to mark the graves of its elite, the Aksumite civilization is best known for the frescoed rock-cut churches of such Ethiopian towns as Axum, Lalibela and Gondar, which resulted from the kingdom's adoption of Christianity around AD325.

Present-day Zimbabwe was the centre of another great empire from the 10th to 15th centuries AD. The ruins of the capital, Great Zimbabwe, once home to 18,000 people, are some of the oldest structures to survive in southern Africa; characteristic of the culture are dry-stone walled conical towers. The city controlled the main trading routes from South Africa to the Zambezi, where Arabic traders would come to buy locally mined gold, copper and precious stones, as well as animal hides, ivory and metal goods.

The slave trade and museum collections

Europe's determination to break the Asian monopoly on the trade in such luxury goods as gold, silver, silk, ivory, pepper and spices led to the first voyages of discovery in the 15th century and the beginnings of direct contact between sub-Saharan Africa and Europe. One tragic consequence was the expansion of the slave trade,

leading to what some archaeologists call the third 'out of Africa' diaspora, because slaves were shipped as a captive labour force first to the newly colonized islands of the Canaries and Madeira, then to the Caribbean and the Americas, and then to the European mainland. Slavery has itself now become a big subject of archaeological research, and because so few historical records survive, the excavation of sugar plantations is one way of recovering the facts about this shameful trade.

Treasures that have been acquired from Africa have helped to foster an appreciation of the often overlooked artistry and skill of Africans. However, they also present museums with an ethical dilemma, as the modern nations of the world ask for the return of cultural treasures that were taken from them in ways that are now considered unfair and unjust.

Above The rock-cut churches of Lalibela, Ethiopia, were inspired by Biblical accounts of the New Jerusalem, home to God and the saints.

Benin Bronzes

Colonial expansion by European powers into Africa led to one of history's great ironies: by conquest and looting, Europeans came to appreciate the African culture. The Benin Bronzes are an example. These detailed sculptures cast in the kingdom of Benin (today's central and northern Nigeria) from the 13th to the 16th centuries were taken by British forces in a 'Punitive Expedition' in 1897. They now occupy pride of place in many archaeological collections, such as that at the British Museum.

Left A ceremonial hip pendant worn by Benin chiefs.

Asia and Australasia

Asia is home to some of the oldest continuous civilizations, with cultures as varied as that of the Tamils of southern India, or of the Han people of China and as old as the ancient Greeks or Romans — yet their civilizations continue to thrive, where other dynasties and empires have passed into dust.

In the past, the focus of much archaeo-logical research in Asia has been limited to the western regions (the ancient Near East), in modern Iran, Iraq, Turkey, Syria and in the Indus Valley region of what is now Afghanistan, Turkmenistan, Pakistan and western India. It is in these regions that agri-culture, metallurgy, cities and settled state societies originated, along with the languages and writing and counting systems that are used by 62 per cent of today's world populations. Here, American and European archaeologists compete to claim older and still older evidence of the defining traits of civilization, but this pattern of research is slowly changing with the develop-ment of indigenous archaeological

Below The widely-studied archaeology of the Indus Valley includes some of the oldest and largest towns of the ancient world.

research programmes, which are showing what a melting pot of king-doms, dynasties and religions this was.

Empires and religion

In India, it has been suggested that there is a continuity between the Indus Valley civilization of 3300BC and the Vedic period of the 2nd and 1st millennia BC. This is when the sacred Sanskrit texts known as the Vedas were composed, laying the foundation of Hinduism and the many independent kingdoms and republics that flourished from about 550BC, contemporary with Cyrus the Great (590–530BC), whose vast Persian Empire spread right to the Indus River.

Other great conquerors, such as Alexander the Great (356–323BC), the ancient Greek king of Macedon, also built extensive empires that reached to the borders of India. However, within

Above Terracotta warriors from the tomb of China's founder, Qin Shi Huang (died 210BC).

India itself, it was Ashoka (304–232BC) who united much of the subcontinent under one ruler and who embraced Buddhism, establishing schools and monasteries; he also placed moral ideals at the core of government. His model of kingship influenced the dynasties of southern India and many South-east Asian countries, including Cambodia, Laos, Myanmar (Burma), Thailand, and Vietnam, as did the twin influences of Hinduism and Buddhism.

The rich archaeological legacy of Angkor Wat, in Cambodia, results from this religious fusion, built in the 12th century AD as a temple to the Hindu deity Vishnu, and beautifully carved with scenes from the Hindu creation myth, then converted to Buddhist use in the 14th century.

The Chinese state

To the north, contemporary with Ashoka, Qin Shihuan (259–210BC) took an entirely different path to the unification of the vast Chinese Empire. Rather than encouraging diversity and tolerance in scholarship and religion, China's first emperor introduced the strong central control that continues to characterize China today — outlawing the ancient Chinese ethical and philosophical systems developed from the teachings of Confucius, with its humanistic emphasis on the civilized individual, and putting in its place the idea of the state as arbiter and the emperor as god. He was known to history as the initiator of such massive

Frozen tombs of Siberia

The nomadic Pazyryk people of Siberia were merchants whose constant journeying on horseback along the trade routes connecting China to Europe from the 5th century BC is reflected in their art. Preserved by the permafrost of Siberia, their frozen tombs have yielded tattooed bodies, saddles, saddle bags, clothing, children's toys of felt, carpets and gilded wooden figurines, all of which demonstrate the assimilation of artistic ideas from the different people with whom they came into contact, from the Vikings of Scandinavia to the Buddhists and Hindus of Asia.

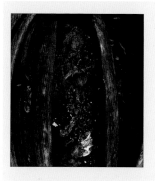

Above Siberian 'Ice Maiden', frozen in her wooden tomb for 2,500 years.

Above This distinctive Lapita pottery marks the cemeteries of the people who set out (perhaps from Vietnam, Taiwan or the Philippines) to colonize the Pacific islands from 1350BC.

infrastructural projects as the Great Wall of China and the national road system. It was not until 1974 that his greatest legacy, the terracotta army, was discovered, buried in a massive mausoleum in China's ancient capital, Xi'an. That underground army, found by farmers digging a well, is estimated to be 8,000 strong, and is now the instantly recognizable international icon for China's past.

Nomads by sea and by land

These huge civilizations, builders of monuments that have become the basis of heritage-based tourism worldwide, can sometimes blind archaeologists to the achievements of ordinary people, whose traces were barely visible in the archaeological record until the recent advent of DNA. This revealed the astonishing journeys that were made in the past, dispelling the belief that people were relatively immobile until the age of cars and aircraft.

For example, the Lapita people (named after the location of archaeological site on the Pacific island of New Caledonia, where their pottery was first recognized) travelled astonishing distances from about 1500BC to colonize the many tiny and remote islands of Oceania. Distinctive Lapita pottery is found in cemeteries on numerous South Pacific islands, buried with or underneath human remains. A distinctive feature of Lapita cemeteries is that the skulls of the deceased are often removed to a ceremonial house, and a shell is placed in the grave where the skull should be. Some of the graves also contain material that has been carried vast distances. A piece of the volcanic, glass-like stone called obsidian, used for toolmaking, was found in a Fijian Lapita grave that had come from a mine on the island of New Britain in Papua New Guinea, some 4,500km (2,800 miles) to the west.

Modern Fijians have a myth that the descendants 'came from Africa', but the study of pig DNA tells a different story. The Neolithic colonizers of the Pacific carried pigs with them, and by comparing the genes of pigs from around the Asia-Pacific region, archaeologists have demonstrated that most of the region's pigs share a common ancestry, which can be traced to Vietnam. Other sources of evidence, including human genetic and linguistic data, support the idea that Pacific colonists first began their journey in Taiwan or the Philippines. This points to a steady migration eastward, with people moving from Vietnam along different routes through islands of South-east Asia, before fanning out on long oceanic journeys into the Pacific.

Long journeys by land and sea are by no means limited to the Lapita people. The Romani people were referred to as Gypsies based on the mistaken belief that they came from Egypt, but DNA studies have now established that they originated in the Punjab and Rajasthan regions of the Indian subcontinent, and that today's Romani, found all over Europe and North Africa, are the descendants of traders who have been journeying between Asia and Europe for more than 1,000 years.

Above The triple lion monument of Ashoka the Great, adopted as India's national monument.

The Americas

Daring seafaring journeys similar to those made by the Lapita people have brought people into the Americas. Others travelled long distances over a land bridge. However, exactly how and when these anonymous Asian people arrived remains the subject of research and considerable debate.

Most likely, many journeys were made rather than one. Some people travelled from Siberia, as big-game hunters tracked their quarry across the dried up Bering Strait and down the ice-free corridor east of the Rockies as the last glaciers began retreating about 13,000 years ago. Others came as seafarers out of the islands of Japan or the Pacific coasts of present-day Russia, hugging the coasts of Alaska and British Columbia as they hunted seals or harvested fish and seafood.

Some archaeologists believe there were even earlier journeys. A British-led team has found what it believes to be 40,000-year-old human footprints in New Mexico. Altogether 160 human footprints were found. Such an early date, derived from tests on the fossilized volcanic ash in which the footprints were found, has added to the tantalizing evidence from gene studies that links some of the people of southern America to indigenous Australians, suggesting that the first migrants to the Americas might have been seafarers from Australia.

The populous and sophisticated societies of pre-Columbian America were probably derived from fewer than 80 individuals, according to gene studies. Although that figure might seem small, bear in mind it probably represented just less than 1 per cent of the number of reproducing adults – about 9,000 – in northern Asia at the end of the ice age.

The rise of complex societies

Like their counterparts in Africa, Asia and Europe, these hunter-gatherer migrants developed agricultural systems. Squash and chilli were domesticated as early as 6000BC. Maize, beans and tomatoes soon followed, as did cotton, yucca and agave, all grown for textile fibres, and tree-borne fruits, including avocado, papaya and guava. Animal bones from food pits show that duck, deer and turkey were raised for meat, as were dogs, whose butchered bones are commonly found in middens dating from 3500BC onward.

Above Detail from the sinister 'games field' of Chichén Itzá, Mexico.

The availability of greater food resources through farming led to the rise of a sequence of complex and impressive cultures, especially in that area of Central America that stretches from Mexico to Costa Rica. This region saw the rise of some of the most advanced cultures of the Americas. They are grouped together as Meso-american cultures not just because they were geographical neighbours, but because they evidently shared ideas and innovations, including writing based on hieroglyphs, counting systems and formalized agricultural systems based on the movements of the sun, moon, planets and stellar constellations. They included the Olmec (1200BC to about 400BC) – which is sometimes described as the 'mother' culture for the later variants: the Teotihuacán (first millennium AD), the Maya (AD150–900), and the Aztec, Miztec and Zapotec (AD600 to the Spanish conquest of 1519).

Above Teotihuacán, the Aztec city in modern Mexico, was the biggest city in the Americas prior to European colonization.

Above The remnants in New Mexico of a settlement built by the Anasazi people (AD700–1130).

Above Excavating an American Indian site in Illinois, searching for evidence of trade, tools, weapons, religion, food and culture.

Above Machu Picchu was built in 1450, and its existence was only revealed to the wider world as recently as 1911.

The Lost City of the Incas

The story of Juanita, also known as the 'Ice Maiden', is that of a 14-year-old girl whose frozen remains were discovered on top of Mount Ampato near Arequipa, Peru, in 1995. Sacrificed around 1445, she is the best preserved of many young children offered to the gods, perhaps because of their purity, by the Inca people. Their empire arose from the highlands of Peru in the early 13th century and, through conquest and assimilation, grew to incorporate a large portion of western South America. Within a few years of the arrival of the Spanish conquistadors in 1532, Inca culture was dead, ravaged by war with the Spanish, and then by smallpox, typhus, flu, diphtheria and measles.

Those few who survived continued to farm the slopes of Machu Picchu meaning 'the Old Peak', and often referred to as 'the Lost City of the Incas'. Lost only to the outside world, it was 'rediscovered' in 1911 by Hiram Bingham, who was shown the secret route to the site by local people, paving the way for this icon of Inca civilization to be designated as a World Heritage Site in 1983 and become the most visited tourist attraction in Peru.

Today, Macchu Picchu illustrates many of the dilemmas that face archaeologists when a site becomes too popular. Visitors and film crews have caused damage to the site, and there is pressure from developers who want to construct a cable car to the ruins, to develop a luxury hotel, shop and restaurant complex and to build a helicopter landing pad. Despite this, the remoteness of Macchu Picchu in the slopes of the Andes, retains its power to evoke a sense both of human insignificance and of the astonishing lengths to which humans have gone to form and shape the world.

Mesoamerican life

Religion and symbolism permeated all aspects of Mesoamerican life, and archaeologists are still discovering the many ways in which buildings and landscape were shaped as a symbolic mirror of the real and mythical cosmos. For example, cities were aligned on the cardinal points of the compass and divided into a northern zone, which was the realm of the underworld where tombs are found, and a southern zone, with its markets and residential zones for the living. At the axis of the two zones, the monumental plaza, with its governmental buildings, defined the crossing point between the two worlds. Towering pyramids topped by temples reach to the heavens.

Long narrow L-shaped ball courts, with high side-walls, were the setting for some form of ritual game. The rules are unknown, but it is thought they might have involved human sacrifice – whether the winners, the losers or all of the participants lost their lives to the gods is far from clear. Plenty of finds demonstrate that human lives were sacrificed to the gods, and one of the great debates in Mesoamerican

Above The jungle still hides many Mayan sites, like the remains of this house in Aguateca, Guatemala, founded around AD100.

archaeology is the degree to which warfare and violence were implicated in the rise and often sudden demise of empires and dynasties.

If violence was implicated in the collapse of the city of Teotihuacán around AD750 or of the decline of the Mayan civilization from between AD800 and 1000, was it internal conflict, political, social or religious upheaval or attack from an external enemy? What is clear of course is that in every case it was the political and religious structures that collapsed. Ordinary people went on surviving, adapting and living in the world that might even have been regarded as a better place without priests and rulers calling for blood letting and sacrifice from time to time.

Case study: Çatalhöyük

Archaeologists in the 19th century presented our prehistoric ancestors as crude, brutish and inarticulate. The excavation of the Neolithic settlement of Çatalhöyük in modern Turkey, reveals just how far from the truth this equation is between prehistoric and primitive.

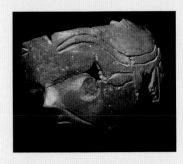

Archaeologists derive much of their information about the origins of agriculture, houses, cities and societies from the excavation of hillocks or mounds called 'tells', that might look natural at first but that are really the result of the accumulation of debris from thousands of years of human occupation on the site. Tells, when excavated, consist largely of the remains of the collapsed mud-brick walls of houses, temples and public buildings, but also of hearths, debris and industrial areas, which archaeologists have systematically excavated, looking for, and finding, the origins of early agricultural communities.

There are some 50,000 visible tells in Asia alone, testifying to the long settlement of the area. Tells are found as far east as the Indus Valley and as far west as Turkey, where the name for such a mound is höyük, as in Çatalhöyük, which means 'Fork Mound', the renowned Neolithic site in central Turkey, south-east of the present-day city of Konya.

Rooftop access

Occupied between 7400 and 6000BC, Çatalhöyük's mud-brick houses are so tightly packed that there are no streets. Rooftops served as a public plaza and people gained access to their homes by climbing down ladders. Each home consisted of a main room for working, cooking, eating and sleeping, and side rooms for storage and food preparation, and each housed a family of five to ten people.

Above One of the Neolithic pots excavated at Çatalhöyük, displaying faces.

Houses were kept scrupulously clean, and the mud-brick walls were coated in white plaster. Refuse was deposited in pits outside the home, and excavating these reveals that wild food (fish, waterfowl and eggs and wild cattle) was a major source of meat for the community, in addition to domesticated sheep and cattle. Food remains from storage bins reveal that wheat, barley and peas were grown, and almonds, pistachios and fruit were harvested from orchards. Pottery and obsidian tools were manufactured, and traded for dates from the Levant, sea shells from the Mediterranean or Red Sea and flint from Syria.

Left Archaeologists restore the red paint daubed on a wall on 'Building 59'.

Above An elevated view of one of the buildings in the southern portion of the site.

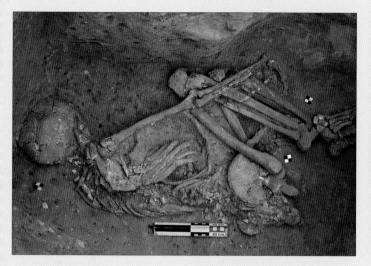

Above The inhabitants buried at Çatalhöyük were often wrapped in woven artefacts, which helped archaeologists to date the remains.

Above A child's skeleton – dated to the later phase of the settlement's history – lies in one of the burial 'hearths'.

Rich symbolism

However, what the excavation also reveals is the extent to which ritual and symbolism dominated people's lives. Instead of religion being concentrated in special buildings, every house seems to have doubled up as a shrine and cemetery. The walls were painted with hunting scenes and images of aurochs (wild cattle), leopards and vultures swooping down on headless figures. The heads of animals, including large horned bulls, were mounted on the walls, where they must have been a constant inconvenience, with their thrusting horns taking up limited interior space.

Stranger still, the people of Çatalhöyük lived with their deceased relatives all around them. The dead were buried in pits beneath hearths and under sleeping platforms, often placed in baskets or wrapped in reed mats. The skulls were occasionally dug up and given plaster faces, painted to recreate eyes and flesh and the appearance of living human flesh.

Every so often the houses themselves were ritually dismantled, leaving just the lower 90cm (3ft) or so of the original walls, which were then filled in with demolition rubble, sometimes taking great care to bury the domed clay oven and hearth in such a way as to protect it from damage. Objects such as stone axes and bone tools were deliberately buried in the fill and in the walls of the new home, as were female figurines modelled in clay or carved from horn and various types of stone. Similar carvings were also placed in food and grain storage bins.

Experimental archaeology

The current excavations at Çatalhöyük, which began in 1993 under the leadership of Ian Hodder (then of the University of Cambridge, now of Stanford University), have been described as the most ambitious excavation projects currently in progress anywhere in the world, partly because the excavators are seeking to pioneer new approaches to excavation in which everyone taking part can contribute to decision-making and to the interpretation of the site. In this sense, the excavation mirrors the structure of the original Çatalhöyük community, which appears to have been democratic to the extent that there are no obvious buildings that can be identified as palaces or temples. The population of Çatalhöyük – up to 8,000 people at any one time – seem to have lived together as genuine equals.

Ian Hodder says of the site: 'a child growing up in such a household would soon learn how the space was organized – where to bury the dead and where to make beads, where to find the obsidian cache and where to place offerings. Eventually, he or she would learn how to rebuild the house itself. Thus the rules of society were transferred not through some centralized control, but through the daily practices of the household.'

This is a site that challenges how archaeologists explain the mindset of Neolithic people, and some have said that it is not typical. Yet there are echoes all over the region of similar practices, especially in the female figurines and in the references to bulls (in Greek legend, the people of Europe are descended from Europa). The more sites archaeologists excavate from this period and in this region, the more evidence is discovered for a cult of skulls and for rituals involving dangerous animals, such as wild cattle, wild boar, leopards, snakes and scorpions. It is a curious paradox that such threatening creatures should be associated with the beginnings of domestication and the taming of nature.

213

SPECIALISMS

Given that archaeology is the study of the material remains of the human past, it follows that all artefacts – physical objects made by human hands – have an archaeology. Archaeologists can identify the earliest known book (as distinct from scrolls or writing tablets), for example, to 3rd-century Egypt (the so-called Gnostic manuscripts, found in 1945 buried in a jar near the Nile). They can use archaeological techniques to date the wooden boards, leather, textiles and paper from which books are made, they can study the techniques employed in their construction and they can excavate workshops or monastic scriptoria where they were made. Archaeology is, thus, a discipline with as many possible subjects as there are archaeologists willing to research them. There are major branches of the subject with a substantial body of literature; most of these specialisms have societies and journals dedicated to providing a forum for specialists to share their techniques and discoveries, and all of them can be studied at university.

Opposite Archaeologists specializing in Polynesian culture prepare to move the famous Easter Island monoliths.

Above Students of buildings' archaeology use a planning frame to record the outer stone structure of a medieval mill.

Above Specialists examine fragments of papyrus – an ancient writing material made from the pith of plants.

Above Archaeologists in Hanoi, Vietnam, restore the excavated ruins of an ancient citadel dating from the 7th century AD.

Industrial Archaeology

The term 'industrial archaeology' is used to mean the study of mining, manufacturing, transport and the other large-scale processes that are associated with the Industrial Revolution. Its origins can be traced to the 16th century, but industrial processes flourished from the late 18th century.

Instead of studying romantic ruins set in beautiful landscapes and excavating small-scale sites to find delicate traces of people living in the natural environment, industrial archaeologists study the remains of processes that left ugly scars across the landscape, reduced human beings to slavery as adjuncts of machines, caused disease, injury and death and have left a legacy of pollution and climate change across the planet. Unsurprisingly, industrial archaeologists have struggled for recognition – it is more challenging to persuade people that a redundant steel works or coal mine represents an important part of our heritage than a medieval abbey.

Industrial accomplishments

Since the 1950s, archaeologists have had an impact by standing up for the preservation and restoration of railways and canals and for the reuse of industrial buildings as loft-style apartments. They have persuaded UNESCO to recognize as World Heritage Sites some of the places that mark milestones in industrial history: in Great Britain these include the Blaenavon Industrial Landscape in south Wales, where steel making was invented; the Cornwall and West Devon Mining Landscapes, where deep-mining techniques were developed that are now practised all over the world; and New Lanark, in Scotland and Saltaire, in Yorkshire, as examples of model industrial towns where mill workers were given decent houses, clean water and education, in contrast to the exploitation they commonly experienced elsewhere. They have also encouraged the study of large landscapes and the connections between the different processes.

Above Excavating large industrial sites usually requires a tentative partnership between manpower and machinery.

Pioneers at Ironbridge

The Ironbridge Gorge landscape, in Shropshire, England, also a World Heritage Site, is an exemplar. It has been dubbed the birthplace of the Industrial Revolution because it was here that Abraham Darby I (1678–1717) perfected the smelting process that opened up an era of cheap iron (later used so effectively by his grandson, Abraham Darby III, who built the famous iron bridge after which the gorge is named in 1779).

When archaeologists studied the area in the 1970s, they pioneered techniques for documenting and preserving the entire community, with all its inter-related activities. They also created a

Above Ironbridge Gorge, birthplace of the Industrial Revolution, survives as an outdoor museum.

Above The Industrial Revolution was built on coal and iron from deep mines, brought to surface by pit head winding gear.

Above Parts of an industrial press for bending and shaping metal from a Russian steelworks.

new form of open-air museum, with multiple sites, as evidence of the messiness and complexity of the region's quarrying, iron-making and ceramic manufacturing industries, but also of the social consequences, preserving examples of workers' housing, shops, chapels and educational institutes. Ironbridge set an example that was rapidly taken up all over the world, and industrial archaeology is now a global activity.

In general, industrial archaeology involves recording landscapes, buildings, machinery and processes, by means of still photography and video film, measured drawings and written descriptions. Industrial archaeologists might record a specific industrial

Below This horse-drawn engine replicates ancient mining conditions in the Wieliczka Salt Mines in Poland.

complex, such as Isambard Kingdom Brunel's 1840s railway works at Swindon, Wiltshire, the factory for the world's first commercial railway, the Great Western Railway, or they might be interested in a specific building type – for example, studies have recently been published on naval dockyards, gunpowder factories, breweries, cotton mills and glassworks, seeking to write the history of an industry through its surviving physical remains.

Human knowledge

A future challenge for the discipline is not just to record redundant buildings and machinery, but also to capture the skills of people who still have the knowledge to keep the machines running and explain how they work. Much effort in industrial archaeology today is spent in gathering data in the form of interviews and video recordings of people working in those countries where historic industrial processes can still be found: Bessemer

(a process named after the English inventor Henry Bessemer) and open-hearth steel-making, long extinct in Sheffield, where the processes were developed, but still practised in the Urals, for example, or textile manufacture in and around Mumbai, using processes that Mahatma Ghandi saw in England in the 1890s but that have long ago disappeared from there.

Industrial archaeology commands political attention because it represents the heritage of many people alive today: people who themselves worked in coal mines, factories or steelworks, or those whose parents and grandparents did. This adds resonance and meaning to industrial heritage, but enormous challenges are involved in preserving industrial heritage and presenting it in any meaningful way because of the scale of industrial monuments, and the costs involved.

In Europe, one solution is the creation of the European Route of Industrial Heritage (ERIH), a network of important industrial sites that have left their mark on European industrial history and that are thought important enough to warrant government funding. At a global level, the International Committee for the Conservation of the Industrial Heritage (TICCIH) has been formed to promote the study, protection, conservation and explanation of the remains of industrialization, and their aims are set out in the Nizhny Tagil Charter for Industrial Heritage of 2003. Its website – www.mnactec. com/TICCIH – is a good starting point for anyone interested in learning more about the subject.

Coastal and Marine Archaeology

Water, although a difficult medium to work in, can be an excellent medium for preserving archaeological remains, from wrecked ships to drowned villages. Finding, excavating and preserving such remains requires a repertoire of highly specialized skills.

Above Recovering the anchor from Henry VIII's sunken flagship the *Mary Rose.*

The discovery of prehistoric villages beneath the lakes of Switzerland and Italy and at Mere, near Glastonbury in Somerset, England, alerted archaeologists as far back as the late 19th century to the exceptional state of preservation that exists in waterlogged sites. The absence of free oxygen in such sites excludes those bacteria that cause organic materials to rot and fade from the archaeological record. These 'anaerobic' or 'anoxic' sites, as they are called, are rich in the objects that give us a much more complete picture of daily life in the past, including

Below Archaeologists at Baia Bay, Italy, recover a marble couch that was once part of the Emperor Claudius's summer home.

complete human bodies – the so-called 'bog people' found in peat deposits in northern Europe.

Special excavation methods

Finding, excavating and preserving such remains requires a repertoire of highly specialized skills. In some cases, the site to be excavated can be drained of water by surrounding it with a coffer dam and pumping the water out. Such sites are often sprayed continually with water, or flooded again at the end of every day. Because stepping on the site will damage precious organic remains, as will the use of the digger's normal repertoire of metal barrow, pick, spade and trowel, the diggers are suspended above the remains on planks, lying

Above Divers survey a ship wrecked in 1025AD at Serçe Limani, Turkey, dubbed the 'Glass Ship', because of the large quantity of glass found in the vessel's cargo.

(uncomfortably) on their stomachs to excavate preserved timbers using plastic spatulas.

Organic finds begin to deteriorate as soon as they are exposed to air, so conservation is a high priority, with artefacts and ecofacts being placed in water tanks for immediate treatment, and eventually being preserved by careful drying and stabilization. In some cases, this involves the slow and expensive process of replacing the water content with wax. Such efforts are rewarded by the quality, nature and completeness of the finds assemblages from waterlogged sites, such as the 1,000 letters written on birch bark found at Novgorod in Russia that tell so much about daily in the city about AD1400, or the leather shoes from London that tell us about medieval fashions, or the beautiful silk cap imported from central Asia that was worn by a Viking settler in York, in the north of England, in the 10th century.

Working underwater

Compared with working on waterlogged sites, working underwater is more challenging still. Even sites lying in only a few feet of water demand diving skills and expensive specialist equipment. Sites further from land need a boat or ship to provide a means of access and support for the activities being undertaken in the water, as well as facilities for conservation. Weather, tides, strong currents and limited visibility provide an ever-changing and

Above Late medieval shoes recovered from a waterlogged site in excellent condition.

often dangerous work environment, but maritime archaeologists are not easily deterred and have developed survey and recording techniques that enable them to overcome such hazards. Unlike commercial salvagers who look for a quick return for their efforts, underwater archaeologists record everything they find – just like a terrestrial archaeologist – even if the process takes far longer and is more costly, because it involves expensive electronic measuring tools.

The history of the ship

Underwater archaeology has long been associated with the finding of historic shipwrecks – from the *Titanic* to the *Mary Rose* – and many maritime arch-aeologists specialize in the study of vessel construction and use, based on the wrecks they can excavate and lift. Not all of them involve diving. The oldest boat yet found, a plank-built vessel used for river transport 4,000 years ago, was found protruding from the peat and clay banks of the River Humber, at North Ferriby in Yorkshire, northern England, while the world's oldest known seagoing vessel, a Bronze Age boat from 1000BC, came from a deep waterlogged hole in the middle of Dover, the coastal town in south-east England. In Pisa, Italy, 16 ancient ships, complete with cargo, ropes, fishing equipment and stone anchors, were found a few hundred metres from the Leaning Tower in the silted up channel of a former river bed.

By contrast, hundreds of Spanish, French, English and American ships lie in waters of varying depth around

Above A diver surveying the remains of the *Mary Rose* underwater.

Mary Rose

Completed in 1511, the *Mary Rose* sank during an engagement with the French fleet in 1545. Her rediscovery and excavation from 1979 led to the pioneering of many techniques now commonly used on similar projects worldwide, as has her lifting from the sea bed on an iron frame on 11 October, 1982. This marked the beginning of a decades-long conservation project to preserve the remains of the hull and the many possessions of the crew that were found on board. These include musical instruments, games, quill pens and inkwells, leather-bound books, navigational and medical equipment; carpentry tools, guns, longbows, arrows, cooking and eating utensils and lanterns.

Finding out more

The following societies and institutes provide training in maritime arachaeology, from one-day introduction courses to advanced diving and archaeology studies:
• Great Britain, the Nautical Archaeology Society brings together professional and amateur archaeologists: www.nasportsmouth.org.uk
• Great Britain, Bristol University: www.bris.ac.uk/archanth/postgrad/maritime.html
• United States, the Institute of Nautical Archaeology based at Texas A&M University: ina.tamu.edu
• United States, the Lighthouse Archaeological Maritime Program (LAMP) in Florida: www.staugustinelighthouse.com/lamp.php
• Australia, Flinders University: ehlt.flinders.edu.au/archaeology/specialisations/maritime

the coastline of both sides of the Atlantic, evidence of European global exploration, the formation of colonial empires, and the development of trans-Atlantic economy. The port of Cádiz in Spain, which played such a key role in the Spanish colonization of the South American continent, is estimated to be the grave for no less than 800 ships that went to the bottom of the sea during the 16th to 18th centuries. The Nautical Archaeology Society has records of an amazing 40,000 historic ship losses around Great Britain's coast, but estimates that there are at least 60,000 more.

Some wrecks are of value to arch-aeologists because of their cargoes, and some because of what they might

reveal about naval architecture and shipbuilding technology, while others have immense historical value. For example, the *Bonhomme Richard*, the 42-gun frigate commanded by John Paul Jones, America's naval hero, who daringly brought the battle right to the shores of his enemy during the war of the American Revolution, winning America's first ever naval victory against a nation that had previously commanded the seas. Scuttled after the battle, Jones's flagship, *Bonhomme Richard*, lies somewhere off the English coast at Flamborough Head, east Yorkshire, where the Naval Historical Center in Washington and the Ocean Technology Foundation are currently scanning the ocean floor to find it.

Churches

Any building that has been altered since its original construction has an archaeology, because its history can be divided into different phases of construction. In the case of churches, some of which are nearly 2,000 years old, that archaeology can be complex.

Above The cross-shaped 13th-century Bet Giyorgis ('St George's church'), Lalibela, Ethiopia, is carved from solid rock.

Churches are among the world's oldest standing buildings. The earliest churches in Europe stand on the sites of pagan temples, and incorporate Roman buildings into their crypts. By the Middle Ages, every parish community in Europe has a church, and most have survived to the present. Churches are not restricted to Europe. Some of the world's oldest churches survive in the Holy Land, in Egypt and Ethiopia, and in parts of Turkey, Syria, Lebanon, Jordan and Georgia – some of them converted to mosques, some surviving as remote rural churches or monasteries.

Over the centuries that have passed since these churches were constructed, they have been altered, remodelled and improved many times, in order to accommodate changing ceremonies and religious ideas, to cope with growing congregations, to keep up with the latest architectural fashion, or to incorporate the chapels and memorials of wealthy donors. Rarely is the church razed to the ground and rebuilt; more often the adaptation affects only part of the building, so that older parts survive, perhaps hidden under plaster or pierced by new windows, arches or doors.

Stratigraphy and style

Unravelling the precise sequence in which the church was built and altered is the challenge that faces church archaeologists, who use techniques like those of the terrestial archaeologist. A church (or any other multi-phase building for that matter) can be analysed by its stratigraphy, using logic to determine that one area of masonry must be older than another because of the way one area overlies the other or is bonded or abutted to it. Just as artefacts can be placed in chronological series, buildings can be phased on the basis of their stylistic details.

Most people are familiar with the names and rough dates of the broad categories of European architecture – classical, Romanesque, Gothic, Renaissance, Baroque, Neo-Gothic, Eclectic, Arts and Crafts and Modern –

but these are broad categories that architectural historians and building archaeologists have been studying and refining for some 300 years. The results of all that research are what enable an experienced church archaeologist to walk around a church, analysing the patterns and discontinuities in the exterior and interior walls and noting diagnostic architectural details, and make a good stab at giving the history of the building and the main phases of its construction and alteration.

New discoveries

Given that churches, from magnificent cathedrals and majestic monasteries to humble rural chapels, have been studied for so long, and given that nearly all of them now have written histories, one might ask whether there is anything left to learn. Most church archaeologists would say that the amount we do not know far exceeds the amount we do know, partly because many of the diagnostic details that enable church archaeology to be studied are hidden in places that are not normally accessible – high up in the soaring roof space or beneath the soil of the church floor – or are disguised by plasterwork or later masonry.

Church archaeology comes into its own once a church is subject to a major restoration programme that might include the introduction of scaffolding or the removal of floors or plasterwork – but the floors and plasterwork might

Above 12th-century San Joan de Casselles church, Andorra, served the spiritual needs of medieval pilgrims.

Above The medieval church at Berkeley Castle, Gloucestershire, UK, might have been built on top of a Saxon palace and nunnery.

themselves be of great archaeological interest and so should never be removed without prior study.

The Tomb of Christ

The importance of studying structures in situ is demonstrated in the restoration of the Rotunda of the Anastasis (the Resurrection), in the Church of the Holy Sepulchre in Jerusalem. It stands over a rock-cut tomb discovered by workers employed by the Roman emperor Constantine the Great in AD325, and has been revered since as the Tomb of Christ.

When the comparatively modern marble structure placed over the site of the Sepulchre was found to be bulging under the weight of its superstructure and in imminent danger of falling down, archaeologist Martin Biddle was allowed to study the structure in minute detail. He found numerous earlier structures, which he compared to an onion, one surviving inside the next. This enabled him to reconstruct the appearance of the tomb at various stages in history, including those periods when medieval pilgrims and Crusader Kings flocked to the Holy Land to visit the Sepulchre. Biddle also examined the remains of the original rock-cut tomb, which he identified as part of a 1st-century BC quarry, re-used as a Jewish cemetery in the 1st century AD. It was the site of a public building – a temple – built after Titus destroyed the city of Jerusalem after the Jewish Revolt of AD70.

This temple, perhaps dedicated to the Roman goddess Aphrodite, was

itself destroyed by Constantine's agents in AD325 as they searched for Calvary or Golgotha, the site of Christ's crucifixion, and the tomb identified as the place of his resurrection. To protect these holy places, Constantine then built the first in a series of magnificent Christian buildings, which have themselves been adapted, altered and repaired many times following their initial construction.

The lessons that emerge from many such exercises in unpeeling the onion of church history is that many such buildings are much older than they look, and that many have hidden

Above A specialist inspects worn stone on Notre Dame Cathedral in Paris, as part of a ten-year restoration project.

Above The masonry of walls and windows may offer clues as to construction dates.

Petrological analysis

Based on the assumption that builders use different materials each time they modify, adapt or extend a building, the history of a building can be revealed by petrological analysis. By examining the structure, it can show a change of stone size or type, or a change in construction technique, from large square-cut stones to small rectangular stones, or from stones laid in a regular pattern to those laid randomly. The methods of construction used for window or door openings can also be dated precisely: for example, the use of small flat stones and tiles set in a hemispherical arch, or the use of a single stone as a lintel. The history of a building can thus be analysed by recording the place, shape and position of the materials making up the fabric of the wall, and their geological type.

This technique, when used to study the eastern wall of the Saxon church at Deerhurst, in Gloucestershire, in the west of England, revealed a patchwork of 19 different types of stone, from the earliest Saxon masonry at the bottom of the wall, to the evidence of roof heightening and restoration work carried out in the 19th century. What interested archaeologists was the evidence of two triangular shapes high up on the wall, which led to the discovery of two panels on the interior with the faint signs of paintwork and of a figure scratched into the stone. Although only visible now under special lighting conditions, the lines were made by a 10th-century artist setting out the outlines before painting in the detail of what would have been vividly coloured saintly figures set in triangular niches.

Below The first church built in the United States, at Jamestown, Virginia.

histories that have yet to emerge. Sometimes, simply turning over a stone can reveal a new chapter to the building's history. This is exactly what happened when church archaeologist Warwick Rodwell was finishing a six-week excavation of the floor of Lichfield Cathedral, in the English Midlands, when a piece of masonry

was lifted to reveal, hidden on the underside, a beautifully carved angel, now known to be part of an 8th-century shrine to the cathedral's founder, St Chad, with much of its original painted decoration still intact. This find gives valuable insights into the possible appearance of the first Saxon church on the site.

Buildings

Some of the techniques used in church archaeology apply to any old or multi-period building, but archaeologists in this field use a huge range of other techniques, involving timber joints and tree-ring dating, door and window styles, brick sizes and bonding techniques and even paint analysis.

If you invite a house 'detective' into your home to analyse its structure, he or she will probably head straight to the attic, because this is where the tell-tale signs are often found that offer clues to the age of the house. Looking at the timbers that hold up the roof and keep the house dry, an archaeologist will gain some idea of the date from the wood itself – whether it is sawn or split, whether it is a relatively modern material, such as pine, or an older local wood, such as oak, chestnut or elm – from the type of truss (the structural framework of wood used to support the rafters and roofing material) and the joints used to join together the different timbers making up the truss.

Other clues include the thickness of the timbers – and whether they are from the branches of the tree or from the main trunk – whether there is any decorative work that might suggest the timbers were intended to be seen as the open roof of a hall, and whether there is any soot or smoke blackening – often the sign of an early house without a chimney. Of course, all of these features can be found, but will not necessarily date your house, because timber was a valuable resource that was often recycled. A buildings archaeologist will look for a range of clues and some degree of consistency – there is always the possibility that recycled timbers came from an earlier house on the same site.

Right When examining walls, archaeologists carefully look for clues that indicate where extensions have been added or alterations made at a later date to the original building.

Truss typology and dateable details

A buildings archaeologist can speak with confidence about dates based on analysing the roof trusses because many years of study by local architectural societies have established that roof trusses and jointing techniques have changed and evolved at regular intervals, depending on fashion, the availability of raw materials and the status of the house. Many of these changes are regional in character – such as the style of the carved ornamentation on door frames, for example, while some are national in character, such as the dimensions of standard house bricks at different periods in time, and the different patterns used for laying those bricks.

Once the dating of such features was broad and approximate, because it depended on being able to date the main construction phases of the building on the basis of written records – letters, diaries, leases, deeds and inventories. However, tree-ring dating (*see* Dendrochronology and Other Dating Methods) is now commonly employed to give much more precise dates to diagnostic features.

Above One of the main objectives of rescue projects is to make a record for posterity of buildings facing demolition.

Specialists within the field

There are some buildings archaeologists who specialize in the field known as vernacular architecture, which is the study of ordinary people's homes, how they developed and what those houses can tell us about living conditions in the past. Yet others specialize in studying the development of a particular building type – be it farmsteads, hospitals, prisons, silk mills, town halls, cinemas, theatres or railway stations. However, perhaps the biggest field of work for those who make a living from the study of buildings is in understanding and conserving what are termed 'polite' buildings, which often take the form of large public buildings, the grand houses of the aristocracy or historic monuments,

Below The depth of a roof beam can be a clue to its age: medieval beams were bigger because large trees were plentiful, but shipbuilding and warfare rapidly reduced the availability of mature timber.

Above 18th-century Kew Palace, London, was restored using clues from scraps of original paint and fabric surviving in attics and behind later panelling.

Above Vermont State House, United States, was painstakingly restored in the 1980s.

such as medieval castles. Many of these are owned by charitable bodies and are open to the public, and their care, conservation and presentation to the public depends on a detailed understanding of their archaeology.

From studying the structure of the building, it is possible to write a detailed history of which parts are the oldest, and what was added or changed over time. Tying those changes into written records then adds a human dimension. Arachaeologists might be able to say who built the library, as well as when. Buildings archaeology can be dry without a vivid sense of what that castle or stately home actually looked like at different stages in its history, and to understand this buildings arch-aeologists can literally 'excavate' the walls for tiny patches of surviving decorative surfaces by peeling away the different layers of paint, plaster or wallpaper to build up a dated sequence of decorative schemes.

Restoring Kew Palace

One recent example was the ten-year restoration of Kew Palace, in west London, which was completed in 2006. Although called a palace, this was a relatively small and intimate home

that served as a country retreat for the royal family in the late 18th century. It was built on the edge of a former royal park, which was developed into the Royal Botanic Gardens when the park was used for planting the many exotic plant specimens that British explorers sent back from their travels in Africa and Australasia.

Astonishingly, large parts of the palace remained untouched from since the time of King George III and Queen Charlotte (1800–1818), so it was possible to piece together the decorative scheme of 1804 by studying small flakes of paint and scraps of paper and fabric that had survived beneath later panelling. Where these had lost their original colour due to fading and ageing, a battery of scientific techniques, including chemical analysis and polarized light microscopy, were used to analyse the minerals and dyes employed in paints and furnishings.

The attics in particular yielded paint finds going back to the very first merchant's house of 1631 that was enlarged to create the palace. To show how the historically authentic decorative schemes were researched, one room has been left in its original state, unrestored, to enable visitors to see the evidence for themselves and compare the room as found with the vibrantly colourful bedrooms, library, boudoirs and reception rooms of the rest of the palace.

Vermont State House

Another classic example of archaeo-logy coming to the aid of a building restoration programme can be seen in the richly arrayed interiors of the Vermont State House, home to the government of the American state of Vermont. This is a fine example of Greek Revival architecture that opened in 1859 and was carefully restored in the 1980s. One of the challenges in building restoration is to decide which of the many decorative schemes in the history of a building should be given priority. In this case, rather than return all the rooms back to one point in time, the archaeologists recovered evidence for over a century of changing fashions and tastes, from the original Neoclassical style, to American Empire, Renaissance Revival, Rococo Revival and Aesthetic Movement.

Finding out more

The following websites are useful for buildings archaeology:
• Great Britian, the Institute of Historic Buildings Conservation: www.ihbc.org.uk
• United States, the National Trust for Historic Preservation: www.nationaltrust.org

Parks and Gardens

The archaeology of parks and gardens — known as 'designed' landscapes as distinct from 'natural' or 'wild' ones — is a recent innovation, but one that has been employed to understand better the views that our ancestors might have enjoyed as they looked out from their cottages, castles or palaces.

Garden archaeology originally began as an extension to architectural history. Researchers turned from the restoration of buildings to ask questions about their landscape setting, based on the knowledge that many grand buildings were designed to be viewed as part of a carefully crafted ensemble of trees, fountains, statuary, flower beds, pathways and vistas.

Historical illustrations, in the form of paintings and engravings, can provide clues to the design and planting schemes of some important gardens, and more general evidence can be derived from literature, wall paintings, tapestries and manuscript illustrations. Fine paintings by Giusto di Utens in the Firenze com'era Museum in Florence, Italy, for example, depict 12 of the palaces of the Medici family. They show what they looked like with such

accuracy that they have been used as the basis for their restoration, as well as for providing a rich visual source for late 16th-century villa gardening in general.

However, artists often flattered their clients by showing a modified scene — much as artists today might 'airbrush out' inconvenient details or add features that might exist only in the imagination. In addition, few topographical paintings go back further than the 17th century, so garden archaeology has become an essential tool for filling in the missing details, especially of the earliest gardens.

Hard features

Gardens are, by nature, fleeting and ephemeral — since the ancient beginnings of poetry and song, gardens have been a metaphor for the transient pleasures of life and of a lost Paradise.

Above Medieval park and gardens restored within a castle complex, Gloucestershire, UK.

Yet some aspects of gardens have endured better than others. Using remote sensing devices (*see* Geophysical Surveys), such as ground penetrating radar, resistivity and magnetometry, archaeologists can often trace paths and borders, and even find the remains of paving materials, decorative edging and areas of soil disturbance or compaction where large trees or hedges once stood. Water pipes can be traced that supplied fountains or ponds, and the bases of walls, and sometimes the decorative masonry of garden buildings, summerhouses, seats and monuments can be recovered from excavation. These so-called 'hard' features help with the reconstruction of the garden's skeleton.

Above When the British took over the running of the Taj Mahal, India, they altered the original landscaping to resemble English lawns.

Right The gardens at Wawel Castle, Kraków, Poland, have had to be reconstructed from old records and archaeology.

Above The 18th-century formal gardens at Versailles Palace, France, were restored with archaeological help after storms uprooted many old trees in 1999.

Above Historically influenced gardens surround the mausoleum of Vietnam's first President, Ho Chi Minh (1890–1969), in Hanoi, Vietnam.

also research the utilitarian gardens that were once a vital source of food when people had to be self-sufficient. For example, the Bayleaf medieval garden at the Weald and Downland museum in Sussex, England, crosses over into experimental archaeology in recreating the appearance and planting of a medieval garden, using the tools and techniques of the period to see just what is involved in a subsistence lifestyle. One of the findings was just how difficult pest control could be if you wanted to have any food fit to eat after the birds, beetles, caterpillars and snails had taken their fill.

Soft features

Reconstruction of the 'soft' elements – the specific varieties of tree, shrub, hedge, herb, fruits, vegetables and flowers – is based on a combination of environmental archaeology, using surviving seeds and pollens as clues, and the study of contemporary eyewitness accounts and botanical books to see what was fashionable.

The result, as at the United States' Colonial Williamsburg, in Virginia, might be a conscious compromise between historical authenticity and modern planting. Contemporary accounts of the gardens in 1777 make it clear that the York River and the James River could be seen from the gardens, but nobody wanted to cut down the large and shady trees that now obscure that view and give the gardens so much of their character just for the sake of historical accuracy. Likewise, the beds are planted with a mix of historically accurate native plants and introduced plants capable of tolerating Virginia's hot and humid summers.

Garden patterns

It helps that many ornamental gardens, from Moghul India to the palaces of Islamic Spain and Portugal and to the palace of Versailles, were strictly geometrical in their layout, occupying a sequence of outdoor rooms. If one small part can be recovered through excavation, it is often possible to predict how the larger scheme might

have looked, and this principal has been used to restore such gardens as the Shakespearian knot gardens at New Palace in Stratford-on-Avon, England, the Great Garden at Het Loo Palace in the Netherlands and some of the great aristocratic gardens of 19th-century Russia, Germany, Poland, Hungary and the Czech Republic.

Gardens of utility and delight

One of the great discoveries of garden archaeologists in recent years is the extent to which the medieval castles of Europe, which we think of as dour defensive buildings, were designed with aesthetics in mind. Moats can be interpreted as defensive, but they also lend romance to the setting, reflecting the building in their still waters. From the castles of the Loire Valley in France to the Bishop's Palace at Wells, western England, or the vineyard backed castle at Bodiam in East Sussex, southern England, archaeologists surveying the landscape have found dams, sluices, embankments and rills that suggest water gardens were an integral part of the castle landscape. Castles were often designed to take advantage of what gardeners call 'borrowed views': distant hills and woodland that lie beyond the garden boundary but form a distant frame or focal point.

As well as seeking to understand the history and appearance of these aristocratic domains, garden archaeologists

Finding out more
Garden history societies are active in Great Britain, Australia and the United States. The website of the Garden History Society – www.gardenhistorysociety.org – has links to similar associations all over the world. Other useful garden archaeology websites are:
• International society, the Society for Garden Archaeology serves as a forum for people involved in the archaeological investigation of gardens and designed landscapes: www.gardenarchaeology.org
• United States, Dumbarton Oaks, Washington DC, part of Harvard University, a leading centre for the history of garden and landscape architecture: www.doaks.org
• United States, former home of Geoge Washington at Mount Vernon, VA: www.mountvernon.org
• United States, former home of Thomas Jefferson at Monticello, VA: www.monticello.org

Below Catalonian gardens in Spain.

Forensic Archaeology

In this emerging science, forensic archaeologists collect evidence for recent criminal investigations — especially in cases involving murder, genocide and war crimes — and also to solve ancient puzzles, such as the identity of Jack the Ripper or the cause of Beethoven's death.

Above Protective white suits must be worn by forensic archaeologists working at sensitive sites to prevent contamination of the evidence.

When human remains need to be excavated in ways that will enable the maximum amount of information to be retrieved about the identity of the deceased — and the causes and circumstances of that person's death — forensic archaeologists have the most experience to perform such a task. Many of the archaeologists who specialize in this field of investigative and legal archaeology have a background in some aspect of biology, such as molecular genetics or taphonomy (the chemical and biological processes that take place when materials decay).

The techniques that these archaeologists use at a crime scene are no different to those they would use to excavate human remains in an archaeological context. What they bring to the forensic process is a detailed knowledge of how to excavate buried remains, what to look for and how to interpret the pattern of evidence found. Where once the police might have used basic techniques to excavate a grave, archaeologists have taught them how to be systematic and precise.

Forensic methods

Called in by the police or by human rights agencies to help locate graves, forensic archaeologists use aerial photography and satellite imagery to survey for disturbed ground that might, for example, be the site of a mass grave, and remote sensing techniques help to refine the area of search. Precise excavation of grave sites follows archaeological principles in labelling and recording precise find spots of objects in and around the grave, using grids and three-dimensional measuring equipment. Soil samples are collected for environmental evidence, such as pollen, plant remains, charcoal, snails and insects and ash, all of which can help a forensic archaeologist to say something about the environment a victim has been in prior to their burial.

Studying human skeletal remains can help determine the age, sex and height of the deceased, and various individual characteristics, including body mass, musculature, state of health and dental imprint, all of which can be matched against health records. These are used not only in murder investigations, but also victim identification following disasters, such as earthquakes, flooding, terrorist attacks, fires or plane accidents. In murder investigations and post mortems, the archaeologists' knowledge of pathology can help distinguish between older injuries, those that might have been the cause of death and those that the body suffered after death.

Forensic archaeologists also look for objects associated with the grave, for instance clothing and footwear,

Left French forensic expert Pascal Kintz proved by the chemical analysis of his hair, shown here, that Napoléon died of arsenic poisoning.

Above Some ancient burial sites can still be regarded as crime scenes. Archaeologists will inspect bones for injuries that reflect foul play.

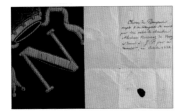

Above Forensic techniques have established that Beethoven was killed by lead in the medicines he was prescribed.

documentation, weapons and other potential evidence. They use their knowledge of the chemical and biological processes involved in decay to explain how long the items might have been buried in the ground and look for the tell-tale evidence of fingerprints, blood, DNA or fibres that can help trace the body to a person or crime scene.

Clues in human hair

Forensic archaeology has been used successfully on numerous occasions to try to identify the cause of death of various historical figures, often based on an analysis of the chemical residues in human hair. By studying both hair and bone fragments, the Viennese forensic expert Christian Reiter was able to determine, for example, that Beethoven's death in 1827 at the age of 57 was caused by lead poisoning. The exposure to lead probably came from treatments that Beethoven was given by his physician, Dr Andreas Wawruch, for cirrhosis of the liver, which was given as his cause of death at the time. Dr Wawruch's diary reveals that he prescribed salts containing lead, and that he rubbed cream containing lead into Beethoven's abdomen.

Professor Martin Warren, a forensic scientist of the University of Kent in England, studied a lock of hair from King George III, which had been kept at the Science Museum in London since the king's death in 1820. He concluded that the king had also taken medication that caused death, rather than cured him. Late in his life, the king had severe attacks of the hereditary illness called porphyria, and was treated with an 'emetic tartar' made from antimony, which contains high levels of arsenic.

In the case of Napoléon Bonaparte, arsenic poisoning was long suspected as the cause of the fallen French emperor's death in 1821, partly because Napoleon's body was found to be remarkably well preserved when it was moved in 1840, and arsenic is a strong preservative. Arsenic levels were indeed found in locks of Napoleon's hair. Some scientists have theorized that he was deliberately poisoned, while others thought his hair tonic contained arsenic, or that it came from the copper-arsenic minerals in the green wallpaper in his room. Now it is thought more likely that it came from antimony potassium tartrate given as a purgative to Napoléon in an attempt to cure stomach cancer, the real cause of his death.

Jack the Ripper

Ian Findlay, Professor of Molecular and Forensic Diagnostics at the University of Brisbane, has concluded that Jack the Ripper, the notorious serial killer who killed at least five women in London, England, in 1888, but who was never caught, could have been a woman. His conclusions came from extracting DNA from the gum on the envelopes and postage stamps of letters sent by 'the Ripper' to the police. They confirm the suspicions of Frederick Aberline, the detective who led the investigation at the time. The prime suspect is Mary Pearcey, who used a similar modus operandi to the Ripper in murdering her lover's wife, and who was hanged for that offence in 1890.

Finding out more
A number of colleges offer courses in forensic archaeology.
• Mercyhurst Archaeological Institute, Erie, Pennsylvania: mai.mercyhurst.edu – website has links to numerous related resources
• The Institute of Archaeology and Antiquity, Birmingham, UK: www.arch-ant.bham.ac.uk/arch/pforensic.htm
• The School of Conservation Sciences at the University of Bournemouth, UK: www.bournemouth.ac.uk/conservation

Above Historic crimes might yet be resolved using forensics: Jack the Ripper's knife is now displayed at London's Police Crime Museum.

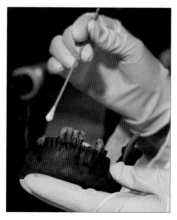

Above Forensic examination of jawbones and other body parts has enabled archaeologists to determine the ages of many victims of Pompeii.

A Face from the Past

One of the skills used in forensic archaeology is the reconstruction of someone's appearance from their skeletal remains. The techniques involved in bringing faces back to life can also be used to visualize historic figures, such as Helen of Troy and Cleopatra.

Above An archaeologist restores a painted wooden sarcophagus found near the famous Step Pyramid in Saqqara, Egypt.

Using anatomical knowledge and computer modelling mixed with the skills of a trained artist and portrait painter, a specialist in facial reconstruction can sculpt the head of a 2,000-year-old Roman soldier, a 1,500-year-old Anglo-Saxon farmer or even a 25,000-year-old Neanderthal.

The same skills have been used to reconstruct famous faces from the past. Shakespeare, Columbus, Cleopatra and Helen of Troy have all been visualized in this way, although in all four cases their reconstructions are based on portraits from coins, paintings, tomb sculptures, painted vases, written descriptions or pure guesswork, rather than on skeletal evidence. Much has been made of the fact that Cleopatra was not conventionally beautiful by modern Western standards, judging by the portraits on her coinage, a fact confirmed by the Roman author Plutarch, who said of Cleopatra that

'her actual beauty was not in itself so remarkable', instead the appeal lay in 'the attraction of her person, joining with the charm of her conversation, and the character that attended all she said or did…it was a pleasure merely to hear the sound of her voice'.

Archaeology has yet to find a way of recovering Cleopatra's voice, but where a skull survives as the basis for facial reconstruction, archaeologists no longer have to imagine or fantasize. Reconstructions are based on relating the distinctive clues provided by the human skull — jaw size, brow shape, nose profile — to the soft tissue that might have formed the living face. Such craniofacial reconstructions are based on a large body of measurements and other data relating to the musculature of the human face and how this varies according to a person's diet, age, gender and race. However, there is still much that is speculative, because the

precise appearance of noses and ears is impossible to predict from skull shape, and these add substantially to the unique appearance of the individual.

Kremlin beauties

Using such techniques, Sergie Nikitin, one of Russia's leading forensic archaeologists, has reconstructed the facial appearances of several of Russia's tsarinas and princesses from the 15th to the 18th centuries. Their remains come from Moscow's Kremlin cemetery, used for the burial of tsars and their families from 1407 to 1731. It was destroyed by Stalin in the 1930s as part of his campaign to break the influence of the Church in Russia. However, encased in stone coffins, the remains of five women, including those of Marfa Sobakina, the third wife of Ivan the Terrible, survived. Marfa was chosen by Ivan from 1,500 potential wives, chosen as the most beautiful women of their day. Their beauty may have been their downfall, as Marfa died two weeks after her marriage — poisoned, it is said, by a jealous rival, but more likely killed by use of toxic cosmetics based on white lead, mercury and arsenic.

The face of Tutankhamun

Putting a real face on the past is such an important technique for engaging the public that large sums have been invested in projects to accompany blockbuster exhibitions. One example

Above The face of Helen of Troy, as sculpted by the Neoclassical artist Antonio Canova.

Above The golden mask of Tutankhamun concealed the boy pharaoh's face for decades.

Above The partially reconstructed face of a Neanderthal woman who lived some 35,000 years ago near Sainte-Cesaire, France.

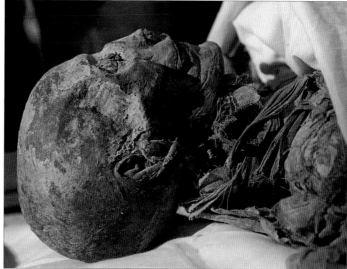

Above Queen Hatshepsut was among the most powerful female monarchs of ancient Egypt. She declared herself pharaoh after the death of her husband-brother Tuthmosis II.

was the reconstruction of the appearance of Tutankhamun, whose tomb has been the subject of enormous public interest since its discovery by Howard Carter in 1922.

The beautiful golden death mask of the boy pharaoh (who ruled from 1333–1324BC) has become an instantly recognizable icon for ancient Egypt, but three teams of scientists – Egyptian, French and American – used a battery of scientific techniques in 2005 to see what Tutankhamun really looked like and to find out as much as possible about his life from his mummified remains.

In reconstructing Tutankhamun's appearance, the three teams worked separately, and from different evidence. The Egyptian team worked from three-dimensional scans of the pharaoh's skull, while the French and American teams worked from casts of the skull; the American team worked blind, with no idea of whose appearance they were reconstructing. The resulting consensus was shown as the front cover of the June 2005 edition of *National Geographic* magazine, and caused some controversy because of the selection of a medium skin tone and hazel coloured eyes, illustrating the limits of current science in determining the precise appearance of genetically inherited characteristics that are difficult to determine from the skull alone.

An untimely death

One theory about the boy's death – that he died from a murderous blow to the head – was discounted through the discovery that loose pieces of bone at the back of the skull were removed as part of the embalming process and did not represent a mortal wound. However, a fractured leg bone – previously dismissed as the result of rough handling by embalmers after death, is now thought to have been caused by a fall from a height during the boy's short life; he also has some missing ribs that were sawn off, archaeologists believe, in an attempt to save the Pharaoh's life. It now looks as if Tutankhamun met his death in a riding or hunting accident, perhaps falling of his horse, resulting in the broken leg, and a kick to the chest that broke his ribs. Such severe injuries, if turning gangrenous, might have killed the young king within hours.

Revealing the boy king

The preserved face – and feet – of a boy king was revealed to the public for the first time in roughly 3,000 years when, in November 2007, the mummy was removed from its golden tomb and the linen covering his skin was removed by archaeologists. The mummy was later placed in a sealed cabinet within the tomb to protect it from the detrimental effects of exposure to humidity and warmth that began with Carter's famous exposition.

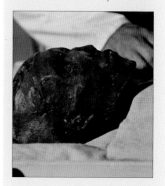

Above At last, the unmasked face of Tutankhamun is revealed to the world.

229

Battlefield Archaeology

As an important component of the world's cultural heritage, battlefields have increasingly become subject to the scrutiny of specialist archaeologists, whose twin aims are to commemorate and honour the war dead and to understand better some of the events on which history has turned.

The story of how battlefield archaeology has developed from a niche interest into a mainstream specialism in such a short time mirrors many other developments in archaeology and society. In its early days, archaeology was often run by military personnel, including Lieutenant-Colonel Thomas Edward Lawrence – perhaps better known as Lawrence of Arabia. His survey of the Negev Desert in 1914, funded by the Palestine Exploration Fund, served the dual purposes of archaeological and military intelligence. Another example is the work of Brigadier Sir Robert Eric Mortimer Wheeler, who ran his digs like a military operation and interpreted the classic sites that he dug – such as Maiden Castle – as massive prehistoric fortifications. Trained in the classics, fed on a literary diet of Greek and Roman war and heroism and with

personal experience of two world wars, it was not surprising that archaeologists of the first half of the 20th century often exaggerated the role of armed and organized conflict in the rise and fall of civilizations.

However, by the second half of the 20th century, and with growing momentum in the 1960s and 1970s, the reaction to war (coinciding as it did with anti-Vietnam demonstrations) led many archaeologists to seek alternative explanations for cultural change. Mortimer Wheeler's Maiden Castle, along with 'hill forts' in general, became market places and ritual sites rather than battlefields, and major developments in art and industry, in architecture and agriculture, were seen as the products of peace, not war, of trade and consumerism, not the imposition of a lifestyle by conquerors on the conquered.

Above A rare World War II 'Alan Williams Turret', designed for machine gun fire and installed to protect airfields.

Ancient violence

From these extreme positions, a middle way is now being sought. The precise extent to which warfare and violence played a part in changing the course of history is a topic that will always be debated by archaeologists, but that debate is increasingly informed by the study of ancient skeletal remains to find injuries that can best be explained as war wounds or evidence for human violence. Recent studies have shown that a surprising number of prehistoric skeletons do bear fractures or cuts that look like the results of lethal violence. The puzzle is whether this represents some form of routine warfare – the constant struggle of one community set against another – or

Above The multiple ramparts of Europe's largest Iron-Age hillfort at Maiden Castle, Dorset, UK, built 450–300BC.

Above Archaeologists survey underground tunnels built for storing precious works of art and top secret documents during World War II.

Above Archaeologists used GPS (Global Positioning Systems) to pinpoint the location of artefacts found on the site of Little Bighorn.

The Battle of Little Bighorn

Further back in time, the historical record might be less rich, or may not exist at all. A pioneering example of battlefield archaeology was the study of the site of the Battle of Little Bighorn on 25 June 1876, when Lt Col George A. Custer and 263 US army soldiers met their deaths in battle with several thousand Lakota Sioux, Cheyenne and Arapaho warriors. Here, metal-detector survey was used to locate and map discarded weapons and ammunition. Excavators discovered 320 historic artefacts connected with the battle, including arrow points, trouser buttons, boot nails, a screw from a Colt revolver backstrap and an assortment of cartridge cases and bullets. By careful analysis of these scant remains, it was possible to begin to construct a model of the placement and movement of people across the battlefield. Despite its mythic significance, almost nothing had been known previously about the precise details of this battle, commemorated in books and film as the site of 'Custer's Last Stand'. The evidence from the archaeology has now enabled a National Monument to be constructed telling the story of all those who took part in this conflict of two cultures.

Above A Colt .45' bullet located on the battlefield using metal detection.

Above Metal detectors survey the front line at Little Bighorn.

Above Locations of finds obtained via GPS were later added to a map of the battlefield.

whether we are seeing a rare event. It is perfectly possible that the remains that come from prehistoric burial mounds represent an elite warrior class, or they might even have been selected for burial in this way because of their heroism in, for example, a dual or a violent ritual.

Elusive battlefields

As well as studying human remains, archaeologists also study battle locations to understand precisely what happened in specific battles and to ensure that battlefields are recognized as important places for society as a whole. One of the first challenges facing battlefield archaeologists is to identify where the battle actually took place. Historically well-documented battles, such as the Battle of Bosworth Field (which led to the ascendancy of the Tudor dynasty on the English throne) or the Battle of Culloden, Bonnie Prince Charlie's attempt to regain the British throne) are surprisingly elusive when it comes to finding evidence on the ground.

Battlefields may only have witnessed events that lasted a mere three hours or so – perhaps a day at most – so there is far less evidence to find than with long-inhabited sites. Looters often searched battlefields after the event, so little survives other than the small items considered of little value. Typical tell-tale finds might consist of something as small as a button from a military uniform, a cap badge, or the remains of weapons and ammunition.

Battlefield archaeologists, therefore, expend a lot of time in field survey work, talking to farmers about any finds they might have made during ploughing and cultivation, looking at collections built up by metal detectorists, and studying the topography to try to match the landscape to historical descriptions of the battlefield.

Commemoration

The aim of this survey work is to locate as precisely as possible the location of historic battle sites, to compile battlefield inventories and to develop management and conservation plans to ensure that such historic places are well-protected from development and their significance is fully understood. Commemorating those who died becomes all the more important with recent battlefields, where archaeologists can identify the soldiers who died, and where there might be war veterans and relatives still alive who knew those men and women. Working on such sites is, in the memorable phrase of leading battlefield archaeologist, Nicholas Saunders, about 'excavating memories', where the emotional relationship between us and the past is far stronger than on most archaeological sites.

In the case of such large conflicts as the two world wars, battlefields can be discovered by accident, often as a result of a new road scheme or development. Battlefield archaeologists are called in to exercise skill and sensitivity in the excavation, recording and recovery of the remains, using historical resources, such as war records, diaries, letters, memoirs and photographs to write the detailed story of the site.

Ethnoarchaeology

From the Greek ethnos, *meaning 'race', ethno refers to a people or culture, thus, the term ethnoarchaeology. Specialists in this field immerse themselves in other people's lives — especially those of people whose way of life is more comparable to that of the prehistoric or medieval past than to modern life.*

Above Ancient lifestyles: canoes provide the main form of transport for Yanomami tribespeople in South America.

One of the most difficult challenges facing any archaeologist is to understand the meaning of artefacts and structures that survive in the archaeological record. To give one example, an archaeologist might be able to deduce that a certain type of pot, or a certain type of decoration, is associated with the dead because its type or decoration is found mainly on pots used in cemeteries and cremations, or from its absence in domestic contexts. However, this glimpse into the meaning of the pot is limited without a knowledge of why that shape or decoration is used in this way. 'If only we could go and ask the makers and users why they did this', is often the unspoken cry of many an archaeologist.

Ethnoarchaeology (also called social or cultural anthropology or ethnography) aims to do exactly that. Its practitioners live among the people of their chosen study group, aiming to integrate themselves to become as unobtrusive as possible, to learn their language and to devote a considerable period of their lives to asking questions and observing how people live.

The diversity of human experience

Perhaps one of the most celebrated of such studies was that of pioneer anthropologist Margaret Mead, whose book called *Coming of Age in Samoa* (1928) looked at the rites of passage associated with the transition from childhood to adulthood. The book was extremely influential in its time, but it was later criticized as being too naive and painting too idealistic a picture, taking too much on trust and not allowing for the fact that the people that she interviewed might not be telling the literal truth.

The methods used by ethnoarchaeologists have thus had to adapt to the fact that people might not want to divulge the detail of complex moral, religious and cosmological systems, so a new method of 'participant observation' was subsequently born in which the researcher gained a close and intimate familiarity with a given group of individuals through living with them over an extended period of time and observing at first-hand their interactions with their natural environment and such domestic and economic activities as food preparation, disposal of refuse and religion and ritual.

More recently, social anthropologists have realized that fundamental truths about human responses to their environments can be found anywhere. Walking down any street with an enquiring mind will suggest a hundred lines of anthropological enquiry about

Above Roma people have been gathering for centuries to honour their patron, Saint Sarah the Black, in the Camargue, southern France.

Left Proud of their roots, Native American Sioux continue to re-enact lost lifestyles in South Dakota, USA.

Above Observing tool use in pre-industrial societies provides valuable clues to the meaning of archaeological finds.

Objects and their meaning

To illustrate how objects can be containers of meaning, a professor once brought a plastic three-dimensional jigsaw puzzle of the globe into his lecture. He broke the jigsaw into its component parts and gave a piece to everyone in the room as he talked, as a souvenir of the lecture. If that piece of jigsaw became an archaeological find, the archaeologist would simply think 'jigsaw'. The archaeologist would not know that that jigsaw piece connected its owner to a specific lecture, on a particular day and at a particular place, and to a group of people who all shared the experience. Much of the material that is found in archaeology might have similar multiple resonances whose meanings can no longer be read without ingenuity and guesswork, and even then, archaeologists might never know what special meaning the object had for its owner.

Above The lifestyles of the Veda people in Sri Lanka may differ little from those of our Mesolithic hunter-gatherer ancestors.

Above Ethnoarchaeologists working with Romani people in Europe have recorded beliefs that reflect very ancient taboos and polarities.

the way that people behave and interact. Anthropologists today no longer work exclusively with the fast-disappearing groups of people who remain unaffected by modernity. Instead, they study all forms of human experience, including nomadic lifestyles and sedentary, conformist and non-conformist.

In the case of ethnoarchaeologists, they specifically look for the way that material culture reflects the manner in which people express gender and ethnicity, race, religion, family life or kinship. They also study such diverse topics as military culture, gang culture, gay culture, tattoo culture, the role of the media in society and popular culture, and the impact of globalization, drug culture, punk culture, Romani culture, the culture of the Japanese 'salaryman' and of the 'geisha'.

Observation as a stranger

The aim for the archaeologist is to try to turn him- or herself into a 'someone from Mars', taking nothing for granted and constantly asking what this means, how the meanings are expressed and transmuted and what impact they have on those who share or reject these cultural phenomena. Attempts to codify the results into some sort of universal system of symbol and meaning led to the rise of structuralism in archaeology in the 1960s and 1970s, built on the desire to place the study of human culture on a scientific and systematic basis.

Structuralism itself borrowed heavily from Freudian psychology, and the idea that polarities – such as black/white, male/female, young/old, inside/outside, clean/dirty, living/dead, summer/winter and famine/plenty – are fundamental to the human psyche. Some practitioners also approached the topic with a Marxist perspective that saw history in terms of immutable processes connected with the control of economic resources, which many critics of such thinking said reduced human beings to agents within a system that was beyond their influence or control, denying their freedom to act on the basis of personal choice.

Multiple resonances

Practitioners today are still happy to generalize about the phenomena they observe, but they are no longer so dogmatic in asserting that all humans

will behave in certain ways under certain conditions, or that all forms of behaviour can be reduced to a set of binary oppositions. Instead, what ethnoarchaeologists now bring to the subject is an awareness of the sheer complexity of human thought and behaviour. Normally in science the rule of Ockham's razor is observed, which says 'always look for the simplest explanation'. In studying human beings, the opposite often applies. What is found in archaeology often hints at the profundity and diversity of human behaviour, as those who study shamanism and the mindset behind rock art and cave paintings will testify. Indeed, even trying to explain in objective terms what a cathedral, church, temple or mosque is all about will quickly dispel any notion that human behaviour can be reduced to simple formulae.

Linguistic Archaeology

Language is key to what distinguishes humans and apes, and like the human evolutionary tree, languages have a genetic history. One of the most fascinating areas of archaeology is the attempt to map that history, working back from today's languages to the origins of languages.

Archaeologists who study human origins argue that it is language that makes us special. Our close relations in the evolutionary tree do not lack intelligence, but their intelligence is specific, based on a profound understanding of the local environment. The ability to think beyond that environment, to make an imaginary leap from the visible world to the worlds that lie beyond vision – whether over the physical horizon or in the supernatural world – are dependent on language, by which is meant not simply the association of a certain sound with a certain object, but a varied, fluid vocabulary, governed by rules of grammar.

Language probably developed as a consequence of social complexity. Primates in the wild live in relatively small groups, stay together and maintain regular physical and visual contact with all the other members of the group by sharing food and grooming. *Homo sapiens* developed language as a tactic for coping with the growth of the social group to the point where it is no longer feasible to know what is happening throughout the group. Like friends staying in touch via a telephone, language is key to sharing experiences that happen outside the immediate field of vision and for extending out knowledge of the world beyond localized understanding.

Songlines and Dreaming

The first language, if we could ever get back to it, might have a vocabulary related to geography and to the ability

Above Stories in stone: hieroglyphs cover the walls of the ancient Egyptian temple of Kom Ombo (150BC).

of people to be able to tell each other where they have been, and what they saw on, say, a hunting or foraging expedition. This is similar to the celebrated songlines, or dreaming tracks, of indigenous Australians, whose orally transmitted song cycles evoke the landscape as created during the primordial Dreaming, when the earth and everything upon it was created. These include such detailed descriptions of trees, rocks, waterholes and other landmarks that indigenous people can use them to navigate large distances through the deserts of Australia's interior.

It has been estimated that there were up to 750 distinct languages or dialects in Australia prior to the arrival of European colonists, and of these, some 200 indigenous languages survive today. How all these languages relate to each other is not at all clear, but attempts are being made to analyse and classify the languages in order to draw up a family tree for language groups and their influence on each other.

Indo-European linguistics

Such complex and difficult work goes back to the 18th century, when linguistic scholars began to recognize similarities in vocabulary between languages spoken in India and Europe. They theorized that people living in a swathe across Asia and Europe once spoke the same proto language – Indo-European – and that the linguistic

Above Some languages and writing systems are based on pictures or symbols, including ancient Egyptian, Chinese and Mayan scripts.

Above The evil spirit Nabulwinjbulwinj features in Aboriginal lore and in rock art at the Anbangbang rock shelter, Kakadu, Australia.

Above The Kharosthi alphabet, widely used in north-west India and central Asia until the 4th century AD, provides clues to even older Aramaic languages.

Above Languages as diverse as Spanish, Hindi, English and Urdu are ultimately derived from a common Indo-European tongue.

Above The Dead Sea Scrolls, displayed in Washington DC, are written in Aramaic, Greek and Hebrew, and are among the only surviving original texts of the Bible.

diversity we now experience is the result of communities developing new vocabularies in isolation, just as the many languages of modern Europe have evolved from Latin.

A purely theoretical language, the Proto-Indo-European language (PIE) was constructed by linguistic archaeologists by looking for words that are common to the modern languages derived from Indo-European, including Spanish, English, Hindi, Iranian, Bengali, Russian, German, French, Italian, Punjabi and Urdu. There are thousands of root words, including many of the words we use for counting and words indicative of a pre-industrial lifestyle, such as sheep, dog, wolf, fire, horse, cow, wife, king, priest, weave and wheel.

Links between languages and archaeology

More recently, linguistic archaeologists have observed that there is a strong correlation between language and genes. In very simple terms, people who speak the same language also share the same distinctive genetic profile. This discovery has revolutionized the study of language evolution, because genetic scientists are able to give approximate dates to the evolution of specific gene types (known as haplotypes), which in turn helps to give a relative date for the language. Linguistic historians can now see which people and languages in Africa, for

example, are related and identify the linguistic characteristics that they share and that might provide clues to the common language they once spoke.

It might be argued that language is not archaeology because it is not material, but language overlaps in many ways with some of archaeology's central concerns, such as the migration of people, the creation of cultural identity (what is more distinctive of a culture than its language?) and the influence of one culture over another (demonstrated by the absorption of new words from one language into another). Linguistic theorists imagine that there are several different ways that languages change and evolve, all of which have archaeological implications. They can affect each other simply through regular contact, by elite dominance, where one group imposes its language on another, or bars access to wealth to those who don't speak the language, or through some form of innovation (such as pottery, metallurgy or farming) that has its own vocabulary, relating to technological practice.

Although the study of linguistic history goes back to the 18th century, it is, in its latest manifestation, still in its infancy, with many questions still to be answered by geneticists, linguists and archaeologists working together.

Basque
Euskara, the language of the Basque people of north-west Spain, has been identified as a relic of a language older than Indo-European, just as DNA studies have identified the Basque people as having a distinctive genetic profile. Numerous attempts have been made to explain why Euskara has become what is known as a 'language isolate' (meaning that it is not derived from nor related to any other language), including the possibility that the Basque people are the remnants of an early migration of people into Europe who survived the ice ages that led to the demise of other early European settlers.

Archaeoastronomy

Many of the world's archaeological monuments incorporate significant alignments that relate to the movements of the sun, moon, planets, constellations and stars. Students of archaeoastronomy devote themselves to understanding what significance these alignments might have.

The 1965 publication of *Stonehenge Decoded*, in which astronomer Dr Gerald S. Hawkins argued that the monument was built to observe lunar and solar events, made a major new contribution to the understanding of the monument. It was followed by *Megalithic Sites in Britain* (1967) by Alexander Thom, Professor of Engineering at Oxford University, whose study of megalithic sites gave evidence for widespread astronomical knowledge in Neolithic Europe.

Simultaneously, research in the Americas established that the planting of crops and the distribution of water, in some of the major civilizations of pre-Columbian Central America, was controlled by a sophisticated calendrical system in which rocks and hilltops were used as markers for charting the passage of the sun and the seasons. Suddenly, it became possible to read whole landscapes, and not just isolated monuments, as evidence of a

sophisticated understanding on the part of our ancestors of cosmic events and their impact on human life.

Lunatic fringe

Ironically, these early studies, although based on meticulous measurements and observations at many hundreds of sites, received a cold welcome among many traditional archaeologists, while being embraced enthusiastically by hippies, pagans and new-age groups seeking to recover pre-Christian wisdom, beliefs and religious practices. Ordinary archaeologists were deterred from engaging with this new evidence because it involved a detailed knowledge of advanced mathematics and astronomy – but evidence continued to grow and it led to the creation of the entirely new (and still thriving) discipline of archaeoastronomy.

One of the main activities of archaeoastronomers is the study of alignments, but they also study objects such as the

Above Many archaeologists now believe that the siting of ancient monuments and megaliths in Europe show ancient astronomical learning.

Nebra sky disc (*see* Metal Detecting) that might have an astronomical significance. Wary of the connection with pseudoscience and 'false' archaeology, many of today's academic archaeoastronomers are concerned with distinguishing between demonstrable facts and coincidences, and the starting point for such studies is the attempt to recreate ancient sky conditions, so that the data from alignment studies can be set in its correct astronomical context.

Some argue that early forays into the discipline were over-enthusiastic and attributed to the builders of stone circles and alignments a knowledge of astronomy that they did not really

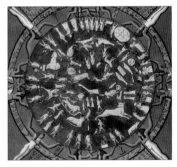

Above Ancient Egyptian people saw the stars forming the shapes of gods in human and animal form.

Left Druids gather at the ancient Neolithic site of Stonehenge, Wiltshire, England, to celebrate the summer solstice.

Above Prehistoric astrological art at Painted Rocks State Park, Arizona. Three points of sunlight cross the panel at the winter solstice.

Right The traditional Inca observations at Cusco continue to this day.

possess. Sophisticated patterns and alignments might simply be inherent properties of certain geometric shapes, rather than planned and conscious markers. Many east to west alignments are simple, and say nothing about the builders than that they wanted to express a sense of connection with the sun, the seasonal cycle, life, death, the ancestors, birth, renewal and fertility – simple connections that don't require deep astronomical knowledge.

Yet, there are real, discernible alignments that are common to many Mesolithic and Neolithic monuments throughout Europe, from the Urals to the west of Ireland and from Orkney to southern Spain. The big question about all these alignments is whether they mark sunrise or sunset, moonrise or moonset, summer or winter solstice. Answering such questions depends in part on other branches of archaeology, not least the study of animal remains from the feasting that took place at these monuments. In the case of Stonehenge, the age of the pig bones points to a winter festival, so the people who turn up at Stonehenge at the solstice (21 June) each year to watch the midsummer sunrise are celebrating a different event from that for which this and many similar monuments were intended – they should be turning up for the winter solstice sunset on 21 December.

New World evidence

In the Old World, archaeoastronomers have to base their investigations on mathematics and statistics. In the New World, they can consult the historical records of early colonizers, such as the 16th-century Spanish missionaries who lived among the people of Central and South America and wrote chronicles that today provide information about calendrical rituals. In August 1570, for example, the chronicler Cristóbal da Molina observed the Situa ritual at Cusco, the capital of the Inca Empire, in Peru, when, at the full moon, 4 groups of 100 warriors ran out of the palace along the kingdom's 4 main roads, aligned on the cardinal points of the compass, ordering everyone in the kingdom to wash their clothes, their tools and weapons in the rivers as a symbolic purification of the whole state.

Some ancient Inca practices survive today. Ethnographers in Peru often record conversations with farmers who still follow an agricultural cycle based on the Inca calendrical system, which uses the lunar cycle matched to the movements of the Pleiades constellation to guide their planting, irrigation and harvesting. It is this combination of practicality – the use of the natural cyclical events as a guide for agricultural activity – and the fascination with the sky and its capacity to fill people with awe, that makes archaeoastronomy an engrossing discipline.

Astronomy and power

Knowledge of the sun's movements can be translated into powerful political and ideological statements, as is explicit in Inca astronomical practices. These were linked to the political operations of the Inca king, who considered himself an offspring of the sun. Inca practice has its roots in much older monuments and religious beliefs: the 13 towers of Chankillo, built in the 4th century BC in the Casma-Sechin River basin, 150km (240 miles) north of Lima in Peru, is one of the oldest observatories for tracking the rising and setting of the sun yet found in South America. It is the equivalent of Stonehenge and hundreds of similar henges, enclosures, stone rows and earthen banks, passage graves, and megaliths built all over Europe during the Neolithic period.

Above The 13 towers of the solar observatory at Chankillo, Peru.

237

Case Study: Recreating Pugin's House

The Grange, the home of the 19th-century architect Augustus Pugin, set the pattern for neo-Gothic domestic architecture in Great Britain and abroad. Understanding the house and recreating its original appearance provides an excellent example of buildings archaeology in practice.

Above The striking wall covering with the Pugin family motto: *En Avant* ('Forward').

The Grange, located in the Kent town of Ramsgate in south-east England, was rescued from redevelopment in 1997 by the Landmark Trust, a charity that specializes in the restoration of historic buildings, which are then rented out as holiday homes. The Trust is selective in what it restores, but recognized in the sorry remains of a once-proud building a house of immense importance in the history of domestic architecture. It was designed by one of the most influential architects and designers of the 19th century, Augustus Welby Northmore Pugin (1812–52), a devout Catholic who did more than anyone to create the internationally ubiquitous Gothic revival, or Neo-Gothic style.

Pugin built many churches, schools, monasteries, convents and country houses, but he is best known as the man who designed the richly furnished interiors of the Houses of Parliament in London, after its medieval predecessor burned down in 1834.

Pugin built few domestic houses, but the house he built for himself in Ramsgate is particularly important because it set the template for much Victorian suburban architecture, not only in Great Britain but from Australia to the west coast of the United States. Restoring the house was an exercise in rediscovering the origins of the English middle-class suburban home.

Back to the original

Many changes had taken place since The Grange was completed in 1844, including various extensions and changes to the internal layout. Archive research enabled the Landmark Trust to locate notebooks and sketches that Pugin made of the original layout of the house. The floorplan has now been reinstated as Pugin intended, oriented to make the most of views of the sea, with three principal ground floor rooms – the drawing room, library and dining room – grouped around a square entrance hall, and a corridor leading off to the kitchen, to a square tower from which Pugin would watch passing ships, and to a private chapel.

If his design seems familiar now, it was radical in its time because it abandoned the classical symmetry of the preceding Georgian and Regency age. Sketches show that the house was designed from the inside out. Pugin thought first about what rooms he wanted and for what purpose, which ones needed fireplaces and which ones

Above Restoring the grand arch in the library using traditional craft techniques.

Left The exterior of the restored Grange. Pugin broke the architectural rules of his day by introducing asymmetry in place of the rigid symmetry of the Regency era.

needed windows, and he let the resulting plan dictate the external appearance. This was the reverse of the practice of the time, in which rooms were placed either side of a central passage, and life adapted to the spaces, rather than the other way around. 'Convenience', was one of Pugin's mantras when it came to domestic design and the asymmetry that resulted has since become the hallmark of English domestic architecture based on the central tenet that 'form should follow function'.

Rich interiors

Recreating the richly wallpapered, painted and panelled interior, furnished with pieces reflecting Pugin's own designs, as well as paintings and objects similar to those that had inspired his work was a bigger challenge. Archaeology came to the rescue here because, despite constant redecoration by subsequent owners, small traces of the original décor remained concealed beneath later work. Pugin also left behind a great deal of documentary evidence, including his own watercolour paintings of some of the rooms.

The covered porch was added by Pugin's son Edward, and opens into a generous hall, where Pugin kept a chest of clothes to give as charity to any beggar who came calling. The hall panelling is of the same simple joinery as was used throughout the house, above which the walls are papered with a red and green pattern based on the words of his family motto – *En Avant*, meaning 'Forward'. The striking diagonal design of the banisters was probably inspired by timber framing in northern France, which Pugin visited often, and the tiles on the floor incorporate Pugun's initials, AWP and family emblem, the black martlet (a heraldic bird, like a swallow).

Living rooms

The appearance of the library – one of the most important rooms in the house, because it was here that Pugin designed the interiors of The House of Lords – had to be recreated from shadowy marks on the walls and floorboards and from clues given in letters that Pugin wrote describing his working habits. These enabled the positions to be worked out of Pugin's desk, his bookshelves and his drawing

chests, as well as the wording of the text friezes that ran around the shelves, consisting of inspiring quotations from the Old Testament Book of Proverbs. The main cornice frieze also bore the names of Pugin's favourite people – saints, friends and clients – and places, designed to inspire him in his work.

In the dining room, original panelling survived that held a clue to the rest of the house, and it was possible to strip layers of paint to recover the original mahogany colour. The medieval look of the room was recreated from documentary as well as physical evidence, the ceiling being stencilled with a design based again on Pugin's initials.

Another Puginesque innovation that we take for granted today was the use of the kitchen for meals – Pugin designed the kitchen to be bright and airy, rather than an inferior room for servants, with large windows framing views of the neighbouring church. Fortunately, the original dresser had survived from the 1840s – the only piece of original furniture in the house.

Below The Grange dining room had its original panelling, but this had to be stripped of its later paint.

Above The restored study, with Pugin's desk and chair in place, and the onrnate frieze that encircled the room with biblical quotations.

Above The restored hallway and stairs have floor tiles and red and green wallpaper with Pugin's martlet (heraldic bird) emblem.

Above The restored dining room as Pugin would have known it when entertaining his London friends.

PUBLIC ARCHAEOLOGY

This final chapter looks at the work of archaeologists who specialize in the management and protection of the heritage, and who strive to engage the public in archaeology through many forms of advocacy, including policy research, political lobbying, educational work and journalism. Their work is rooted in questions about who owns the heritage – whether it is a universal resource that belongs to all humanity or it belongs to the person who own the land on which potentially valuable objects are found.

If, as most archaeologists agree, archaeology is an activity carried out in the public interest, in the pursuit of knowledge about our collective past, it follows that archaeology should be rooted in public involvement – at the least, archaeologists have a duty to explain their work to the public, and at best, archaeology should be a community activity. So here are some suggestions for ways that you can get involved in research, fieldwork and digging, and in more formal and structured learning about archaeology.

Opposite TV and podcast archaeology is now regularly broadcast to satisfy public demand.

Above Volunteers at a summer archaeology school practise the meticulous cleaning of sites during excavation.

Above Re-enactment has strong links to ethnoarchaeology: here we see the dress of 17th-century Jamestown, Virginia, USA.

Above Families visiting a heritage site are taught how to perfect their observation skills through drawing what they can see.

Promoting Archaeology

Why do archeaologists do archaeology at all? If it is just to indulge our personal curiosity, what right has archaeology to be paid for by public funds? And why are there laws that protect the heritage from destruction — why not let people do what they like with their own land and homes?

Archaeology can sometimes come across as an arcane discipline, of little relevance to today's modern world, a subject that is of interest to only a few academics. True, archaeology furnishes the objects that make such compelling exhibits in museums, but so does tomb robbing, treasure hunting, metal detecting and the art and antiquities trade. So what makes archaeology so special that it deserves massive funding from governments, developers, universities, charities and volunteer donors, especially if the result is an excavation report of immense interest to no more than 100 people and meaningless to the rest of humanity?

There are no simple answers to these questions, and some archaeologists wrestle with them every day. These are the archaeologists who specialize in the field of advocacy, lobbying and public policy. Their aim is to find ways of influencing decision makers and the public at large to support archaeology, so that the framework of law, funding and decision making within which archaeologists operate is as favourable to archaeology as possible.

What that means in simple terms is that archaeology should be taught in schools, that planning decisions should protect the best of our archaeology and heritage and not destroy it, and that archaeology should be funded.

Fighting for archaeology

If governments are to take notice of these requests, they have to be underpinned by some robust arguments about the value of archaeology to society in terms of directly measurable benefits — such as the amount that archaeology contributes to employment and tourism — and less tangible benefits, such as the pleasure that

Above London's heritage is preserved in the conversion of Bromley Hall into office premises.

people get from archaeology as a hobby, the degree to which conservation improves people's quality of life, and the role of archaeological methodology in training people in problem solving and team building skills.

The asking and answering of such questions has had a direct impact on what archaeologists do in practical terms. For example, archaeologists no longer see the excavation report as the only end product of archaeological fieldwork or research. The knowledge gained from fieldwork can be used to enrich people's lives through museum displays, special exhibitions, visitor attractions, magazine and newspaper articles, television, books, lectures, festivals and dramatic re-enactments, storytelling and novels.

Above Archaeology festivals and open days encourage archaeologists of the future to have a go and get involved.

Above To replicate the excitement of archaeological discovery, this sand pit is carefully seeded with pots, toy jewellery and bones.

Outreach work

Today, archaeology is more popular and democratic than it has ever been. The discipline is no longer the preserve of leisured aristocrats digging burial mounds on their private estates or of antiquaries and aesthetes building their private museum collections, or of intrepid explorers heading into unknown lands. Today, archaeologists take seriously the concept that what they do is 'for the benefit of the nation' (these words are from the Parliamentary Act of 1895 that created the National Trust in Great Britain, one of the world's first conservation charities), and they work hard to give something back in return for popular support.

Archaeologists do this in part by helping to conserve the historic land-scapes, villages, towns and cities that form the background to people's lives and that are the basis for the global tourism and leisure industry. They are also active in running museums, taking archaeological materials into schools and encouraging school groups to visit historic sites, in skills development and in community archaeology projects.

Celebrating archaeology

Archaeologists in Great Britain have pioneered a number of ways of engaging people in archaeology. There are now no less than three major annual festivals that are the biggest of their

Above Volunteers on a live 'local archaeology' dig explore the remains of houses similar to their own.

kind in the world in terms of the number of participants: National Archaeology Week takes place each summer, when families are encouraged to visit sites of archaeological and historical interest or museums, heritage and resource centres, to see archaeology in action and to take part in activities on-site. In September, Heritage Open Days celebrates Great Britain's rich architectural heritage, with free access to properties that are usually closed to the public, from castles to factories, town halls to tithe barns, and parish churches to Buddhist temples. In the United States many states have archaeology awareness months. In 2007 The US Department of Defense issued their soldiers with archaeology awareness playing cards to educate them about the importance of respecting ancient sites in Iraq and Afghanistan. In Australia, the country has a National Archaeology Week, partly to persuade more aspiring archaeology students into further education.

Involving the community

The Heritage Lottery Fund distributes money raised from the sale of lottery tickets to community archaeology projects, enabling people to research the history and archaeology of their locality. The principle behind this scheme is that people are more likely

Above Young people are encouraged to develop an understanding of the past and the lessons it can teach us.

Above Many people learn about the past by attending re-enactment events recreating past lives and heroic battles.

to value and care for their heritage if they understand it, especially if their understanding derives from their own research endeavours. Also successful is the Portable Antiquities Scheme, which employs a network of community archaeologists all over the country to help people identify the finds that come from their gardens, from metal detecting or beachcombing. In this way many finds that would otherwise go unreported are now logged and can lead to some spectacular discoveries.

Most archaeological organizations work to engage the public through regular lectures and open days. Some have pioneered webcasts and dig diaries to share the experience of digging a new site with enthusiasts around the world, and there are many worldwide video clips that can be seen on the Archaeology Channel, at www.archaeologychannel.org.

There are many career opportunities for people who want to combine arch-aeology with skills in teaching, film or communication, or as managers of visitor attractions or as museum curators. This is a rewarding field, with opportunities for people to discover how enriching archaeology can be.

Conservation and Research

The idea that heritage belongs to everyone has led to the establishment of different schemes for identifying, protecting and conserving the best of the past. This involves achieving an effective balance between what archaeologists preserve and what is allowed to be developed.

Above Restoration of the burned Brittany parliament, France.

Since the mid-19th century, when writers and thinkers such as John Ruskin and William Morris began to argue for the protection of the best buildings from the past, many books have been written on conservation philosophy, many of which argue that governments worldwide need to take better care of the heritage, to put more money into archaeological conservation and research, and to frame policies that protect archaeology. In reality, this is far from easy. Archaeology is everywhere and to protect it all would be, to use a phrase favoured by the opponents of conservation, 'to preserve everything in aspic'.

Conservation also sits ill with the idea that private owners have the right to do whatever they like with their land and property. In reality, that is not true, and we all accept restrictions on our rights in the interests of a greater good – such as agreeing to obey traffic laws to prevent chaos on the roads. Heritage laws have been framed in many parts of the world that seek to balance the short term interests of private owners with the wider public interest in a heritage that belongs to the nation (or the human race) as a whole, and is worthy of protection for future generations.

A finite resource

The sheer volume of the material left by the some of the world's classical civilizations means that many people are faced by the remains of the past every day. Farmers in parts of Turkey,

Iran and Iraq describe their lands as 'pottery fields', because of the sheer amount of ancient material they turn up with their ploughs, and digging the garden in any city or town that was founded by the ancient Romans is likely to turn up pottery, tile, brick and nails from 2,000 years ago.

With such abundance, it is easy to be complacent, but archaeologists have realized over the last century that the survival of this rich legacy cannot be guaranteed. It is under threat from many forces, including looting and the effects of conflicts in areas such as Iraq, Afghanistan, Ethiopia and Nepal, to name just a few. In other places neglect is the problem: in Italy, Greece, north Africa and Turkey there is so much archaeology that governments cannot fund its conservation, or guard it against theft or damage.

Above Centuries-old agricultural methods in Turkey are better for preserving buried archaeology than modern farming techniques.

Even in countries where war and looting are not endemic, construction projects or simple changes in agricultural practice can destroy precious archaeology. This occurred in Great Britain, for example, when cattle farmers devastated by foot and mouth disease, ploughed up pasture to grow potatoes. In the process they eradicated thousands of years of buried archaeology. Another example is when big office developments in the City of London involved the excavation of large holes that contained the record of the city's history.

Above Some excavation sites host tours to encourage visitors to learn about the historic treasures hidden beneath their city streets.

Left World Heritage status helps protect these 7th-century Buddhist carvings at the Longmen Caves, Henan province, China.

Above Medieval Tallinn, capital of Estonia, has survived numerous wars to become a World Heritage Site in 1997.

Monument protection

In response to such threats, arch-aeologists have long aspired to creating comprehensive lists of archaeological sites – and that term includes standing buildings, historic landscapes, gardens and battlefields, as well as buried archaeology – so that they can be fenced and protected from develop-ment. In some countries and states (but by no means all), these lists serve as the basis for legislation to protect heritage at every level, from internationally important sites to local heritage.

At the bottom of the pyramid are conservation areas, districts within cities, towns and villages where owners are encouraged to maintain the historic character of their properties and must apply for permission for alterations or extensions that might then have to be carried out using traditional materials – timber windows, rather than plastic, or stone walls and roof tiles instead of concrete. At the next level are sites that are regarded as nationally important, and that are protected from all forms of development, being conserved as prime examples of historic property. Then there are conventions that are regional in scope and that aim to protect not just buildings and buried archaeology, but whole landscapes. These are often protected by being

The origins of monument protection

The very first archaeological inventories date from the early 19th century in France, where the Comité Spécial des Arts et Monuments was set up in 1837 and charged with the task of drawing up a list of ruins and buildings worthy of state protection. Prosper Mérimée was appointed to the post of inspector-general of historical monuments, but he was sceptical of the enterprise, which he described as 'naive administrative romanticism'. He predicted that to catalogue all of France's archaeology would 'take 200 years and fill 900 volumes'. Mérimée was a pragmatist, and decided that the list of monuments to be protected should bear some relationship to the scale of the budget available for their conservation. He eventually produced a list of 59 monuments (the state allocated a mere 105,000 francs for their restoration).

designated as national parks – in the United States and Canada, national park status is the primary means by which outstanding natural and archaeological landscapes are conserved.

World Heritage Sites

At the apex of the pyramid are World Heritage Sites, designated by the World Heritage Committee of UNESCO (the United Nations Educational, Scientific and Cultural Organization); these consist of sites that are considered to have 'outstand-ing universal value'. The list currently includes 830 sites, in 138 countries, ranging from well-known heritage icons, such as the Taj Mahal, Angkor Wat, Chichén Itzá and the Egyptian

pyramids, to transnational sites such as the Frontiers of the Roman Europe, which includes sites such as Hadrian's Wall and the Upper German-Raetian border wall that stretches from the Atlantic coast of northern Britain, through Europe to the Black Sea, and from there to the Red Sea and across North Africa back to the Atlantic coast.

The aim of the World Heritage Committee is to designate those sites that genuinely have resonance for all the people of the world. They should help to reinforce the idea of common humanity that underlies efforts toward world peace and multiracial harmony – an example of heritage having a value above and beyond the purely academic.

Re-enactment and Experimentation

Some archaeologists firmly believe that the best way to engage the public and to understand the past is to try to recreate it as accurately as possible, for example, by trying to make beer using ancient Egyptian techniques and ingredients or by building prehistoric houses using the tools of the period.

Above Making a Bronze-Age tool from flint requires practice and skill.

New forms of archaeology have been pioneered by the re-enactment movement, which first began as a way to make museums more interesting to visitors. Historians have traced the fashion for 'living museums', with actors and interpreters helping to explain the exhibits, as far back as the mid-19th century and the Great Exhibition, when tableaux illustrated life thoughout the British Empire. In 1881, Scandinavia pioneered the open-air museum dedicated to traditional building types and folk crafts with King Oscar II's museum at Oslo in Norway.

Left Henry Ford's Greenfield Village, in Michigan, USA, pioneered the concept of a living history museum.

In the United States, Henry Ford's Greenfield Village in Dearborn, Michigan, which opened in 1928, was intended to encompass the whole of American history, but it was more of a theme park, especially compared to the country's current generation of living museums, represented by Mystic Seaport, Plimoth Plantation and Fortress Louisbourg. Worthy of note, Canada's Black Creek Pioneer Village and Britain's Blists Hill Victorian Town use actors to impersonate people from the past in order to be as historically accurate as possible.

Learning by doing

It was in the United States – specifically at Colonial Williamsburg, which opened in 1934 – that re-enactment and archaeology came together for the first time, the objective being not just to entertain and inform visitors, but to gain new knowledge of past crafts and activities by doing them.

Since then, re-enactment has moved out of the museum and into the community with groups of like-minded people coming together to recreate past processes and understand them better by adopting past ways of life. Members of the Roman Military Research Society (Legio XIIII Gemina Martia Victrix), for example, recreate the life of a Roman soldier on the

march to understand better what it feels like to march 30km (20 miles) a day in sandals carrying a bag of armour, dig a defensive bank and ditch around your temporary encampment at the end of the day and cook meals using ingredients and equipment typically found on excavations of Roman forts.

Re-enactment societies represent a hidden mass of heritage enthusiasts, and some re-enactment societies – such as the Sealed Knot (recreating English Civil War armies and battles) and the American Civil War Society – have thousands of members worldwide that outnumber the memberships of some national archaeological societies.

Some re-enactors charge for their services, and see their work as an extension of their careers as artists, educators, eco-warriors, actors, storytellers and musicians. They might also work as advisors to television and film companies on the authenticity of sets or costumes. Others do everything for love – however, they are no less professional in their attitude and are often more passionate about historical authenticity than the professionals.

Experimental archaeology

A further stage beyond the re-enactment of lifestyles is to reconstruct the past using the original post holes (or an exact template copied from a real site) and replica tools, as has been done in England in recent years in building a reconstruction of a Bronze Age trackway at the Peat Moors Centre near Glastonbury, Iron-Age circular houses at the Butser experimental farm in Hampshire, or Saxon longhouses at West Stow in Suffolk.

This form of re-enactment is perhaps better referred to as 'experimental archaeology', because the aim is to answer some very specific research questions. Among them are how efficient is a Bronze Age axe for forest clearance; how long does it take to construct an Iron Age home; how many people can comfortably live in it; how effectively does smoke disperse from the central hearth; how often does it need rethatching; what advantages are there to the suspended floors that typify Saxon homes; why did our ancestors store grain in underground pits rather than in jars (answer: because they are more effective at preventing fungal growths that destroy the grain or result in food poisoning); what happens when buildings, pits and ditches are abandoned – how quickly do they collapse or fill, and what does the resulting stratigraphy look like compared to what we find on real archaeological sites?

Some re-enactments are ambitious in scale. For example, one attempt to find out how the stones used for building

Above A thatched Iron-Age house at Westhay, Somerset, UK, based on those discovered at the abandoned Glastonbury Lake Village.

Stonehenge were transported from their source in south Wales to the Salisbury Plain in south England ended in disaster when the boat built to carry the stone sank soon after setting sail. However, attempts to recreate a typical circular henge monument, with timber circle, ditch and bank, raised all sorts of interesting questions such as whether or not henges originally had roofs.

Above A skilled ceramicist re-enacts ancient kiln-firing techniques to learn how prehistoric pottery was made.

Above Heyerdahl's balsa raft used in the Kon-Tiki expedition.

Voyages of discovery

Among the best-known examples of re-enactment are the adventures of the late Thor Heyerdahl (1914–2002), the Norwegian adventurer who built an international reputation for his oceanic journeys in reconstructions of ancient craft. Heyerdahl was so determined to prove that prehistoric people were capable of navigating huge distances that he risked his life to sail from Peru to the Tuamotu Islands in French Polynesia on a raft of balsa wood, a distance of 7,000km (4,300 miles).

The Kon-Tiki expedition was inspired by descriptions of Inca boats recorded by Spanish chroniclers and by Inca myths that Heyerdahl interpreted as evidence of contact between the peoples of South America and the Pacific. From studying the DNA of pigs, we now know that the islands of the Pacific were not colonized from South America, but from Vietnam via Taiwan and the Philippines (see *Asia and Australasia*). However, Heyardahl's main point remains valid: we should not underestimate the ability of ancient people to navigate the oceans.

Getting Involved

Being passionate about their discipline, archaeologists want to share their interest. As a result, amateur involvement is warmly welcomed, and there are many doors through which one can enter if he or she wants to find out more.

Above Many archaeological summer schools are crying out for volunteers – and some may offer the opportunity to travel abroad.

Undoubtedly the best way to learn about archaeology is to take part in an excavation. Working for two weeks on a dig will introduce you to basic field techniques and let you decide whether two weeks of digging is more than enough for one lifetime or whether you want to devote the rest of your life to the discipline.

Field schools

There is no one single comprehensive source of information about archaeology field schools, a good place to start, however, is the Archaeological Fieldwork Opportunities Bulletin (www.archaeological.org/webinfo.php ?page=10015), published by the Archaeological Institute of America annually. This institution also has an online database of fieldwork projects in which volunteers can participate: www.archaeological.org/webinfo.php ?page=10016. In Great Britain, there is a web-based service on the site of the Council for British Archaeology: www.britarch.ac.uk/briefing/field.asp.

Many universities run field schools that are designed for training the students enrolled at that institution, but that often accept a small number of guest diggers. It is worth looking at the website of your nearest university,

Below Dutch students excavate and record the medieval walls of Utrecht, in the Netherlands, looking for evidence of the city's buried Roman origins.

going to the school's department of archaeology and seeing what might be available. For example, the Bristol University Field School (www.bris. ac.uk/archanth/fieldschools) offers opportunities to work in England, France and the Caribbean, on field survey, excavation and underwater archaeology. You must expect to pay to take part in any of these projects, and in return for a small weekly fee, you can expect basic accommodation (perhaps a camp site), training, and the occasional evening lecture or excursion to other sites in the area.

Training digs

There are also a limited number of organizations that run field schools undertaking important research almost staffed by paying volunteers (the usual ratio is one experienced archaeologist to two or three beginners). The standard of training on these courses is high, but they are also more expensive than university field schools. You can find out more by following the links on the About Archaeology website (http://archaeology.about.com) or by investing in a copy of the publication called *Archaeo-Volunteers: the World Guide to Archaeological and Heritage Volunteering* (greenvolunteers.com). Archaeological summer schools and training excavations in Europe are listed on the Archaeology in Europe website (www.archaeology.eu.com/ weblog/index.html), and the website for the magazine *Current Archaeology* (www.ilovethepast.com) has useful feedback from people who have been on training excavations, telling you what to expect and providing reviews of the good and the not so good archaeological training experiences.

Alternatively, you can visit the website of the Earthwatch Institute (www.earthwatch.org), an international environmental charity that promotes the involvement of volunteers in fieldwork projects in all the sciences. The organization runs some 140 projects in over 50 countries, and some are suitable for families and children, with projects ranging from excavation in Peru, to cave art research in Europe, to the recording of historic buildings in Armenia.

Themed travel

Of course, if you prefer archaeology without the hard work, several excellent travel companies provide holidays based on archaeology, where participants are introduced to the subject by leading specialists who offer a privileged insight into the subject as they give guided tours and lectures. They often take you to places that are perhaps not normally accessible

Below A student learns to excavate and record the foundations of a prehistoric building on a training excavation.

to tourists. Andante Travels (www. andantetravels.co.uk) is one of the best specialist tour operators in this field, and is perhaps the only such company in the world that is owned and run by archaeologists. The American-based Archaeological Tours (www. archaeologicaltrs.com) offers a similar international programme of tours led by leading American scholars. Another firm, Ancient World Travel (www.ancient.co.uk) specializes in trips to archaeologically rich destinations led by people who have, in many cases, directed the excavations that you will visit. The company also organizes weekend conferences at which top archaeologists provide an introduction to the many different aspects of the world of archaeology.

National and local societies

Yet another way in which to become involved in archaeology is to join a national archaeological society, or one of the literally hundreds of local archaeological and historical societies that exists around the world. In Great Britain, there is a comprehensive list of local societies, which can be found on the website of the Council for British Archaeology (www.britarch.ac.uk/ info/socs.asp). You can search for organizations in other parts of the world by using the links on the Archaeology on the Net website (members.tripod.com/~archonnet/).

National, regional and international societies exist to promote the study of just about any archaeological topic you can dream up, from the archaeology of specific materials, such as glass or building materials to the big themes of prehistoric, Roman or medieval archaeology. By typing in the relevant words – for example, 'glass' and 'archaeology' and the county in which you live – a search engine should quickly enable you to locate relevant societies via the internet.

If you join a society, expect a lecture programme, newsletter and field trips. The best societies run their own research projects, which you can join and learn from. In time you might feel

Above As well as being intellectually challenging, archaeology is also great fun and a healthy and sociable outdoor activity.

confident about embarking on your own project, in which case society membership is a good way of finding a mentor. Just as importantly, you can use the society to tap into the archaeological network and find out what is going on in your field of interest. It is a network that anyone can join. Every day all over the world there are public lectures being delivered in museums, universities and society meetings that anyone can attend.

Papers in archaeological journals are increasingly accessible on the internet, and if the books and papers that academics produce are sometimes written in language that looks more like social science or linguistic philosophy, there are also many popular books written by knowledgeable academics that will serve as a way in to the more abstruse parts of the archaeological spectrum.

Learning More

If you want to take your interest in archaeology a step further, colleges and universities offer a great range of study opportunities. In addition, there are the opportunities for self-guided learning through books, specialist magazines, television programmes, lectures and websites.

Above Simply visiting ancient sites, like Rome's Colosseum, is a great way to learn.

Archaeologists are great enthusiasts for their discipline, and they often write books and articles or appear on television programmes to explain their discoveries. This means that there is no shortage of sources for formal and informal learning.

Formal learning

Many schools, colleges and universities provide evening classes and extramural courses, along with lifelong learning opportunities built around archaeology. In Great Britain, you can study for formal qualifications in GCSE and A Level archaeology (see the Council for British Archaeology website at: www.britarch.ac.uk/cba/factsht7.shtml), or you can buy the standard textbooks that support this subject and work through them on your own. *The Archaeology Coursebook*, by Jim Grant, Sam Gorin and Neil Fleming, is written by teachers and is packed with links to relevant websites, along with tasks and exercises for consolidating your learning. Another book is *Archaeology: an Introduction*, by Kevin Greene, which is used by many adult students and undergraduates as their basic primer.

At the time of writing, online learning is still under development as a way of learning about archaeology in your own time. Oxford University's Department of Continuing Education offers two online learning courses, in the 'Origins of Human Behaviour' and in 'Ritual and Religion in Prehistory', and further modules are being tested by organizations in Great Britain such as the Archaeology Training Forum

(www.archaeologists.net/modules/icontent/index.php?page=41). In the United States, the Archaeological Institute of America also provides a website (www.archaeological.org/webinfo.php?page=10260). When they are fully developed, they will offer a step up from simply reading about the subject, with structured approaches to the subject and the opportunity to share ideas and develop critical arguments through online interaction with tutors and fellow students.

Degree study

Typically, if you choose to study archaeology at university, you can expect to spend the first year in learning about core concepts, basic techniques and the broad outlines of world archaeology. Often you will be expected to take part in fieldwork as an intergral part of the degree. In the second year, you might be able to select specialist topics from a range of modules and in the third year you

Above More formalized learning in Sudan, where univeristy students are being taught the techniques of drawing and analysing pottery.

might be encouraged to undertake a piece of original research, writing it up as a dissertation.

Archaeology provides an entry into many professions because it develops a good training in scientific method, team work and problem solving and clarity of thinking and expression. Those archaeology graduates who stay in the profession can study further to equip themselves to work in museums, education or fieldwork. Around 5 per cent of those who complete their archaeology degrees will go on to do post-graduate study for three years, during which time they will produce a thesis – a written piece of original research – while beginning to develop skills as a teacher and lecturer, enabling them to be qualified for junior lecturer posts and to begin to work their way up the academic ladder to the ultimate goal: the title of professor.

Above Archaeology at degree level offers students the chance to develop their skills in team building and problem solving.

Self learning

However, learning about archaeology need not be structured or academic. You can share in the sheer excitement of archaeological discovery in scores of less formal ways. One is to subscribe to one of the leading archaeology magazines that are written for non- specialists and that do an excellent job in reporting on the latest thinking, finds and projects in the subject. Magazines such as *Archaeology* (www.archaeology.org/), *Current Archaeology* and *Current World Archaeology* (www.archaeology.co.uk/) and *British Archaeology* (www.britarch.ac.uk/BA/ba.html) all publish part of their content on their websites, so you can browse before deciding whether or not to subscribe.

In addition, there are some excellent websites that aim to capture archaeological news stories from around the world and provide links to the source, or succinct summaries. You can easily keep up to date with all the latest discoveries and ideas by spending 15 minutes a day browsing the daily news pages of the Archaeological Institute of America (www.archaeology.org/online/news/index.html) or the Archaeologica website (www.archaeologica.org/), both of which have links to the newspapers and journals in which the stories originally appeared.

Above Archaeologists are often rewarded by finding objects, like this Viking hairpin, that provide direct contact with past people.

Above Excavating cremated bone with a spoon to ensure none gets lost.

Lectures

For live lectures, a good starting place is the local museum, where the curatorial staff often give free lectures, as do invited specialists. This is an often overlooked aspect of museum activity. National museums in particular offer outstanding lectures related to their special exhibitions, where you might be fortunate to hear the world expert on the subject give a free lunchtime lecture or lead a personal guided tour of the galleries.

Some archaeological organizations also use blogs and webcams to communicate with fellow enthusiasts so that you can follow the progress of excavations on a daily basis and share the way that interpretations often change as the dig develops. By this means, you can keep in daily contact with what is going on at key world archaeology sites such as Çatalhöyük (*see* Case study: Çatalhöyük) at www.catalhoyuk.com/ or Stonehenge (*see* *Complex Societies*) at www.shef.ac.uk/archaeology/research/stonehenge, or on the Archaeological Institute of America's interactive dig website: www.archaeology.org/interactive/index.html.

Television

There are plenty of television stations that will provide a programme about a specific project or a series covering archaeological themes, such as human origins, or cave art. One long-running British series that is also broadcast on cable channels in different parts of the world is 'Time Team', which is well worth watching because, unlike most

Above Sieving soil at the site of the first Russian-American fort, Kodiak Island, Alaska, USA.

televion archaeology, it shows you what archaeologists do and how they make deductions from what they find. 'Time Team' reflects the processes of archaeology, rather than just the discoveries that are the staple fare of the many archaeological shows that are broadcast regularly on cable television stations devoted to history.

Further reading

For the places where you are likely to find the very latest in archaeological research results, you can try reading the archaeological journals, such as *Antiquity* (antiquity.ac.uk/) and *World Archaeology* (www.tandf.co.uk/journals/rwar). If you feel ready for truly indepth material, you can also try reading the science-based periodicals such as *Science* (www.sciencemag.org/) or *Nature* (www.nature.com/index.html) – but be aware that these latter magazines can be heavily technical and difficult to understand without a grounding in the subject.

To obtain such a grounding, there are two outstanding books, both of which are encyclopaedic in scope and written with lucidity and a thorough knowledge of the subject: *The Human Past*, edited by Chris Scarre, and *Archaeology: Theories, Methods and Practice*, by Colin Renfrew and Paul Bahn. These two books contain comprehensive cross references to the more advanced specialist books on the many topics that they address, making them the ideal starting point for exploring the many different branches of the archaeological family tree.

Case Study: Jamestown/Colonial Williamsburg

Jamestown and Colonial Williamsburg are nearby neighbours in the American state of Virginia, and together they exemplify all that is best in community archaeology and the presentation of the past to the public through living history re-enactment.

Above A reconstructive model of the Jamestown fort 'cottage'.

Jamestown (originally also called James Towne and Jamestowne) was the site of the first permanent British colony in North America. It was officially founded on 14 May 1607 and named after the reigning British monarch. James I (1603–25). The early colonists built their first settlement on site on an island in the James River for defensive purposes, however, this mosquito-ridden swampy outpost lacked good farming land and drinking water. The colonists eventually relocated their capital to higher ground a short distance away in 1699, building the

Below This montage shows what the very first Jamestown homes and stockades might have looked like.

new town named Williamsburg (because by this time, it was William III (1689–1702) who was reigning on the British throne).

The members of the first colony included John Rolfe, whose experiments in growing tobacco led to the colony's eventual economic survival. He also married Pocahontas, daughter of Wahunsunacock, Chief of the Powhatan Confederacy, establishing a period of peace with Native Americans in the region.

By the 20th century, it was assumed that all archaeological evidence of that first historic colony had been lost to the scouring tides of the James River. In 1994, the Association for the Preservation of Virginia Antiquities

(APVA), the charity that now owns the site, set up a project called Jamestown Rediscovery to test this theory. Within days of beginning work, a team of volunteer archaeologists, under the direction of Project Director Bill Kelso, began to recover early colonial artefacts. In 1996, the team successfully located the site of the original settlement, which was within its original triangular palisade walls.

Below (Top) Newly cast lead shot as it emerged from a 17th-century mould, with the runner still attached.

Below (Bottom) The corroded remains of a Scottish 'snaphaunce' pistol, used for personal protection by one of Jamestown's early settlers.

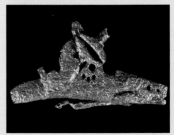

Living archaeology

Since then, thanks to the water-logged conditions of the ground at Jamestown, hundreds of thousands of artefacts have been recovered, including the remains of several houses and wells, and the graves of several of the early settlers. What makes this site so exceptional is the huge effort that has gone into involving visitors, enabling them to observe archaeologists in action and ask questions about the progress of research at the site.

The spectacular discoveries from the site include arms and armour, medical instruments, ceramics, tools, coins, trade items, clothing, musical instruments, games and food remains. They are displayed in a museum called 'the Archaearium', an unusual word that Bill Kelso has coined from the Greek *archeo* ('ancient') and the Latin *arium* ('place'). It consists of a glass building that covers parts of the site of the archaeological excavation, linking the history and the finds directly to the 'ancient place' where they were found. As well as reconstructing the appearance of the fort 400 years ago, digital technology is used to show visitors precisely where the objects

Below The excavation of a boiler jar, dated to 1610. Analysis of this precious find suggests that the first Jamestown settlers distilled their own alcohol, not only to drink, but also as a medical antiseptic and anaesthetic.

were recovered from the site, along with videos showing them being unearthed and conserved, thus involving those visitors who cannot take part in the dig with a sense of what it is like to be the archaeologist who makes the discovery.

The wider landscape

Historic Jamestown (the island itself) is now part of a wider historic landscape that takes in the port, fields, waterways and subsidiary settlements – such as Martin's Hundred and Henricus – built by the growing colony as it expanded along the banks of the James and York Rivers. Some of these sites have been excavated, while others remain to be excavated, protected from development by the designation of the whole area as the 'Historic Triangle'. This historic area is managed by the National Park Service and takes in the Colonial Williamsburg living history museum and Yorktown, where General Cornwallis surrendered to George Washington in 1781, ending the American Revolution, plus recreations of a Native American village and replicas of the sailing ships that brought the early colonists to America.

Colonial Williamsburg stands on the high ground between the James and York Rivers, where it was to evolve into the centre of government, education and culture for the colony of Virginia. Today, the clock has been turned back by the removal of buildings later than

1780 to create a living history museum that aims to be as authentic as possible with its recreations of colonial life and crafts. It literally meets the people and shares the life of the colony's 17th and 18th-century inhabitants.

Like archaeology in the wider world, which has grown to embrace the whole sweep of human history and experience, including the human tragedies of slavery, imprisonment and war, Colonial Williamsburg has responded to criticism that it neglected the role of African Americans in colonial life (in the 1950s, African Americans were allowed to visit Colonial Williamsburg only one day a week). New programmes have been added to explain slavery and present a more rounded picture of the people and the era.

Finding out more

Up to the minute accounts of work in progress at Jamestown can be found on the Historic Jamestown website, (www.historicjamestowne.org/index.php), and the whole story of Bill Kelso's quest for the site of the original colony is told in his book, *The Buried Truth*. For the people of Colonial Williamsburg, and details of conferences, educational activities and events, see the Colonial Williamsburg Foundation's website at www.history.org/.

Below A complete, if corroded, iron breastplate emerges from the now-dry moat surrounding the Jamestown fort.

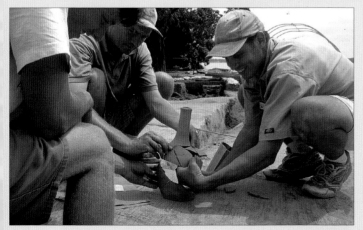

A HISTORY OF
ARCHAEOLOGY

Image Monolithic stone heads, called moai, have stood sentry over the coast of Easter Island for almost 1000 years.

Understanding the Past through Archaeology

Archaeology allows us a privileged look at the way our ancestors lived, and it is this desire to learn more about our inherited cultural history that drives archaeologists to delve deeper into our past. Here we explore some of the greatest archaeological discoveries and the people who uncovered them.

Above The vast Pyramid of the Sun in Mexico's Teotihuacán or 'city of the gods'.

This part of the book will take you on a journey back in time to different cultures and landscapes. The first section looks at the lives and work of many of the great archaeologists – the men and women whose commitment to uncovering the secrets of the past has brought us face to face with our ancestors.

This second section focuses on some of the world's best known archaeological sites and finds, looking in detail at the fascinating civilizations behind them and the story of their rediscovery and excavation.

The archaeologists

The names of archaeologists such as Hiram Bingham, the discoverer of the lost Inca city of Machu Picchu, still seem to epitomize archaeology's spirit of adventure and unstinting quest for knowledge of the past.

The foundations for the professional and scientific archaeology that is practised today were laid in the 19th century by a small group of amateur scholars for whom curiosity about the remote past became an abiding passion.

Below An aerial view of Angkor Wat Cambodia. In recent years, radar data has enabled archaeologists to detect hitherto undiscovered areas of the vast Angkor complex.

The early days of archaeology brought a succession of intrepid, often colourful scholars and adventurers. Among them were Arthur Evans and Heinrich Schliemann who gave the modern world its first glimpse of both the Minoan and Mycenaean civilizations. There were also early Egyptologists, Giovanni Belzoni and Auguste Mariette; Max Uhle, the father of South American archaeology; and Augustus Pitt Rivers whose meticulous approach to excavation put field work on a more professional footing. The first of the true professional archaeologists began to emerge in the early 20th century. Their pioneering work led to many significant breakthroughs: Alfred Kidder's excavations at Pecos, New Mexico; Dorothy Garrod's studies at the Palaeolithic caves of Mount Carmel; and, in 1922, perhaps the greatest discovery of them all – the tomb of Tutankhamen in Egypt's Valley of the Kings by the English archaeologist Howard Carter.

As the 20th century progressed, archaeology became primarily a field for highly qualified specialists, who had access to new and ever more sophisticated techniques for dating, excavation and survey. The ground-breaking excavations of several generations of the Leakey family in Africa, for example, have had a considerable impact on our collective understanding of the origins of man. In Peru the tireless dedication of Maria Reiche ensured that the Nasca lines were brought to the attention of the wider world.

Right A family shrine (*lararium*) found in the House of the Vettii in the ruined city of Pompeii. Excavations have brought us face to face with a remarkable Roman city frozen in time since the 1st century AD and have allowed us a unique glimpse of what everyday life was like for a Roman citizen. The city has revealed a bakery, a laundry, a theatre and even a snack shop.

The archaeological sites

In a book of this size, it is impossible to do more than provide a glimpse of some of the myriad of important sites and finds from around the world. Any period or region of the globe could easily fill several such volumes. The sites that have been selected will, however, provide a unique insight into many of the world's great archaeological treasures – from the Temples of the Far East to the cave paintings of Europe, and from the enigmatic cities of Mesoamerica to China's incomparable Terracotta Army.

This fascinating journey begins in Africa, from the pyramids of Egypt in the north to the prehistoric caves in the south. Next comes a sample of some of the ancient sites of the Middle East, including some of the world's oldest cities, such as Uruk and Susa.

The sections on Europe and the Mediterranean reveal spectacular finds, including the Anglo-Saxon ship burial at Sutton Hoo in England and the Ulu Burun shipwreck off the coast of southern Turkey. The sites of the Far East stretch from Harappa in the west to Nara in the east, while the Easter Island statues are among the jewels of Oceania. The Americas features sites as diverse as the Viking settlement of L'Anse aux Meadows in Newfoundland and the magnificent royal tombs at Sipán in Peru.

That new exciting discoveries are still to be made in many parts of the world is a certainty. Large parts of Africa, for instance, remain practically untouched by archaeologists. And advances in science mean that archaeologists can now extract more information from less material, for example, a single fragment of a pot can be dated, analysed for its constituent materials, its firing temperature, its decorations and even, from traces on its inner surface, what it used to contain.

Another trend in the world of archaeology is that the dates for the origins of different phenomena, such as the invention of pottery, the ritual burying of the dead or the cultivation of plants, keep getting pushed further back, while the place of origin may also move around as new discoveries start to modify our understanding. This is one of the many reasons why archaeology is such a compelling subject – new discoveries such as The Iceman, found in the 1990s in the Tyrolean Alps, can turn up unexpectedly and radically alter our cumulative picture of the ancient world.

Left Emperor Qin Shi Huangdi's incredible terracotta warriors lay undisturbed for over 2000 years before they were discovered.

This timeline presents a selective list of significant milestones and events in the history of places and civilizations featured in this book.

7 million BC	**Africa**	* Our oldest known ancestor: Sahelanthropus tchadensis, found in northern Chad in 2002.
3.2 million BC	**Africa**	* 'Lucy' (*Australopithecus afarensis*) found in Ethiopia's Awash Valley in 1974.
2.5 million BC	**Africa**	* The first stone tools.
1.5 million BC	**Africa**	* The earliest evidence for controlled fire use from fossil hearths and burnt animal bones from sites in Kenya and from the Swartkrans Cave in South Africa.
800,000 BC	**Africa**	* Archaic hominins begin to spread from East Africa as part of the first 'out of Africa' wave of migration.
500,000 BC	**Far East**	* 'Peking Man', *Homo erectus pekinensis*, is found at Zhoukoudian, near Beijing (Peking) in 1923, cousin to the 'Java Man' *Homo erectus* remains found in Indonesia in 1891.
300,000 BC	**Africa**	* The first evidence of body art: stone tools from Zambia used for the grinding of pigments.
150,000 BC	**Africa**	* *Homo sapiens sapiens* develop as a species.
100,000 BC	**Africa**	* *Homo sapiens* begins to migrate out of Africa into Asia and Europe. Shell beads of this date found in Israel and Algeria.
71,000 BC	**Africa**	* The first known art: an ochre block marked with an abstract design from South Africa's Blombos Cave.
50,000 BC	**Australia**	* The first Homo sapiens reach Australia; stone tools from Lake Mungo and rock art at Dampier.
39,000 BC	**Europe**	* Oldest known musical instrument: bone flute made by *H. neanderthlenisis*.
33,000 BC	**America**	* The date when geneticists believe the first humans might have arrive America, though there is no undisputed physical evidence for this.
21,000 BC	**Africa and Europe**	* Seeking refuge in caves around the Mediterranean and Atlantic coasts, modern humans manage to survive the ice ages, while Neanderthals succumb to the cold.
18,000 BC	**Europe, Asia, and Americas**	* The Mesolithic: a period during which the climate begins to warm; today's seas, coastlines begin to form and people begin to evolve new languages and cultures.

16,000 BC	Americas	* The probable date at which humans arrived in America across the frozen Bering Straits from Siberia. Later migrants arrived 13,000 years ago by boat from Japan.
13,000 BC	Europe	* The people of Mezhirich in the Ukraine build shelters out of mammoth bones.
9000 BC	Asia and Europe	* The Neolithic: the beginnings of agriculture, pottery and permanent settlement.
5500 BC	Africa	* 5500-2500 Saharan rock art is created.
5000 BC	Far East	* Mehrgarh in Pakistan has become a prosperous town and centre of industry.
4800 BC	Asia	* Copper tools from Mehrgarh, in modern Pakistan, indicate early metal-working on an industrial scale.
4000 BC	Middle East	* The Uruk society reaches its height in the 4th millennium.
	Far East	* Harappa in Pakistan is an important centre of the local Harappan Bronze Age culture.
3800 BC	Europe	* The first long barrows and ceremonial enclosures are built in Europe, land cleared and farmed.
3500 BC	Asia	* The first written records in the form of cuneiform clay tablets from lower Mesopotamia (modern Iraq). The first city states with a priestly governor or king, living in a temple/palace.
3300 BC	Europe	* The Iceman found in the Ötztaler Alps lives around this time.
3100 BC	Middle East	* Development of proto-Elamite script begins at Susa. * The Sumerians develop cuneiform in the late 4th and early 3rd millennia.
	Europe	* Henge monuments, such as Stonehenge, Woodhenge and Durrington Walls, suggest astronomical knowledge and large winter solstice gatherings.
3000 BC	Africa	* 2975-2950 Distinctive dynastic mastaba tombs are built at Saqqara and Abydos.
2700 BC	Europe	* Minoan civilization on the Aegean island of Crete based on large palaces with central control over food and other resources.
	Africa	* Djoser (ruled 2668-2649) commissions Egypt's first stone building.
2650 BC	Africa and Asia	* The Great Pyramid of Khufu, Egypt's first pyramid. Wheeled sledges and bullock carts in India.
2600 BC	Asia	* Towns in the Indus Valley, with piped water. Wheel-made pottery in China.

2600 BC	Africa	* Khufu (ruled 2551-2528) built his Great Pyramid at Giza, the site of many later monuments, such as the Great Sphinx.
2000 BC	Asia	* Abraham, the father of the Jewish people, is thought to have lived around this time; the Exodus of the Jewish people from Egypt to the Promised Land probably took place between 1444 and 1290bc.
1800 BC	Europe and Asia	* Early iron-working in Asia, but iron only supplants bronze when tin supplies are disrupted from about 1200bc.
1700 BC	Far East	* Foundation of the Shang Dynasty in China.
	Mediterranean	* The New Palace at Knossos is built by the Minoans of Crete in the 16th century.
1500 BC	Mediterranean	* The Mycenaeans of Greece come to prominence.
	Asia Pacific	* The Lapita people, boat-borne migrants from Taiwan, Vietnam and the Philippines, begin to colonize the islands of the Pacific.
1400 BC	Africa	* Tutankhamen (ruled 1333-1324) is interred in the Valley of the Kings.
	Mediterranean	* A Bronze Age ship sinks off the cape of Ulu Burun in Turkey in the 14th century.
1300 BC	Africa	* Ramesses II (c.1290-1224) builds the twin temples of Abu Simbel.
1200 BC	Americas	* First Mayan cities and ceremonial centres established along the coast of Mexico.
1194 BC	Europe	* Probable date of the events described in Homer's Iliad, based on burnt layers at the city of Troy.
800 BC	Europe	* The Iron Age in Europe (characterized by Celtic metalwork), which ends as Rome begins to expand and develop its empire from 340bc.
776 BC	Europe	* Olympic Games established at the sanctuary of Zeus, in the ancient Greek city of Olympia.
700 BC	Mediterranean	* The first temple at Delphi is probably built in the 7th century.
	Europe	* The Celtic kingdoms of central Europe begin to show Mediterranean influence.
	Americas	* Occupation begins at Tikal, a Mayan city in Guatemala.
600 BC	Middle East	* Construction of Persepolis begins under Darius the Great.
500 BC	Mediterranean	* The Temple of Zeus at Olympia is constructed.
	Far East	* Rich burials of horse-riding nomads in natural icebox tombs begin in the Altai mountains of Siberia.
	Americas	* Construction of the Great Pyramid at Cholula begins.

330 BC	**Middle East**	* Alexander the Great destroys the vast stone palace of Darius the Great at Persepolis.
210 BC	**Far East**	* Qin Shi Huangdi, the first Chinese emperor, was buried with over 7000 life-size terracotta soldiers.
200 BC	**Mediterranean**	* Eumenes (ruled 197-159) built the Altar of Zeus at Pergamon.
146 BC	**Mediterranean**	* 146 Carthage is destroyed by the Romans.
AD 64	**Mediterranean**	* 64 Nero constructs the Domus Aurea after a fire in Rome.
AD 79	**Mediterranean**	* 79 Mount Vesuvius erupts destroying Pompeii and Herculaneum.
AD 1-100	**Americas**	* The Moche culture emerges in coastal northern Peru.
AD 500	**Americas**	* The Central Mexican city of Teotihuacán reaches its height in the 6th century.
	Europe	* The burial mounds at Sutton Hoo, on the coast of Suffolk, are in use from the late 6th century.
AD 600	**Americas**	* The Ancestral Puebloan (Anasazi) Indian society flourishes at Mesa Verde, meaning 'green table', in south-west Colorado.
AD 800	**Americas**	* Occupation begins at the city of Chichén Itzá in Mexico which served as the ceremonial centre for the Mayan empire.
AD 1000	**Americas**	* A group of Scandinavians settle at L'Anse aux Meadows in Newfoundland, Canada, they were the first Europeans to settle in the New World.
AD 1350	**Oceania**	* Shag River Mouth in New Zealand is occupied for about 50 years with a population of around 200 people.
AD 1400	**Americas**	* The Chimú are conquered by the Incas and the assimilation of their culture, including their advanced statecraft, engineering and religious practices, greatly influences the course of Inca civilization.
AD 1492	**Americas**	* The first voyage of Columbus is taken as the start of the modern era in archaeology and history, and the beginning of the process of globalization.
AD 1700	**Oceania**	* HMS *Pandora* sinks in Australia's Great Barrier Reef in the 1790s, the ship lays undiscovered until 1977.
AD 1800	**Americas**	* 1876 The Battle of Little Bighorn takes place.

ARCHAEOLOGISTS

'It was a thrilling moment for an excavator, quite alone save his native staff of workmen, to suddenly find himself, after so many years of toilsome work, on the verge of what looked like a magnificent discovery – an untouched tomb.'

HOWARD CARTER

The following chapters chart the lives and achievements of archaeologists such as Howard Carter – shown in the foreground of this photograph taken in 1923 – who have changed the face of archaeology and our understanding of the past.

FOUNDERS OF ARCHAEOLOGY

During the 19th century, adventurers and antiquarians realized that the secrets of the past lay beneath their feet. A cast of sometimes colourful, mostly self-taught amateurs populated archaeology in those years. Each had his style, from the hell-for-leather pursuit of the spectacular find of Schliemann, to Belzoni, who uncovered the Great Temple at Abu Simbel (facing page), and from the single-minded application of Champollion in his quest to decode Egyptian hieroglyphs, to the meticulous, analytical approach to excavation of Pitt Rivers, for whom the everyday was as important as the exotic. Whatever their ways and means, all of these men helped lay the foundations for today's scientific discipline of archaeology, whether by establishing methods, by capturing the public's imagination or simply by inspiring others to follow in their footsteps.

Opposite The twin temples at Abu Simnel are adorned with four colossal figures of Pharoah Ramesses II.

Arthur Evans On the island of Crete, Evans found the remains of Europe's oldest literate civilization, which he named 'Minoan'.

Ephraim George Squier The enigmatic Squier meticulously catalogued the work of the mid-West's so-called Mound Builders.

Max Uhle Known as the father of South American archaeology for his work at Pachácamac and other sites in the Andes.

Giovanni Belzoni

(1778-1823)

After a colourful early career, which included a stint as a strongman in an English circus, this 2m (6ft 7in) giant of a man, Italian by birth, went on to become one of the pioneering figures of Egyptology. Among other achievements, Belzoni uncovered the Great Temple at Abu Simbel.

Born the son of a barber, in Padua in north-eastern Italy, Giovanni Battista Belzoni was peripatetic from the start. At one time he wanted to become a monk, joining a Capuchin monastery, then changed his mind and turned his attention to hydraulic engineering. By his mid-twenties, he was married and living in London, where poverty led him to exploit his exceptional height and strength by working in fairs and

Below Egyptian workers under Belzoni haul the top part of the statue of Ramesses II from the Ramesseum in 1816. The lower section of the seated figure remains in situ.

circuses. Also at this time, he first met his future patron, the painter, traveller and antiquarian Henry Salt.

Arriving in Egypt

Belzoni never gave up his interest in hydraulics, however, and in 1815 he visited Egypt, with the aim of selling a new design of water wheel to the pasha (ruler), Mohammed Ali. When this project failed, Belzoni started to work for Salt, recently appointed British consul-general in Cairo.

His first commission was to retrieve the upper section of a colossal statue of Ramesses II for the British Museum

in London, where it remains today. The Italian's engineering skills came into play as he carefully removed the detached head-and-shoulders portion of the figure from the courtyard of the Ramesseum, on the Nile's west bank, opposite modern Luxor, and had it shipped back to England. He then sailed south to visit Abu Simbel. Back in Luxor, he carried out excavations at the Karnak Temple and discovered the tomb of Ay, Tutankhamen's successor.

In February 1817 Belzoni cleared away the deep blanket of sand under which the Great Temple at Abu Simbel had remained buried. In October he

entrance he had discovered hidden on the north face. He inscribed a message dating his discovery – 2 March 1818 – on the internal wall of the pyramid.

After a journey to the shores of the Red Sea, where he identified the ruins of the Greco-Roman port of Berenice, Belzoni travelled south to the island of Philae, located in the Nile near Aswan, to recover a fallen obelisk on behalf of Englishman William John Bankes. In spite of an altercation with the French Consul, Drovetti, who claimed the column for France, Belzoni succeeded in acquiring it. Bankes erected the obelisk in his garden at Kingston Lacy, Dorset, where it still stands. Belzoni then set out into the Western Desert towards Libya, where he hoped to find the oasis of Jupiter Ammon.

Into print

In 1820 Belzoni published his *Narrative of the Operations and Recent discoveries within the pyramids, temples, tombs and excavations in Egypt and Nubia; and of a journey to the coasts of the Red Sea, in search of the Ancient Berenice; and another in the oasis of Jupiter Ammon*. The work was a bestseller and was followed by a successful exhibition of his finds in the recently completed Egyptian Hall in Piccadilly, London.

In 1822 Belzoni travelled to Russia, where he met Tsar Alexander I. His last adventure was an attempt to reach the fabled city of Timbuktu. But he made it only as far as Benin in modern Nigeria, where he died of dysentery on 3 December 1823, aged 45.

Belzoni operated before the age of scientific archaeology and, judged by its precepts, his methods were open to question. He was more interested in finding monuments than in recording or studying them, and he often caused irreparable damage in the process. He has also been accused of being little more than a 'tomb robber', someone who hunted treasures in order to sell them to European collectors. Even so, his discoveries were groundbreaking and he was an inspiration to future generations of Egyptologists, assuring his place as a pioneer in the field.

Above Nineteenth-century travellers pose before the ruins of the Ramesseum. The complex, the mortuary temple of Ramesses II, one of Egypt's longest-reigning pharaohs, lies in western Thebes, opposite modern Luxor.

made a string of remarkable finds in the Valley of the Kings: the unfinished tomb of Prince Mentuherkhepshef (a son of Ramesses IX), the tomb of 19th Dynasty founder Ramesses I and the beautifully decorated tomb of his son, Seti I, father of Ramesses II.

Belzoni next worked at Giza, where in 1818 he became the first person in modern times to reach the interior of the Pyramid of Khaefre, the second largest of the pyramids at Giza, whose

J.F. Champollion

(1790-1832)

Champollion was the brilliant young scholar who in the early 1820s cracked the code of the Rosetta Stone. In doing so, he made it possible to solve one of the great academic mysteries of the age — how to decipher the lost language of ancient Egypt — and opened up a new era in Egyptology.

Jean-François Champollion was born less than a year after the start of the French Revolution and grew up in the town of Figeac in south-west France. He was a precocious child and enjoyed studying foreign languages, becoming proficient in many, including Italian, English, Latin, Greek, Arabic, Coptic and Chaldean. In 1809, when only 19, he was appointed assistant professor of history at the Lyceum of Grenoble, where he had been a student.

Given his interest in languages, it was natural that Champollion should become involved in the attempt to decipher ancient Egypt's hieroglyphic script. The French discovery, in 1799, of the Rosetta Stone, a stela (inscribed tablet) dating from the Ptolemaic era, offered a realistic chance of doing that, since it bears a decree written in two languages – Egyptian and Greek – but laid out in three texts. The Greek version uses Greek characters, but the Egyptian text is inscribed in both hieroglyphs and demotic script.

Slowly but resolutely, Champollion pieced together the different portions of the puzzle. By late 1821 he had proved that demotic was a late, much simplified version of hieroglyphs. He had also demonstrated that individual hieroglyphs did not necessarily stand for individual words, suggesting that they had a phonetic component – that some, at least, stood for particular sounds or groups of sounds. He knew too that royal names were written in cartouches (flattened ovals). The latter provided an important

Below The Rosetta Stone, discovered in Rosetta, Egypt, in 1799 by French troops, was the primary key to decoding Egyptian script. This is a detail of its hieroglyphic inscription.

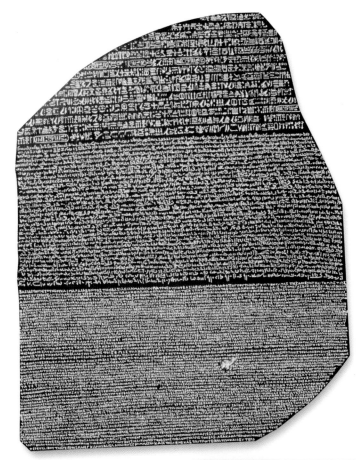

Right The bilingual inscription on the Rosetta Stone dates from 196 BC during the reign of King Ptolemy V of Egypt. The stone has been held by the British Museum since 1802.

lead, enabling Champollion to read 'Ptolemy' on the Rosetta Stone, both 'Ptolemy' and 'Cleopatra' on the obelisk recovered by Belzoni from the island of Philae and 'Alexander' on an inscription from the Karnak Temple. In this way Champollion was able to create an alphabet of 12 hieroglyphs, each one representing a sound, that could be applied to all Greco-Roman names written in Egyptian.

The puzzle completed

This phonetic solution to hieroglyphs worked with non-Egyptian names, but it was far from clear whether it held for Egyptian ones. The breakthrough came on 14 September 1822. While working on texts from the temples at Abu Simbel, which were 1500 years older than the inscriptions on the Rosetta Stone, and thus old enough to contain traditional Egyptian names, Champollion came across a cartouche that ended in a repeated hieroglyph. According to his phonetic alphabet, the symbol represented the sound of the letter 's', so he surmised that the royal name set down in the cartouche ended in a double 's'. Turning to the remaining two hieroglyphs in the cartouche, he postulated that the disc-shaped symbol at the beginning might represent the sun. In Coptic, a form of ancient Egyptian now used only by the Coptic Church, the word for sun is 'ra'. He then deduced that the second symbol in the cartouche stood for 'm' and that the name was Ramesses.

Fame at last

Champollion immediately presented his discoveries to the Academy of Inscriptions in Paris. Two years later he published a more comprehensive work, *A Summary of the Hieroglyphic System of the Ancient Egyptians*, in which he showed that hieroglyphs could represent sounds as well as concepts, depending on the context. The book

made him a celebrity and was the foundation upon which all further decoding of hieroglyphs was based.

In 1826 Champollion was named curator of the Egyptian collection of the Louvre Museum in Paris, then in 1828 began a year-long tour of Egypt, his first and only visit to the country. Champollion was created professor of archaeology at the Collège de France in Paris in March 1831 but died from a stroke a year afterwards. His ancient Egyptian grammar and dictionary were published posthumously, in 1836 and 1841 respectively.

Right This cartouche represents the name of Seti I. Cartouches similar to this but containing Greco-Roman names set Champollion on the road to deciphering hieroglyphs.

Sir Arthur Evans

(1851-1941)

On Crete, Arthur Evans discovered the remains of Europe's oldest literate civilization and believed that he had found the palace of the legendary King Minos. His interpretation has been derided as wish-fulfilment, yet Evans' methods mark him as a founder of modern field archaeology.

Arthur Evans first visited the island of Crete in 1894 to look for prehistoric coins and seals (clay tablets). As a boy in Hertfordshire, England, Evans had been fascinated by the inscriptions on ancient coins and artefacts collected by his father, Sir John Evans, who was a noted numismatist (coin specialist) and antiquarian. Sir John was also a successful businessman whose wealth enabled his son to first study modern history at Oxford and afterwards tour the Balkans. In 1876 Arthur Evans became special correspondent in the Balkans for *The Manchester Guardian*, and between then and 1882, when he was expelled from the region on political grounds, he identified the sites of several Roman roads and cities in Bosnia and Macedonia.

Below This fresco from 1700-1400 BC, found at Knossos, depicts bull-vaulting, believed to be a religious ritual among the Minoans.

In 1884 Evans took up a post as a keeper of the Ashmolean Museum in Oxford. He believed that a script, as yet undeciphered, on Aegean Bronze Age coins in the collections belonged to the Mycenaeans. He visited Athens to search for similar inscriptions and learnt that on Crete, peasants often unearthed inscribed seals, coins and gemstones when cultivating their fields.

Travels in Crete

Accompanied by a young student, John Myres (later celebrated for his archaeological excavations on Cyprus), Evans travelled through Crete in 1894-5, searching for sites and inscribed artefacts. The two nurtured the idea that the Greek myths were based on historical fact. The previous year Myres had applied for a licence to dig at the tell (artificial

mound) at Kephala (Knossos), where in 1878 the Cretan archaeologist Minos Kalokairinos had uncovered sections of a great building. Evans and Myres were not the only ones interested in digging at Kephala at around this time. Heinrich Schliemann was among the others who applied. All were unsuccessful although in 1895 Evans, with money and all the credentials and contacts of a journalist and antiquarian, was allowed to buy part of the site.

Kephala

Arthur Evans began his excavations at 11 a.m. on Friday, 23 March, 1900. He was assisted by David Hogarth and Duncan MacKenzie, experts in archaeological methods, and also by Theodore Fyfe, a specialist in ancient architecture. MacKenzie kept meticulous records of the excavations in his day books. The chambers and storerooms that the team uncovered and the artefacts they discovered there told them that the site was the palace-city of an early literate civilization. However, Evans's interpretations of the finds at the mound were controversial. Basing his deductions on the Homeric myths and

Above This is the smaller of two cult figurines from c.1500 BC discovered close to the central shrine at Knossos. Both figurines hold serpents and may have been snake goddesses.

on coins found at the site, which bore images of labyrinths, minotaurs and of Ariadne, daughter of King Minos, Evans declared that he had found the palace of the mythical Cretan king, who had kept the Minotaur (half man, half bull) in a labyrinth.

Some repair of the site's crumbling walls, stairs and foundations proved necessary for safety and for access to some parts of the complex. However, Evans rebuilt walls and reconstructed rooms using reinforced concrete, rebuilt timber structures and painted his 'reconstitutions', as he referred to them, in pink and terracotta; he also decorated rooms with reproduction frescoes. Evans declared one chamber to be the Throne Room of King Minos and restored it in what he considered to be appropriate style. Archaeologists today avoid such 'over-interpretation' and use of modern materials.

Evans excavated most of the palace complex in four years but lived and worked at Knossos for some 30 years, publishing his findings in four volumes between 1921 and 1931. His views on the site were widely accepted at first,

Above Minoan pillars, unlike Greek columns, are wider at the top than the bottom. Evans had many rebuilt and painted to match the plaster he found on some floors and walls.

and in 1911 he received a knighthood. However, his chronology for Minoan civilization clashed with the findings of other archaeologists working in the field and later investigations of the site concluded that the connection with the mythical King Minos was fanciful.

Evans's legacy

Some archaeologists have condemned Evans as a falsifier of history. Yet his achievements outweighed the errors he committed and he was no treasure-seeker. Evans discovered a previously unknown, literate civilization, which dated back beyond the Mycenaeans to the 3rd millennium BC and dominated the Aegean from 1900 to 1300 BC. He remains a towering figure in the development of archaeology, and the names he gave to the site at Kephala that he excavated, 'Knossos', and to the civilization that built it, 'Minoan', continue to be used today.

Above This fresco, known as 'the Prince with Lilies' or 'Priest-King', shows a figure wearing a headdress of lilies and peacock feathers. The fragments of this fresco were discovered beneath the Corridor of the Processions in the south section of the complex at Knossos.

271

Henry Layard

(1817-1894)

Layard was responsible, along with Frenchman Paul Emile Botta, for the first serious excavations in Mesopotamia (Iraq) and the rediscovery of the Assyrians. Display of his finds in the British Museum and his descriptions of his digs stimulated public enthusiasm for Near Eastern archaeology.

Born in Paris, Layard was the son of an official in the colonial civil service of Ceylon (Sri Lanka). After receiving an education in Europe and Britain, he entered a solicitor's office in London but left six years later with the aim of taking up a post in the Ceylon Civil Service himself. Travelling eastwards overland, Layard got only as far as the Middle East, which he explored thoroughly, visiting numerous ancient sites, including in Iraq various tells (artificial mounds) hiding the ruins of ancient Mesopotamian cities. The tells and the ruins they held fascinated Layard and he developed a desire to

excavate and study them for himself. It was in Iraq that he met Botta, who began excavating in the area of Mosul, in the north of the country, in 1842. That same year Layard's travels took him to Constantinople (Istanbul), the Ottoman capital, where he remained, carrying out unofficial diplomatic tasks for the British envoy, Stratford Canning, until he could fulfil his wish of returning to Iraq to excavate.

Uncovering Assyria

In 1845 Layard secured a gift of £100 from Canning and went back to Iraq to undertake his own excavations.

He began at a site called Nimrud, a tell situated near the banks of the Tigris, 30km (19 miles) south-east of Mosul. On the very first day Layard came across the ruins of an Assyrian palace, and a short time afterwards unearthed a second palace.

During two years of digging, Layard uncovered portions of half a dozen palaces decorated with the limestone wall-reliefs characteristic of Assyrian royal buildings, the colossal statues of human-headed winged bulls that guarded palace portals and numerous smaller works of art. Among the latter was the so-called Black Obelisk, which dated from 825 BC and depicted the military exploits of the Assyrian king Shalmaneser III, including the submission of Jehu, king of ancient Israel, to Assyrian dominion. Layard originally believed that he had found the remains of Nineveh, the Assyrian capital from c.700 BC until its fall in 612 BC. In fact the ruins were those of Kalhu, the biblical city of Calah, which had been the capital of the empire from the 9th century BC until Sargon II moved it north to Dur-Sharrukin (Khorsabad) in 717 BC.

Layard returned home to England in 1847, where his discoveries initially met with mixed reviews. Many people disparaged the aesthetic qualities of

Left A force of local workers moves an Assyrian winged bull statue at the site of Nimrud in 1849. This engraving is taken from Henry Layard's work *Discoveries in the Ruins of Nineveh and Babylon.*

Assyrian art, and the subject was even raised in Parliamentary committee, where the suitability of Layard's finds for display in the British Museum was discussed. Others, meanwhile, among them Layard's patron Canning, were elated. Layard himself sought popular support: his book *Nineveh and Its Remains* (1848-9) placed emphasis on the adventure of archaeology and the biblical associations of his results.

French competition

In 1846 the Louvre Museum in Paris had opened a display of Assyrian finds recovered by Botta, who three years previously had unearthed Sargon II's capital at Khorsabad. Some eminent British figures were not slow in seeing a challenge. Stratford Canning, for one, expressed in a letter to Prime Minister Robert Peel a belief that Layard's Assyrian finds 'will beat the Louvre hollow'. Persuaded by such appeals, the British Museum provided the then considerable sum of £2000 for the archaeologist to ship his finds back to London and continue his work in Mesopotamia. Layard arranged for the artefacts, including carved wall-reliefs and massive winged bulls, to be transported to Britain via India, where curiosity-seekers opened many crates awaiting passage on the quayside. The British Museum opened its Nineveh Gallery in 1853 to popular acclaim.

Layard used the remaining funds to excavate the tell at Kuyunjik, which lay to the east of the Tigris, opposite modern Mosul. In 1849 he uncovered the palace of Sennacherib and tens of thousands of clay tablets from the library of Assurbanipal. The latter find included Mesopotamian literature, dictionaries and other materials that would open the Mesopotamian world to scholarly study. This time there was no mistake: Layard had discovered the ancient city of Nineveh.

In 1849-50 Layard shifted his focus southwards, where he briefly explored Babylon, near modern Al-Hillah, and other mounds. However, used to the immediate results he had enjoyed with the Assyrian tells and unfamiliar with

the technical demands of excavating mud-brick architecture, Layard found these southern sites disappointing. Nevertheless, Layard again presented his findings to a fascinated public in *Discoveries in the Ruins of Nineveh and Babylon*, published in 1853.

A break with the past

Two years previously Layard had left Iraq and abandoned archaeology. In 1852 he entered British politics as Member of Parliament for Aylesbury, subsequently rising to Under Secretary

Above The ruins of the final Assyrian capital of Nineveh were unearthed at Kuyunjik, near Mosul in northern Iraq. Frenchman Paul Emile Botta was the first to excavate at the site, but the breakthrough was made by Layard.

for foreign affairs and being appointed privy counsellor. He served as an MP until 1869, when he traded politics for diplomacy, becoming ambassador first to Spain and later to the Ottoman court in Constantinople, the position formerly held by Layard's one-time patron Stratford Canning.

Auguste Mariette
(1821-1881)

As first Director of Egyptian Monuments, appointed in 1858, Mariette was the most influential Egyptologist of his generation. His achievements included bringing order to the hitherto largely unregulated excavation of the country's antiquities, and the founding of the Egyptian Museum.

A native of Boulogne-sur-Mer on the north coast of France, Mariette spent a brief period in his late teens working in England, first as a schoolmaster and then as a designer for a ribbon-maker. In 1840 he returned to France to complete his education and then took up a teaching position in Boulogne. His fascination with ancient Egypt was triggered in 1842, when he was asked

Below Mariette's first great discovery was the Serapeum. Here is one of the huge granite sarcophagi in which the bulls were buried.

to put in order the papers of the recently deceased archaeologist and draughtsman Nestor L'Hôte, a relative who had accompanied Champollion on his 1828 expedition to Egypt. After years of private study of the Coptic and Egyptian languages, in 1847 Mariette published a catalogue of the Egyptian collection in the Boulogne Museum. Two years later, he obtained a junior post at the Louvre Museum.

In 1850 Mariette visited Egypt to collect Coptic manuscripts for the Bibliothèque Nationale. However, he

Above Ka-aper was a chief lector-priest during the reign of Userkaf (2465-2458 BC). Mariette's workers found the statue near the king's pyramid at Saqqara in 1860.

found manuscripts in short supply and turned instead to archaeology. His first excavation at Saqqara resulted in the discovery of the Serapeum – the galleries where the sacred bulls of the Apis cult were buried. Mariette went on digging at Saqqara for a further four years before returning to France.

Route to the top

By now an assistant conservator in the Louvre's department of Egyptology, and an archaeologist of some repute,

Right Egyptian workers haul sarcophagi (stone cases) from a tomb, watched over by Mariette (far right). His appointment as the first Director of Egyptian Monuments brought some regulation to the export of artefacts.

Mariette went back to Egypt in 1857 to help to prepare for a visit by Prince Napoleon, a cousin of the French Emperor Napoleon III. He launched a series of excavations at Giza, Saqqara, Abydos, Thebes and Elephantine, where his workmen busily sought out antiquities, which they then reburied so the prince could 'discover' them. The next year the Ottoman viceroy of Egypt, Said Pasha, appointed Mariette to the newly created post of Director of Egyptian Monuments, giving him effective control of the country's antiquities. From then until the end of his life, Egypt was Mariette's home.

Using his near-absolute powers, the new director restricted the selling and export of Egypt's antiquities. In 1859 Mariette persuaded Said Pasha to set up a museum at Bulaq, near Cairo, where they could be preserved. These collections were the basis for today's Egyptian Museum in Cairo, which was eventually opened on its current site in 1902. Mariette also embarked on a massive countrywide programme of simultaneous excavations, employing a force of almost 3000 workers. His projects included the first digs to take place at the Karnak Temple, situated in modern Luxor, as well as a 20-year excavation in the Nile Delta at Tanis, the biblical city of Zoan and a capital of ancient Egypt. In 1859 Mariette's workers found a virtually intact tomb in the necropolis of Dra Abu'l Naga, on the west bank of the Nile at Thebes (opposite Luxor). The treasure-filled coffin within belonged to Ah-hotep, mother of Ahmose I, founder of the 18th Dynasty, among whose pharaohs were Tutankhamen and Akhenaten. The next year Mariette began clearing the temple at Edfu, situated some 96km (60 miles) south of Luxor. The temple had developed into a village over the centuries, with houses having been built even on the sanctuary roof.

Nevertheless, though he nominally excavated at least 35 sites, Mariette was rarely on the spot to supervise his workforce, and the standard of his digs was not high. Additionally, many of his written records were lost when his house at Bulaq flooded in 1878.

Rank and honour

Mariette published a vast range of books and papers, including *Catalogue of the Boulaq Museum* (1864-76), *The Serapeum of Memphis* (1857) and *Karnak* (1875). He also received numerous honours, among them the Légion d'Honneur in 1852 and acceptance into the Académie des Inscriptions et des Belles-Lettres in 1878; in Egypt he was elevated to the rank of bey and later to that of pasha. In addition to his many accomplishments in Egyptology, he also collaborated on the libretto of Verdi's Egyptian-themed opera, *Aïda*, first performed in 1871 in Cairo.

Mariette died in 1881, having been in poor health for some years, and was interred in a sarcophagus at Bulaq. With the completion of the Egyptian Museum in Cairo in 1902, the coffin was moved to the building's forecourt and remains there, surmounted by a bronze statue of the former Director of Egyptian Monuments, which was unveiled in 1904.

Jacques de Morgan

(1857-1924)

Frenchman de Morgan began his working life as a mining engineer but combined this work with a strong and growing interest in archaeology. He eventually abandoned engineering when he accepted the appointment of Director-General of the Egyptian Antiquities Service.

The son of a mining engineer, Jacques de Morgan was born near the town of Blois in north-western France. His father bequeathed him not only his professional leanings but also his avid interest in prehistory. De Morgan graduated from the School of Mines in 1882 and began a career that took him to many parts of northern Europe and Asia. While managing a copper mine in Russian Armenia, he studied early

Below A photograph taken in the 1950s of the 1897 French excavation site at Susa. The project unearthed some remarkable finds, but the approach used meant that all archaeological context was lost.

metallurgy in the Caucasus. He then headed a scientific mission to Persia (Iran), where he combined geological studies – he was the first person to recognize the presence of petroleum in the south-west of the country – with archaeological inquiry.

Late in 1891 de Morgan returned to France but the following year took up the post of Director-General of the Egyptian Antiquities Service, which he held until 1897. While in Egypt, he founded the Greco-Roman Museum in Alexandria and laid the cornerstone of the Cairo Museum. He also carried out some field work, including a brief exploration of Naqada, a prehistoric

site about 24km (15 miles) north of modern Luxor, and the excavation of several pyramids at Dahshur, where he found a trove of royal jewellery dating from ancient Egypt's Middle Kingdom (*c.*1975-1640 BC).

A move to Persia

In 1897 de Morgan was appointed director of the Délégation en Perse, a permanent mission formed to exploit the archaeological research monopoly that Persia had granted France two years earlier. He decided to focus on the ancient city of Susa in the winters and pass the summers in north-west Iran exploring prehistoric cemeteries. His work in the Caucasus shows he could be a competent prehistorian, but he was not prepared for Susa. Deciding that stratigraphic excavation (layer-by-layer analysis) would not be possible, he treated Susa as a 'strip-mining' exercise. Employing a team of 1200 labourers, he removed huge quantities of earth – according to one estimate, 2.45 million cubic metres (86.5 million cubic feet) in less than a decade. As a result, he recovered some superb pieces of Mesopotamian art, including the Victory Stela of Naram-Sin and the Law Code of Hammurabi, but entirely without archaeological or architectural context.

In 1907 he turned over direction of the Susa dig and in 1912 resigned from the Délégation. Returning to France he devoted the remainder of his life to writing such works as the three-volume *La préhistoire orientale*.

Edouard Piette

(1827-1906)

Edouard Piette was a pioneering prehistorian in 19th-century France, who ruined himself financially with his excavations of Palaeolithic cave sites in the south-west of the country. He also amassed the finest collection of Ice Age portable art objects, including the 'Lady of Brassempouy'.

Piette was a lawyer by profession and worked as a provincial magistrate for most of his life. Born at Aubigny in the Ardennes, in north-eastern France, he developed a strong interest in geology at an early age. While a student of law in Paris, he was able to indulge this passion by attending geology lectures at the Sorbonne and at the School of Mines. From geology, his scope soon spread to archaeology and prehistory, especially in the French Pyrenees.

Cave sites in the Pyrenees

Although he carried out important work on tumuli (burial mounds) and monuments of later prehistory, Piette is especially remembered for his pioneering excavations at much earlier sites, such as the caves at Lortet, Arudy, Gourdan and, in particular, Le Mas-d'Azil – all of which are in or near the Pyrenees. At Le Mas-d'Azil, in the foothills of the central part of the range, he first identified a phase in prehistory between the end of the Ice Age and the start of the Neolithic period. Characterized by flat bone harpoons and small pebbles decorated with red dots and stripes, the culture came to be known as the Azilian.

Like other scholars of the period, Piette did not excavate himself but employed workmen to do it, checking them from time to time. He was, nonetheless, a pioneer in many other ways. Not only was he the first scholar to help fill the 'hiatus' after the Ice Age, but he was also one of the first

to find sites by searching systematically in suitable parts of the landscape. He was remarkably open-minded, willing to explore concepts such as the possibility that Palaeolithic people had already started cultivating plants and had succeeded in at least semi-domesticating horses. Piette was one of the very few prehistorians to believe Sanz de Sautuola's claims that figures of

animals in the Altamira cave in northern Spain were painted during the Palaeolithic period. He was also largely responsible for introducing the young Abbé Henri Breuil to the field of prehistory: Piette employed Breuil to produce illustrations of some of his portable art objects.

The beautiful 'Lady'

Piette died in 1906, shortly before the publication of *L'Art Pendant l'Age du Renne* (1907), a magnificent volume devoted to his collection of Ice Age portable art. Even though his research and excavations had left him ruined financially, Piette bequeathed his art collection to the French nation. As well as numerous fine pieces that he had found himself, it also contained items he had acquired from others. Among its best-known pieces is the 'Lady of Brassempouy', a tiny but exquisite carving of a female head, fashioned from a mammoth tusk. Dating from about 21,000 BC, it was found in 1894 in the Grotte du Pape, a cave at Brassempouy in the foothills of the Pyrenees. The statuette can be seen at the National Museum of Antiquities at Saint-Germain-en-Laye near Paris.

Left The 'Lady of Brassempouy', also known as the 'Lady with the Hood', is a statuette standing 3.6cm (1½in) high. It is one of the earliest known examples of a sculpture of the human face – a generalized representation rather than the portrait of an individual.

Augustus Pitt Rivers
(1827-1900)

Nearly 40 years in the British army equipped Pitt Rivers with a military precision, which he brought to the field of archaeology. He established new standards in excavations, insisting on keeping meticulous records of exactly where artefacts were found and the prompt publication of results.

Archaeological excavations during the 19th century were largely unscientific affairs. Diggers often paid little attention to recording the positions of artefacts in the ground, and haphazard methods of excavation prevented accurate logging of the soil layers and the collection of other key information. Furthermore, published documentation was very scarce. It took a retired

Below Pitt Rivers (standing on the top of the mound) supervises the excavation of Wor Barrow on his estate in 1893-4. This long barrow was a Neolithic burial site.

British army general, known to us by his inherited name of Pitt Rivers, to begin to place archaeological field research on a professional footing.

A military career

Pitt Rivers was born Augustus Henry Lane Fox in Hope Hall, Yorkshire, the son of a British military officer. In 1841 he entered the Royal Military Academy at Sandhurst and embarked on his own army career, receiving a commission in the Grenadier Guards in 1845. He was a soldier for almost 40 years, serving in England, Canada,

Ireland, the Crimea and Malta. Lane Fox retired in 1882 with the rank of lieutenant general.

During his military service, Lane Fox began to collect artefacts from the places in which he was stationed. He started by acquiring weapons and then extended his collecting to a broader range of objects, both practical and decorative. His interest went beyond simple acquisition; he was concerned with charting the development down through the ages of practical objects, among them the rifle, a field of study he described as 'typology'.

Left Pitt Rivers was an avid collector throughout his adult life. The items shown here were all found by the 'father of scientific archaeology' and are a jar from London, a Bronze Age axe (below left) and a Neolithic flint axe from Farnham, Dorset.

name of Pitt Rivers; they also enabled him to retire comfortably. His estate spread out over a large expanse of chalk downland in the south of England. Called Cranbourne Chase, it lies where the counties of Hampshire, Dorset and Wiltshire meet.

As his army career went on, Lane Fox also began to excavate archaeological sites and to make detailed notes about his work. Beginning in Ireland in the early 1860s, when he was in his 30s, he investigated sites of many different periods in Brittany, southern England, Wales and even Denmark. In general, Lane Fox worked alone or with a few chosen companions and, from time to time, with hired workers.

In 1880, in his early 50s, Lane Fox inherited an estate of 3500 ha (8650 acres) as well as a large annual income of about £20,000 under the will of his great uncle, Henry Pitt, the second Lord Rivers. The terms of the will required Lane Fox to assume the

In medieval times, the area had been a royal hunting ground and, until the 19th century, farming there was strictly limited, which meant that any archaeological sites on the estate, such as barrows (burial mounds), had survived largely untouched.

Excavating the Chase

Recognizing the archaeological riches of his land and the neighbouring parts of Cranbourne Chase, Pitt Rivers devoted the rest of his life to their meticulous excavation. He worked on dozens of Bronze Age barrows, as well as investigating several Bronze Age, Iron Age, Roman and Romano-British enclosures. To help him, he had a staff

of draughtsmen, surveyors, foremen, excavators and clerks — all labouring under the retired general's demanding and eccentric personality. Pitt Rivers's techniques were ahead of their time, setting standards for documentation and publication that established the foundations upon which archaeology developed in the twentieth century. The results of this work appeared in four imposing volumes, *Excavations in Cranbourne Chase*, published between 1887 and 1898.

Safe pair of hands

When the appointment of Inspector of Monuments was introduced in 1882, Pitt Rivers became the first to hold it, and approached the task of cataloguing and protecting Britain's archaeological sites with customary meticulousness. Despite the fact that his own archaeological research was overshadowed by spectacular finds made elsewhere during his lifetime, such as those of Schliemann at Troy and Mycenae, which had not benefited from such a painstaking approach, Pitt Rivers's contribution to archaeological method came to be appreciated in the decades after his death. A particular disciple was Sir Mortimer Wheeler, himself a military man, who hailed the excavation principles used by Pitt Rivers as the inspiration for his own field work. Pitt Rivers died on 4 May 1900, at the age of 73.

The Pitt Rivers Museum

In 1884, sixteen years before his death, Pitt Rivers gave a collection of about 20,000 archaeological and ethnographic artefacts to the University of Oxford. Today, the Pitt Rivers Museum is one of the world's most remarkable museums, organized by artefact function rather than period or region. This means that all artefacts with a particular purpose can be seen together. The museum's collections have now expanded to include more than 250,000 objects.

Above The fascinating collections at the Pitt Rivers Museum in Oxford give the visitor an insight into how different cultures overcame similar problems.

Above Like the items at the top of the page, this Anglo-Saxon pot, found by Pitt Rivers, is part of a collection that was acquired by the Salisbury and South Wiltshire Museum in 1975.

Henry Rawlinson

(1810-1895)

Soldier, politician and Orientalist, Henry Creswicke Rawlinson was also a noted linguist, whose work from the 1830s to the 1850s on the inscriptions at Behistun helped to decode the cuneiform scripts and make possible the study of the writings of the ancient Mesopotamian world.

Born in the north Oxfordshire village of Chadlington, Rawlinson joined the East India Company as an officer cadet in 1827. Five years later he was posted to Persia (Iran) to help reorganize the Shah's army. During his two years in Persia, he acquired and developed the fascination with cuneiform scripts that would last the rest of his life.

Until the 1830s comparatively little progress had been made in decoding cuneiform scripts, partly for lack of a key like Egypt's Rosetta Stone, a text in several languages, one of which could already be read. Rawlinson and a number of other scholars eventually created that key with their work on the long cuneiform texts that the Persian king Darius I (reigned 521-486 BC) had had inscribed on his tomb near Persepolis and on a cliff at Behistun in western Iran. This text was written in three tongues: Elamite (the language of Susa), Akkadian (the language of Babylon and the Assyrians) and Old Persian. Rawlinson began copying the Behistun inscription in 1835 but had completed only the Old Persian and Elamite versions of the text when tensions between Britain and Persia obliged him to leave.

Another in the field

Rawlinson was not the only scholar attempting to decipher the cuneiform scripts, but he undertook much of his early work in isolation. In 1838 he published the still incomplete results of his work on the Old Persian text from Behistun, unaware of the more successful efforts of the Irish cleric Edward Hincks, who was the first to present the Old Persian cuneiform alphabet. In 1840 Rawlinson went to Kandahar in Afghanistan as political agent but gained a transfer to Turkish Arabia, where he was British Resident in Baghdad from 1843 to 1849. From Baghdad, Rawlinson was able in 1847 to copy the Akkadian text at Behistun, and in 1851 he published a translation of the first column of the Akkadian version, plus the systematic reading of 246 signs. This was a stunning and decisive breakthrough.

The Akkadian cuneiform was more complicated than the Old Persian. It was a syllabic script, with numerous logograms (signs representing whole words). Sceptics doubted the claims of Rawlinson and others that they had decoded it. In 1857 the Royal Asiatic Society put these doubts to rest. The society placed a newly discovered text before four scholars, among them Rawlinson and Hincks, who returned basically similar translations.

Though known chiefly as a linguist, Rawlinson also undertook some field archaeology. In 1851, having given a collection of Near Eastern antiquities to the British Museum, he received funding from the museum to continue Henry Layard's explorations in Iraq. Retiring from the East India Company in 1855, Rawlinson served as a crown director of the company. He also held a number of diplomatic and cultural posts, including a trusteeship of the British Museum, and was an MP in the 1850s and 1860s.

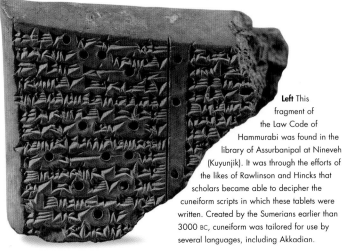

Left This fragment of the Law Code of Hammurabi was found in the library of Assurbanipal at Nineveh (Kuyunjik). It was through the efforts of the likes of Rawlinson and Hincks that scholars became able to decipher the cuneiform scripts in which these tablets were written. Created by the Sumerians earlier than 3000 BC, cuneiform was tailored for use by several languages, including Akkadian.

Sanz de Sautuola

(1831-1888)

Don Marcelino Sanz de Sautuola will forever be linked with the cave of Altamira in Cantabria, northern Spain, whose huge coloured wall and ceiling decorations dating from the Ice Age led him to realize that Palaeolithic people had produced great works of art.

Born in the coastal city of Santander, the capital of the region of Cantabria in northern Spain, Sanz de Sautuola trained as a lawyer. Nevertheless, as a prominent landowner, he did not need to work and was able to devote his time to his numerous interests, among them geology, botany and prehistory.

The marvellous find

In 1876 Sanz de Sautuola paid a visit to a hill called Altamira, which lay on land owned by his family. He had been informed of the existence of a cave by local farmer Modesto Cubillas, who while out hunting eight years earlier had followed his dog into an opening in the hillside, only to discover a series of chambers and passages. During his 1876 visit Sanz de Sautuola noticed some black painted signs on a wall but paid them little attention. In 1879 he returned to do some excavating, and while he was digging in the cave floor for prehistoric tools and portable art of the kind he had not long ago seen displayed at a Paris exhibition, his five-year-old daughter Maria was playing in the cavern. Suddenly, she spotted a number of coloured paintings of animals on the ceiling.

Her father was utterly dumbstruck. He found that the figures seemed to have been created with a fatty paste and noticed the similarity in style between these huge depictions (the red deer is 2.2m/7ft 3in long) and the smaller portable figures he had seen in Paris. He therefore deduced that both types of art were of a similar age, but when he attempted to convince the academic establishment, his ideas met with widespread rejection. Indeed, so well preserved were the paintings that he was even accused of forgery. In 1902 academia recanted and declared that Sanz de Sautuola had been right. Sadly, the news came too late for the Spaniard, who died in 1888, a sad and disillusioned man.

Below The Altamira paintings date from c.14,000-12,000 BC. The animals depicted include bison, horses and deer.

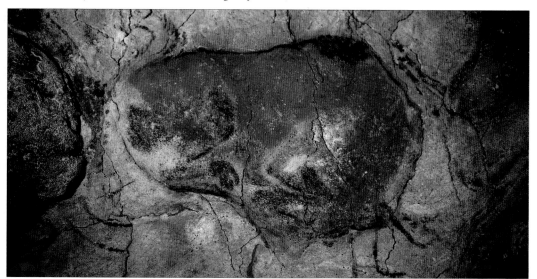

Heinrich Schliemann

(1822-1890)

Self-made businessman and self-taught archaeologist, Schliemann defied the opinions of experts and proved that places described by Homer had existed. By 1873 he had unearthed the site of Troy, and in 1876 he brought to light the Bronze Age civilization of Mycenae.

Schliemann was born into the large family of a poor Protestant minister in the Duchy of Mecklenberg-Schwerin in northern Germany. He mantained that his father imbued in him a love of Homer, which seeded his desire to find the ruins of Troy. This claim may have been wishful thinking, because records show that after the death of Schliemann's mother, his father sent him away, aged 11, to a fee-paying school in a neighbouring duchy. Only months later, though, he had to leave, his father having been accused of embezzling church funds. He then attended a vocational school until, at 14, he was apprenticed to a grocer.

At the age of 19, Schliemann signed on as a cabin boy to work his passage to the Americas but was shipwrecked and washed up in Holland. He was taken on by a commodities company and later by an import/export firm, where he displayed acute judgement and a flair for languages. He was sent to St Petersburg as an agent, then in 1851 sailed for California, where he set up in banking, buying and reselling gold dust from prospectors. In 1852 he returned to Russia, cornered the market in indigo, then moved into munitions when the Crimean War began. By his early forties, having made his fortune three times over, he had retired from business.

Troy and Mycenae

Free of the need to work, Schliemann travelled widely and, in 1868, while on a visit to Ottoman Turkey, he met

Frank Calvert, a British archaeologist and consular official. Some historians surmise that Schliemann's obsession with proving the historical existence of Troy, then thought to have existed only in legend, may have emerged at this point. For 20 years Calvert had believed that a tell (artificial mound) at Hissarlik in Turkey was the site of Troy but could not raise the funds to excavate it. Schliemann became his financial partner and, after writing a thesis in support of Calvert's ideas, took over his excavations. He began

Below Schliemann's second wife, Sophia, wears the 'Jewels of Helen', part of the cache known as 'Priam's Treasure', found in the 1870s at Level II of the excavation at Troy.

digging in 1871 and soon found that several cities lay beneath the mound at progressively lower levels. Reasoning that Homeric Troy must be the city at the bottom, Schliemann dug through the ruins of later cities – destroying much archaeological evidence as he went. Later Wilhelm Dörpfeld would divide the site at Hissarlik into nine levels, with Level I, the oldest, at the bottom. In the event, Schliemann got down to Level II, and believed he had uncovered Homeric Troy.

Priam's Treasure

By 1873 Schliemann had unearthed not only the remains of a fortified city but also a spectacular treasure of gold and jewellery. This he believed to be the treasure of King Priam, ruler of Troy during the war against Greece, immortalized in Homer's epic *Iliad*. However, controversy overshadowed his discovery of the treasure, since Schliemann, possibly with Calvert's cooperation, smuggled it out of the country. Schliemann published an account of his excavations in 1874. It was met with a mixture of acclaim and scepticism: archaeologists disparaged both his destructive methods and his fanciful theories. Indeed, Level II at Hissarlik was later dated to about 2500-2300 BC, a thousand years too early for the Troy of the *Iliad*, which has been placed at Level VI/VII.

Schliemann, meanwhile, had a new project. He determined to prove the claim of Pausanias, a geographer of the 2nd century AD, that Agamemnon, who led the Greek attack on Troy, was buried at the hilltop site of Mycenae. He selected a site just inside the gate of the citadel and in August 1876, under the supervision of the Greek Archaeological Society, began digging. Within a month he had uncovered the first of several tombs of Bronze Age chieftains in what is now labelled 'Grave Circle A'. Five wore gold face masks and each had been buried with spectacular weapons, ornaments and vessels of precious metals. Schliemann announced that he had discovered the tombs of Agamemnon, Cassandra and Eurymedon, and the finest of the five masks became known as 'the face of Agamemnon'. Once again, however, these finds were later found to be too old, this time by 300 years.

Troy and Mycenae were not the whole sum of Schliemann's projects. In 1868 he excavated on Ithaca, the legendary island home of Odysseus in the Ionian Sea, and in 1884 he dug at

Tiryns, the Mycenaean hill fort whose ruins Pausanius had visited. Yet Schliemann went back time and again to reopen his site at Troy: in 1878 when he found two more small caches of treasure; again in 1882; and finally in 1888, two years before his death in Naples from an ear infection.

Schliemann's reputation suffered as a result of his damaging excavation methods, dubious site interpretations, lawsuits resulting from his theft of ancient grave goods, and the untruths in his autobiographical writings. He has even been accused of forging some of the treasures he claimed to have found and has often been dismissed as a treasure-seeker. Yet archaeologists today grant his claim to have 'opened up a new world for archaeology' and pay tribute to his determination, energy and dedication – he funded all his excavations – in furthering and publicizing archaeology.

Above This gold chalice with rosette decoration was recovered from Tomb IV of Grave Circle A at Mycenae in Greece and has been dated to the 16th century BC.

Below This photograph from the turn of the 20th century shows sightseers examining Grave Circle A, uncovered by Schliemann in 1876 amid the ruins of Mycenae.

Ephraim Squier

(1821-1888)

Employed variously as journalist, political official and diplomat, Squier is one of the most enigmatic figures in the history of American archaeology. His major work was to catalogue and classify for posterity the prehistoric earthen mounds of the mid-West, many of which are now lost.

Born in Bethlehem, New York, Squier was the son of a Methodist minister. After flirting with civil engineering, education and the law, he became a journalist, editing various publications in New York State, Connecticut and Ohio. He then entered the political world as clerk to the latter state's House of Representatives. While living in the mid-West, Squier became one of the best-known antiquaries in America for his work on the 'Mound Builders'.

The mid-Western states are famous for the many earthen mounds that dot the landscape. These mounds reach back to the prehistoric period, some as far back as the 4th millennium BC,

and had a variety of functions: some were burial sites, for instance, while others were religious in nature. The site of the ancient city of Cahokia in Illinois, inhabited from about AD 700-1400, has mounds of many shapes, the largest of which is believed to have supported the chief's residence; Great Serpent Mound in Ohio is, as its name suggests, in the shape of a snake.

Enter Ephraim Squier

Squier's contribution to the discussion over the origins of these earthworks was the publication in 1848 of *Ancient Monuments of the Mississippi Valley*, a landmark in American scientific research whose byline he shared with

local antiquarian E.H. Davis, although he was responsible for most of the writing. This volume was unique in its comprehensiveness and its accuracy in describing and drawing the mounds, for its meticulous classification of the different categories of mounds and the detailed descriptions of the artefacts and their art styles. Squier felt that the mounds had been built by a lost race of Mound Builders – not the ancestors of contemporary Native Americans as some had postulated. Indeed, it was the prevailing view at the time that the forerunners of the Native Americans would have been incapable of such feats of engineering. The book made him a household name. Furthermore, since so many of the sites he described have since disappeared as a result of development, the volume is invaluable to modern archaeologists.

In 1848 Squier's support for newly elected president Zachary Taylor led to his being appointed US chargé d'affaires in Central America. While he was there, he published works on the region's monuments as well as on its peoples. Squier was able to extend his study of ancient monuments to South America when President Lincoln sent him to Peru as US commissioner in 1862. He returned to New York six years later and in 1873 was divorced. During his life he suffered periodic bouts of mental illness until his death in 1888.

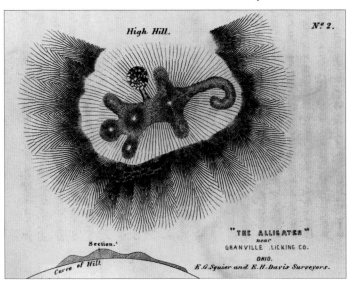

Left The Alligator in central Ohio is one of a number of mounds in the shape of an animal.

Thomsen and Worsaae

(1788-1865 and 1821-1885)

Long before the age of scientific archaeology, Christian Jurgensen
Thomsen, curator of the Danish National Museum, and his one-time
assistant Jens Jacob Asmussen Worsaae instigated and developed the
Three-Age System, still the framework for organizing Eurasian prehistory.

Thomsen was born in Copenhagen, Denmark, following his father into the family wholesale business. When his parents died, he sold up and devoted himself to his antiquarian interests. In 1816, despite his lack of training, he was entrusted with the curatorship of the nation's Collection of Northern Antiquities, later to develop into the Danish National Museum.

His appointment occurred because by the start of the 19th century, it was clear to scholars throughout most of

Below This burial site north of Alborg, Denmark, dates back as far as the Germanic Iron Age (AD 400-800), which was the final phase of the Iron Age in Northern Europe.

Europe that ancient objects lay in the soil. Collections of artefacts began to develop as the activities of farming and industry disturbed many sites. With a view to conserving its wealth of material, Denmark set up a Royal Committee for the Preservation and Collection of National Antiquities, which in turn appointed Thomsen.

Based in the loft of Trinitatis Church in Copenhagen, Thomsen sought to bring order to the chaotic collections and figure out a logical way to display them. He chose to classify the cutting tools according to the material used to make them: stone, bronze and iron. This way of working was not new, but Thomsen extended the classification

Above This cremation urn lid, from Bronze Age Denmark, is thought to depict the marriage of the god and goddess of fertility.

to the other materials that were found along with the tools. Certain types of pottery, for example, were associated only with stone implements, while glass beads were found only with iron tools. In this way Thomsen was able to impose order on the collections and propose a chronological scheme: the Stone Age, succeeded by the Bronze Age, followed by the Iron Age. Today we call this the 'Three-Age System'.

One step further

Worsaae, born in Vejle, Denmark, was an assistant to Thomsen from 1838 to 1843 and his successor as the National Museum's curator. Worsaae extended the Three-Age System from museum displays into the field, using layer-by-layer excavation to demonstrate its validity. Some have called Worsaae the 'first professional archaeologist' for his analytical approach to excavation and the study of finds. As a result of his work Thomsen's Three-Age System was adopted throughout Europe.

The Three-Age System still survives as a convenient organizing principle of Eurasian prehistory, and the Stone and Iron Age categories are also applied in Africa. While it is not considered to be an inevitable progression of cultural and technological development, and many of the most interesting times straddle the ages, it still provides a set of basic chronological markers.

Max Uhle

(1856-1944)

It is impossible to study the ancient civilizations of the Andes without coming across the work of Max Uhle. He brought scientific methods to South American archaeology and formed the basis for our understanding of the relationships of the region's ancient peoples.

Uhle was born in the city of Dresden in eastern Germany. Archaeology did not exist as a discipline when he was growing up and studying, and in 1880 he received his Ph.D. at the University of Leipzig in linguistics; his thesis was on Chinese grammar. Uhle then found work in a Dresden museum, where he came into contact with archaeological objects from around the world. In particular he got the chance to study a range of pieces from the Andes, which were flowing into Germany at that time along with people fleeing the 1879-1884 War of the Pacific between Chile, Bolivia and Peru. Meanwhile, a geologist friend, Alphons Stübel, provided him with data from the ruined city of Tiwanaku (Tiahuanaco) in Bolivia, including photographs and moulds, as well as measurements of architectural features.

After studying the Americas from afar and publishing on Tiwanaku and other aspects of the archaeology of the region, Uhle eventually visited South America in the early 1890s. It was the beginning of a prolific career as a field archaeologist during which he became one of the most important figures in the study of the ancient civilizations of the Americas. Uhle's work was critical both to establishing a number of the main stylistic sequences of Andean archaeology, including those of Nasca

Below Uhle was instrumental in showing that Tiwanaku, Bolivia was a pre-Inca site. This is the ruins' Kalasasaya mound.

and Tiwanaku, and to our knowledge of the archaeological sequence of Andean South America.

First studies

Uhle's early archaeological projects included explorations in Argentina, Bolivia and Chile. His research at Tiwanaku helped establish it as one of the most important pre-Inca cities in the region, and also convinced the Bolivian government to protect what is now one of their most important tourist destinations. It was his analysis of the styles and content of the images on the stonework at Tiwanaku, based on the material brought back by his geologist friend Stübel, that showed that the site predated the Inca. Uhle's identification of similar styles in pottery and other artefacts found at Pachácamac and other sites in coastal Peru laid the groundwork for the timeline of Andean archaeology in use today, although that has been greatly refined in the past century.

Another of Uhle's analyses that has withstood the test of time is his 1917 classification of the mummies of the ancient Chinchorro people, a small-scale society of fishers and hunters of the coastal Atacama desert. Uhle came across the mummies during a visit to northern Chile and he arranged them into three types – simple, complex, simple but clay-covered – a system which is still in use. Since chronometric dating techniques were not available to Uhle in those days, he had no idea how old the mummies were. Later work showed that they are the world's oldest artificially prepared mummies, predating those of ancient Egypt by around 2000 years.

Above These human remains were unearthed in 2005 in an Inca cemetery in Pachácamac, a sacred site first excavated by Uhle in 1896.

However, Uhle's best-known work was on the site of Pachácamac, now an important tourist destination around 40km (25 miles) south of Lima, Peru. A vast settlement built of mud brick but with some stone architecture, it housed one of the most sacred shrines of the Andes under the Inca. Uhle's excavations at Pachácamac included painstaking analysis and documentation of the soil layers, in which he was able to identify several different styles of pottery. He argued that the variations in style represented different periods of occupation. This work was not only a rich source of data but also produced fabulous and important archaeological collections. Furthermore, it laid the groundwork for the ongoing study of Pachácamac and the chronological and geographical relationships of different archaeological cultures.

Widely considered to be the 'father of South American archaeology', Uhle nevertheless published little. His few works include *The Ruins of Tiahuanaco in the Highlands of Ancient Peru* (with Stübel, 1891) and *Pachácamac: Report of the William Pepper, M.D., LL.D., Peruvian Expedition of 1896* (1903).

Left Among the artefacts given up by Tiwanaku is this incense burner in the form of a puma, for use in religious ceremonies.

PIONEERS OF ARCHAEOLOGY

The early 20th century saw the emergence of a new breed of archaeologists, the first true professionals. Their methods were fast becoming more rigorous and careful than those of their predecessors, and they laid the foundations for the scientific approach of our own times. Many of the scholars of the period are among the greatest names in the history of the subject; some of archaeology's most famous discoveries, such as Machu Picchu, the tomb of Tutankhamen, the burials of Ur and the Indus city of Mohenjo-Daro (facing page), are owed to their skill and luck. The first great women archaeologists also came to the fore – Dorothy Garrod and Gertrude Caton-Thompson, for example. The arsenal of techniques available for studying the past also expanded dramatically, with the arrival of aerial photography, pollen analysis and eventually radiocarbon dating.

Opposite Mohenjo-Daro, or Mound of the Dead, was one of the largest cities of the Indus civilisation.

Henri Breuil During his lifetime, this French archaeologist was considered the foremost authority on Palaeolithic cave art.

Gertrude Caton-Thompson Her excavations at Great Zimbabwe were to challenge western notions of African culture.

Max Mallowan The husband of Agatha Christie. He made important contributions to Mesopotamian archaeology.

Hiram Bingham

(1875-1956)

One of the best-known names in Andean archaeology, Hiram Bingham brought Machu Picchu to the attention of the world. Today, the once lost city of the Inca, perching on the eastern slopes of the Andes, is the most visited site in South America.

Hiram Bingham III was born and raised in Hawaii, the son and grandson of missionaries. He attended Yale University as an undergraduate and then returned for a time to Hawaii. He began graduate studies at the University of California before moving to Harvard, where he studied History and Political Science, obtaining a Ph.D. in 1905. Bingham returned to Yale as an adjunct professor in 1907.

In 1899 Bingham had married Alfreda Mitchell, an heiress and granddaughter of Charles L. Tiffany, founder of the New York jewellery and luxury goods store. His wife's wealth would be important in allowing him to pursue his research interests in South America.

Bingham first travelled to South America in 1906, visiting historical sites in Venezuela and Colombia, and then Argentina and Peru. He attended the first Pan-American Scientific Congress in Chile in 1908, later visiting Cuzco, Peru, the ancient capital of the Inca. He became interested in the early colonial Inca and particularly in finding the lost Inca city of Vilcabamba, where Inca royalty had held out against the Spanish Conquistadors for several years.

A spectacular discovery

Bingham set out for South America again in 1911. With the help of local historians he studied colonial documents and began exploring archaeological ruins along the Urubamba Valley (now known as the Sacred Valley of the Inca) outside Cuzco. On 24 July 1911 he was led by a local guide through the jungle and up a steep path to a spectacular set of Inca ruins located in a spot known as Machu Picchu (Old Mountain Peak). Believing he had found the ruins of Vilcabamba, Bingham announced the discovery of the site and received funding from the National Geographic Society for additional research.

Bingham assembled a team of scholars and scientists to assist him in a multidisciplinary study of the important site. On two subsequent expeditions he cleared, documented and excavated the site. Although his excavation methods were limited, he produced a great deal of data and important collections that continue to be studied. A portion of the collections were taken to the Peabody Museum at Yale, where they remain today. Extensive analyses were done by Bingham and his colleagues and the project received a great deal of publicity. The National Geographic Society devoted the entire issue of their April 1913 magazine to Bingham's discovery. His story of trekking through the wilderness to discover a lost Inca city captured the public's

Left Located near the Main Plaza at Machu Picchu is the sacred Intihuatana, or 'hitching post of the Sun', which was used in Inca religious festivals. It is unique as the Spanish destroyed all other such stone structures as evidence of idolatry.

Above A panoramic view of Machu Picchu, with Mount Huayna Picchu towering in the background. The Inca builders constructed their remarkable buildings from stones cut to fit tightly together without mortar.

imagination. In one account he describes his first view of the site, 'We rounded a knoll and suddenly faced tier upon tier of Inca terraces rising like giant stairs. Each one, hundreds of feet long, was banked by massive stone walls up to ten feet high.'

Bingham abandoned archaeology after the Machu Picchu project, serving in the US military during World War I before entering into politics. He was elected as a member of the US Senate in 1924.

Royal estate

Although it was Bingham who put Machu Picchu on the map, most of his ideas have since been superseded by new information. We now know that Machu Picchu, far from being the last outpost of Inca royalty, had actually been abandoned by the time the Spanish arrived in Peru in 1532. Spanish colonial documents studied by the American archaeologist John Rowe and his students indicate that the site had in fact been built as a royal estate for the Inca ruler Pachacuti (AD 1438-71).

Machu Picchu was inhabited for most of the year by a relatively small group of retainers, with the palaces and other spectacular buildings reserved for seasonal use by the ruler and his entourage. The archaeological materials that Bingham recovered consist largely of everyday items used by those who lived at the site year-round, and not the fabulous luxury goods of the Inca elite. The materials found in the burials indicate that Machu Picchu's retainers came from throughout the Inca Empire, from the coast to the rainforest. Why the city was eventually abandoned, however, remains a mystery.

The site today

Bingham's theories about Machu Picchu may not have endured, but his legacy has, both in the US and in Peru. Archaeological exploration has continued at the site since Bingham's day and in 1983 it was listed as a World Heritage Site by UNESCO.

A recent exhibition entitled *Machu Picchu: Unveiling the mystery of the Inca*, organized by Yale University, toured the United States to great acclaim, sparking renewed interest and increased US tourism to Peru. The Peruvian government cooperated with Yale in the development of the exhibition, but it also requested that Yale return the Machu Picchu collections permanently to Peru.

Henri Breuil

(1877-1961)

Henri Edouard Prosper Breuil was one of the towering figures in the study of Old World prehistory during the first half of the 20th century, and was the pioneer of the study of Ice Age cave art. His views on Palaeolithic art were considered definitive by a whole generation of archaeologists.

Although the French archaeologist Henri Breuil trained as a priest in his youth, and remained one until his death, it was only a title – he was allowed to devote his whole existence to studying prehistory; he undertook virtually no religious duties, and made almost no contribution to the reconciliation of prehistory's findings with religious teachings.

Awakening

The son of a lawyer, Breuil was born and grew up in northern France, a place that infused him with an intense love of nature, especially of insects, and entomology remained a lifelong interest. An important early influence was his relative, the well-known geologist and archaeologist Geoffroy d'Ault du Mesnil, who showed Henri his collection of fossils and took him to the ancient sites of the Somme region. Here he met Louis Capitan, who introduced him to the study of prehistoric tools. Breuil also had the supreme good fortune, as a young man

with a talent for drawing animals, to make the acquaintance of Edouard Piette and Emile Cartailhac, two of France's greatest prehistorians at the turn of the century, when they needed help with the study and illustration of Palaeolithic portable and cave art.

Breuil was to go on to become the world's leading authority on Palaeolithic art until his death. He discovered many decorated caves or galleries himself, and copied their art – by his own reckoning he spent about 700 days of his life underground.

Although now seen as excessively subjective and incomplete, his tracings are nevertheless recognized as remarkable for their time. For some caves they constitute our only record of figures that have since faded or disappeared. Breuil concentrated not only on Palaeolithic art, but also on the megalithic art of France and (during World War I) the Iberian peninsula. In World War II he began a long campaign of copying rock art in parts of southern Africa.

Breuil's greatest contributions to tool typology were made in France, where he set out the first detailed description of the characteristic tools of each French Palaeolithic period, dividing the Magdalenian into six phases on the basis of changing tool types. This scheme was both durable and influential, but has now been replaced by a simpler and more flexible

Early/Middle/Upper Magdalenian. In the same way, Breuil conceived of two cycles in the development of Palaeolithic art, the 'Aurignaco-Perigordian' followed by the 'Solutreo-Magdalenian' – two essentially similar but independent cycles, each progressing from simple to complex forms in engraving, sculpture and painting. This system, however, was inconsistent and unsatisfactory, and was eventually replaced by the four 'styles' of André Leroi-Gourhan, themselves now in the course of abandonment.

Breuil saw Palaeolithic art primarily in terms of hunting magic, and he generally considered decorated caves to be accumulations of single figures, unlike Leroi-Gourhan who saw them as carefully planned compositions.

An irascible and egotistical man, Breuil nevertheless had a lasting influence on numerous devoted friends and pupils. So ingrained was his image as the 'Pope of Prehistory' that he was often thought virtually infallible. It is only in recent years that it has become possible in France openly to criticize and re-examine his work like that of any other scholar. His huge legacy of publications and tracings has been found to contain many errors, but equally an abundance of insights that are now supported by new finds.

Left A drawing of a bison from the cave of Altamira, in Spain. Breuil copied and published hundreds of examples of rock carvings and paintings from Europe and Africa.

Howard Carter

(1874-1939)

The discovery of the tomb of Tutankhamen in Egypt's Valley of the Kings in the 1920s is one of the great events in archaeology. The story behind this magnificent find by the English archaeologist Howard Carter continues to fire the imagination.

Howard Carter was born in London on 9 May 1874. Art was a major influence in his youth. His father, Samuel John Carter, was an artist known for his paintings of animal scenes. The young Howard's educational interests, however, led him down the route of history and archaeology. At the age of only 17, he started his Egyptological career, working as assistant to Percy Newberry in the rock-cut tombs of Beni Hasan and el-Bersha.

Early career

After a brief spell with Flinders Petrie at Amarna, Carter worked at the Delta site of Mendes. He then worked with Edouard Naville at the Deir el-Bahari mortuary temple, Thebes, until in 1899 he was offered a permanent position with the Egyptian Antiquities Service.

After five happy years working in Luxor, Carter was transferred to Saqqara. Here he became involved in a diplomatic incident. A party of drunken Frenchmen had attempted to force their way into the antiquities holdings, and Carter had allowed his workmen to defend themselves. Owing to the subsequent row, in which Carter sided with his local workers rather than with the Europeans, he resigned in October

1905 to become an artist and antiquities dealer. He would soon return to archaeology, however.

In 1909 Carter came under the patronage of Lord Carnarvon, who had made a visit to Egypt in 1905 and had been inspired to pursue some archaeological work there. Rather than permit Carnarvon himself to work unsupported, however, the Antiquities Service appointed Carter as the expert.

Three years' work in the Theban necropolis was followed by a brief excavation at Xois and a mission to Tell el-Balamun. The war years were spent working for the War Office in

Cairo, although Carter continued to undertake a series of small-scale digs at various sites.

Carter was convinced that the 18th Dynasty king Tutankhamen still lay in the Egyptian Valley of the Kings. However, as Theodore Davis had been granted sole permission to excavate in the Valley, Carter could only watch and wait. When, in 1914, Davis gave up his concession, the war prevented any new field work.

Royal tomb

In 1917 Carter began to clear the Valley. It was slow and expensive work, and Lord Carnarvon started to

Right A wall painting depicts Tutankhamen, riding on a chariot and firing arrows at the Nubian enemy. The vultures act as protective guardians over the king.

Above A throne found in the tomb of Tutankhamen, made from ebony and ivory with gilt features on the sides.

Tut.ankh.Amen's insignia distinctly I would have fervently worked on and set my mind at rest ...'

Three weeks later work resumed. Soon it was possible to read the name of the tomb owner: 'Tutankhamen'. The doorway was dismantled, and the entrance corridor cleared.

By 26 November Carter had entered the antechamber, a storeroom packed with grave goods. A second chamber in the western wall, the 'annex', held more grave goods, while the northern wall included the sealed entrance to the burial chamber. It was to take the team seven long weeks to empty the antechamber. Each object had to be numbered, photographed, planned and drawn before it could be moved. On 17 February 1923 the wall sealing

doubt the existence of the tomb. Eventually, it was agreed that there would be one last season. On 1 November 1922 workmen started to clear rubbish lying beneath the tomb of Ramesses VI. Three days later they discovered 16 steps leading to a blocked doorway. Carter rushed to the telegraph office to call his patron.

The drama of such moments was captured in Carter's journals, which he maintained throughout his work in the Valley. The following extract was written on Sunday, November 5: 'Though I was satisfied that I was on the verge of perhaps a magnificent find ... I was much puzzled by the smallness of the opening in comparison with those of other royal tombs in the valley. Its design was certainly of the XVIIIth Dyn. Could it be the tomb of a noble, buried there by royal consent? Or was it a royal cache? As far as my investigations had gone there was absolutely nothing to tell me. Had I known that by digging a few inches deeper I would have exposed seal impressions showing

the burial chamber was demolished and an enormous gilt shrine was revealed. Inside was another gold shrine, then another, and another.

Later that month, however, Lord Carnarvon was bitten on the cheek by a mosquito. He sliced the scab off the bite while shaving, and started to feel unwell. Blood poisoning set in, and pneumonia followed. Lord Carnarvon died in Cairo on 5 April 1923.

Sarcophagus

On 3 January 1924, the doors of the innermost shrine were opened, revealing the sarcophagus. On 12 February, the cracked lid was hoisted

Below Howard Carter (left) stands holding a crowbar, having opened the doorway to the chamber of Tutankhamen's tomb. Arthur Mace of the Metropolitan Museum is on the right.

Above Wall paintings around Tutankhamen's sarcophagus. The Burial Chamber was the only part of the complex to contain wall paintings.

off the quartzite base. The next day the wives of the archaeologists were to be allowed a viewing of the coffin. The government objected, however. Carter was furious. Work stopped, and did not resume until early 1925.

Tutankhamen had been buried in three coffins – the outer pair made of gold-covered wood, and the inner coffin of solid gold. A gold mask had been placed over the mummy. Resin-based unguents had been poured over the dead king and they had hardened, gluing the king into his coffin. The golden mask, therefore, had to be removed using hot knives.

Carter spent a decade recording and preserving the tomb. Yet before he could complete the publication of his greatest work, he died in London on 2 March 1939.

King's burial

Tutankhamen's burial followed the funerary orthodoxy of ancient Egypt. Body fluids were purged, internal organs were removed and placed in canopic jars and the body was treated with the preservative natrum, the complete process lasting a required 70 days. The body was then wrapped in 13 layers of treated linen, into which were inserted 143 assorted amulets and charms. Tutankhamen's preparation was completed with a magnificent solid-gold death mask covering the head and shoulders. Objects found around the body included items of jewellery and flowers.

Right One of the two wooden and painted sentry statues posted in the antechamber at the sides of the walled door that led into the king's burial chamber.

G. Caton-Thompson

(1888-1985)

Gertrude Caton-Thompson is a towering figure in the history of African archaeology. Her work at Great Zimbabwe would cause an ideological storm in western academia, upsetting many of the racially motivated preconceptions about Africa prevalent at the time.

Born in London in 1888, Gertrude Caton-Thompson enjoyed a privileged upbringing and education. From Newnham College, Cambridge, she proceeded to the British School of Archaeology in Egypt, training under the eminent Egyptologist, Sir Flinders Petrie. With Elinor Gardner, she initiated the first archaeological survey of the northern Faiyum and served as a field director for the Royal Anthropological Institute. After further work on predynastic sites in Egypt, Caton-Thompson undertook work at the site of Great Zimbabwe, in modern Zimbabwe.

Great Zimbabwe

The extensive ruins in Africa had first been excavated by Theodore Bent in 1891, and then by R.N. Hall as part of the imperialist programme of Cecil John Rhodes. Hall, whose abilities as

an excavator were questioned even in his own time, proposed that Great Zimbabwe was the site of the legendary goldfields of Ophir. He argued that Great Zimbabwe had been made by a highly civilized society that (almost by definition) could not be indigenous to Africa.

The British Association for the Advancement of Science sent David Randall-McIver to investigate. He concluded that the site was medieval in date and African in origin. When Caton-Thompson took over the excavations in 1929, she was able to demonstrate that Randall-McIver's ideas about Great Zimbabwe were valid. Working with two female assistants, she conclusively established the site's African origin.

Her findings challenged colonial prejudices about African inferiority and caused furore in an ongoing

controversy about the intellectual capacity of African peoples and their place in colonial societies. Caton-Thompson, resolute in her findings and her scientific detachment, declared that she was quite 'unconcerned with speculations'.

Legacy

Caton-Thompson is remembered for her intrepid life and formidable personality as well as for her archaeological researches, which continued apace after her Zimbabwean work. In the early 1930s she conducted important excavations at the Egyptian site of Kharga Oasis, later working also in south-west Asia. In later life she was vice-president of the Royal Anthropological Institute, president of the British Prehistoric Society, held offices at the University of London and was a Fellow of Newnham College.

Her autobiography, *Mixed Memoirs*, was published in 1983 when she was in her mid-nineties. In it she describes herself as 'not easily alarmed'. Others have described her as 'fearless', 'fastidious' and possessed of 'extraordinary energy and powers of leadership'. She once listed her favourite recreation as 'idleness'. However, there is little evidence of her indulging in it. Gertrude Caton-Thompson retired in 1957 and died in Worcestershire in 1985.

Left The Great Enclosure, which was built in several stages, is the largest and most impressive structure at Great Zimbabwe.

Li Chi

(1896-1979)

Li Chi was one of the pioneers of modern Chinese archaeology. His familiarity with western methods of research gave him a fresh perspective on China's archaeological finds, and had a major impact on the quality of his field work, most famously at Anyang.

Regarded as the father of modern Chinese archaeology, Li Chi was born on 12 July 1896 in Zhongxiang, Hebei province. In the west he is best known for his excavation of the city of Anyang, Henan province, and his research on the so-called 'oracle bones'.

Although he had a Chinese education, Li Chi belonged to the first generation of Chinese archaeologists to be trained by leading scholars in universities and colleges in western Europe and the United States and, as such, was open to new methods of archaeological investigation. Li Chi studied anthropology and received a Ph.D. from Harvard in 1923.

In China Li Chi began working on Neolithic materials and soon became involved with the Academia Sinica's Institute of History and Philology, becoming its first director in 1928.

New research

At the beginning of the 20th century, field archaeology had been brought to China as a new western discipline. The Swedish geologist J.G. Andersson (1874-1960) discovered the first Neolithic site in China – the cave of Peking Man. Li Chi was the first Chinese archaeologist to apply western techniques on the first scientific excavation of Xiyincun, Anyang, carrying out field excavations in situ. A major focus of this new generation of Chinese archaeologists was to search for the origins of Chinese civilization and also to stop the looting of Chinese relics.

Old bones

In 1899 hundreds of bones inscribed with Chinese characters came to light in today's city of Anyang. They had been dug up by peasants and were being ground into medicine. It is said that in that year an official under the last of the Chinese dynasties, the Qing (1644-1911), fell ill and was prescribed 'dragon bones'. These bones, both tortoise shells and cattle shoulder blades, dated from about 3000 years earlier.

In 1928 the Academia Sinica decided to undertake excavations in Anyang at a site called Yin, the city that proved to be the last capital of the historical Shang Dynasty (1700-1027 BC) and the most important Bronze Age site in East Asia.

Between 1928 and 1937 a total of 15 seasons of excavations were carried out in Anyang under Li Chi's leadership. By 1937 archaeologists had excavated more than 100,000 objects, including thousands more inscribed bones, which they recognized as tools of divination. The ancient texts inscribed on the bones provide invaluable information about rulers, battles, folk religion and religious rites.

Excavations were halted by the outbreak of the Sino-Japanese war. Li Chi and his fellow research colleagues, together with their collection, were evacuated to western China. Publications and research continued and finally, in

1948, the Academia Sinica moved to Taiwan. Li Chi continued the work there and also trained young archaeologists, such as Kwang-Chih Chang (1931-2001), who finally brought the archaeology of China to the attention of the western world. In 1950 Li Chi became the head of anthropology and archaeology at the National University in Taipei and began directing publication of his remaining Anyang materials. He published a number of books, including *The Beginnings of Chinese Civilization* (1957) and *Anyang* (1977).

Li Chi died on 1 August 1979 in Taipei, Taiwan.

Above A food vessel cast in bronze with relief designs found at Anyang and dating from *c.*1300-1000 BC shows a high-quality of workmanship.

Dorothy Garrod

(1892-1968)

An important figure in prehistoric studies, Dorothy Garrod conducted important excavations at the Palaeolithic caves of Mount Carmel in Israel, where she was able to identify the longest stratigraphic record in the region, spanning about 600,000 years of human activity.

The archaeologist and prehistorian Dorothy A.E. Garrod was the first woman to be appointed a professor at the University of Cambridge, holding the Disney Chair of Archaeology from 1939 to 1952. Garrod was the only daughter in a distinguished medical family, and the loss of her three brothers in World War I inspired her determination to achieve a life worthy of the family tradition, though in a different field. She was taught at Oxford by the prehistorian R.R. Marett and subsequently in France by Abbé Henri Breuil, who encouraged her research for her first book on the Upper Palaeolithic in Britain. Thereafter her work centred mainly on the Palaeolithic, with notable success.

Garrod owed her first major excavation (in 1926) to Breuil, who had identified the Devil's Tower site in Gibraltar. There she found a Middle Palaeolithic flint industry and the skull fragments of a Neanderthal child.

Rising reputation

The excavation and the publication of her findings established Garrod's place in Palaeolithic studies. Her lasting reputation was determined largely in Palestine during the years 1928-37, first by her excavation of Shukbah Cave in the Wadi en-Natuf. There she found human remains associated with a previously unknown Epipalaeolithic culture, which she named 'Natufian', whose people were apparently taking early steps towards agriculture. In a deeper level she recognized traces of Neanderthal occupation.

After a brief period in southern Kurdistan (where she identified further evidence of Middle and Upper Palaeolithic occupation), she returned to Palestine to begin the major work of her career in archaeology at the

Left Human remains at a Mount Carmel cave site. Garrod's excavations at Mount Carmel in the 1930s helped expand the anthropological picture of the Middle East.

Mount Carmel caves. In el Wad Cave she again found the Natufian culture, though in a later and richer phase than at Shukbah, with decorated burials and more complex lithic (stone) and bone industries.

Tabun Cave

In Tabun Cave, deepest of the group, the uppermost level corresponded to the lowest in el Wad, with a further seven levels descending to a pre-handaxe lithic industry. Garrod's skill in typological analysis enabled her to identify a cultural succession in the caves spanning some 600,000 years of human occupation. At different periods in history, Tabun and the nearby Skhul Cave 2 (which was excavated by her American colleague T.D. McCown) were occupied by two Palaeolithic human populations – Neanderthal and Anatomically Modern People – now known to have genetic differences.

Academic advance

Garrod's final report on the Mount Carmel excavation (*The Stone Age of Mount Carmel, vol.1*, 1937) established a new standard for its time, earning her a D.Sc. from Oxford University. When the Disney Chair at Cambridge became vacant, Garrod didn't think she stood much chance. She told a friend at the time, 'I shan't get it, but I thought I'd give the electors a run for their money'. Her election on the eve of World War II was an important landmark in higher education for women. In 1942 she was recruited to the RAF Medmenham Unit for Photographic Interpretation (staffed by several archaeological colleagues) for the duration of the war.

Returning to Cambridge, she worked to raise the status of archaeology as an academic subject in the university; it became part of the full Tripos and degree scheme in 1948.

Final work

Long vacations were devoted to excavation with French colleagues at the French sites of Fontéchevade and Angles-sur-l'Anglin. In 1952, four

years after women were admitted as full members of the university, she retired from Cambridge and settled permanently in France. In 1958 (aged 66) she resumed work in the Levant.

Garrod devoted this final phase of her working life to the eastern Mediterranean, where ancient caves and beaches preserved evidence that related Quaternary sea levels to the Ice Ages of Europe. Thus, when no absolute dating methods existed, their

Above As much as in Garrod's time, the Mount Carmel site is an enormous challenge to any archaeologist. The range is 26km (16 miles) long and reaches 7.2km (5 miles) wide.

respective prehistoric sequences could be correlated. However, the prolonged and difficult excavation, which ran from 1958 to 1963, was to take its toll on her health. She was awarded a CBE in 1965 three years before her death in Cambridge.

William Grimes

(1905-1988)

William Grimes devoted much of his career to the archaeology of both his native Wales and the city of London. His expertise in handling fragile sites saw him busily employed around the bomb-damaged capital during and following World War II. He is famous for his work on the London Mithraeum.

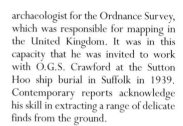

Born in Pembrokeshire, Wales, Grimes studied classics at the University of Wales in Cardiff and was employed in the National Museum of Wales. This brought him into contact with the prehistoric and Roman antiquities of Wales and his subsequent career reflects this dual interest. One of his first projects was the publication of material from the legionary workshops at Holt in north Wales, which had served the fortress at Deva (Chester). He worked on a number of prehistoric sites in Wales in the 1930s and in 1939 published a catalogue of prehistoric antiquities in the National Museum.

Grimes had developed an expertise in working on waterlogged sites that had preserved organic material. In 1938 he went to work as an archaeologist for the Ordnance Survey, which was responsible for mapping in the United Kingdom. It was in this capacity that he was invited to work with O.G.S. Crawford at the Sutton Hoo ship burial in Suffolk in 1939. Contemporary reports acknowledge his skill in extracting a range of delicate finds from the ground.

Wartime work

During World War II, Grimes was responsible for excavating many archaeological sites before their development as military locations, such as airfields. One of the more famous excavations conducted at this time was the Iron Age temple on the site of what is now Heathrow airport to the west of London.

In 1945 he was appointed director of the London Museum and was responsible for a number of rescue excavations in the city, which had been devastated by enemy bombing. In 1954 he famously excavated a Roman Mithraeum on a bomb site off Walbrook in central London. He succeeded in salvaging many of its finds, including marble statuary.

Grimes was appointed the director of the Institute of Archaeology in London in 1956 and subsequently served on many national bodies, where his archaeological expertise was much in demand.

Left Excavations at the Roman temple to the god Mithras in London. This photograph was taken on the site's public open day.

David Hogarth

(1862-1927)

Born in Lincolnshire into a clergy family, David George Hogarth went on to have a distinguished archaeological career. He conducted excavations at many locations in southern Europe and the Middle East, including Cyprus, Crete, Ephesus, Melos, Egypt and Syria.

As a young man Hogarth studied classics at Oxford and was the first student from that university to be admitted to the newly opened British School at Athens. One of his interests was in Greek inscriptions, which were seen as an important supplement to classical literary and historical texts. While at Athens he studied the inscriptions of Thessaloniki, then part of the Ottoman empire.

Ottoman Journey

In the late spring of 1887, Hogarth joined the archaeologist and biblical scholar William Mitchell Ramsay for a journey across Anatolia from Smyrna (Izmir) on the Aegean coast to Cilicia in the south-east. This was to be the first of a series of such travels in the Ottoman empire, and it included a survey of the upper Euphrates Valley. Hogarth's introduction to the world of archaeological excavation came on the island of Cyprus as part of the British project to record some of the classical sites there.

Hogarth's archaeological expertise took him to Egypt, initially to work on the Greek and Latin inscriptions found by Flinders Petrie. One of the projects in Egypt was a survey of Graeco-Roman Alexandria. In the mid-1890s he worked on a survey of the Faiyum in search of papyri that, it was hoped, would provide new examples of classical literature.

In 1897 Hogarth was appointed director of the British School at Athens. During this period there was

continuing work at the Bronze Age site of Phylakopi on Melos, and in 1899 Hogarth returned to the western Nile delta to work at the Greek trading station of Naukratis. With the removal of Crete from the control of the Ottoman empire, Hogarth turned his archaeological attention to the island, working on a number of sites including Knossos and Kato Zakro.

Hogarth next directed the British Museum excavations at Ephesus and in 1908 he returned to the Euphrates Valley to initiate work at Carchemish, where one of the excavators was T.E. Lawrence ('of Arabia'); the two men

Above Hogarth conducted an excavation of the Temple of Artemis at Ephesus between 1904 and 1905, publishing *The Archaic Artemisia of Ephesus* in 1908.

worked together during World War I when Hogarth ran the Arab Bureau in Cairo. In 1908 Hogarth was appointed Keeper of the Ashmolean Museum in Oxford. After war service in the eastern Mediterranean as part of the military intelligence community, Hogarth returned to Oxford where he developed his interest in the Hittites, publishing *Kings of the Hittites* in 1926. He remained keeper of the Ashmolean until his death in 1927.

Alfred Kidder

(1885-1963)

*Alfred Vincent Kidder is still rightly regarded as one of the most
important and influential American archaeologists, his reputation built on
both his technical innovations in excavation and his contribution to
theory, especially in the area of chronology building.*

Alfred Kidder grew up in New
England and originally wanted to
become a physician. However, after
entering Harvard he found himself
uninspired by medical training and
after taking a short course in
anthropology became consumed by
the subject, developing a particular
interest in archaeology.

After working on sites in the
American Southwest, mainly in
Arizona and Utah, he changed his
major and in 1914 received a Ph.D.
in anthropology (concentrating on
ceramics); he was only the sixth
person in the United States to receive
a doctorate that concentrated on this
sub-discipline.

Chronologies

At the time American archaeology was
still desperately trying to organize the
burgeoning amount of data from
excavations into some coherent
system. Even in the Southwest, the
technique of tree-ring dating was still
in its infancy, and the most pressing
concern there, as elsewhere on the
continent, was to establish baseline
chronologies. Kidder was well aware of

this when, in 1915, he initiated
excavations at the Pecos Ruins in
northern New Mexico, which at the
time was the largest archaeological
undertaking in the United States. This
large complex prehistoric ruin was
perfect for the application of
stratigraphic excavations, whereby
different levels in a variety of sites in
a region could be identified by

Below The interior of a kiva (a dug-out used for
religious ceremonies) at the Pecos ruins. Kidder
was director of excavations at Pecos from
1915 to 1929.

Above An exterior view of a kiva at Pecos with the ruins of a mission in the background. Kidder's work helped the development of a cultural chronology of the American Southwest.

men', Walter Taylor. He argued that Kidder and his generation had held archaeology back for concentrating too much, in Taylor's view, on the construction of cultural history rather than investigating the processes by which cultures changed. In this, Taylor's critique presaged the revolution in archaeology of the 1960s called the 'New Archaeology', a revolution that explicitly advocated the scientific method to answer why and how cultures change through time and space. Kidder and others of his generation were, in Taylor's view, guilty of concentrating too much on the artefacts of the past, rather than trying to learn about the people who made and used them.

Despite this criticism, which stung Kidder personally, his place in the pantheon of American archaeologists is assured. The Society for American Archaeology, for instance, calls its most prestigious award after him.

diagnosing their material culture. The temporal sequence could then be checked through excavation at other sites and then applied on a region-wide basis, so that a relative chronology between the sites could be established.

The sheer quantity of material coming out of Pecos, as well as from other archaeological excavations in the Southwest, led Kidder to convene the first Pecos Conference in 1927. The result was the so-called 'Pecos Classification', by which South-western prehistory was organized into a series of stages that quickly became time periods, each one recognizable by particular pottery styles and architectural forms. The selection of a relatively small number of temporally diagnostic artefacts per period is reminiscent of the geological process of identifying type fossils unique to a particular stratum. It is also similar to the 'chest-of-drawers' archaeology used for European prehistory. The Pecos Classification, with some modification, is still the primary time-space framework for the northern part of the American Southwest.

Theoretical attack

In 1929 Kidder took up a prestigious position with the Carnegie Institution in Washington, being appointed the director of the Division of Historical

Research. Beginning in the 1930s, Kidder switched his practical interests to Central America and conducted excavations at Mayan sites such as Chichén Itzá, among others. Kidder employed a team of inter-disciplinary scholars to try to portray as holistic a picture of the past as possible.

In 1950 Kidder retired from the Peabody Museum and Carnegie Institution, although he remained active in the field of archaeology up until his death in 1963. However, towards the end of his career Kidder became the target of an attack by one of archaeology's first 'angry young

Below An 800-year-old painted pottery bowl made by Anasazi Indians at Pecos, where Kidder excavated a large collection of pottery fragments.

Winifred Lamb

(1894-1963)

The classical archaeologist Winifred Lamb carried out pioneering excavations in Greece, the Aegean islands and Anatolia. She rose to become the honorary keeper of Greek Antiquities at the Fitzwilliam Museum, Cambridge.

Winifred Lamb was born in London, the only child of a colliery owner and Liberal Member of Parliament. She read classics at Newnham College, Cambridge. Upon completing her studies in 1917 she joined the Naval Intelligence Department (Room 40) at the Admiralty in London, where one of her colleagues was the Oxford archaeologist Sir John Beazley. It may have been at his prompting that she purchased Greek pottery from the Hope sale at Christies in 1917, which included part of the 18th-century collection formed by Sir William Hamilton. Lamb's first published article appeared in the *Journal of Hellenic Studies* in 1918.

Recognition

In 1919 Lamb was invited to become the honorary keeper of Greek and Roman Antiquities at the Fitzwilliam Museum, Cambridge. For nearly 40 years she fulfilled this role against a background of active field work in Greece and Turkey.

She was one of the first people to be admitted to the British School at Athens after World War I. One of her responsibilities was to work on the excavation of the Bronze Age palace at Mycenae under the direction of Alan Wace. Her interests in Greek prehistory are reflected by her creation of a prehistoric gallery back at the Fitzwilliam Museum.

Lamb became involved in pioneering excavations in Macedonia and she was keen to show a link between the Balkans and north-west Anatolia. She also worked with the British School's resumed excavations at the historical site of Sparta, where she published some of the small bronzes. Lamb had a strong interest in this category of antiquities and published one of the defining studies of Greek and Roman bronze statues.

The death of her father in 1925 gave Lamb the financial means to direct her own excavations and through the late 1920s and '30s she worked on a series of sites on the island of Lesbos, most notably Thermi. From Lesbos she looked to Anatolia and was one of the first women to excavate in the new republic of Turkey at the site of Kusura.

Lamb was badly injured in London during World War II when a German V2 rocket hit her lodgings, killing her housemates. Although this restricted her activities, she continued to travel in Turkey and was a moving force behind the creation of the British Institute of Archaeology in Ankara in 1948. She retired in 1958 and died of a stroke on 16 September 1963.

Left The theatre at Sparta, one of Winifred Lamb's excavation sites during the 1920s. She conducted her work at Sparta under the auspices of the British School at Athens, where she was admitted in 1920 and was in attendance there into the early 1930s. In 1931 she was given the title Honorary Student by the School.

Sir Max Mallowan

(1904-1978)

Better known to the wider world as the husband of the mystery writer Agatha Christie, Max Mallowan made lasting contributions to Mesopotamian archaeology. His work established the basic outline of the prehistoric and early historic cultures of northern Iraq and Syria.

Max Edgar Lucien Mallowan was born in London on 6 May 1904. The seeds of his interest in archaeology were planted at New College, Oxford, where he read classics. Following his graduation, Mallowan began an archaeological career at Ur, where he worked as an assistant to Leonard Woolley from 1925 to 1930.

Aged 26, he met Agatha Christie at Ur when she visited in 1930 and the two were married in Edinburgh six months later. Woolley, however, banned spouses from the field, and so Mallowan left Ur and worked with R. Campbell Thompson at Nineveh in 1931 and 1932.

At Nineveh Mallowan developed a stratigraphic sequence for that long-occupied site; the sequence survives today in the name Ninevite 5, in reference to an early 3rd-millennium BC pottery style.

Major projects

Mallowan launched his first independent project in 1933, at Arpachiyah in northern Iraq. He would spend the best part of a year at the site, and during his excavations there he exposed remains of Halaf (6th millennium BC) and of Ubaid (5th millennium BC) occupations. Arpachiyah remains an important reference site for the Halaf culture, known for its elaborately painted pottery and circular *tholos* houses.

Mallowan then moved his field work to Syria during the remainder of the 1930s. At Chagar Bazar he found a

Below A Middle Eastern sculpture from the 3rd millennium BC depicts a bull's body with a human head. Mallowan found many such zoomorphic images during his work in Iraq and Syria. Tragically, many of the Nimrud ivories discovered under Mallowan's direction were looted or damaged in Baghdad during the fighting of 2003.

cultural sequence beginning with Halaf materials and continuing into the 2nd millennium BC. At Tell Brak he uncovered the Uruk-period Eye Temple (c. 3500-3100 BC), so named for the many small stone idols with prominent eyes found there, and a palace belonging to the Akkadian king Naram Sin (2213-2176 BC). In the Balikh Valley he undertook a survey and soundings at several sites.

Knighthood

In 1949, having been recently named director of the British School of Archaeology, Baghdad (a position he kept until 1961), Mallowan resumed the long-interrupted excavations at

Nimrud, which he continued until 1957. The project focused on the domestic quarters and administrative wing of the North-west Palace, and also explored the remains of Fort Shalmaneser, along with other palaces, temples and private houses near the city wall. The most spectacular result was the discovery of the Nimrud ivories.

Mallowan garnered many academic positions during his career, including president of the British Institute of Persian Studies between 1961 and 1978, and received a knighthood in 1968. He wrote his autobiography *Mallowan's Memoirs* in 1977, a year before his death.

Sir John Marshall

(1876-1958)

John Marshall's defining work was at Taxila in India, to which he committed over 20 years of research and investigation. Marshall also directed excavations at Mohenjo-Daro, work that would alter the historical understanding of the Indian subcontinent.

John Hubert Marshall was born on 19 March 1876 in Chester. Having attended Dulwich College as a young man, he then proceeded to King's College, Cambridge, where he undertook a Classical Tripos between 1898 and 1900.

Early work

Marshall gainied invaluable experience of excavation and archaeological exploration at the British School in Athens, where many of Britain's foremost archaeologists would cut their teeth. In 1902 he was appointed Director-General of Archaeology in India, a post that had been in abeyance for more than a decade. India's long and varied history had left a wealth of art and architecture whose preservation had been sadly neglected, and little of its rich prehistory had been investigated. Marshall devised and initiated appropriate conservation measures for known monuments and began a programme of excavations.

Among his main foci were the Early Historic cities and Buddhist monuments located by Sir Alexander Cunningham, who had retired as director-general in 1885 after decades of exploring sites known from early Buddhist literature.

Marshall's principal excavation, begun in 1913 and continued until 1936, was at Taxila, a long-lived

Above Here is the famous 'Priest King' of Mohenjo-Daro, discovered by Marshall during his work there in the 1920s. Note the ornamentation around the forehead and the broad trefoil sash.

trading, political and cultural centre, but he and his officers also investigated other Early Historic cities, including the site of Pataliputra. Equally important was the clearance, survey, excavation and restoration of Buddhist monasteries and stupas (relic mounds). Between 1912 and 1919 Marshall also worked at Sanchi, where the Mauryan emperor Ashoka had built a stupa to house relics of the Buddha. This had been enlarged and several others were constructed by later kings, along with monasteries. Marshall concentrated

Left Mohenjo-Daro has produced some of the finest archaeological finds in the Indian sub-continent, and at one time had an estimated 35,000 occupants.

on the Great Stupa, revealing its magnificent gateways, lavishly decorated with reliefs depicting scenes from the Buddha's life, as well as figures from folk tradition.

A few prehistoric Indian sites were known, but the Early Historic cities that emerged in the mid-1st millennium BC were thought to have been the first flowering of Indian civilization. This picture was changed dramatically in 1922, when investigations by Archaeological Survey officers at Harappa and Mohenjo-Daro in the Indus valley unexpectedly revealed the remains of two great cities with distinctive and previously unknown material that was clearly considerably older than the Early Historic period.

Marshall publicly announced their discovery in 1924; Mesopotamian scholars were immediately able to demonstrate that the Indus Civilization, as it was now called, had been contemporary with Sumer, the first civilization in the Near East.

Mohenjo-Daro

Marshall took personal control at Mohenjo-Daro for the major excavation season of 1925-6, assisted by senior staff and with more than a thousand labourers.

The excavations revealed a huge and well-planned city with brick drains and many public wells. Often the houses had bathrooms and private wells. The city was divided into two parts – the residential Lower Town, and a higher Citadel Mound, soon identified as the locus of important public buildings. These included the Great Bath, a large rectangular tank of baked brick made watertight with bitumen, probably for ritual bathing.

One part of the Lower Town yielded a quantity of jewellery, including a fine necklace of extremely long

carnelian beads. Etched carnelian beads were found widely within the city, as were pottery vessels decorated with fishscale, geometric and animal designs. There were many steatite seals also bearing animal designs, particularly the unicorn, along with a few signs in what was now identified as the Indus script. In one building was discovered a rare piece of sculpture, depicting the head and upper torso of a bearded man wearing a garment decorated with trefoils – the now-famous 'Priest-king'.

After one season Marshall returned to his work at Taxila, but excavations continued at Mohenjo-Daro until 1931. Outstanding finds included the lively bronze statuette, known as the 'dancing-girl', and the so-called 'Proto-Shiva' seal, which bears a design showing a three-faced horned deity surrounded by wild animals.

Marshall officially retired as director-general in 1928, but continued to work until 1934 when he returned to England. There he

Above A steatite seal from Mohenjo-Daro, depicting an elephant and assorted monograms and dating from around 2500 BC.

worked on the mammoth report on his excavations at Taxila, which finally emerged in 1951.

The list of publications he left at the time of his death on 17 August 1958 included *The Monuments of Sanchi* (reprinted 1983), a large three-volume work which he co-authored with Alfred Foucher.

Right The Great Stupa at Sanchi (the dome rising in the background) was the focus of one of Marshall's great studies. An elegantly carved gateway (torana) depicts scenes of Buddhist worship.

Pierre Montet

(1885-1966)

Pierre Montet is most closely associated with the one-time royal capital, Tanis, in the northern Nile Delta. Here, just before and after World War II, he discovered a series of magnificent burials dating from the 21st and 22nd Dynasties in the 11th-8th centuries BC.

Born at Villefranche-sur-Saône in the Beaujolais region of central France, Montet first studied Egyptology at the University of Lyon, where he was taught by Victor Lore, a former head of the Egyptian Antiquities Service. He then moved to the French Institute of Eastern Archaeology in Cairo until the outbreak of World War I.

Royal tombs

From 1921 to 1924 Montet excavated at the Lebanese site of Byblos, where he discovered a temple and a series of tombs belonging to local rulers. This early work sparked a lifelong interest in the connections between Egypt and her eastern neighbours. In 1929 he began work in the Nile Delta at Tanis, the Egyptian capital during the 21st and 22nd Dynasties. It was also the favoured burial place of the monarchs of these dynasties, who abandoned the royal necropolis in the Valley of the Kings in favour of the better-guarded precincts of the temples there. The French archaeologist Auguste Mariette carried out excavations at the great Amen temple of Tanis in 1859, discovering a series of 12th- Dynasty royal sculptures; now Montet cleared the temple area, uncovering yet more royal statuary.

His greatest finds, however, came from a temple dedicated to the goddess Mut (known elsewhere in the eastern Mediterranean as Anta or Astarte), where in February 1939 he discovered a multi-chambered royal tomb (labelled Tomb I) lying beneath ruined Ptolemaic buildings. Buried there were King Osorkon II and his son Prince Hornakht.

In a neighbouring tomb (Tomb III), which he entered in March 1939, he found the disturbed burial chamber of Psusennes I and the mummies of Sheshonq II and Siamun, along with the undisturbed chambers of Psusennes II and Amenemope (who had usurped a chamber originally prepared for Queen Mutnodjmet).

The outbreak of World War II brought the work at Tanis to a halt, but as soon as peace returned Montet was back. In February 1946 he discovered the burial chamber of General Wendjebauendjedet, also in Tomb III. Today, the contents of these magnificent burials are displayed in Cairo Museum.

Montet was Professor of Egyptology at the University of Strasbourg (1919-48), then at the Collège de France, Paris. He published many books and articles, including *La Nécropole Royale de Tanis* (1958), *Everyday Life in the Days of Ramesses the Great* (1958) and *Eternal Egypt* (1964). He also founded the journal *Kêmi*. He died in Paris on 19 June 1966.

Left An overview of the arrowhead fortification wall at Byblos. Systematic excavations of the ancient Phoenician city did not begin until the 1920s.

André Parrot

(1901-1980)

André Parrot helped shape our cultural and historical understanding of the Middle East. His archaeological career stretched from the 1920s to the 1970s, and he is best known for his 40-year directorship of the excavations at Mari in Syria.

Parrot was born on 15 February 1901, the son of a minister, Charles Parrot. Like his father, Parrot seemed destined for a religious career, studying Protestant theology at the Sorbonne. However, a series of art history courses at the École du Louvre, then a year of antiquity sciences at the École Biblique et Archéologique Française in Jerusalem, expanded his interests to include archaeology, particularly that of the Near East.

Between 1926 and 1933 Parrot undertook numerous excavations, first at Nerab in northern Syria then Baalbek in the Lebanon, before moving to the Mesopotamian sites of Telloh (originally Girsu, capital of Lagash state) and Tell Senkere (Larsa). He directed excavations at Telloh and Tell Senkere from 1961 to 1967.

Life achievement

In 1933 Parrot began excavations at Tell Hariri in Syria, formerly ancient Mari. He was director of work there until 1972, during which time the site yielded constant riches, including over 20,000 cuneiform clay tablets and the Old Babylonian palace of Zimri-Lim (1782-1759 BC). Parrot commented that 'each time a vertical probe was commenced in order to trace the site's history down to virgin

soil, such important discoveries were made that horizontal digging had to be resumed'.

Parrot's work in the Middle East ran alongside professional advancement in France. He became the Inspecteur Géneral des Musées in France in 1965, and the Louvre's director between 1968 and 1972. He held numerous other institutional and honorary academic posts. Parrot was also a prolific author, his works including *Sumer* (1960), *Assur* (1961) and *L'aventure archéologique* (1979). Many of his writings explored the relationship

Above A haunting figure from the Mari Temple of Ishtar, created from alabaster, gypsum and lapis lazuli.

between biblical scripture and archaeology, Parrot believing that the latter threw a 'powerful light ... upon the religion and beliefs of a people in search of supernatural forces'.

Right Parrot remains the central figure behind the excavations at Mari, to which he dedicated much of his working life. He probed its history back to its foundations in around 2900 BC.

Sir Flinders Petrie

(1853-1942)

The British Egyptologist Flinders Petrie transformed both our knowledge of ancient Egypt and the techniques of field archaeology. In particular, he developed sequence dating, a method of reconstructing the histories of ancient cultures on the basis of their pottery and other remains.

Surveying was in the blood for Flinders Petrie. His father was an engineer and surveyor, and his grandfather was the navigator Matthew Flinders, who first charted large parts of the coast of Australia. Flinders Petrie was still only in his late teens when he started recording the prehistoric monuments of southern England. Later, with his father's assistance, he made the most accurate survey of Stonehenge at that time.

The Great Pyramid

In 1880, aged 26, he made his first trip to Egypt to survey the Great Pyramid at Giza. At the time, many believed that the pyramid had been built using a divinely inspired 'pyramid inch' as the basic unit of measurement – some even thought this was related to the cubit used to build Noah's Ark and the Tabernacle of Moses. Petrie wanted to find out the truth. Employing just one workman,

he spent two seasons on the survey and structural examination. The end result, so accurate that Petrie's survey is still used today, showed that the 'pyramid inch' theory was false.

In 1883 he started working for the newly founded Egypt Exploration Fund, with excavations at Tanis (modern San el-Hagar) in the Nile

Below A view of the Great Pyramid, one of the Seven Wonders of the Ancient World.

Delta. This was followed by a season at the Greek trading centre Naucratis (el Nibeira). Later, with the support of two wealthy private backers – the Manchester businessman Jesse Haworth and the collector Martyn Kennard – he moved to Hawara in the Faiyum region, south-west of Cairo. Here, on the north side of the Middle Kingdom pyramid of Amenemhat III, he found a large Roman cemetery, which yielded a series of mummies with beautifully painted wood-panel faces. Next, he moved to Illahun (Lahun), also in the Faiyum region, where he excavated some 1800 rooms in a village that had been built for pyramid construction workers.

After a brief interlude working in Palestine, Petrie returned to Egypt, working first at the pyramid cemetery of Meidum, then at Akhetaten (modern Amarna). In Akhetaten he was denied access to the royal tombs, so he excavated in the central city instead, uncovering a beautiful painted gypsum pavement in the Great Palace.

Devising sequence dating

In April 1892 Petrie was appointed Professor of Egyptology at University College, London. From then on, he taught for half the year and spent the winter months in Egypt.

At Koptos (ancient Gebtu, modern Quft), Petrie discovered a series of statues, including three prehistoric colossal sculptures representing the fertility god Min. At Tûkh, close to the southern town of Nagada, he investigated a curious cemetery housing many hundreds of prehistoric graves – the remains of the peoples who had lived in the Nile valley before Egypt became one unified country. There were no texts with these graves, and so Petrie had to devise a new way of dating them, which came to be called sequence dating. This involved identifying the different types of pottery associated with the different burials, and using these to arrange the burials into successive chronological phases.

Above The Sphinx at Memphis excavated by Petrie in 1912. The Sphinx, 8m (26ft) long, is carved from a single piece of alabaster.

Excavations at Luxor, Qurna, Deshasha and Dendera followed. Petrie then moved to Abydos, where he was principally interested in the tombs of the 1st and 2nd Dynasty kings. He re-investigated 13 royal tombs, which allowed him to join his prehistoric Nagada grave sequence to the beginning of Egyptian history. He continued his field work at Giza, where he discovered 2nd Dynasty tombs which confirmed that Giza had been used as a cemetery long before Khufu built his Great Pyramid. In a cemetery at another site, Tarkhan, he found amazing quantities of textiles.

Then, in 1914, the Egyptian government imposed a change in archaeological protocol. All future excavations were to be under strict state control.

The old practice of dividing finds on a more or less 50:50 basis between the excavator and the Egyptian state was abolished; from this point on, all discoveries would automatically remain in Egypt unless the authorities chose to make an exception. These new regulations caused problems for Egyptologists like Petrie, whose private backers expected to receive some material reward for their funding. As a result, Petrie left Egypt after World War I to work in Palestine instead. He retired from University College, London, in 1933 and died in Jerusalem on 29 July 1942, at the age of 89.

Julio C. Tello

(1880-1947)

The Peruvian Julio C. Tello was one of those rare archaeologists whose work shaped the way an entire nation perceived itself. He expanded Peru's understanding of its pre-Columbian past, and also invested much of his time and effort training future generations of archaeologists.

Julio C. Tello is considered the Father of Peruvian Archaeology by most Peruvians. His work was central to establishing the importance of the early civilizations of Peru among academics, the public and, significantly, among Peru's political class. His work synthesizing and summarizing the sequence of ancient civilizations of the Andes, as well as at specific sites such as the famous Chavín de Huantar, inspired a generation of young archaeologists.

Tello was to become the first academically trained Peruvian archaeologist. His career included service as the director of the National Museum, as a professor at Peru's most important universities and even in the Peruvian congress. He established major museum collections, trained dozens of Peruvian archaeologists and promulgated laws to protect Peru's archaeological sites and resources. He also helped establish Peru's pre-Columbian past as an important part of her history.

Below The ruins of a wall at the site of Chavín de Huantar, Peru.

Right A carved stone nail head (Cabezas Clavas) at Chavín de Huantar.

Early promise

Tello was born and raised in the highlands of Huarochiri, outside Lima. He went to Peru's capital to study, working for the famous Peruvian intellectual Ricardo Palma and becoming interested in archaeology. He studied medicine, graduating from San Marcos University with a thesis on syphilis in ancient Peru in 1908. He then earned a scholarship to Harvard, where he did his post-graduate studies. During this time he worked with the famous physical anthropologist Ales Hrdlicka. Upon his return from the United States, Tello focused his work largely on pre-Inca civilizations in Peru. His work at Chavín de Huantar and other sites was extremely influential.

Scientific archaeology was in its infancy at the beginning of Tello's career, and many scholars at the time believed that civilization had emerged in only a few places, then spreading, or diffusing, to far-reaching areas. Peru was viewed, by the German scholar Max Uhle among others, as part of a larger American civilization that had its roots in Central America rather than locally. Tello disputed this idea, and much of his work was focused on establishing the local origins of Andean civilization. His work at Chavín de Huantar was particularly important.

Challenging ideas

Radiocarbon dating and other chronometric methods had yet to be invented, and stylistic analysis and stratigraphy were the main methods of assigning relative dates to, and establishing the relationships in time and space among, archaeological cultures and materials. Tello argued that Chavín greatly pre-dated Inca and other later Andean civilizations, and that it formed the original, or matrix, civilization of the Andes. More recent work has demonstrated that the origins of Peruvian civilization

pre-date even Chavín. The Chavín were, however, one of the first groups whose style spread widely across the Andean region. The influence of the Chavín style can be seen in architecture, pottery and other objects made throughout a wide area of Peru about 2500 years ago.

Archaeologists now believe that Chavín de Huantar was a major political and religious centre with trading relationships that extended from Peru's desert coast to the jungle. Tello published widely, writing books and newspaper articles during his lifetime, and he left reams of unpublished notes (some have been published posthumously).

While many of his ideas have been updated or modified by more recent studies, new techniques and more detailed analysis, Tello's influence is still felt today in several ways. First, Tello was correct in his assertions that Peruvian civilization developed locally, and we now know that the cultural sequence of the Andes extends back well over 12,000 years. Second, Chavín de Huantar was, as Tello believed, one of the most important early sites in the Andes, although it was neither the first nor the only early centre of civilization. Finally, Tello and some of his contemporaries shifted the perspective of Peru's intellectual and

political communities concerning the nature of Peruvian history and the importance of the pre-Columbian past and the indigenous civilizations. Peru's ancient civilizations and local traditions are now viewed by many educated Peruvians as a significant part of their country's past, and as something to be claimed as heritage by all Peruvians.

Below A relief sculpture covers the ruins of a monolith at Chavín de Huantar, Peru. Tello's work revealed much about the sophistication of early Andean culture.

Alan Bayard Wace

(1879-1957)

One of Britain's foremost archaeologists working in Greece and the Mediterranean in the first half of the 20th century. He was director of the British School at Athens from 1914 to 1923 and held positions at the Victoria and Albert Museum in London and Cambridge University.

Alan John Bayard Wace was born on 13 July 1879, the son of a Cambridge mathematics fellow. The young Wace later studied classics at the same university as his father. At Pembroke College he developed a strong interest in the sculpture of the Hellenistic period and on graduation went to Greece to continue his research at the British School in Athens. His interest in sculpture brought with it an invitation from Henry Stuart-Jones, director of the British School at Rome, to contribute to the study of sculpture in the civic collections there, and Wace worked as a librarian in the school from 1905. Thus, Wace

would spend part of each year in the Italian capital working on museum collections, and the other part in Greece undertaking field work.

In Greece, Wace participated in the British School's excavation and survey in and around Sparta. However, he had a long-standing interest in Greek prehistory and was soon involved in a major survey of Thessaly in central Greece, hunting for prehistoric mounds; sites at Theotokou and Zerélia were excavated.

In 1914 Wace became director of the British School at Athens. Although working in part for naval intelligence, he also undertook excavations with

Carl Blegen of the American School at Korakou. Their close friendship underpinned the post-war excavations at Zygouries and the British work at Mycenae. Blegen and Wace challenged the view of the supremacy of Crete held by Sir Arthur Evans and instead promoted the influence of the mainland Mycenaean Greeks.

Major positions

Wace, who was a recognized expert in Greek island embroideries, returned to London to work as a curator of textiles at the Victoria and Albert Museum. In 1934 he was appointed to the Laurence chair of Classical Archaeology at Cambridge.

He then returned to excavate at Mycenae in 1939, but World War II intervened. Following the Allied evacuation of Greece, he ended up in Egypt. Here he served as the chair of Classics and Archaeology in the Farouk I University at Alexandria. This post allowed him to return to his earlier Hellenistic interests and he worked on some of the Ptolemaic sites. Returning to Mycenae in 1950, he was responsible for discovering Linear B tablets in the city. His writings include *Mycenae: an Archaeological History and Guide* (1949).

Left Wace was as passionate about his academic instruction as about his field work. Here he lectures a group of students about a statue of Leonidas, the king of Sparta, where he conducted excavations with the British School at Athens.

Sir Mortimer Wheeler

(1890-1976)

Sir Mortimer Wheeler was not only a renowned archaeologist in his own right, he was also passionate about the development of new generations of researchers and helped create programmes and institutions that trained dozens of future archaeologists.

Robert Eric Mortimer Wheeler was born in Glasgow, Scotland, the son of a journalist. He studied classics as a student at University College London, where he was introduced to archaeology by Ernest Gardner, a former director of the British School at Athens. He graduated in 1910 and continued his studies by working on Roman pottery from the German frontier. Wheeler later joined the Royal Commission on Historical Monuments in 1913, but this job was interrupted by war service in the Royal Artillery; he was awarded the Military Cross in 1918.

Roman forts

Wheeler was appointed as the Keeper of Archaeology at the National Museum of Wales; he was later promoted to director (1924). During this period he excavated a number of Roman forts across Wales, including Caernarfon (Segontium), Y Gaer near Brecon and the amphitheatre at the legionary fortress at Caerleon (Isca) in south-east Wales.

As excavations were underway at Caerleon, Wheeler moved to the London Museum as keeper. Over the next decade he worked with his wife, Tessa, to create an institute to train future archaeologists. The Institute of Archaeology was opened as part of the University of London in 1937; sadly Tessa died of a heart attack the year before it opened. Together 'the Wheelers', as they were affectionately known, had excavated at a series of Romano-British sites, notably Lydney Park in the Forest of Dean, Gloucestershire, and the major city of Verulamium near St Albans.

War past and present

Wheeler's interests then turned to the Iron Age societies that faced Rome during the invasion of Britain in the 1st century AD. He conducted a major excavation at the Iron Age hillfort at Maiden Castle in Dorset. Just outside one of the gates he found the corpse of one of the defenders who had been killed by a piece of Roman artillery; the bolt from the ballista was still sticking in the spine. On the eve of World War II he excavated Iron Age hillforts in northern France, shedding light on the settlements described by Julius Caesar.

Wheeler returned to military service and served in North Africa and then in the invasion of Sicily. Before he could get involved in the Italian campaign, however, he was transferred to the Archaeological Survey of India. After partition, Wheeler returned to London as professor of the archaeology of the Roman provinces; however, he maintained links with Pakistan, acting as adviser to the new archaeological service and ran a training excavation at Mohenjo-Daro. In Britain, Wheeler returned to his earlier interests in Iron Age and Roman archaeology by excavating the major Iron Age site at Stanwick in Yorkshire.

He was dedicated to supporting British archaeology around the world through the development of the British Academy and the creation of foreign institutes of archaeology. Wheeler was knighted in 1952 and after numerous appearances on radio and TV was named British TV Personality of the Year in 1954.

Below Maiden Castle is the largest hillfort in Europe, covering an area of 19ha (47 acres).

Sir Leonard Woolley

(1880-1960)

Leonard Woolley received international acclaim in the 1920s with the discovery of the 'Royal Cemetery' at Ur in southern Mesopotamia. While spectacular, the Royal Cemetery was but one of many important finds at Ur, and Woolley undertook several major projects during his career.

Leonard Woolley, born in Upper Clapton in England, was the son of a clergyman. At first he intended to take up his father's calling, but on leaving New College, Oxford, he accepted the advice of the warden and pursued a developing interest in archaeology.

Woolley served his apprenticeship on excavations in Egypt, Italy and England, and then at Carchemish in Syria, where he headed up the excavations beginning in 1912. T.E. Lawrence was another member of the Carchemish project, and the two also collaborated on a survey of Wadi Arabah south of the Dead Sea.

After World War I (part of which he spent as a prisoner-of-war), Woolley undertook a final season at Carchemish and another at Tell el-Amarna in Egypt, before heading the excavations at Ur from 1922 until 1934. He initiated his third major project in 1937 at Tell Atchana and the nearby Mediterranean port of al-Mina in north-west Syria, a project that was to run for seven seasons until 1949.

Carchemish and Ur

Carchemish, on the banks of the Euphrates river just south of the current Turkish-Syrian border, is an immense mound with a very long history of occupation. Woolley's excavations

Above From Ur, the god Ningirsu depicted as a lion-headed eagle.

uncovered remains of a local Neo-Hittite (9th-8th century BC) capital, including palaces, temples and fortifications. At the time, the Neo-Hittite kingdoms were particularly enigmatic (indeed, the kingdoms remain inadequately studied), and Woolley's excavations provided good information about Neo-Hittite architecture, art and general culture.

Ur, in the deep south of Mesopotamia, was first settled in the 5th millennium BC and was occupied more or less continuously until around 200 BC. During his 12 seasons at Ur, Woolley excavated remains from every period of this long history. The most prominent results include: traces of the earliest village at Ur, covered by an alluvial silt that Woolley equated with Noah's flood; the ziggurat of the Ur III period (*c.*2112-2004 BC) when Ur was the capital of a strong regional kingdom; and residential districts belonging to the same period and to the Old Babylonian period (*c.*1800 BC). Because Near Eastern archaeologists traditionally focus on public monuments, the residential districts provide all too rare evidence for ordinary life in ancient Mesopotamia.

Left A detail from the 'Standard of Ur' found by Woolley and dating from *c.*2500 BC. It was found in a grave in the Royal Cemetery.

Right The staircase of the monumental stepped ziggurat at Ur, which Woolley excavated in 1923.

Royal cemetery

Of Woolley's results, the Royal Cemetery attracted by far the most attention. For roughly 500 years the residents of Ur buried thousands of their dead in a cemetery near the main temple of the city. Of the several thousand tombs that Woolley excavated there, most were simple interments accompanied by few grave-goods. But some tombs (Woolley identified a total of 16 tombs used for royal burials) were elaborate chambers entered through ramps, containing thousands of objects, plus the bodies of retainers sacrificed to accompany their masters in death.

Among the objects placed in the tomb are some of the most famous pieces of ancient Sumerian art ever found: the golden royal helmet of King Meskalamdug; the 'Standard of Ur', a plaque showing scenes of warfare and ritual rendered in nacre and lapis lazuli inlay originally on a wooden frame; lyres and 'ram in a thicket' statues ornamented with gold, silver, lapis and nacre; and intricate headdresses of gold and silver. Even the more 'ordinary' objects could be luxurious, such as weapons made of gold or silver, containers made of expensive stone or metal, toiletry kits of precious metals, and a variety of other jewellery. These extravagantly rich royal tombs date to around 2600 BC.

A forgotten kingdom

After the splendours of Ur, Tell Atchana is something of an anticlimax, but even so the site gave Woolley important results. His excavations uncovered palaces and temples from the Middle and Late Bronze Ages (c.2000-1200 BC). Archives of cuneiform tablets, plus a long inscription on the statue of a king, identify Tell Atchana as ancient Alalakh, and these texts remain today among the most important available sources for north-west Syria during these periods. The concurrent excavations at al-Mina found structures, perhaps warehouses, dated to the 8th-4th centuries BC. The Greek pottery and other objects associated with these structures remain a central reference in discussions about Greek commerce in the east.

Woolley was also a prolific writer. During his lifetime he published over 25 books, many of which expressed his love of archaeology as much as the findings of his work. His work includes *Spadework: Adventures in Archaeology* (1953) and *Excavations at Ur: A Record of 12 Years' Work* (1954). Woolley was knighted for his services to archaeology in 1935.

Right Ornate jewellery and hair ornaments found in burial pits by Woolley at Ur.

MODERN ARCHAEOLOGISTS

It is probably fair to say that few of the archaeologists of the mid- to late-20th century became household names. The increasingly scientific nature of the subject has brought relative anonymity. Nevertheless, the quality of the work carried out has constantly improved in tandem with the battery of new techniques available for dating, analysis, excavation and survey. The great archaeologists of the 20th century, including Ignacio Bernal, Rhys Jones, Kathleen Kenyon, Michael Ventris and others featured here, have dramatically deepened our understanding of human civilization. The scope of subject areas and locations has been incredibly diverse, ranging from the decipherment of Linear B to excavations at the ancient Zapotec capital of Monte Albán (facing page), and from new interpretations of Palaeolithic art to pioneering studies in Aboriginal Australia.

Opposite The Zapotec capital of Monte Alban was a political and economic centre for almost 1000 years.

Meave Leakey Continuing the Leakey family tradition, her work has helped to redefine our understanding of human evolution.

Maria Reiche Her life's work was devoted to the Nasca lines etched into the face of the Peruvian desert.

Spyridon Marinatos He excavated an ancient city preserved under volcanic rock on the island of Thera (Santorini).

Manolis Andronikos

(1919-1992)

The discovery of rich royal tombs from the 4th century BC at Vergina in Greece — which Andronikos identified with the Macedonian king Philip II, father of Alexander the Great — marked the pinnacle of a long, prestigious career in archaeology.

Manolis Andronikos was born in Prousa (the Turkish city of Brusa) on 23 October 1919, the son of Greek parents who had settled in Salonica (or Thessaloniki) after World War I.

At the age of 17 he joined the excavations of the Macedonian royal palace at Vergina, which were being undertaken by K.A. Rhomaios. These uncovered an impressive series of sumptuous dining rooms that gave views over the great western plain of Macedonia. Andronikos's career was interrupted by the German occupation of Greece during World War II. After serving with the Greek forces in the Middle East, he later resumed his studies at the Aristotelian University of Thessaloniki, receiving his doctorate in

1952. From there he went to Oxford where he worked with Sir John Beazley, whose expertise lay in the field of Greek, and especially Athenian, figure-decorated pottery.

Vergina

From Oxford Andronikos returned to Thessaloniki, first as a lecturer and then as professor of archaeology. He next worked on a series of excavations in Macedonia, eventually returning to the royal palace at Vergina in 1962, where his interest in archaeology had begun. He also turned his attention to the Iron Age burials around Vergina, and in particular to the Great Mound that lay at the heart of an extensive mound cemetery around the modern

Above A small ivory head of a bearded man, which Andronikos identified with Philip II, was excavated from Tomb II.

town. Excavations were initiated in 1976 and Andronikos uncovered two burials, one of which remained intact.

Tomb II was particularly rich, with a series of silver drinking vessels and jugs, an ivory-inlaid couch, elaborate armour and a stone sarcophagus, which held a solid gold burial chest, or larnax. The British scholar Nicholas Hammond had proposed that Vergina was the site of the ancient Macedonian capital of Aegae, which led Andronikos to conclude that he had opened the grave of one of the members of the Macedonian royal family. He also believed that the plate and pottery from the tomb should be dated to the third quarter of the 4th century BC. On this evidence he concluded that this must be the burial of Philip II of Macedonia, who had been assassinated in the theatre at Aegae.

The cremated remains found in the larnax in Tomb II were those of a middle-aged man. A team of professional forensic archaeologists from the University of Manchester have attempted a reconstruction based on known images of Philip II.

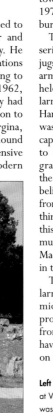

Left The site of the Macedonian Royal Palace at Vergina. In 1993 an underground building was constructed to enclose and protect the royal tombs. The treasures found in the tombs have been on display since 1997.

Above The Rhomaios Tomb at Vergina is broadly contemporary with other royal burials found by Andronikos at the site.

Tomb III contained a beautiful silver hydria (a Greek water jar) decorated with a gold wreath. This had been used as the container for the cremated remains of an individual who was aged about 14. A likely candidate is Alexander IV, who was murdered around the year 309 BC.

Disputed finds

Scholars have now started to question the date of Tomb II and therefore the identification with Philip II. The Attic black-glossed 'saltcellars' may be as late as the early 3rd century BC, and the barrel-vaulted style of the tomb may have been introduced to Macedonia after the eastern conquests of Philip's son, Alexander the Great. The Lion Hunt frieze that decorated

the front of Tomb II also seems more in keeping with the iconography of Alexander and his successors.

Recent re-examination of all the skeletal evidence from the tomb has suggested that the body had been cremated some time after the person had died, which makes it unlikely to be that of Philip II. Moreover, questions have been raised about the identification of damage to one of the

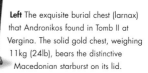

eyes that had convinced many that this was indeed Philip, who was known to have been blinded in one eye by an arrow injury. It has now been proposed that Philip II was, in fact, buried in (the robbed) Tomb I adjacent to a hero shrine that is likely to have been associated with a religious cult linked to Philip II.

Andronikos continued his work at Vergina, and subsequently revealed many more royal tombs. He wrote up his findings in *The Royal Graves at Vergina* (1978) and *Vergina: The Royal Tombs and the Ancient City* (1984). He received the Order of the Phoenix from the Greek government, Greece's highest civilian honour, just prior to his death on 30 March 1992.

Left The exquisite burial chest (larnax) that Andronikos found in Tomb II at Vergina. The solid gold chest, weighing 11kg (24lb), bears the distinctive Macedonian starburst on its lid.

321

Ignacio Bernal
(1910-1992)

One of the giants of Mexican archaeology, Ignacio Bernal devoted his long and distinguished career to unravelling the archaeological history of the Oaxaca valley of southern Mexico, and in particular the Zapotec capital of Monte Albán.

Although he was born into a distinguished family of historians, Bernal did not turn to archaeology until he was in his early thirties, when he began working with the great archaeologist Alfonso Caso at Monte Albán. Thus began a close collaboration with Caso and a life-long commitment to the archaeology of Oaxaca. Very little was known about the Zapotecs prior to Caso and Bernal's work, but based on their extensive archaeological explorations, and those of subsequent scholars, Oaxaca is now among the best-known regions of Mesoamerica.

Below A spectacular view across the ruins at Monte Albán. By AD 300 the population of the city numbered around 50,000.

Bernal received his Ph.D. in 1950 from the National Autonomous University of Mexico (UNAM) and enjoyed a diverse career that included both administrative posts directing the National Institute of Anthropology and History (1968-71) and the National Museum of Anthropology (1962-68 and 1970-77). He served as a cultural attaché in Paris, and as president of the Society for American Archaeology (1968-69). In addition to his active service, he was a charismatic instructor both at the UNAM (1948-76) and at Mexico City College (1951-59).

Monte Albán

Bernal worked at Monte Albán from 1942 to 1944 and again between 1946 and 1953. His initial research

Above The oldest carved stones at the site are the so-called *danzantes* (dancers), depicting the contorted figures of slain captives. These slabs were displayed on façades and bear some of the earliest hieroglyphs known in Mesoamerica.

considered the Formative era of Monte Albán (500 BC to AD 200), while his dissertation was based on the late Classic period (AD 500-800), spanning the rise and decline of the great city.

He also branched out from Monte Albán to explore other areas both within the valley of Oaxaca and in the mountainous Mixteca region to the west. His projects at Coixtlahuaca and Tamazulápan were among the first scientific investigations of the Mixtecs, a cultural group of great interest to his colleague Caso.

Bernal also led a long-term project at Yagul (1954-62), where a Postclassic palace complex revealed the final phase of pre-Hispanic Oaxaca. The interaction of Mixtec peoples in the Zapotec region of Oaxaca was documented in colonial histories, and Bernal sought to apply archaeological rigour to test the chronicles. Between 1966 and 1972,

Bernal returned to his interest in Formative Oaxaca, directing an extensive project at the site of Dainzu, contemporary with the founding of Monte Albán, where carved stones depict the pre-Columbian ballgame.

Lifetime's work

Bernal's prolific publication record was documented on his 80th birthday, when it tallied 267 books and articles. Notable contributions include a book on the funerary urns of Oaxaca (with A. Caso), *Mexico Before Cortes* (1975; originally published in Spanish in 1959), an exhaustive bibliography of Mesoamerican archaeology and ethnography with 30,000 entries, a comprehensive volume on the ceramics of Monte Albán (with A. Caso and J. Acosta), which is popularly referred to as the 'blue bible', and *A History of Mexican Archaeology* published in 1980.

As is demonstrated by the tremendous scope of Bernal's publications, as well as his active service to Mexican archaeology and to

training archaeology students, Bernal was passionate about his craft and tirelessly committed to sharing his passion with academic and popular audiences alike. France awarded him the Légion d'Honneur in 1964 and Britain the Royal Order of Victoria in 1975. Similar honours were also

Above The ballcourt at Monte Albán. There are no stone rings and the court is shaped like a capital 'I'. Some experts think that the sloping walls were used in the game, not for spectators.

bestowed on him by countries including Germany, Italy, Belgium, Denmark and the Netherlands.

Monte Albán

The capital of the Zapotec empire between 500 BC and AD 800, Monte Albán (which means 'white mountain' in Spanish) was arguably the first urban centre in Mesoamerica. Located on a series of ridges, the city looms 300m (1000ft) above the valley of Oaxaca. Its acropolis was artificially modified into an enormous plaza surrounded by pyramids and civic-ceremonial buildings. Hieroglyphic texts, many of which remain undeciphered, represent the earliest known writing system in the Americas, and low-relief carvings embedded in the architectural façades depict sacrificial victims and imperial conquest.

While much of the initial reconstruction was directed by Caso and Bernal, research has continued through intensive survey of the 2000+ residential terraces, excavations of elite and commoner residences, and archaeo-astronomical interpretations of the enigmatic Building J. Together with the settlement-pattern surveys of the valley surrounding the city and investigations at many of the subordinate sites in the region, Oaxaca is one of the best-known regions for interpreting pre-Columbian Mesoamerica.

Alfonso Caso

(1896-1970)

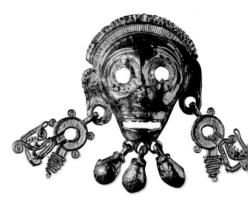

The Mexican archaeologist Alfonso Caso made important contributions to pre-Columbian studies in Mexico. His most celebrated discovery was Tomb VII at Monte Albán, which presented components of both Zapotec and Mixtec cultures.

Born in Mexico City in 1896, Alfonso Caso was one of the foremost Mexican archaeologists of the 20th century. He shaped the direction of the Mexican archaeological and anthropological institutions, while also making numerous major contributions to the interpretation of the pre-Columbian cultures of Mesoamerica. Caso's early training

Below An impressive view across the Grand Plaza at Monte Albán. Building J, in the foreground, may have been an observatory.

was as a lawyer, but early on his imagination was captured by the ancient cultures of his country and he began studying at the School of Advanced Studies under renowned scholars, such as Eduard Seler, Hermann Beyer and Manuel Gamio. He was later awarded an honorary doctorate from the National Autonomous University of Mexico.

Over the course of his career, Caso founded many of the cornerstones of Mexican archaeology, including the *Revista Mexicana de Estudios*

Above A gold bead, beautifully carved in the shape of a mask, shows the sophistication of pre-Columbian metalworking.

Antropológicos (Mexican Journal of Anthropological Studies), the National Institute of Anthropology and History, the National School of Anthropology and History and the National Indigenous Institute. Particularly in the second half of his career, he was deeply committed to the development of the discipline of anthropological archaeology.

Oaxaca

Caso is best known for his archaeological investigations in central Mexico, particularly in the state of Oaxaca. His long-term excavation at Monte Albán, the capital of the Zapotec civilization, added important breadth to a pre-Columbian history dominated at the time by Maya and Aztec cultures.

In addition to clearing and restoring numerous monumental structures on the ceremonial acropolis, Caso and his team also explored 180 tombs in elite residential compounds. The most famous of these was Tomb VII, where over 500 elaborately worked precious objects of gold, silver, jade, turquoise, alabaster and shell were found in association with a shrine to an earth/fertility goddess. Prominent among the grave offerings were carved weaving battens, inscribed with texts using the Mixtec hieroglyphic writing. Spurred on by these discoveries, Caso gained further

Above An ornate gold pendant excavated from Tomb VII at Monte Albán. This and other treasures from the tomb are now kept in the Oaxaca regional museum.

renown by making significant strides in the practical decipherment of this complex writing system.

Above A section of a pre-Columbian codex, named the Codex Zouche-Nuttall and now in the British Library in London. It is one of three codices that record the genealogies, alliances and conquests of several 11th- and 12th-century rulers of a small Mixtec city-state in Oaxaca.

Legacy

The inter-relationship of archaeology and epigraphy was a trademark focus of Caso, who also published works on Aztec and Tarrascan calendar systems. His several books on the Aztecs, notably *People of the Sun* (1958), remain among the most important treatments of the subject. His other publications include *Thirteen Masterpieces of Mexican Archaeology* (1938).

A true 'Renaissance-style' scholar, Caso's interests were diverse and his approach to research rigorous. In recognition of his profound influence on Mexican archaeology, he was buried in 1970 in the Rotunda of Illustrious Men in Mexico City.

Rhys Jones

(1941-2001)

Welsh-born archaeologist Rhys Jones was a true pioneer of modern Australian archaeology. Through his extensive field work he was able to reshape the chronology of Australia's prehistory and advance our knowledge of the Aboriginal culture.

Rhys Jones belongs to a group of several young archaeologists, many of them Cambridge-trained, who took up positions in Australia as part of the expansion of universities there in the 1960s. This period saw an explosion of knowledge in Australian archaeology as archaeologists tackled questions such as the age of human settlement, the impact of people on the environment and the role of ethnography in interpreting the past. The relatively new technique of radiocarbon dating dramatically extended the beginnings of Aboriginal occupation of Australia from 10,000 to 40,000 years ago in just over a decade of research. Rhys Jones's contribution to answering these questions cannot be overstated. He was also an excellent teacher and an eloquent communicator.

Jones was born into a Welsh-speaking family in north Wales, attended grammar school in Cardiff and went on to read Natural Sciences and Archaeology at Cambridge University. He took up a Teaching Fellowship at the University of Sydney

Below Jones's observations of modern Aboriginal life helped to inform his interpretations of their prehistory.

Left A rock formation in Kakadu National Park, Arnhem Land.

in 1963, where he completed a Ph.D. Jones then moved to the Research School of Pacific Studies at the Australian National University in 1969, where he would spend the remainder of his career.

Tasmania and Arnhem Land

Jones's first field research in Australia focused on Tasmania, where his excavations at the Rocky Cape site confirmed that occupation there predated the separation of Tasmania from the mainland due to rising sea levels. He also conducted a study, via their records, of the early French explorers' encounters with Tasmanian hunter-gatherers. Jones's fascination with the Tasmanian story and the tragedy of their encounter with European society led to a collaboration with Tom Hayden on the film *The Last Tasmanian*.

In the 1980s Jones also played a key role in the discovery of an Ice Age occupation in south-west Tasmania and successfully campaigned to save these important sites from being drowned by the damming of the Franklin River for hydroelectric power.

In Arnhem Land (Northern Territory) he worked with his long-term partner and fellow archaeologist Betty Meehan, documenting the lives of the Anbarra people of the Blyth River area. From them he gained an insight into Aboriginal life and culture. The use of ethnography as a source of models for interpreting the historical past strongly informed his work.

Much of Rhys Jones's work focused on broad questions of chronology and also on the impact of human colonization on the Australian environment. He promoted the development of new dating methods based on luminescence, resulting in claims for the age of Australian human colonization as far back as 60,000 years and establishing the age of rock art through dating the sediments trapped in mud wasps' nests.

Firestick farming

Jones studied the issues of Aboriginal transformation of the natural environment through the use of fire, and developed the concept of 'firestick farming'. He first coined the term in 1969 after he observed how the Aborigines used controlled burnings to clear land for hunting and to change the local plant species. Firestick farming symbolized a change in attitude to Aboriginal people, and hunter-gatherers in general, as active managers of their environment, rather than random wanderers at the mercy of nature.

He had a flair for the dramatic, once famously announcing his land claim over Stonehenge as a Welshman and thus an indigenous person and true descendant of the builders of the sacred

Above A young Aboriginal woman deliberately sets fire to grasses as a precaution against more dangerous fires during the dry season in Arnhem Land.

British place. He believed passionately in the importance of Australian archaeology, both in terms of its contribution to the broader human story and the potential it held for the development of important theories in the study of hunter-gatherer societies. He made full use of the media and film to project his knowledge of Aboriginal studies and succeeded in putting Australian archaeology firmly on the international stage.

He died on 19 September 2001 at the age of 60 and was buried at Bungendore cemetery wearing his well-worn bushman's hat.

Kathleen Kenyon

(1906-1978)

An eminent British archaeologist of the ancient Near East whose excavations at Jericho during the 1950s made landmark discoveries, especially for early Neolithic periods. She also excavated at Samaria and Jerusalem, and published influential studies of Levantine archaeology.

Kathleen Kenyon was born in London on 5 January 1906, the daughter of Frederic Kenyon, a biblical scholar of high reputation, director of the British Museum and also president of the British Academy. This background clearly influenced her choice of future career. She read history at Somerville College, Oxford, where she became the first woman president of the Oxford University Archaeological Society.

She gained her first archaeological experience in 1929 when she worked as a photographer on Gertrude Caton-Thompson's famous expedition to Great Zimbabwe in Africa.

During the 1930s Kenyon devoted much of her time to Roman Britain: she was a regular participant in the excavations carried out by Mortimer and Tessa Wheeler at Verulamium (St Albans), and she conducted her own

excavations at Jewry Wall (Leicester). Kenyon also assisted the Wheelers in establishing, in 1934, the famed Institute of Archaeology at the University of London. Mortimer Wheeler was at this time developing and applying his method of careful stratigraphic excavation (exploring a site in strata), and Kenyon's association with him deeply influenced her own approach to archaeological excavation.

During World War II Kenyon served as a divisional commander of the Red Cross, in Hammersmith, London, and also as the acting director of the Institute of Archaeology. When she resumed archaeological field work after the war, Kenyon initially pursued her Roman interests, with work in Britain and in Libya. But she soon launched the work in the Near East that would make her famous.

Apprenticeship at Samaria

Kenyon had received initial experience in the field of Near Eastern archaeology in the early 1930s, when she assisted in the excavations headed by John Crowfoot at Samaria, the capital of the biblical kingdom of Israel. The site had been heavily destroyed at the end of the 8th

Left Kenyon's work at Jericho took her back to the very beginnings of human civilization. The Pre-Pottery Neolithic stone tower dates to c.8000 BC. The tower, built of solid stone and standing 9m (30ft) high, was entered through an internal staircase.

century BC and then reoccupied through Roman times – its stratigraphy was very challenging. Kenyon's contribution to that project was a stratigraphic section through the site that extended from the Iron Age II (c.1000-600 BC) through the Roman periods.

Ancient Jericho

After the war Kenyon returned to the Near East where she was involved in the reopening of the British School of Archaeology in Jerusalem. Such is Kenyon's place in the life of this centre of learning that in July 2003 the British School was officially renamed the Kenyon Institute.

In 1952 Kenyon launched excavations at Jericho (Tell al-Sultan), which she continued until 1958. Jericho, a mound in a spring-fed oasis west of the Jordan river, had been the object of excavations by John Garstang during the 1930s. Kenyon's thorough excavations produced results that far exceeded those of the earlier work, making landmark contributions to regional and even world archaeology.

She exposed a Pre-Pottery Neolithic (roughly 8300-6200 BC) settlement protected by a massive stone wall and tower – a very early example of the coordination of community labour. The plastered skulls and plaster statues at the site were part of a mortuary cult characteristic of the period.

The subsequent Pottery Neolithic period (c.5800-4500 BC) levels contained pit houses, as well as pottery that helped elucidate this still poorly known period. The Early Bronze Age (mid-3rd millennium BC) town had been surrounded by a wall with towers, while the Middle Bronze Age (c.2000-1550 BC) town had been enclosed by earthen ramparts. Cemeteries situated around the mound contained collective burials in caves, the mortuary assemblages of which helped to refine significantly the chronology of Bronze Age material culture.

A Jerusalem finale

After Jericho Kenyon shifted her attention to Jerusalem, where she carried out the first modern excavation in the 'City of David' just south of Temple Mount. Begun in 1961 and brought to a close by the 1967 Six-Day War, the Jerusalem excavations must be counted as less successful than those at Jericho. Kenyon did find remains of the Iron Age II (1000-600 BC) capital of Judah, including traces of the town wall and of houses constructed on terraces up the hill slope, and also remains of later periods of occupation. However, these results are largely superseded by the work of Israeli archaeologists, who have been conducting many further excavations since 1967.

An influential figure

Kenyon's contribution to Near Eastern archaeology was not limited to the technical publication of results that are a necessary conclusion to any field project. She also wrote important overviews of Levantine archaeology, such as *Archaeology of the Holy Land* (1960), which helped shape a framework and questions that are still pertinent today. In addition, she encouraged several generations of budding archaeologists with her *Beginning in Archaeology* (1952), in which she explained the techniques and goals of archaeological field work. Other publications include: *Jerusalem - Excavating 3000 Years of History* (1967) and *Royal Cities of the Old Testament* (1971). In 1962 she was appointed Principal of St Hugh's College, Oxford and on her retirement in 1973 was made a Dame of the British Empire. Kathleen Kenyon died on 24 August 1978, in Wrexham, Wales.

Below A statue, fitted with remarkable shell eyes, from Jericho, dated to the 7th millennium BC. Kenyon also discovered plaster models made by sculpting the plaster over human skulls (these proved difficult to excavate).

The Leakey Family

(1903-present)

The Leakey family has had a huge impact not only on archaeology, but
also on the general understanding of how the human species has evolved.
Several generations of Leakeys have conducted research in Africa,
exploring finds related to early human and proto-human life.

Louis and Mary Leakey formed a legendary partnership in the history of African archaeology and in the founding of the modern science of palaeoanthropology. The Leakey name is synonymous with human origins research in East Africa, though the couple's contributions also shaped many adjacent fields of academic study, such as primatology.

African investigation

Kenyan-born Louis Leakey (1903-1972) studied archaeology and anthropology at Cambridge University, graduating in 1926. Suspecting that Africa was the cradle of human evolution, he returned to East Africa and began seeking hominid fossils. He later met Mary Douglas (1913-1996), an English archaeologist and illustrator, whom he married in 1937. In early work, Louis Leakey explored the existing idea that Africa had experienced intermittent wet periods (known as pluvials) that corresponded to the European Ice Ages. In this model, culture and change were explained by correlating archaeological industries and sequences and palaeoclimatic episodes.

The popularity of the pluvial hypothesis waned, and Louis devoted himself to palaeoanthropological studies. There were few early

breakthroughs, but in 1948 the couple made a notable find near Lake Victoria of an 18-20 million-year-old Miocene primate named *Proconsul africanus*. It is not ancestral to humans, but its discovery heralded remarkable future finds, assisted by what became known as 'Leakey's luck'.

Olduvai Gorge

Work in Olduvai Gorge, in northern Tanzania, focused world attention on the Leakeys' quest for human origins. Olduvai is a ravine 48km (30 miles) long and 91m (300ft) deep. Partly an ancient lake basin, it is made up of a

series of beds, representing a build-up of layers of lava, volcanic ash and water-borne sediments. The hominid fossil-bearing beds had accumulated over approximately 2 million years.

Assuming that different artefact cultures might be associated with different early human species, the Leakeys set out to find the fossil remains of the makers of the stone-tool industries found in Olduvai Gorge. Correlating hominid species and artefacts recalls the idea of the 'pluvial hypothesis', in which cultural materials were linked to climatic episodes. Mary Leakey meticulously

Right Meave Leakey (b.1942) has continued the family tradition of African research. Her work in the Turkana Basin in Kenya produced some of the oldest surviving hominid remains.

classified the Olduvai artefactual industries as the Oldowan, Developed Oldowan and Early Acheulean.

The Olduvai Gorge work bore fruit in 1959 when Mary discovered a hominid cranium in Bed II. They named it *Zinjanthropus boisei* (in honour of Charles Boise, whose

funding had enabled the work). *Zinjanthropus*, now known as *Australopithecus boisei*, was a robust (heavily built) species of australopithecine (a species of extinct hominid). It is now known that it lived in different East African locations between 2.3 and 1.2 million years ago.

At the time of the discovery, scientists believed that humans had most likely evolved in Asia, and at a much later date. The australopithecines are now regarded by most palaeoanthropologists to have been in the direct line of human ancestry. However, neither Louis, Mary nor their son Richard, also an eminent palaeoanthropologist, endorsed this interpretation. The excitement generated by the discovery of 'Zinj' attracted funding from the National Geographic Society, which allowed the Leakeys to continue and deepen their important research.

In 1960 their searches revealed a mandible and other bones that came to be named *Homo habilis* ('handy man'). The Leakeys believed this was the first tool-making hominid and probably a direct human ancestor. It may have given rise to *Homo erectus* fossils, another species found at Olduvai. (Early African specimens are also named *H. ergaster*.)

In time, Richard Leakey's team at Koobi Fora and Lake Turkana would reveal many more *H. ergaster* specimens, as well as individuals of a species named *Homo rudolfensis*, contemporary with *H. habilis*. Anatomical studies aside, the existence at Olduvai of in situ (undisturbed) materials, including 'home bases' and butchery locations, has been proposed but also contested. Such sites offer opportunities for investigating early human behaviour and society.

Fossil footprints

In later years Mary remained in East Africa with her beloved dalmatians while Louis travelled the world, giving lectures and raising essential funding. Louis died in 1972. Mary continued working in East Africa and in 1976-77 made a unique and important find. A volcanic eruption approximately 3.6 million years ago,

Left An anthropologist examines Laetoli footprints during a 1995 excavation. The hominid prints discovered at Laetoli were accompanied by dozens of animal prints.

Above The Olduvai gorge has produced a wide range of rich archaeological finds, ranging from 2.3 million to 15,000 years old.

at Laetoli in northern Tanzania, had rained ash over two, and probably three, sets of footprints – perhaps 70 prints in all. Initially stamped in soft ground, they were preserved by the hardening ash. Scientific examination suggested a pattern of movement and weight-transference characteristic of a creature walking upright. Mary believed they were made by early *Homo*, but most now attribute them to *Australopithecus afarensis* – the same species as the famous 'Lucy' – from Ethiopia. The significance of the Laetoli footprints lies in the light the find may shed on human evolution. Formerly it had been thought that the hominids before *Homo* had not been bipedal and that tool use may have preceded upright walking techniques.

The Leakey legacy

Though best known for their East African discoveries, and their many books and monographs, the Leakeys' influence went further. Studies by the primatologists Jane Goodall, Dian Fossey and Birute Galdikas-Brindamour of chimpanzees, gorillas and orang-utans, respectively, were made possible by Louis Leakey's support. Mary Leakey is also remembered for recording Tanzanian rock art, dating to the more recent African past. She diligently worked on, almost until her death in 1996 at the age of 83.

The Leakeys' studies have helped many researchers to rethink existing ideas about a single line of human descent. Instead, it seems that some of the hominid species had evolved in parallel with each other. Most of all, their work truly established the importance of Africa as the place where our species evolved.

The work of the Leakey family in the field of human evolution is perpetuated by the Leakey Foundation and by scores of independent and associated international researchers. They include Richard Leakey's wife, Meave, whose work has brought new species of hominid to light and, most recently, their daughter Louise.

Below The skull of *Australopithecus boisei*, discovered at the Olduvai Gorge, Tanzania.

André Leroi-Gourhan

(1911-1986)

Leroi-Gourhan's abiding interest was in the Palaeolithic period, particularly in the study of cave art. He saw a sophistication in the distribution of art around a cave not previously observed, and he produced one of the defining books on the interpretion of this primitive art form.

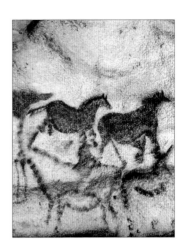

Above Leroi-Gourhan interpreted Palaeolithic art as structured and composed, rather than as a random collection of images.

André Leroi-Gourhan was a French archaeologist who made enormously important contributions to the excavation of Palaeolithic sites as well as to the study of Ice Age art. Born in Paris in 1911, he spent his early student years learning Russian and Chinese, after which he turned to ethnology and archaeology. He was involved in setting up Paris's Musée de l'Homme, of which he was a sub-director, and he was later professor at the Collège de France (1969-82).

Leroi-Gourhan carried out many major excavations, first in the caves of Arcy-sur-Cure – where he discovered the first known examples of ornaments made by Neanderthals – and subsequently at the late Ice Age open-air site of Pincevent near Paris, a camp of reindeer hunters. Here he pioneered techniques of horizontal excavation, the minute study and moulding of occupation floors, and ethnological reconstruction of the life of stone-age people.

Interpreting cave art

Leroi-Gourhan's huge book *Préhistoire de l'Art Occidental* (1965) embodied his revolutionary approach to Palaeolithic art. Previously, cave art had been seen as simple accumulations of figures (most notably by the Abbé Breuil) and interpreted through simplistic use of supposed analogies to modern cultures. Leroi-Gourhan, together with Annette Laming, strove to avoid such analogies, and saw the figures as purposefully arranged within each cave. He found that horses and bison dominated the art numerically, and tended to cluster in the central parts of the caves. He believed that horses were male symbols, and bison female, even when the bisons were clearly bulls.

Leroi-Gourhan was also the first to tackle the enigmatic 'signs' in Palaeolithic art, deciding that, like the animal figures, they constituted a dual system for exploring and explaining the world, which might perhaps be interpreted in the sexual terms of vulvar signs and phallic signs.

Subsequent work inevitably modified or cast doubt on much of this approach, but it nevertheless remains the single greatest contribution to the interpretation of Palaeolithic art.

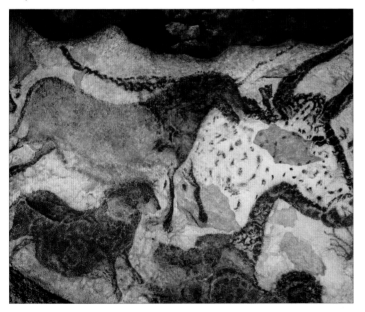

Left A detail from one of the reproduction cave paintings at Lascaux II, a facsimile site opened in France in 1983.

Spyridon Marinatos
(1901-1974)

A Greek archaeologist with an international reputation, Marinatos excavated several famous sites of the Aegean. One of his greatest finds was the remains of an ancient Minoan city entombed beneath volcanic rock on Thera, wiped out by a cataclysmic volcanic eruption around 1500 BC.

Spyridon Marinatos was born on the Greek island of Kefalonia on 4 November 1901, a time when the earlier discovery of Mycenae and Knossos had heightened world interest in archaeology. At the age of 19, while still an undergraduate reading archaeology at Athens University, he was appointed an inspector of antiquities.

In 1929, after postgraduate study in Germany at Berlin and Halle, he became director of the Archaeological Museum of Heraklion, Crete. Here his excavations at the Villa of the Lilies (so called because fragments of frescoes found there depicted red and white lilies), and other buildings in the nearby settlement of Amnissos, gave him a valuable first-hand experience of Minoan archaeology.

The Thera volcano

Like other Minoan sites on Crete, Amnissos had been struck by an earthquake, then rebuilt, and was later mysteriously abandoned after a fire. Pumice found in a seafront building is said to have led Marinatos to think of the Cyclades island of Thera – modern Santorini – situated 100km (62 miles) to the north of Crete, which had been torn apart by a massive volcanic eruption. In 1939 Marinatos published in the journal *Antiquity* his theory that this eruption had actually taken place around 1500 BC, and had caused such devastation that it had brought about the demise of the flourishing Minoan civilization.

Marinatos proposed excavating on Santorini where, during the late 1800s, artefacts had been exposed by minor earthquakes and during quarrying. French, German and Greek archaeologists had dug around the village of Akrotiri, exposing the remains of ancient buildings. However, the outbreak of World War II and then the Greek Civil War made work impossible and Marinatos busied himself with other projects. In 1946 he travelled abroad in search of antiquities stolen by occupying forces, and during the 1950s he excavated the Minoan settlement and palace complex at Vathypetro, Crete, where he found a wine and olive press and a potter's kiln. Intending to turn Vathypetro into a museum, Marinatos had the remains reconstructed, for which he was criticized by his peers, since this made further excavation and interpretation difficult.

Left A view of the ancient city of Akrotiri, Thera, as it has emerged from the volcanic rock. Despite its great age, the site has been impressively preserved, with many staircases still standing alongside numerous pithoi (storage jars) and the framework of a sophisticated drainage system.

Excavating Akrotiri

Geologists had been sceptical about Marinatos's 1939 theories, arguing that earthquakes occurring on Santorini were never as powerful as he claimed. In the 1960s, however, American scientists from Columbia University found thick ash deposits in ooze that was dredged up from the Mediterranean. The ash was found to be from the Thera volcano and it covered so vast an area that the eruption that produced it must have been of the magnitude of the 1883 eruption of Krakatoa, Indonesia. Interest revived and in 1967 the Greek Archaeological Society licensed Marinatos, then General Inspector of Antiquities, to excavate on Santorini near the village of Akrotiri.

Marinatos's team chose a point on the southern tip of the island, where the tephra (solidified ash) was thinnest, and at about 30m (98ft) they uncovered streets, squares, multi-storey dwellings and workshops of the most important Minoan port outside Crete. The earliest pipes and water closets ever discovered showed that the port was inhabited by an advanced civilization that used cold water and hot (from thermal springs). Jars in ancient storerooms contained traces of olive oil and other food – but there were no skeletons, indicating that people had prior warning of the eruption and had fled.

Some of the dwellings excavated at Akrotiri displayed delicate, well-preserved Minoan frescoes. One depicts saffron-gatherers presenting their harvest of stamens to a seated figure, perhaps a goddess. In another two youths are shown boxing.

From 1968 Marinatos published annual reports of his findings at Akrotiri. His team uncovered just a corner of Akrotiri, however, and excavations continue to this day. Geologists have also recovered evidence that suggests that the Thera

eruption may have been many times the magnitude of Krakatoa, creating a dust cloud so great that it blocked out the sun for a prolonged period.

Marinatos also made other highly significant excavations that yielded important archaeological finds. In 1966 he unsuccessfully searched the seafloor for the fabled drowned city of Helike, but in the early 1970s he

located the site of the Battle of Thermopylae and excavated the ancient burial mound constructed after the Battle of Marathon.

Marinatos was killed in an accident at Akrotiri in October 1974 when an ancient wall collapsed on him. At the site a fitting memorial marks his immeasurable contribution to the archaeology of the Aegean.

Right One of the most beautiful frescoes at Akrotiri is this young fisherman holding his catch on a string.

Harald Pager

(1923-1985)

Harald Pager was one of the most accomplished and dedicated rock art researchers of our time. His name is synonymous with Ndedema Gorge in southern Africa where he uncovered and meticulously recorded thousands of cave paintings.

Born and brought up in a small town in Czechoslovakia, Harald Pager settled in Austria after World War II, where he trained as an industrial designer and artist at an art college in Graz.

He emigrated to South Africa in 1956 where he worked as a commercial artist before embarking upon the recording of rock art made by the San (Bushmen), a Stone Age hunter-gatherer people.

Ndedema Gorge

In 1971 Pager's work was published in a large volume entitled *Ndedema*. This work is perhaps the most significant

book on rock art ever produced. It documented five years' work with his wife Shirley-Ann, who always assisted him, locating and recording the rock paintings of one richly painted valley – Ndedema (now known as Didima) – in the Drakensberg Moutains, KwaZulu-Natal, South Africa. The couple found 17 sites in the 5.5-km (3.4-mile) long valley and meticulously recorded each of the almost 4000 individual images painted on the walls of the rock shelters.

The work was a milestone in South African rock-art research. Only in the 1950s had A.R. Willcox effectively

and systematically first used colour photography in recording. Previously, recorders had relied on freehand drawings, watercolour copies and, later, monochrome photographs.

Only photography, with its total faithfulness to detail, reproduced the all-important details of the rock face, and only colour reproductions conveyed the palette on which the images rely for their visual impact. Pager, who was both visually and scientifically trained, recognized that colour photography was problematic in recording less well-preserved images. To accommodate this, he developed an innovative technique that entailed first photographing the paintings in black and white. The couple then returned to the site and painted onto the photographs with oil paints, which were carefully colour-matched.

Professor Raymond Dart's enthusiastic foreword to *Ndedema* hailed the book as the 'first and only' publication to be directly modelled on archaeological and scientific principles. Pager's precision recording included plotting every mark and compiling quantitative data, not only on subject matter but also on composition, perspective, technique and postures. The quantitative data are

Left Harald Pager at work copying a panel of three tall hunters and eland (Africa's largest antelope) at Botha's Shelter, Ndedema Gorge. The pigments used in the cave paintings were mainly black, white and orange, although there is great depth in this palette.

integrated into a detailed discussion of the archaeology of the Drakensberg San peoples and the environment of the region. Colour plates and line drawings of true virtuoso quality complete the tour de force.

Before relocating to Namibia, Pager published another important book on South African rock art, *Stone Age Myth and Magic*, comprising an extended discussion of the significance of the paintings.

Pager and rock art

Today, some researchers question the value of science for understanding art and culture. However, though in *Ndedema* Pager chose to suspend the question of aesthetics, his appreciation of visuality underpinned his approach. The shamanistic model, which subsequently emerged, reverted to analysing the art almost exclusively in terms of subject matter. That model has been widely criticized, for example by art historians, better equipped than anthropologists to appreciate Pager's close attention to the visual characteristics of the rock paintings.

Pager's visual acuity, and his vast and empathetic familiarity with the materials, enhanced his insights into San rock-art traditions. He was, for example, sceptical of the claim that the imagery derived from the hallucinations of 'shamans', noting that the shamanistic explanation was insufficiently tied to the paintings themselves and their visual attributes.

Namibian rock art

In 1978 Pager embarked on another, perhaps even more, ambitious recording programme, this time in the Brandberg Mountains, Namibia. There, together with two Namibian field assistants, he recorded nearly 900 sites containing over 40,000 figures. Five volumes have been

published so far, covering the Amis Gorge, Hungorob Gorge, the Southern Gorges, Umuab and Karuab Gorges, Naib Gorge and the Northwest. Regrettably, the economics of publishing demanded reliance on line drawings rather than colour reproductions, but Pager's efforts have nevertheless resulted in a truly monumental record of the colour and vibrancy of Namibian art.

Harald Pager died prematurely in 1985. Though remembered for his recording, his legacy lies also in the domains of conservation and in raising awareness of African rock arts.

Right A crowded panel from Sebaaini Shelter, Ndedema Gorge. Many paintings are superimposed on other older paintings. There were 1146 paintings in all at the site when Harald Pager was there to copy them.

Tatiana Proskouriakoff

(1909-1985)

Proskouriakoff was one of the 20th century's pioneering researchers into Maya peoples and cultures. Training as an architectural artist enabled her to bring ruins to life in her published work, while her new interpretation of Maya hieroglyphics changed the way inscriptions are studied.

Born in Tomsk, Siberia, on 23 January 1909, Tatiana Proskouriakoff moved to the United States in 1916 where her chemist father was posted to oversee munitions production for the Russian war effort. She received a Bachelor of Science in Architecture from Pennsylvania State University in 1930. Lack of work as an architect during the Depression led her to take a job as illustrator at the university museum.

First expedition

Her work at the museum attracted the attention of archaeologist Linton Satterthwaite, who invited her to join his 1936 expedition to the site of Piedras Negras, Guatemala. So began her illustrious career as ethnologist and archaeologist. During her time at Piedras Negras, Proskouriakoff would create some of the best-known archaeological reconstructive drawings from sites all over the Maya world.

While studying the hieroglyphic inscriptions on monuments at Piedras Negras, Proskouriakoff noticed a repetitive pattern of dates and signs which she identified as a succession of seven rulers spanning 200 years. From this she demonstrated that Maya texts spoke of rites of passage and the major accomplishments of rulers, rather than – as had previously been believed – purely astronomical and calendrical knowledge. This work, on which current knowledge of epigraphy (study of inscriptions) is based, won

Above A Mayan stela (carved stone slab) from Piedras Negras. Many of the stone carvings depicted either rulers or local deities.

Proskouriakoff the Alfred V. Kidder Medal (which she herself had designed) in 1962.

Over the course of her career, Proskouriakoff published numerous pioneering works, including *An Album of Maya Architecture* (1946), *A Study of Classic Maya Sculpture* (1950), *Portraits of Women in Maya Art* (1961) and *Jades from the Cenote of Sacrifice, Chichén Itzá, Yucatan* (1974). In addition to the Kidder Medal, she was awarded Pennsylvania State Woman of the Year (1971), honorary degrees from Tulane and Pennsylvania State Universities, and the prestigious Order of the Quetzal from the people of Guatemala (1984). Her friends and family remember her as a disciplined scholar and free-spirited individual, who was not afraid to follow her ideas and contradict those of her colleagues. She died on 30 August 1985.

Left Maya hieroglyphs on a stela from Tikal, Guatemala. The complex writing system is made up of hundreds of unique signs, or glyphs, in the form of humans, animals, supernaturals, objects and abstract designs.

Maria Reiche

(1903-1998)

For over 50 years the German-born Maria Reiche devoted her life to exploring the Nasca lines in Peru. Her work revealed some of the secrets of the lines, while also helping to preserve this amazing archaeological phenomenon for future generations.

No major archaeological site is perhaps more closely linked with a single name and personality than the Nasca (Nazca) lines of Peru. These huge lines form designs etched into the desert between the Nasca and Ingenio river valleys, several hours' drive south of Lima. They would almost certainly have been destroyed long ago had it not been for the work of Maria Reiche.

Reiche was born in Dresden, Germany, in 1903. Her father, a judge, died in World War I, and her mother, who had studied in England as well as Berlin, taught and did other work to support the family. Reiche spoke and read several languages, and she studied mathematics at Hamburg and Dresden and became a teacher. In 1932 she left Germany to accept a position as governess to a family in Cuzco, Peru, later moving to Lima where she made a living teaching and working as a translator at San Marcos University. It was through her academic connections there that she was eventually drawn to Nasca.

Desert lines

The Nasca lines had been virtually unknown until commercial air traffic began in Peru during the 1920s. Pilots for Faucett, the first company to run flights between Lima and the southern city of Arequipa, noticed huge lines, triangles and other markings on the desert pampa to the north of the town of Nasca.

The Peruvian archaeologist Toribio Mejía Xesspe conducted the first formal study of the lines in 1927, publishing an article in which he suggested that the lines were ancient ceremonial pathways. In 1941 the American historian Paul Kosok, who had come to Peru to study ancient irrigation canal systems and the origins of Andean civilization, became interested in the Nasca lines. He observed that some of the lines

Left This glyph of a dog is one of the most complex of the Nasca figures.

Above An aerial photograph of the outline of a hummingbird. Like other Nasca lines, it can be recognized as a coherent figure only from the air.

marked the winter solstice from a central location and theorized that the lines might have been used to make astronomical and calendrical observations. Kosok had hired Reiche to make translations for him, and he inspired her to begin researching the Nasca lines in her own right.

The Nasca lines consist of a huge complex of gigantic figures etched into the surface of the desert across nearly 40km (25 miles) of the south coast of Peru. Most of the lines form geometric designs, including loops, triangles and other forms, but some 30 or so of the designs on the Nasca plain itself are figures, mostly animals.

The many lines were made by removing rocks and sand that had been blackened by centuries of exposure to the elements (forming the surface known as 'desert varnish'), leaving lighter coloured lines on the surface of the plain. The designs, and the pottery associated with the lines, indicate that they were made by the ancient Nasca, a civilization known for its spectacular polychrome pottery and masterful use of underground water resources for irrigation of the desert. The Nasca culture thrived during what is known as the Early Intermediate Period, beginning roughly 2000 years ago and lasting for approximately 600 or 700 years.

Left The Nasca monkey with its huge spiral tail was first recognized by Maria Reiche in 1946. Such is the scale of the artworks, that they probably took several hundred years to complete.

A life's work

Reiche's work on the Nasca lines began after the end of World War II, when she was allowed to move freely in Peru after a period of severe restrictions on German citizens ended. She spent virtually all of her remaining years living there, mostly in primitive conditions, studying the lines and working for their preservation. Although she received some funding, and occasional support (particularly in the area of aerial photography) from the Peruvian military, plus the attention of scholars and intellectuals inside and outside of Peru, she worked largely alone. She battled to save the lines from destruction due to increasing traffic from the Panamerican highway and other development. Peru's National Cultural Institute declared the lines an intangible zone in 1970, laying an important foundation for their protection. It was Maria Reiche, however, who hired and paid the guards that protected the lines.

Regarded for many years as a somewhat eccentric foreigner by the local people, Reiche eventually became a revered member of the community as tourism, based largely on the fame of the lines, began to take off in the 1970s. She spent the latter years of her life installed in the relative luxury of the Tourist Hotel in Nasca, becoming one of its major attractions herself. By the 1980s she was suffering from glaucoma and Parkinson's disease, but she continued to give daily lectures to visitors and to advocate her theory that the lines had been made by Nasca astronomers to mark major calendrical events.

Maria Reiche believed strongly in her own theories of the Nasca lines, paying little attention to the work of other scholars, and she saved the lines and carefully documented them. Scientific studies of the lines have demonstrated that some do mark major calendrical events, such as the summer and winter solstice, but many do not. Current theories about their significance focus on Andean cosmology and posit that some may have served to guide pilgrimages, ceremonial processions and other rituals. The lines have drawn the interest of scientists and pseudo-scientists for the past 50 years. Although many scholars disagree with Reiche's theories about the purpose of the lines, they all acknowledge that without her they would not be there today for us to study.

Below The surface of the Nasca desert (one of the driest in the world) consists of rock, not sand, hence the Nasca lines have been preserved.

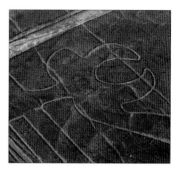

Above The Nasca lines, including this impressive parrot, were declared a UNESCO World Heritage Site in 1995.

John Howland Rowe

(1918-2004)

His total dedication to accurate research and his vast knowledge of the history of South America made John Rowe a world authority on Andean culture and history. His seminal 1946 paper on the Inca at the time of the Spanish Conquest remains an international standard reference.

John Howland Rowe is one of the most important figures in the development of Andean archaeology as an academic discipline in the United States. His work is likely to have a deep and lasting importance over archaeological debate for years to come. While many American archaeologists focused on field work and techniques of analysis in archaeology, and worked in multiple areas applying basically similar approaches to different regions, Rowe emphasized a different approach – deep expertise in a single region. Furthermore, instead of applying one academic approach to multiple regions or sites, he applied approaches from multiple disciplines – including archaeology, history and linguistics – to the study of the Andean past, and especially to the history of the Inca. Unsurpassed in his knowledge of the Inca for more than a generation, his

Below The carved rock 'Inca throne', one of the key features of the Inca temple (or fortress) overlooking Cuzco at Sacsayhuaman, Peru.

Left John Rowe developed an intimate knowledge of the linguistic systems of the ancient Andean peoples. These knotted and coloured strings, called *quipu*, were used by the Inca to record information about such things as population and to keep track of harvests and livestocks.

interpretations of Inca history and archaeology formed the basis for virtually all research on the Inca in the late 20th century.

Beginnings

Rowe stated that he had been interested in archaeology from the time he was three years old. He was born on 10 June 1918, in Sorrento, Maine. His father, Louis Earl Rowe, had spent a single field season in Egypt, an experience that left him with a lifelong interest in the ancient past which he passed on to his son.

John Rowe studied classical archaeology at Brown University before moving to Harvard to study anthropology, receiving his master's degree in 1941. From there he went to Peru, where he conducted research and taught in Cuzco before serving with the US Combat Engineers in Europe between 1944 and 1946. He later returned to Harvard, where he received his Ph.D. in Latin American History and Anthropology in 1947. Rowe was hired by the University of California at Berkeley in 1948 and he spent the rest of his career there, teaching and building the anthropology library at one of the premier anthropology departments in the United States.

Rowe's scholarship was greatly influenced by his background in classical studies. The study of classical archaeology required proficiency in ancient languages, as well as in history, art styles and archaeology. Rowe's linguistic abilities and training enabled him to master Spanish easily and then to learn Quechua, the language of the Inca that was still widely spoken in Cuzco and other areas of Peru. He was also able to read and understand Spanish colonial records of many

kinds. His application of art historical techniques of stylistic analysis led to a rigorous approach to definition and classification of the iconographic and artistic styles of archaeological cultures of the Andes, an approach that he passed on to his students.

Study method

Rowe believed in studying data in great detail. He read colonial documents thoroughly and assessed their relevance and also the accuracy of their information based on his knowledge of Inca history and archaeology. His reliance on historical evidence, and particularly on those sources that he viewed as reliable, led him to discredit many other previously well-regarded sources, or at least portions of what they said.

His most influential body of work is his description of Inca civilization before the Spanish conquest, as well as his interpretations of the impact of the Spanish on the indigenous culture during the early colonial era. His most widely read paper is called 'Inca Culture at the Time of the Spanish Conquest', published in the multi-volume *Handbook of South American Indians* in 1946. In this and related works, Rowe synthesized his knowledge and interpretations of Inca civilization and provided a picture of Inca society that scholars, tour guides and interested lay persons could grasp.

A lasting contribution

Rowe left an important legacy to archaeology in the students he trained both in the United States and Peru, the scholarly organization he founded, with its academic journal dedicated to Andean studies, and the anthropology library he founded at the University of California. His scholarly papers and editorial productions number more than 300 from 1940 to 2005, with a large proportion in Spanish.

His emphasis on detailed knowledge and deep understanding of the available data set high standards that have helped Andean archaeology to grow as a discipline. His interpretations of the

Inca remain important, even as the details of the Inca civilization are clarified and modified by new research. Rowe retired in 1988, but continued research work until his death in Berkeley in 2004.

Below A figurine depicting one of the 'chosen women' (often called 'Virgins of the Sun'), who were concubines of the Inca emperor and given to seal political marriage alliances between Inca and other societies.

Sir J. Eric Thompson

(1898-1975)

The English archaeologist John Eric Sidney Thompson is widely regarded as the pre-eminent scholar of the pre-Columbian Maya civilization of the first half of the 20th century. He made a lasting contribution to the decipherment of Maya.

Thompson was born in London on 31 December 1898. He was sent to Winchester College in 1912, but at the outbreak of World War I he joined the army under the assumed name Neil Winslow, giving false information about his age. An injury ended his army career with the Coldstream Guards in 1918. After working as a gaucho in Argentina, he went on to study anthropology at Cambridge University.

Researching the Maya

In 1926 Thompson went to Chichén Itzá, Mexico, to work with the celebrated Mayanist Sylvanus Morley of the Carnegie Institution. During his time with the Institution, Thompson was sent to numerous sites around the Maya world. Most notable were his travels through the British Honduras (Belize). His work there involved some of the first excavations of smaller sites beyond elite ceremonial centres, focusing on the lives of 'common' Maya. During this time he also gathered information from many modern Maya people, recognizing the continuity of certain beliefs and practices that dated all the way back to pre-Hispanic times.

Thompson was also sent to the Maya site of Coba in Mexico, and his report of the large ruined city and its many hieroglyphic inscriptions

Above A detail of a carving at the ruined Maya city of Coba. Thompson published a detailed description of the site in 1932.

prompted Sylvanus Morley to carry out a more thorough investivation of the remote site.

Thompson's work produced a correlation between the Maya calendar and the Gregorian calendar that remains in use to this day. During the 1940s he also conducted considerable work on the decipherment of Maya hieroglyphics, developing a numerical cataloguing system for the glyphs that survives in the modern discipline.

Thompson was a prolific writer and was passionate about transferring his knowledge to the wider world. His incredible corpus of respected publications includes *The Civilisation of the Mayas* (1927), *Ethnology of the Mayas of Southern and Central British Honduras* (1930), *Maya Hieroglyphic Writing: Introduction* (1950), *A Catalogue of Maya Hieroglyphs* (1962), *Maya History and Religion* (1970), and also an amusing autobiography entitled *Maya Archaeologist* (1963).

Thompson received many honours in recognition of his work and was knighted in 1975, shortly before his death in Cambridge that year.

Left An aerial view of the ruins at Coba. Thompson made his first visit through the jungle by mule while on his honeymoon.

Michael Ventris

(1922-1956)

By the time he was 30, Michael Ventris had deciphered Europe's oldest written language, which had been found half a century before in engravings on clay tablets at Knossos. He proved what experts had refused to consider: that Linear B writing was an archaic form of ancient Greek.

Michael Ventris was a 14-year-old schoolboy when he attended a lecture and exhibition on Minoan civilization given in London by the 86-year-old archaeologist Sir Arthur Evans. On display were tablets engraved with a script which, Ventris was told, no one could decipher. When excavating Knossos, the Minoan palace-complex on Crete, in 1901, Evans had excavated more than 3,000 tablets and had identified their faint engravings as writing. Evans distinguished a hieroglyphic script and two scripts composed of glyphs and other symbols, which he named 'Linear A' and 'Linear B'. Certain that they were examples of Minoan writing, Evans devoted the next several decades to their decipherment but to no avail.

Ventris, who had learned Polish from his mother, French and German during his childhood in Switzerland, and studied Latin and Greek at his English prep school, resolved to decode the hieroglyphics of Linear B. At 18 he published his first conclusions – that Linear B was the script of the Etruscans – in the *American Journal of Archaeology*, which aroused academic interest.

Background

Rather than read classics at university, however, Ventris trained as an architect, enrolling at the Architectural Association School of Architecture in 1940. In 1943, with World War II at its height, he joined the RAF and flew as a navigator but continued his professional training after the war. He also worked diligently on deciphering the elusive Linear B in his spare time.

Leaps in the dark

An American philologist Alice Kober had already prepared some of the groundwork for the decipherment of Linear B by working out a grid expressing the relationships between vowels and consonants in the script. After Kober's death in 1950, Ventris built on her work. Inspired guesses speeded his progress. For example, he assumed that the most common symbol was the vowel 'a'; that certain symbols followed by glyphs were women's names and others men's; and that commonly occurring symbols on the tablets found on Crete, but not on others excavated on the Greek mainland, were town names.

As he deciphered more of the hieroglyphics, Ventris noticed a connection between Linear B and the ancient Greek language. A link with Greek had been firmly rejected for 50 years, but in 1952 Ventris publicized this idea in a BBC talk. Afterwards, he received an offer of assistance from John Chadwick, a recognized specialist in archaic Greek.

The two men deciphered the tablets more completely and in 1953 they jointly published their conclusions: Linear B, they announced, was a written form of the ancient Greek used by the first Greeks – the Mycenaeans – and was used from around 1450 BC. The discovery met first with scepticism, then with acclaim. Yet for Ventris it marked the end of his obsession with Linear B.

Having solved the problem, his interest waned. He returned briefly to architecture but, dissatisfied with his achievements, soon abandoned it. Always a loner, he had little to fall back on: his marriage had failed; his children had become strangers. On 6 September 1956, he died in a car accident at the age of just 34.

Below A clay tablet from the Mycenaean Palace at Pylos, in Greece. The Linear B tablets revealed financial records and lists of livestock and agricultural produce, tableware, textiles and furniture.

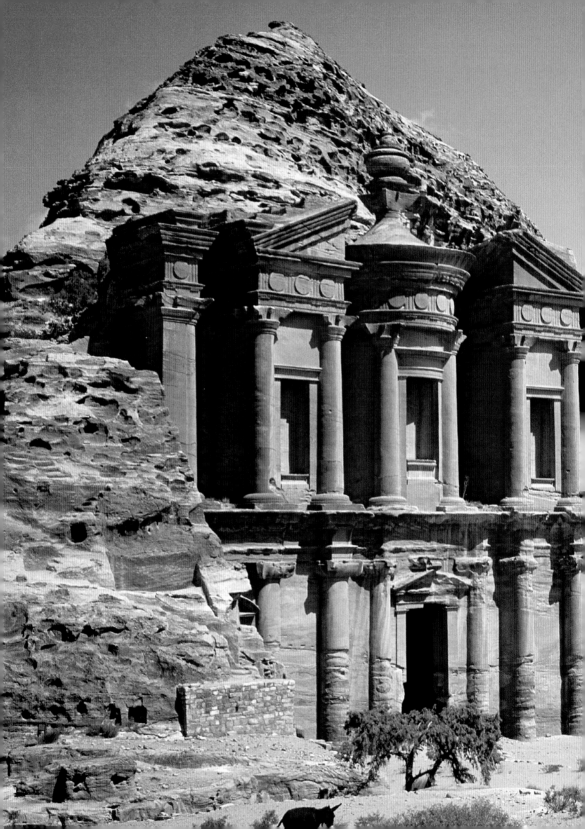

ARCHAEOLOGICAL SITES

'Match me such marvel save in Eastern clime,
A rose-red city half as old as time.'

J.W. BURGON (1845)

The beautiful rock-hewn tomb façades of Petra, a desert city rediscovered in 1812, stand as an enduring testament to the skill and vision of our ancestors. Other equally impressive sites from across the ages and continents are explored in the following chapters.

Saqqara This vast necropolis contains an array of monuments, including mastaba tombs and pyramids.

Giza The royal pyramid complex includes the Great Pyramid of Khufu, one of the Wonders of the Ancient World.

Karnak From the New Kingdom, this complex was the most important religious establishment in the Egyptian empire.

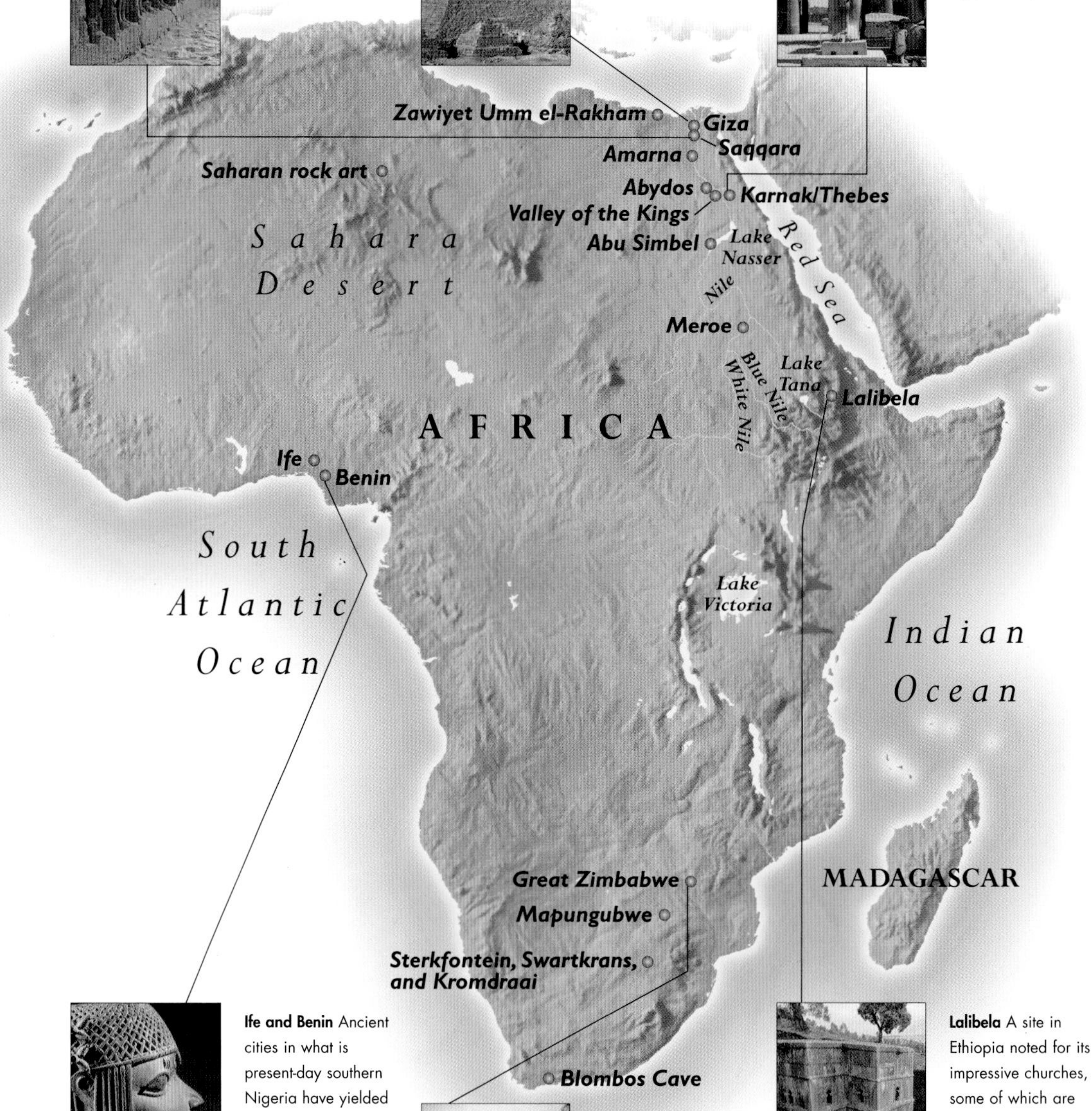

Zawiyet Umm el-Rakham ○

Giza ○

Saqqara

Amarna ○

Saharan rock art ○

S a h a r a
D e s e r t

Abydos ○

Valley of the Kings

Karnak/Thebes

Abu Simbel ○ *Lake Nasser*

Nile

Red Sea

Meroe ○

Blue Nile
White Nile

Lake Tana

Lalibela

A F R I C A

Ife ○ ○ **Benin**

South Atlantic Ocean

Lake Victoria

Indian Ocean

MADAGASCAR

Great Zimbabwe ○

Mapungubwe ○

Sterkfontein, Swartkrans, and Kromdraai ○

Ife and Benin Ancient cities in what is present-day southern Nigeria have yielded a remarkable series of sculptures.

Blombos Cave ○

Great Zimbabwe A Late Iron Age site dating back around 1000 years. Once the capital of a vast Shona empire.

Lalibela A site in Ethiopia noted for its impressive churches, some of which are cut from solid rock.

THE GREAT SITES OF AFRICA

This vast continent contains some of the most spectacular and important archaeology in the world. There is the stunning prehistoric rock art of the Sahara, for example, with its depictions of crocodiles and elephants bearing witness to more clement and humid times in that region; and the equally beautiful but different rock art found in southern Africa. In South and East Africa are the numerous sites that have yielded many fossil specimens of our earliest ancestors – the hominids. The continent also has astonishing and impressive structures, such as the rock-cut churches of Lalibela and the tower of Great Zimbabwe. Above all there is Egypt, whose temples and tombs have enchanted the world for centuries and whose ancient remains have given rise to an entire branch of archaeology.

Large parts of this continent remain virtually unexplored archaeologically, so there are bound to be many more exciting discoveries still to be made.

Rock art The Tassili N'Ajjer range in the Sahara is known for rock art made over a long period.

Valley of the Kings Egypt's New Kingdom rulers were buried in rock-cut tombs.

The Great Sphinx The colossal statue guards the entrance to the mortuary complex at Giza.

Sterkfontein, Swartkrans and Kromdraai

The fossil sites of Sterkfontein, Swartkrans and Kromdraai, north of Johannesburg, South Africa, are known as 'the cradle of humankind' and have been accorded World Heritage Site status. These sites are especially rich in australopithecine fossils.

The cave system at Sterkfontein has revealed a sequence of deposits with fossils dating from 3.5 to 1.5 million years ago. Between 1936 and 1947 excavations were carried out by Dr Robert Broom. He was following in the footsteps of Raymond Dart, who in 1924 described the first *Australopithecus* specimen – the Taung child – in South West Province, South Africa. In 1936 Broom found the first adult *Australopithecus africanus* fossil at Sterkfontein. In 1938 his work revealed more *A. africanus* specimens at Kromdraai.

Excavations at the nearby Swartkrans cave provided evidence of another species of australopithecine. It was

Right Mrs Ples is the most complete cranium of an *Australopithecus africanus* **ever** found in Africa.

named 'Paranthropus', but it is now usually classified as *Australopithecus robustus*, because of its heavier, more muscular build. It differs from other australopithecines, as well as humans, on account of its larger teeth and jaw and the presence of a sagittal crest – a ridge of bone along the top of the skull to which powerful jaw muscles were attached.

One of Broom's most celebrated finds was a well-preserved skull, around 2.7 million years old. It was discovered at the Sterkfontein Caves in 1947 and was originally classified by Broom as belonging to the genus *Plesianthropus*, (meaning 'almost human'). The skull was dubbed 'Mrs Ples' by the media. Today it is recognized as *Australopithecus africanus*. It is also thought that the skull may, in fact, have been that of a young male. Working at Swartkrans with John Robinson, Broom also discovered *Homo erectus* (or *ergaster*) remains. *Homo habilis* fossils have also been identified at Sterkfontein.

Further finds

Researchers have built on the work of Broom and his contemporaries. Almost two decades of work at Swartkrans by Dr Bob Brain have been celebrated in both the scientific arena and in the popular imagination – for example in Bruce Chatwin's book *The Songlines*. Brain's finds included over 120 hominids belonging to the genera of *Australopithecus* and *Homo*.

Brain's careful analysis of the australopithecine bones revealed a pattern of tooth marks. The shape and

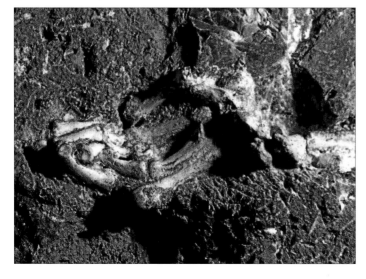

Left These are the hand bones of a 3.3 million-year-old australopithecine fossil, found at Sterkfontein in 1998.

Left The hand (top), arm (middle) and skull (bottom) of Clarke's 3.3 million-year-old find, embedded in the rock at Sterkfontein.

The first use of fire

Brain and his colleagues also noticed that a number of the bones from Swartkrans had been burnt. Using a technique known as electronic spin resonance, they were able to estimate the temperatures at which the bones were burnt. Some of the bones were burnt at the high temperatures often associated with campfires, rather than at the low temperatures normally linked to bushfires. So the Swartkrans bones may represent the earliest hominid use of fire, although it is not clear which of the species present at Swartkrans — *A. robustus* or *H. erectus* — might have been responsible.

'Little Foot'

In 1994 Dr Ron Clarke was examining boxes of fossils excavated from Sterkfontein in the 1970s, when he discovered four australopithecine foot bones that fitted together. The bones displayed both human and ape-like features. Clarke and his colleagues concluded that this hominid (Stw 573) might have been adapted for both bipedal (upright) walking and tree-climbing. The boxes contained several more foot and leg bones from the same individual, and Clarke wondered whether the remainder were still in situ in the cave.

Amazingly, a search located more bones from the individual, including an arm, hand and complete skull. It is likely that a near-complete skeleton may be assembled. The hand bones seem to confirm the idea that the creature was at least partly adapted for arboreal (tree) living. This important fossil is probably around 3.3 million years old.

The deposits at Sterkfontein, Swartkrans and Kromdraai are of international importance in studies of human evolution. Continuing work will no doubt reveal further exciting finds that shed light on our ancestors and their way of life.

spacing of the puncture holes were consistent with their having been made by the canine teeth of a large leopard-like carnivore. Brain hypothesized that these australopithecines had been killed by large cats, such as leopards and sabre tooths. Like leopards today,

the animals probably dragged their kill into trees. The bones are thought to have fallen into sinkholes, where they became part of the bone-bearing breccias ('breccia' refers to rock composed of sharp-angled fragments within a fine-grained matrix).

351

Blombos Cave

Excavations at Blombos Cave, a site on South Africa's south coast overlooking the Indian Ocean, have uncovered Stone Age finds of international interest. Preservation is unusually good because limestone caves are conducive to the survival of organic materials such as bone.

The deposits, more than 4m (13ft) deep in some places, date mainly to the Middle Stone Age. The uppermost levels indicate that the site was used by Later Stone Age hunter-gatherers in the last two millennia.

Ancient finds

A team of researchers, led by Dr Christopher Henshilwood, have been working at Blombos Cave since 1991. The artefacts found in the Middle Stone Age levels include the oldest known bone tools, such as projectile points and awls; bifacial tools (shaped on both sides); and perhaps the earliest evidence for fishing. The most exciting finds are pieces of engraved pigment (ochre) and perforated shells that may be the oldest known jewellery.

Modern human behaviour

These important finds at Blombos Cave have contributed to debates about 'modern human behaviour'.

Above Some of the oldest known bone tools have been found in unusually large numbers at the Blombos Cave.

Modern humans, at least anatomically, originated in Africa probably between 120,000 and 150,000 years ago. Some researchers believe that modern human behaviour formed gradually, alongside anatomical evolution, but others believe that there was a more abrupt change, with modern human consciousness emerging only about 40,000 years ago. Researchers regard the capacity for 'symbolic thought' as fundamental to modern human behaviour. In archaeological terms, it is indicated by the making of visual art, decoration of the person (body painting and jewellery suggesting a new awareness of selfhood) and ritual behaviour (for example, attention to death and burial).

The Blombos Cave discoveries suggest that modern human behaviour was in place about 75,000 years ago. The finds include tens of thousands of pieces of red ochre (an iron ore used worldwide as a pigment). Two ochre slabs from Blombos Cave are marked with incised lines. Some researchers believe that this is 'art' – evidence of an emerging human capacity to think abstractly, using symbols. Others remain more sceptical about regarding the marks as 'art' and as evidence for prehistoric peoples intentionally forging symbolic 'meanings'.

Excavations have also revealed a remarkable collection of shells, which seem to have been deliberately perforated, from a tiny species of mollusc that lived in a nearby estuary. The shells, which carry traces of red ochre and show signs of wear, may be the world's oldest known beads.

The Blombos Cave finds have raised new questions about the timing of the emergence of modern human behaviour and its relationship to the evolution of the body and brain.

Left The early artist decorated pieces of ochre with an array of carved lines. Many experts regard these markings as being early evidence of the human ability to think symbolically.

Saharan rock art

The Sahara Desert is extremely rich in ancient rock paintings and petroglyphs (rock carvings). This rock art is testimony to a time when the environment of the region was wetter and the landscape was home to hunting and herding peoples.

There are tens of thousands of rock-art sites in the moutainous areas, with Algeria's Tassili N'Ajjer range being particularly rich in paintings and Libya's Messak range in engravings.

Subjects and dating

These paintings and petroglyphs are among the most spectacular in the world; however, they are difficult to date. Paintings seldom contain sufficient amounts of carbon for radiocarbon dating, and the technique cannot be applied to petroglyphs. Accordingly, the dating of Saharan rock art has depended largely on subject matter and style, which are correlated with environmental and economic changes.

Above The sandstone outcrops of the Tassili N'Ajjer range present a barren scene today, but once this was savannah landscape, populated with an abundance of animals.

The subjects chosen by the ancient rock artists are diverse, although – as in other African rock-painting traditions – human figures and animals predominate. A few specialists believe that some of the images date to the end of the last Ice Age, more than 10,000 years ago. Most, however, attribute the earliest figures to the Bubalus period, from the late 6th to the mid-4th millennium BC. Subjects from this period include animals that are now extinct, such as the buffalo *Bubalus antiquus*. The Cattle period follows, a period lasting to the mid-2nd millennium BC, and linked to the introduction of pastoralism (herding). The images feature not only cattle but also various wild animals. The next phase has been dubbed the Horse period, and in later phases camels are also depicted, as are chariots and charioteers. It is hoped that this general chronological scheme will eventually be refined by direct dating.

Interpretations

As with rock art elsewhere, interpreting these images has been difficult. A variety of strange and fanciful ideas have been applied to Saharan rock art, from the existence of 'Martians' in the Tassili to recent notions about 'shamans', 'trance' and hallucinogenic mushrooms. It is far more sensible and plausible, however, to relate the images to mythologies and rituals, such as rites of passage.

Above A rock painting from the 2nd millennium BC, featuring people and cattle.

Giza

The three pyramids at Giza represent the pinnacle of tomb architecture. King Khufu's Great Pyramid is the oldest and last-surviving Wonder of the Ancient World. For more than 4000 years it was the tallest monument ever built. To this day it is still the largest stone monument in the world.

The Giza cemetery lies on a plateau by the Old Kingdom capital, Memphis. First used in Early Dynastic times, it became a royal necropolis when the 4th Dynasty King Khufu (Cheops), who reigned from 2551 to 2528 BC, chose the site for his pyramid complex.

The Great Pyramid

Khufu's Great pyramid has sides that vary by less than 5cm (2in) and the base is almost completely level. The pyramid was once cased in Tura limestone, but it was removed in the Middle Ages and reused in the building of Cairo.

The 12th-century writer Abou Abdallah Mohammed Ben Abdurakim Alkaisi claimed that the first modern pyramidologist, Caliph El Ma'mun, forced his way into the pyramid with a battering ram and discovered Khufu's mummy. However, the pyramid had been looted centuries ago, so this is unlikely. The first significant investigation was led by the astronomer John Greaves, who published his results in 1646. In 1763 Nathaniel Davison explored the well that dropped from the Grand Gallery, and in 1817 Captain Giovanni Battista Caviglia connected the well to the descending passageway.

The chambers

Three chambers inside the pyramid are linked by passageways. From the entrance on the north face a steep passageway drops to enter the Subterranean Chamber, an unfinished underground room of ritual significance. The ascending passageway leads to the Grand Gallery, a corridor with walls made from seven layers of limestone blocks. The west wall of the Gallery includes the entrance to the horizontal passageway leading to the Queen's Chamber. This chamber had a ritual purpose but was not used for a queen's burial. The Grand Gallery leads upwards to an

Below The three pyramids dominate the skyline to the west of Cairo. The original casing stones are still visible at the top of Khaefre's pyramid (centre).

antechamber, then to the red granite burial chamber, known as the King's Chamber. 'Air-shafts' (long, narrow passageways), which are orientated towards the northern pole star and the constellation of Orion, lead from the King's and the Queen's Chambers.

Boat pits

Khufu's pyramid was surrounded by a narrow courtyard defined by a limestone wall. The only access to this area was via a walled causeway, which linked the pyramid mortuary temple to the valley temple – now lost under the modern suburb of Nazlet el-Simman. Five boat-shaped pits were excavated close to the causeway and mortuary temple, but these were empty when opened. Two narrow, rectangular pits dug parallel to the south side of the pyramid outside the enclosure wall, discovered in 1954, held dismantled wooden boats. One boat remains sealed in its tomb, but the other boat has been conserved and fully reassembled, and it is displayed in a museum near the pyramid.

Queens' pyramids

A small satellite pyramid lay outside the enclosure wall to the south-east of Khufu's pyramid. Three larger queens' pyramids, with mortuary chapels, lay to the east of this satellite pyramid. All three were robbed in antiquity, but a shaft discovered to the east of the Great Pyramid in 1925 has yielded the burial equipment and jewellery of Queen Hetepheres, mother of Khufu. Although the shaft held Hetepheres's canopic jars and sarcophagus, there was no sign of the queen's body.

Khaefre's pyramid

Khufu's son, Khaefre (reigned 2520-2494 BC), built his mortuary complex to the south of the Great Pyramid. His pyramid is smaller than Khufu's but is built on higher ground, and this, together with its steeper angle, makes it appear the larger of the two. Khaefre's pyramid had a subterranean burial chamber that was built, lined and roofed in a large, open trench before the pyramid was erected on top. The entrance, about 11m (35ft) up the northern face, was well hidden. In 1818 Giovanni Battista Belzoni realized that the entrance was not in the centre of the northern face. When he

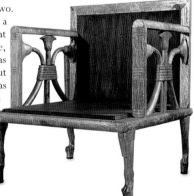

Right An armchair, adorned with gold, was included in the grave goods provided for Queen Hetepheres.

Left The Great Sphinx faces due east, the direction of the rising sun. The statue is crumbling today because of the wind, humidity and the smog from Cairo.

Beyond this a horizontal passage, guarded by three granite portcullises, leads to a rectangular antechamber that may have once been intended to serve as a burial chamber. A descending corridor drops from the anteroom floor to the burial chamber and a ritual 'cellar'. From the northern wall of the antechamber, directly above the entrance from the horizontal passage, a corridor led up through the bulk of the pyramid before petering out, unfinished, in a rough upper chamber.

Human remains

The burial chamber yielded a basalt sarcophagus carved with elaborate panelling. In 1838 it was dispatched to the British Museum in London, but it was lost when the ship carrying it foundered off the Spanish coast.

The sarcophagus had been empty when rediscovered, but the chamber at the end of the blind upper passage yielded a wooden coffin with some human remains: a pair of legs, a lower

reached the burial chamber he found a graffito scrawled by 'The Master Mohammed Ahmed, stonemason'.

Today, Khaefre's complex (pyramid, mortuary temple, causeway and valley temple) is the most complete of the Giza three and is the only one to retain some of its Tura limestone casing.

The Great Sphinx

Looking towards the rising sun, the Great Sphinx crouches beside Khaefre's Valley Temple. It is an awesome 72m (236ft) long and 20m (65ft) tall and is Egypt's largest statue. Its human head, which is perhaps Khaefre's own, is about 22 times life-size, with eyes 6ft (2m) high. Today, the Sphinx is clean-shaven, but it would have sported a long, plaited, curved beard of the type worn by gods and deified kings. As the Great Sphinx is carved from a natural rocky outcrop covered in places with a stone block veneer, the statue has sustained differential weathering due to the three limestone strata in its body.

Menkaure's pyramid

Khaefre was succeeded by his son Menkaure (reigned 2490-2472 BC), who also chose to build at Giza. His pyramid was aligned with those of Khufu and Khaefre but, as space was now somewhat limited, it was built on a smaller scale. To compensate, the bottom layers of the pyramid were cased in expensive red granite. The pyramid casing was removed by Mohammed Ali Pahsa (1805-48); the first European to enter the pyramid was Colonel Howard Vyse (1837).

From the pyramid entrance on the north face, a passageway drops down through the masonry and into the bedrock before opening into a chamber.

Below A papyrus dating from about 1000 BC shows workers dragging a shrine towards a tomb. The workmen who built the pyramids at Giza would have used a similar dragging technique to move large blocks of stone.

ANCIENT EGYPT TIMELINE

Periods/dynasties	Dates
Late Predynastic Period	3100-2950 BC
Early Dynastic Period (1st-3rd Dynasties)	2950-2575 BC
Old Kingdom (4th-8th Dynasties)	2575-2150 BC
1st Intermediate Period (9th-11th Dynasties)	2125-1975 BC
Middle Kingdom (11th-14th Dynasties)	1975-1640 BC
2nd Intermediate Period (15th-17th Dynasties)	1630-1520 BC
New Kingdom (18th-20th Dynasties)	1539-1075 BC
3rd Intermediate Period (21st-25th Dynasties)	1075-715 BC
Late Period (26th-30th Dynasties, 2nd Persian Period)	715-332 BC
Greco-Roman Period (Macedonians, Ptolemies and Romans)	332 BC-AD 395

Above A statue of Menkaure with the goddess Hathor on his right and a goddess representing the seventh nome (administrative district) of Upper Egypt on his left.

torso, and some ribs and vertebrae wrapped in cloth. These remains have been dated by radiocarbon analysis to the Roman Period. The wooden coffin, which is inscribed for 'Osiris, the King of Upper and Lower Egypt, Menkaure, living forever' has been dated, based on stylistic grounds, to the 26th Dynasty Saite Period. The coffin is more than half a millennium older than its bones, and neither is dated to the time of Menkaure.

Khentkawes's tomb

The late 4th/early 5th Dynasty Queen Khentkawes I built her tomb to the south of Khaefre's pyramid and connected it by a causeway to Menkaure's valley temple. This imposing structure, complete with its associated 'pyramid village', was initially misclassified as a pyramid. Further investigation has revealed it to be a mastaba-style superstructure perched on top of a natural rock base, cased in fine Tura limestone.

Inside Khentkawes's tomb a granite-lined chamber allows access to a descending passage leading to the antechamber, burial chamber and a series of storerooms. Here were recovered the fragments of a smashed alabaster sarcophagus but no other signs of burial. A granite doorway names Queen Khentkawes, lists her titles and then adds a cryptic phrase which can, with equal validity, be translated either as 'King of Upper and Lower Egypt and Mother of the King of Upper and Lower Egypt' or as 'Mother of the Two Kings of Upper and Lower Egypt'. It is clear that Queen Khentkawes was an important woman, who was rewarded with a regal-style burial close to Egypt's most prominent funerary monuments.

Saqqara

The extensive necropolis at Saqqara, situated near the cult centre of the sun god Re of Heliopolis, was built in the western desert of northern Egypt near Memphis, capital of the Old Kingdom. Sculptural reliefs in the underground chambers provide a rich source of information on life in the Old Kingdom.

During the 1st and 2nd Dynasties, Egypt's elite built their mastaba tombs at Saqqara. Named after the Arabic word *mastaba*, meaning 'low bench', these were low, flat, mud-brick super-structures covering burial chambers that were cut deeper and deeper until they passed through the desert sand into the bedrock. Although occasionally packed solid with sand and gravel, the super-structures were usually filled with storerooms for the grave goods needed in the afterlife.

By the end of the 1st Dynasty the number of rooms had been reduced in favour of more subterranean storage galleries. Eventually, the mastaba became a solid mound with two false doors at each end of the eastern wall. Around the largest mastabas were single rows of smaller, brick-lined tombs. These tombs were built for the artisans who worked for the deceased.

The Step Pyramid

Djoser, who was first king of the 3rd Dynasty, raised his mortuary complex on the high ground of the Saqqara

Above This is a statue of Imhotep, the legendary architect of Djoser's pyramid. Imhotep was also revered as the founder of Egyptian medicine.

Right Djoser's six-step pyramid was the prototype of the more sophisticated pyramids built by his successors of the 4th Dynasty.

358

cemetery. This was Egypt's first stone building. Working in limestone, the royal architect Imhotep designed an unusual square, solid mastaba-like structure with corners orientated to the points of the compass and a burial shaft cut beneath. This structure was subsequently extended on all four sides and upwards until, after several stages, it evolved into an impressive six-step pyramid. Today this pyramid is 60m (197ft) high and has a ground plan of 121m x 109m (397ft x 358ft).

The Step Pyramid's interior was explored by Napoleon's soldiers, von Minutoli and Segato (1821), John Shae Perring and Colonel Vyse (1837), and Richard Lepsius (1842). It was not until 1924, when Pierre Lacau and Cecil M. Firth started to excavate around, rather than beneath, the Step Pyramid that the true complexity of the site was realized.

The substructure was accessed by a shaft descending from the courtyard of the mortuary temple that ran along the lower step of the northern pyramid wall. The burial chamber lay at the base of a wide shaft that dropped from the centre of the original mastaba. The compact granite-lined burial chamber could be entered only via a 1m- (3ft-) wide hole in the ceiling; after the funeral, this hole was sealed with a stone plug.

The burial chamber lay at the centre of a maze of corridors and rooms. In the 'king's apartment' over 36,000 blue-green tiles were stuck onto sculpted limestone to replicate the ridged reed walls of Djoser's palace. Shafts for the burial of lesser members of the royal family were provided along the original mastaba, but they were abandoned when the building extension covered their entrances.

Around the pyramid was an enclosure defined by a limestone wall, measuring more than 1600m (5249ft) long and 10.5m (34ft) high. The wall was equipped with 14 false doors, plus one true entrance. The best-known and most fully restored buildings in the complex are in the southern and eastern sections of

the enclosure, and in the area around the pyramid. Here were built a series of inaccessible symbolic buildings — replicas of Egypt's most important shrines whose carved stone doors could never be opened.

The Apis burials

A further 14 royal pyramids from the Old and Middle Kingdom were raised at Saqqara. From the New Kingdom until the Ptolemaic Period the mummified sacred Apis bulls were buried in the Saqqara Serapeum, or bull cemetery. Before the 19th Dynasty reign of Ramesses II, the carefully selected bulls were interred in individual tombs; subsequently, they were buried in enormous stone sarcophagi in underground galleries. The Serapeum became a place of pilgrimage for late dynastic Egyptians. It was rediscovered by Auguste Mariette in 1851.

Above The interior of the mastaba of Irukaptah – a court official, one of whose titles was Head of the Butchers of the Great House – houses figures of his family in the niches.

Below A limestone statue of an Apis bull from the 4th century BC was found in Saqqara's bull cemetery.

Abydos

As cult centre of the god of the underworld Osiris, Abydos became an important 'national' cemetery and place of pilgrimage, with a wealth of tombs and monuments. The vast necropolis is situated on the desert edge on the west bank of the Nile in Upper Egypt.

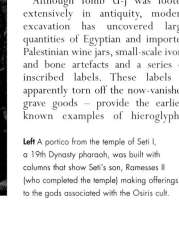

The Abydos graveyard was used for over 3000 years, from Prehistoric times until the Roman age. Initially, it had been used by all, irrespective of rank or wealth. By late Predynastic times, however, the part of the necropolis known today as the Umm el-Qa'ab had evolved into one of Egypt's most exclusive burial grounds, where Egypt's early kings built their tombs. As many generations of Egyptians continued to build tombs and occasional temples, Abydos developed into a rich multi-period archaeological site.

Abydos has been the site of virtually unbroken excavation from the first serious work conducted by Auguste Mariette (in 1859) onwards. Archaeologists from the German Archaeological Institute in Cairo, led by Gunther Dreyer, are currently involved in a thorough long-term reappraisal of the site and are discovering much that was missed by its early excavators.

Early writing

The most impressive of the late prehistoric tombs, which measures almost 67sq m (721sq ft) in area, is a 12-chambered structure known today as Tomb U-j. Traces of a wooden structure (possibly the remnants of a shrine) in the burial chamber, plus the discovery of an ivory crook-style sceptre, suggest that this is the tomb of a regional king.

Although Tomb U-j was looted extensively in antiquity, modern excavation has uncovered large quantities of Egyptian and imported Palestinian wine jars, small-scale ivory and bone artefacts and a series of inscribed labels. These labels — apparently torn off the now-vanished grave goods — provide the earliest known examples of hieroglyphic

Left A portico from the temple of Seti I, a 19th Dynasty pharaoh, was built with columns that show Seti's son, Ramesses II (who completed the temple) making offerings to the gods associated with the Osiris cult.

Left Plant motifs traditionally adorned the capitals of Egyptian columns. The column shafts were originally designed to look like a tree trunk or a bundle of plant stems.

Below An ivory statuette of an unknown king of the 1st Dynasty was found at Abydos. The king is wearing the crown of Upper Egypt.

writing. Some of these brief texts have been translated; they mention agricultural estates and the Delta settlements of Buto and Bubastis.

Tombs of the first kings

Umm el Qa'ab, or 'Mother of Pots', was so named because of the heaps of shattered ancient pottery found covering the ground. It was here that Egypt's first kings built their mud-brick mastabas (flat-topped, free-standing tombs).

Both Émile Amélineau (in 1897) and Flinders Petrie (in 1899) excavated here. They discovered that Cemetery B on the Umm el Qa'ab housed three double-chambered tombs dated to the Dynasty 0 kings Iri-Hor, Ka and Narmer, plus the tomb complex of the 1st Dynasty King Aha. The remaining kings of the 1st Dynasty built their tombs to the south of Cemetery B.

These tombs all shared a similar plan. The underground burial chamber was surrounded by storage chambers and covered by a low, brick-covered mound that was hidden beneath a larger mound. Above ground, two stelae (upright slabs or pillars) recorded the name of the deceased king.

Early excavators considered the Abydos tombs of the 1st and 2nd Dynasty kings to be disappointingly small. So small, in fact, that it was speculated that they were cenotaphs rather than actual burials. It is now realized that the tombs were merely one element in the kings' much larger funeral complex. Less than 2km (1¼ miles) to the north-east of their Umm el Qa'ab tombs, closer to the cultivated land, they built massive rectangular ritual enclosures defined by mud-brick walls. The precise purpose of these funerary enclosures is unknown.

The 1st Dynasty tomb complexes included long, narrow trenches subdivided into subsidiary graves. These were provided, not for the royal family, but for the king's personal retinue: his servants, minor courtiers, harem women and, occasionally, favourite animals, including dogs and lions. The deceased – partially mummified in a cloth coated in natron (a carbonate salt) – were buried in short wooden coffins with their own grave goods. Their names were engraved on small, crude limestone stelae. The funerary complex of King Djer included 318 of these subsidiary graves. Of the 97 surviving stelae, 76 bore women's names. As most of the subsidiary burials were disturbed in antiquity, it is impossible to determine how these women died. But it seems likely that they were human sacrifices – servants who were either murdered or persuaded to commit suicide at the time of the king's death. If this is the case, it was only a short-lived ritual. The 2nd Dynasty tomb complexes of Peribsen and Khasekhemwy lack any form of subsidiary burial.

Hidden in a hole in the wall of the tomb of Djer, Petrie found the earliest known example of mummification – a linen-covered arm dressed with four gold and bead bracelets. The arm was subsequently lost in Cairo Museum, but the bracelets survive to testify to the skill of the ancient craftsmen.

Later royal monuments

Khentamentiu, 'Foremost of the Westerners', was the original, local god of the necropolis. His temple was an important religious site during the earliest dynasties. By the late Old Kingdom, however, Khentamentiu had become identified with Osiris, and the Umm el Qa'ab had become

recognized as the burial place of Osiris, with the 1st Dynasty tomb of King Djer being transformed into the god's tomb.

Ideally, every pious Egyptian would have liked to be buried close to Osiris, but that was clearly impossible. Instead, Abydos became an established place of pilgrimage. Many ordinary Egyptians visited the necropolis to witness the 'mysteries of Osiris', which included a re-enactment of the god's violent death and subsequent rebirth. The pilgrims dedicated either statues or *mahat* (mud-brick shrines holding limestone stelae that could act as small-scale cenotaphs or dummy burials). Today, these stelae, which have survived in their hundreds, are our most important source of information for the funerary beliefs, occupations and family connections of non-royal Egyptians living during the Middle Kingdom. The statues were placed in the cult temple of Osiris, while the

mahat were set up overlooking the processional way linking the temple of Osiris to his 'tomb'.

Kings, too, established *mahat* at Abydos, although their monuments were on a far larger scale. The 12th Dynasty king Senwosret III built a cenotaph temple that may even have replaced his pyramid as his final resting place. The 18th Dynasty king Ahmose continued this tradition by building a cenotaph for his grandmother, the 17th Dynasty queen Tetisheri, and other New Kingdom monarchs followed suit.

The most impressive surviving *mahat* are the temples built by the kings of the early 19th Dynasty. Seti I built a small *mahat* for his father, Ramesses I, and an enormous one for himself. His son, Ramesses II,

Below The falcon-headed sky god, Horus, is depicted offering life to the dead pharaoh Ramesses II.

completed Seti's temple and built his own smaller version. Seti's Abydos temple has Egypt's best-preserved King List. Here the Ramesside scribes recorded an unbroken line of kings stretching from Menes, the legendary founder of the 1st Dynasty (who is probably to be equated with Narmer), down to Seti himself. The heart of the Seti temple incorporated seven sanctuaries dedicated to Osiris, Isis, Horus, Amen-Re, Re-Harakhty, Ptah and the deified Seti.

Immediately to the west of his temple, Seti excavated a dummy tomb. This was a curious subterranean structure whose central hall, roofed in granite, was accessed by a descending corridor. This structure is today known as the Osireion. Although the Osireion never housed the king's mummy, a room opening off the central hall was shaped and decorated like an enormous sarcophagus. A channel surrounding the hall acted as a moat for ground water, and perhaps allowed the hall to symbolize the mound that rose up from the sea of chaos at the moment of creation.

Karnak

The toponym Karnak is a modern one, referring to the site of a series of temples built in the northern part of the southern Egyptian city of Thebes. The Egyptians called this site Ipet-Swt, 'most select of places', since it was the home of Amen-Re, the great imperial god of New Kingdom Egypt.

The Amen-Re temple is the heart of the Karnak site. Its impressive remains were never lost (early explorers mistakenly believed that Karnak was a great royal palace), and they have been the subject of almost ongoing exploration and excavation from the early days of Egyptology, which has involved the work of many people.

Colossal monuments

There was almost continuous building works at Karnak from the early Middle Kingdom up to Roman times – a period of almost 2000 years – as successive kings expanded and re-modelled the temple complex. Karnak grew into an extensive, multi-period site of bewildering size and complexity, representing the achievements of many ancient builders.

Above A relief from the White Chapel of Senwosret I, showing the king paying homage to Min, the god of fertility.

Below This 19th-century view of the ruins at Karnak was painted by the Italian archaeologist Giovanni Battista Belzoni.

Much of what is now visible was erected during the three centuries covering the period from the early 18th Dynasty to the mid 19th Dynasty (*c.*1550–1250 BC). In order to demonstrate their piety to Amen-Re, the Theban kings enlarged and embellished the god's house with impressive colossal structures. Especially notable in this context are the monolithic granite obelisks erected in the early 18th Dynasty by Tuthmosis I, Hatshepsut and Tuthmosis III, the multiple pylon gateways built by Amenhotep III in the late 18th Dynasty, and the hypostyle hall decorated by Seti I and Ramesses II in the early 19th Dynasty. Most of the stone for this huge building programme came from the riverside sandstone quarries upriver at Gebel el-Silsila.

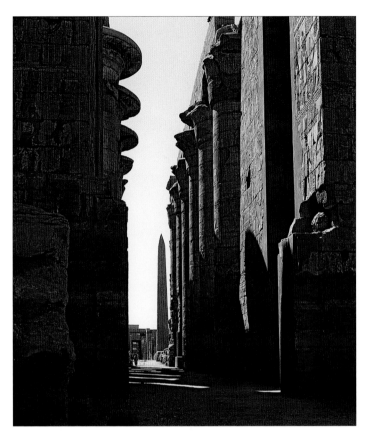

the Amen-Re temple via a series of courtyards and pylons. A branch of this southern axis also bypassed the Mut enclosure and ran along a sphinx-lined road southwards, to Amen-Re's 'Southern Harim' temple at Luxor.

Later building works

Later kings were unable to build on the same vast scale as their New Kingdom predecessors. Their interest in Karnak, however, prompted them to carry out minor works of repair and improvement in most parts of the temple structure, and they erected smaller temples for 'guest' deities within the Amen-Re enclosure. The last major building project at Karnak seems to have been the replacement of the central sanctuary of Amen-Re with one built by the Macedonian king Philip Arrhidaeus, who reigned from 323 to 316 BC.

Below A colossal statue of Ramesses II, with the diminutive figure of a princess, possibly one of his daughters, standing at his feet.

Above These two rows of columns once supported the roof of an immense hall in the temple of Amen-Re. There are 134 columns in all, arranged in 16 rows.

Demolition and reuse

In order to build, many kings demolished the monuments of their predecessors. The most striking evidence for this can be seen in the pylon gateway (pylon three) built by Amenhotep III. The rubble fill of his pylon included blocks of exquisitely carved, fine limestone taken from a dismantled chapel originally erected by the Middle Kingdom monarch Senwosret I. This chapel, the White Chapel, is the most significant remnant of the large, and now almost entirely lost, Middle Kingdom temple. Like other examples of dismantled but recovered buildings at

Karnak (most famously the quartzite Red Chapel built by Hatshepsut), the White Chapel now stands, rebuilt, in the open-air museum within the Amen-Re enclosure.

The main axis of the Amen-Re temple was aligned westwards, so that it formed part of a processional route linking Karnak with the royal mortuary temples situated on the Theban west bank.

It is from the reign of Amenhotep III that the intention to develop the Amen-Re temple as the nucleus of a series of related, satellite structures becomes most clear. To the south of the Amen-Re enclosure, Amenhotep III enlarged a temple enclosure for Mut, divine wife of Amen-Re. Mut's temple enclosure was joined to the Amen-Re enclosure by a second processional axis running south from

The Valley of the Kings

Egypt's New Kingdom monarchs (Dynasties 18-20) were southerners loyal to the god Amen of Thebes. Abandoning the northern pyramid cemeteries favoured by the kings of the Old and Middle Kingdoms, they were buried in the cliffs on the west bank of the Nile, opposite the Karnak temple of Amen.

The kings' funerary monuments were divided into two separate elements. A highly visible mortuary temple was built on the edge of the cultivated land. Here the cults of the dead kings could be maintained for all eternity. Meanwhile, their rock-cut tombs were hidden in a remote dry valley known today as the Valley of the Kings (Biban el-Moluk). The elite workmen employed to construct these tombs lived in the purpose-built village of Deir el-Medina.

The royal mummies

As the New Kingdom plunged into economic decline, thieves targeted the rich royal burials. Eventually, the High Priests of Amen emptied the tombs, stripping the kings of their grave goods and storing their mummified bodies in caches dotted about the necropolis. Two major royal caches have been discovered – one in a tomb in the Deir el-Bahari cliffs (DB320) and one in the Valley tomb of Amenhotep II (KV35).

The royal tombs

The classical historian Diodorus Siculus, writing in the 1st century BC, suggested that there might be as many

as 47 tombs in the Valley. However, it was not until 1707 that Claude Sicard recognized the true nature of the royal necropolis. The first significant work in the Valley was conducted by Belzoni who, in 1816, found the tomb of Tutankhamen's successor Ay (WV23). The following year he discovered the tombs of Mentuherkhepshef (KV19)

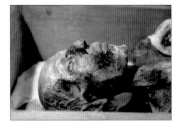

Left The mummy of Ramesses II, who died at the age of 92. His mummy was discovered at Deir el-Bahari in 1881.

Above The Valley of the Kings today. The monarchs' tombs were made by boring into the limestone walls of the valley's cliffs.

and Seti I (KV17). Commencing excavations in 1898, Victor Loret discovered the tomb of Tuthmosis III (KV34), the cache in the tomb of Amenhotep II, the tomb of Tuthmosis I (KV38), and 14 private tombs.

Theodore Davis, a wealthy, retired American lawyer, was determined to find an intact tomb. In 1902-3, working with Howard Carter, he discovered the tomb of Tuthmosis IV (KV 43). They then excavated KV20, the tomb of Tuthmosis I and his daughter Hatshepsut. On 5 February 1905 Davis, this time working with James Quibell, discovered the almost intact double burial of Yuya and Thuyu (KV46), who were the parents of Queen Tiy, wife of Amenhotep II. On 6 January 1907, working with Edward Ayrton, Davis found KV 55, a secondary Amarna burial. In 1908 Davis and Ayrton discovered KV57, the tomb of Horemheb who succeeded Ay.

During their excavations, Davis's team were able to uncover several components of Tutankhamen's burial: a faience cup (1905-6); a small pit holding the remains of the king's embalming materials (1907); a small chamber that yielded a model servant figure; and the gold foil from a chariot harness, which was inscribed with the names of Tutankhamen and Ay (1909).

On 1 November 1922 Howard Carter, financed by Lord Carnarvon, discovered the tomb of Tutankhamen himself (KV62). More recently, the 1989 rediscovery of KV5 by the Theban Mapping Project, led by American Egyptologist Kent Weeks, has led to the identification of an enormous tomb prepared for the burial of the sons of Ramesses II. Work on the tomb is still in progress; so far more than 100 chambers built on different levels have been revealed.

The Valley of the Queens

Also known as 'the Place of Beauty', the Valley of the Queens was the last resting place of many New Kingdom queens, princesses, princes and nobles. The cemetery was first recorded by Robert Hay in 1826, although official excavations did not start until 1903, when Ernesto Schiaparelli, Director of Turin Museum, set to work. Schiaparelli opened several tombs in the Valley, but his most important discovery was made in 1904, when he found the

empty, but beautifully decorated, tomb of Queen Nefertari, who was the consort of Ramesses II (QV66). The paintings on the tomb walls depict the queen's journey after death to the afterlife, guided by various guardian-spirits and deities, including Isis, Hathor and Osiris.

Left The gold mask ot Tutankhamen, one of the priceless treasures discovered in his tomb by Howard Carter and his team in 1922.

Below Part of the hall from the tomb of Seti I in the Valley of the Kings. The ceiling shows the stars and constellations of the northern sky.

Amarna

The city of Amarna (ancient Akhetaten) was a purpose-built capital in Middle Egypt designed by the 18th Dynasty pharaoh Akhenaten (c.1353-1335 BC) as a suitable home for his favoured god, the Aten. Excavation has revealed a wealth of secrets from the New Kingdom.

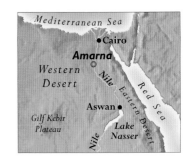

The city, situated on the east bank of the Nile, almost equidistant between the southern capital Thebes and the northern capital Memphis, was defined by a series of massive inscriptions carved into the limestone cliffs of the east and west banks.

Amarna was occupied for little more than 25 years before being abandoned during the reign of Tutankhamen. The site has been excavated by a series of archaeologists including Flinders Petrie, Ludwig Borchardt and John Pendlebury. The workmen's village is currently being investigated by the Egypt Exploration Society, led by Barry Kemp. Norman de Garis Davis recorded the tombs of the nobles, and Geoffrey Martin has recorded the royal tomb.

The city

Amarna may be divided into three disparate areas: the main city, the workmen's village, and the tombs. The city was laid out along the Royal Road, or Sikket es-Sultan, a long, fairly straight road that ran parallel to the river. The Royal Road linked the North Riverside Palace, the fortified private home of the royal family, to the southerly Maru-Aten cult centre.

The southern suburb, home of some of Amarna's most luxurious villas, was also the site of a large glass factory and the sculptors' studios. One of the sculptors who worked here was Thutmose, who created the painted limestone bust of Akhenaten's wife, Nefertiti. This masterpiece of Egyptian sculpture was discovered by Borchardt in 1912 and is now housed in the Berlin Museum.

Left This is the bust from a colossal statue of Akhenaten, one of a series from the Great Temple of the Aten.

Right A touching depiction of Akhenaten holding his daughter on his lap and kissing her, but the statue was never finished.

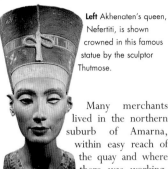

Left Akhenaten's queen, Nefertiti, is shown crowned in this famous statue by the sculptor Thutmose.

Many merchants lived in the northern suburb of Amarna, within easy reach of the quay and where there was working-class housing. The city centre housed the Great Palace, administrative buildings and two significant temples: the Great Temple to the Aten and the Lesser Temple. The King's House was opposite the Great Palace and linked to it by a mud-brick bridge that passed over the Royal Road. Surrounding the House were the offices and archives of the civil service. It was here, in 1887, that a local woman discovered the 'Amarna letters' – a series of clay tablets representing the remains of Akhenaten's diplomatic archive.

The workmen's village

A valley in the cliffs to the east of the main city was the location for the workmen's village. The houses were for the labourers employed to cut the elite tombs. In contrast to the city proper, the village was laid out with a strict regularity and enclosed by a wall with a single gate. Within the complex each workman was given a small unit, measuring 5m x 10m (16ft x 33ft), and 63 houses stood in six straight terraced rows facing onto narrow streets.

The tombs

The main cemetery – the one that was provided for the ordinary people of Amarna – lay to the north of the city; the investigation of this cemetery is currently in progress. A separate small cemetery was associated with the workmen's village.

The royal tomb, and a series of subsidiary royal graves, lay in a dry valley, or wadi. It was discovered by locals sometime during the early

Above Akhenaten and members of his family present offerings to the Aten. The relief comes from the Great Palace at Amarna.

1880s; when archaeologists entered the tomb, they found that it had been thoroughly looted. Two groups of rock-cut tombs were provided for Amarna's elite, with 18 tombs lying to the north and 27 tombs to the south of the royal wadi. Only 24 of the elite tombs were inscribed and none has yielded a mummy, suggesting that few of the tombs, if any, were ever occupied. The elite decorated their

tombs with images of the royal family going about their daily duties. The most elaborately decorated tomb was built for Ay, father of Queen Nefertiti. This tomb contains the lengthy poem known today as *The Great Hymn to the Aten*.

369

Abu Simbel

The twin temples at Abu Simbel, which were carved out of the mountainside and adorned with colossal statures, were built as a triumphant statement to the power of the 19th Dynasty pharaoh Ramesses II (c.1290–1224 BC) and his favourite queen, Nefertari.

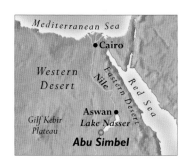

The Great Temple and the Small Temple, as the twin temples are known, project from a vertical rock face at Abu Simbel, on the west bank of the Nile, in Nubia, 64km (40 miles) north of the Second Nile Cataract. They were re-discovered by the explorer Johann Ludwig Burckhardt, and cleared of sand by Giovanni Battista Belzoni (1817).

The Great Temple

The façade of the Great Temple is adorned with two pairs of colossal seated statues of the king. Each statue is about 22m (72ft) tall. An earthquake during Year 30 of Ramesses' reign caused the statue to the north of the entrance to lose an arm (later restored) and the statue to the south to lose its upper body. Above the doorway stands the god Re-Herakhty. To his left is the goddess Maat and to his right

is the sign for 'User', so that the statue is a rebus reading 'User-Maat-Re', the throne name of Ramesses II.

The Great Temple extends 48m (157ft) into the cliff. The first pillared hall is decorated with scenes of Ramesses displaying his military triumphs. The second hall includes images of the divine Ramesses. Beyond the halls, four gods sit in a niche in the sanctuary: Ptah of Memphis, Amen-Re of Thebes, Re-Herakhty of Heliopolis and Ramesses of Per-Ramesse. Twice each year (on the 20th February and the 20th October), the rising sun would illuminate the four statues.

The Small Temple

A local form of the goddess Hathor, the sacred cow, was strongly identified with Ramesses' consort Nefertari, and

Left A statue of Ramesses depicted as the god Osiris, from the interior of his Great Temple.

Above The four colossal figures of Ramesses II flank the entrance to the Great Temple. The smaller figures between his legs are members of the royal family.

the Small Temple was dedicated to the goddess. The façade shows two colossal figures of Nefertari and four of Ramesses. The images on the internal walls include scenes of temple ritual and of Hathor and Taweret, protectors of women in labour.

Rescue mission

When, in 1954, the decision was taken to build the Aswan High Dam, the Abu Simbel temples had to be moved clear of the water. Between 1964 and 1968 the temples and statues were dismantled and reconstructed on higher ground at a site nearby.

Egypt's fortress

Located on Egypt's Mediterranean coast, 280km (174 miles) to the west of Alexandria, Zawiyet Umm el-Rakham is the largest and best-defended fortress to survive from Egypt's imperial age, the New Kingdom. It was designed to intimidate local Libyan tribes.

This large fortress-town was founded by the pharaoh Ramesses II in around 1280 BC in order to defend Egypt from the growing incursions of Libyan tribesmen, and to protect international trade routes in the eastern Mediterranean.

Fortified staging post

It was discovered by chance in 1948, and the site has been excavated since 1994 by a team from the University of Liverpool, led by Dr Steven Snape. A combination of seasonal rainfall and the large-scale use of mudbrick by Ramesses' architects has meant that little of the fortress has survived above ground level. However, the site has produced a series of important structures, together with artefacts, which are either unique or of outstanding quality.

The site was built with impressive fortifications, and among them there is a single, heavily defended gateway. Notable structures were also found within the fortress walls, which includes the 'Governor's Residence'. This multi-functional building served as both a production and an administrative centre, as well as being the private quarters of Neb-Re, who was 'Troop Commander, Overseer of Foreign Lands'.

Discoveries indicate that the huge garrison was sustained by a combination of self-sufficiency – a major bakery/brewery has been excavated, as have a series of wells – and exchange with local nomads, which can be attested by finds of animal bones and ostrich egg shells. The role of Zawiyet Umm el-Rakham as a defended staging post for international trade in the Late Bronze Age is confirmed by a range of ceramic vessels originating from many points on this trade circuit, including Canaan, Mycenae and Cyprus.

Above The remains of some of the mud brick enclosure walls at Zawiyet Umm el-Rakham still survive today. The walls were originally 5m (16ft) thick.

Abandonment

The fortress was abandoned, probably early in the reign of Ramesses II's successor, Merenptah, as a result of increased pressure on the part of the Libyans. Today, Zawiyet Umm el-Rakham has the 'frozen-in-time' character of sites that have been suddenly destroyed, such as the near-contemporary Ulu Burun shipwreck off southern Turkey. On-going investigations at Zawiyet Umm el-Rakham will no doubt reveal much more about life in the garrison.

Right In this statue of Neb-Re, he is holding a standard bearing the lion head of the goddess Sekhmet.

371

Meroe

Although the memory of Meroe was preserved in the Bible and by the classical authors who recorded a land ruled by a 'Queen Candice', the city remained lost until, in 1772, the explorer James Bruce came across ancient remains near the village of Begarawiya in the Nile Valley.

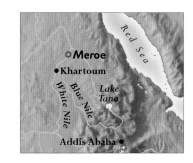

The second independent kingdom of Kush (Upper, or southern, Nubia) lasted for more than 1000 years. Although one political and cultural continuum, the period is divided into two phases on the basis of the royal burial ground.

In the Napatan empire (c.900-300 BC) burials were made south of the 4th Nile cataract at Gebel Barkal, Kurru and Nuri. During the Meroitic empire (c.300 BC-AD 300) burials were carried out further south, beyond the 5th cataract on the east bank of the Nile at Meroe, in present-day Sudan.

Taking advantage of a period of Egyptian weakness, the Kushite kings were able to rule Egypt as the 25th Dynasty. However, eventually Meroe fell to Ezana of Aksum, and the city was abandoned and forgotten.

The Royal City

In 1910 John Garstang excavated the 'Royal City', the walled royal residential quarter of Meroe. He discovered what had been a prosperous industrial city, whose temples were dedicated to a mixture of Egyptian and

non-Egyptian gods. Chief among the latter was the lion-headed hunter god Apedemak. The imposing Temple of Amen included a large outer court and a series of pillared halls. The Sun Temple featured a pylon gateway and a sanctuary that was walled and floored with blue-glazed tiles.

The cemetery

More than 40 kings and queens of Meroe were interred in rock-cut burial chambers beneath small, steep-sided pyramids. Accompanying the royal family into the afterlife were

Above These gold panels engraved with Egyptian hieroglyphs were part of a piece of Kushite jewellery.

Above The steep-sided pyramids that mark the tombs of the kings and queens of Meroe were built on a smaller scale than their Egyptian counterparts.

hundreds of sacrificed servants. In 1834 the Italian doctor turned archaeologist Guiseppe Ferlini partially dismantled the pyramid of Queen Amanishakheto to recover a collection of grave goods, including gold and beaded jewellery. The pyramid cemetery was subsequently formally excavated by George Reisner (1920-23).

The Zimbabwe tradition

The Later Iron Age sites of Mapungubwe and Great Zimbabwe represent the first two phases of the Zimbabwe Tradition in South Africa. These sites provide evidence for the emergence of complex societies that developed into large and powerful states almost 1000 years ago.

Sites in the Limpopo River Valley, South Africa, dating to the last centuries of the 1st millennium, were typical of the Late Iron Age economy, founded on cattle-keeping and agriculture. The Limpopo River linked these settlements to east coast commerce and its important trading hubs, such as Sofala.

Findings from excavations – such as ivory and glass beads, and later gold items – suggest that subcontinental and intercontinental trade became increasingly important to the economy of the Limpopo Valley.

Mapungubwe

The hill site of Mapungubwe, which was rediscovered in 1932, lies in the Northern Province of South Africa, close to the borders of Zimbabwe and Botswana. Mapungubwe provides evidence of a stratified society that had both elite and commoner classes. Many researchers consider it the centre of southern Africa's first 'state'. The elite occupied stone structures on the summit. The ordinary classes lived in homesteads at the hill's foot and on the surrounding plateau. Excavations of the hilltop burials of the elite have revealed prestige goods, including items of copper and gold. Most famous is a golden rhinoceros, a small wooden sculpture clad in thin sheets of gold foil.

Mapungubwe was established by the early 1200s and flourished in the 13th century. Yet it was abandoned by the mid-14th century. Its decline has been attributed to a colder climate and to the limited capacity of the local environment to sustain a population of several thousand people. Changes in the city's place within the trading networks of the time may have been a factor too. Precisely as Mapungubwe waned, Great Zimbabwe, in the southeast of contemporary Zimbabwe, was on the rise.

Great Zimbabwe

At its pinnacle, Great Zimbabwe had become the capital of a vast Shona empire. The word *Zimbabwe* is from the Shona term meaning 'stone houses', or 'venerated houses'. The stone structures at Great Zimbabwe are

Right The Great Enclosure is one of the most impressive of Great Zimbabwe's remains. With walls up to 12m (39ft) high and 6m (20ft) thick, the Great Enclosure is Africa's largest single ancient structure south of the Sahara.

The walling would have enclosed *daga* (mud and grass) huts and structures, and perhaps maintained separation between categories of person, distinguished by class, kinship and gender. Several types of walling, including a decorative style that incorporates a herringbone design, have been identified from different time periods.

Early investigations

Portuguese travellers were the first Europeans to visit the site in the 16th century. In the 1870s a German geologist named Karl Mauch revealed the ruins of Great Zimbabwe to the western world and in 1891 Theodore Bent carried out the first excavations.

These late-Victorian visitors speculated that it was the work of Phoenicians, Sabaeans and other incomers into the subcontinent, fuelling romantic myths about 'lost cities'. They denied that it could be the work of indigenous peoples, supporting contemporary prejudices about the inability of African peoples to produce great civilizations and justifying European colonization.

Archaeological work sponsored by the British Association for the Advancement of Science provided

Above Two rows of chevrons adorn the top of the Great Enclosure's outer wall, an example of the fine craftsmanship of the stonemasons.

reminiscent of those at Mapungubwe, but the site is larger, covering an area of about 50ha (124 acres). Like Mapungubwe, it comprises settlements on a hilltop as well as in the fertile valley below. It was the centre of a greater state, with scores of smaller *zimbabwes* linked to it. Occupation of Great Zimbabwe precedes and post-dates the distinctive stone walling, much of which dates to the city's heyday in the 14th and 15th centuries.

Rather than serving a defensive purpose, the dry-stone walls are thought to have delineated both functional and social spaces within the complex. The walls, creating a series of passages, were not built according to a preordained design, but were apparently added to as circumstances required – joining living areas, demarcating cattle enclosures and perhaps protecting areas of special social or symbolic importance.

another view. In the 1900s David Randall-McIver investigated both Great Zimbabwe and similar smaller settlements in the area. Although he failed to provide irrefutable archaeological evidence for his findings, he was convinced that the site dated to the earlier part of the 2nd millennium and was an indigenous African settlement. He was succeeded in the late 1920s by Gertrude Caton-Thompson, whose own excavations provided firm evidence to support Randall-McIver's findings.

Caton-Thompson's work provided crucial links between structures and finds in the deposits and located in situ materials. Aided by further analysis of datable imported goods, such as Chinese ceramics, she was able to revise earlier chronologies. Caton-Thompson argued that far from being the work of Phoenicians, 'Every detail in the haphazard building, every detail in the plan, every detail in the contents, apart from the imports' indicated that Great Zimbabwe was an African achievement. However, myths about the 'mystery' of Great Zimbabwe persist to this day.

From the Eastern Enclosure, which is associated with the hill settlement – and hence the city's elite – came the discovery of six of eight carved soapstone birds that stood atop carved pillars. Their symbolic significance is unknown, but they may have symbolized chiefly strength and authority, and/or the power of the ancestors. Today, the Zimbabwe bird is the emblem of the contemporary Zimbabwean nation.

Decline and fall

Like Mapungubwe, Great Zimbabwe was a trading centre with a population of skilled farmers and craftsmen, but on a far larger scale than its more southerly predecessor. At its zenith, Great Zimbabwe's population has been estimated at 10,000, or perhaps even twice that – at least double the size of Mapungubwe. Yet by the middle of the 15th century Great Zimbabwe had declined, as had Mapungubwe before

it. Again, environmental factors have been invoked as an explanation. Did the population density exhaust local resources, such as the wood needed for the kilns? Were pastures over-grazed and degraded? Had the goldmines been exhausted? Alternatively, was there some upset in the trading network in which the success of Great Zimbabwe was embedded? Excavations at other sites indicate that the centre of trading moved north and, over the next two centuries, to sites in the south-west.

In contemporary Zimbabwean archaeology, researchers lament the fact that romantic myths about Great Zimbabwe still circulate. Current archaeological interest focuses more pointedly on understanding the cultural and social lives of the Great Zimbabweans, rather than on neutral description or on the establishment of dates and sequences. The scientific studies of many archaeologists, from Caton-Thompson to the more recent work of Peter Garlake and Tom Huffman, among others, have laid the foundations for new questions to be addressed by a new generation of researchers.

Below This conical tower may represent a grain bin, symbolizing the king's key function of ensuring a reliable supply of grain.

Ife and Benin

The cities of Ife and Benin, in the south-west of present-day Nigeria,
are known for their extraordinary sculptures, principally in terracotta
and metal. Both cities flourished before the arrival of the first Europeans
in the late 15th century.

Archaeology in Nigeria is a recent development and has focused on artefacts of artwork. The most significant findings are from early 2nd millennium sites at Ife and Benin.

Ife

The city-state of Ife is of great importance in the traditions and origin myths of the Yoruba people. Ife

no doubt owed a great deal to its trade networks, with the domestic economy probably based on yam cultivation. The people of Ife were producing their artworks by the 12th century, though the site had been inhabited for some centuries previously.

The Ife artworks are known for their naturalism, exemplified by magnificent sculpted heads and human figures, but they also include more stylized works. Some sculptures were associated with Ife royalty, but others may have been placed in domestic shrines.

Benin

The kingdom of Benin dates to the late 12th century. Although associated with the Edo peoples, rather than the Yoruba, the first oba (king) was said to be descended from the founder of Ife. Metal-working, as well as sculpting in ivory, was carried out for the oba and his court. The art of Benin changed over time. Portuguese influence was felt in the late 15th century, and it was at about this time that Benin metal-working reached its greatest heights. Late pieces included new themes, such as Portuguese soldiers. 'Benin bronzes', as they are known – although they are brass – were made using the lost-wax technique, where the sculptor makes a wax model, which is encased in clay. When heated the wax melts, leaving a mould that can be filled with molten metal. When cool, the clay mould is smashed, revealing the metal sculpture.

As well as finely made metal heads of the oba and queen mothers, Benin is also known for the hundreds of brass plaques portraying courtly life, which once adorned the columns of the oba's palace. In 1897 the British sacked Benin, removing thousands of works, exiling the oba and effectively bringing the art tradition to an end.

Left This superb bronze head depicts one of the kings of Benin.

Lalibela

Situated near Lake Tana in Ethiopia, Lalibela is famous for its churches, hewn from the pink-coloured volcanic rock of the Lasta mountains. The site is principally associated with the Zagwe dynasty and named after one of its rulers, who reigned in the late 11th to the early 12th century.

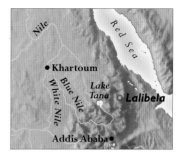

Recent work at the site by the eminent British archaeologist David Phillipson has provided a new perspective on the history of Lalibela. The site is thought to have come into being in the 7th or 8th century, at a time when the power of Axum to the north was in decline and the political environment was unstable. Some structures dating to this phase, namely the churches of the Ethiopian saint Merkurios and of the archangel Gabriel, may have been part of a fortress and palace complex.

A second developmental phase probably dates to the 10th or 11th century. The buildings – or, more properly, sculptures – of this time are unquestionably inspired by Christianity. These later churches self-consciously utilized features that refer to the architecture, and by implication, the legendary power that

Axum had enjoyed. Churches dating to around the late 12th century and early 13th century are attributed to King Lalibela. As with other African sites there has been unwarranted speculation that Lalibela's churches were not built by indigenous peoples, but were the work of foreigners, such as the Knights Templar.

Lalibela's vision

According to legend, Lalibela was poisoned by his brother and fell unconscious for three days. During that time he travelled to heaven, where he saw churches cut from the rock. Another explanation is that he travelled to Jerusalem and was

Left The Bet Giyorgis church, built in a deep pit with perpendicular walls, can be reached only by a tunnel.

Left One of the 12 apostles was carved into the rock in the church of Golgota-Mikail.

inspired to recreate it. Whether or not Lalibela aimed to create a 'New Jerusalem', the references to the Holy City are abundant. A stream running through the site was named after the River Jordan and Lalibela himself is said to be buried beneath the church of Golgota-Mikail, named after Golgotha (the hill of Calvary where Jesus was crucified).

The structures

Some of the churches are free-standing, detached from the rock on all sides. Others remain attached to the mountain from which they have been carved, and yet others extend underground. The rock churches and their courtyards are joined by a labyrinth of tunnels and passages, with catacombs and hermit caverns. Externally, churches such as that of Bet Medhane Alem – the largest monolithic church at Lalibela – are surrounded by trenches that separate them from the natural landscape.

Two of the churches contain remarkable artworks. Inside Bet Golgota are life-size, bas-relief sculptures of human figures, probably saints. In the same church is a painting of St George, Ethiopia's national saint, slaying the dragon. The rock church of Bet Giyorgis, constructed with a cross-shaped floor plan, is set apart from the others. It was allegedly constructed for St George himself after he complained to Lalibela that no church had been built for him.

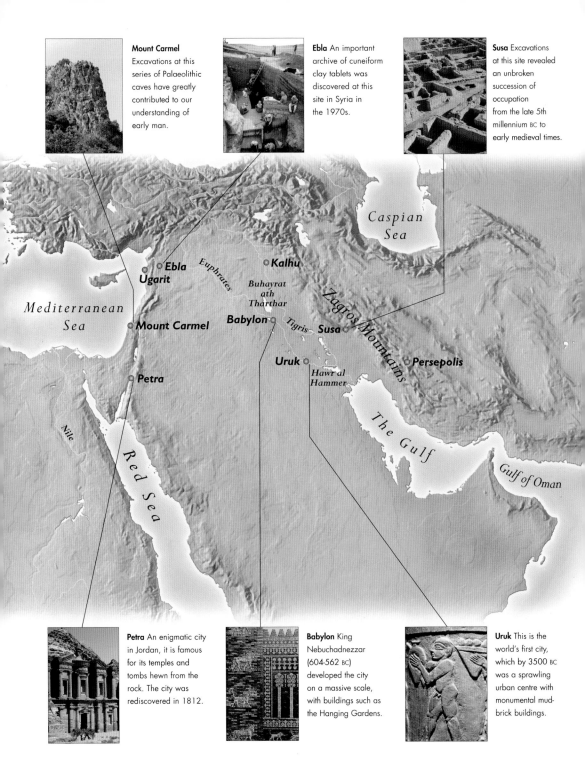

Mount Carmel Excavations at this series of Palaeolithic caves have greatly contributed to our understanding of early man.

Ebla An important archive of cuneiform clay tablets was discovered at this site in Syria in the 1970s.

Susa Excavations at this site revealed an unbroken succession of occupation from the late 5th millennium BC to early medieval times.

Caspian
Sea

Ebla
Ugarit
Euphrates
Kalhu
Buhayrat
ath
Tharthar
Zagros Mountains

Mediterranean
Sea

Mount Carmel
Babylon
Tigris
Susa

Uruk
Hawr al
Hammer
Persepolis

Petra

Nile

Red Sea

The Gulf

Gulf of Oman

Petra An enigmatic city in Jordan, it is famous for its temples and tombs hewn from the rock. The city was rediscovered in 1812.

Babylon King Nebuchadnezzar (604-562 BC) developed the city on a massive scale, with buildings such as the Hanging Gardens.

Uruk This is the world's first city, which by 3500 BC was a sprawling urban centre with monumental mud-brick buildings.

THE GREAT SITES
OF THE
MIDDLE EAST

Asia's contribution to world archaeology was initially centred on the Middle East, where work concentrated on exploring the Bible lands for links with the great religions, as well as on understanding the rise of civilization, cities and writing. The pioneering work of archaeologists Layard and Botta in the Assyrian cities revealed a previously unknown culture to the world, with its impressive reliefs and huge winged bull figures. Names such as Ur, Nineveh, Babylon and Sumer lived once again as archaeologists uncovered layers of major settlements. The reconstruction of Babylon's Ishtar Gate in Berlin is testimony to the splendour of these early cultures. Sadly, conflicts in this war-torn region have caused a great deal of destruction. Its museums have been pillaged and many sites have been ransacked.

Ugarit A cosmopolitan Late Bronze Age port in Syria, it occupies a strategic position in the eastern Mediterranean.

Kalhu Excavations at this ancient Assyrian capital in modern-day Iraq have produced a wealth of spectacular finds.

Persepolis Extensive bas-reliefs testify to the importance of this city built by Persian kings during the 6th and 5th centuries BC.

Mount Carmel

Caves and rock shelters along this low limestone range in northern Israel provided habitation sites for early humans. The local fauna and the resources of the coastal plain and sea enabled intermittent occupation over a period of some 800,000 years or more.

Mount Carmel extends south-east for some 32km (20 miles) from the port of Haifa at its northern end. The Palaeolithic cave sites of Tabun, el-Wad, Skhul and Kebara have long since attracted archaeological excavation and are important areas for prehistoric excavation and research.

Excavation

The site's archaeological importance was first recognized in 1928 by Charles Lambert's discovery of the first prehistoric art object to be found in the Levant – a bone animal carving from el-Wad cave from what is known as the Natufian culture (around 10,000-12,500 years ago).

Subsequent excavation in this and other cave sites in the Wadi (1929-34), under the direction of Dorothy Garrod, revealed the Carmel's unique value. Garrod established that the strata in el-Wad and Tabun Caves combine to form a cultural sequence spanning the length of human occupation and activity in the Levant, from the Lower Palaeolithic Acheulian (hundreds of thousands of years ago) to the Natufian.

The discovery of skeletal remains of Neanderthal and Anatomically Modern Humans, in Tabun and Skhul caves respectively, provided the first direct evidence for the intermittent presence of both these Mousterian (Middle Palaeolithic, *c.*180,000-30,000 years ago) populations in the Near East.

Kebara Cave in southern Mount Carmel was first excavated by Stekelis (in 1927) and briefly by Garrod and McCown (in 1928). Then the Natufian, Kebaran and Aurignacian levels were excavated by Turville-Petre in 1931. With absolute dating of the site available, the Israeli archaeologist Bar-Yosef and others (excavating from 1982-89) shed further light on the Levantine Mousterian with the discovery of a Neanderthal burial. This was an adult male who lived around 62,000 years ago and whose intact hyoid (at the base of the tongue) and throat bones implied this species' capacity for speech.

Excavation at the Mount Carmel sites continues, mainly under the auspices of the University of Haifa.

Below Exposed limestone can be seen in this view of Mount Carmel. Cave sites such as Tabun, el-Wad and Skhul have occupation deposits inside the cavern and at the top of the talus slope that formed at the cave's entrance.

Uruk

Located on a branch of the Euphrates River in southern Mesopotamia (Iraq), Uruk was continuously inhabited for nearly 5000 years, until the early centuries AD. The remains at Uruk provide evidence for the emergence of the world's first cities.

The first excavations at Uruk in the mid-19th century produced scattered results, but a prolonged German project – begun in 1912 and continued through much of the 20th century – revealed the city's development and history. The investigations uncovered many important 'late' monuments, including the palace of a local king of the early 2nd millennium BC, an unusually decorated temple from the later 2nd millennium BC and a New Year's Festival temple built in the 6th century BC.

Excavations also yielded archives of cuneiform tablets – a writing system of wedge-shaped characters pressed into clay slabs – that belong to these periods. These monuments, texts and other finds are important, in some cases providing unparalleled glimpses into these late periods.

The world's first city

In Mesopotamian legends, the city of Uruk (Warka in Akkadian, Erech in the Bible) was associated with the development of urban life and civilization. Archaeology tells the same story. Uruk initially was a scatter of villages established in the 6th millennium BC, which began to coalesce around 4000 BC. Already by 3500 BC Uruk covered 250ha (618 acres) and by 2800 BC the urban sprawl covered 550ha (1360 acres) enclosed by a city wall, which Mesopotamian stories attributed to the semi-legendary King Gilgamesh.

Excavation in two temple precincts, the Eanna ('the House of Heaven'), associated with the goddess Inanna (Ishtar), and the ziggurat of the god Anu, provided a detailed view of the pivotal period of urbanization (the Uruk period, *c.*3800-3100 BC).

Left A detail of the Uruk Vase (*c.*3300 BC) shows a file of naked men presenting offerings to the goddess Inanna. The alabaster vase was stolen from the Baghdad Museum in April 2003, but it was returned two months later.

Above An overview of the massive ziggurat in the Eanna precinct.

During this relatively brief span, the residents of Uruk created the monumental religious architecture characteristic of Mesopotamia, including the ziggurat (superimposed terraces supporting a temple). Administrators developed a system of writing, which was initially for recording economic transactions, and used cylinder seals to authenticate their documents. Artisans produced sophisticated works of art in stone, terracotta and other media; the 'Uruk Vase' and the 'Warka Lady' are justly famous, while many cylinder seals are masterpieces in miniature.

Craftsmen developed techniques of mass-production to satisfy the now large market; one form of pottery – the 'bevelled rim bowl' – appears in great quantity and may have been used for doling out rations to workmen.

Ugarit

From around 1550-1200 BC Ugarit was the capital of a Late Bronze Age kingdom in north-west Syria. Ugarit was deeply involved in the international politics and commerce of the time. An early alphabet was used for texts in the local language.

Known today as Ras Shamra, Ugarit lies a short distance from the Mediterranean coast of Syria. This strategic location gave Ugarit access both to the eastern Mediterranean sea lanes and to overland caravan routes.

The long-term archaeological project, begun in 1929 by Claude Schaeffer, shows that Ugarit was first settled in early Neolithic times (before 6000 BC) and grew to become a walled town by the middle of the 3rd millennium BC. Ugarit's foreign

Below The palace quarter, now just ruins, had numerous courtyards, pillared halls and a columned entrance gate.

connections, especially with Egypt, were already evident during the 3rd millennium BC and continued through the 2nd millennium BC.

Two main sources of evidence are available to reconstruct everyday life in Ugarit: the archaeological remains and thousands of cuneiform tablets.

A prestigious centre

The earlier settlements are important in their own right, but the Late Bronze Age town is much better known. This town covered over 22ha (54 acres) and had up to 8000 residents. The acropolis – the mound formed by earlier occupations – held

the tower-like temples of Baal and Dagan. The royal palace at Ugarit was laid out around five interior courtyards surrounded by suites of rooms with varied public or private functions; the dead kings were buried in underground chambers beneath the palace. The residential quarters were arranged in irregular blocks laced with lanes, each block encompassing households of different size, apparent wealth and occupation.

Cuneiform tablets from the palace and some private houses reveal Ugarit's political and diplomatic history, social organization, economic structure and foreign trade, as well as other aspects of daily life. Other texts relate myths, religious poetry and cultic rituals that strongly echo practices reported in the Bible. While most texts are written in Akkadian, the lingua franca of the day, many were written in a cuneiform version of the Canaanite alphabets of the Late Bronze Age Levant.

The texts make clear Ugarit's cosmopolitan nature, as does its material culture. Egypt's influence on local art was pervasive, and numerous Egyptian objects also appeared in Ugarit. Imported pottery and artefacts show connections in other directions, including Cyprus, Minoan Crete and Mycenaean Greece.

The Late Bronze Age world of the eastern Mediterranean came to an abrupt end around 1200 BC, with the cataclysmic upheavals associated with the movements of the 'Sea Peoples'. Invaders sacked the town and the site was not reoccupied.

Susa

From around 4200 BC this ancient city in Iran was a major point of interaction between the Mesopotamian world and the resource-rich uplands to the east. The site provides important evidence for the emergence of civilization in the region.

Susa is an enormous mound, sprawling across an area of 550ha (1359 acres) and rising over 35m (115ft) above the surrounding plain, on the Shaur River in Khuzistan in south-west Iran. This location, in the blurred cultural boundary between Mesopotamia and the mountains of western Iran, gave Susa enduring strategic importance. The city in fact looked mainly to Mesopotamia during some periods and to the Iranian highlands during others, but it always maintained ties with both.

Exploration of Susa began in 1884, with the discovery of an Achaemenid Persian *apadana* ('pillared hall'). Excavation resumed in 1897 when a permanent French mission, headed initially by Jacques de Morgan, began its investigation; the French mission continued at Susa, with interruptions for world wars, until 1979.

Above There are mud-brick remains of the Elamite settlement at Susa.

Gateway city

The excavations reveal an unbroken succession of occupation for some five and a half millennia, from around 4200 BC until the Mongol conquest in the 13th century AD. The first occupations (c.4200-3500 BC) contained elegant painted pottery with highland ties. Of equal significance were burials discovered both in and near a large mud-brick platform; this kind of burial ceremonialism is associated with emerging social complexity in many prehistoric cultures.

The material culture of the period – c.3500-3100 BC – displays very close similarities with the Uruk culture of southern Mesopotamia, including styles of mass-produced pottery, cylinder seals and early writing. Then in around 3100-2700 BC, Susa returned to its mountain orientation – developing a system of writing ('proto-Elamite') found in various sites around the Iranian plateau and enjoying commercial and cultural associations with eastern Iran,

Left Statuettes made of precious metals depict worhippers bearing offerings. This finely executed gold figure – made 13th to 12th century BC – is carrying a kid. It was discovered at the site in 1904.

western Afghanistan and Turkmenistan. From the mid-3rd millennium BC until the late 7th century BC, Susa was the major city of the Elamites, a people inhabiting south-west Iran from the southern Mesopotamian borderlands to Fars. The city then passed into the hands of imperial powers; the Achaemenid Persians kept Susa as a major administrative centre and the Seleucids perhaps implanted a colony of Greeks. Susa's importance declined with the establishment of new regional centres, however, and it was reduced to a village during the early centuries AD.

Ebla

The site of Tell Mardikh, ancient Ebla in north Syria, gained fame in the mid-1970s after the discovery of a large archive belonging to a previously unknown 3rd millennium BC kingdom. The city was also a significant regional centre during the Middle Bronze Age (c.2000-1550 BC).

Tell Mardikh covers an area of approximately 60ha (148 acres). It consists of a lower town and an inner citadel mound rising some 22m (72ft) above the surrounding plain. An Italian team led by Paolo Matthiae began excavating at Ebla in 1964, and work at the site has continued ever since. Although the depth of later deposits obstruct a good view of the early occupations at Mardikh, it is known that the site was first settled late in the 4th millennium BC. By about 2400 BC Ebla had grown to become the capital of a west Syrian kingdom.

Above Many cuneiform clay tablets were found at the site, which provide valuable information about life in the ancient city.

The archive

Knowledge of this kingdom comes mostly from the discovery of an archive of 17,000 tablets and tablet fragments recovered from the royal Palace G on the slope of the citadel mound. The larger tablets had originally been stored on shelves, but they had fallen onto the floor when the palace was destroyed. However, the excavators were able to reconstruct their original position on the shelves and it soon appeared that the tablets were originally shelved according to subject. Unfortunately, the excavations have not yet been able to expose much of the palace, due to the overburden of subsequent occupations at the site.

Left The many excavations have yielded a wealth of archaeological material, including palaces, temples and large religious precincts, tombs and defences.

The texts were written in a cuneiform script borrowed from Mesopotamia but adapted to express a west Semitic language. The archive records a palace economy based on obligatory labour gangs issued food and clothing in exchange for their work, on commercial transactions, and on storage of agricultural and manufactured goods. In addition, the archive reports on the attendance of students at scribal schools in Mesopotamia; gift exchanges of valuable goods between kings and also skilled craftsmen; international agreements to secure trade relations; gifts given to visiting foreign merchants; and other affairs of state.

Revival

Palace G was destroyed during an invasion from southern Mesopotamia, probably around 2300 BC. Ebla's inhabitants rebuilt the city, but around 2000 BC invaders again destroyed it. Revived once more, the city then entered a renaissance during the Middle Bronze Age. The settlement expanded in size and its residents erected a massive rampart wall, some 3km (2 miles) long, around their city. The wall was surmounted by fortresses. The social elites occupied large palaces, often located near temples and funerary cult buildings above royal tombs. Ebla's architecture during this period, notably the ramparts and several temples, has parallels in contemporary sites of the southern Levant, and artefacts indicate frequent interactions with that region and also with Egypt.

Kalhu

One of the first Mesopotamian sites to be excavated, Kalhu was the capital of the Assyrian empire during the 9th and 8th centuries BC. The city had numerous palaces ornamented with elaborate stone wall-reliefs and filled with sumptuous furnishings; underground chambers held royal graves.

Kalhu, the Biblical Calah, was the capital established by the Assyrian king Assurnasirpal II (883-859 BC), near the Tigris River in northern Iraq. Its modern name Nimrud derives from an imagined association with Nimrod the 'mighty hunter before the Lord' whom the Bible (Genesis 10:8-12) credits with founding Nineveh, Calah and other Assyrian cities.

Expansion

The location was first occupied in prehistoric times, but the oldest cuneiform texts mentioning the place belong to the 13th century BC. King Assurnasirpal greatly expanded the city in the 9th century BC when he laid out the imperial Assyrian capital as a walled enclosure. This covered an area of 360ha (890 acres), with a separate walled citadel in the south-west corner and an arsenal (Fort Shalmaneser) in the south-east corner.

After the Assyrian capital was moved to Khorsabad at the end of the 8th century BC, Kalhu remained a provincial capital until late in the 7th century, when invaders brought the Assyrian empire to an end.

Rediscovery

In 1820 Claudius James Rich, who was the East India Company's resident in Baghdad, visited and provided the first modern description of Nimrud.

Below Layard's vision of what the city of Nimrud might have looked like was presented in this lithograph by James Ferguson.

However, it was Sir Henry Austen Layard, who in 1845 began the first large-scale excavations of the site. It was his results that sparked strong British interest in Mesopotamian archaeology. With the assistance of Hormuzd Rassam, and using local workmen, Layard made significant discoveries, including the walls and southern part of the North-west Palace, including the colossal gateway figures and impressive bas-reliefs that adorned the walls of the palace. He also unearthed the first of the spectacular Nimrud Ivories.

After World War II, the British School of Archaeology in Iraq sponsored renewed excavations at Nimrud under the direction of Sir Max Mallowan – the archaeologist husband

Nimrud Ivories

Excavations have revealed a vast cache of elaborately carved ivory pieces. Originally, much of the carved surface of the ivory would have been covered in gold leaf, which had long been removed. Some particularly fine pieces were found at the bottom of two wells in the southern wing of the North-west Palace, where they had been discarded by looters. Many of the ivories would have been presented to the city as tribute from vassal states to the west of Assyria, where elephants were native.

Above This ivory sculpture, known as the Mona Lisa of Nimrud, was one of the pieces found in the wells.

Above Sculpture decorates the base of an archway at Nimrud.

of Agatha Christie – who discovered important archives of cuneiform tablets and many beautiful carved ivories in the royal precinct.

British teams worked on all areas of the acropolis and also at Fort Shalmaneser, where a large number of ivories were found. From 1987 to 1989 an Italian team of achaeologists surveyed the site and excavated at Fort Shalmaneser. Iraqi restoration work, which began in the mid-1950s, has also revealed significant discoveries.

These excavations carried out over the past 150 years have uncovered portions of over a dozen palaces, temples and administrative centres, but they have touched only small areas of more ordinary residential quarters.

The North-west Palace

Excavations in all the palaces and public buildings at Kalhu have produced some spectacular finds, including works of art, administrative archives and records of state, such as the vassal treaties of Esarhaddon (ruled 680-669 BC). But perhaps most impressive of all is the North-west Palace, built by Assurnasirpal and probably completed between 865 and 869 BC. The palace's inauguration was celebrated with lavish festivities attended by about 70,000 people from all over the empire. An inscription lists what the guests were given to eat and drink, including 1000 ducks, 500 geese, 500 gazelles, 10,000 doves, 10,000 skins of wine and large quantities of beer, fish, eggs and nuts.

The palace lay at the western edge of the citadel, adjacent to that structure's massive mud-brick walls, which were around 15m (49ft) high and 3.7m (12.1ft) thick. The private apartments and possibly the harem were housed in the south wing of the palace, while the administrative offices and storerooms were in the north wing.

The largest of the palace's audience halls was the Throne Room. It was here that the king received foreign visitors, so it was designed to impress. Enormous bas-reliefs, which would have stood about 2.2m (7ft) above the ground level, adorned the walls of the Throne Room.

The North-west Palace has yielded many important discoveries, including the so-called 'Banquet Stela' relating the king's conquests, building projects and the inaugural feast for the palace itself; bronze artwork in the styles of Syria and Phoenicia; and ivory furniture inlays rendered in multiple regional styles. Cuneiform tablets discovered in rooms in the north wing of the palace reveal interesting

Right The Assyrian sphinx, shown on this beautiful ivory plaque, had a human head and the body of a winged lion.

information about the administrative and economic organization of the Assyrian empire.

Fort Shalmaneser

Assurnasirpal's son Shalmaneser III (859-825 BC) built his arsenal along the same lines as a royal palace. The overall architectural plan of the fort is preserved along with the stone foundations of the wall that encircled the 30-ha (74-acre) complex. Archives discovered at the fort provide important details about the Assyrian army's troops, horses and arms. Other records deal with tax collection and legal affairs.

Royal tombs

Between 1988 and 1989 a team of Iraqi archaeologists unearthed the tombs of 9th and 8th century BC queens in vaulted chambers beneath the private apartments of the North-west palace. Three of these tombs contained enormous masses of jewellery and ornaments of gold and semi-precious stones, including a royal crown. Other items included

vessels, seals and ornaments. These rich burials – known as the Nimrud Treasure – give a vivid illustration of Assyrian wealth, amassed through conquest, loot and tribute.

Below A bas-relief from Assurnasirpal's palace includes a figure (left) that represents a protective winged genie, a prominent feature of Assyrian art. Here the genie holds a cone in his right hand and a bucket in his left – both objects are associated with purification and the power to protect.

Babylon

The city, located on a now-dry branch of the Euphrates River in central Iraq, reached its largest and most elaborate state under the kings of the Neo-Babylonian empire (626-539 BC), when the splendour of its buildings surpassed all others of its time.

Its Biblical associations – from the Tower of Babel to the Babylonian exile – ensured that Babylon never faded entirely from memory, but the location of the city was long uncertain. The British Resident in Baghdad, Claudius Rich, presented the first detailed description of the site at the beginning of the 19th century, and visiting archaeologists later in that century added some details.

Excavations

The first systematic exploration of the site was carried out by the German archaeologist Robert Koldewey, who excavated almost continuously from 1899 until 1917, when he retired from the field in the face of the invading Indian army. Koldewey's team published many detailed reports about their work, but some of their results

even now remain unpublished. The Germans returned to Babylon during the 1960s and 70s to investigate several specific questions, and the Iraqi government launched a reconstruction programme for parts of the site. However, Koldewey's work remains the baseline for understanding this capital of the Mesopotamian world.

The remains of early Babylon are deeply buried beneath the abundant later construction of the city and there is a high water table, so Koldewey was prevented from digging deeply into

Below In 1982 the Iraqi President Saddam Hussein began reconstructing the 600-room palace of Nebuchadnezzar on top of the original ruins, much to the disapproval of archaeologists. Some of the bricks, which were inscribed with Saddam's name, began to crack after just ten years.

History

Babylon existed by the mid-3rd millennium BC, when the name appears in several cuneiform texts. After the period known as the Old Babylonian dynasty (1894-1595 BC), Babylon was racked with intermittent periods of crisis, occupation and rebuilding for around the next thousand years. In 626 BC the Neo-Babylonian revival began with the expulsion of the Assyrians, who had conquered Babylon a century earlier. The Neo-Babylonian kings, particularly Nebuchadnezzar (604-562 BC), launched massive building projects in Babylon, their imperial capital. This golden period came to an end when Babylon was captured by Achaemenid Persians in 539 BC and the city passed forever under foreign rule. Babylon slowly receded into the backwaters of history and was largely abandoned during the early centuries AD.

the city, apart from one area where he reached an Old Babylonian residential quarter. So Koldewey focused on large exposures of the ceremonial heart of the Neo-Babylonian city.

The city

Neo-Babylonian Babylon covered an area of 8.5 sq km (3.3 sq miles) and had a population of around 150,000 residents. The city, which was surrounded by a massive wall and moat 18km (11 miles) long, spread along both banks of the Euphrates River; fortresses constructed around the edges of the city strengthened its defences. The two parts of the city were connected by bridges. Koldewey documented the piers of one stone bridge that stretched over 100m (328ft) across the river.

An inner city, surrounded by its own rectangular wall on the left bank of the river, formed the civic centre of the Neo-Babylonian empire. The main ceremonial entrance to the inner city was the famed Ishtar Gate – the most spectacular of eight gates that ringed the city's perimeter. This gate was a barrel-arch between pairs of square towers faced with blue-glazed baked bricks moulded with images of bulls and dragons. A walled Processional Way, running along a 15m- (49ft-) high embankment parallel to the river, passed through the Ishtar Gate and into the Inner City.

Once inside the Inner City, the Processional Way first passed Nebuchadnezzar's palace, then blocks of religious architecture that included the temples of the war goddess Ishtar, the wisdom god Nabu, and several other gods. Next came the Etemenanki containing the famed ziggurat of Marduk, and finally the E-sagila, the temple proper of Marduk.

Monumental buildings

The city was famed for two architectural features in particular: the Greek historian Herodotus counted the Hanging Gardens as one of the marvels of the ancient world, while according to the Biblical story God caused people to speak mutually unintelligible languages after seeing the hubris of the Tower of Babel. When Koldewey excavated Nebuchadnezzar's palace, he found massive vaulted chambers constructed of baked bricks laid with natural asphalt. He thought that these were the foundations for the Hanging Gardens – the asphalt protecting the structure

against water seepage from the plants above. However, many scholars today are sceptical of this interpretation.

According to Herodotus, the ziggurat of Marduk was like a stepped pyramid built with six levels, with the seventh level at the top being a temple of Marduk. Only the base of the ziggurat survived until Koldewey's day, so these details cannot be confirmed. The ziggurat was square, about 91m (298ft) to a side at its base, and constructed as a solid core of unbaked bricks covered with a mantle of baked

Above A reconstruction of the Ishtar Gate – built with bricks excavated at the site – is housed in the Pergamon Museum, Berlin. The top of the gate is crenellated (notched) and would have provided cover for archers defending the city.

bricks. The mantle was looted through the ages, leaving only a flattened mound. Koldewey's investigation showed that the Assyrians rebuilt an older ziggurat in the 7th century BC, and that Nebuchadnezzar renewed the ziggurat during the following century.

Left The head of a dragon sculpted in bronze represents Marduk, Babylon's patron god. The bronze is in the Louvre Museum in Paris.

Persepolis

The royal seat of the Achaemenid (Persian) empire, Persepolis was founded by Darius the Great (522-486 BC). The impressive palace complex, built on an immense terrace, was later destroyed by Alexander the Great in 330 BC during a drunken party in celebration of his conquest of that empire.

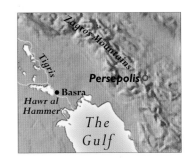

To create his new palace at Persepolis (in south-west Iran) — and for building another massive palace at Susa — Darius ordered that skilled craftsmen and valuable materials be assembled from all parts of the empire.

Persepolis became the ceremonial centre of the Persian dynasty, and although the kings spent much of their time in other cities, such as Susa and Babylon, they carried out state ceremonies at the new dynastic capital. Persepolis was a vast complex, and Darius did not live to complete its construction, a task that fell to his son Xerxes (486-465 BC) and grandson Artaxerxes (465-423 BC).

Excavating the site

Major excavation work to uncover the half-buried city began in 1930. Among the stonework archaeologists uncovered graphic bas-reliefs that reveal much about the religious and social hierarchy of the city.

In 1935 the first of a series of pioneering aerial survey flights was carried out under the directorship of Professor Erich Schmidt, then field director of the Persepolis expedition. Hundreds of aerial photographs were taken of the site and its environs, at different seasons and at different times of day, giving a valuable overview of the excavations. Documentation and mapping helped to identify areas of the site where digging could begin.

Right An overview of the complex shows the columns of the *apadana* in the background. Although impressive, the ruins only hint at the scale and splendour of the actual city.

Architectural showpiece

The great complex of halls and palaces at Persepolis was built on a vast stone terrace built against a hill slope at the edge of the vast Marv Dasht plain. This terrace covered an area of 450 x 300m (1476 x 984ft) and was 14m (46ft) high. The visitor reached the top of the terrace via a monumental double-return staircase ornamented with depictions of the royal guard. The platform supported a dense array of imposing buildings, the most magnificent of which was the *apadana* (a high pillared audience hall) built by Darius. The *apadana*, elevated upon its own platform overlooking the plain, was built of finely polished stone and mud brick encased in cedar; colossal columns, each 19m (62ft) high, carried the weight of the ceiling. Its entry staircase is decorated with the famous reliefs portraying emissaries bearing tribute gifts from all corners of the Achaemenid empire.

Next to the *apadana* is the Throne Hall, or the Hundred-Column Hall, which was started by Xerxes. The northern portico of the building is flanked by two colossal stone bulls. Along with other pillared halls, there were also harem quarters and a

treasury; these once-sumptious buildings are represented today mainly by rows of stone pillars.

In addition to some important government archives recorded on clay tablets, Persepolis was also a source of trilingual inscriptions – in Old Persian, Akkadian and Elamite.

These inscriptions greatly aided the decipherment of the cuneiform script in the first half of the 19th century.

Although Alexander the Great's men had plundered the city, archaeologists have found many artefacts, including weights, tools, weapons, bowls and bottles sent as tribute from Egypt.

Royal tombs

Darius and three of his successors were buried in tombs cut into the cliff face at Naqsh-i Rustam, about 13km (8 miles) north of Persepolis. The tomb entrances were carved as the façade of a columned building, with relief and inscription overhead. The tombs have long since been looted of their treasure.

Right The capture of the Roman emperor Valerian by the Persian king Sharpur I in AD 260 is commemorated in this relief.

Petra

The Nabataeans, an Arabic-speaking people of north-west Arabia, made Petra, in southern Jordan, their capital. By the first century AD the city had become a thriving centre, with magnificent temples and tombs hewn from the rust-coloured rocks.

The Nabataeans first appeared in history during the late 4th and 3rd century BC, when they were already middlemen in the caravan trade – their location giving them control of the major routes connecting the Mediterranean Sea with Arabia and the Indian Ocean.

Access to the Mediterranean world meant that the Nabataeans were open to Greco-Roman architectural and artistic influences, which they incorporated into some of their buildings at Petra. The spectacle of classical façades carved into the red stone enchanted European travellers, beginning in 1812 with the Swiss-born and British-sponsored Johann Burckhardt. Although Petra attracted increasing numbers of visitors during the 19th century, the first systematic study came only in 1898 with the work of the German R.E. Brünnow. The first real excavations began in 1929 and have continued ever since. In recent years field work has been carried out by, among others, British, American, Swiss and Jordanian teams.

Desert city

Petra lies within a knot of dry water courses, called wadies, deeply incised into the sandstone of southern Jordan. This location enjoys little rainfall, yet Nabataean engineers created a complex system of dams, cisterns, pipes, aqueducts and other water-control devices. One aqueduct brought water from the Musa (Moses) spring

Below The Monastery is the largest tomb façade in Petra. It consists of two storeys and is topped by a magnificent urn.

Above Two of Petra's rock-cut tombs are the Palace Tomb (left) and the Corinthian Tomb.

into the city through the famous Siq – a gorge up to 200m (656ft) deep and in places only 3m (10ft) wide.

The first sight to greet visitors emerging from the Siq is the magnificent Khaznah (the Treasury), a two-storeyed pillared façade carved into the cliff face, giving entrance to four chambers. The structure was a tomb or, less probably, a temple.

The Siq opens up into a large open area through which run several wadis from the surrounding rugged heights. The Nabataean builders carved many tombs into rock faces along these wadis and upon the hills from which the wadis descend.

This central area housed Petra's urban centre, with its civic heart along the Colonnaded Street – a formal road lined with columns and flanked on either side by temples, markets and other public spaces. A fountain marked one end of the street, and at the other

end a monumental triple arch gave entrance to the great temple known as Qasr al-Bint. This large complex, constructed in the mid-1st century AD and remaining in use until the 6th century, is distinctive for the elephant

heads that ornamented the pillar capitals on the lower platform. The Temple of Winged Lions, a structure built upon vaulted foundations, is named for the lions that decorated the capitals of that building. Recent exploration of the market immediately adjacent to the Southern Temple shows that this open space in fact held a garden with a large pool; the other two 'markets' remain uninvestigated.

The rise north of the Colonnaded Street hosted a cluster of three Byzantine churches and chapels. A building adjacent to the basilica yielded the 6th-century AD personal archive – contracts, wills, sermons and lectures – of a certain archdeacon Theodoros.

Recent excavations on top of a hill south of the Colonnaded Street uncovered the dwellings of well-to-do families, including a mansion decorated with elaborate wall paintings.

Left Visitors to Petra in the 19th century included the painter David Roberts (1796-1864), who captured the city's ethereal beauty.

Ostia Excavations at this ancient port have revealed fascinating details about urban life at the height of the Roman Empire.

Delphi The 4th-century BC remains of the Temple of Apollo lie at the heart of a complex of ancient buildings.

Göbekli Tepe A site containing elaborate stone structures carved by hunter-gatherers in about 9600 BC.

E U R O P E

Black Sea

Tarquinia
Ostia
The Domus Aurea in Rome
Pompeii and Herculaneum

Pergamon

Göbekli Tepe

Mediterranean

Delphi
Olympia
Athenian Agora
Mycenae

Carthage

Knossos

Ulu Burun

Sea

Cyrene

Masada

A F R I C A

Red Sea

Mycenae This fortified city was one of the major centres of Greek civilization in the 2nd millennium BC.

Ulu Burun The oldest shipwreck ever found has provided a wealth of information about Mediterranean trade in the 14th century BC.

Masada This fortress-palace at the southern end of the Dead Sea was the last outpost of Jews in the Jewish Revolt of AD 66-73.

THE GREAT SITES OF THE MEDITERRANEAN

As the cradle of European civilization, the Mediterranean has yielded a rich variety of archaeological sites. The discovery of Pompeii and Herculaneum in the 1740s was one of the major events affecting knowledge of, and curiosity about, the Roman world. Later, as archaeology was able to extend its investigations back in time, earlier cultures such as those of the Etruscans, Mycenaeans and Minoans were uncovered, thanks to work by pioneers such as Schliemann and Evans. More recently, the Mediterranean Sea has proved a plentiful source of shipwrecks, most notably Ulu Burun, with the latest technology making it possible to detect and study wrecks at great depths.

From the prehistoric site of Göbekli Tepe in Turkey to the exquisite frescoes at Knossos on Crete, the Mediterranean is one of the world's foremost archaeological regions.

Pergamon Successive Attalid kings developed this Turkish city into one of the jewels of the Hellenistic world.

Carthage Founded in 814 BC, this Phoenician colony become one of the leading trading centres of the western Mediterranean.

Pompeii Excavations have revealed a city – its buildings and people – frozen in time after the eruption of Vesuvius in AD 79.

395

Göbekli Tepe

A ceremonial site of hunter-gatherers, Göbekli Tepe is remarkable due to the fact that its builders used massive blocks of limestone as architectural elements. Even more amazing is that these structures are dated to about 9600 BC, just before the dawn of farming in the Near East.

The low mound of Göbekli Tepe in south-east Turkey was first discovered in the 1960s during a survey. However, it was not until 1994 that Klaus Schmidt of the German Institute of Istanbul realized that it was a prehistoric site and began excavations.

Prehistoric architecture

Using nothing more than flint tools and perhaps fire and water, the builders of Göbekli Tepe carved out blocks of limestone that weighed up to seven tonnes from the local bedrock. They then transported these huge blocks a short distance and set them upright within circular stone buildings cut into the bedrock. At least four such semi-subterranean buildings are known, while others may still lie beneath the hillside. Two pillars were erected in the centre of each building, and several others were placed around the walls.

Each pillar is wider at the top than at the bottom, with some even having a 'T' shape, up to a height of almost 3m (10ft). In the nearby quarry, an unfinished pillar was discovered that dwarfed even those found in the buildings, suggesting that the Göbekli Tepe architects had something more impressive planned.

Images of wild animals, including foxes, boar, cattle, gazelle, herons, ducks and snakes, are carved into the pillars. One even shows a snarling lion. Some of the reliefs have been deliberately erased; perhaps this was in preparation for new pictures.

Hunter-gatherers

There are no traces of domesticated plants or animals among the deposits of animal bones and plant remains. Everything came from wild species, such as gazelle, wild pig, wild cattle, almonds and wild wheat. Thus, the

builders of Göbekli Tepe were hunter-gatherers. Moreover, it appears that there was no human habitation at the site, for no traces of houses, hearths or storage pits were revealed.

So what were hunter-gatherers doing at Göbekli Tepe if they did not live there? Klaus Schmidt believes that the site was a ritual centre to which people came to visit. The Göbekli Tepe carvings and architecture show similarities with those at Jerf el Ahmar, about 100 km (62 miles) away in Syria, which suggests a possible range for the people using the site. The question is whether it was a single group or a number of different groups connected through a common belief system.

The archaeologist Stephen Mithen, developing ideas first proposed by the French prehistorian Jacques Cauvin, has suggested that ritual activity of the kind that appears to have taken place at Göbekli Tepe was a catalyst in the emergence of agriculture. In the late 1990s, geneticists identified wild wheat not far from Göbekli Tepe as the closest wild relative of domesticated wheat, thus making the area a strong candidate for the origin of wheat domestication. Mithen hypothesizes that those taking part in the ceremonial rituals at Göbekli Tepe and other nearby sites may have taken seed grain back to their distant homes, where they planted it and thus began domesticating the grain.

Left The pillar carvings at Göbekli Tepe presage the depiction of animals in cave paintings, such as these found at Çatal Hüyük in central Turkey, a Neolithic site dating to about 7000 BC.

Knossos

The labyrinthine palace at Knossos on the island of Crete was the largest and most important of the palatial complexes built by the Minoans during the 2nd millennium BC and is the most thoroughly excavated. Archaeology has revealed delicate wall paintings and unearthed thousands of artefacts.

The Minoans were not Greeks, but their Bronze Age culture became part of Greek history. They settled on Crete during the 3rd millennium BC and became prosperous traders. From about 1900 BC they began to build grand houses and palaces.

Excavations

The first archaeologist to dig at Knossos was Minos Kalokairinos, a Cretan merchant and antiquarian, who in 1878 excavated the west façade and two storerooms and found many artefacts. The person most closely associated with Knossos,

however, is the English archaeologist Arthur Evans, who began excavations in 1900. Work at the site was interrupted in 1912-14 by the Balkan Wars but was resumed in 1922 and continued until 1931, when the investigation of the West Court and the Minoan town was completed.

Minoan palaces

Like Kalokairinos, Arthur Evans was certain that he had found the seat of Minos, the legendary king of Crete, and named Knossos the 'Palace of King Minos'. 'Palace' is a misnomer, however, since the site may have been

a temple-city dedicated to the cult of the bull. Carvings and images of bulls appear on buildings and artefacts.

Settlements on Crete were frequently destroyed by earthquakes and new ones were built on top of them. Archaeologists have been able to excavate successive settlement layers at Knossos, dating back some 7000 years to Neolithic times. During the 1600s BC earthquakes destroyed the

Below The frieze in the main room of the Queen's apartments depicts dolphins. Marine life was a favourite theme in Minoan art, appearing on pottery as well as frescoes.

first Minoan palaces. This stimulated a phase of rebuilding, and new, larger and more complex palaces arose on the sites of the old. At Knossos, the New Palace effaced its predecessor almost completely and covered an area of 2ha (5 acres). Grand houses and tombs are found beyond its perimeter.

The New Palace

Like other Minoan palace-complexes, Knossos was built around a central Great Court, surrounded by rooms. It also has a West Court – a surviving feature of the Old Palace – and a monumental west façade. There are two storeys below ground and there were perhaps two or more upper storeys. The layout is disorientating: few passages lead directly from A to B but follow a circuitous route and emerge in unexpected places.

The walls of the palace were made of unbaked brick. Wood was also widely used for columns,

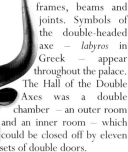

Right A rhyton (drinking horn) made from steatite in the shape of a bull's head from Knossos, c.1700-1600 BC. The horns are gilded, the eyes made of rock crystal and the muzzle is crafted from mother of pearl.

doors and window frames, beams and joints. Symbols of the double-headed axe – *labyros* in Greek – appear throughout the palace. The Hall of the Double Axes was a double chamber – an outer room and an inner room – which could be closed off by eleven sets of double doors.

On the west side is the Throne Room with stone benches and a high-backed chair built into the wall. Arthur Evans believed this to be the throne of King Minos, but it may have been the seat of a high priestess. Rooms on a floor situated above the Throne Room may have been used for ceremonies.

A number of storerooms (many with storage jars and vessels, and shrines) have been excavated. The complex also had a theatre, banqueting halls and craft workshops, and an intricate plumbing and ventilation system. There were also grain mills and wine and oil presses.

A number of annexes were built onto the main palace, including the Little Palace and the Royal Villa. To the south of the palace lies the Caravanserai, which was interpreted as a reception hall and hospice. Some of the rooms are equipped with baths and are decorated with wall paintings.

Frescoes

The Minoans decorated their interiors with charming wall paintings, many depicting animals and plants. Visitors conducted from the West Door along the Corridor of the Procession Fresco may have been awed by paintings depicting court ceremony, while today's visitors may be delighted by the replica Dolphin Fresco, which Arthur Evans installed in what he thought were the Queen's apartments on the

Left The walls of the Throne Room are adorned with colourful replica frescoes depicting mythological beasts, such as griffins.

Restoration

Arthur Evans's excavations between 1900 and 1931 eventually revealed 1300 rooms in the palace complex. However, his practice of restoring the palace while excavating aroused controversy. He hired teams of builders to roof some of the rooms and reconstruct the palace walls with modern materials, such as concrete. He also commissioned skilled artists to reconstruct some of the damaged frescoes, including those in the Throne Room. While this work has been dismissed by some as being inaccurate, for others the restoration has made the complicated site easier to understand, helping the visitor to appreciate the scale and grandeur of the original complex. Certainly, some restoration was necessary – for example, the rebuilding of the collapsed Grand Staircase in the Central Court in order to access two storeys below ground level. In recognition of his discovery of and insights into Minoan civilization, Evans's bust stands in the Central Court.

Above The west portico of the North entrance to the palace was reconstructed. The red columns were typical of Minoan architecture. Unlike Greek columns, they were made of wood and were wider at the top than the bottom. They had round, pillow-like capitals (tops).

lower floors. The Bull Chamber, near the north entrance, has a replica relief fresco of a charging bull. One of the most famous frescoes at Knossos shows a young man vaulting over a bull.

Ancient writing

Arthur Evans discovered many discs and seal impressions of Minoan writing. Archaeologists call this script 'Linear A' and recognize that the writing of the Mycenaeans, 'Linear B', developed from it. Linear A has never been deciphered.

Conundrums

More than a century of excavation at Knossos and other similar sites has raised questions about the Minoans.

Above Storage containers called *pithoi* were found in a storeroom. Food, grain, wine and oil were stored in these jars. Ropes were threaded through the handles to move them.

Archaeologists disagree, for example, on whether they were warrior people. Knossos has no fortifications, but its position – just inland on a low hill in a valley – is defensive. Many types of swords and axes have been found, but some specialists think they may be ceremonial weapons.

There has also been much debate about whether Minoan civilization was in fact a matriarchal society. The key figure at Knossos may have been a high priestess, with the king acting merely as a figurehead.

Mycenae

The city-states of the Bronze Age Mycenaean civilization, of which the ancient Greek city of Mycenae in the north-east Peloponnese was the richest and largest, were distinguished by fortifications so monumental that later peoples called them 'Cyclopean', after the one-eyed giants of myth.

From about 1500 BC the Mycenaeans, a merchant-farmer-warrior people, dominated trade in the Mediterranean. They began to build a network of palace-citadels on the Greek mainland, of which Mycenae was probably the first to be built. The Mycenaeans eclipsed the Minoans of Crete to become the dominant power in the eastern Mediterrannean.

Palace-citadel

Mycenae occupied a strong, defensive position on a hill that overlooked gorges. It was fortified mainly in the 14th century BC. Its curtain wall was 1km (0.6 miles) in circumference,

with two portals and a smaller exit gate. A great ramp led up the hillside to the great Lion Gate, through which visitors entered the citadel. The lions carved above the 3m- (10ft-) high gate symbolized the power of the rulers of Mycenae, and they may once have had heads made of metal and staring eyes of a reflective stone. In case of siege there was a hidden cistern that was supplied via a concealed aqueduct with water from a spring.

The Mycenaean acropolis enclosed a hilltop palace, with a great open court at its centre. The Great Court faced a columned portico, which led into the 'megaron' – the main hall with a vestibule and a huge central open hearth. Four columns positioned around the hearth supported the roof.

Excavations at Mycenae during the 20th century revealed a temple in which were found pottery idols carrying cult objects, a bathing room containing a water jug, a shrine and a cult room. The remains of colourful frescoes adorned the walls of these and other rooms. Recent work has focused on houses in the town that surrounded the citadel, which covers some 32ha (79 acres) and was built mainly in the 13th century BC.

Grave goods

The citadel was built on the site of older settlements. Two grave circles from a cemetery in use between 2000 and 1650 BC lie within and outside its

Above The actual door of the Lion Gate was made of two wooden leaves, which opened inwards.

Cyclopean architecture

The terrace wall supporting the great ramp leading into the citadel, the curtain wall and bastions, the monumental gates and the underground passage to the secret cistern are all examples of the Cyclopean building style of the Mycenaeans. They were constructed using massive stones averaging 6-7m (20-23ft) thick in places, and enormous lintels, which were hauled up the hillside or along earth ramps. The large, irregular blocks of stone were roughly finished and laid uncoursed. Small rocks and stones were inserted between them for stability. The curtain wall ranged in height from 4.6m (15ft) to 17m (56ft) on the south-west side.

Above A gold funeral mask dating from the 16th century BC, found in one of the shaft graves at Mycenae.

walls. It was here that Schliemann, the archaeologist who rediscovered Mycenae, began to dig in 1876. The site had long been known, but it was Schliemann who first excavated the site. He was searching for the place, according to Homer's *Iliad*, from where 1000 ships had set sail for Troy under Agamemnon's command.

Schliemann concentrated his search on the deep deposits just beyond the Lion Gate. He soon discovered the shaft graves – deep pits cut through the rock and earth – where the early Mycenaen rulers from the 16th–13th century BC were buried in spectacular style. Here Schliemann unearthed a wealth of gold, silver, bronze, ivory and pottery artefacts, including death masks, diadems, vessels of precious metals and daggers and swords of bronze. The city which Homer had described as 'a city of gold', was living up to expectations.

Schliemann also excavated the large, circular, dome-shaped tholos (or beehive) tombs. The entrance passages to these tombs were cut into the hillside and led into a tall, circular chamber. The most impressive of these tholos tombs is the so-called Treasury of Atreus, constructed in the 13th century BC.

Below Grave Circle A is inside the north-west corner of the citadel walls of Mycenae.

Ulu Burun

A sponge diver working off southern Turkey in 1982 found a shipwreck.
It was a late Bronze Age merchant ship with a cargo of precious commodities.
The excavation of the ship has provided information about seafaring life,
international trade and shipbuilding in the late 14th century BC.

The merchant ship was resting on a slope on the sea floor about 44m (144ft) deep. It had been carrying a cargo of precious commodities, which included copper ingots, ebony logs and ivory tusks, and has provided more than 1200 artefacts. Analysis of its cargo, including jars containing food such as fish, figs, grapes and pomegranates, olives and olive oil, and *pithoi* (storage jars) for carrying water, indicates that the ship may have originally sailed from Egypt or an eastern Mediterranean port such as Ugarit in Syria. From here it then travelled to Cyprus to load its main cargo of copper. The ship may then have headed to the lands of Asia Minor, which at this time were ruled by the Hittites. It was off the Ulu Burun promontory, which is about 8km (5 miles) south-east of Kas, in modern Turkey, that the ship must have run into unfavourable conditions, such as strong winds, and sunk.

Although most of the ship's timbers had been eaten away, computer modelling suggests that to carry its 20-tonne cargo, including up to six oarsmen, 1 tonne of ballast stones for stability, and 24 anchors, the ship must have measured around 15 x 5 x 2m (49 x 16 x 6ft).

Marine excavation

The difficult task of excavating both the shipwreck and its scattered cargo at depths of 44-61m (144-200ft) under water took 11 dive programmes, each one lasting several weeks, carried out between 1984 and 1994. The work was directed by

Copper and tin

Among the objects found scattered on the seafloor around the wreck were what Mehmet Cakir, the sponge diver who discovered it, described as 'metal biscuits with ears'. Marine archaeologists suspected that these were copper ingots with carrying handles.

The Ulu Burun shipwreck was found to carry more than 10 tonnes of copper ingots from copper mines on Cyprus. Also on board was about 1 tonne of tin.

Copper was the basis of the Bronze Age economy: a mixture of nine parts copper to one part tin melts at a lower temperature than pure copper, is easier to cast and the end product – bronze – is a harder metal for tools and weapons. The ship's cargo of copper and tin would have been enough to make almost 11 tonnes of bronze.

Above Each ingot found around the Ulu Burun shipwreck was between 70 to 80cm (28 to 31in) in length. They were made of copper, which was an important metal during the Bronze Age.

US professors George F. Bass, founder and director of the Institute of Nautical Archaeology (INA), and Cemul Pulak. To avoid the bends (nitrogen narcosis) at these depths, the divers were able to work for only 20 minutes at a time.

Treasure trove

The Ulu Burun wreck has yielded the largest and richest collection of Late Bronze Age trading goods and artefacts found to date. Most of the ship's cargo consisted of commodities, notably Cypriot copper ingots, the earliest ingots of glass ever found, and almost 150 jars of resin, perhaps for burning as incense. There were great logs of cedar and Egyptian ebony, elephant tusks, hippopotamus teeth (for carving), ostrich eggshells (for containers) and tortoise carapaces (to make musical instruments).

Among the manufactured goods on board were bronze and copper containers, pottery jars and cups, vessels of tin and fine faience and ceramics. There were many commercial weights, some in the shape of animals, including cows, bulls, lions, a sphinx, ducks, a frog and a housefly. The ship was also loaded with bronze woodworking tools and fishing implements, and weapons such as swordheads and arrowheads, daggers and swords.

Priceless commodities

The Ulu Burun ship is most famous for its precious cargo of gold, silver and electrum metal and ornaments; beads of glass and semi-precious

stones, such as agate, carnelian, quartz and amber; and jewellery, including bracelets and pendants. These goods came from far and wide – jewellery and pottery from Canaan (the eastern Mediterranean), fine pottery originating from Cyprus, animal products from tropical Africa and amber from northern Europe.

Some of the most valuable commodities and artefacts of gold, silver and electrum were Egyptian.

One of the most precious items salvaged from the wreck is a gold scarab, which is inscribed with what is believed to be the only surviving cartouche of Queen Nefertiti, wife of Pharaoh Akhenaten. Seals from the royal houses of Egypt, Assyria and Syria have also been found in the wreck. These have inspired a theory that the wreck was once a 'royal ship', perhaps under the patronage of the Egyptian pharaohs. However, other

Above An archaeologist works on a row of copper 'oxhide' ingots, one of four rows in situ. A total of 354 of these ingots have been found on the shipwreck.

objects found that belonged to the crew indicate that the men were from Canaan, Cyprus and Mycenae. These objects and the wide-ranging origin of the cargo suggest to others that the Ulu Burun ship carried commercial and private goods.

Olympia

Located in a fertile valley in the north-west of the Peloponnese in southern Greece, Olympia was the cult centre of Zeus, to whom the Olympic Games, first held in 776 BC, were dedicated. Today, the ruins of Olympia have provided an insight into the glory of the games.

Excavations at the site, which had been covered in silt brought down by the River Alpheios, began in 1875 by archaeologists from the Prussian Academy of Science; this marked the first permit issued to archaeologists from outside Greece. A major series of excavations resumed at Olympia in 1952, which are still continuing.

Sacred site

The understanding of the topography of the sanctuary has been helped by the descriptions of the 2nd-century AD Roman travel writer Pausanias. At the heart of the sacred space lay the Temple of Zeus, which was built during the second quarter of the 5th century BC. Excavations have uncovered marble figures from the two triangular pediments at either end.

The temple housed the gold and ivory cult statue of Zeus, one of the Seven Wonders of the Ancient World. The statue, which stood 15m (50ft)

high, has long disappeared (after being removed to Constantinople). However, the German excavators discovered the

Above A circular design from the interior of a 6th-century BC Athenian drinking cup shows a long jumper using weights.

workshop of the sculptor Pheidias to the west of the sanctuary (later turned into a Christian basilica). Inside were tools, moulds and materials used to craft the statue of Zeus.

To the east of the sanctuary, and joined to it by a tunnel, was the stadium in which some of the races for the original games took place. Remains of the stone starting line have been located. On the stadium's southern slope there is a stone platform for the *hellanodikai* (the judges). Bases for statues of the winners in the competitions have been found across the site. Other finds include a number of tripods decorated with griffins; some are likely to have been given as prizes in the events held within the sanctuary of Zeus.

Below Athletes practised boxing, wrestling and long jumping in the *palaestra*, an annexe of the gymnasium. This was surrounded by colonnades providing shelter from the sun.

Cyrene

The Greek colony of Cyrene, in Cyrenaica, a region in north-east Libya, was established in the late 7th century BC by people from the island of Thera. Today, the many ancient ruins speak of the city's 1000-year period as a flourishing trading centre.

The city was visited by European travellers from the early 18th century, but the first systematic survey was made by British army officers, Robert M. Smith and E.A. Porcher, during 1860-61. Richard Norton made the first scientific exploration by the Archaeological Institute of America. He was granted a permit by the Ottoman authorities in 1910. There appears to have been opposition from Italian interests in the archaeological sites, however, and one of Norton's colleagues was shot and killed. Norton started the exploration of the extensive necropolis of the city of Cyrene and recovered terracotta figures from an extra-mural sanctuary.

The agora

In September 1911 Cyrenaica was annexed by Italy and much of the initial survey work in the region was conducted by Federico Halbherr, who had earlier worked on Crete. The Italians concentrated their work on the main public space of the city – the agora. Remains of the council chamber, or *bouleuterion*, have been uncovered, as well as a shrine sacred to Battos, the founder of the colony. The agora was the area for the display of public monuments, such as a statue celebrating a Ptolemaic naval victory in the mid-3rd century BC.

The Roman influence

As Cyrenaica formed part of the Roman Empire, so the city attracted a series of benefactions. Among them was the construction of a temple to house the imperial cult. Other areas

explored by archaeologists include the Temple of Apollo, lying to the north of the acropolis and whose origins lay in the earliest time of the colony. The temple was rebuilt during the reign of Emperor Hadrian after the Jewish revolt of AD 115-117. The *propylaeum*, or monumental gateway, dates to the time of Emperor Septimius Severus (ruled AD 193-211). In 2005 Italian archaeologists discovered 76 intact

Below Carved figures of Herakles and Hermes are from the gymnasium at Cyrene.

Roman statues, dating from the 2nd century AD, which had remained undiscovered since an earthquake occurred in AD 375.

Other discoveries

American excavations have continued at the extra-mural sanctuary of Demeter and Kore to the south of the city on the Wadi Bel Gadir. Substantial amounts of archaic (7th and 6th century BC) material have been found revealing contacts between the city and other parts of the Aegean world.

Delphi

Archaeologists have unearthed the oracle of Apollo at Delphi, the most important oracle in the Ancient World. At its peak in the 6th century BC people came from all over Greece and beyond to have questions about the future answered by the priestess Pythia, who spoke on behalf of Apollo.

The village of Kastri, which had occupied the area of the sanctuary of Apollo since medieval times, had to be relocated several kilometres away before excavations by the French School in Athens, first directed by Théophile Homolle (1848-1925), could begin in 1893. After the removal of huge quantities of earth, the remains of two sanctuaries, dedicated to Apollo and Athena, were uncovered. Outside the sanctuary, the gymnasium, the stadium, the settlement of Delphi and its cemeteries were also excavated.

The Temple of Apollo

The focal point for the sanctuary was the Temple of Apollo. The present remains date from the 4th century BC. However, at least two other temples have been identified. It is thought that the first was probably constructed in the 7th century BC but was destroyed by fire in the mid-6th century BC. Marble pedimental sculpture from this temple, depicting the epiphany of Apollo, has been recovered.

The temple was constructed on a large terrace supported by a massive retaining wall running along the contours. This formed the rear of a long colonnade, known as the Stoa of the Athenians. An inscription

indicates that booty from the Persian wars of the early 5th century BC was placed on display here.

The treasuries

The sanctuary was approached by a sacred way that snaked its way up the hill to the temple. This was lined by dedications and small buildings known as treasuries, which were dedicated by individual cities and housed gold, silver and priceless works of art.

Among the treasuries was one of the Greek island of Siphnos, which was mentioned by the Greek historian Herodotus (*c*.484-420 BC). It has been identified as the structure with caryatids (columns carved in the shape of clothed, standing young women) at the front of the building. Work on the treasury is still ongoing.

At the corner of the sacred way, in a prominent position, stood the treasury of the Athenians, thought to have been erected after the Athenian victory over the Persians at the battle of Marathon in 490 BC. The treasury was decorated with a series of metopes (reliefs) depicting the deeds of Herakles, and the new Athenian hero, Theseus. This building, which was restored by the French excavators in 1903-6, is the best-preserved on the site.

The *kouroi*

Herodotus mentioned the gift of a pair of statues by the people of Argos during the 6th century BC. These have sometimes been associated with the pair of striding male statues, or *kouroi* (plural of *kouros*, the Greek for 'a youth'), which were recovered by the French. A study of the inscriptions on the statues shows that they had indeed been made by sculptors from Argos, and that they represented the *Anakai*, the Argive cult associated with the sons of Zeus (and called the *Dioskouroi* elsewhere in the Greek world).

Now on display at the museum at

Opposite A scene from the continuous frieze around the Siphnian Treasury shows the battle between the gods and the giants (gigantomachy). A lion pulls the chariot.

Above Doric columns are at the eastern end of the Temple of Apollo. The monument was partly restored 1938-41. Excavations are still being carried out at the site to this day.

Delphi, these 2.2m- (7ft-) tall statues may originally have been displayed in an open-plan structure whose architectural elements have been found reused in other buildings at Delphi. There appears to have been a frieze showing scenes from the life of the *Dioskouroi/Anakai*. Researchers believe this building may have been damaged or dismantled when the sanctuary was rebuilt in the 6th century BC.

Bronze tripod

Just east of the temple the base of a bronze tripod, supported by twisted snakes, was discovered. A head of one of the snakes was found in nearby excavations, but the tripod itself had been taken to Constantinople in Late Antiquity, where it remains today. The tripod had been dedicated by the Greek cities that had fought against Persia during the invasion of mainland Greece in 480-479 BC.

Bronze charioteer

One of the most stunning sculptural finds made by the French excavators was the life-size bronze of a charioteer, which seems to have been toppled during an earthquake and landslide. Parts of the base have been discovered, showing that the bronze formed part of the victory monument of Polzalos, the tyrant of Gela on Sicily, who had won the chariot race in the Pythian games during the 470s BC. The group itself would have originally included the four horses pulling the chariot, and possibly two out-riders. The sculpture depicts the charioteer at the moment when he presents his horses to the spectators in recognition of his victory.

Left The statue's eyelashes and lips are made of copper, while the eyes are made of onyx. He is wearing the long chiton worn by all charioteers during a race.

The Athenian Agora

Lying to the north of the Acropolis, the Agora, or marketplace, first became the commercial, political, religious and cultural centre of life in Athens in the early 6th century BC. The large open square was surrounded by shops, banks, council buildings, law courts and the mint.

In 1890-91 a deep trench cut for creating the Athens-Piraeus Railway revealed extensive remains of ancient buildings. Systematic excavations on the site of the Agora first began in 1931, under the auspices of the American School of Classical Studies at Athens. The location of the Agora had already been known, thanks to the topographical description given by the 2nd-century AD Roman travel writer Pausanias.

The heart of democracy

Excavations have uncovered buildings associated with Athenian democracy along the west side of the Agora. These include the *bouleuterion*, or council chamber, where 50 members of each of the 10 tribes of Attica met. Next to it was the *tholos*, a circular building where the presiding tribe for each of the months resided. In front of these buildings was a long stone base surmounted by statues of the heroes, after whom each of the Athenian tribes was named (more were added in the Hellenistic and Roman periods), and alongside which notices relating to each tribe could be displayed.

On the hill behind the public buildings is the well-preserved Temple of Hephaistos. The discovery of planting pits dating from the 3rd century BC indicate that the grounds of the temple were fully landscaped.

On the north side of the Agora was the 'Royal' stoa, or colonnade, where the laws of Athens were placed. Next to it was another stoa decorated with painted panels, showing scenes from the famous Athenian victory at the battle of Marathon in 490 BC. Remains of one of the law courts have been found, including ballots for making decisions in trials.

The Agora received a number of benefactions in the Hellenistic period, including the stoa given by Attalos II, a king of Pergamon. The Romans added a concert hall (the *odeion*) to the open square at the end of the 1st century AD, and Emperor Augustus seems to have moved a redundant temple of Ares, the god of war, from the countryside round Athens and reconstructed it in the open space.

Left The reconstructed Stoa of Attalos, built in about 150 BC, is now a museum.

Tarquinia

Beautiful frescoes adorn some of the 6th-century BC burial tombs found in Tarquinia, in modern Tuscany. These scenes, which include figures playing sports, hunting and banqueting, provide an important insight into the culture of the Etruscans, who dominated the area north of Rome.

The cemeteries of Etruria drew increasing interest in the 19th century. The rock-cut tombs were opened and their contents – bronzes and fine figure-decorated pottery, such as the Athenian pottery with local metalwork found by Signor Rispoli in the late 1880s – were transported to museums.

The excavations of the Monterozzi cemetery (1958-63) was sponsored by the Lerici Foundation. It uncovered some 5500 tombs of the 6th and 5th centuries BC. The Foundation also backed excavations of the Hellenistic Villa Tarantola cemetery in the 1960s.

Excavations in the cemeteries suggest that there was contact with the eastern Mediterranean from the 8th century BC. One of the tombs had a faience vase bearing the cartouche of the Egyptian pharaoh Boccohoris (late 8th century BC); a scarab of the same pharaoh was found in a grave on the island of Ischia in the Bay of Naples.

In recent years archaeologists have carried out photographic probes of the tombs at Tarquinia, by inserting a camera into a small hole dug into the tomb. This provides a photographic record of the contents of the tomb before they are exposed to the light.

Painted tombs

A burial chamber of the mid-6th century BC, known as the Tomb of the Bulls, includes a fresco depicting the ambush of Prince Troilus by Achilles during the Trojan War. Sporting events, including discus-throwing, are portrayed on the walls of the Tomb of the Olympic Games. The natural

Above A banqueting scene in the Tomb of the Leopards shows one man holding an egg, the symbol of life after death. All are wearing crowns of laurel for the festive occasion.

world is represented in the decoration of the Tomb of Hunting and Fishing, dated to about 520 BC, which includes scenes of birds and dolphins and fishermen casting their nets. The Tomb of the Leopards (early 5th century BC) shows a banqueting scene.

One of the features of the tombs was the inclusion of false architectural details, so that the tombs resemble the rooms of a house. This technique can be seen in the Tomb of the Augurs (late 6th century BC), where a double door is flanked by two figures with arms outstretched.

Left This gold Etruscan earring is dated to the 3rd century BC. Etruscan goldwork was of an exceptionally high standard. One technique was granulation, which involved the soldering of tiny beads of gold.

409

Pergamon

In the 3rd to 2nd centuries BC, Pergamon, in north-west Turkey, developed into a major power. Successive Attalid kings transformed the city into one of the most important architectural and cultural centres of the Hellenistic east. Its library was second only to Alexandria's.

The city of Pergamon was established by Philetairos in 283 BC and continued down to 133 BC when King Attalos III bequeathed it to Rome. It stands on a steeply sloping hill, with the royal buildings at the highest point. With its combination of monumental sculptures, Temple of Athena and

theatre, the acropolis at Pergamon seems to have been designed to evoke the acropolis at Athens.

The Altar of Zeus

Antiquities had been removed from the site since the 17th century. The first scientific investigation was instigated

by Carl Humann in the 1870s. He worked with the support of the Royal Museums in Berlin and came to an agreement with the Ottoman authorities that one-third of the finds could be removed. Humann's initial focus was on the monumental Altar of Zeus at the south end of the site. The altar, which measured 36.4 x 34.2m (119 x 112ft), had been constructed by Eumenes II (197-159 BC) to commemorate the defeat of the Gauls, who had arrived in Anatolia in the early 2nd century BC. The altar was surrounded by a continuous 120m- (394ft-) long marble relief frieze – perhaps inspired by the frieze on the Parthenon at Athens – showing a gigantomachy (battle between the Greek gods and giants). The iconography of the frieze also included scenes about Telephos, the mythical forefather of the Attalids.

The precinct of Athena

To the north of the altar was the Doric temple of Athena. This was surrounded by a series of colonnades, or stoas, which carried relief carvings of the weapons of the defeated enemies of Pergamon. The bases of a number of sculptural groups were found in the open space before the temple. These may have included the famous statue groups known from ancient classical authors, such as Pliny the Elder, which commemorated the defeat of the Gauls. It is likely that the

Left In 1871 the front of the Altar of Zeus was shipped to Germany, where it has been reconstructed in the Pergamon Museum, Berlin.

'Dying Gaul' and a group showing the suicide of a Gaul after killing his wife, which were known from Roman copies, were derived from Pergamene originals displayed in this area.

The library

The north stoa of the precinct of Athena also provided access to the celebrated library of Pergamon. Study of the holes for mounting the shelving has allowed scholars to estimate that the reading room alone would have stored some 20,000 papyri, perhaps one-tenth of the total for the library. Inside the reading room was a colossal statue of Athena, which may have been a copy of the Athena Promachos from the Athenian acropolis.

The Trajaneum

At the northern end of the acropolis was the Trajaneum. Built in the Corinthian style with 6 x 9 columns, this temple was the focus for worship of the deified Roman emperor Trajan, completed by his successor Hadrian (ruled AD 117-138). In the excavation of the site, remnants of sculptures of both emperors were found.

Above Only ruins survive of the Trajaneum, which originally stood 18m (60ft) tall.

Theatre of Dionysos

On the western slope of the acropolis, below the Temple of Athena, was located the steeply raked Theatre of Dionysos, god of wine. The top row was some 36m (118ft) above the level of the actors. The theatre provided a focal point for the acropolis to anyone approaching the city from the west. The 80 rows of seats would have held an audience of about 10,000 people. The bottom of the theatre was level with a long terrace, which provided access to the Temple of Dionysos. Plays were performed on a portable wooden stage, which was removed between performances and stored in the theatre terrace's lower floors. Three rows of quadrangular holes remain in the floor of the theatre terrace that once held the wooden support beams for the temporary stage.

Sanctuary of Asklepios

In the lower city there was a major Sanctuary of Asklepios, the healing god. This seems to have been established in the 4th century BC and was one of the three main healing centres of the god in the Aegean, alongside Kos and Epidauros. The sanctuary received a number of benefactions during the Roman period. One of the most notable was the domed temple itself, given by the Roman consul Lucius Cuspius Pactumeius Rufinus in the middle of the 2nd century AD. The design appears to have been based on the Pantheon at Rome.

Below An aerial view of the acropolis shows the Trajaneum at the centre, with the columns at the rear outlining the northern portico.

Carthage

*Founded as a Phoenician colony on the Tunisian coast near Tunis, ancient
Carthage rose to become one of the great powers of the Mediterranean
and Rome's most dangerous rival. In 146 BC the city was destroyed by
Rome. However, archaeologists have still been able to make discoveries.*

The site was excavated by Charles
Ernest Beulé from the 1850s. In 1925
Francis W. Kelsey excavated the *tophet*,
the sanctuary sacred to the deities Tanit
and Baal Hammon, and found it to
contain the remains of children who
had been sacrificed. This was the
subject of a series of rescue excavations
in the 1970s supported by UNESCO.

The German archaeologist F. Rakob
uncovered the earliest levels relating to
the Phoenicians. These date to the 8th
century BC, which roughly corresponds
to the traditional foundation date of
814 BC given in ancient texts.

The city

Details about the range of religious
temples has come from Punic
(Phoenician) inscriptions, although
the evidence of religious structures
is slight and reflects the efficiency of
the Roman destruction of the city.
Rescue excavations have revealed
information about the housing. Some
of the wealthier buildings, for example,
had internal colonnades.

The cemeteries of the Phoenician
city were discovered by the Frenchman
Father Delattre in 1878. Some of these
were accessed by vertical shafts and the

lowest levels can be more than 30m
(98ft) underground. Further work on
the cemeteries is being undertaken by
the University of Georgia.

The harbours

The western Phoenicians spread across
much of the western Mediterranean.
Their strength lay in their ships and
there were two main harbours for the
city. The circular harbour appears to
have been used for the war fleet.
British excavations there have revealed
evidence for activity as early as the
5th century BC. The second rectangular
harbour seems to have been used for
commercial shipping. Other significant
Punic harbour facilities have been
excavated at Motya, in western Sicily,
which was destroyed by the people of
Syracuse in the early 4th century BC.

Roman Carthage

By the middle of the 1st century AD,
Carthage was established as a thriving
Roman colony. Named Colonia Julia
Carthago, after Julius Caesar, it
became the hub of the prosperous
Roman province of North Africa, with
a population peaking at approximately
500,000. Among the remains of the
Roman city are elements of a massive
bath complex, which appears to have
been constructed in the middle of the
2nd century AD. The Romans also
built an aqueduct stretching over
130km (81 miles) to supply the city's
demand for water.

Left Stone stelae, such as these in the *tophet*
sanctuary, were set up over urns containing the
ashes of human sacrifices.

The Domus Aurea

Following a devastating fire in Rome in AD *64, Emperor Nero seized a large area of the ruined city to create a huge palace. Named the Domus Aurea, or Golden House, because of its gold-covered façade, its extravagance shocked the citizens of Rome and amazed the archaeologists who later excavated it.*

The remains of Nero's extravaganza remained buried until the late 15th century, when some chambers were discovered by accident. The scale of the project to the north-east of the Palatine was vast: conservative modern estimates suggest it may have covered at least 50ha (124 acres). It included pavilions, reception rooms, gardens and an artificial lake. At the entrance, Nero placed a colossal statue of himself that was intended to evoke the Colossus of Rhodes. The palace was described by the Roman biographer Suetonius, who mentioned ivory fittings and inlaid jewels in the ceilings. The Domus Aurea was probably the intended setting for works of art that Nero had removed from various cities and sanctuaries in the empire.

After Nero's suicide in AD 68, successive emperors attempted to obliterate the Golden House. The main parts were filled in with earth and built over. Part of the western end is covered by the Baths of Trajan. The artificial lake was drained and became the site of the Flavian Colosseum.

A palace fit for a feast

Excavations beneath the Baths of Trajan have revealed parts of Nero's building. Just over half of the length of the building has been explored, and originally it must have been approximately 400m (1312ft) long. One of the major features of the palace was the provision made for huge banquets. Some 50 dining rooms have been found arranged round a rectangular courtyard in the western end of the complex.

Above The Domus Aurea still lies under the ruins of the Baths of Trajan.

Below The octagonal room has smaller rooms that radiate from it.

At the centre of the western wing was an octagonal courtyard covered by a concrete dome with a central oculus (opening) to let in light. This was surrounded by five dining rooms, each with a water feature. On either side would have been two polygonal courtyards; the western one, which still survives, is itself surrounded by 15 dining rooms.

Although the palace was stripped of its treasures by subsequent emperors, fine frescoes and mosaics on the walls and ceilings have survived, and they provided inspiration for Renaissance artists such as Raphael. One of the long connecting corridors had apparently just been plastered, probably in preparation for a fresco, when the palace was abandoned.

Ostia

Located at the mouth of the River Tiber, Ostia became Rome's principal port in the 1st century AD. Many of its buildings, including apartment blocks, amphitheatre, shops and baths, remain to this day, providing important clues to urban life in the Roman Empire.

Rome's growing population meant that it became increasingly reliant on imported foodstuffs, especially grain. The harbour at Ostia was too shallow for the larger ships to enter, so their goods had to be transferred to smaller vessels to be brought on shore. Grain convoys waiting to be unloaded were occasionally wrecked, leading to shortages and the threat of political unrest. In AD 42, during the rule of Emperor Claudius, work began on the construction of a new permanent and secure harbour, which was completed by his successor Nero (AD 54-68).

The port's facilities underwent further improvements under Emperor Trajan, who ruled AD 98-117, with the construction of a hexagonal harbour. There was space for at least 100 ships, and cargoes could be offloaded into

Below A mosaic shows ships entering the harbour of Ostia, represented by the central lighthouse. The inscription reads: 'Here ends every pain'.

a series of warehouses built behind the harbour front. Grain and other materials could then be transported to the city of Rome via a specially constructed canal, which has been identified by a geophysical survey conducted by British archaeologists from the University of Southampton.

With the end of the Roman Empire, Ostia fell slowly into decline and was effectively abandoned in the 9th century AD. The city became a source for building materials and its marble was used in the construction of St Peter's basilica in Rome.

Renewed interest

In the late 18th century Ostia attracted the interests of dealers in antiquities — among them the Scotsman Gavin Hamilton — who supplied the European elite on their Grand Tour. As Ostia was part of the papal possessions a series of studies were made during the 19th century, initially at the prompting of Pope Pius VII. One of the

first scientific excavations at Ostia was conducted by Rodolfo Lanciani in the 1870s. The first series of major excavations was conducted from 1907 by Dane Vaglieri. Mussolini encouraged extensive work at Ostia from 1938 in anticipation of the proposed world fair of 1942. The outbreak of World War II, however, meant that scientific excavations did not resume until 1953.

The city revealed

At the heart of the city lay the Piazzale delle Corporazioni. This square was surrounded by a series of small offices for the merchants who used the port. Many of them are named in a series of mosaics. Thus, it has been possible to identify links with Alexandria in Egypt, Carthage in North Africa and Narbonne in Gaul. A theatre, which probably belongs to the early imperial period, was adjacent to the complex. Major public buildings included extensive bath complexes, such as the Maritime Baths. Excavations between

Above The Capitolium, dating back to the 2nd century AD, was built on an unusually high podium so it dominated its surroundings. Six columns used to stand in front of it.

1997 and 2001 by archaeologists from the University of Augsburg have made a study of one of the *macella*, or meat markets, of the city.

The excavations have also revealed aspects of domestic arrangements in a Roman city. A number of housing blocks have been explored. These differ from the traditional houses found in Roman cities, and reflect the growing pressure on space in the expanding urban areas of the imperial period. These structures were usually three storeys high, a height restricted by Roman legislation in the face of poor building. Elsewhere, numerous shops, taverns, workshops and some of the city's communal latrines have been uncovered.

Numerous temples have been discovered, some sacred to standard Roman deities, others to cults introduced from the provinces of the empire. One of the central temples was the Capitolium (Temple of Jupiter, Juno and Minerva). Among the earliest cults to be introduced was that of the Anatolian female deity Cybele, who arrived at the end of the 3rd century BC. A number of *Mithraea* (temples dedicated to the worship of the Persian god, Mithras) have been found in the city. Part of the initiation rites of Mithraism included the ceremonial killing of a bull. Evidence for Egyptian cults, such as Serapis and Isis, have been found, reflecting the close links between Italy and Egypt generated through the trade in grain.

One of Ostia's cemeteries on Isola Sacra – a sacred artificial island – was excavated by G. Calza from 1925-40. The anthropological study of the human remains now forms part of a major project by La Sapienza University in Rome.

Below Traders and craftsmen are buried in tombs in the Isola Sacra cemetery.

Pompeii

Excavation of the ruined city of Pompeii has provided an extraordinary snapshot of Roman life in the 1st century AD. Streets, houses, shops and even people have been frozen in time, just as they were on the fateful summer day in AD 79 when Mount Vesuvius erupted.

Pompeii lies to the south-east of Mount Vesuvius alongside the Bay of Naples in the Italian region of Campania. The city had been buried under ash during the catastrophic volcanic eruption and the site was effectively lost for 1600 years. Many neighbouring communities, most famously Herculaneum, were also destroyed or damaged.

Rediscovery

Remains of the city came to light in 1748 when the first of a series of excavations of the site began. One of the first buildings to be recognized was the Temple of Isis, which had been restored following an earlier earthquake at Pompeii in AD 62.

The first scientific excavations of Pompeii were conducted by the Italian Giuseppe Fiorelli. He had already prepared studies of the history of excavations at Pompeii, and had made a plan of the city, dividing it into *regions* – a system still used today. It was Fiorelli's expertise that brought about the creation of a School of Archaeology at Pompeii (1866-75). Fiorelli was also responsible for the reorganization of the finds from the excavations at Pompeii in the museum at Naples.

Life in a Roman town

The excavated town has revealed much about everyday life. The Forum, the baths, the many shops, taverns and houses, and some out-of-town villas,

Below The oldest known amphitheatre, built in 80 BC, could hold 20,000 spectators. The 2-m (6-ft) parapet would originally have been painted with fighting and hunting scenes.

Above A fresco from the Villa of the Mysteries shows a young woman in bridal yellow arranging her hair, while Cupid holds a mirror.

such as the Villa of the Mysteries, are remarkably well preserved. There are also workshops and markets, complete with the types of objects that were used in them. Elsewhere there is a laundry and even a snack bar (*thermopolium*), where archaeologists discovered a cloth bag containing the previous day's takings. A bakery has loaves of bread still in the oven.

One of the structures excavated is the amphitheatre, which is known from historical texts to have been the site of riots between the citizens of Pompeii and one of its neighbours, Nuceria, in AD 59. Nearby were located the barracks that housed the gladiators who performed at the *ludi*, or games. The city also had two theatres for the performance of plays whose origins lay with the Greek people who had settled in Campania. The largest theatre could accommodate an audience of 5000 people in the open air.

Casts of victims

One of Fiorelli's techniques, first used in 1870, was to take casts of the victims' bodies that had been sealed in the ash. The decomposed bodies had left spaces into which Fiorelli injected plaster to create lifelike models.

These casts show men, women and children at the exact moment that tragedy struck. One man was buried so quickly that he died before he had a chance to lie down. A family carrying their gold jewellery and prized possessions were found in the cellar of the Villa of Diomedes, located outside the walls of the city.

There is even a cast of a guard dog, still wearing its collar and its head pulled by the chain that attached it to the wall.

Above A plaster cast of a man who has slumped down against a wall, covering his face in a desperate attempt to avoid breathing in ash and poisonous gases. Casts have also been made of furniture, food and the roots of plants.

417

Left Like all prosperous Roman cities of the time, Pompeii and Herculaneum had bath houses where people could go to bathe and socialize. The bath houses at Herculaneum were particularly elaborate, with beautiful tile floors, frescoes, marble fountains and sinks, and statues.

paintings that have since been lost. A series of paintings from the Villa of the Mysteries is decorated with scenes showing an initiation ceremony in a cult probably related to Dionysos, god of wine. The decorative schemes of private houses are enhanced by the display of sculptures, including family portraits, and small bronzes.

Writing on the wall

The walls of Pompeii are marked with numerous examples of the Roman custom of wall writing – messages for the public to read. One person wrote: 'I am surprised, oh wall, that having to carry so many stupid writings, you can still stand up'. The walls also featured political messages. Some 2800 political slogans have been collected to date, which provide a

Below The honorary arch of Tiberius or Germanicus is at the north side of the forum. Statues would have been set in the two niches.

Wall paintings

The burial of Pompeii meant that wall paintings, which do not normally survive from antiquity, could be studied. Following the devastating earthquake of AD 62, a number of houses in the city were undergoing redecoration when the AD 79 eruption struck. The art collection of one resident was found stored in a room, to keep it safe while building work was being carried out.

It has been possible to identify a sequence of decorative styles – first analyzed by August Mau in 1882 – which have been used to date late republican and early imperial wall paintings. There was use of fantastic architectural forms and an attempt to evoke a range of exotic marbles. Many of the paintings appear to copy Greek

valuable insight into Roman politics at the time. The city was controlled by a series of magistrates, such as *duoviri* and *aediles*, who were elected on an annual basis. One study has reconstructed the list of candidates for office for the nine-year period prior to the eruption. Some of the texts show that individuals supported a package of candidates for office.

The latest research

Recent geological work has been able to explain the pattern of the volcanic eruption and the sequence for the series of flows of volcanic fragments (pyroclastic) that swept down onto the city. This enhances the contemporary eyewitness accounts by the Younger Pliny whose uncle, Pliny the Elder, died during the disaster.

The initial cloud that came up from the mountain contained ash and pumice, and it seems that debris was deposited towards the south of the eruption. Pliny's account mentions that individuals had to tie pillows to their heads to try to protect themselves from the debris, or lapilli.

As ash accumulated at Pompeii, rows of houses would have collapsed, thereby denying the occupants any sense of protection. The earliest pyroclastic flows hit Pompeii on the morning of 25 August, destroying the villas that were situated outside its walls. Around 7.30 a.m. a further surge broke over the city. As many of the bodies were found above the 2.5m- (8ft-) deep layer of pumice, it has been estimated that approximately 10 per cent of the city may have been killed at this point.

One relatively modern approach to the study of Pompeii has been through the work carried out by Wilhelmina Jashemski on the gardens of the city. She was able to study the remains of plant roots alongside pollen analysis to reconstruct the range of plants used in the 1st century AD. Excavation revealed that parts of some of the gardens at Pompeii were given over to the cultivation of vegetables and vines. There is also evidence of the cultivation of citrus trees.

Herculaneum

The neighbouring town of Herculaneum had been buried by a series of pyroclastic flows – ground-hugging avalanches of hot ash, pumice, rock fragments and volcanic gas – in the early hours of the morning of 25 August. There was little warning, and it may have taken as little as four minutes for the flow to travel from the slopes of Vesuvius to the town.

Remains at Herculaneum were first discovered in 1711 when a well was being dug at a depth of 15-18m (50-60ft). Early excavations were conducted by cutting a series of horizontal tunnels and extracting whatever antiquities had been found. Some of the earliest exploration was in the area of the theatre; among the early finds was the larger-than-life-size bronze statue of Lucius Mammius Maximus, who appears to have been a freedman (a slave who has been given his freedom). Excavations were conducted sporadically throughout the 19th century.

The intense heat of the pyroclastic flows had caused rapid carbonization (partial burning). Herculaneum has yielded some of the best examples of organic remains, including timber, furniture, cloth and even loaves of bread. In 1982 excavations by the seafront in a series of boat-sheds uncovered remains of the bodies of victims who had sought refuge during the eruption. Careful excavation has shown how they were smothered as the pyroclastic flows hit the city. Evidence of flying debris was discovered in fractured bones. Studies of the bodies has revealed significant information about the lifestyles and ages of the individuals. This find has challenged earlier theories that few people had been killed in Herculaneum; renewed estimates suggest that thousands may have died in the eruption.

Excavations have uncovered remains of one of the main bath complexes as well as the edge of the forum area. Among the private residences was the Villa of the Papyri, so-called because of the discovery of more than 1000 carbonized papyrus rolls from the library of Lucius Calpurnius Piso Caesonius, an elite member of the community.

Above The excavated buildings at Herculaneum can be seen with Mount Vesuvius looming in the background. Much of the city remains unexcavated.

Masada

The fortress-palace of Masada, built by Herod the Great (ruled 37-4 BC), is famous as the last stronghold of Jews in the Jewish Revolt of AD 66-73. Facing Roman invasion after a six-month siege, over 960 Jews — men, women and children — committed mass suicide on the rock in AD 73.

Roman activities at Masada were recorded by the Jewish historian Josephus (AD 37-c.100) in his account of the Jewish War. The site, on the edge of the Judean Desert at the southern end of the Dead Sea, was first identified in 1838 by the American scholars Edward Robinson and Eli Smith. In 1867 the site was surveyed by Charles Warren, on behalf of the Palestine Exploration Fund.

Herod's fortifications

An important survey of Masada was made in 1955-56, on behalf of the Israel Exploration Society. This led to

Below The remains of the defensive wall on the plateau of the rock, which rises about 440m (1444ft) above the Dead Sea.

a major excavation made by the Israeli archaeologist Yigael Yadin (1963–65). Among the buildings uncovered was Herod's stunningly constructed palace at the north end of the rocky outcrop.

The palace effectively hangs above the ravine and gives views northwards over the Dead Sea and the Judean Desert. Massive terraces had to be put into place to support the palace.

The decoration of the palace, in Roman style with Corinthian columns and wall paintings imitating panels of fine marble, indicates the strong links between Herod and the Roman world. On the uppermost terrace Yadin discovered a Roman-style bath house — further evidence of how far Roman cultural customs had begun to be adopted by the ruling elite in Judea.

A synagogue was discovered on the western side of the plateau. This had four tiers of plastered benches along the walls and two rows of columns in the centre. Also unearthed were fragments of Old Testament scrolls, containing parts of the books of Deuteronomy and Ezekiel.

The occupation period

During the siege in AD 73 by the 10th Roman legion, Masada was completely encircled by a series of Roman siege walls supported by eight forts. These had been plotted in the 1920s by the British Royal Air Force. Further detailed study was conducted by the British scholar Sir Ian Richmond, who was able to produce a detailed map of the structures.

Qumran

In 1947 the unexpected discovery of biblical scrolls, often called the Dead Sea Scrolls, encouraged the exploration and excavation of a series of caves on the eastern edge of the Judean Desert at the north-western end of the Dead Sea. Nearby was located a complex at Khirbet Qumran, which was excavated by Roland de Vaux from 1951 to 1956.

By the end of 30 BC the site seems to have been the location for a Jewish religious community, which has been linked to a Jewish sect known as the Essenes. Coins dating from the time of the Jewish Revolt suggest that the settlement had been abandoned in AD 68.

Pottery found at Qumran appears to be the same as that found in the caves where the scrolls were discovered. It has been suggested that the scrolls may have been prepared at the main site, where there is apparent evidence of a scriptorium, or writing room, on what must have been an upper floor. Parts of the cemetery have been excavated, which was found to contain the bodies of both men and women; this has raised issues about the prevailing view that this was an all-male community.

Above Fragments of one of the scrolls, known as the Rule of the Community.

The Romans erected a controlling fortress on a plateau immediately opposite the palace; this is likely to have been the camp from where the Roman governor Flavius Silva controlled the operations. Each of the forts was protected by special gateways with an inturned entrance. A massive siege ramp was constructed from the west, protected by the positioning of Roman siege artillery behind it.

Josephus described the drama and tragedy of the mass suicides in AD 73. Rather than fall into Roman hands, first men killed their wives and children, then drew lots to kill the rest of the garrison. However, relatively few bodies have been discovered. Radiocarbon tests on textiles associated with a group of approximately 25 skeletons suggest a date broadly in keeping with the capture of Masada. The presence of pig bones, however, has suggested that these bodies may be linked to the Roman garrison that was located at the site for some time after the suppression of the revolt.

Stonehenge A major complex of prehistoric monuments whose purpose is still shrouded in mystery.

Sutton Hoo An Anglo-Saxon burial ship with a wealth of artefacts discovered in England in 1939.

Biskupin A fortified lakeside settlement of timber-built buildings dating back to the 8th century BC.

Skara Brae

North Sea

Baltic Sea

Newgrange

Biskupin

Mezhirich

Sutton Hoo

Stonehenge

E U R O P E

Carnac

Heuneburg

Bay of Biscay

The Alps

The Iceman

Bl a Se

Lascaux

Adriatic Sea

Pyrenees

Lascaux A cave, rediscovered in 1940, with the most spectacular collection of Palaeolithic wall art yet found.

The Iceman The body of a prehistoric man, with some of his belongings, frozen in time for around 5,300 years.

Mezhirich These extraordinary Ice Age dwellings were constructed from the bones and tusks of the woolly mammoth.

422

THE GREAT SITES OF EUROPE

Archaeology as a subject really began in Europe, as educated people tried to learn more about impressive monuments, such as Stonehenge in England. As the world of scholarship in the mid-19th century began to realize that humankind had a very ancient past, the study of prehistoric sites got underway, including the decorated caves of the last Ice Age. We now know that there were people in parts of Europe, such as Atapuerca (Spain), up to a million years ago, so the time scale of the continent's prehistory is immense.

Europe is home to a fascinating and diverse range of important sites and material – from the unsurpassed cave paintings of Lascaux to mysterious stone circles, and from mammoth-bone houses to Iron Age forts. These discoveries – as well as the magnificent ship burial at Sutton Hoo in England and the wonderfully preserved Iceman found in the Tyrolean Alps – provide important clues about our past and ancestors.

Carnac The landscape of this region is studded with impressive Neolithic monuments, including alignments of standing stones.

The Heuneburg The site of a Celtic fortress provides a fascinating glimpse of life in Iron Age Europe.

Skara Brae A unique Neolithic settlement of stone-built houses on Orkney, preserved for thousands of years beneath the sand.

Mezhirich

The Ice Age inhabitants of Mezhirich, in the Ukraine, built their dwellings from the bones and tusks of the woolly mammoth. These extraordinary mammoth-bone houses — along with others discovered at sites in Eastern Europe — represent the world's oldest human architecture.

We often think of the Ice Age people of Europe as having lived in caves, and it is true that when caves were available they were usually the first choice. In many parts of Europe, however, there were few or no caves, and the Palaeolithic (literally meaning 'old stone age') hunters had to live in the open. This required the construction of shelters from whatever materials were available. Although trees were scarce on the steppes of southern Russia and Ukraine, fortunately the bones of mammoths were plentiful, and the Ice Age inhabitants used them

Below The plan shows the mammoth bones at the excavation of Mezhirich Dwelling 4. The long tusks are clearly visible.

to build substantial shelters, which have been described as the most ancient ruins on earth.

The mammoth-bone houses of this treeless plain were built after the last maximum deep freeze of the Ice Age that took place about 20,000-18,000 years ago. Since the number of individual mammoths represented by the bones in these sites is immense, it seems unlikely that they were obtained solely as the result of hunting. Instead, most were probably gathered from the natural accumulations of bones that were found on the periglacial landscape as mammoths died natural deaths over the centuries. When people reoccupied the area as the ice sheets retreated northwards, around 17,000 years ago,

they would have found the bones lying about and selected the ones most suitable for construction. Jaws, tusks, shoulder blades and long bones were lugged back to the settlement sites — no mean feat since mammoth bones can be extremely heavy.

The bone-house dwellers

Along with mammoths, the inhabitants of Mezhirich also hunted bison, bear, reindeer, horse, hares and Arctic fox, along with rodents and birds. They either ranged over vast areas or had a wide network of trading contacts, for crystal, ochre and amber found at Mezhirich came from dozens — even hundreds — of kilometres away. Bone and ivory were worked into beads and pendants, and some of the mammoth bones had traces of paint.

Archaeologists believe that the mammoth-bone houses at Mezhirich and other sites in the Dnieper and Don valleys served as base camps during the long winter on the periglacial steppe. About 25-50 people may have lived at each of these sites for several months at a time. During the short summer, their inhabitants probably dispersed to temporary camps in pursuit of game. As well as serving a functional purpose, these mammoth-bone structures would have provided a strong visual signal about the presence of their inhabitants on the landscape.

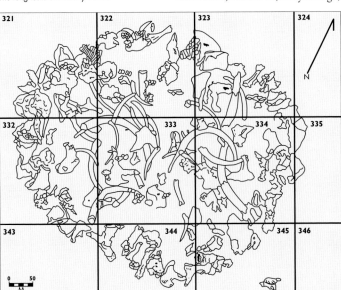

The Mezhirich site

Located along a tributary of the Dnieper river southeast of Kiev, Mezhirich is one of the best-studied and best-preserved Ice Age sites. The mammoth-bone houses here were built about 15,000 years ago.

In 1965 a farmer digging his cellar, almost 2m (6ft 6in) below ground, struck the massive lower jaw of a mammoth with his spade. The jawbone was upside down and had been inserted into the bottom of another jaw.

A year later, the first of several excavation campaigns at the site revealed the traces of four circular structures, each measuring between 6m and 10m (20ft and 33ft) in diameter, plus associated hearths, pits and habitation refuse. Other structures may be present in unexcavated parts of the site. The presence of refuse

Above It is thought that the red design on this painted mammoth skull may represent the flames and sparks of a fire.

layers and hearths confirms the residential nature of these structures.

When excavated the structures appear as jumbles of bones, but careful mapping and study permit the reconstruction of the architecture. Jaws were stacked up to form walls, supplemented by long bones. In one house, 95 mammoth jaws were carefully piled several deep to make an interlocking herringbone pattern of structural bone. Tusks and shoulder blades formed the roof framing, which was probably covered over by hides. Such shelters would have been necessary to protect the inhabitants from the bitter winds that swept across the steppes at

Above This reconstruction is of a Mezhirich mammoth-bone dwelling.

the end of the Ice Age. A hearth inside each hut kept the occupants warm and permitted the cooking of meat.

Spadzista Street

The remains of mammoth bones were also found at a somewhat earlier site in southern Poland, named Spadzista Street B. Recent studies have shown, however, that there are key differences between this site and Mezhirich. At Mezhirich, large bones useful for building were selected from natural accumulations. At Spadzista Street, however, many small bones from extremities, skulls and tails were found. As it seems unlikely that people would have transported such small bones any distance for construction, Spadzista Street has now been interpreted as the site of a mammoth butchery site, possibly a killing site.

Lascaux

Discovered in 1940 by four teenage boys, the cave of Lascaux, situated on a hill above the town of Montignac in Dordogne, France, houses one of the biggest collections of Palaeolithic figures, including about 600 painted animals and abstract signs and almost 1500 engravings.

No proper excavation was ever carried out in Lascaux, and much of the archaeological layer was lost when the floor was lowered and the cave adapted for tourism. Nevertheless, it is clear that this was never a habitation site, and people merely made brief periodic visits for artistic activity or ritual. Charcoal fragments have provided radiocarbon dates around 15,000 BC.

Dazzling imagery

The Palaeolithic entrance of the cave may have been close to the modern artificial entry leading into the great Hall of the Bulls, whose walls are covered in painted figures. They were apparently outlined, and then their infill was done by spraying or with a pad and dampened powder.

The hall's frieze is dominated by a series of four enormous black aurochs bulls (now extinct), over 5m (16ft) in length, as well as smaller horses and tiny deer. The frieze begins at the left with an enigmatic imaginary animal, with two straight horns, known oddly as the 'Unicorn'.

The hall is prolonged by the Axial Gallery, which has a keyhole shape in cross section, and whose upper walls and ceiling were decorated with more paintings of cattle, deer and horses, as well as dots and quadrilateral signs. The figures include the so-called Chinese horses (named because of their superficial resemblance to the style of horses in some Chinese art) and a jumping cow.

Right A detail from one of the paintings of aurochs bulls at Lascaux.

Above The painter of the back-to-back bison has managed to convey a sense of movement.

At the far end is a falling horse, painted upside down around a rock; photographic reproduction has revealed that, although the artist could never see the whole animal at once, it is in perfect proportion. The Lascaux artists also conveyed perspective simply and cleverly by leaving the far limbs of the animals unattached to the bodies.

Leading off to the right from the Hall of the Bulls is the Passage. Here there are almost 400, often small, engravings, dominated numerically (like all of the cave's art) by horses, depicted in the same style as the other paintings. To one side is the Great Apse, which contains over 1000, often superimposed, engravings.

Within the Apse is the entrance to the shaft, 5m (16ft) deep, containing the famous scene of a bird-headed man (the cave's only human figure). He has an erect phallus and is falling backwards in front of an apparently speared bison with its entrails spilling out; a bird on a stick stands nearby, and a rhinoceros painted in a different style walks off to the left.

Beyond the Apse is the Nave, with its frieze of five black deer heads, each 1m (3ft) high and usually described as swimming; the nave also has two painted male bison, facing in different directions, with overlapping rumps. The cave ends with the narrow, 25-m (82-ft) long 'Gallery of the Felines', into which one can only crawl; it is covered in engravings, including six felines.

Techniques

Stone tools suitable for engraving were found only in the engraved zones. Many lamps were recovered. The cave contained 158 mineral fragments, together with crude mortars and pestles stained with pigment. There are scratches and signs of wear on many of the mineral lumps. Black dominates, followed by yellows, reds and white. Chemical analysis revealed sophisticated uses of heating and mixing of different minerals to produce a variety of hues.

For much of the decoration, ladders or scaffolding must have been used. In the Axial Gallery there are sockets cut into the rock on both sides, which probably held branches forming joists for a platform, to provide access to the upper walls and ceiling.

Although seen in recent decades as a homogeneous cave, whose art was produced within a few centuries of 15,000 BC, Lascaux is currently undergoing reappraisal. Its history now seems far more complex, with a number of decorative episodes, possibly scattered through millennia.

Motivation

Many different theories have been put forward to explain the phenomenon of Ice Age cave art, from being used as hunting magic to depicting fantasies involving shamans and trance imagery. There is no doubt that some cave art – though by no means all – had a strong religious motivation of some kind, and much of it was probably linked to mythology, and the transmission of information of different kinds.

Lascaux II

The cave opened to the public in 1948, but it had to be closed again in 1963 when it was realized that the numbers of visitors (eventually reaching 100,000 per year) were having a radical effect on the cave's micro-environment, and causing the proliferation of algae and bacteria. These problems have now been largely overcome, and although the public is no longer admitted, a facsimile of the cave and its paintings has been made nearby. Opened in 1983, Lascaux II receives 300,000 visitors per year.

Stonehenge

Located on Salisbury Plain in Wiltshire in southern England, Stonehenge is Britain's most famous and enigmatic prehistoric monument. The original purpose and meaning of this complex structure of stone and earth, which first began to be built around 5000 years ago, is still shrouded in mystery.

Excavations and radiocarbon dating carried out at the site over the years have revealed that Stonehenge is the remnants of at least three different circles. The first monument, dated to about 2950 BC, was a simple circular enclosure – an earthen bank with a ditch on the outside, and two entrances at north-east and south. Such ritual structures, called 'henges',

are well known in Britain, although their ditch is usually on the inside. The depth of the Stonehenge ditch was about 2m (6ft 6in), and the chalk excavated from it was piled up to form the interior bank, which was also about 2m (6ft 6in) high.

A circle of 56 holes was dug within the henge. These holes are known as Aubrey holes, after their 17th-century

discoverer, John Aubrey. The holes do not seem to have contained posts or upright stones, and they were later filled in – many contained cremation ashes. Also at this time, two great stones were erected at the entrance. One of them, known as the heel stone, still survives.

The second and third stages

In around 2600 BC the so-called bluestones were erected in a circle, after probably being transported 322km (200 miles) from the Preseli Hills of South Wales. Some specialists insist that the bluestones arrived in the vicinity of Stonehenge as erratics, through natural glacial action during the Ice Age. However, there is a total absence of such rocks in Wessex except in prehistoric monuments. So unless one argues that prehistoric people used every single large bluestone in the area, the only other explanation is that the rocks were brought to the area through human transport, despite the great distances and efforts required.

Finally, around 2300 BC, the great blocks of sarsen stone (a hard sandstone), weighing 25 to 45 tonnes, were hauled by hundreds of people more than 32km (20 miles) to the site. These enormous sarsen stones were set up as a ring of uprights with their unique lintels. Within this circle was an inner horseshoe setting of five trilithons ('three stones'), each

Left The inner horseshoe arrangement of towering trilithons is clearly visible in this aerial view of Stonehenge.

Above The standing stones and trilithons cast shadows across the surrounding grassland of Salisbury Plain.

comprising two uprights with a horizontal stone on top. The lintels, weighing 9 tonnes, were held in place with mortise and tenon joints.

In 1953 some petroglyphs (carvings on rock) of prehistoric daggers and axe-heads were discovered on one of the sarsen uprights in the horseshoe, and more were detected recently, thanks to laser scanning.

Excavations at Stonehenge have recovered an abundance of sarsen 'mauls', battered round stones ranging from tennis- to soccer-ball size. These were used to bash and

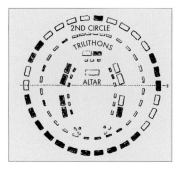

Above This 19th-century engraving shows a plan of Stonehenge, during a time that saw many, often damaging, excavations by amateurs.

shape the surface of the sarsens and bluestones, and to carve the mortises and tenons.

The monument, approached by an 'avenue' of twin banks 12m (39ft) apart and 2.5km (1¹/₂ miles) long, was abandoned in about 1600 BC, after 1400 years of continuous use. The finished monument would have been visible from kilometres around, and many of the clusters of Bronze Age round barrows (burial mounds) were placed on ridges that were visible from the ceremonial site.

What was it for?

Nobody knows who built these monuments or why. In the 12th century the English writer Geoffrey of Monmouth claimed that Merlin had removed the stones from Ireland and rebuilt them in England. The 17th-century architect Inigo Jones saw it as a Roman temple, while in the 18th century the antiquarian William Stukeley attributed it to the Druids — as do many people today. Yet Druids had nothing to do with building the monument, since they emerged in Britain more than 1000 years after Stonehenge was finished.

Stonehenge was likely a ritual site for ceremonialism. It had some astronomical or calendrical function, since the sun rises over the heel stone on midsummer's day and the

monument's north-east/south-west axial alignment is upon the midwinter sunset. In the 1960s and '70s the astronomical aspect was exaggerated by astronomers who thought the monument had been a sophisticated eclipse predictor. These claims have been criticized by recent researchers.

A monumental landscape

Stonehenge was surrounded by a monumental landscape of tombs, enclosures and ceremonial sites, including the famous megalithic tombs known as the Kennet long barrows, and Silbury Hill, the greatest prehistoric mound in Europe. But above all, there is Avebury, 32km (20 miles) away from Stonehenge. The largest stone circle in Europe, enclosing an area of 11 hectares (28 acres), Avebury comprised numerous 20-tonne sarsen stones, which were erected about 5000 years ago in a circle within a massive circular ditch and bank earthwork. The monument was under construction and in use for about 1500 years, and the whole of Stonehenge could easily be fitted inside either of Avebury's inner circles. Like Stonehenge, Avebury defies attempts to unlock its mysteries.

The Iceman

In 1991 a German couple hiking in the Tyrolean Alps spotted a yellow-brown human body emerging from the ice near the Similaun glacier in the Ötztaler Alps. The Iceman, Similaun Man, or 'Ötzi', as the body was named, is the oldest fully preserved human to have survived from prehistory.

The corpse, which lay at an altitude of more than 3200m (10,500ft), was crudely excavated because nobody had any idea of its age or importance. It was taken to Innsbruck University, Austria, while the many objects and garments later found in the vicinity were taken to Mainz, Germany, to be preserved. Because measurements taken at the spot proved that the body

Below The desiccated body of the Iceman was photographed at the spot where he was discovered in 1991, near the Similaun glacier.

had been lying 93m (305ft) inside the Italian border, in 1998 Ötzi was transferred to a museum in Bolzano, where he is displayed today in a chamber with constant humidity and a temperature of -6°C (21°F), along with all his restored equipment.

The first assessment of the Iceman's axe was that it had a bronze blade, and that the body was probably 4000 years old. Subsequent examination, however, showed that the metal was almost pure copper, and radiocarbon dating of the body, of grass from its

garments and of artefacts placed the Iceman to about 5350 to 5100 years ago, the Copper Age (Late Neolithic) in this region.

Clothes and toolkit

Analyses of the Iceman's well-preserved equipment and garments have revealed much about the tremendous range of materials and techniques used in prehistoric life. For example, 18 types of wood have been identified in the 70 artefacts. These include a flint dagger with an ashwood

shaft in a woven grass sheath and an unfinished yew-wood long-bow. The Iceman's axe, 60cm (24in) in length, had a yew-wood handle and a copper blade glued in place with birch pitch and leather straps. A deerskin quiver held 14 arrows of viburnum and dogwood. Two sewn birch-bark containers held what may be embers for starting a fire, while a short rod of linden wood, with a piece of antler embedded at one end, was probably used for working flint tools. Two round pieces of birch fungus, attached to leather slips, are thought to have some medicinal purpose. There was a marble disc with a perforation at its centre, which was attached to a leather strip and a tassel of leather thongs. The Iceman was also carrying what could have been a fur backpack with a frame of hazel and larchwood.

Microscopic analysis of the tool surfaces revealed traces of animal hair, blood and tissue, suggesting that the Iceman had recently killed or butchered a number of animals, such as chamois, ibex and deer. Deposits of large, partly cooked or heated starch grains on the axe blade imply that one of his last acts was to repair or refit the shaft while eating porridge.

The Iceman's clothing comprised much-repaired leather shoes (with bearskin soles and deerskin uppers) stuffed with grass for insulation; goat-hide leggings and loincloth; a calfskin belt and pouch; a cape of woven grass or reeds; a coat made up of pieces of tanned goat hide, sewn together with animal sinews; and a bearskin cap. The supposed backpack may, in fact, be the remains of one snowshoe.

How did he die?

Much speculation concerns the Iceman's identity and his cause of death. DNA analysis of his intestinal contents revealed that his last meal consisted of red deer meat and possibly cereals, while earlier he had also eaten some ibex. Hornbeam pollen in his stomach shows that he probably died in June. The pollen (inhaled about six hours before his

death), as well as the kinds of flint in his equipment, show that he came from the Katarinaberg area, to the south in Italy.

The man was in his mid- to late 40s (quite old for the time), dark-skinned, around 1.57m (5ft 2in) in height, and weighed about 50kg (110lb). He was not in good shape. His lungs were blackened by the smoke from fires; he had hardened arteries; his teeth were worn (probably from coarsely ground grain); his toes showed traces of frostbite; and some of his ribs had been fractured and healed. There are small tattoos – short lines and a cross – on his lower back, knees, ankles and left wrist, which were made by rubbing charcoal into small cuts. These marks may be therapeutic, aimed at relieving arthritis.

One of the Iceman's fingernails was recovered, and dark lines in it have revealed that the man suffered regular periods of severe disease or malnutrition (which affects nail growth) during the months before his death. So he was an already enfeebled individual, perhaps caught by a storm on the mountain, who succumbed to the elements.

Above The Iceman's well-preserved belongings – including his well-worn shoes packed with grass for insulation – have provided a unique time-capsule of the kinds of objects made from organic materials that were used by prehistoric man.

A CT scan taken in 2001 revealed the presence of a stone arrowhead in the Iceman's upper left shoulder, but it is unclear whether this arrowhead was responsible for killing him – if it did, where is its shaft? His own arrows were beautifully preserved, so why did the shaft of this one disappear? Could it be the vestige of an old hunting accident?

Two deep wounds have also been detected on the Iceman's right hand and wrist, and it appears that something sharp penetrated the base of his right thumb, causing a serious wound not long before he died. These marks have led to speculation about hand-to-hand fighting.

In short, even after 15 years of study, the Iceman is still presenting us with enigmas and surprises, and we still do not know exactly how he died, let alone what his occupation was or why he was on the mountain.

Carnac

The landscape around the French seaside resort of Carnac, on the Morbihan coast of southern Brittany, is studded with Neolithic ritual monuments. The region has the greatest concentration of megalithic monuments, including spectacular standing stones, in all of Europe.

The area, covering around 300 sq km (116 sq miles), is filled with a profusion of long mounds, passage graves and standing stones known as menhirs, which occur singly and in groups. Yet the archaeological fame of this area comes from the remarkable parallel rows of standing megalithic stones that stretch in some cases for over 1km (0.6 miles).

The Carnac stones had long been the subject of myth, but it was a Scottish antiquary, James Miln, who made the first extensive excavations from around the 1860s.

Carnac mounds

Some of the earliest megalithic monuments to be built at Carnac were the great menhirs and the long mounds, which date from before 4000 BC. The long, low Er-Grah mound was almost 200m (656ft) long when it was built, while Carnac's most impressive mound, Saint-

Below A section of the alignment of standing stones at Le Menec. The stones are smaller at the eastern end, at around 1.5m (5ft), rising to around 4m (13ft) at the wider western end.

Michel, is still 125m (410ft) long today – large enough for a chapel to be built on top of it. Along with several others, they form a distinctive regional type of monument known as 'Carnac mounds'. The mound at Er-Grah originally lacked a central stone chamber, but one was added later, while Saint-Michel contained a small stone cist. Excavations at Saint-Michel, which first began in 1862, yielded remarkable grave goods, including 39 stone axes. Several of the stone axes were made from jadeite, which comes from the Alps.

The Grand Menhir Brisé

Adjacent to the Er-Grah long mound is the Grand Menhir Brisé, a huge granite pillar that stood 20m (66ft) high when it was upright. Now toppled, its four pieces weigh a total of 356 tonnes, making it the largest standing stone known from prehistoric Europe. On one of the pieces is a carving of an enigmatic object that archaeologists have called an 'axe-plow', although recently it has been suggested that this figure, which is repeated on other Carnac megaliths, might represent a whale of the sort seen in the nearby ocean. Archaeologists found a number of holes close to the Grand Menhir Brisé where other large menhirs had stood, although the stones themselves are now missing.

Passage graves

Carnac's great menhirs were pulled down during the 4th millennium BC. The Grand Menhir Brisé was simply too large to be reused, but fragments of others found their way into the next type of monument to be constructed in the Carnac area – the passage graves. Two of the most famous are La Table des Marchand, which is adjacent to the Er-Grah long mound and the prostrate Grand Menhir Brisé, and Gavrinis, which is on a small island just offshore.

The remarkable fact is that pieces of the same menhir found their way into both of these megalithic monuments. Observant archaeologists noticed that horns that had been carved on the enormous stone slab, which formed the roof of the Gavrinis tomb, matched the body of an animal carved on the capstone of La Table des Marchand tomb. Closer examination showed that the broken edges of the stones matched, proving that they were originally one enormous stone, possibly one that had stood near the Grand Menhir Brisé.

The Gavrinis tomb is further known for the profusion of carvings on its stones, including curved lines and concentric semi-circles.

Alignments

The long mounds, great menhirs and passage graves were merely a prelude to the crowning achievement of the Carnac megalith builders – the rows of standing stones known as alignments. These are multiple rows of irregularly spaced menhirs, each several metres tall, which were erected starting just before 3000 BC and ending around 2500 BC. Over the years many of the stones have disappeared, and others have fallen over, but the surviving menhirs give a

Above The passage of the Gavrinis tomb is extensively decorated with patterns of concentric semi-circles and parallel lines.

good impression of how these monuments would have looked to their Neolithic builders.

There are several alignments at Carnac, and several more elsewhere in Brittany, but the most important are Le Menec, Kermario and Kerlescan. At Le Menec, 1050 menhirs stand in ten slightly converging rows that stretch for about 1.2km (0.75 miles) from west to east and are 100m (328ft) across at their widest point, while at Kermario 1029 surviving stones run in seven rows for over 1km (0.6 miles). The Kerlescan alignment is shorter, about 350m (1148ft), but it contains approximately 300 stones in 13 rows.

The purpose of the alignments is unknown. Suggestions that they held astronomical significance have not been widely accepted, as the stones are irregularly spaced and the rows bend slightly. More probable is the theory that they were processional paths that led to stone enclosures in which rituals occurred.

Left A carved stone from La Table des Marchand tomb highlights the artisan's skills.

Newgrange

The Neolithic inhabitants of Ireland constructed enormous burial monuments from large stones (megaliths) that were then covered with smaller stones or earth. The Boyne valley is particularly rich in prehistoric tombs, of which the huge mound of Newgrange is the most famous.

Such megalithic tombs take different forms, but some of the most impressive are the passage tombs, in which a burial chamber is entered by going through a narrow tunnel-like corridor. Passage tombs are found in many parts of Ireland, and they often occur in clusters that form vast cemeteries. In the Boyne valley, the tombs of Knowth, Dowth and Newgrange are the focal points of a huge mortuary and ceremonial complex that existed around 3000 BC.

Newgrange

The tomb was first rediscovered in 1699 by labourers who were looking for building stones. It was at this time that the entrance to the tomb was discovered. A major excavation and restoration project was carried out between 1962 and 1975.

The circular mound is around 85m (279ft) across and 11m (36ft) high. The perimeter is marked with 97 large stones, many of which are decorated with engraved spirals. A passage 19m (62ft) long and lined with upright stone slabs leads into the main burial chamber. The central part of the chamber is roofed with flat stone slabs in circular courses, each one set closer to the centre to form a beehive-shaped ceiling, which reaches its peak 6m (20ft) above the chamber floor. Smaller chambers open off the central part of the chamber to form a cross-shaped plan.

Every year, at the time of the winter solstice, on 21 December, the sun shines directly along the passage into the chamber for about 17 minutes as it rises. The alignment is too precise to have occured by chance. The sun enters the passage through a specially contrived opening, known as a roofbox, directly above the entrance.

Not much was left for archaeologists to find in the chamber other than a few cremated human bones. Based on evidence from other Irish megalithic cemeteries, the chamber would have contained the cremated remains of multiple individuals, along with pottery and other artefacts. The area in front of the entrance would have been the scene of communal ceremonies, while the whole tomb would have been visible from a great distance to reflect the importance of the ancestors whose remains it contained.

Below An impressive façade of white quartz, using stone found at the site, greets the visitor to Newgrange, although its reconstruction has been the subject of archaeological debate.

Skara Brae

Farmers first settled the Orkney Islands off the northern tip of Scotland around 3700 BC. By 3100 BC a large settlement was established at Skara Brae. Scarcity of timber meant the settlers built their houses and furniture of stone, much of which has survived to this day.

After being occupied and rebuilt for centuries, the sandstone houses at Skara Brae – on Mainland, Orkney's largest island – were abandoned and slowly covered over by drifting sand and turf. In the 1920s the eminent prehistorian V. Gordon Childe cleared the sand and exposed the houses in one of his rare excavation projects. The remarkable architectural detail he revealed resulted in Skara Brae becoming one of the most famous Neolithic settlement sites in Europe.

The houses

A trash dump, or midden, had existed on Skara Brae before the Neolithic farmers built their houses. The farmers scooped large pits in the midden, which they then lined with sandstone slabs to form at least eight houses. Each house had a rectangular open area 4m to 6m (13ft to 20ft) across and 3m (10ft) deep. In the centre of each house was a sunken, stone-lined hearth, which would have been used for heating and cooking. Some of the houses had alcoves that open from the central area, and tunnels roofed with stone slabs joined the houses. We do not know how the open areas were roofed. It has been suggested that whale ribs covered with hide were used in place of timber.

Furniture

Stone slabs and blocks were stacked to form shelf units that appear to have been used for storage. Larger bins along the sides may have been filled with straw and furs to make beds. Stone-lined square pits in the house floors had their seams packed with clay to make them watertight, perhaps for storing shellfish.

Above A shelved stone 'dresser' was positioned on the wall opposite the doorway.

Life at Skara Brae

The inhabitants of Skara Brae kept cattle, pigs, goats and sheep, and they fished. They also cultivated barley and wheat on a small scale. Deer and stranded whales yielded additional meat, and sea-bird eggs were gathered.

Bone was used to make beads for necklaces and awls for working hides. Some of the most distinctive artefacts at Skara Brae and other Neolithic sites on Orkney are carved stone balls, which may have served as symbols of status and prestige.

The windswept Orkney landscape has yielded several other such sites of this period, although none as well preserved as Skara Brae. Circles of standing stones and immense passage graves complete the dramatic Neolithic scenery.

Left Each of the dwellings shares the same basic layout, with a central hearth.

The Heuneburg

Situated along the upper Danube in south-west Germany, the Heuneburg was a prosperous early Iron Age hilltop fortress. The powerful chiefs who ruled there controlled the trade with the Greeks in the region. The mud-brick fortifications were evidence of contact with the Mediterranean.

Beginning around 800 BC, central Europe was inhabited by the Celts, whose lands were divided into complex chiefdoms. Between 650 and 450 BC the Celtic chiefdoms in west-central Europe began trading with Greek merchants. This led to remarkable accumulations of wealth and demonstrations of status. One especially prosperous chiefdom was Heuneburg. Built on a hilltop, its fortification system – begun in the late Bronze Age – enclosed an area of 3.3ha (8 acres). Systematic excavations, which began in 1950, have yielded an exceptional amount of artefacts relating to the Celts on the Upper Danube.

The hillfort

During the early Iron Age, around 650 BC, a substantial part of the wall was constructed with Mediterranean-style, sun-dried mudbrick, which ostentatiously demonstrated that the chief had contacts with distant lands and could imitate their building style. The mud-brick wall was suddenly and violently destroyed late in the 6th century BC. Apparently, the hillfort was then rebuilt under new leadership using the standard Celtic method of timber framework and stone.

The interior of the hillfort had the remains of structures that housed the local nobility and specialized pottery and jewellery workshops. Imported goods included Greek black-figure pottery, coral and amphorae (large jars) from the region of Massilia (Marseille), which had contained wine brought up the Rhône valley. An outer settlement covering about 20 hectares (49 acres) stood outside the ramparts. Many of the structures in this settlement were houses, while others were workshops for working bronze and weaving cloth.

The fortress succumbed to a great fire in about 450 BC, after which it seems to have been abandoned forever.

Burial mounds

Further afield, and dating back to the same time as the hillfort, lie several burial mounds where Celtic chieftains were interred. Among these is the Hohmichele tumulus, which at a height of 13m (43ft), is one of the largest in central Europe. Excavations at Hohmichele began in 1936. In the centre was a large burial chamber built of massive oak beams. Although this had been looted in antiquity, archaeologists found grave goods, including a bronze cauldron, a four wheeled-wagon, numerous small ring beads of green glass and even a piece of silk, probably from China.

Below The hillfort has revealed important clues about life in a Celtic settlement over time.

Biskupin

The lowlands of northern Poland are dotted with lakes connected by streams. It was by one of these lakes, at Biskupin 60km (37 miles) north-east of the city of Poznan, that the waterlogged remains of a fortified settlement dating to the 8th century BC was uncovered.

In 1933 a local schoolteacher named Walenty Szwajcer noticed timbers sticking out of the peat at Biskupin. Szwajcer had heard of the famous Swiss Lake Dwellings and thought these might be the traces of a similar find. He reported his discovery to the museum in Poznan and excavations, led by Professor Józef Kostrzewski, began the following summer.

The settlement

Over the following several years, Kostrzewski's excavations revealed the waterlogged remains of a large settlement in which the outlines of timber houses along log streets were clearly visible. A rampart constructed from timber boxes filled with earth and stone surrounded the settlement. At its base, a breakwater of oak logs prevented the lake water from

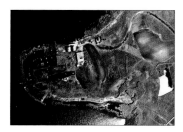

undermining the walls. A gate in the rampart provided the main entrance to the settlement.

The houses at Biskupin were set in continuous rows. They were strikingly uniform. Each consisted of a large central area with a stone hearth, which was entered through a vestibule with a storage area. If there were 7 to 10 inhabitants per house, and a total of about 100 houses, then the population of Biskupin was somewhere between

Left Excavations at Biskupin were technically advanced for their time. In 1935 aerial photographs of the peninsula were taken from a balloon borrowed from the Polish army.

700 and 1000 people. Narrow streets made from timbers ran between the rows of houses, with a larger open area situated just inside the gate.

The inhabitants of Biskupin grew mainly millet, wheat, barley, rye and beans. Pigs provided most of their meat, but they also kept cattle for milk and pulling wagons and ploughs. Wooden wagon wheels and plough-shares have been found in the waterlogged sediments, along with a range of items made from wood, cloth and other perishable materials. The inhabitants of Biskupin were also part of a trade network that extended as far as Italy and Ukraine.

Dating

Accurate dating of Biskupin has been provided by the study of the tree rings of the timbers. Virtually all the trees used in the construction of Biskupin were cut between 747 and 722 BC, and over half of them were cut during the winter of 738-737 BC. The actual duration of the settlement is unclear, but there were several episodes of reconstruction.

Right Reconstruction of the rampart and some of the streets and houses began in 1968. The interiors of the houses have been furnished to show how the inhabitants lived.

Sutton Hoo

The excavation of mounds at Sutton Hoo near the English Suffolk coast in the late 1930s unearthed an Anglo-Saxon boat burial, with a spectacular number of preserved grave goods. Sutton Hoo remains the richest burial site ever discovered in Britain.

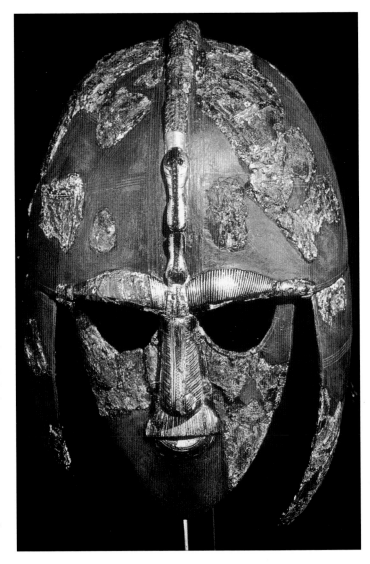

The round burial mounds were on the estate of Mrs Edith May Pretty, who had an interest in the past. She hired a local antiquarian, Basil Brown, to excavate them, and in June 1938 he and two helpers began opening the mounds. Although the first three that they excavated had been robbed in ancient times, enough remained in them to show that the mounds contained cremation burials from the Anglo-Saxon period. In addition, Brown found a number of iron objects that he identified as the rivets used to hold together the planks of ships.

Discovery of the ship

Another excavation campaign in 1939 was concentrated on a single large mound. Here Brown discovered row upon row of iron rivets. He quickly deduced that he had found a buried boat, whose wood had decayed but whose regular pattern of rivets survived. The boat had been used as the tomb of an elite individual. He traced the rows of rivets downward

Above This exquisite gold buckle would have been used to fasten the king's waist belt.

Right This is an extremely rare example of an Anglo-Saxon helmet. It was fitted with decorative foil panels of tinned-bronze, which depict animal motifs as well as scenes from German and Scandinavian mythology. The nose has two small holes cut into it to allow the wearer to breathe freely. The bronze eyebrows are inlaid with silver wire and garnets.

and found that the boat had been 27 m (88ft) long. Word of this discovery spread, and several professional archaeologists soon arrived to give Brown help in documenting the find.

Burial goods

Work proceeded to the central burial chamber in the middle of the boat. Over 17 days of excavation in July and August 1939, an astonishing collection of 263 burial objects was found. Armour and weapons included an iron helmet, a coat of mail, a wooden shield with bronze decoration, a hammer-axe and a sword. Textiles had been preserved, including wall hangings and cloaks. There were gold ornaments and coins; silver bowls, dishes and spoons; bronze hanging bowls; wooden tubs and buckets; and drinking horns with silver decoration. Even traces of a wooden lyre encased in a beaver-skin bag were recovered. The artefacts showed connections with Gaul, Byzantium and North Africa.

Further excavations

Archaeologists have returned to the Sutton Hoo cemetery several times since 1939. More mounds were excavated between 1965 to 1970 and 1983 to 1992, and additional burials have been found recently on the site. A reinvestigation of one of the mounds, originally excavated by Basil Brown in 1938, showed that it too had once contained a ship burial. Some of the burials were cremations with the burnt bones in bronze bowls, while others were uncremated. Under one mound, a young man lay in a coffin in one pit, while his horse lay in another. Several uncremated burials found in the early 1990s are intriguing in that they appear to have met violent deaths – by decapitation or hanging – and were buried face-down.

It was initially supposed that the person buried in the Sutton Hoo ship burial was Raedwald, king of East Anglia between AD 599 and 625, and many scholars continue to accept this attribution. Raedwald had been

baptized into Christianity, but he soon reverted to paganism. While this specific identification is far from certain, the subsequent excavations have established that the Sutton Hoo mounds were indeed a cemetery for the Anglo-Saxon elites between the late 6th and late 7th centuries. After

Above This photograph was taken when the Sutton Hoo ship was under excavation in 1939.

the period of elite pagan burial, the site may have been used as a place for executions, which may account for the victims of violent deaths.

439

Harappa A great city of the Harappan (Indus) civilization, it flourished during the 3rd millennium BC.

Mount Li The life-size Terracotta Army discovered here has been described as the Eighth Wonder of the World.

Peking Man The first skullcap of *Homo erectus* was discovered in 1929 at a Palaeolithic site near Beijing (Peking).

Pazyryk

Altai

Peking Man

Nara

A S I A

Huang (Yellow River)

Mount Li

Taxila

Indus

Himalaya

Chang (Yangtze)

Harappa

Mehrgarh

Brahmaputra

Sanxingdui

Ganga

Dholavira

Pataliputra

Pacific

Ocean

Bay of Bengal

South China Sea

Mekong

Angkor

Mehrgarh Excavations at this site in Pakistan have revealed the earliest evidence for farming in South Asia.

Angkor This vast complex of temples and other buildings in modern Cambodia was once the capital of the mighty Khmer empire.

Nara The many ancient temples, shrines and other buildings reveal Nara's importance as a former capital of Japan.

THE GREAT SITES OF THE FAR EAST

The lands of the Far East are studded with monuments to past civilizations. Archaeologists had long been aware of the importance of many of the region's sites, but other jewels of the Far East have remained hidden until relatively recently. The chance discovery in 1974 of China's Terracotta Army sparked one of the great ongoing archaeological investigations of all time. Most recently, Japan has become prominent not only in exploration of its own past, but also in funding archaeological work in other parts of the world. So much of this vast region – including large areas of Siberia, Mongolia, Central Asia and China – remains relatively unexplored archaeologically. Exciting new discoveries are sure to await us, possibly even including the very timing and location of human evolution. In the meantime, some of the world's most impressive sites – such as the stunning temples at Angkor – bear witness to the awe-inspiring scale of human enterprise in this area of the globe.

Pazyryk Tombs in Siberia have revealed the frozen bodies and possessions of nomads who lived in the 5th to 3rd centuries BC.

Pataliputra By the 4th century BC, this city in northern India had become the spectacular capital of the Mauryan dynasty.

Taxila A World Heritage Site of considerable archaeological importance, it is located in a fertile valley of northern Pakistan.

Peking Man

In the early 1920s two human teeth were found in a cave near the village of Zhoukoudian, not far from Beijing (Peking). Further excavations led to the discovery a few years later of a complete human skullcap. These were the remains of a new genus of human, given the popular name of Peking Man.

Between 1921 and 1966 six nearly complete human crania, or skullcaps, numerous fragments of skulls, 157 teeth, pieces of humerus and various other bone fragments were unearthed from the hills around Zhoukoudian, 42km (26 miles) south-west of Beijing

Below Anthropologists and local workmen dig near the original cave where the Peking Man skull was discovered. The walls are marked in chalk in numbered sections to keep track of what is found.

(Peking). The area had long been a source of ancient animal bones – referred to by local people as 'dragon bones' – which were used in Chinese medicine, and it had therefore attracted the attention of geologists and archaeologists.

Human remains

In February 1918, Johan Gunnar Andersson, a Swedish geologist and mining adviser to the Chinese government, made his first visit to

Zhoukoudian, lured by the rumours of 'dragon bones'. He explored the gullies and caves in the area, and in 1921 he discovered bones and teeth, together with some quartzite cutting tools, which suggested human activity. He sent the collection to Sweden for investigation, and in 1927 announced that two human teeth, one of them a molar, had been discovered among the remains.

The discovery caught the attention of the scientific world as at that time no such human fossils had been discovered in China or any other country in Asia. The Canadian anthropologist Dr Davidson Black, head of the Peking Union Medical College's department of anatomy, identified the find as a previously unknown hominid group, *Sinanthropus pekinensis*, or 'Peking Man'.

More extensive excavations at the Zhoukoudian site began, and in 1929 the Chinese geologist Wenzhong Pei discovered a complete skullcap of Peking Man. Just after this discovery, a second skullcap was found. By 1932 excavation in the area had expanded and employed more than 100 workers. In 1936 another three complete skullcaps were unearthed.

These fruitful excavations came to a halt in 1937, however, when Japan invaded China. They did not restart until 1951.

Who was Peking Man?

Peking Man was classified as a type of *Homo erectus* (upright man) that had inhabited the Zhoukoudian area around 500,000 to 230,000 years ago,

Left Inside one of the caves at Zhoukoudian, archaeologists have identified 13 layers in the excavated deposits.

or charcoal, and researchers concluded that the bones were charred by fire caused by lightning.

The lost fossils

During World War II the more notable fossils, including the five skullcaps, were dispatched to the USA for safekeeping. They disappeared during the journey, however, and have never been recovered. In July 2005 the Chinese government founded a committee to find the bones.

Excavations since World War II have brought to light many more fragments of the Peking Man species, including parts of a skull all from the same person. The pieces were reassembled into a skullcap, and it is now the only original one.

To protect and conserve the site, the State Council of China announced Zhoukoudian to be one of the first State Key Cultural Heritage Units under Protection. The site was placed on UNESCO's World Heritage List in 1987, and since 1997 a joint UNESCO-China project has been set up to preserve Zhoukoudian.

Below A reconstruction of Peking Man's skull shows that his teeth were larger and more robust than those of *Homo sapiens*.

during the Middle Pleistocene. Based on pollen analysis, scientists decided that Peking Man lived at this site during an interglacial period. The climate was a little warmer than it is today, and the area was covered with grassland and trees. Hazelnut, pine, elm and fruit were all part of Peking Man's diet.

Peking Man was a hunter, gatherer, toolmaker and cave-dweller. The discovery of stone scrapers and choppers, as well as several hand axes, indicated that he used a variety of tools for different tasks. Scientific research revealed that the average capacity of his brain was 1088ml (nearly 2 pints). That of a modern man is 1400ml ($2^{1}/_{2}$ pints). He was up to 1.56m (5ft) tall.

Early excavators of the site also claimed to have uncovered hearths, and they were convinced that Peking Man had learned to use fire for cooking. As a result, scientists redated the earliest human mastery of fire from 100,000 to more than 400,000 years ago. However, in the 1990s new discoveries and research revealed no evidence for hearths, ash

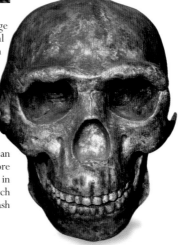

Mehrgarh

In the 1970s a French team excavating at Mehrgarh in western Pakistan discovered the remains of a village that had been occupied in the 7th millennium BC. Three decades later, Mehrgarh is still the only farming settlement of this antiquity known in South Asia.

The settlement lay above a gorge cut by the Bolan River on the Kachi plain, where the mountains of Baluchistan meet the Indus plain. As part of their work the French team examined ancient deposits in the side of the gorge. They were excited when they found traces of material unlike anything previously known in the Indian subcontinent.

The settlement

The people who lived at the settlement had hunted local game, but they also cultivated wheat and barley and raised sheep and goats, like the farmers whose communities were emerging in contemporary West Asia, Iran and the Caspian region. They also domesticated local zebu cattle.

Archaeologists are still debating whether the people who settled at Mehrgarh originated from West Asia or were local people who had acquired West Asian domestic plants and animals through trade links. Shells from the Arabian Sea and turquoise from Turkmenia found at the site are both evidence that there were wide-ranging exchange networks.

The originally dwellings on the site were simple mud houses, but the buildings took on a semi-permanent nature by 5000 BC, when they were made with mud bricks. By 5500 BC the people of Mehrgarh had begun to make pottery. Mehrgarh's inhabitants were skilled artisans who made beads from many materials, including shells, bone, lapis lazuli, steatite (soapstone), calcite and limestone. One bead has been found made of native copper.

Recently it has been discovered that the tiny stone drills used to perforate their beads had another, surprising, purpose – they were also used for treating toothache. Researchers at the Univeristy of Missouri-Columbia, led by Andrea Cucina, were cleaning the jaws and teeth of fossils found at Mehrgarh when they discovered small holes in some of the teeth. These holes were drilled to relieve the pain in decayed teeth and were probably filled with an organic material.

By the 4th millennium BC the settlement had grown into a major town, becoming a centre of industries that included metal-working and the manufacture of terracotta figurines. These figurines often wear elaborate headdresses and strings of beads

Above The excavated remains at the site include a complex of large, compartmented mud-brick structures, which were probably used as storerooms.

around their necks and waists. Some are shown holding a baby and they are often interpreted as mother goddesses.

During the Harappan (Indus) period (c.2500-1900 BC), however, Mehrgarh appears to have been abandoned for the nearby town of Nausharo.

In the early 2nd millennium BC, burials at Mehrgarh reflected the presence of outsiders, probably from the prosperous culture that had developed in Bactria and Margiana. Similar material was found at Pirak, a new town that developed after the decline of the Harappan civilization.

Harappa

Excavations at the city of Harappa in the Punjab region of Pakistan have yielded a wealth of information about the still largely enigmatic Harappan (Indus) Bronze Age culture, the first great civilization of the Indian subcontinent.

The city of Harappa in the Indus Valley was visited several times by the 19th-century archaeologist Sir Alexander Cunningham. He published a selection of finds from the site, including a steatite stamp seal, although he had no inkling of its great antiquity. Unfortunately in the 1850s the site was used as a brick quarry to provide ballast in the construction of the Lahore to Multan railway.

A large quantity of Harappa's ancient mud bricks had been removed and it was a sadly reduced site when excavations, under the British archaeologist Sir John Marshall, started in the 1920s and its importance began to be realized. A modern town covering part of the settlement has also restricted work here. In spite of these problems, excavations at Harappa and Mohenjo-Daro – the other great city of the Indus Valley, which lay 644km (400 miles) to the south – have provided important clues about the Harappan civilization.

The apparently sudden emergence of the Indus civilization has always been something of a puzzle. Recent discoveries, however, have shown that Harappa evolved gradually from a village settlement established in the mid-4th millennium BC into a thriving town, where the beginnings of a script and a system of weights reflected a growing complexity. Unlike many other contemporary Indus towns, Harappa was not destroyed or rebuilt in the crucial Transition period (2600-2500 BC), but it continued to grow, eventually becoming a city of around 150ha (370 acres).

The city

Excavations in the Marshall era exposed brick-built houses. As at Mohenjo-Daro, these were laid out along streets with excellent drains, although Harappa, located beside the river Ravi (a tributary of the Indus),

Below The streets of Harappa were laid out following the cardinal directions, and the houses were built of bricks of uniform size.

Above A series of working floors built of characteristic Harappan bricks were located north of the citadel. It is thought that the platforms were used for threshing grain. A recently excavated example may have had a wooden mortar in its centre.

had few wells. As at Mohenjo-Daro there was a raised mound ('citadel') where in the 1940s Sir Mortimer Wheeler excavated massive walls and gateways. The buildings that had once graced the mound's summit had, however, been destroyed. North of the citadel Wheeler also uncovered a large ventilated storage building, which was dubbed 'the granary', but it was more probably a palace or public building. He also discovered a series of circular working floors and small buildings, which he interpreted as the mean dwellings of downtrodden workers. More recent work suggests that these were in fact workshops.

A combined Pakistani and American team conducted modern scientific excavations and field work at Harappa between 1986 and 2001. Their investigations revealed that the city

included at least three, and probably more, separately walled mounds in the Mature Harappan period (c.2500-1900 BC). The massive walls, with their sophisticated gateways, formed part of brick platforms that raised the city above the level at which there was risk of flooding from the nearby river. The gateways gave the authorities control over who came into and out of the city and were probably used as customs posts to extract taxes or duties on goods brought into or leaving the city.

Several cemeteries were uncovered south of the city. In the Mature Harappan period people were placed in graves that were sometimes lined with bricks, often with a layer of pottery vessels. Some burials had shrouds and wooden coffins. The deceased had few grave goods apart from pottery but the women often wore shell bangles, and some individuals had strings of beads. The

Left Terracotta 'mother-goddess' figurines such as this were a distinctive feature of Harappan culture.

Dholavira

Contrary to earlier theories that the Harappan civilization gradually expanded south into India's Gujarat region, recent discoveries have revealed early Harappan farming settlements there. Among these was Dholavira, which by 2600 BC was a town surrounded by a substantial stone and brick wall. This grew into a great city, with industrial quarters for shell-working, potting, bead-making and other crafts.

The site, rediscovered in the 1960s, has been under excavation by the Archaeological Survey of India since 1990. Dholavira initially had a raised citadel and a walled Middle Town with a grid pattern of streets and lanes. After a serious earthquake it was rebuilt and extended, creating a Lower Town in the east. An area of the Middle Town adjacent to the citadel was cleared to form a large, open public space. The citadel was divided into two separately walled parts – the lower 'Bailey' and the higher 'Castle', which had a gateway in each wall, and was probably accessible only to the privileged few. A ramp led up to a terrace in front to the main – north – gate.

Local water supplies were inadequate for the city's 5000-10,000 inhabitants, who excavated 16 massive water tanks along the inner face of the city wall. These collected rainwater and were filled by damming two seasonal streams.

One of the most significant discoveries are the remains of a wooden signboard in one of the side rooms of the northern gateway. This board, which would probably have been placed originally above the gateway, was set with ten gypsum signs in the Indus script. Despite decades of study this script still cannot be deciphered, so the board's message is unknown. Its existence, however, shows that writing was an integral part of life.

Left This charming Harappan terracotta is a model of a bird in a cage.

were worked; beads were crafted from many materials; and steatite was cut into seals.

The city was well placed to procure resources from areas to the north, including timber from the Himalayas, which was floated downriver. Some was shipped to Mesopotamia with which the Harappans enjoyed flourishing trading relations. The Harappans established a trading outpost at Shortugai on the Amu-Darya (Oxus) River in northern Afghanistan to access the region's rich mineral resources. These included tin, gold and lapis lazuli, the beautiful blue stone that was one of the most highly prized commodities in the ancient world.

Harappa's location also made good use of local resources: agricultural land in the river valley, pasture for its cattle on the adjacent higher ground, and fish in the river. In addition, it could draw on the produce of other parts of the Harappan realms; for instance, dried marine fish were brought here from the Arabian Sea coast, some 885km (550 miles) away.

There is still much to be learned about the site, most of which remains unexcavated. In 2005 plans to redevelop a site adjacent to the ruins were cancelled when a large quantity of new artefacts was discovered.

other cemetery, where the graves contained beautiful painted pottery, belonged to a later period when the city was in decline.

A flourishing economy

Harappa was a major industrial centre, with craft activities that were concentrated particularly in the south-eastern mound. Here, pottery was made and fired in sophisticated updraught kilns and decorated with a tin glaze; copper, gold, shell and stone

Below The Indus people used solid-wheeled, ox-drawn carts to transport goods. This unusual terracotta model from Mohenjo-Daro suggests that they also travelled in ox-drawn chariots.

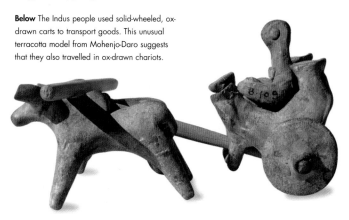

Pazyryk

In the frozen ground of the Altai mountains in Siberia, a group of burial mounds have yielded some exceptionally well-preserved remains from the 5th to 3rd centuries BC: human bodies frozen in the ice along with their possessions, including horses, textiles and leather, gold and silver objects.

During the first millennium BC the treeless grasslands that lie among the Altai mountains in Central Asia were home to horse-riding nomads who buried their chiefs and other important members of society in timber chambers under large earth mounds. Owing to the area's climate, the contents of the tombs became encased in ice and thus preserved, providing archaeologists with an extraordinary amount of information on this prehistoric society. 'Pazyryk' is the local word for 'burial mound' and it was applied to a series of tombs excavated in the Ust'-Ulagan valley between 1929 and 1949. In the 1990s, several more burial mounds were excavated on the Ukok plateau, near the Chinese border.

Natural iceboxes

The Pazyryk tombs at Ust'-Ulagan were discovered by the Russian archaeologist Sergei Rudenko in 1924. He began work on them five years later. This cluster of tombs consisted of five large and nine small, low earthen mounds covered with stones. The large mounds were 36-46m (118-151ft) in diameter, while the small ones were 13-15m (43-49ft) across. Under the centre of each mound was a shaft 4-6m (13-20ft) deep, filled with logs and stones. At the base of each shaft was a chamber constructed of logs, containing the burial and grave goods.

The secret to the preservation of the contents of the tombs lies in the fact that warm, moist summer air was trapped in the chamber at the time of burial. This warm air rose, and the moisture condensed on the stones in the shaft, trickled back down and saturated the corpse and grave goods. Additional moist air entered from the outside through the earth mound. The following winter, this moisture froze solid inside the tomb. The mound of earth prevented the ice from thawing, and thus the tombs became natural iceboxes.

A double burial

In one of the large Pazyryk tombs, the burial chamber is lined with felt and contained the embalmed bodies of a man and woman. Their coffin was decorated with cut-out leather figures of deer, while the bodies inside were wrapped in a woollen rug. Tattoos on

Left A felt appliqué figure of a horseman was found on a wool wall-hanging in one of the tombs. The horse's tack, trimmed mane and braided tail matched those of the real horses excavated at Pazyryk.

Above A detail on the edge of a Pazyryk carpet shows a horse and rider.

Above The chief's right arm from the wrist to the shoulder is decorated with a series of six fabulous animals, their hindquarters twisted around and with branchy horns.

the man depicted animals such as griffins, rams, birds, snakes and deer. Around the coffin were items of clothing and objects made from leather, wood, gold and silver, including some remarkable mirrors. The Pazyryk tombs also contained horse burials – between 7 and 14 horses per tomb – along with immaculately preserved bridles, saddles and cloth coats.

Recent tree-ring and radiocarbon dating of the Pazyryk timbers suggest that the tomb containing the double burial was constructed between 325 and 275 BC.

Ice maiden

In 1993 the archaeologist Natalya Polosmak found a frozen Pazyryk-type barrow at Ukok. It contained the tattooed body of a young woman, about 25 years old, in a log coffin. Outside the burial chamber were six horses, each killed by a blow to the head. Their manes, and even their felt saddle-covers, were well preserved. Stylized images of deer and snow leopards carved in leather decorated the outside of the coffin. In 1995, Polosmak and her husband, Vyacheslav Molodin, excavated another frozen tomb, this time of a man. No further Pazyryk-type burials have been excavated since then. The government of the autonomous Altai Republic passed a law barring further excavation because the finds were being taken to distant research institutes.

Ancient riches

The contents of the Pazyryk and Ukok tombs reveal the tremendous wealth of the nomadic aristocracy, while the textiles also demonstrate their contacts with distant lands, such as Persia and China.

Pataliputra

Occupying a strategic position on the south bank of the Ganges River in north-eastern India, Pataliputra became capital of the vast Mauryan empire under Emperor Chandragupta. Accounts of the glittering city give us an impression of the largest South Asian city of its time.

Pataliputra (modern-day Patna) was founded in the 5th century BC by the kings of Magadha, one of the principal *mahajanapadas* (great states) of the time. Magadha gradually gained control of neighbouring states until in the 4th century BC its ruling dynasty, the Mauryas, united most of India in a great empire, with its capital at Pataliputra, the meeting place of major trade routes to the north-west, north, south and south-west.

Imperial city

Little remains of the city, but clues can be found in carvings on Buddhist monuments known as stupas, especially those at Sanchi in central India.

Eyewitness accounts also help to throw light on the city. An envoy named Megasthenes described Pataliputra in around 300 BC as being long and narrow, enclosing richly furnished palaces. It was fortified by a moat and had timber walls pierced with arrowslits, with 570 towers and 64 gateways.

Kautilya, advisor to the first Mauryan emperor Chandragupta, described his ideal city in a treatise, the *Arthashastra*. Many of the features excavated at Pataliputra in the early 20th century show that Kautilya's vision was based on contemporary urban architecture.

A massive wooden rampart matching Megasthenes' description was uncovered, its timbers preserved by waterlogging. It was built of two parallel lines of huge wooden posts, more than 7m (23ft) high, with a floor of wooden beams between them.

The remains of an open pillared hall, perhaps from one of the palaces mentioned by Megasthenes, were discovered within the city. With its 84 polished sandstone pillars in ten rows, set into a wooden plinth, the hall resembled the public buildings of Achaemenid (Persian) palaces. Ash and other burnt material suggest there had been a massive wooden roof, destroyed by fire. A wooden stair connected the hall with a canal. Other discoveries include brick houses with tiled roofs and soakwells for drainage built of columns of massive terracotta rings.

Left Carvings on the Great Stupa at Sanchi give an impression of early Indian cities.

Taxila

Since the 1st millennium BC, the Taxila valley in northern Pakistan has been a major crossroads for trade and communications between South Asia and the regions beyond the mountains, the Iranian plateau and the west, Central Asia and China. It has provided details about many religious cultures.

The successive cities of the Taxila valley and their associated religious establishments attracted the attentions of many distinguished antiquarians and archaeologists, including Sir Alexander Cunningham, Sir John Marshall and Sir Mortimer Wheeler. Today Taxila is a World Heritage site.

Bhir Mound

Although settlement here dates back to the Neolithic period, it was in the 1st millennium BC that Taxila rose to prominence. In the 5th century BC a settlement known today as the Bhir Mound was founded by people under Achaemenid rule who had strong cultural ties to the emerging states of the Ganges valley. Later, in the 4th century BC, the region was incorporated into the Mauryan empire and Taxila became its provincial capital. The majority of excavated buildings belong to this period, including houses, shops and a pillared shrine.

Sirkap

In the 2nd century BC the valley came under the control of Bactrian Indo-Greeks, who constructed a new walled city at Sirkap. This was laid out in Greek 'chequerboard' fashion, with a walled acropolis and several palaces. Shrines and monasteries constructed in the city and the surrounding valley reflect the diversity of religions practised by Sirkap's cosmopolitan inhabitants under the Indo-Greeks and their Shaka and Parthian successors. These include Buddhist monumental shrines (stupas), a Zoroastrian fire-temple and an Indo-Greek shrine.

Sirsukh

Valuables concealed in the city reflect the troubled period in the 1st century AD when the valley fell to the Kushans, Central Asian nomads, who built a new walled city, named Sirsukh. The Kushans became great patrons of Buddhism, endowing monasteries and encouraging art. Under their rule the famous Gandhara art style, which successfully mingled Indian and Western traditions, reached its apogee. But around AD 460 the valley was overrun by the White Huns, from whose ferocious attacks it never recovered.

Below Beautifully decorated votive stupas at the Jaulian site, which is situated in the hills surrounding the Taxila valley. The main stupa and monastery at Jaulian are among the best-preserved buildings at Taxila.

Mount Li

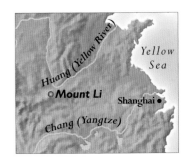

In 210 BC the First Emperor of China, Qin Shi Huangdi, was buried in a vast burial mound close to Mount Li. Not far away, hidden underground, were more than 7000 life-size terracotta soldiers, together with horses and chariots, to guard him after death. They lay undisturbed for 2000 years.

Born during the Warring States Period (453-221 BC), when ancient China was divided into a number of contending kingdoms, Shi Huangdi became king of the state of Qin in 246 BC. Having ruthlessly obliterated the other states, in 221 BC he unified the whole country under his own rule and gave himself the title of First August Emperor of China.

He established his capital at Xianyang, near present-day Xi'an in Shaanxi province in the heart of China. Here, in an area of about 12 sq km (4½ sq miles), he had a number of large brick palaces constructed. Unfortunately, the city was set alight by a rebel army in about 206 BC, during the late Qin Dynasty. It is said that the fire lasted three months and destroyed the whole district. Scientific excavation, which started in 1933, yielded hollow bricks and iron, bronze and ceramic objects that testify to the enormous wealth and might of the First Emperor.

The written record

These excavations are not the only source of information about the First Emperor. The historian Sima Qian (c.143-85 BC) recorded that the First Emperor had a huge mausoleum built for himself near Xianyang, with a tomb at its heart laid out like a small universe. This aroused the curiosity of archaeologists, and in March 1974 the first excavations of the area were conducted by Shaanxi Provincial Institute of Archaeology.

The mausoleum

Located north of Mount Li, the mausoleum is 35km (22 miles) east of Xi'an. Its plan is rectangular, with the

Below The terracotta soldiers, discovered in pits not far from the mausoleum, vary in height, uniform and hairstyle, according to rank. This is Pit 1, which contains the largest number of soldiers and horses.

long axis oriented north-south. The mausoleum compound contains several buildings, laid out like the Emperor's palace at Xianyang. It was originally enclosed by an outer and an inner wall made of pounded earth. Except in a few places, the walls have been completely destroyed over the centuries, but remnants indicate that they were 8-10m (26-33ft) high and 8m (26ft) thick. The outer wall measured 2165m (7100ft) north to south, and 940m (3085ft) east to west; the inner wall 1355m (4445ft) north to south and 580m (1900ft) east to west. Gates were set into the walls, and there were watchtowers at each corner.

The tomb itself, which is covered by a mound of earth, or tumulus, has not yet been excavated, but the rest of the compound has been excavated step by step, including side pits, buildings and attendant tombs. Bricks and tiles provide evidence of the various types of building on the site.

Only 53m (174ft) north of the tumulus are the foundations of a great temple hall. In the north-west corner of the walled area are foundations of smaller, private rooms. On the west side, the remains of three buildings have been excavated and inscriptions on the tiles identify them as provisions offices. The excavation has also revealed a workshop where the stones for the tomb were prepared.

Only 20m (66ft) west of the tomb excavators found two bronze chariots, each drawn by four bronze horses. Large quantities of hay had been placed

Above One of the army's cavalrymen is wearing a breastplate and leading his horse by a copper bridle.

with them, as if the horses were alive. The chariots were badly destroyed but could be restored. They are about half the size of real chariots of the time and illustrate the techniques of chariot-building and harness-making.

Shi Huangdi's tomb

Although the tomb is untouched, again we know something about it from the historian Sima Qian. Excavation and building work had begun at Mount Li as soon as the First Emperor had become King of Qin. By the time he had become emperor, 700,000 conscripts from all parts of the

country were at work there. They dug through three subterranean streams and poured molten copper for the outer coffin; the tomb was filled with models of palaces, pavilions and offices, as well as fine vessels, precious stones and other treasures, including pine trees carved out of jade.

Sima Qian describes fascinating details about the tomb's decoration:

'*All the country's streams, the Yellow River and the Yangzi were reproduced in quicksilver (mercury) and by some mechanical means made to flow into a miniature ocean. The heavenly constellations were shown above and the regions of the earth below. The candles were made of whale oil to ensure their burning for the longest possible time.*'

Crossbows were erected to ensure that any thief breaking in would be shot. And as another precaution, the middle and outer gates were closed to imprison all the artisans and labourers, so that they could not divulge any secrets of the tomb. Trees and grass were planted over the mausoleum to make it seem like a hill.

Perhaps archaeologists have been deterred from excavating the tumulus by the historian's description of booby-traps and rivers of mercury. It is also possible that the tomb itself, like the side pits, was robbed and destroyed with the capital in 206 BC.

The Terracotta Army

In 1974 local farmers drilling a well discovered what was to be one of the world's greatest archaeological treasures – the Terracotta Army.

The spectacular life-size clay figures were found in a cluster of four pits located about 1.2km (³/₄ mile) east of the outer wall of the mausoleum. Pit 1 contains the main battle formation, consisting of more than 6000 clay soldiers and horses. Pit 2 contains cavalry and infantry units and war chariots with horses. The much smaller Pit 3 contains high-ranking

Left This is one of the kneeling archers. Each soldier was given a real weapon, such as a spear, sword or crossbow.

China and its dynasties

For nearly 4000 years, China was ruled by emperors from a succession of dynasties. The first dynasty, the Xia, came to power in c.2000 BC and marks the point when one clan or family took control of every aspect of life in the country. During this dynasty a governing structure and legal system were developed. In 1911, nationalist forces declared China a republic and the Qing dynasty was overthrown.

2000-1500 BC	Xia
1700-1027 BC	Shang
1027-771 BC	Western Zhou
770-221 BC	Eastern Zhou
221-206 BC	Qin
206 BC-AD 6	Western Han
6-25	Hsing (Wang Mang interregnum)
25-220	Eastern Han
220-280	Three Kingdoms
265-316	Western Chin
317-420	Eastern Chin
420-588	South and North Dynasties
580-618	Sui
618-906	T'ang
907-960	Five Dynasties
969-1279	Song (Sung)
1279-1368	Yuan
1368-1644	Ming
1644-1911	Qing (Ch'ing) or Manchu

Right An infantryman with his hair wound into a distinctive topknot is wearing a loose tunic belted at the waist.

officers and represents the command post. Pit 4 is empty and was probably unfinished at the time of the emperor's death.

Pit 1 is the largest of the four and measures 230 x 62m (755 x 203ft). Warriors and horse chariots were placed in 11 columns, separated by stamped earth walls. The walls supported wooden roof beams, which were covered with layers of matting. A layer of earth measuring 3m (10ft) deep was placed over the matting to conceal the army's location. The floor was covered by some 256,000 tiles. It has been calculated that 126,940m³ (4.5 million cu ft) of earth had been moved in order to create the pit and 8000m³ (282,520 cu ft) of timber was used in its construction.

The warriors were placed in the pits when the wooden roofing was finished. As the figures are so heavy, it is possible that they were assembled in the pits, so no one at the time would have seen the army in its entirety.

An ancient production line

Clay is found in loess (a fine-grained silt), which covers large areas of northern China, providing an almost unlimited supply of a raw material that can easily be modelled. The craftsmen of the imperial workshops were divided into teams, with a foreman controlling around ten men. The names of 85 different foremen have been found on 249 figures.

Each part of the warrior's body – head, arms and hands, body and legs – was modelled separately, using standardized castes. Next, the face and hands were individually sculpted and features such as hair and moustaches were added. Then the parts were fitted together. Once the figure was assembled, craftsmen used additional clay to shape details such as those on the shoes or the armour.

The figure was then fired in a kiln. For the process to be successful, the different parts had to be fitted together while the clay contained exactly the right amount of moisture, so correct timing in making and assembling the figure was essential.

Finally, lacquer was used to colour the figures and paint the facial features. Working in this way, the craftsmen maintained a consistent quality of work, while producing several thousand terracotta figures, all with individual features from their faces to the soles of their shoes. It is an army that replicates the First Emperor's guard in his lifetime.

Archaeological excavations are still ongoing. So far over 8000 figures have been found.

Nara

The city of Nara, 40km (25 miles) south of Kyoto, was Japan's capital from AD 710 to 784, when it was called Nara-no-miyako or Heijo-kyo. It formed the core of a centralized state, which thrived under the influence of China's T'ang dynasty. The site has revealed many details of city life.

The site now lies within the central part of the present-day city of Nara. Numerous excavations have been carried out here, which have revealed features of the residences of both noblemen and common people, as well as roads and an abundance of artefacts of different kinds.

The city

Measuring over 4km (2¹/₂ miles) from west to east, and almost 5km (3 miles) north to south, the city was built on the Chinese grid pattern, with avenues running west to east and streets north to south.

The central thoroughfare, Suzaku Boulevard, was 84m (275ft) wide; at its southern end was the principal gate to the city, while at its northern end was the Imperial Palace. It is thought that at its height almost 200,000 people inhabited the city. The grounds of the Imperial Palace covered an area of about 1.25 sq km (¹/₂ sq mile), and contained the Imperial Residence, the Halls of State (including the Great Audience Hall) and various government offices and bureaux. This was the political nucleus of the Japanese nation-state, and it provided direct employment for around 10,000 officials and public employees.

Palace grounds

The grounds of the Imperial Palace were first precisely surveyed by archaeologists at the start of the 20th century, when their extent and layout were ascertained. The first excavations were carried out between 1924 and 1932, but major work began in the 1950s and has continued ever since. Hundreds of thousands of square metres have been uncovered in hundreds of excavations, and these have been thoroughly documented by archaeologists. An earthen wall ran around the palace compound. This was 2.7m (9ft) wide at its base and perhaps 6m (19ft) high, with 12 gates opening out of it.

In 1975 a 1200-year-old imperial villa garden was discovered by archaeologists. Excavations uncovered many features such as buildings, fences, gutters and wells, all located around a magnificent S-shaped pond. Among the artefacts were eaves-tiles of the same kind as those used at the Imperial Palace, and wooden tablets with letters written in ink still visible on them. In fact, tens of thousands of such tablets have been recovered, providing an important written

Below The Buddhist Todai-ji Temple was built on the orders of Emperor Shomu (reigned AD 724-49). The main hall (Daibutsuden) is still the world's largest wooden building, even though it was rebuilt in 1709 at only two-thirds of the original size.

Preservation and tourism

In 1906 the Heijo-kyo Preservation Society was formed, with private donations helping to acquire and conserve parts of the site. The Japanese government designated the whole area of the palace a 'Historic Site' in 1963, and they began to buy and preserve it. Since 1970 the Nara Cultural Properties Research Institute has been in charge of repairs, conservation and presentation of the site to the public, and have exhibited the excavated materials.

record of life in Nara. They comprise documents accompanying the movement of people or goods; government records, accounts and memoranda; and labels, including baggage labels on taxed goods.

A number of the garden's excavated buildings have been reconstructed at the site, some of which have pillars set directly into the ground without base-stones. They all faced east, in order to admire the pond and the view to the mountains. Water is thought to have come from the Komo River, which flowed along the east side of the garden site. A receiving reservoir stood to the north of the pond; from there water flowed into a stone-lined pool through a 5-m (16-ft) wooden conduit, and then overflowed into the pond. At the southern end was a 2.5-m (8-ft) wooden conduit and a stopcock.

Above The bronze Great Buddha is housed in the Todai-Ji Temple. The huge seated figure is 15m (49ft) tall and weighs 500 tonnes.

Ornamental water plants seem to have been grown along the pond's edges, since square wooden planting frames were found there. Rocks – gneiss, granite and andesite – were laid out with great skill, vertically and obliquely, along the banks.

Angkor

The immense complex of temples and other buildings that formed the city that is now called Angkor, in modern Cambodia, was one of the great wonders of ancient Asia. Today, despite years of neglect and damage caused by warfare, it is still one of the world's most impressive tourist destinations.

Rediscovered by a French missionary in 1850, Angkor was studied quite intensively in later decades, and the French colonialists eventually established major programmes to research the archaeology of what was then called Indochina. A restoration programme under the direction of the Ecole Française d'Extrême-Orient began in 1907, which worked to clear away the forest, repair foundations and install drains to protect the buildings from water damage.

In the early 1970s, the Angkor region was captured by the Khmer Rouge, who carried out a 20-year period of neglect and destruction, with sculptures being destroyed or illegally sold, and vegetation allowed to encroach on the buildings.

Restoration work began again after the end of the civil war. Some temples have been carefully taken apart and reassembled on concrete foundations.

The Khmer empire

In the early centuries AD, there seem to have been important political, religious and commercial links between China and India. By the 6th century Chinese records give the name 'Zhenla' to the region of the Middle Mekong River.

Zhenla appears to have denoted a series of regional chiefdoms, each with large, defended settlements, and with temple architecture that displayed a strong Indian influence. Many other elements of Indian culture were also adopted, and the Hindu and Buddhist religions were incorporated. Indian styles of religious art and

architecture became widespread, with new forms and local characteristics also developing at the same time.

By the 9th century AD Zhenla seems to have been consolidated into a single, powerful Khmer empire by King Jayavarman II. At the end of that century King Yasovarmon I moved the capital to Angkor, and from here the empire was the dominant force in South-east Asia until the early 15th century, when Angkor was pillaged by troops from neighbouring Siam (modern Thailand).

Above The towers of the Bayon temple in the heart of Angkor Thom are crowned with massive serene faces.

The Angkor complex

Although the word 'Angkor' comes from a Sanskrit term for 'holy city', Angkor itself was not a city at all, but rather a huge, sprawling complex of temples, monuments, reservoirs and canals that developed in different stages over the centuries. It is not really known to what extent ordinary people lived inside the complex.

The spatial layout of Angkor was based on Indian religious concepts. It was oriented around a central pyramid temple built on Phnom Bakheng, the only natural hill in the area. This temple was linked with Mount Meru, the central mountain in traditional Indian cosmology.

Successive Khmer kings founded temples in which, at first, the central object of worship was the lingam (stylized phallus) of the Hindu god Siva; this also represented royal authority. Gradually, the emphasis of Angkor's iconography changed from the Hindu cult of Siva to Mahayana Buddhism; nevertheless, the constant concern was the desire of Khmer rulers to construct monuments to their own immortality.

Angkor Thom

The Khmer kingdom reached its greatest extent under Jayavarman VII, who built the huge complex of Angkor Thom in the 12th century and which probably remained the Khmer capital until the 17th century. This complex covers 9 sq km ($3^1/_2$ sq miles), and is enclosed by a wall of 3 sq km (1 sq mile). Each side is pierced by a great gateway, which features a tower carved

Above The wonderful bas-reliefs at the Bayon temple capture scenes from everyday life. This relief shows a harvesting scene with workers collecting fruit into baskets.

Below Dedicated to the Hindu god Vishnu by King Suryavarman II, the magnificent temple of Angkor Wat was constructed over a period of 30 years.

with four faces pointing to the four cardinal directions; each gate is approached by an impressive avenue of carved gods (at one side) and demons (at the other) carrying a giant serpent across the moat.

The complex contains a few residential structures (doubtless most dwellings were of wood and thatch and have not survived), but there are numerous temples from various centuries. The most magnificent of these, and one of Angkor's greatest buildings, is the Bayon where the four entrance roads converge.

The Bayon probably began as a Hindu monument, but was converted into a Buddhist sanctuary before being completed, probably in the late 12th/early 13th century. It is characterized by its famous 54 towers, each with four beatifically smiling faces of an Avalokitesvara (a future Buddha), and its extensive bas-relief carvings. These incredible carvings show scenes from Khmer everyday life, as well as events in Khmer history, including great naval battles. The details are highly evocative and include scenes of people cooking, bartering and playing chess, as well as weapons, vessels and cock fighting.

To the north of the Bayon stands the great carved Elephant Terrace, 3m (10ft) high and 300m (984ft) long, with its numerous bas-relief elephants as well as other figures, and many smaller temples.

Angkor Wat

Another very successful monarch was Suryavarman II, who, in the 12th century, built the most famous temple complex of all, Angkor Wat. Situated about 1km (0.6 miles) south of Angkor Thom and covering an area of about 81ha (200 acres), Angkor Wat is the largest and best-preserved temple at the site. This great temple blended Hindu cosmology and architecture with pre-existing Khmer beliefs. The enclosure symbolizes the Hindu cosmos, while the temple itself stood for the five peaks of Mount Meru, the abode of the gods.

One of Angkor's great advantages was its location on the shore of Tônlé Sab, the biggest lake in Southeast Asia. In the wet season, water from the Mekong River flows back into the lake and more than trebles its surface area. The lake provided not only a supply of fish, but also water for irrigation. An elaborate complex of reservoirs, canals and moats was dominated by two huge man-made reservoirs. It is known from Chinese

Below An aerial view of Angkor Wat shows the quincunx of towers at its centre. Today, the temple is a symbol of Cambodia, appearing on its national flag.

Above A scene from a Bayon relief depicts the Khmer army going to war against the invading Cham (from Vietnam).

visitors in the 13th century that the people of the Angkor region had three or four rice crops per year, so clearly they had a large agricultural surplus.

Downfall

It also seems likely that a fall in this agricultural surplus – of unknown cause – may have been a factor in the downfall of Angkorian civilization, along with the military expansion of the Siamese. Another possibility is an increase in the incidence of malaria, because if warfare had led to the paddy fields being less well maintained, then the water could have become clear and calm, which is ideal breeding grounds for the most dangerous kind of mosquito.

After the sack of Angkor in 1431, most of the complex was abandoned. However, Angkor Wat was taken over by Buddhist monks, and became a major pilgrimage centre.

Angkor today

As a major international tourist destination, Angkor has many visitors, and five-star hotels proliferate in the nearby town of Siem Reap. This is in stark contrast to the poverty in the neighbouring villages, and the tragic results of the thousands of landmines that were laid in the region. The temple of Ta Prohm is currently one of the most popular tourist destinations in the complex, because its walls are still enveloped by the giant, twisting roots of fig trees, a sight that characterizes the romantic notion of ancient ruins integrated with nature. Another, more remote site is Kbal Spean, a place unique in the world, where rock art occurs within the bed of a flowing river – numerous bas-reliefs of lingams, and figures such as Vishnu and Siva, were carved into the very bed of a river near the top of a hill.

Left Enormous fig trees stretch their roots over the ruins in the central courtyard of the temple of Ta Prohm. When restoration work began at Angkor in the early 20th century, the authorities decided that Ta Prohm should be left as it was. Tourists can still enjoy the beauty of these trees.

461

HMS *Pandora*
This late 18th-century shipwreck has yielded some remarkably well-preserved contents.

Nan Madol
A mysterious ancient complex of man-made lakes separated by a network of canals.

Easter Island
This remote volcanic island is studded with hundreds of stone statues called *moai*.

PHILIPPINES

North Pacific Ocean

Pacific Ocean

AUSTRALIA

Easter Island

I N D O N E S I A

Nan Madol
Pohnpei Island

MICRONESIA

MELANESIA

PAPUA NEW GUINEA

○ **Wreck of HMS Pandora**

○ **Dampier Archipelago**

New Caledonia

Lapita ○

A U S T R A L I A

Darling

Lake Mungo ○
Lachlan

South Pacific Ocean

Southern Ocean

NEW ZEALAND

○ **Shag River Mouth**

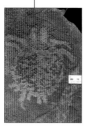

Dampier Archipelago
This region is home to probably the largest collection of rock art in the world.

Lake Mungo
This now-dry lake in New South Wales has revealed evidence of human occupation dating back 50,000 years.

Shag River Mouth A site rich in cultural material dating back to the earliest days of settlement in New Zealand.

THE GREAT SITES OF OCEANIA

Parts of this vast region were among the last in the world to be settled, but the colonization of the far-flung Pacific islands is arguably the greatest exploit in human history. The islands produced some remarkable cultures, such as those of Hawaii or New Zealand, but the most extraordinary of all was that of Easter Island, with its stone statues, rich rock art and many other archaeological features. Australia itself has proved a land of great archaeological surprises since its early prehistory was first unearthed only a few decades ago. Often wrongly considered to be very primitive, the Aborigines were in fact extremely well adapted to the often harsh environments in which they lived, and were responsible for some notable cultural achievements, including a wealth of rock art. Archaeologists have also learned a great deal from Aborigines and inhabitants of Papua New Guinea, who still make stone tools and other implements in traditional ways.

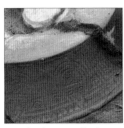

Lapita bowl An example of distinctive Lapita pottery, which is named after one of the sites in New Caledonia.

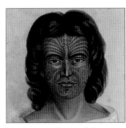

Maori tattoos The art of skin marking – called *ta moko* – has always been an important part of Maori culture.

Ahu Tongariki Easter Island statues were mounted on stone platforms, known as *ahu*. This is the island's largest platform.

463

Lake Mungo

The now-dry Lake Mungo is part of the Willandra Lakes system in the far west of New South Wales in Australia. The area is rich in archaeological sites and provides an extraordinary picture of Aboriginal occupation stretching back many millennia.

Fifty thousand years ago, the Willandra Lakes had been filled by fresh water from the Lachlan River. Then around 40,000 years ago the climate began to dry out, and the human inhabitants of the region had to adapt their way of life to increasing drought conditions. By 20,000 years ago the lake system was completely dry. Nevertheless, the region does not seem to have been totally abandoned. Although archaeologists have focused mainly on the older sites, evidence of younger sites allows them to explore human adaptation to changing environments over a 50,000-year period.

Cremation

In 1968 environmental scientist Jim Bowler, from the Australian National University, came across burnt bones eroding from dunes at Lake Mungo, where he was studying ancient climates. The remains proved to be those of a young woman, perhaps 19 years old. She had been cremated on the shores of the lake. Her bones had then been gathered and smashed, and finally interred in a small pit. This remarkable find remains the world's oldest evidence of ritual cremation.

Mungo Man

In 1974 a second burial was found nearby. The body of a 50-year-old man had been laid in a shallow grave and covered with red ochre. The original radiocarbon dates suggested that the burial occurred about 30,000 years ago, and the young woman's cremation about 25,000 years ago. In 1999 researchers using new dating

Above The near-complete skeleton of a 50-year-old man, who had been carefully laid on his back with his hands clasped.

methods controversially suggested Mungo Man could in fact be more than 60,000 years old. However, more detailed study of the finds and their context now suggests an age of about 40,000 years for both burials, and dates the earliest human presence in the area, shown by stone tools, at about 50,000 years ago.

Life around the lakes

Hearths and earth ovens, middens, scatters of stone artefacts, and stone quarries around the lakes provide a vivid picture of what life must have been like when they were full. People hunted a range of large and small animals and collected frogs, freshwater mussels and crayfish. They also fished for Murray cod and especially golden perch, which were probably caught using nets.

Stone from local quarries was used to make tools for chopping, cutting and scraping. Analysis of microscopic wear traces on some of these tools shows that they were used for scraping meat from bone and cleaning plant tubers.

The impact of the finds

Lake Mungo occupies an important place in the history of Australian archaeology. The first discoveries there came at a time when archaeologists had only recently demonstrated Ice Age occupation of Australia. The findings firmly established the dispersal of fully modern humans into Australia and provided an unusual insight into the beliefs of ancient people. Surveys and excavations have continued there ever since, and human remains, the bones of extinct animals and camp sites continue to be discovered.

The skeletal evidence remains significant in broader debates about the dispersal of modern humans, as well as the nature of the people who first colonized Australia, while the extraction of ancient DNA from Mungo Man offers new possibilities.

In 2003 the discovery of 20,000-year-old fossilized human footprints added yet another dimension to the archaeological record of the area. This was the first time fossil footprints had been found in Australia. There are at least 124 prints making eight trackways. Study of the sizes and characteristics of the prints suggest they were made by adults and children, some running and some walking. Other marks and indentations are still being studied, but some are thought to be the marks of tools such as spears and digging sticks dragged over the surface.

Indigenous peoples worldwide are concerned about controlling their history and how archaeologists research their past. Lack of respect for human remains has been a particularly contentious issue, and in Australia there has been considerable debate and even conflict between archaeologists and Aboriginal communities. In 1992 the remains of Mungo Lady were formally returned to the care of local Aboriginal communities. This event is an example of increasing partnership between Aboriginal groups and archaeologists in Australia generally.

Left Steve Webb of Bond University, Queensland, examines a series of animal bones – perhaps the remains of a meal – in a 20,000-year-old fireplace.

Below The spectacular crescent-shaped dune formations, which run for 30km (19 miles) along the eastern shore of Lake Mungo, are known as 'The Walls of China'.

The rock art of Dampier

The rugged terrain of the Dampier Archipelago, on the north-west coast of Australia, contains what is probably the largest concentration of rock art in the world. Archaeologists estimate that there may be up to 250,000 individual petroglyphs (carvings made into the rock face).

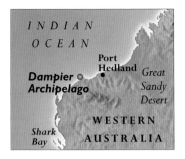

The art at Dampier is extraordinarily diverse both in its subject matter and technique, including human and animal figures as well as a wide range of geometric motifs. Rock art is always difficult to date, but the large number of marine mammals and fish represented at Dampier suggests that much of the art dates to the last 6000 years, when the sea reached its present level and the islands of the archipelago were formed.

Many of the rock motifs can be linked with contemporary Aboriginal ceremonial practices in the wider Pilbara region. However, some heavily weathered designs, such as face motifs, may be much older. They resemble art from elsewhere in Australia, which is thought to date back to the earliest settlement of the continent, up to 50,000 years ago. As well as art, there is also a range of other sites, including shell middens, campsites, quarries and workshops, and stone arrangements.

Threat of destruction

Despite the richness of the area, Dampier is also one of the world's most endangered heritage sites. Industrial development began in the 1960s and continues to this day. Many decorated boulders have been destroyed or moved from their original locations. Those that survive are under threat from future development and emissions from the industrial estate. There is still no proper inventory of the archaeological sites or comprehensive heritage management plan.

Below Tumbled boulders adorned with petroglyphs are a distinctive feature of the landscape of the Dampier Archipelago.

Figures from the Dreaming
The Yaburara Aborigines inhabited the Dampier archipelago and groups from the mainland also visited seasonally. Beginning with the arrival of American whalers in the 1840s, local Aboriginal communities were devastated by European settlement. The impact of introduced diseases and raiding for forced labour for the pearling and pastoral industries was particularly severe. The Yaburara were effectively wiped out in 1868 in the Flying Foam Massacre. Aboriginal communities in the Pilbara today still feel responsible for caring for Yaburara land. They believe that the Dampier petroglyphs were all made by the ancestral creator spirits, or *marga*, during the Dreaming, which they call the 'time when the world was soft'.

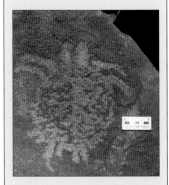

Above Turtles are common in the most recent art phase and are often shown mating, as here, or with eggs.

Nan Madol

Known as the Venice of the Pacific, the mysterious Nan Madol is perhaps the most spectacular site in all Oceania. Situated on the volcanic island of Pohnpei in the Caroline Islands, it is a vast ancient complex of artificial islets linked by a network of canals.

In all there are 93 artificial islets at Nan Madol. These are constructed of massive basalt stones with coral and rubble fill. The whole site covers an area of about 81ha (200 acres) of sheltered reef and is protected from the sea by massive sea walls.

Mapping the site

The first map of Nan Madol was produced in 1910. Since then, archaeological research at the site, most recently led by Bill Ayres, has produced detailed maps of archaeological remains of more than 20 of the islets. Excavations have enabled archaeologists to compile a chronology of the development of Nan Madol, which can be related to the historical accounts in Pohnpei oral traditions.

History

Nan Madol seems to have been the ceremonial and administrative centre of a single state, uniting the whole population of Pohnpei under a single ruling dynasty. The artificial islets

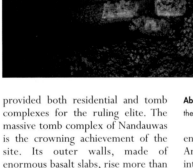

provided both residential and tomb complexes for the ruling elite. The massive tomb complex of Nandauwas is the crowning achievement of the site. Its outer walls, made of enormous basalt slabs, rise more than 7m (23ft) above the level of the canal. These surround a central tomb

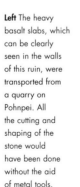

Left The heavy basalt slabs, which can be clearly seen in the walls of this ruin, were transported from a quarry on Pohnpei. All the cutting and shaping of the stone would have been done without the aid of metal tools.

Above An aerial view of Nan Madol reveals the network of artificial islets and canals.

enclosure within the main courtyard. An impressive portal marks the entry into Nandauwas.

Nan Madol was first occupied about 2000 years ago. By AD 1000 the first artificial islets had been constructed. Most of the massive monumental architecture, such as the Nandauwas tomb complex, dates to the period AD 1200-1600. According to Pohnpei oral history, this was the period when Pohnpei was united under the rule of the Saudeleur dynasty. Centralized Saudeleur rule seems to have collapsed about AD 1600, to be replaced by regional chiefdoms. Nan Madol thus lost its role as a political centre and by the time Europeans visited Pohnpei in the 19th century, the vast complex had been abandoned.

The Lapita culture

A distinctive type of highly decorated pottery marks the appearance of a new cultural complex on several islands in the western Pacific. This cultural complex, which began about 3500 years ago, is called Lapita, after an archaeological site in New Caledonia.

The Pacific Ocean covers about one third of the earth's surface. The settlement of this vast area, with its hundreds of remote islands, involved remarkable feats of voyaging. The western rim of the Pacific, including New Guinea, Australia and the western Melanesian islands, was occupied by about 30,000 years ago. The colonization of the more remote islands of Oceania began around 1500 BC and seems to have been very rapid. How it was achieved has been debated since the earliest European voyages to the South Pacific in the 18th century.

Lapita pottery

Archaeologists first recognized the pottery in 1909 on Watom Island, off New Britain. Lapita sites are widely distributed from the Bismarck Archipelago, off the north-west coast of New Guinea, as far as Fiji, Tonga

and Samoa. The Lapita cultural complex spans a period of about 1000 years and is often linked to the expansion of speakers of Austronesian languages into the region.

Lapita pottery is handmade and poorly fired but is usually very highly decorated, although plain wares were also made. The designs were most commonly stamped into the damp clay using a comb-like tool. Sometimes the potter used a sharp stone or shell to cut

Above Archaeologists excavate a pot-burial site at Teouma. The pots are clearly visible.

Left A flat-bottomed Lapita bowl, decorated with a repeat design of stylized faces.

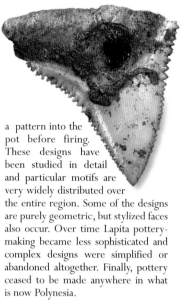

a pattern into the pot before firing. These designs have been studied in detail and particular motifs are very widely distributed over the entire region. Some of the designs are purely geometric, but stylized faces also occur. Over time Lapita pottery-making became less sophisticated and complex designs were simplified or abandoned altogether. Finally, pottery ceased to be made anywhere in what is now Polynesia.

Lapita settlements

Most Lapita sites are coastal settlements. Marine resources, such as fish, seabirds, turtles and shellfish, made an important contribution to the economy. Lapita colonists introduced domestic pig, dog and chicken to the areas they settled and cultivated tuberous plants and tree crops. Some settlements seem to have been built on piles over the water. As well as the distinctive pottery, Lapita sites often contain shell ornaments and fishhooks, files, bone awls, tattooing needles, and shell and stone woodworking tools known as adzes.

A feature of the Lapita cultural complex is evidence for long-distance exchange between communities. The best indication of the transport of particular materials comes from the study of obsidian, a distinctive volcanic glass. There are several known sources of obsidian in the Bismarck Archipelago, especially on Manus and New Britain. Obsidian from Manus is found as far away as Vanuatu, while obsidian from New Britain is very widely distributed from Borneo to Fiji.

Above and above left Artefacts include this drilled shark tooth and shark vertebra.

Origins of the Lapita

It is widely agreed that the descendants of the Lapita people were the Polynesians. Their culture seems to have developed from the Lapita culture of the Fiji, Tonga and Samoa area. There is, however, considerable disagreement about the origins of the Lapita cultural complex. Some archaeologists argue for local development in the Bismarck Archipelago, while others favour an origin in a South-east Asian island.

The site of Teouma in central Vanuatu is one of the most important Lapita sites and will help to answer these questions. Discovered accidentally in 2003, subsequent excavations at Teouma have revealed a cemetery which, at 3200 to 3000 years old, is the oldest known in the Pacific region. The site is unique in other ways. The distinctive Lapita pottery found there is extraordinarily well preserved. There is evidence of complex burial rites in the form of burials, with the heads removed and the interment of skulls and other human bones in large pots. Such pot burials are unique in the Pacific, but occur from about 5500 years ago in island south-east Asia. Study of these bones, and of DNA extracted from them, will give important clues to the origins of the Lapita people.

Right This fragment of Lapita pottery, which was discovered in 2001, has a unique three-dimensional sculpted face. The stamped designs visible on the face may represent tattoos.

469

Easter Island

Easter Island is one of the most remote pieces of inhabited land in the world, so remote that it is extremely unlikely that it was ever colonized more than once. Certainly the archaeological record indicates a single unbroken development of culture from the first settlers until the arrival of Europeans.

Easter Island

Santiago

South Pacific Ocean

The 166 sq km (64 sq mile) volcanic island is the easternmost inhabited island of Polynesia. It is situated some 3700km (2300 miles) from South America and 2200km (1367 miles) from Pitcairn Island.

Colonization

People first arrived here in canoes in the early centuries AD. Contrary to the theory of Norwegian Thor Heyerdahl (who in 1947 sailed from Peru to Polynesia in the *Kon Tiki*), the colonists did *not* come from South America, but rather from eastern Polynesia. This is confirmed not only by archaeology and language, but also anthropology, blood groups and genetics.

Once on the island, the colonists were trapped, and it constituted their whole world. Their first known contact with others came on Easter Sunday 1722, when the Dutch navigator Roggeveen encountered and

named the island. The Dutch were the first to leave us written descriptions of the inhabitants.

Analyses of pollen from the sediments at the bottom of the freshwater lakes in the island's volcanic craters led British palaeobotanist John Flenley in the 1980s to discover that the island was originally covered by a rainforest dominated by a species of huge palm tree.

It was on this island, which looked totally different from that of today, that the voyagers arrived, bringing with them the domestic animals (chickens, rats) and food plants (bananas, sweet potatoes, taro) with which they transformed the environment of many Polynesian islands.

Constructions

During the initial phase, the islanders seem to have constructed small, simple *ahu* (stone platforms) of

normal Polynesian type, with small and relatively crude statues upon or in front of them.

In the middle phase of Easter Island's prehistory (*c.*AD 1000-1500), enormous effort was poured into the construction of bigger ceremonial platforms and hundreds of large statues. As the population grew, there was a need for ever-increasing quantities of food. The decline of the forest, as land was cleared, can be seen in the pollen from the craters. The increasing quantity of statue carving required more timber for rollers and levers to transport the statues.

More than 800 *moai* (statues) were carved, mostly in the soft, volcanic tuff of the Rano Raraku crater, with basalt hammerstones. They depict a human with a prominent nose and chin, and often elongated ears containing disks. The bodies, ending at the abdomen, have arms held to the sides, and hands held in front, with long fingertips meeting a stylized loincloth. They represent ancestor figures.

Over 230 *moai* were transported from the quarry to platforms around the island's edge, where they were erected, backs to the sea. At the most prestigious platforms, the statues were given a *pukao*, or topknot, of red scoria (burnt lava), raised and placed on the head; and white coral eyes, inserted at certain times or ceremonies to 'activate' the statues' *mana* (spiritual power).

Left One of the many *moai* that remain in and around the quarry at Rano Raraku, buried up to their necks in sediment.

The statues on platforms ranged from 2 to 10m (6½ to 33ft) in height, and weighed up to 83 tonnes. The biggest platform on the island was Tongariki, with 15 statues.

The quarry at Rano Raraku still contains almost 400 statues on its slopes, in every stage of manufacture. Finished statues on the slopes are covered by sediments up to their necks, but they are all full statues down to the abdomen.

Collapse

The final phase of the island's prehistory saw a collapse: statues ceased to be carved, cremation gave way to burial, and 1000 years of peaceful coexistence was shattered by the toppling of statues, and an abundant manufacture of *mataa* – spearheads and daggers of obsidian. The conflict was resolved by abandoning the earlier religion and social system based on ancestor worship, in favour of one featuring a warrior elite. An annual chief, or 'birdman', was chosen each year at the ceremonial village of Orongo, perched high on the cliff separating the great Rano Kau crater from the ocean. Each candidate had a young man to represent him. Every spring these young men had to descend the sheer cliff, 300m (984ft) high, then swim over a kilometre (0.6 mile) on a bunch of reeds to an islet. Here they would await the arrival of the sooty tern, in order to find its first egg. The winner swam back with the egg in a headband, and his master would become the new birdman. Orongo's rock art is festooned with carvings of the birdmen, sometimes holding the egg which symbolized fertility. This system ended with the arrival of missionaries in the 1860s.

The causes of the island's decline were probably complex, but the major factor was clearly human colonization. From at least 1200 years ago one can see a massive reduction in forest cover until, by the time Europeans arrived, there were no large trees left. The imported rats fed on the palm fruits and helped prevent regeneration. Without timber, statues could no longer be moved and ocean-going canoes could no longer be built, thus cutting the population off from a supply of deep-sea fish. Chickens became the most precious source of protein. Deforestation caused tremendous soil erosion, which damaged crop-growing. Starvation gave rise to raiding and violence, perhaps even to cannibalism.

Right This statue has been given a separate topknot of red scoria and eyes of white coral.

Above The 15 statues on the Tongariki platform, which were restored in the 1990s, stand facing inland, their backs to the sea.

471

Shag River Mouth

The Shag River Mouth site, located in Otago on the east coast of New Zealand's South Island, was first discovered in 1872. The site, which has a long history of investigation, occupies an important place in New Zealand archaeology because of the richness and diversity of the cultural remains.

Excavations at the site in the late 19th and early 20th century uncovered a rich and diverse artefact assemblage. Large quantities of the bones of the large, flightless moa, and other faunal remains, were also found, as well as evidence for hearths, houses and refuse areas. The site was generally interpreted as a long-term village site, dating from the earliest period of settlement in New Zealand, and played an important role in early debates about the nature and antiquity of moa hunting and the role of Polynesian settlers in the extinction of the birds.

The settlement

Modern excavations in the 1980s have shown that the site was a short-lived permanent settlement, occupied for about 50 years in the mid-14th century AD. The economy of the site was originally based on the specialized exploitation of large game, such as larger species of moa and fur seals. The focus on big-game hunting seems to have caused depletion in the local resources and later midden deposits indicate that the emphasis later shifted to fishing.

The settlement at Shag River Mouth had a central butchery and cooking area surrounded by midden dumps. Dwellings and workshop areas were clustered in groups around the central area. The excavators estimate a population of 100 to 200 people.

The range of artefacts recovered from the site is remarkable and reflects the diversity of activities that were

carried out at the site. As well as fishing and hunting gear, and plant processing equipment such as grindstones and pounders, there is evidence of bone and stone working. Shell beads and a greenstone tattooing chisel provide evidence of personal adornment. Shag River Mouth is an example of how modern methods of archaeological excavation and analysis can shed new light on old interpretations.

Above Finds of tattooing chisels at sites such as Shag River Mouth show that the distinctive Maori custom of tattooing was part of the culture that the first settlers brought with them to New Zealand.

Left The skull and neck of a moa, one of several species of flightless bird hunted to extinction by the first Polynesian settlers. This bird was mummified in the dry atmosphere of a central Otago cave.

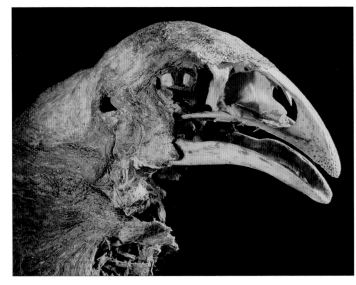

HMS *Pandora*

On-going explorations of the wreck of HMS Pandora, *which sank in the deep waters of Australia's Great Barrier Reef in the 1790s, are gradually unearthing a treasure trove of well-preserved artefacts, providing an extraordinary snapshot of life on board at the time.*

The 24-gun frigate set sail from England in 1790 to track down the *Bounty* mutineers and bring them to justice. Her captain, Edward Edwards, caught up with the 14 mutineers who had remained in Tahiti. He failed to find the other mutineers, who had sought refuge on Pitcairn Island, and headed for home with his prisoners. However, the ship struck submerged coral and sank on 29 August 1791 trying to negotiate the Great Barrier Reef. Most of the crew survived, along with ten of the mutineers who were subsequently tried in England.

Excavation

The ship was rediscovered in 1977 and preliminary archaeological surveys showed that she was remarkably well preserved. Much of the ship's hull had been very quickly covered with sand when she sank and therefore survived intact. Systematic excavations began in 1984, led by Peter Gesner of the Queensland Museum.

Excavation work on the *Pandora* has been expensive, difficult and dangerous because it is so remote, and the depth of the wreck allows only relatively short dives. Consequently, only a small part of the site has been excavated so far.

Many of the artefacts found come from the officers' cabins and storerooms on the lower deck. These have yielded a wealth of personal items and equipment, such as surgical instruments, which presumably belonged to George Hamilton, the ship's surgeon. A pocket watch found in the same area

was probably also Hamilton's. Future excavation work in the bow area will reveal details of the lives of ordinary seamen on board the ship.

Below The Pacific claimed many ships at the height of the 18th-century explorations. This painting shows the *Astrolabe*, which sank two years before HMS *Pandora*.

Souvenirs

Among the items found on board are a number of local curiosities that crew members had picked up on their journey. These would have been collected either as souvenirs to take back home or perhaps to sell on to European collectors. These artefacts – including such things as Polynesian clubs and poi pounders, which were used to pound fruits – provide a valuable insight into Pacific culture at the time. First Lieutenant John Larkin seems to have collected many of these curiosities.

Left Many curiosities, such as this whalebone carving of a Polynesian god, were sold on to collectors in Europe.

Little Bighorn
Excavations begun in 1983 have uncovered previously unknown details about this famous American battle.

Mesa Verde
This location in Colorado is famous for its Anasazi structures, including remarkable many-roomed cliff dwellings.

Chichén Itzá
The impressive ruins of this Maya ceremonial centre include a huge stepped pyramid, an observatory and a ballcourt.

Tikal The largest of the ancient ruined cities of the Maya civilization, it included monumental buildings such as step pyramids.

Chan Chan A great mud-brick city in the Moche Valley, it was divided into huge, rectangular compounds by its pre-Inca builders.

Moche Outstanding pots representing life-like people and other subjects provide important clues about the Moche culture that produced them.

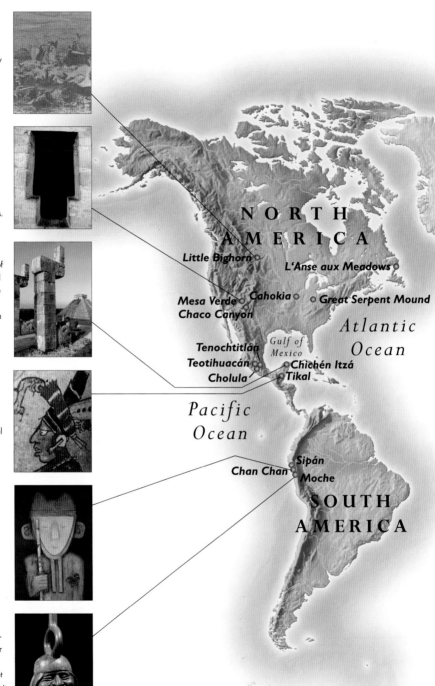

NORTH AMERICA

Little Bighorn

L'Anse aux Meadows

Mesa Verde   Cahokia   Great Serpent Mound
Chaco Canyon

Atlantic Ocean

Tenochtitlán   *Gulf of Mexico*
Teotihuacán   Chichén Itzá
Cholula   Tikal

Pacific Ocean

Sipán
Chan Chan   Moche

SOUTH AMERICA

THE GREAT SITES OF THE AMERICAS

Although the earliest-known excavation took place at Huaca de Tantalluc on the coast of Peru in 1765, the New World was otherwise something of a latecomer to archaeological research. But the amazing monuments and cultures of both Mesoamerica and South America soon established the huge importance of this continent to the history of humans. Today, study of the Maya rivals that of Ancient Egypt and the Classical World in popularity and importance. A huge amount of archaeological work has also been carried out in North America – from the Anasazi dwellings of Chaco Canyon in the west to the Viking settlement of L'Anse aux Meadows in the east.
In the next few years new discoveries, together with genetic data, should also shed fresh light on how and when the New World was first colonized.

Teotihuacán Archaeologists are still not sure why this once monumental city of Mesoamerica was abandoned.

Great Serpent Mound The precise significance of this huge earthen mound in Ohio is shrouded in mystery.

Tenochtitlán The once vast capital of the Aztec empire is buried beneath modern day Mexico City.

Cholula

One of the most important economic and ceremonial centres of pre-Columbian Mesoamerica, the Mexican city of Cholula is the oldest continuously occupied city in the Americas. The Great Pyramid is the largest in the world by volume.

Situated in the highland Puebla Valley, Cholula first rose to prominence during the Middle Formative period (1000-500 BC), and it continued to thrive through the pre-Columbian era. The city became one of the most important regional centres in pre-Hispanic Central America, and it was also the centre of the cult of the deity Quetzalcóatl.

Archaeological investigations have been ongoing at the site for the last 100 years, with most of the attention focused on the Great Pyramid, which is almost completely buried beneath a layer of soil and vegetation. Due to its long history and monumentality, and the fact that much of the ancient city is covered by modern construction, Cholula remains one of the great enigmas of ancient Mesoamerica.

Prime location

The Puebla Valley, situated between Mexico City and the Gulf Coast, is surrounded by snow-capped volcanoes that supply the alluvial plain with reliable run-off water for intensive agriculture. Located near the convergence of several perennial rivers and a marshy lake, Cholula enjoyed an advantageous environment; colonial Spanish accounts describe it as the most productive zone in New Spain. Another resource was the high clay content in the sub-soil, making it ideal for pottery production. Cholula polychrome pottery was widely traded, and it was noted that the Aztec ruler preferred dining on the beautiful dishes of Cholula. The city is also located on crossroads connecting the highland valleys with the Gulf lowlands, and with the southern highlands of Oaxaca, making it an entrepôt for long-distance exchange.

Early visitors

When the Spanish conquistador Hernán Cortés and his army entered Cholula in 1519, they were amazed at the grandeur of the city, comparable to the Spanish cities from which they had come. The Great Pyramid was taller than the Great Temple of Aztec Tenochtitlán and the marketplace featured an array of exotic goods from throughout Mesoamerica, brought by the long-distance merchants known as the *pochteca*.

Numerous colonial chroniclers described the economic, political and religious organization of Cholula, providing valuable information to complement the archaeological finds. Cholula was also the source of the Mixteca-Puebla stylistic tradition, exemplified in a series of pictorial manuscripts (codices) known as the Borgia group (after the Borgia Codex, which was saved from destruction by Cardinal Borgia and is now housed in the Vatican Library). With their array of gods, kings, mythical creatures and

Left A view of the east side of the Patio of the Altars shows a large head sculpture in the foreground.

abstract designs, these codices depict pre-Hispanic perspectives on the city and its religious groups.

The Great Pyramid

Referred to as the Tlachihualtepetl ('artificial mountain') in Colonial sources, the Great Pyramid at Cholula has been an important religious site for 2500 years, including its current use as the base for a prominent Catholic church.

Dedicated to Quetzalcóatl, work on the Tlachihualtepetl was begun in the Late Formative period (500 BC-0), and construction continued into the Early Postclassic period (AD 900-1200) in at least four major building phases, until it measured over 400m (1312ft) on a side and 65m (213ft) in height. The Great Pyramid was built around sacred principles, oriented to the setting sun at the summer solstice (25 degrees north of west), and standing over a spring, which represents passage to the underworld.

The construction history of the Great Pyramid was explored via 8km (5 miles) of tunnels dug by archaeologists from the 1930s to the 1960s. These excavations revealed different façades and staircases, which had been buried as the pyramid was enlarged and modified. Archaeologists have reconstructed one side of one of the lower segments of the pyramid.

Other excavations have exposed the ceremonial platforms and patios around the base of the pyramid, especially the Patio of the Altars where 10-tonne slabs of onyx form two stela-altar groups oriented towards the setting sun on the longest day of the year. On the platform façade of the patio is the Drunkards Mural, depicting over 100 life-size revellers partaking of hallucinogenic drink and transforming into their animal co-essences.

Other areas

Pre-Hispanic mounds have been found in other parts of the site, although only a few have survived urban development; Cortés counted more

than 400 mounds when he first rode into the city. Salvage excavations have documented residential areas of the ancient city, including changing ethnic patterns as Cholula adapted to the turbulent political events that caused the rise and decline of neighbouring cities, such as Teotihuacán, Tula, Monte Albán and Tenochtitlán. In the

face of these changes, it is significant that Cholula was able to maintain its importance for 3000 years.

Above Full excavation and restoration of the pyramid has been restricted due to the fact that the Catholic church, built at the top by the Spanish in 1594, is a designated colonial monument and place of pilgrimage.

Tikal

Deep in the jungles of what is now Northern Guatemala, the Maya built an astonishing city that was to become one of the largest and most important of the Classic Maya period. The scale of some of its buildings, including steep-sided pyramids, is to this day awesome.

Tikal's roots date back to the Middle Preclassic period (*c.*700 BC), although the nature of this early site is not well understood, as it had been covered by later construction. The city began to grow in the Late Preclassic period (*c.*350 BC to AD 250), with the most impressive architecture located in the *Mundo Perdido* ('Lost World') complex, including a large temple pyramid at its centre. It continued to be important into the Early Classic period (*c.*AD 250-600). The pyramid was modified at the beginning of this period and shows architectural similarities to structures from the Central Mexican city of Teotihuacán. Tikal flourished in the Classic period (*c.*AD 250-900) and then, in common with other Maya cities, went into decline.

For centuries the city had been effectively lost to the jungle until its rediscovery in 1848. Archaeologists later confirmed Tikal to be one of the Maya's main political and ceremonial centres. The first large-scale excavation

Below The Great Plaza at Tikal is dominated by the great step pyramids of Temple I and Temple II (shown here).

Right This detail is from a painted vase, made in Tikal in around AD 700.

and mapping project at the site was carried out by the University Museum of the University of Pennsylvania between 1956 and 1970.

Architecture

Maya construction was accretionary – with new layers added to existing buildings. As a result, the majority of Early Classic architecture at Tikal has been built over by later construction efforts. Much of the architecture that is visible at the site today was constructed during the Late Classic period (AD 600-900). This includes the massive palace complexes (most notably the central acropolis), much of the funerary architecture (Temples I-V and much of the North acropolis), and also the site's ballcourts and *sacbeob* (raised roadways). The area around Tikal also flourished at this time so that at its peak the central district and its rural hinterlands came to encompass an area of over 50 sq km (19 sq miles), much of which is still to be cleared and excavated.

Below Relief carvings on a stela depict a man wearing a ceremonial headdress.

Collapse
Tikal collapsed sometime during the 9th century AD, and the majority of the site was abandoned, with a small squatter population remaining in the area. The last stela, known as Stela II, has the date AD 869. This collapse was part of the broader phenomenon referred to as the Classic Maya Collapse that is represented by a large-scale depopulation throughout the southern Maya lowlands. The cause of this collapse is widely debated, with suggested causes including warfare, internal dissent, disease, drought and famine. Excavated skeletons at the cemetery certainly indicate that disease and malnutrition were widespread.

Teotihuacán

From around AD 100 to 600, Teotihuacán — meaning 'city of the gods' — was the largest city of the Americas. The vast central Avenue of the Dead is still flanked by impressive ceremonial architecture, including the monumental Pyramid of the Sun.

Located in the Basin of Mexico in the central highlands, approximately 40km (25 miles) north-east of Mexico City, Teotihuacán quickly grew to prominence due in part to a volcanic eruption in the southern basin that destroyed the early site of Cuicuilco, its major competitor during the pre-Classic period.

The pre-Columbian Basin of Mexico was filled with an extensive network of lakes that facilitated transportation and supported a diverse biosphere, which included fish and waterfowl. The people of Teotihuacán were able to exploit this environment by using intensive agriculture, hunting and gathering of wild resources. They also mined locally available obsidian for stone tool manufacture.

At its height Teotihuacán had become a thriving economic centre with a population estimated at about 150,000 people.

Abandonment

The ceremonial precinct in the urban core was destroyed by fire in about AD 600. By the time the first Spanish conquistadores arrived in 1519 the pyramids were in ruins and the vast city overgrown except where it was under cultivation. However, this was never a 'lost city' — in fact, the continued agricultural productivity of the surrounding lands meant that it was never even completely abandoned. The ruins of Teotihuacán were well known to the local people and were a place of pilgrimage in Aztec times. Historical accounts suggest that the Aztec king Moctezuma visited an oracle at Teotihuacán to learn of the strange bearded men (the Europeans), as the conquistador Cortés and his army approached their city.

Minor archaeological excavations were carried out in the 19th century, and in 1905 major excavation and restoration work began under archaeologist Leopoldo Batres; the Pyramid of the Sun was restored to celebrate the centennial of Mexican Independence in 1910. An important mapping project led by René Millon produced detailed maps and plans of the city. Archaeological work at the site continues to this day.

A well-planned city

The layout of the city is a marvel of urban planning and monumental construction. In about AD 100 the city underwent intensive urban renewal, with the streets organized by a strict grid system arrayed around the principal Avenue of the Dead. Stretching for approximately 2.3km (1¹/₂ miles) and 40m (130ft) wide, this causeway was probably used for

Left A view along the Avenue of the Dead from the Pyramid of the Moon extends towards the vast Pyramid of the Sun.

Another important feature of the ceremonial centre is the Pyramid of the Feathered Serpent (Quetzalcóatl) located within the *ciudadela* (Citadel) enclosure. The pyramid, which was first excavated between 1917 and 1922, was originally covered with a carved façade of undulating feathered serpents, an important supernatural entity found in many Mesoamerican cultures. Excavations into the rubble core of the Pyramid have found nearly 200 sacrificial burials of male and female warriors and attendants, many killed with their hands bound behind their backs and attired in elaborate jewellery of human teeth.

Enigmatic city

In contrast to the contemporaneous Maya, Teotihuacán lacked a well-developed writing system, so little is known of its dynastic histories. The cause for Teotihuacán's abandonment remains one of the great mysteries of the ancient capital. Theories include climatic change, invasion and even internal unrest, but so far the precise reason for the city's demise is unclear.

ritual processions to the many important religious buildings that flanked the avenue.

The largest and most impressive monument was the Pyramid of the Sun, which measures about 280m (918ft) wide at the base and soars to a height of about 65m (213ft). It would have been surmounted by a temple made of perishable materials, which would have extended it much higher. Excavations carried out directly under the pyramid in 1971 revealed a ceremonial cave.

At the northern extreme of the Avenue of the Dead is the equally impressive Pyramid of the Moon. Excavations carried out at the pyramid since 1998 by a team of archaeologists led by Saburo Sugiyama have revealed a great deal of material, including human burials. The Pyramid of the Moon is fronted by a large plaza surrounded by administrative platforms and the Palace of the Feathered Butterfly (Quetzalpapalotl), perhaps the most extravagant of the residential palaces.

The names and significance of these pyramids are unknown – and in fact the actual language of the inhabitants of Teotihuacán remains a source of scholarly debate – but again we owe the names to the Aztecs who continued to worship at these shrines when they were encountered and recorded by the Spanish.

The Moche

Beginning in the first century AD a civilization known as the Moche emerged on the north coast of Peru that could rival any in the world for wealth and power. The Moche were skilled craftsmen who, among other things, created wonderful pots that record many aspects of their way of life.

The major Moche settlements were located in the massive river valleys that cut through the desert coast. Here they farmed vast tracts of land, harvested huge quantities of resources from the ocean and controlled herds of camelids. Large numbers of specialized labourers produced pottery, metalwork, textiles and other luxury items. The Moche constructed enormous adobe (mudbrick) pyramids and developed sophisticated irrigation systems and road networks.

Moche religion and ritual life were spectacular, filled with pageantry, drama and violence. Ritualized warfare, the capture and display of prisoners, and human sacrifice were its hallmarks.

Moche society

Each major Moche settlement was ruled by a set of hereditary rulers who held political and religious power. At one of the settlements, San José del Morro, studied by archaeologist Luis Jaime Castillo, women held the most important religious posts, although elsewhere it was men. Below the rulers in this hierarchical society was a vast group of retainers and administrators, who held many specific roles in religious, political and economic life. Thousands of commoner families supported the Moche state with their agricultural work, or by fishing or herding. Upon their deaths Moche people were buried in cemeteries or elaborate tombs, with their placement determined by their social and economic positions in life.

Below Despite its history of erosion and destruction during the colonial period, the monumental stepped Pyramid of the Sun (Huaca del Sol) still towers above the surrounding plain. Overlooking the Pyramid is the Temple of the Moon (Huaca de la Luna).

Moche artisans were highly skilled, living in segregated sections of major settlements or in their own towns. One set of specialists were the potters, who produced a huge range of moulded, sculptural pottery bottles depicting animals, plants, buildings, scenes from everyday life and, most famously, people. They produced pottery known in Peru as the *huacos eroticos* (erotic pots) that show men and women engaged in a wide range of sexual acts and related activities, as well as many other types of pots. Fineline pottery, with detailed drawings of Moche rituals, is among the rarest and has been important in revealing details about Moche religion and ritual.

The Moche artisans were also expert metalworkers. Jewellery and other ornaments of gold, silver, copper and alloys were often inlaid with turquoise and lapis lazuli. They also crafted metal tools, such as chisels, spear points and fishhooks.

Warriors held a special position in Moche society, living well until at least some of them suffered a gruesome end. We know this because of careful study of Moche pottery and other art, especially the ceramic vessels known as portrait pots. These three-dimensional sculptured images of the faces of Moche warriors and others on the outside of mould-made

Above A depiction in copper and gold shows the sacrificer god holding a knife in one hand and the head of one of his victims in the other.

ceramic bottles have provided important clues about the lives of ancient Moche warriors.

Building works

The major Moche settlements were dominated by huge adobe (mud-brick) pyramids with platforms, temples and huge spaces, decorated with friezes depicting Moche deities, scenes of processions of prisoners and other huge murals. Tombs of rulers and other important people were placed inside the pyramids in elaborate ceremonies that are depicted on Moche fineline pottery. The residences, workshops and cemeteries of the vast majority of Moche people were situated in compounds adjacent to the major pyramids and in towns up and down the river valleys.

The Moche built huge complexes of canals to irrigate the vast agricultural fields required to feed their people. However, catastrophic rains brought on periodically by El Niño destroyed the irrigation systems, causing widespread disruption in food supplies that may have had long-term consequences for the Moche economy.

They also appear to have prompted the Moche to sacrifice groups of young men, probably in the hopes of appeasing the gods who they believed brought on the devastating rains. The recent discovery by archaeologist Steve Bourget of the skeletal remains of at least 34 sacrificed adult males resting in layers of mud on the edge of the Pyramid of the Moon attest to the Moche practice of large-scale human sacrifice.

Pyramid of the Sun

Moche archaeological studies have advanced greatly in the last two decades, but there is still much to learn. The spectacular wealth of the ancient Moche has been one of the biggest challenges, because Moche sites have been subject to 500 years of looting. When the Spanish arrived in

Below The facial features and expressions depicted on portrait pots are so lifelike that they probably represented real Moche people. Musicians were a popular subject for moulded pots.

Below A gold funerary mask with lapis lazuli eyes was found in one of the royal tombs.

Below Although they had no written language, many aspects of the Moche culture are depicted in their pots, including ritual human sacrifice, as shown here.

Above Archaeologists have been working on the excavation of the temple tomb at Sipán.

Peru they looted all the gold and silver they could extract from the Inca Empire, but they also turned their attention to Moche Pyramids containing rich tombs. The most spectacular and tragic example is the Pyramid of the Sun along the Moche river, the focus of a recent long-term study project. This truncated pyramid structure was made of some 140 million adobe bricks, most of them imprinted with the mark of the community that provided them in some form of tribute. The Pyramid of the Sun was the largest adobe structure ever built in the Americas, but only an estimated one-third of it remains today. During the Spanish colonial era the Moche river was actually diverted in order to wash the structure away so that the treasure inside could be mined. The Spanish were after gold and silver, which they melted down and shipped back to Spain.

We will never know what was inside the destroyed portions of the pyramid, or what clues about

Moche civilization were lost forever. Looting still continues today, and archaeologists and Peruvian officials are engaged in a constant battle to preserve Moche sites as tourist destinations and as repositories of information and local heritage.

Moche mummy

In 2005 archaeologists discovered the mummified body of a young Moche woman at the El Brujo archaeological site on Peru's north coast near Trujillo. The mummy, which was dated to around AD 450, had complex tattoos and was remarkably well preserved. A young girl with a rope around her neck had been buried alongside her. The presence of gold jewellery and other artefacts, including a headdress, indicated that the woman had been a member of the Moche elite. Archaeologists also excavated various military artefacts, including war clubs and spear throwers.

Sipán's tombs

The dramatic story of the discovery of royal tombs at the Moche site of Sipán began on the night of 16 February 1987. Walter Alva, the archaeologist in charge of what was then a small regional museum on Peru's north coast, was awakened by a call from local police. A group of local looters had been digging illegally at Sipán and began to fight over the rich spoils of their labours. One or more of them went to the local police, who recovered a few spectacular gold objects and asked Alva to inspect them. Alva confirmed that they were pre-Columbian objects and, on a tip-off from one of the looters, he went to Sipán to search for their source.

Over the course of the next few months, and under constant threat of attack from the looters, Alva studied the site, confirming that the confiscated items had been taken from Sipán. He then mounted a project that was eventually to uncover the most magnificent burial ever found in the Americas. The tomb contained the remains of a man wearing spectacular ritual regalia, including textiles, featherwork, beaded items, gold and silver necklaces, staffs and hundreds of pottery vessels. The items had been layered on top of the body of the man who had been buried deep inside a huge mud-brick pyramid. This was the first scientifically excavated tomb of a Moche ruler. The painstaking excavation, which took months to conduct, would be the key to huge advances in our understanding of the ancient Moche.

Christopher Donnan, an archaeologist who had spent decades amassing an illustrated archive of Moche pottery, had published a number of papers on the scenes depicted on Moche fineline pots. These rare vessels were completely covered with elaborate drawings of rituals, such as burial ceremonies and sacrifice. Although Donnan and his colleague Donna McClellan had identified a series of figures that appeared repeatedly in the scenes found on the pottery, they had never seen evidence that such figures had actually existed in Moche society. The newly excavated Sipán tomb provided such evidence. Donnan was able to identify object after object found buried in the tomb as the same items depicted in the drawings of the costume and paraphernalia associated with one of the figures from the pots. This finding revolutionized the study of the ancient Moche, and subsequent finds at Sipán and other major Moche sites confirmed that the rulers of different Moche settlements had been the figures in the fineline drawings on the pottery. The fineline drawings depicted gruesome scenes of ritual sacrifice, and the discovery of one of the key figures in the drawings suggested that these rituals had actually occurred.

The ability to match iconographic scenes to the bodies of real individuals who lived nearly 2000 years ago was an incredible advance in archaeology. Since that first discovery, Moche studies have proliferated up and down the north coast of Peru. The remains of Moche rulers have been found at several other sites and have led to a much more in-depth understanding of Moche political economy and ritual organization. Archaeologists now believe that hereditary rulers of each of the major Moche cities came together periodically to perform the spectacular rituals depicted on the fineline pots.

Below The central coffin containing the body of the Lord of Sipán is surrounded by the bodies of sacrificed retainers.

Chichén Itzá

The importance of Chichén Itzá as a Maya ceremonial centre is reflected in its architecture, which includes a massive stepped pyramid, an observatory, a great ballcourt and the Sacred Cenote, which was a natural well into which offerings and human sacrifices were made.

Chichén Itzá is located in the state of Yucatán in Mexico, far to the north of the Classic Maya heartland, which contained cities such as Calakmul and Tikal. Chichén Itzá was occupied during the Terminal Classic and Early Postclassic periods (around AD 800-1200), flourishing at a time that roughly coincided with the collapse of the large centres of the southern and central Maya lowlands. Once one of the largest cities of Mesoamerica, today the ruins extend over an area of 5 sq km (2 sq miles).

The American John Lloyd Stephens visited the ruins in 1840 and published an account of his findings. From 1895 Edward H. Thompson began a 30-year exploration of Chichén Itzá, which included dredging the first artefacts out of the Sacred Cenote. The Carnegie Institution and the government of Mexico began a 20-year restoration and excavation project in 1924. Further work has been carried out at the site since the 1980s.

Architecture

The architecture at Chichén Itzá is organized around a series of ambient outdoor spaces, called plazas, in a pattern that is seen throughout the Maya area. Chichén Itzá is divided into two main areas of settlement, one of which is traditionally considered to be Terminal Classic (*c.*AD 800-900) Maya, while the other is ascribed to an Early Postclassic (AD 900-1250) Maya-Toltec hybrid culture. The earlier settlement, located on the south of the site, contains architecture that is traditionally associated with the Maya,

whereas the architecture in the newer part shows strong influences from central Mexico, with buildings reminiscent of those at Tula (the Toltec capital). However, the cultural and

Above Two pillars in the form of a feathered serpent stand at the entrance to the Temple of the Warriors. At the top of the stairway in front of the two serpent statues is a reclining *chacmool* figure.

Above The interior of the Castillo houses King Kukulcán's Jaguar Throne, which is made of stone and painted red with jade spots.

chronological distinctions between these two areas of the site are becoming increasingly blurred as new research is conducted on the site.

The Castillo

One of the site's most important monuments, in the 'Toltec' part of the city, is the Castillo. This square-based, stepped pyramid is about 25m (82ft) high and each of its four sides has a staircase of 91 steps. The Castillo is decorated with snake iconography, most notably along the balustrades of the staircases. Scholars Linda Schele and Peter Mathews have suggested that the structure might represent a 'snake mountain', an important location in Mesoamerican religion. At the spring and autumn equinoxes the sun's shadow creates the illusion of a serpent

moving down the pyramid. Excavations at the Castillo has revealed evidence of an earlier construction.

The Great Ballcourt

There are other smaller ballcourts at Chichén Itzá, but the Great Ballcourt is the largest in Mesoamerica, measuring about 166 x 68m (545 x 223ft). It is also notable for its well-preserved murals and elaborate architecture, with temples at either end. The sides of the

Below Astronomers made observations of the stars from the tower of the Caracol.

interior of the ballcourt are lined with sculpted panels depicting teams of ball players. While the actual rules of the ballgame are still shrouded in mystery, it appears to have been an activity steeped in both political overtones and religious imagery.

The observatory

The astronomical observatory, known as the Caracol ('snail' in Spanish) in reference to its spiral staircase, is the only round structure at Chichén Itzá. It features an observation tower built on two rectangular platforms.

Chaco Canyon

A thousand years ago, Chaco Canyon in New Mexico was home to a remarkable prehistoric society that lived in multi-storey villages, developed irrigation systems that enabled them to grow crops in the desert environment, and built an extensive road system.

Chaco Canyon National Historical Park is, with Mesa Verde, one of the most important archaeological sites in North America. The canyon is a seasonal wash that cuts through the dry deserts of northern New Mexico. Its dryness, coupled with long winters and a short growing season, hardly made it a promising location for the flowering of such a remarkable culture. And yet, between around AD 850 and 1250, the Ancestral Puebloan (Anasazi) Indians built several large villages here, with buildings designed for residential, ceremonial and public use.

As at Mesa Verde, Chacoan potters produced beautifully painted and technologically sophisticated ceramic vessels. As well as pieces of pottery, excavations have also unearthed other examples of their craftsmanship, including baskets and turquoise jewellery.

Chaco Canyon reached the height of its influence in the 11th century AD. After this it declined, and was finally abandoned in the middle of the 13th century AD.

Apartment living

The sites in Chaco Canyon were first viewed by Europeans in the mid-19th century, and excavation began at the end of the century. A series of large and smaller villages are scattered through a section of the canyon, approximately 20km (12 miles) in length. The largest, of which there are 13, are known as great houses. Each consists of several hundred inter-connected rooms built on several levels, arranged around public plazas. Some housed families, while others were used as storerooms.

The buildings were constructed using timber, sandstone and adobe, and are interspersed with roughly cylindrical masonry structures known as kivas. These chambers, which are partly sunk into the ground, were

Below This Chacoan white-ware pitcher is decorated with a typical geometric design, which was applied with a yucca brush. The colours were achieved using plant dyes.

used for meetings and ceremonies, as similar chambers are by Puebloan Indians today. The canyon also contains larger versions of the kiva, called great kivas, which have astronomical significance. Casa Rinconada is the best example.

Archaeologists have found evidence of well-engineered water-diversion systems such as dams and ditches. These collected as much run-off water from the cliffs above as possible and transported it to fields in the canyon around the great houses, where crops such as corn and squash were grown.

Sections of the canyon walls still contain rock art, and carved handholds and steps that the inhabitants would have used to climb to the mesa tops above. Although most archaeologists believe that the canyon was occupied all year round, some have speculated that it was used only at certain times of the year, perhaps in the cycle of some religious ceremony.

Pueblo Bonito

The largest and best-known great house in Chaco Canyon, known as Pueblo Bonito ('pretty village' in Spanish), was excavated by Neil Judd on behalf of the National Geographic Society during the 1920s. Arranged in a 'D' shape, the buildings originally stood four to five storeys high and were built of high-quality, shaped masonry that has withstood the test of time remarkably well. Analysis of tree rings in the wooden beams has revealed that construction

began in the 900s, with the major work being carried out between 1075 and 1115. Pueblo Bonito comprises over 300 individual rooms at ground level; some estimates put the total number as high as 650. It also contains at least 32 kivas and two great kivas, the biggest almost 20m (66ft) across.

Ancient networks

Chaco was at the centre of a network of over 645km (400 miles) of well-constructed roads that fanned out over the surrounding countryside for as far as 160km (100 miles). Many of the roads connected the canyon to more than 150 so-called Chacoan outliers – smaller habitation and ceremonial sites that were part of the overall Chacoan network. The roads facilitated trade but may also have connected individual ceremonial sites into the wider network. One example is Chimney Rock, 150km (93 miles) north of the canyon, in the pine forests of southern

Above An aerial view of the Chaco Canyon ruins shows Pueblo Benito in the foreground. The connecting road network is clearly visible.

Colorado. Some archaeologists have suggested that Chimney Rock served as a centre for harvesting lumber, meat and hides, which were then transported back to Chaco for use there or for redistribution. Others have suggested that because Chimney Rock was probably built in the 11th century AD, at the time of a lunar standstill, its purpose was primarily religious.

Artefacts, such as copper bells and macaw skeletons, have been discovered at Chaco Canyon, suggesting trade connections with other contemporary Mesoamerican cultures. However, the intensity of this trade connection is not clear. The presence of these items might be the result of sporadic contact, rather than the existence of a formal trading and exchange system between the two areas.

Satellite images

In the 1980s NASA conducted a series of infrared satellite scans of Chaco Canyon, and these revealed a remarkable feature that was undetectable by conventional archaeological methods at ground level or from aerial photography. They showed an extensive network of roads with the canyon at its centre. The most surprising feature of these roads was that they are absolutely straight, even going across obstacles in the terrain rather than around them. The reason for this uncompromising straightness is not known, but it could have been practical: as the Chacoans went everywhere on foot, and did not use pack animals or vehicles, they could take the most direct route. Alternatively, it could have had a symbolic significance.

Mesa Verde

Located in south-west Colorado, Mesa Verde National Park contains some of the best-preserved archaeological sites in North America. Chief among these is an incomparable collection of sites where the Ancestral Puebloan (Anasazi) Indians lived, dating from approximately AD 600-1300.

Mesa Verde, which means 'green table' in Spanish, is a series of flat-topped mountains (mesas) – a common feature of the western United States. Although there is evidence of human occupation in the area from as early as 10,000 years ago, the most remarkable remains are those associated with the Ancestral Puebloan Indians – so called because they were the ancestors of the modern Pueblo people.

The archaeological remains were first brought to public attention in 1888 by Richard Wetherill, a young Colorado cowboy. An early visitor to the site was Gustaf Nordenskjöld, who in 1893 published *The Cliff Dwellers of*

Below Cliff Palace is the largest of the cliff dwellings, built into an alcove 27m (89ft) deep and 18m (59ft) high. The circular kivas can be seen in the foreground.

the Mesa Verde, the first scholarly study of the site. In 1906 the area was established as a national park to preserve the extensive remains, which had been ransacked and damaged by looters. It was designated a World Heritage Site in 1978.

Thousands of different sites have been discovered, including semi-subterranean pithouses and masonry roomblocks, both of which were

of the complex contains some original plaster, which had been painted with abstract designs.

Abandonment

The Ancestral Puebloans occupied these cliff dwellings for only the last 75 to 100 years of their occupation of the Mesa Verde region, and archaeologists speculate that they may have been located where they were for defensive purposes. Their inhabitants abandoned the region over the period of a couple of generations at the end of the 13th century, possibly forced out by drought.

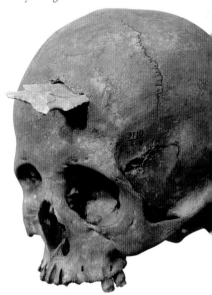

places where people lived. There are also circular, underground kivas, which were used for ceremonial purposes. Extensive masonry water reservoirs were part of the complex water irrigation systems that the Ancestral Puebloans built in this arid region. They also grew corn and produced beautiful pottery of different shapes and designs.

Cliff Palace

The most spectacular sites at Mesa Verde are the multi-storeyed, many-roomed pueblos ('villages' in Spanish) that were built into the natural cliff alcoves on the sides of the mesas. Of these, the most famous is Cliff Palace,

Above The cliff dwellings feature distinctive key hole doors.

which contains upwards of 200 rooms and 23 kivas. The primary building materials were sandstone slabs, mortar and wooden beams. Dwelling rooms were lined with plaster, which was often painted. Specially cut stairs allowed the inhabitants to reach their fields on the mesa top. There are several multi-storey round and square towers at Cliff Palace. The interior of a four-storey tower at the south end

Right The skull of a 20-year-old woman was excavated at Mesa Verde. The flint that killed her is still lodged into the front of the skull.

L'Anse aux Meadows

When Norwegians Helge and Anne Stine Ingstad excavated L'Anse aux Meadows in Newfoundland in 1961, they found astonishing proof that the first Europeans to settle in the New World were Scandinavians in the 11th century AD — some 500 years before Columbus.

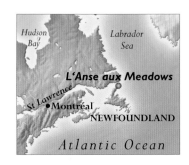

Ancient Norse sagas told of the Viking hero, Erik the Red, who was banished from Norway in AD 982 and ultimately established a series of colonies in a forest-covered land called Vinland. Later generations identified Vinland with North America. However, there was no evidence of Viking occupation there until the Ingstads, tipped off by a local fisherman, started work on L'Anse aux Meadows, which lies on Epave Bay near the northernmost tip of the island of Newfoundland. For the next nine years the Ingstads led an international team of archaeologists in the excavation of the site. Major excavations were continued by Parks Canada from 1973 to 1976.

These excavations unearthed the remains of eight houses (of wood and sod construction), smaller buildings, a smithy and a charcoal kiln. The buildings were of the same kind as those used in Iceland and Greenland just before and after the year AD 1000. Artefacts found in the ruins of these buildings included typical Viking objects of the 11th century AD, such as iron rivets, a bronze pin and a spindle whorl. Radiocarbon dates supported the artefact chronology.

Viking settlement

In every characteristic the site differs from contemporary American Indian settlements in the area, and it can be plausibly linked to the story of Erik the Red in the so-called Vinland Sagas. The climate was too severe for cultivating grapes, so the term Vinland may refer to the making of berry wine from the wild berries found nearby.

The shallowness of the middens indicates that the site was only occupied for a relatively brief period of time, perhaps about 30 years. It is unclear why it was abandoned so soon after it was settled. The climate may have been unsuitable for long-term reliance on agriculture. Or perhaps its isolation simply made it too dangerous.

Below Three Norse sod houses have been reconstructed at the site.

Cahokia

During the 11th century AD a great metropolis arose on the fertile flood plain of the Mississippi River. A major centre of the Mississippian Culture, Cahokia is a leading candidate for a true pre-Columbian city in North America. The site is the focus of ongoing archaeological research.

Cahokia is located just east of St Louis, Illinois, in an area known as the American Bottoms, where the confluence of the Missouri, Mississippi and Illinois rivers has created one of the most fertile regions on the continent. The site, which was inhabited from AD 700-1400, covers an area of about 15 sq km (6 sq miles).

In the early 19th century journalist and explorer Henry Marie Brakenridge studied the site and described it in a letter to Thomas Jefferson. His findings aroused little attention, however, for although Cahokia is named after the local Indian tribe, for most of the 19th century Euroamerican settlers refused to believe that a site as complex as this could have been built by ancestors of contemporary American Indians. Many fanciful stories circulated as to who had built this and other mounds, including the lost tribe of Israel, the Egyptians, even a band of Welshmen. Early relic-hunters and archaeologists did not realize the significance of their finds, and full-scale scientific excavation did not begin until the 1960s.

A well-planned city

Excavations at the site have revealed a 3km- (2 mile-) long wooden stockade encircling the inner part of the site, which almost certainly served as a defensive wall. Inside the stockade are the remains of plazas, earth mounds and communal buildings. Houses were built around the plazas and arranged in rows within the stockade. The remains of suburbs outside the stockade and satellite villages have also been found.

Above Monk's Mound is the largest man-made mound in North America.

The largest structure at the site is Monk's Mound, a rectangular, terraced earth mound that overlooked a large plaza at the centre of the city. Carbon dating has revealed that this mound was started in around AD 950 and took over 200 years to reach its current size. Its base covers 6ha (15 acres), and it reaches about 30m (98ft) high. The flat top of the mound originally supported some sort of wooden structure, possibly a chieftain's house or a religious building. Smaller mounds at the site were used as burial sites for prominent individuals.

During excavations of one burial mound (Mound 72), archaeologists found the body of an important man in his 40s, along with a cache of arrowheads from different parts of the region buried nearby. Over 250 other skeletons were also found in Mound 72, many in mass graves and some with their heads and hands missing.

At its peak Cahokia was at the centre of a wide-reaching trade network that extended from the Gulf of Mexico to Hudson Bay and from the Atlantic coast to the Great Plains. Archaeologists are unclear as to why the city fell from power, but AD 1200 marked the arrival of a period of severe drought, which may have undercut the population's ability to produce food.

Woodhenge

In the early 1960s archaeologist Dr Warren Wittry identified some large pits at the site that seemed to be arranged on the arcs of circles. Noting that wooden posts set in these pits would have been oriented to the rising sun, he suggested that the circular structure served as a calendar, and named it Woodhenge. Further excavations revealed that there were as many as five post circles at the site.

Great Serpent Mound

Winding along the crest of a ridge overlooking Bush Creek Valley in southern Ohio is a giant earthwork construction. Aerial views of the site show the unmistakable shape of a spectacular serpent curving for some 400m (1300ft).

Great Serpent Mound (or Serpent Mound) is the world's largest extant example of the so-called effigy mound, the term given to prehistoric earthen constructions that represented animals and which are found throughout the American Midwest.

The mound is constructed from earth built onto a clay and rock base; it is about 6-7.5m (20-25ft) wide and, on average, about 1.5m (5ft) high. Its creators worked with artistry and skill to create a sinuous snake whose three

Below The mysterious oval mound at the serpent's head can be seen in the top right-hand corner of this aerial photograph.

coils appear to be evenly sized and spaced, as if representing a symbolic pattern. Some archaeologists interpret an oval mound at the head end as an egg in its open mouth. Others see it as the eye of the serpent.

Dating

The site was first recorded by Ephraim Squier and Edwin Davis in *Ancient Monuments of the Mississippi Valley*, their monumental study of the earthen mounds of the Midwest published in 1848. The first excavations were undertaken by archaeologist Frederic Putnam of Harvard University in the late 1880s. In 1901 an engineer named

Clinton Cowan mapped and carried out geographical surveys of the site. This work, along with Putnam's excavations, have been the basis for modern investigations of the mound.

Archaeologists have found the mound difficult to date accurately because so far no artefacts or human remains have been found in it. The historical view was that it was created during the so-called Adena Culture – a predominantly hunter-gatherer society that inhabited present-day Ohio, Kentucky and West Virginia between 500 BC and AD 200. Burial mounds in the surrounding area have been definitely attributed to the Adena people, so the connection seems plausible. However, it is possible that the Serpent Mound is much later. A burial mound and village site close to the serpent's tail date to about AD 1000, which places them within the Mississippian Culture. And pieces of charcoal recently recovered from a previously undisturbed part of the Serpent Mound have been radiocarbon-dated to the same time.

As with so much prehistoric imagery, it is almost impossible to determine exactly what the mound meant to its builders, or how it fitted into contemporary religion and iconography. Burial data from Adena and Mississippian contexts provide some insights into prehistoric religion and iconography, so if a firmer date could be determined for the Serpent Mound, archaeologists would have greater leeway in trying to understand its purpose.

Chan Chan

Until the 15th century AD Chan Chan, on the north-west coast of Peru, was the impressive capital of the Chimú civilization. Today, the ruins of the enormous pre-Inca city make up one of the largest and most important archaeological sites in the New World.

Chan Chan is the largest known adobe city in the Americas and it was named a UNESCO World Heritage Site in 1986. It has also been listed as one of the world's most endangered archaeological sites because of natural and human threats posed to the site.

Much of what we know about Chan Chan today is due to the massive archaeological research project directed by Michael E. Moseley and his colleagues during the 1970s, known as the Chan Chan-Moche Valley project. This project, which included archaeological surveys and excavations, as well as environmental studies, produced huge amounts of archaeological data. In addition, a number of now well-known North American archaeologists conducted their graduate research on the project. Ongoing research at Chan Chan and throughout the north coast of Peru continues to produce new discoveries and to build on the foundations laid by the project.

Adobe city

Chan Chan covers an area of roughly 6 sq km (2 sq miles) along the Moche River Valley. The city comprises at least nine huge compounds, known as *ciudadelas* (citadels), that contain the remains of palaces and administrative complexes. The huge decorated adobe walls of the compounds are 10m (33ft) high and protected vast networks of storage rooms, as well as courts, royal residences, a reservoir and burial chambers. Each compound was accessible only through a single

doorway. There are also vast areas of residences, workshops and cemeteries. The city was supported by a huge complex of irrigated agricultural fields, as well as by fishing and herding.

Left A statue stands sentinel in the Tschudi Complex, which is the best preserved of the city's *ciudadelas* and also features friezes, courtyards and some original walls.

Chan Chan was meticulously planned and built by the ancient Chimú civilization, which controlled much of northern Peru before the Inca conquest. The Chimú civilization arose beginning around AD 1000 and became increasingly powerful until the mid-15th century, when they were conquered by the Inca. Chimú statecraft, engineering and religion were incredibly advanced, and they greatly influenced the technology and culture of Inca civilization.

Below A view of part of the core of the city shows fragile adobe ruins. They are vulnerable to natural erosion, as they become exposed to air and rain, and require careful conservation.

Tenochtitlán

Excavations under present-day Mexico City have periodically uncovered the remains of Tenochtitlán's walled precinct, including the Great Temple, which was the ceremonial heart of the once vast capital of the Aztec empire from AD 1325 to the arrival of the Spanish in 1521.

Located on an island in the lake system of the Basin of Mexico, Tenochtitlán grew rapidly to become the largest city of the ancient Americas, a thriving hub of political, economic and religious activity with a population of 250,000.

Following the Spanish conquest, however, much of the the ancient city was destroyed to make way for the capital of New Spain. Fortunately, much is known about the Aztecs and their capital city from the colonial period histories collected by Spanish chroniclers using native informants. The most important of these was the *General History of New Spain*, compiled by Fray Bernardino de Sahagún in the mid-16th century. Other useful sources of information include legal documents from land disputes in the early colony, and pictorial manuscripts produced by indigenous scribes.

Most of the city remained buried until the year 1790, when excavation for water pipes uncovered two Aztec sculptures. A few sections of the city's Great Temple, or Templo Mayor, were unearthed in the first half of the 20th century. However, it was not until the 1970s that a major excavation project was undertaken.

Expansion

The city was founded in the 14th century by Nahuatl-speaking migrants from the north, who settled on an unpopulated island. The Aztecs met the challenge of island life by constructing causeways to the mainland. They also expanded their space by building floating gardens (*chinampas*) of reed mats covered with a thin layer of lake silt and anchored into the shallow lakebed by the roots of corn plants. Over time, these floating gardens became increasingly solid, to the point where they could be used for housing.

After the initial years as poor fishermen and mercenary soldiers employed by more powerful city-states, in 1420 the Aztecs formed an alliance with neighbouring groups to conquer and control the Basin of

Left While it suffered cataclysmic destruction during the Spanish conquest, the rapid metamorphosis into Mexico City has in some ways preserved the foundations of the Aztec city, with remarkable finds such as the Great Temple still awaiting discovery.

Above A symbolic sculpted eagle was found within the sacred precinct.

Mexico. This alliance quickly grew through military conquest and coercion until it commanded tribute from throughout the central highlands and the Gulf Coast.

The Great Temple

Tenochtitlán's ceremonial precinct of monumental buildings was dominated by the Great Temple, a massive dual pyramid dedicated to both the Aztec patron deity Huitzilopochtli, and the storm god, Tlaloc.

Archaeological excavations at the base of the temple demonstrate that it was built as a symbolic re-enactment of the birth of Huitzilopochtli. According to myth, the pregnant goddess Coatlicue was attacked by her jealous daughter, the moon goddess Coyolxauqui, while on Serpent Mountain (*coatepec*). Decapitated, Coatlicue still gave birth to her son, Huitzilopochtli, who dismembered Coyolxauqui, whose body rolled to the base of the mountain.

When, in 1978, workers employed by the Electric Light Company discovered the huge Coyolxauqui sculpture – depicting a naked, dismembered woman – archaeologists knew that they had found the base of Serpent Mountain and the ritual centre of the Aztec empire.

Right The base of the skull rack (*tzompantli*) is decorated with sculpted skulls. The rack would have been used for the public display of human skulls, typically those of war captives or other sacrificial victims.

The mammoth excavation project, headed by the Mexican archaeologist Eduardo Matos Moctezuma, required the demolition of several city blocks in the centre of Mexico City, adjacent to the Cathedral and National Palace. Clearing the architectural rubble caused by the destruction of the temple by the Spaniards revealed six stages of construction, as the temple was sequentially expanded, perhaps by each Aztec ruler.

The second stage of the Great Temple pyramid was small enough that it survived, even preserving some of the stone temple structures on the pyramid base. A multi-coloured *chacmool* sculpture of a reclining warrior was found in the Tlaloc temple, and a sacrificial stone was unearthed in the Huitzilopochtli temple. Additionally, serpent heads decorate the preserved pyramid and the surrounding walls, to represent the mythical Serpent Mountain.

Over 100 caches of valuable and symbolically charged objects have been found buried in and around Tenochtitlán's Great Temple, including artefacts of gold, jade and other precious materials.

Also of note are the hundreds of animal skeletons from sea, land and sky, along with artefacts from previous Mesoamerican civilizations, which were buried in an attempt to make the Great Temple a symbolic *axis mundi*, or world axis of creation.

Above The reclining *chacmool* figure has a sacrificial tray on his lap. The statue is unique as it is the only one ever found with its original colouring.

In addition to the Great Temple itself, archaeologists have also uncovered a warrior's compound and a *tzompantli*, or skull rack, in the ceremonial compound. Other construction excavations have yielded remnants of the ancient city, including the famous Calendar Stone, which is decorated with calendrical signs representing the sacred cycle of time.

During the building of the Metro system, archaeologists accompanied construction teams to recover and preserve evidence of the ancient city wherever possible. One area that has been extensively excavated and preserved is the city's Tlatelolco district, where Aztec pyramids, colonial cathedrals and modern high-rises are juxtaposed in what is known as the Plaza of the Three Cultures.

Little Bighorn

On 25 June 1876, General George Armstrong Custer rode to his death against a force of Sioux and Cheyenne Indians. Custer's Last Stand passed into American legend, but many of the details of the battle remained a mystery until archaeologists started working on the site in 1983.

Custer and 647 men of the 7th Cavalry were taking part in a US army campaign to force Sioux and Cheyenne Indians back onto the Great Sioux Reservation of South Dakota. On 25 June they inadvertently stumbled onto a mass Indian village of as many as 7000 inhabitants, located along the banks of the Little Bighorn River in Montana.

Unaware of, or perhaps deliberately ignoring the size of the force confronting him, Custer charged the village. At the end of that day, he and 210 men under his command lay dead. About 60 Indians had died. However, perhaps because the dead tell no tales, and the Sioux and Cheyenne were never asked, for over

a century little was known about the actual sequence of events. We still don't know with certainty, for example, how Custer died.

Below The site was first preserved as a national cemetery in 1879. In 1890, the marble blocks that dot the battlefield were added to mark where the soldiers fell.

Revealed by fire

It was not until 1983, when a grassland fire bared the prairie, that archaeologists were able to unravel many of the battle's secrets. From then until 1996, archaeologists, led by Dr Douglas Scott of the National Park Service, have conducted surveys of the land. Scott's team visually identified the physical remains of the battle and used metal detectors to locate spent bullets and other metallic objects (ten iron arrowheads were also found).

Careful analysis of the artefact distribution showed that Custer split his command into three elements. This was an accepted tactic when cavalry attacked a village, but it may have been a factor that hastened his defeat.

Scott's groundbreaking work encouraged others. For example, one of Scott's colleagues, Dr Richard Fox, identified individual combat positions and plotted the movements of both soldiers and Indians as they moved across the battlefield. Fox concluded that the location of Custer's so-called 'last stand', Custer's Hill as it is called today, was not actually the last place where fighting took place. Rather, the last American casualties came after the soldiers had fled the hill.

Fox concluded that although the Americans had arrived at the battle well-organized and tactically prepared to fight, as the battle progressed they gradually lost discipline, ultimately succumbing to a fatal panic that destroyed their cohesion as a fighting unit. It seems that archaeology has destroyed at least one segment of the Custer legend. The excavations carried out by Scott and his team have also pioneered the archaeological investigation of battlefields in other parts of the world.

Right A pile of bones is all that remains on the battlefield of Little Bighorn in this photograph looking towards the Indian village, taken around 1877.

Skulls

Of great interest are the forensic studies commissioned by Dr Scott on the skeletal remains of some of the troopers, who fell and were subsequently buried on the battlefield itself. Analysis revealed that skull fragments had been smashed while the body was still alive, or very soon after death – confirmation of Indian accounts of the troopers being finished off with clubs and axes. Other remains showed evidence of mutilation. One individual aged about 25 had been shot in the chest by a repeating rifle. He had then been shot in the head, had his skull smashed in, been pierced with arrows and then had his front and rear torso slashed. Other skeletons tell of similarly grisly ends.

Glossary

Absolute dating A date for an object, structure or occurrence that is accurate to a specific year. Absolute dates for some archaeology can be secured using scientific techniques such as radiocarbon dating.

Acheulian A tradition of tool-making associated with *Homo erectus* in the Lower Palaeolithic period.

Acropolis From the Greek meaning 'the high point of the city', the upper citadel of an ancient Greek city.

Adobe Mudbrick made by drying mud in the sun and used for building.

Adze A stone tool made of flakes or pebbles used for woodworking.

Agora An open public space at the centre of an ancient Greek city.

Amphora A large storage jar.

Anthropology The biological and cultural study of humanity.

Apadana The pillared audience hall of an ancient Persian palace.

Aridity Extreme dryness with little moisture, typical of the conditions found in desert regions. Aridity prevents bacteria from growing and preserves organic remains.

Below The Pyramid of Khafre is the second largest of Giza's great pyramids.

Above Electronic Distance Equipment (EDM) is used to accurately plot excavations.

Artefact An object that has been found during excavation that is the result of human activity.

Assemblage A collection of artefacts or ecofacts found in the same context, such as all the objects found buried in a grave.

Aurignacian Cultural assemblages associated with *Homo sapiens sapiens* as they replaced *Homo neanderthalensis* lasting about 12,000 years from around 40,000 years ago.

Australopithecine A general term for the species that make up the pre-human hominid genus *Australopithecus* found in Africa between 4 and 1 million years ago.

Australopithecus africanus One of the earliest direct ancestors of modern humans, dating back to 3 million years ago.

Barrow A mound of earth and/or stones over a grave or graves. Also known as a tumulus.

Benchmark Any fixed point that serves as a reference point for other measurements.

Biface A stone tool that has had flakes removed from both faces.

Bronze Age The second age of the Three Age System in which bronze was the primary material for tools and weapons.

Canopic jars Clay containers used to hold the internal organs removed from a body when it was mummified in ancient Egypt.

Carbon-14 dating A method of dating organic remains such as seeds, based on the fact that living things absorb the isotope carbon-14 when they are alive, and then release it again at a constant rate after death.

Caryatid A column in the form of a female figure.

CAT scanning A Computerized Axial Tomography scan combines X-ray images to create a three-dimensional view of an object.

Cenotaph From the Greek meaning 'empty tomb', cenotaphs were tombs built for ceremonial purposes and never intended to hold human remains.

Cenote A naturally formed well.

Centuriation The process of dividing the countryside surrounding new towns into equally sized square allotments which were then allocated to the occupants of the colony.

Below The excavated ruins of a Celtic fort at Castro de Barona, Spain.

Above A view through the mysterious standing stones at Stonehenge.

Codex A manuscript formed from leaves bound together recording political or religious information.

Corpus Everything ever discovered from a particular culture.

Cuneiform An early script developed by the Sumerians in about 3000 BC. It was written using a wedge-shaped tool known as a stylus which was impressed into wet clay.

Cylinder seal A Mesopotamian carved seal that was rolled across a clay seal to produce an impression.

Datum point A set point from which measurements are taken for a specific project.

Dendrochronology A method of dating based on the analysis of tree-ring sequences.

Earthworks Any grass-covered earthen features in the landscape that result from human activity such as castle mounds.

Effigy mound A prehistoric mound in the form of an animal.

Egyptology The study of the ancient Egyptians through archaeology and discovered artefacts.

Excavation The removal of soil deposits in the reverse order in which they were laid down enabling archaeologists to work back chronologically from the present day to the earliest surviving remains.

Faience A non-clay ceramic glaze used for figurines and jewellery in ancient Egypt and the Near East.

Geochemical Scientific analysis of the elements in an object, to calculate where the materials from which it was made originally came from.

Hellenistic The period between the accession of Alexander the Great and the establishment of the Roman empire.

Hieroglyphs A complicated form of writing that uses pictographic and ideographic symbols that was used in ancient Egypt and Mesoamerica among other places.

Henge A usually circular ritual enclosure consisting of a bank and ditch system sometimes enclosing a circle of stones or wooden posts.

Hominid All the species in the Hominidae ('great apes') family, living and extinct, including closely related primates such as chimpanzees and gorillas, as well as humans.

Homo sapiens The biological name given to our own species, modern humans.

Hydria A type of three-handled Greek jar used for carrying water.

Below Gloves are used during the excavation of human remains to prevent contamination.

Above The great Pyramid of the Sun at the ancient American city of Teothuacan.

Hypostyle hall From the Greek meaning 'bearing pillars', a hall with a flat roof supported by pillars.

Infrared film Photographic film that is sensitive to infrared radiation, which is not visible to the naked eye, but that indicates slight differences in temperature.

Intrusive material Material that has found its way into a deposit where it is too recent by comparison with other material in the same deposit.

Iron Age The third age of the Three Age System in which iron became the main material for tools and weapons.

Kiva A circular underground room in a Pueblo Indian village.

Kouros From the Greek meaning 'a youth', a standing nude male statue. The female (fully clothed) equivalent is called a kore.

Lararium A household shrine in ancient Rome.

Light detection and ranging (Lidar) technology A scanner that is mounted in an aeroplane and used to scan large areas of the landscape, picking up tiny variations in contour.

Linear A The syllabic script used by the Minoans of Crete.

Linear B The syllabic script used by the Mycenaeans and Minoans.

Magnetometer An instrument that measures magnetic variation which can be used to detect objects or features buried beneath the soil.

Mahat Mudbrick shrines that held limestone stelae found at the ancient Egyptian site of Abydos.

Map regression Working backward from the most recent map to the earliest, noting changes at each stage, to analyse how the landscape has evolved over time.

Mastaba tomb An ancient Egyptian royal tomb consisting of a freestanding, rectangular mudbrick superstructure over a burial chamber.

Megalith A large stone. A megalithic monument, such as Stonehenge, is one that is made from large stones.

Megaron A rectangular, freestanding hall usually with a centrally located hearth entered through a two-columned porch. Associated with Aegean architecture.

Menhir A single standing stone.

Mesoamerica Term for different civilizations in the region between central Mexico and Northern Honduras characterised by shared cultural phenomena.

Mesolithic Middle Stone Age.

Metallurgy The study of metal objects to understand how they were made and used.

Mesolithic period Literally 'middle stone' age, meaning the period of transition between the Paleolithic (Old Stone Age) and the Neolithic (New Stone Age).

Mesopotamia The region between the rivers Tigris and Euphrates.

Midden A rubbish dump or accumulation of human, domestic waste products.

Moche Pre-Columbian culture of the Moche Valley, Peru.

Mousterian A term for stone tool assemblages associated with the Neanderthals in the Middle Palaeolithic.

Multi-variate analysis Analysis that examines more than one or two variables within an assemblage.

Mummification A technique developed by the ancient Egyptians to maintain the lifelike appearance of a dead body.

Neolithic period The New Stone Age is defined as the point at which we began to live in permanent settlements.

Below A student of archaeology carefully records data at a university sponsored dig.

Necropolis A cemetery, from the Greek meaning 'city of the dead'.

Neolithic New Stone Age.

Obelisk A four-sided stone pillar that tapers towards a pyramidal point. Usually carved from a single piece of stone (a monolith).

Obsidian A sharp volcanic glass used to make tools and jewellery.

Ossuary A container such as a chest for the bones of the dead.

Palaeoanthropology From the Greek meaning 'study of ancient man'. The multidisciplinary study of human evolution focusing on examination of the fossil record.

Palaeolithic period The Old Stone Age accounts for more than 90 per cent of human history, from about 2.6 million years ago to about 15,000 years ago.

Papyrus An early form of paper made from the pith of the papyrus plant.

Parch mark Marks caused by lack of rainfall that reveal buried features because grass or crops grow shorter or turn yellow sooner over shallow soil where walls or floors lie beneath the soil, or because they grow taller or remain greener longer over deep water-retentive features, such as pits or ditches.

Passage tomb A tomb that is approached via a narrow passage.

Petroglyph a carving made into a rock face.

Phasing Placing datable finds in chronological order to work out how the landscape has been used over time.

Pictogram A system of writing using pictures to represent words.

Pithos A large storage jar originally used for keeping oil and wine.

Pleistocene A geologic period denoting the most recent Ice Age that began about 1.8 million years ago and ended about 10,000 years ago.

Polychrome pottery Pottery that is decorated with more than two colours.

Prehistory The period of human history before written records.

Punic Of or relating to Carthage, its people and language.

Radiocarbon dating A method of dating carbon-bearing materials including wood, bone, peat and shell based on the radioactive decay of the Carbon-14 isotope.

Relative dating A system of dating archaeological remains in relation to each other which does not produce an absolute date for objects.

Below A Viking stone ship, typical of Scandinavia, marks a burial site.

Above Thorough archaeological excavation demands painstaking attention to detail.

Relief A carved stone slab with projecting decoration. Also bas-relief (low relief).

Residual material Something that is far older than the other material found in the deposit.

Resistivity meter A device that detects variations in electrical resistance and conductivity in the soil.

Sarcophagus A stone chest used to contain a corpse.

Scarab An ancient Egyptian seal type that was shaped like a dung beetle and incised with a design that was stamped onto the seal.

Slip A solution of very fine coloured clay in water, into which pots are dipped; when fired, it produces a coloured glossy surface.

Spoil tip The place where excavated soil is stored during an archaeological dig, after it has been sieved (sifted), ready to be replaced after the dig.

Stela An upright slab of stone, often carved with funerary reliefs and used as a grave marker.

Stone Age The first age of the Three Age System covering the period from the first production of stone artefacts to the first production of metal artefacts.

Strata Layers of earth or levels on an archaeological site.

Stratigraphy A method of dating that involves placing deposits in sequence according to the stratified layer in which they are found.

Stupa A Buddhist monument, temple or shrine.

Stylistic dating A method of dating that involves placing artefacts in a sequence according to a perceived development in form or decoration.

Tell A long, low mound caused by the accumulation of mud, brick and refuse over time.

Tesserae The basic units that make up a mosaic.

Theodolite A surveying tool for measuring height above sea level.

Tholos A round tomb with a rectilinear entrance passage.

Tumulus An artificial mound of earth and stones, usually covering a burial or burials.

Typology Method of placing objects in a dated series, starting from the oldest to newest.

Ziggurat
A stepped pyramidal temple tower built across ancient Mesopotamia.

Below Bronze age carvings adorn the rocks at Tanumshede, Sweden.

Acknowledgements

Above The careful tagging of artefacts is an essential part of any dig.

AUTHOR'S ACKNOWLEDGEMENTS

A book like this could not have been produced without drawing on the fieldwork and research of countless archaeologists all over the world. We are very grateful to every one of them, and especially to those who have generously shared their photographs and contributed to the case studies. In particular we owe an enormous debt to Tim Darvill, Professor of Archaeology in the School of Conservation Sciences at Bournemouth University, and to his colleagues and students, for allowing our photographer free access to excavations during the summer of 2007, where much of the location photography was taken. Similarly, Mark Horton, Reader in Archaeology at the University of Bristol, allowed us to photograph buildings archaeology work and churchyard excavation. We hope that everyone who was involved in the making of this book will feel that the effort was worthwhile, particularly if it encourages more people to join us in that fascinating and collective endeavour that is archaeology.

PICTURE ACKNOWLEDGEMENTS

(b: bottom, l: left, m: middle, r: right, t: top). Anness Publishing Ltd would like to thank the following people for location photography: **Wiggold Summer School,** Abbey Home Farm, Cirencester, UK, to Will and Hilary Chester-Master at Abbey Home Farm and Professor Timothy Darvill at the School of Conservation Sciences, University of Bournemouth, UK, and **Berkeley Castle Summer School,** Berkeley, Gloucestershire, UK, to Dr Stuart Prior and Dr Mark Horton of the Department of Archaeology and Anthropology, University of Bristol, UK, in conjunction with the Berkeley Castle Charitable Trust, for granting permission to photograph these ongoing arachaeological projects. Thanks also to the students of the School of Conservation Sciences and those who attended the summer school, many of whom feature in the photographs; **Bristol Harbourside Excavation,** thanks to Jim Dyer of Crest Nicholson South West Ltd, Bristol, for granting permission to photograph the excavation, and to the employees of Wessex Archaeology (www.wessexarch.co.uk) for featuring in the photographs. The following photographs are ©**Anness Publishing Ltd** 15b, 38t, 41r, 44t, 45l, 45tr, 45ml, 45mr, 46t, 47b, 56bl, 56br, 56mr, 58t, 59bl, 59br, 59mr, 62, 63m, 69t, 70b, 71t, 72bl, 75bm, 75bl, 76br, 77t, 78t, 78br, 78bl, 79b, 83t, 83b, 85tl, 86t, 87tl, 87tr, 87ml, 87mr, 88b, 89tl, 90br, 90bl, 91tl, 91tm, 92t, 93b, 95tr, 95tl, 95b, 99b, 100t, 100b, 101tl, 101tm, 101tr, 101bl, 101bm, 101br, 103r, 106tr, 106bl, 106br, 107tl, 108t, 108bl, 108br, 112bl, 117tl, 117b, 121tr, 121tl, 121mr, 121ml, 121br, 121bl, 126t, 127tl, 127tm, 127b, 146t, 148bl, 148br, 168t, 180bl, 215l, 216t, 220br, 222bl, 224t, 226br, 241l, 249t **Robert Aberman** 348bm, 373, 374, 375 **akg-images** 259b, 262, 263, 269t, 275, 369l and r, 404t, 417r, 422tm, 423m, 436, 438r, 441r, /ullstein bild 265r, 286t, 319r, 334t, /Erich Lessing 280b, 281b, 353b, 384t, 399t, 406, 433b, /Gerard Degeorge 440bm, 461t, /Nimatallah 446t, /Laurent Lecat. 452, 455 **Alamy** 29b **Amsterdam University Library, Special Collections** 23t, 23b **Ancient Art and Architecture Collection** 268b, 282t and b, 306b, 325t, 328b, 329, 330t, 345b, 348tm and br, 349l, 353t, 354b, 356b, 358l, 363l, 366b, 377t and b, 378tm, 384b, 394br, 395br, 404b, 408, 409t and b, 410, 416, 418b, 420, 422bl, 427, 429t and b, 438l, 440tl and br, 441l, 443b, 445t, 457, 462tr, 463br, 476, 495b, /Danita Delimont, 295t, 370t, 470, 471t and b, /Archaeological Mus. Mexico City 8, /Prisma 281t, /G Tortoli 334b, /Hermitage Mus. St Petersburg 448, 449t and b **Anthony Duke (based on original drawings by Fiona Haughey)** ©**Anness Publishing Ltd** 30b, 51b, 54bl, 54bm, 54br, 76m, 76bl, 93tl, 93tm, 93tr, 99tr, 134b, 140bl **Anthony Duke** ©**Anness Publishing Ltd** 149t, 152b, 183t, 185b, 187b **Antiquity Publications Ltd** 31t **APVA Preservation Virginia** 252t, 252m, 252bl, 252br, 253bl, 253br **Archaeological Computing Laboratory, University of Sydney** /Andrew Wilson 24t, 32t, 32b, 33tr /Damian §§§Evans 33tl, 33bl, 33br **The Art Archive** 258t and b, 266b, 301b, 364b, 372t, 397, 440tm, /Neil Setchfield 459b, /Dagli Orti 261t and r, 271t, 349m, 358r, 360, 366m, 370b, 379l and r, 382, 390, 394tm and bl, 398b, 400r, 401, 407t, 453, 454, 475l and r, 478, 481, 482, 487t, 496, 497l, /Bibliotheque des Arts Decoratifs, Paris/Dagli Orti 266t, 272b, /Musee du Louvre, Paris/Dagli Orti 268t, 309t, 359b, 362, 383b, 389b, /Heraklion Mus./ Dagli Orti 270m, 271b, 398t, /British Mus./ Dagli Orti 272t, /Musee des Antiques St Germain en Laye/Dagli Orti 277b, /National Archaeological Mus. Athens/Dagli Orti 283t, 400l, 503/Culver Pictures 293t, 294b, /Egyptian Mus. Cairo/ Dagli Orti 293b, 294t, 295b, 500/Beijing Institute of Archaeology/ Laurie Platt Winfrey 297m, /National Mus. Karachi/Dagli Orti 307r, 445b, /National Mus. Damascus/Dagli Orti 316m, /Archaeological Mus. Salonica/Dagli Orti 320t, 321b, /Mireille Vautier 322t, 459r, /Museo de las Culturas, Oaxaca/Dagli Orti 325b, /Museo di Anthropologia ed Etnografia, Turin/Dagli Orti 333b, /Archaeological Mus. Tikal, Guatemala/Dagli Orti 338b, /Rijksmuseum voor Volkenkunde, Leiden/Dagli Orti 348bl, 376, /Mus. of Anatolian Civilizations, Ankara/Dagli Orti 396, /Archaeological Mus. Delphi/Dagli Orti 407b, /Christopher Lay 458, /Naval Mus. Genoa/Dagli Orti 462tl, 473t, /George French Anglas 463bm, 472t, /Lucien Biton Collection, Paris/Dagli Orti 473b, /Archaeological Mus. Lima/Dagli Orti 474b, 483r, /Bruning Mus. Lambayeque, Peru/Mireille Vautier 483l **Paul Bahn** 277t, 425t **Gareth Beale, Archaeological Computing Research Group, University of Southampton** 60t, 61b **Stuart Bedford** 167m, 167b, 209tr, 463l, 468t and b, 469tl and tr **University of Bergen** 352 **The Berkeley Castle Charitable Trust** 36b **Berkeley Historic Maps and Images, University of Bristol** 36ml, 36mr **Bibliotheque de l'Ecole des mines de Paris** 276t **Caroline Bird** 462bl, 466 **Blombos Caves Project** 186t **Bridgeman Art Library** 198bl **British School at Athens** 301t, 304t **Charlene Brown** 46b ©**Buckinghamshire County Council** 151b **Göran Burenhult** 168br, 186bl **The Cambridgeshire Collection, Cambridge Central Library and the Principal and Fellows, Newnham College, Cambridge** 296t **Çatalhöyük Research Project** 103m, 114t, 120b, 212t, 212bl, 212br, 213tr, 213tl **Christopher Catling** 25mr, 42b **Corbis** 12t, 13t, 13b, 14br, 16, 19bl, 20b, 21b, 28t, 34t, 35b, 43t, 43b, 45b, 53tr, 74b, 77b, 81t, 96br, 103l, 104t, 104b, 111tr, 111b, 124t, 137tr, 138b, 139bl, 140br, 141b, 141tr, 143t, 145m, 145t, 147b, 149b, 150b, 151t, 154br, 154t, 154bl, 156t, 156b, 157t, 159bl, 160br, 161t, 161b, 164t, 168t, 169b, 169tl, 169tr, 174, 176br, 176t, 177b, 177t, 178br, 178bl, 179b, 180t, 181t, 184t, 184br, 186br, 187t, 188t, 188b, 189b, 192br, 192bl, 196t, 197b, 199tr, 199b, 201tl, 204bm, 204t, 205br, 206t, 207bl, 209tl, 218bl, 218br, 221t, 226bl, 227t, 227bl, 228bl, 232t, 232bl, 232br, 233bl, 233br, 235tl, 235tr, 235b, 236bl, 236br, 237tl, 237tl, 244t, 245tl, 247br, 250bl, 251tr, 251bl, 280t, 284b, 302t, 391b, 440bl, 444, 474t, 499, /Penny Tweedie 326, 327, /Philippe Giraud 423, 432, /epa/Eduardo Herran 339b, /Chris Lisle 281, 286b, /Jeremy Horner 310b, /Sygma/Pierre Vauthey 330z, 426, /Hulton-Deutsch Collection 9, 401, 270t, 283b, 308t, 310t,

Below The Church of St. George in Ethiopia is carved directly from the rock that surrounds it.

/Christopher Loviny 257, 460, /Historical Picture Archive 264, /Bettmann 267, 289m and r, 290, 292b, 296, 305t, 315t, 316t, 319m, 328t, 331t, 339t, 442, /Nik Wheeler 273, 381, 386b, /Roger Wood 274t and b, 378tr, 383t, /Ted Spiegel 285b, /Reuters/Pilar Olivares 287t, /Hanan Isachar 298b, 299b, 378tl, 380, /Visions of America/Joseph Sohm 302b, /David Muench 303t, /Buddy Mays 303b, /Gianni Dagli Orti 305b, 338t, 381b, 387t, /Lindsay Hebberd 307b, /David Bartruff 311, /Charles and Josette Lenars 312b, 313b, 395m, 412, 441m, 450, 474t, 477, 479t and b, /Kevin Schafer 313t, /Michael Freeman 318, /Sygma/ Robert Campbell 319l, 331b, /Richard A. Cooke back cover tr, 322b, 475m, 494, /Danny Lehman 323, /Archivo Iconografico, S.A. 324t, /Eric and David Hosking 333t, /Werner Forman 342t, 386l, /Peter M. Wilson 344t, 405, /Yann-Arthus Bertrand 344b, 395bl, 411b, /Alison Wright 346, 347, 392, /Reuters 350b, 351, /Alison Wood 378bl, /Christie's Images 379m, 387b, /Stapleton Collection 385, /Historical Picture Archive/David Roberts 393b, /Jonathan Blair 402, /Mimmo Jodice 418t, /Sandro Vannini 419, /West Semitic Research/Dead Sea Scrolls Foundation 421b, /Jason Hawkes 422tl, 428, /Paul Almasy 422tr, 437b, /Sygma 422bm, 430, /Sygma/Vienna Report Agency 431, /Richard T. Nowitz 434, /Dean Conger 440tr, 443t, /Craig Lovell 456, /Keren Su 461b, /Jim Sugar 462tm, 467t, /Dave G. Houser/Post-Houserstock 462bm, 465b, /epa/Alan Thorne 464, /Michael Amendolia 465t, /Douglas Peebles 467b, /Angelo Hornak 480, /epa/Jorge Gonzalez 481b, /Dewitt Jones 489, /Carl and Alan Purcell back cover tl, 490, /Wolfgang Kachler 492, /Michael S. Lewis 493, /Kevin R. Morris 498 **Corbis: Gerald Cubitt** 350m **The Cultural Resources Program, Fort Bragg** 112br **Dale Croes** 105t, 105ml, 105mr **The Daily Telegraph** 189tr **Professor T Darvill, University of Bournemouth** 38b **Lucy Doncaster** 26b **Dries Dossche** 68t **Peter Drewett** 153t, 153m **The Flag Fen Bronze Age Centre** /John Byford and Mike Webber 111tl, 196b, 198t **Professor Vince Gaffney, Institute of Archaeology and Antiquity** 190b **Getty Images** 12b, 18b, 21t, 27b, 28b, 39b, 53tl, 67b, 73b, 80bl, 86b, 92b, 102, 106t, 122b, 123br, 123bl, 123t, 124bl, 124br, 125t, 125b, 126br, 127tr, 130, 131m, 132b, 136bl, 138t, 150t, 153b, 159tl, 160bl, 167t, 179m, 184bl, 210br, 211b, 214, 215m, 215r, 230t, 229b. 229tr, 229tl, /Time Life Pictures 289l

Below An archaeologist conducts a thorough excavation of a residential building site.

292t, 297t, 312t, /Roger Viollet 276b, /National Geographic 332, /Express/Hulton Archive 345t **David Gill** 320b, 321t **Gloucestershire Archives** 25ml **Gloucester City Museums** 25t **GUARD, Glasgow University** 74t, 116br, 119tl **Tehmina Goskar** 36t **Guildhall Library, City of London** 19t **Robert Harding** 288, 306t, 441r, 446b, 451, /John Ross 268b, /Vanderhart 296b, /Lorraine Wilson 304b, /Ursula Gahwiler 308b, /Michael Jenner 309b, /Adam Woolfitt 315b, 433t, /Richard Ashworth 317t, /Gina Corrigan 324b, /Gavin Hellier 335, /Odyssey 340b, /Sylvain Grandadam 345t, 421t, /Walter Rawlings 363r, /Upperhall Ltd 367t, 393t, /Evy Thouvenin 388, /Marco Simoni 399b, /Travel Library 411t, /Cubo Images 413b, /Robert Francis 474m, 495t, /Panoramic Images 487b **Fiona Haughey** 68b, 82t, 90t, 94b **Institute of Nautical Archaeology** 394bm, 403 ©**iStockphoto.com** 9b, 47tl, 201tr, 204bl, 209b, 217t, 224br, 225b, 230bl, 234br /Alan Crawford 243t /Alessandro Oliva 225tl /Andy Pritchard 197tl /Björn Kindler 26t, /cenap refik ONGAN 244bl /Chris Ronneseth 224bl /Christina Hanck 245tr /Claudio Giovanni Colombo 220bl /Clifford Shirley 17r, /Cornelia Schaible 246b /Darren Hendley 22t /David Pedre 200bl /Diana Bier 204br /Fabio Bianchini 202br /hazel proudlove 195tl /Hedda Gjerpen 250t /Jamo Gonzalez Zarraonandia 211t /Jan Rihak 234t /Javier Garcia Blanco 198br /John Brennan 195tr /John Leigh 221b /Joseph Justice 241m /Leslie Banks 200t /luca manieri 233t /Luis Seco 210t /Lukasz Laska 47tr /Mark Scott 210bm /Mary Lane 223l /Matt Trommer 197tr /Merijn van der Vliet 248b /Michael Fuery 201b /Natalia Bratslavsky 196m /Neil Sorenson 202t /Oleksiy Kondratyuk 217b /Paul Kline 202bl /Rich Legg 49br /Robert Bremec 207tr, 220t /Roberto A Sanchez /Simon Podgorsek 203 /Steve Geer 216bl, 216br /Steven Allan 24b, 210bl /Steven Phraner 223r /Tan Kian Khoon 208t /Timur Kulgarin 225tr /Volkan Ersoy 200br /Wojciech Zwierzynski 208b /Wolfgang Feischl 58b **Professor Simon Keay, British School at Rome/Graeme Earl, University of Southampton** 60b, 60m, 61t, 61ml, 61mr **The Landmarks Trust** 238t, 238bl, 238t, 239bm, 239br, 239bl, 239tr **Latin American Library/Tulane University** 263m, 282t **Pietro Laureano, 2005** 34m, 34bl, 34br **Macphail, R. I. and Crowther, J. 2004** 115r **Sturt W Manning, Aegean Dendrochronology Project** 172t, 172b, 173t, 173bl, 173br **Vance McCollum, field volunteer, South Carolina State Museum** 110b **Martin Millet** 97t **The Mary Rose Trust** 218t, 219tr **Margot Mulcahy** 27t **Natasha Mulder** 25b ©**Museum of London** 170t /Derek Lucas 170br **Museum of London Archaeology Service** 89bl, 96bl, 113tr, 117tr, 118br, 126bl, 139t, 170bl, 171b, 219tl, 243bl, 298t and b/Andy Chopping 65b, 105bl, 114br, 116t, 128bl, 129tl, 129tr, 129bl, 129br, 131l, 132t, 133tl, 135t, 147tr, 170bm, 205t, /Jan Scrivener 160t /Jon Bailey 146b /Maggie Cox 109b, 109t, 115l, 119b, 128t, 242t, 243br /Trevor Hurst 113tl **Dani Nadel** 193tr, 193tl, 193tl, 193br **Katharina Neumann** 113b **Dr Susan O'Connor, Research School of Pacific and Asian Studies, Australian National University, Canberra** 185t **The Ordnance Survey** (reproduced from 1909 Ordnance Survey map) 22bl **Den Y Ovenden** ©**Anness**

Above The Observatory temple in the Mayan city of Chichen Itza, Mexico.

Publishing Ltd 182b ©**Oxford Archaeology North** 155b /MLA 137tm **The Oxford Archaeological Unit Ltd** 87, 15t, 17m, 19br, 20t, 44b, 49bl, 50b, 59t, 64b, 68b, 69b, 70t, 71b, 72t, 75br, 80br, 84b, 88t, 94t, 96t, 97b, 98t, 98b, 110t, 114bl, 122t, 131r, 134t, 135b, 137tl, 137bl, 137br 148t, 221m, 226t, 230bm, 230t, 244br **Pitt-Rivers Mus. University of Oxford** 279bm **Mr G. A. Pitt-Rivers. By kind permission of Salisbury and South Wiltshire Mus.** 278t and b, 279t and br **Dominic Powlesland, Landscape Research Centre** 55 **Poznan Archaeological Mus. Poland** 437t **Scarborough Museums Trust** 189tl **Jonathan Reif** 193bl **Clive Ruggles** 237b **Science Museum/Science and Society Picture Library** 163b **Science Photo Library** 52bl, 140t, 142t, 143bl, 143br, 144b, 144t, 145b, 157b, 164b, 168bl, 178t, 179t, 180br, 181bl, 182t, 183b, 227br **Sheffield City Archives** 22ml, 22mr **K. Sklenar** 425b **Steven Snape** 371t and b **O. Soffer** 424 **Robin Torrence** 469b **Jonathon Tubb** 165b **Erica Utsi** 57t **University of Reading** 107b **Bob Reece, Friends of Little Bighorn** 230br, 231l, 231m, 231r **The Wace Archive** 64 **Werner Forman Archive** 158t, 158b, 162t, 162br, 163t, 165t, 199m, 207br, 256, 348tl and tr, 349r, 355t, 356t, 359t, 364m, 365t and b, 367b, 391t, 394tl, 413t, 414, 415t and b, 417l, 423r, 435, 474t, 486, 491t, /Nick Saunders 290b, 291, 340t, 341t, 342b, 484t, 485, /British Mus. London 316b, 317b, 361b, /National Mus. Copenhagen 285t, 500l, /Mus. fur Volkerkunde, Berlin 287b, 484b, /David Bernstein Fine Art, New York 343, /Egyptian Mus. Cairo 355b, 357, 368l and r, /Sudan Archaeological Mus. Khartoum 372b, /State Mus. Berlin 378bm, 389t, /National Mus. of New Zealand, Wellington 462br, 472b, /Royal Mus. of Art and History, Brussels 483t, /Maxwell Mus. of Anthropology, Albuquerque, New Mexico 488, /Mesa Verde National Park Mus. 491b **Wessex Archaeology** 14bl, 39t, 40, 41m, 41l, 32t, 46m, 48t, 48b, 51t, 52t, 52br, 54t, 56t, 57bl, 57br, 63l, 63r, 64t, 65t, 66t, 67mr, 67t, 67ml, 72m, 72br, 73t, 76t, 79t, 81b, 82b, 84t, 85tr, 85b, 87b, 89br, 89tr, 91tr, 105br, 112t, 116bl, 118bl, 118t, 119tr, 120t, 133tr, 133br, 136t, 136br, 139br, 142b, 147tl, 151tr, 151tl, 159tr, 159br, 162bl, 166bl, 166br, 190t, 191t, 191b, 222t, 222br, 240, 241r, 242br, 242bl, 246t, 247t, 247bl, 248t, 249b, 251tl **George Willcox** 194t, 194br, 194bl, 195b **www.lastrefuge.co.uk** /Adrian Warren 29t 30t /Dae Sasitorn 17l, 31b, 80t **www.webbaviation.co.uk** 22br

Index